The Times

HISTORY

OF

THE WAR

VOL. V.

PRINTING HOUSE SQUARE.

PRINTED AND PUBLISHED BY "THE TIMES,"
PRINTING HOUSE SQUARE, LONDON.

1915.

CONTENTS OF VOL. V

CHAPTER LXXX.

THE INTERVENTION OF ITALY.

ORIGIN AND HISTORY OF THE TRIPLE ALLIANCE—ITALY'S POSITION AND RELATIONS WITH OTHER POWERS—THE TRIPOLI AND BALKAN WARS—ITALIAN POLICY IN 1914—HER PROTESTS AGAINST AUSTRO-GERMAN ACTION—HISTORY OF THE NEGOTIATIONS WITH AUSTRIA—REASON OF THEIR FAILURE—END OF THE TRIPLE ALLIANCE—OPINION IN ITALY—THE GIOLITTI INTRIGUES—ITALY JOINS THE ALLIES—PUBLIC ENTHUSIASM.

FOR a dozen years at least before the Great War it had been one of the commonplaces of European politics that the Italian alliance with Germany and Austria was unnatural, and against the best interests of Italy. The old unforgotten enmity with Austria and the persistence of the Irredentist problem were alone enough to prevent anything more than a formal bond between Rome and Vienna. Italy, moreover, was a democratic State, in a sense perhaps even more democratic than republican France, while the Central Empires were politically unfree, still based essentially upon royal and aristocratic domination of the people. Ties of race and of culture suggested France as a natural ally. Great Britain, France, and Italy held, broadly, similar ideals of liberty and progress. Between Great Britain and Italy there existed a long tradition of sympathy and friendship, which was strengthened by the factor of common interests in the Mediterranean.

Such arguments were sound as far as they went, but they ignored the history of the Triple Alliance and the events which led up to it. They ignored, moreover, the dangers which threatened Italy if she should endeavour to resume liberty of action.

During the ten years which followed the occupation of Rome by the troops of united Italy, the foreign policy of Italy was directed rather to preserving good relations with all her neighbours than to cultivating special friendship with any one Power. The party of the Right, which fell in 1876, had always maintained its Francophil tradition, though the attitude of France under Thiers had put a severe strain upon the relations between the two countries. The accession to power of the Left, under Depretis, might have been expected to bring about a change in Italian foreign policy. For ten years the Left had advocated an alliance with Prussia, and Bismarck had on more than one occasion practised the policy of maintaining direct relations with the Italian opposition, which was to prove so disastrous to German influence when attempted in the hour of crisis that saw the final exit of Italy from the Triple Alliance.

The Left disappointed the expectations of Berlin and Vienna. Depretis adopted an extremely conciliatory attitude towards France, in spite of the provocation given by French Clericalism on the still living question of the Temporal Power. The idea of the Left seems to have been that Italy could rely upon the rivalry of her neighbours to secure her own interests. The results of the Berlin Congress might well have shattered the dream, for the Austrian occupation of Bosnia and Herzegovina and the Anglo-Turkish agreement, which placed Cyprus in the hands of Great Britain, were both in clear opposition to Italian policy. But the

1

THE KING OF ITALY.   [*Guigoni & Bossi.*]

dream persisted for a few years more. Though Italy had long had her eyes fixed on the North African littoral, her rulers could not see that she was in danger of being anticipated. They went so far as to refuse the suggestion of Austria, Germany and Russia that Italy should occupy Tunis, and perhaps believed that this offer practically amounted to an Italian lien upon the Regency. They did not know their Bismarck. The suggestion was inspired by the idea of embroiling Italy and France, and when Italy declined to follow his advice, Bismarck turned round and made the same proposal to France. Before the Berlin Congress broke up, Tunis was lost to Italy. A verbal agreement had been made between Lord Salisbury and M. Waddington that France should be free to occupy Tunisia, "when convenient."

During the years immediately following Italy had fair warning of French intentions regarding Tunis, and it was even indicated to

the Italian Ambassador in Paris where she might look for compensation. In July, 1880, Freycinet spoke very clearly : " Why will you persist in thinking of Tunis, where your rivalry may one day cause a breach in our friendly relations ? Why not turn your attention to Tripoli, where you would have neither ourselves nor anyone else to contend with ? "

Cairoli and Depretis, who shared power between them during this period, failed to recognize the inevitable trend of events. In the spring of 1881 France sent an expedition to Tunis on the pretext of punishing the Krumir tribe for an attack upon a French force on the Algerian frontier, and on May 12 the signature of the treaty of Bardo established a French protectorate over Tunisia.

Italian resentment was naturally very keen. Tunis had long been regarded, by informed opinion in Italy, as a legitimate sphere of Italian influence. More than 50,000 Italians

THE QUEEN OF ITALY.   [*Guigoni & Bossi.*

had settled in the Regency, and Italy's claim to eventual annexation, or to the declaration of a protectorate, was certainly stronger than that of France, which was founded upon the necessity of protecting the Algerian frontier from real or fancied disturbance.

The Cairoli Government fell immediately. The policy of isolation had proved a disastrous failure, and the conviction rapidly grew that the only way to safeguard Italian interests was to cultivate close relations with Germany and Austria. Depretis, who had succeeded Cairoli, perceived the necessity of a move in this direction, but he was loth to relinquish his belief that Italy could at the same time maintain cordial relations with France. The strongest line was taken by the centre, a small group led by Sidney Sonnino, who maintained that Italy's best course was to conclude a definite alliance with the Central Empires, and at the same time come to an understanding

with Great Britain regarding the Mediterranean. This policy was first put before the public on May 29, 1881, in the *Rassegna Settimanale*, in an article attributed to Sonnino himself.

Mancini, Foreign Minister in the Depretis Cabinet, was for a time unwilling to alienate France by a definite adhesion to the Austro-German alliance which had been formed in 1879. But the policy of isolation, of equal friendship with all the Powers, daily became more clearly untenable. The Tunis question seemed to make a *rapprochement* between France and Italy impossible, but Bismarck feared that Gambetta, who had succeeded Ferry, might take steps to conciliate Italy. He arranged for a German Press campaign in favour of reopening the Roman question, and though the Italian Government faced the threat with spirit, the conviction grew that an alliance with Germany and Austria was the only means of securing the position of Italy in

A REGIMENT OF BERSAGLIERI IN ROME.

The troops on the famous Garabaldi statue, cheering their King and Country.

4

Europe. Such an alliance would put an end to the possibility of attack from Austria ; above all, it would prevent further aggression on the part of France.

Advances were first made to Germany, but Bismarck is reported to have said to Count de Lannay, the Italian Ambassador in Berlin, that the way to Berlin lay through Vienna. Early in 1882 conversations were opened in Vienna, at the instance of the Austrian Foreign Minister, but they did not progress favourably, owing to the unwillingness of Count Kálnoky to guarantee to Italy the possession of the Papal territories, and to an equal unwillingness on the part of Mancini to acquiesce formally in the Austrian tenure of Trieste and the Trentino. Mancini, moreover, desired the support of the Central Empires for Italian interests in the Mediterranean, a proposal which Kálnoky declined to consider. Bismarck finally interposed. The principle of reciprocal territorial guarantees was accepted, but Italy had to relinquish the idea of any pledge of support in the Mediterranean, though it was agreed that the contracting parties should act in friendly consultation with one another in all questions touching their special interests. The Treaty of Alliance was signed on May 20, 1882, but its existence was not made public till March, 1883.

It is often maintained that at first no new alliance was made, but that Italy simply adhered to the existing agreement between Germany and Austria, which was eventually published by Bismarck in 1888. Of late years it has been believed that the alliance was subsequently converted into three separate pacts, between Germany and Austria, Germany and Italy, and Italy and Austria, but the publication of various provisions of the alliance after Italy's declaration of war against Austria on May 23, 1915, shows that it eventually became a single treaty. It is said that the alliance consisted of three separate parts : a general treaty between the Governments for a definite period of years ; a confirmatory pact between the Sovereigns, which required to be signed afresh by each successor to the throne ; and a military convention.

The first term of the Triple Alliance brought little comfort to Italy. France remained resolutely hostile, while the new allies seemed far from friendly. Italy's value in the alliance was largely discounted by the Treaty of Skierniewice, signed on March 21, 1884, by which Bismarck secured the benevolent neu-

trality of Austria and Russia in the event of Germany being forced to make war upon a fourth Power. Italy was treated as a very junior partner, whose admittance into the firm had begun to be regretted by the seniors. She had undertaken certain obligations, but the real object of her entrance into the alliance was in no way assured to her. In Crispi's words, she "still stood alone in defence of her own interests."

The natural result was an attempt to come to an understanding with Great Britain in regard to the Mediterranean. By the autumn of 1886 Bismarck had convinced himself that the renewal of the Triple Alliance was desirable, but Count di Robilant, who had become Foreign Secretary a year earlier, declined to consider a renewal on the original terms. He is supposed to have secured a more satisfactory form of partnership in the treaty which was signed on March 17, 1887. His most important achievement was the negotiation of a parallel understanding with Great Britain, which is believed to have provided for common action by the British and Italian fleets in the Mediterranean in the event of war. In any case, from 1887 onwards the British and Italian Governments acted in perfect accord over Mediterranean questions. The policy advocated by Sonnino six years before had definitely triumphed.

Italy was now in a position to play an important part in Europe. The alliance with Germany and Austria and the understanding with England made her able to face France fairly, on an equal footing, and the knowledge of this fact on the part of both Powers was a necessary prelude to the establishment of satisfactory relations. Again, as the link between Great Britain and the Central Powers, Italy had a value for her allies that promised greater consideration for Italian interests at their hands. Crispi seized the opportunity, and under his guidance Italy began to realize her future. When Crispi fell, a Radical campaign was started against the renewal of the Triple Alliance, but in June, 1891, nearly a year before the expiry of the second term, it was renewed, on the initiative of Berlin, for a period of twelve years. On this occasion the Italian Prime Minister, Rudini, endeavoured to insert the proviso that if Great Britain should be one of the Powers whose declaration of hostilities against Austria or Germany meant involving Italy in war, Italy should be released

GENERAL COUNT LUIGI CADORNA,
Commander-in-Chief of the Italian Armies.

[Morano-Pisculli.

from the obligations of the treaty. Germany declined to include this as a clause of the treaty, but the proposal was recorded and filed with the treaty as a protocol.

This period saw the gradual establishment of better relations with France. The Commercial Treaty signed in 1898 put an end to a tariff war that had lasted for ten years, and in 1900 Visconti Venosta succeeded in establishing a *détente* with France regarding the vexed question of the Tripolitan hinterland.

Two years later his successor, Prinetti, negotiated the agreement which gave Italy a free hand in Tripolitania in return for a recognition of French predominance in Morocco, an agreement which was followed shortly afterwards by a definite understanding with Great Britain regarding Tripolitania.

There were various rumours regarding the two years which preceded the third renewal of the Triple Alliance in 1902. The most interesting is that which asserts that for nearly two years after his accession to the throne the present King of Italy declined to put his signature to the " dynastic agreement." Ultimately, however, the alliance was renewed at Venice in June, 1902, for a further period of twelve years, and the protocol regarding Great Britain was destroyed.

But circumstances were changing. Germany had no mind that Italy should claim an equal partnership in the Triple Alliance, and Italy, now firmer on her feet, was not content with a position in which her obligations seemed to outweigh her advantages. Her allies had shown little inclination to support her Mediterranean ambitions, and she had been forced to look elsewhere in order to safeguard her interests in this quarter. Nor had the alliance wrought any real improvement in her relations with Austria. The Italians in the " unredeemed " provinces were the object of continual petty persecutions on the part of the Austrian authorities, and the question was made more acute by Austrian encouragement of the Slavonic element to the detriment of the Italian. A further cause of friction lay in the Austrian attitude to the Vatican. French clericalism, and the danger it constituted to the Italian State, had died out. Austrian clericalism threatened to take its place. Austria had succeeded France as " Eldest Daughter of the Church," and though the relations between Vatican and Quirinal had greatly improved, there were still chances for mischief-makers. A third point at issue was the Balkan question. On this rock the leaking barque of the Triple Alliance was finally to split, but for a number of years it had been clear that Italian and Austrian interests in the Balkans were growing more and more divergent. It was known that there was an agreement, a self-denying ordinance, in regard to Albania, and it was afterwards revealed that there were definite engagements concerning the whole of the Balkan question. But Austria behaved as though these engagements did not exist. In Albania particularly, a diligent Austrian propaganda was carried on. In self-defence Italy followed suit, and the remarkable spectacle presented itself of two allied Powers, bound both by general and by special engagements conducting rival campaigns of " peaceful penetration " in territory which both had agreed that neither should occupy.

The Mürzsteg agreement of 1903 was a blow to Italian interests in the Balkans, for the establishment of Austrian and Russian financial agents in Macedonia was a definite " score " for Austria, though the appointment of General de Giorgis as Commandant of the international Macedonian gendarmerie was recognized as affording some compensation to Italy. But the light in which the question was regarded and discussed showed clearly that Italy and Austria looked upon one another more as rivals than as allies.

The Morocco crisis of 1905–6 showed another divergence of view between Italy and her allies. While Austria played the part of a " brilliant second " to Germany, Italy's refusal to support German policy gave rise to the famous phrase about " extra dances." At the Algeciras Conference, where the veteran Visconti Venosta was a prominent figure, it was seen that Italy's Mediterranean agreements outweighed the claims of the Triple Alliance. Her allies had no grounds for complaint. They had declined to have anything to do with Italy's Mediterranean interests, and it was Bismarck himself who had suggested to Italy where she should look for support. He had not, of course, foreseen that the understanding with Great Britain would lead to an agreement with France, and the lesser men who followed him had failed to take any steps to divert the trend of Italian policy.

Italy was now on bad terms with both her allies, and the rift was further widened by the Austrian annexation of Bosnia and Herzegovina. The announcement of the annexation was made without any previous notice to the Italian public, though a meeting had just taken place between Baron Aehrenthal and Signor Tittoni, the Italian Foreign Minister. Signor Tittoni's position was made the more difficult from the fact that he had subsequently made a speech in which he declared that " Italy might await events with serenity, and that these would find her neither unprepared nor isolated." The keenest indignation was aroused throughout the country. There was talk of an expedition to Tripoli, where Italian intervention was expected. Indirect compensation, however, was provided by the withdrawal of Austria from the Sanjak of Novibazar, and by her renunciation of the right to police the Montenegrin coast and prevent Montenegro from owning warships.

The withdrawal from the Sanjak was a renunciation only in seeming. Austrian military opinion had decided that the corridor of the Sanjak was not a convenient way of approach to European Turkey. It was too narrow and

BERSAGLIERI ON THE MARCH.

too easily commanded from either side. The opinion was openly expressed that the only possible route to Salonika lay through the Serbian plain, and the withdrawal from the Sanjak meant simply that the plans of the Austrian General Staff for an eastern advance were definitely based upon war against Serbia.

Germany held that the only way of securing her hegemony in the alliance was to prevent the establishment of a real accord between Italy and Austria-Hungary. Count Golu-chowski, who, during his last years of office, had striven to establish better relations between Rome and Vienna, was driven from office by German intrigue. Germany was always on the watch against too close a *rapprochement* between her two allies, and not the least gain to Germany arising out of Aehrenthal's action during the crisis of 1908 lay in the fact that it widened the gulf between Austria-Hungary and Italy.

There were to be other efforts, during the few years that remained before the final break, to improve Austro-Italian relations. It would seem that Aehrenthal had begun to realize, before his death in 1912, that a better under-standing with Italy was necessary to the success of his ambition to secure for Austria-Hungary a greater independence of Germany. Perhaps

if he had lived, a different spirit might have animated the alliance. But it is hardly likely. German interests seemed to lie the other way, and German influence at Vienna was too strong to be resisted. And the history of subsequent events shows that Austrian opinion was in no way ready for the *rapprochement* with Italy that policy should have dictated.

From 1908 to 1911 the unpopularity of the Triple Alliance increased among Italians. It gave no support to Italian aims in the Medi-terranean; it had failed to hold the balance between Italy and Austria in the Balkans; it seemed to promise nothing for the future save a doubtful immunity from Austrian attack—a doubtful immunity, for the military party in Austria talked openly of " a promenade to Milan." Italians began to ask more fre-quently whether Italian interests might not be better safeguarded by a different partner-ship, and when the war with Turkey broke out the renewal of the Triple Alliance in 1914 seemed far from being a certainty.

When Italy made her descent upon Tripoli in the autumn of 1911, Italians were ready for hostile criticism on the part of their allies. It was widely reported that Germany actually brought forward the question of Tripoli during the Moroccan negotiations, and made the suggestion that as "compensation" for her recognition of the French position in Morocco she should be granted a free hand in the territories which had long been regarded as an Italian sphere of influence. What is beyond doubt is that Germany was beginning to develop commercial interests in the Tripoli-taine at a time when Italian interests were being consistently thwarted by Turkey. The example of Morocco had shown the world how the assertion of commercial interests was the immediate prelude to political claims, and the Italian occupation of Tripoli cut short what was no doubt regarded in Berlin as a promising development of policy.

There was a further reason why Italy's action was unwelcome to Germany. It threatened seriously to compromise her position at Constantinople. German diplomacy had assured the Turk that his interests were best secured by German protection, and that he could count upon German support against the aggression of other Powers. Now for the second time in three years an ally of Germany showed that German protection did not extend very far. Germany was naturally irritated by events which threatened to spoil the German game.

From Austria nothing but hostility was expected. A lack of sympathy for Italian interests was the normal attitude at Vienna; and in this case there was some reason for the cold eye turned upon Italian enterprise. War between Italy and Turkey threatened to hasten, and did actually hasten, events for which Austria was not adequately prepared.

The northern members of the Triple Alliance soon showed their displeasure. The withdrawal of the Duke of the Abruzzi's squadron from the coast of Epirus, after the successful little action at Prevesa, was due to the direct veto of Germany and Austria upon any further operations in those waters. Aehrenthal complained of "the embarrassing situation in which Austria had been placed," and the German Ambassador in London told the Italian Ambassador, Marquis Imperiali, that if Italy continued the operations she would have to deal with Austria. The veto was more widely extended. On November 5, 1911, Aehrenthal declared that "Italian action on the Ottoman coasts of European Turkey or the Ægean islands could not be permitted either by Austria or Germany, as being contrary to the Treaty of Alliance." This prohibition followed

A GROUP OF ITALIAN OFFICERS.

General Cadorna, Commander-in-Chief of the Italian Armies, is the third figure from the left ; and
General Porro, Sub-Chief of General Staff, is on the Commander-in-Chief's left.

[Guigoni & Bossi.

GENERAL COUNT PORRO,
Sub-Chief of General Staff of the Italian Army.

upon a report that Italian warships had been using searchlights near Salonika. Two days later, on November 7, Aehrenthal informed the Italian Ambassador at Vienna that he " considered the bombardment of ports in European Turkey, such as Salonika, Kavalla, etc., contrary to Article VII. of the Alliance." A further protest was made by Count Berchtold some months later (April, 1912). He complained that an Italian squadron, when fired on by the forts at the entrance to the Dardanelles, had returned the fire and done some damage. He suggested that if the Italian Government " wished to resume its liberty of action " the Austro-Hungarian Government could do so equally. He declined to admit the right of Italy to make any attack upon Turkey in Europe, and gave an explicit warning that further action might have " serious consequences."

During the first months of the war the expectations that France also would make difficulties were happily disappointed. French opinion showed itself more friendly to Italy than that of any other country. When the greater part of the European Press was publishing grossly distorted versions of events in the Tripolitania, and particularly of the repression which followed the Arab revolt in the oasis of Tripoli, French newspapers, taken as a whole, printed fair and unbiased accounts of the action of the Italian troops. There was some little friction between French and Italians in Tunis, where the old feud had never died out. Some Italians did not fully appreciate the difficulties which beset the French authorities owing to the effects of the invasion upon the Arabs of Tunisia, and after a time there were murmurs against the trade in "contraband" which was alleged to go on between Tunis and Tripoli. But on the whole it may be said that during the last months of 1911 Italo-French relations were actually improved.

The situation changed with startling suddenness. On January 15, 1912, the French mail steamer Carthage was stopped on her way from Marseilles to Tunis and escorted to Cagliari in Sardinia, on the ground that there was included in her cargo an aeroplane destined for the Turkish Army. Considerable excitement was aroused in France, and three days later the capture of a second steamer, the Manouba, greatly increased the tension. This case was more serious than the first. Signor Tittoni, now Italian Ambassador in Paris, had informed the French Government that a Red Crescent Mission, which was to travel by the Manouba, was believed to include several Turkish officers. It was agreed that Italy should not interfere, but that an investigation should be held by the French authorities in Tunis. Unfortunately, the telegram announcing this agreement arrived too late. Italian cruisers had been under orders to stop the Manouba, and as no countermanding telegram arrived, these orders were carried out. The Manouba incident assumed serious proportions.

After a period of tension and discussion the disputes were finally referred for settlement to the Hague, where it was decided that Italy had been justified in exercising the right of inspection in the case of both vessels. But Franco-Italian relations had been seriously prejudiced. French action in Tunis was regarded henceforward with extreme suspicion. The old distrust between the two countries was revived, and it seemed as though the patient work of various far-seeing statesmen had been undone. Resentment against Germany and Austria was largely forgotten in the supposed realization that France was still an enemy. The tendency to drift away from the Triple Alliance was abruptly arrested.

This change of feeling was greatly assisted by the fact that for the first time since the unification of Italy Italians were struck with a doubt as to the reality of British friendship. When Italy declared war upon Turkey, and proceeded to the occupation of Tripoli, British comment was generally unfavourable ; in the case of some newspapers it was very markedly hostile. The nerves of Great Britain, like those of other countries, were suffering from the strain of the Morocco crisis. War had come very near to Europe in the summer of 1911, and the newspapers, occupied with graver matters, had not followed the development of the Tripoli question. War of any kind was resented by people who had just emerged from the shadow cast by the threat of a European struggle. And British relations with Islam furnished another reason for the marked coolness displayed by British opinion towards the Tripoli enterprise.

British criticism caused disappointment and resentment in Italy, but a better understanding would have been quickly re-established by a fuller consideration of each nation's point of view if the situation had not been prejudiced by the disgraceful calumnies levelled at the Italian Army by a large section of the British Press. Official relations between Great Britain and Italy were happily undisturbed by any friction, but the special value of the friend-

DUKE OF GENOA,   [*Rossi.*
Uncle of the King of Italy. Appointed "Lieutenant-General" for the King during His Majesty's absence at the Front.

ship between the two countries had always lain in the fact that it was based on the sympathy of public opinion. This sympathy seemed suddenly broken. Italians felt they had suffered disillusionment. They had expected other treatment at the hands of their traditional friends, though they had counted on neither support nor sympathy from their allies.

Germany was quick to take advantage of the situation. Nor is it likely that Italy showed any reluctance to meet her allies half-way. The rising tide of feeling against the Triple Alliance had not greatly affected the convictions of Italy's political leaders, who still saw in the alliance the best means of preserving peace in Europe and at the same time insuring that Italy's particular interests should not be disregarded. The alliance inspired no enthusiasm. Its drawbacks for Italy were manifest. But it still seemed to serve the interests of peace.

The Triple Alliance was renewed for the fourth time on December 7, 1912, eighteen months before the date of expiry, and owing to the alteration in public opinion the renewal was not greatly criticized in Italy.* For a time it seemed as though the alliance was actually more solid than it had been for a decade. Yet recent revelations have made it clear that during the twenty months which elapsed between the renewal of the alliance and the outbreak of the European War Italy

MARQUIS IMPERIALI,

The Italian Ambassador to Great Britain, and his wife on the balcony of the Embassy in London.

* Although Austro-German diplomacy thus scored a success, its need for haste involved the abandonment of the German intention to amend the terms of the alliance by requiring Italy to assume definite *naval* as well as military obligations.

AT THE BASE HOSPITAL.
Princess Di Bango, assisting with the Red Cross work, with Count Delle Schaglia, President of the Italian Red Cross Society.

was almost unbrokenly engaged in combating the policy of Austria-Hungary. For Austria-Hungary was determined to alter, as Italy was determined to maintain, the balance of power in the Balkans. Italy worked for peace; Austria-Hungary seemed bent on war.

Certain provisions of the Triple Alliance were disclosed in 1915 for the first time. The contents of the first article of the alliance were disclosed in a Note sent by Baron Sonnino to Italian representatives abroad, on May 24, 1915, for communication to the Powers. According to this Note Article I pledged the contracting parties to an exchange of ideas regarding all general political and economic questions which might present themselves. " From this it followed," the Note proceeds, " that none of the high contracting parties was free to undertake without previous accord any action whose consequences might give rise, in the case of the others, to any obligation contemplated by the alliance, or touch their most important interests."

Articles III., IV., and VII. were published in an Austro-Hungarian Red Book towards the end of May, 1915. They were as follows :

CLAUSE III.—In case one or two of the high contracting parties, without direct provocation on their part, should be attacked by one or more Great Powers not signatory

of the present Treaty and should become involved in a war with them, the *casus foederis* would arise simultaneously for all the high contracting parties.

CLAUSE IV.—In case a Great Power not signatory of the present Treaty should threaten the State security of one of the high contracting parties, and in case the threatened party should thereby be compelled to declare war against that Great Power, the two other contracting parties engage themselves to maintain benevolent neutrality towards their ally. Each of them reserves its right, in this case, to take part in the war if it thinks fit in order to make common cause with its ally.

CLAUSE VII.—Austria-Hungary and Italy, who have solely in view the maintenance, as far as possible, of the territorial *status quo* in the East, engage themselves to use their influence to prevent all territorial changes which might be disadvantageous to the one or the other of the Powers signatory of the present Treaty. To this end they will give reciprocally all information calculated to enlighten each other concerning their own intentions and those of other Powers. Should, however, the case arise that, in the course of events, the maintenance of the *status quo* in the territory of the Balkans or of the Ottoman coasts and islands in the Adriatic or the Ægean Seas becomes impossible, and that, either in consequence of the action of a third Power or for any other reason Austria-Hungary or Italy should be obliged to change the *status quo* for their part by a temporary or permanent occupation, such occupation would only take place after previous agreement between the two Powers, which would have to be based upon the principle of a reciprocal compensation for all territorial or other advantages that either of them might acquire over and above the existing *status quo*, and would have to satisfy the interests and rightful claims of both parties.

The success of the Balkan allies in the war against Turkey was a heavy blow to Austria-Hungary, and through her to Germany. The way to the East was blocked by young and vigorous States bent upon progress, and Serbian aggrandizement threatened to complicate the Slav problem within the Hapsburg dominions. As soon as it became evident that the war would result in an accession of strength and territory to Serbia, Austria-Hungary began to move. In November, 1912, she approached Italy with a plan for hampering Serbian development. The fact was revealed by Signor Tittoni in the following words :

Austria-Hungary turned to Italy and requested her adhesion to the Austro-Hungarian programme, which consisted in permitting Serbia her extension of territory on the condition that she should give Austria-Hungary certain guarantees. Italy, in giving her adhesion, declared expressly that she subordinated it to the condition that such guarantees should not constitute a monopoly, to the exclusive profit of Austria-Hungary, and that they should not diminish the independence of Serbia. Austria-Hungary expressed the intention of studying these guarantees and communicating them to us, but she made no subsequent communication, perhaps because she was gradually preparing and substituting for this pacific plan the plan of aggression.*

When the terms of peace between the Balkan Powers and Turkey began to be discussed, Austria-Hungary opposed a direct negative to the Serbian desire for access to the sea.

* Speech at the Trocadéro, Paris, June 24, 1914.

Italy supported her ally in the ill-starred design of an independent Albania, though public opinion was almost certainly against the action of the Government. For public opinion in Italy recognized the justice of the Serbian claim for a port on the Adriatic, and realized that such an outlet would bring great commercial benefit to Italy.

But while the Italian Government was ready to support Austro-Hungarian policy up to a certain point, a very definite limit was drawn beyond which they would not go. They were willing to help in thwarting Serbian ambitions by the establishment of a puppet principality in Albania. They were willing to back up their ally in demanding that the Montenegrins should be deprived of Scutari, though this action was very unpopular in Italy. But Austria-Hungary pressed her programme too far. In April, 1913, when the fate of Scutari had not yet been decided on by the Powers, Austria-Hungary threatened an occupation of Montenegro. On April 30 the Italian Foreign Minister, the late Marquis di San Giuliano, telegraphed to Signor Tittoni asking his views on the question, suggesting that if Austrian troops attacked Montenegro Italy should disembark an expedition on the Albanian coast, and expressing the opinion that if this solution did not meet with Austrian approval Italy would be compelled to follow an opposite policy to that of her ally. Signor Tittoni's reply deserves to be quoted in full :

If Austria wishes to occupy Montenegro, wholly or in part, we must go to Durazzo and Vallona, even if she does not consent. In fact, if Austria were to occupy Montenegro she would perform an action which is not necessary to the carrying out of the decisions of the Powers regarding Scutari, and would therefore put herself first of all outside the decisions of the Powers, acting on her own account without sufficient cause, and disturbing the balance in the Adriatic to our disadvantage ; for even a temporary occupation disturbs this balance. There is no force in the quibbles to which the Austro-Hungarian and German Ambassadors have recourse regarding the letter of Article VII. in the Treaty of the Triple Alliance. The spirit of that article is clear, and for the rest, any disturbance of equilibrium between Italy and Austria would strike not only at Article VII., but at the whole Treaty of Alliance. The day on which Austria should claim to upset, in any way or to any extent, the equilibrium in the Adriatic, the Triple Alliance would have ceased to exist.

Austria-Hungary refrained from action, but her threats, together with the knowledge that Germany stood behind her, induced the other Powers to acquiesce in the programme which refused to Serbia, Greece, and Montenegro the rewards of their efforts in the west. But the second Balkan War ran a different course from that expected by the Central Empires. In a month Serbia and Greece established their superiority. The result was gall to

FUTURIST ARTISTS FOR THE FRONT.
They volunteered as cyclists in the Italian Army.

A BATTERY OF ITALIAN FIELD ARTILLERY.

Austria-Hungary, and on August 9, the day before the Treaty of Bukarest was signed, she made the shameful proposal that Italy should consent to her attacking Serbia. Italy declined flatly to countenance any such action. The incident was not disclosed till December 5, 1914, when Signor Giolitti related to an astonished Chamber of Deputies the story of the Austrian suggestion and Italy's refusal.

It was now evident to Italy that the Triple Alliance stood on a very uncertain foundation, for Austria-Hungary was plainly bent upon attacking Serbia when opportunity offered. Within a year the chance was provided and the opportunity was seized.

When Austria-Hungary sent her ultimatum to Serbia, Italy took action at once. Besides warmly supporting the British proposal for a conference, and pressing upon Germany the necessity of employing every means to preserve peace, the Marquis di San Giuliano made the Italian position very clear to the two allies of Italy. On July 5 a meeting took place between Signor Salandra, the Marquis di San Giuliano and Herr von Flotow, the German Ambassador, and on the same day the Foreign Minister telegraphed the substance of the conversation to the Duke d'Avarna, the Italian Ambassador in Vienna, in these words :

Salandra and I called the special attention of the Ambassador to the fact that Austria had no right, according to the spirit of the Triple Alliance Treaty, to make such a move as she has made at Belgrade without previous agreement with her allies. Austria, in fact, from the tone in which the Note is conceived and from the demands she makes, demands which are of little effect against the pan-Serb danger, but are profoundly offensive to Serbia, and indirectly to Russia, has shown clearly that she wishes to provoke a war. We therefore told Flotow that, in consideration of Austria's method of procedure and of the defensive and conservative nature of the Triple Alliance, Italy is under no obligation to help Austria if as a result of this move of hers she should find herself at war with Russia. For in this case any European war whatever will be consequent upon an act of aggression and provocation on the part of Austria.

These were plain words, and when Austria-Hungary persisted in her action against Serbia, and proceeded to a declaration of war, the Italian Government definitely took up the position which it maintained throughout the long months of intrigue and uncertainty which followed. Notes were dispatched to Berlin and Vienna, on July 27 and 28 respectively, which raised the question of the cession of Austria's Italian provinces and declared that if Italy did not receive adequate compensation for Austria's disturbance of the Balkan equilibrium, "the Triple Alliance would be irreparably broken."

When the fire lighted on the banks of the Danube leapt east and north and west, Italy was able to hold back from the flames. She had already made her position perfectly clear to the other members of the Triple Alliance. To the world at large it was not possible to be so explicit. The Italian Government made an open declaration of neutrality on August 4 pointing out that the *casus foederis*, which would have placed her in the field with Germany and Austria-Hungary, had not arisen. No further step could well be taken, and no further announcement made, until it was known whether her allies would recognize the claim for compensation due under the terms of the alliance. The situation was complicated by the fact that the Giolitti Government had left the Army in a deplorable condition as regards munitions and equipment. Italy was in no position to take the field, or to back her legitimate demands by the force which, she knew well, was the only argument her allies would recognize. She was forced to wait and prepare.

It has been seen that very early in the crisis Italy raised the question of the Italian provinces of Austria-Hungary, and indicated that it was here she looked for compensation. From that position the Italian Government never receded. There may have been moments of uncertainty as to how far it was possible to go, and by what means it was feasible to assure the " redemption " of the Italian provinces outside the kingdom of Italy, but the aim was fixed. At a private conversation in September, 1914, Signor Salandra declared himself convinced that now was the time to solve the Irredentist problem. In all probability negotiations with Austria-Hungary would have been opened sooner than they actually were if it had not been for the illness and death (October 16) of San Giuliano. San Giuliano had in preparation a Note which was to state the Italian case in detail, and Signor Salandra has told how his sole regret, as he faced death, was that he had not seen the day of Italy's entrance into complete national unity.*

Baron Sonnino came to the Foreign Office in November, and on December 9 he addressed a Note to the Duke d'Avarna for communica-

* Speech at the Capitol, June 2, 1915.

tion to Count Berchtold, the then Austro-Hungarian Minister of Foreign Affairs. The opening sentences of the Note give the broad foundation of the Italian case :

The actual military advance of Austria-Hungary in Serbia constitutes a fact which must be an object of examination by the Italian and Austro-Hungarian Governments on the basis of the stipulations contained in Article VII. of the Triple Alliance. From this article derives the obligation of the Austro-Hungarian Government, even in the case of temporary occupations, to come to a previous agreement with Italy and to arrange for compensations. The Imperial and Royal Government ought, therefore, to have approached us and come to an agreement with us before sending its troops across the Serbian frontier.

The Note goes on to recall the Austro-Hungarian resort to the stipulations of Article VII. during the Libyan War, and points out the prime importance to Italy " of the full integrity and of the political and economic independence of Serbia." No " stable pledge " had been given that Austria-Hungary would not acquire Serbian territory, but apart from this point Article VII. provided for compensation in the event of the Balkan equilibrium being upset otherwise than by territorial acquisitions. Baron Sonnino pressed for an immediate exchange of views and for an early entrance upon definite negotiations. He pointed out that public opinion was increasingly occupied with " Italian national aspirations," and suggested that the moment was propitious for coming to an agreement which would remove long-standing causes of friction and ill-feeling.

Count Berchtold replied that the Austro-Hungarian occupation of Serbian territory was " neither permanent nor temporary, but

ITALIAN INFANTRY MARCHING THROUGH THE STREETS OF ROME.

SIGNOR TITTONI,
Italian Ambassador in Paris.

BARON VON MACCHIO,
Austrian Ambassador in Rome.

DUKE D'AVARNA,
Italian Ambassador in Vienna.

momentary." This was only the most startling of various quibbles. He refused to admit
the precedent of the Libyan War on the ground
that Italian operations against European
Turkey would have threatened the *status quo*
in the East, whereas Austro-Hungarian action
against Serbia was undertaken for purely defensive reasons, to secure the integrity of the
Monarchy. Baron Sonnino brushed aside these
arguments. He declared that Italy must
press the rights assured to her under Article
VII., and insisted upon the danger of further
delay in accepting the principle of discussion on
the basis of the Article. His insistence bore
fruit, for Count Berchtold agreed to exchange
views on the question of compensation, and
accepted the general Italian argument.

At this stage Prince Bülow appears upon
the scene. Since his dismissal from office
in 1909 the late Imperial Chancellor had lived
in Rome. As a last hope the Kaiser now put
him in charge of the German Embassy, in
place of Herr von Flotow, who took "sick
leave." His first interview with Baron
Sonnino took place upon December 19, and in
the course of conversation he said that the
object of his mission was to explain the Italian
point of view to Berlin and the German point of
view to Rome. He said that he was aware of
the Italian proposal to Vienna, and had already
expressed the opinion that the Italian contention
was justified. He believed that this would
have its effect in Vienna.

But Hungary here intervened. The mas-
terful Count Tisza obtained the dismissal
of the Austrian Foreign Secretary, Count
Berchtold, and the appointment of his own
nominee, Baron Burian. Baron Burian
adopted a much more intransigeant position,
and though a former Ambassador, Prince
Wedel, was sent from Berlin on a special
mission to Vienna, with the object of inducing
Austria-Hungary to surrender the Trentino,
all the old objections were raised by the new
Minister of Foreign Affairs. Meanwhile Prince
Bülow was trying to clear the ground at
Rome. He began by assuming that the
cession of the Trentino would satisfy Italian
claims, but Baron Sonnino at once replied
that he " did not consider that Italian popular
sentiment would be contented with the Trentino
alone ; that a stable condition of accord
between Austria and Italy could not be effected
except by the complete elimination of the
Irredentist formula 'Trent and Trieste.'"
Prince Bülow seemed to be taken aback.
He said that Austria would certainly prefer
war to the cession of Trieste (he might have
added that Germany shared Austria's preference), and gave it as his opinion that he
" could succeed with the Trentino, but not
with anything more."

Baron Burian continued to vary his line
of argument between a disinclination to
accept the Italian point of view at all and
the suggestion that Italy should be content

with compensation in Albania. Speaking on behalf of Vienna, Prince Bülow urged that Italy should formulate her demands, but Baron Sonnino declined to make any proposals until Austria-Hungary should definitely accept the basis of discussion and cease to oppose "objections of principle." The only basis of discussion which Italy would agree to was "the cession of territories actually in possession of the Monarchy." Until Austria-Hungary accepted this demand Baron Sonnino would neither define nor exclude anything—"neither the Trentino, nor Trieste, nor Istria, nor anything else." He had already explained that, in his opinion, discussion regarding territories belonging to other belligerents would compromise Italy's neutral position, as such discussion "would be equivalent to taking part in the contest." He now pressed for an early decision, pointing out that delays might render an agreement more difficult.

Baron Burian continued to fence, bringing up the question of the Italian occupation of the Dodecannesus, which had apparently been settled with Count Berchtold, in May, 1912, and on February 12 Baron Sonnino withdrew the Italian proposal for discussion, and addressed a grave warning to Austria-Hungary. He declared that any military action undertaken by Austria-Hungary in the Balkans against

[*Elliott & Fry.*

SIR RENNELL RODD,
British Ambassador in Rome.

either Serbia or Montenegro, without previous agreement with Italy, would be considered an open infringement of Article VII. of the Triple Alliance. He added that a disregard of this declaration would lead to grave consequences, for which the Italian Government henceforward declined all responsibility. Five days later he repeated the warning, and said that his previous communication had "the precise significance of a veto opposed by us on any military action by Austria-Hungary in the Balkans until the conclusion of the agreement for compensation in accordance with Article VII. It is necessary to state very clearly that any other procedure on the part of the Austro-Hungarian Government could only be interpreted by us as an open violation of the terms of the treaty, and as clear evidence of its intention to resume its liberty of action ; in which case we should have to regard ourselves as being fully justified in resuming our own liberty of action for the safeguarding of our interests."

This dispatch had a certain special importance apart from its effect upon the course of the long discussion regarding the interpretation of Article VII. Italy's veto assured for Serbia a temporary immunity from attack at a time when there was much talk of a fresh invasion with German assistance.

[*Lafayette.*

THE LATE MARQUIS DI SAN GIULIANO,
Former Italian Minister of Foreign Affairs.

SIGNOR ANTONIO SALANDRA,
President of the Council and Minister of the
Interior in Italy.

The strong position taken up by Italy spurred Germany to fresh effort at Vienna. For a considerable time Baron Burian held firmly to his contention that it was impossible to settle the question of compensation until it had become clear how Austria-Hungary's enterprise in Serbia would fare. The fact that the Treaty of Alliance provided for *previous* agreement as to compensation did not appear to trouble him at all. He argued that it would be most inconvenient for Austria to let military action wait upon diplomatic discussion, and that Baron Sonnino must surely see how awkward it was. The terms of a signed treaty meant no more to Austria-Hungary than they did to Germany. Baron Burian twisted and turned and brought up one new argument after another to show why Austria-Hungary should avoid the obligations of Article VII. Each argument was based upon the plea of expediency ; each argument attempted to show cause why a pledged word should not be kept. Baron Sonnino never swerved an inch. He met every argument by a patient but firm reiteration of Italy's rights under the treaty, and by a refusal to be led away from the text of Article VII.

On March 10 Baron Sonnino put forward three conditions which he considered essential as preliminaries to any negotiation.

First : that absolute secrecy should be preserved. " Any indiscretion regarding the existence and progress of the negotiations would force the Italian Government to withdraw their proposals and break off negotiations."

Second : that the terms of the agreement should immediately be carried into effect.

Third : that the agreement should cover the whole period of the war in so far as any possible invocation of Article VII. was concerned.

Baron Sonnino suggested further that a

DUKE OF THE ABRUZZI,
Commander-in-Chief of the Royal Italian Navy.

period of two weeks should be set aside for discussion, and that if no agreement were arrived at within that time all proposals should be withdrawn.

Difficulties were promptly raised at Vienna. Baron Burian went back to several of his previous arguments, but the chief obstacle lay in Baron Sonnino's second condition, that the cession of territory should follow immediately upon the conclusion of the agreement. Baron Burian flatly refused to accept this condition, and for a few days it looked as though negotiations would not take place at all.

Prince Bülow stepped once more into the breach, and sought to persuade Baron Sonnino that his insistence upon the immediate carrying out of any eventual agreement was not reasonable. He feared that Austria-Hungary would never accept such a condition, and hinted at " the terrible consequences of a rupture between Germany and Italy." Baron Sonnino was immovable, and replied that he would take no further initiative and make no proposals. Prince Bülow offered the guarantee of Germany. Baron Sonnino reaffirmed the essential condition, and when pressed on the point of Germany's guarantee he recorded his opinion, in an identical Note to the Italian Ambassadors in Berlin and Vienna, that at the end of the war Germany might not be in a position to carry her guarantee into effect.

It was not until March 27 that actual negotiations were begun by a rather vague offer made by Baron Burian to the Duke d'Avarna. This offer spoke of the cession of "territories in South Tyrol, including the city of Trent." Various suggestions were made regarding payments to be made by Italy as part of the

ADMIRAL VIALE,
Commander of the Italian Fleet.

Austrian public debt and as indemnification for public works, railways, etc. Baron Burian hoped that the offer might be regarded as a basis for negotiation, but Baron Sonnino's reply was disconcerting. Putting aside for the moment the question of immediate cession, he found the proposals both too vague and too meagre. They did not settle the Irredentist problem ; they did not make any appreciable improvement in Italy's military frontier ; and they did not represent adequate compensation for the freedom of action which Austria-Hungary would enjoy in the Balkans. "A

strip of territory in the Trentino " would not satisfy any of Italy's requirements.

On April 2 Baron Burian became more explicit. He said that Austria-Hungary was willing to cede the districts (*Politische Bezirke*) of Trento, Rovereto, Riva, Tione (except Madonna di Campiglio and the neighbourhood) and Borgo. The frontier line would cut the valley of the Adige just north of Lavis. Baron Burian explained that these districts were far from being only "a strip of territory," and hoped that Baron Sonnino would change his opinion about the importance of the cession offered. Four days later, no reply having been received from Rome, Baron Burian asked for counter-proposals. These were sent to the Duke d'Avarna on April 8.

Italy's demands were as follows :

I. The Trentino, with the boundaries fixed for the kingdom of Italy in 1811. (This boundary line would leave the existing frontier at Monte Cevedale (Zufallspitze) ; run along the mountain ridge between Val Venosta and the valley of the Noce down to Gargazone in the Upper Adige Valley ; thence in a straight line to Chiusa (Klausen) across the mountains and the Val Sarentina ; thence to join the existing frontier between Monte Cristallo and the Tre Cime di Lavaredo (Dreizinnen), including the Ampezza valley, but leaving out the Gadera and Badia valleys (Gaderthal and Abteithal).)

II. A new eastern frontier, to include Gradisca and Gorizia. The line to run from Trogkofel eastwards to Osteruig ; thence *via* Saifritz between the valley of the Seisera and the Schlitzato to the Wischberg ; thence along the existing frontier to the Nevea Saddle, whence

REAR-ADMIRAL ENRICO MILLO,
Italian Minister of Marine.

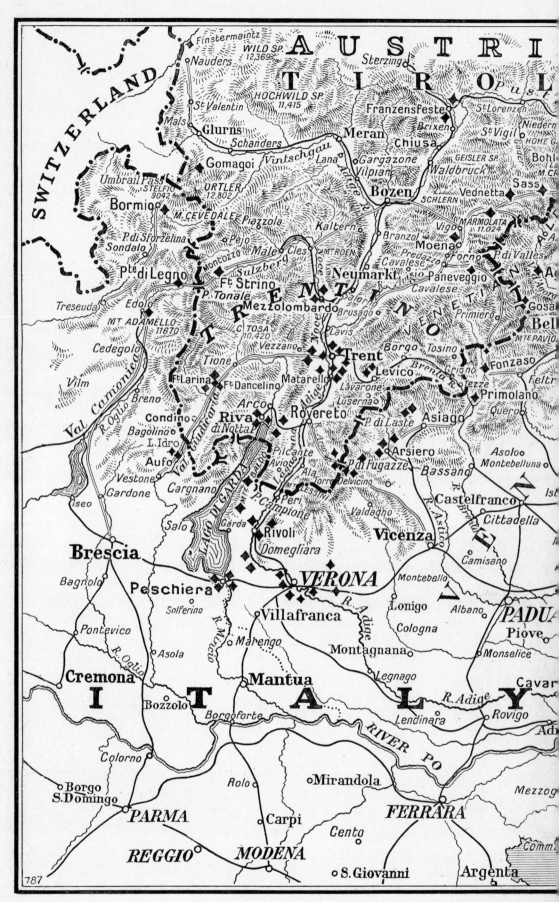

ALIAN FRONTIER.

SIGNOR GIOLITTI,
Former Italian Premier.

it would drop to the Isonzo east of Plezzo (Flitsch); thence along the Isonzo to Tolmino, whence it would run *via* Chiaporano and Comen to the sea, which it would reach near Nabresina.

III. Trieste and its neighbourhood, including Nabresina and the judicial districts of Capo d'Istria and Pirano, to be formed into an autonomous State, with complete independence from Austro-Hungarian rule. Trieste to be a free port.

IV. The cession by Austria-Hungary of the Curzolari Islands off the coast of Dalmatia.

V. The immediate occupation by Italy of the ceded territories and the immediate evacuation by Austria-Hungary of Trieste and the neighbourhood.

VI. The recognition by Austria-Hungary of Italian sovereignty over Vallona and district.

VII. The renunciation by Austria-Hungary of any claims in Albania.

VIII. A complete amnesty for all political or military prisoners belonging to the territories mentioned in I.-IV

The next three articles provided :—

1 (Art. IX.) that Italy should pay to Austria-Hungary as indemnification for loss of government property, as a share of the public debt, and against all money claims, the sum of two hundred million lire.

2 (Art. X.) that Italy should pledge herself to maintain neutrality throughout the war. This applied both to Germany and Austria-Hungary.

3 (Art. XI.) that Italy should renounce any further claims under Article VII. of the Triple Alliance, for the whole duration of the war ; and that Austria-Hungary should renounce any claim to compensation for Italy's occupation of the Dodecannesus.

At this time there were persistent rumours of a separate peace between Austria-Hungary and Russia. Baron Sonnino pressed for an early answer to his proposals and Baron

Burian's reply arrived on April 17. It was wholly unsatisfactory. Articles II., III., and IV. were entirely rejected. Article V., which provided for the immediate transference of the ceded territories, was met by the old objections. Articles VI. and VII. were practically refused. Article VIII. was accepted. As regards Article IX., Baron Burian declared that the sum offered was totally insufficient, but suggested that the question of " pecuniary indemnity " should be referred to The Hague. He claimed that the pledge of neutrality offered in Article X. should be extended to Turkey, as the Ally of Austria and Germany, and requested the insertion of an extra clause in Article XI., providing that Italy's renunciation of further claims under Article VII. of the Triple Alliance should cover all such advantages, territorial or otherwise, as Austria-Hungary might gain from the treaty of peace which should terminate the war.

On only a single cardinal point did Baron Burian offer any concession. The frontier he proposed for the Trentino followed a more reasonable course than that of his original

GENERAL VITTORIA ZUPELLI,
Italian Minister of War.

offer. Leaving the existing frontier near
Monte Cevedale it followed the watershed
between the Upper Adige and Noce valleys
as far as the Flenenspitze and reached the
Noce valley by way of the Pescara. From
there it followed the boundary of the district
of Mezzolombardo to the Adige valley, which
it crossed south of Salorno (Salurn). Thence
it followed, roughly, the watershed between the
Adige and Avisio valleys as far as the Latemar.
Descending from the Col Canon it reached
the valley of the Avisio between Moena and
Forno, and thence followed the ridge
between the San Pellegrino and Travignolo
valleys to the existing frontier at Cima di
Bocche.

Baron Sonnino's reply, sent from Rome on
April 21, pointed out that the increased concessions in the Trentino, the only advance
on Austria-Hungary's original proposals, did
not "repair the chief inconveniences of the
present situation, either from the linguistic

BARON BURIAN
(On left) Austrian Minister of Foreign Affairs.

and ethnological or the military point of view."
As Signor Salandra was to point out later,
"the doors of the house remained open."
Austria-Hungary was determined to keep the
positions that were a perpetual threat to Italy.
But the main stumbling-block lay in Baron
Burian's refusal to admit the principle of
immediate cession.

There were three more conversations between
Baron Burian and the Duke d'Avarna before
negotiations were broken off. The Duke
d'Avarna told his Government that he saw
no prospect of an accord. Baron Burian's
sole concession in regard to Article V. was
the suggestion that the immediate appointment of a mixed Boundary Commission would
be sufficient guarantee that the territorial
transfer would eventually be carried out.
On April 29 the Duke d'Avarna telegraphed
that Baron Burian practically opposed a
negative to all the Italian demands, especially to those contained in the first five
Articles.

On May 3 Baron Sonnino sent to Vienna
a formal denunciation of the Italo-Austrian
Alliance.

In Italy the disclosures of the Government
laid many doubts to rest. The provisions
of the Triple Alliance were secret. There
was no clear idea of the obligations upon

PRINCE BÜLOW
(On left) Acting German Ambassador in
Rome.

either side. The declaration of neutrality made it evident that Italy was not required to join her Allies, but between holding aloof and entering the field against them seemed a long step. Public opinion was very uncertain during the early period of the war. A number of Italians had originally been in favour of joining the Central Empires, influenced partly by the feeling that it was only fair to assist the Allies of thirty years' standing, partly by a genuine admiration for Germany which counteracted the old enmity against Austria-Hungary, and partly by the conviction that Italian interests could only be secured by intervention. This tendency was not much

ment. It must be remembered that Signor Salandra had not yet proved himself. He had held office and shown himself a capable administrator. He had been in close association with Baron Sonnino for thirty years. He had never taken part in the intrigues which had disfigured Italian politics for so long. There was no question of his ability and dexterity, and his character commanded trust. But he was largely untried and his position was very difficult. He had accepted the task of forming a Government when Signor Giolitti retired, but the followers of Signor Giolitti constituted the majority of the Chamber, and the experience of those who had taken office in similar cir-

ITALY'S NEW ARMY.
Recruits on their way to be equipped.

in evidence after the declaration of neutrality, but a strong pro-German current continued to oppose itself to the rising tide of feeling in favour of intervention on the other side. All through the winter the greatest uncertainty prevailed. At one time, early in the autumn, the popular feeling in favour of intervention on the side of the Entente Powers rose very high, and threatened to embarrass the Government. It is not unjust to the memory of San Giuliano to say that his death, and the arrival of Baron Sonnino at the *Consulta*, had something to do with stemming this tide. His Austrophil record was known to all; it was not yet known that he had taken up a firm stand on behalf of Italy's full rights. With Baron Sonnino in charge of the Foreign Office the country had fuller confidence in the Govern-

cumstances on other occasions was not encouraging. Part of his Cabinet was "Giolittian," and the situation called for unusual skill and strength of purpose. Though the country had confidence in Signor Salandra, there was still the feeling that he was untried, and that the circumstances might conceivably be too much for him. The arrival of Baron Sonnino greatly strengthened Signor Salandra's position. He had now at his right hand the close friend and political ally of thirty years. More than that, he had now as Foreign Secretary the man whom all Italy recognized as an example of unswerving rectitude and commanding ability. Baron Sonnino's intellectual endowments had been fully proved, his character not less so. Bluntly straightforward, uncompromising to a fault, he had failed as a parliamentarian. But his very failures had shown him to his countrymen, and to all who knew him, as a man to be trusted. Now was no day for mere parliamentarians; the hour for statesmen had struck. At last Baron Sonnino was to come to his own, and Signor Salandra was to show that all the hopes which had been formed of him were less than the reality.

Before Parliament rose in December, 1914, Signor Salandra pronounced a phrase that deserves to be remembered. There was a certain uneasiness in the country at the prospect of great issues being decided and great changes effected without any profit to Italy, and a senator made the suggestion that Italy should have asked a price for her neutrality. Signor Salandra's reply was striking: "If we had bartered our neutrality, we should also have dishonoured it" (*Se la neutralità noi l'avessimo negoziata, l'avremmo anche disonorata*).

But for many months the position of Italy was liable to misinterpretation. The necessity of preserving secrecy regarding the line of action taken by the Government made this inevitable. The necessity of secrecy bore hard upon the people, and it is a tribute both to Government and governed that the long months of anxiety passed in such relative quiet. Two strong currents of opinion were noticeable. There were those who maintained that the interests of Italy and of civilization alike demanded intervention against Austria and Germany. These grew steadily in number. There were others, a numerous and powerful body, who were very strongly against war. There were many who were oppressed by the thought of Germany's immense military strength,

BARON SONNINO,
Italian Foreign Minister.

and held that Italy ought at all costs to refrain from opposing the Colossus. There were others who argued that Italy was unable to stand the strain of modern war "on the grand scale," that even victory would be too dearly bought. They spoke of the cost at which Italy had maintained her hard-won place among the Great Powers. They said that for more than forty years she had been attempting a stride that was almost beyond her compass, and that the vast efforts intervention demanded would break her down. Some of them went so far as to contend that it was better for Italy to content herself with first position among the lesser nations than to struggle to preserve her place as a Great Power. They talked of revolution and ruin. They feared the temper of the people and did not guess its greatness.

ITALIAN INFANTRY ON THE MARCH.

SIGNOR MARCONI,
The inventor of wireless telegraphy, serving
as Lieutenant in the Italian Army.

Between the interventionists and the neutralists there stood the great mass of Italian
opinion, which had not been able to make up
its mind on the question of peace or war,
and was content to leave the matter in the
hands of the men whom it trusted. It was
widely felt that public opinion did not possess
the material to form a reasoned judgment
on the very difficult problem with which Italy
was faced. There was much discussion in the
Press, and the argument of the interventionists
that Italy's place in Europe depended upon
her taking sides with the Entente Powers, that
neutrality meant isolation, slowly gained ground.
The neutralists were encouraged in their efforts
by a letter from Signor Giolitti to one of his
chief henchmen, Signor Peano, a letter which
was to become historic. In this letter, which
was written on February 2, Signor Giolitti
expressed himself as being unfavourable to
intervention, and declared his belief that
Italy might secure " a good deal " (*parecchio*)
by diplomatic means.

As the spring wore on opinion hardened,
and a new feeling arose—a feeling against
Germany. The terrible story of Belgium
came slowly home to Italians ; very slowly,
for Italians had good reason to be sceptical

regarding atrocity stories. For long the
reports of German "frightfulness," in so far
as they applied to savagery, and not merely
to destructiveness, were simply disbelieved.
But in the end the evidence proved too strong
for most Italians. The eloquent words of the
Belgian Socialist Deputy, M. Jules Destrée,
who told the story of his country's martyrdom
in all the chief towns of Italy from Piedmont to
Sicily, did much to make the truth sink into
the minds of the people. And German propaganda helped to blacken the German name.
For, as the prospect of war seemed to increase,
German agents went about threatening that
German soldiers would work a greater horror
upon Italy than Belgium ever saw. They
gave the items of their programme : destruction, murder, rape. They thought to terrorize
Italians ; they only made them set their teeth.

All through April the tension was great.
Parliament had risen on March 22, and a vote
of confidence in the Government had twice
been recorded, only the Official Socialists
recording their dissent from the motions
which carried with them the request for the
vote. On March 28 the rumour ran through
Rome that an agreement between Italy and
Austria-Hungary was practically concluded,
and that only a few finishing touches were
required before agreement would be complete.
This rumour was circulated from the Embassies
of Austria and Germany, and it is interesting
to note that it was put about just at the
moment when Baron Burian made his first
offer of concessions in the Trentino. The
incident shows how much the Austrian pledge
of secrecy was worth. The rumour fell flat,
and within a fortnight the expressions of
confident hope were replaced by ill-concealed
uneasiness. Once again the leak was from the
Austrian side. Baron Sonnino telegraphed
his counter-proposals on April 8. They were
presented to Baron Burian on April 10, and two
days later they were the subject of comment
in Rome, in certain circles at least. Austrians
and Germans expressed resentment at what
they considered the excessive nature of the
demands and showed the greatest anxiety.
The neutralists fought hard, though there were
some signs of weakening. An attempt was
made to emphasize the existence of " a Slav
Peril," an attempt which was greatly aided
by some articles in the Russian Press which
pushed Slav claims in the Adriatic very far
north. The *Novoe Vremya* went so far as to

say that "if Russia permitted Italy to have Trieste it would be a scandal. Trieste is absolutely Slav." But it was too late to talk of a Slav peril. Italy was waking to a knowledge of the German peril, a knowledge which her wisest statesmen already possessed.

By the end of April the Italian people was braced for war. During the first days of May hearts were stirred by the preparations for the unveiling of a monument to Garibaldi and The Thousand, on the rock of Quarto, whence the expedition had started. The King and the Premier were to be present, and Signor Gabriele D'Annunzio was to deliver an oration. Moreover, there was a general feeling that before May 5, the date of the ceremony, the fate of the negotiations with Austria-Hungary would be decided. So it turned out, though at the time it was not known that negotiations had been broken off. On May 3, the day that Baron Sonnino instructed the Duke d'Avarna to denounce the alliance with Austria-Hungary, the news was published that the King and his Ministers would not leave Rome " in view of the political situation." It is a matter of history now that the Alliance had ceased to exist, and that Italy had already, to all intent, thrown in her lot with Great Britain, France, and Russia ; but at the time no explanation was given of the sudden crisis that kept the King from going to Quarto.

On May 8 the news came that the Lusitania had been sunk. The effect upon the populace was quite extraordinary. For the first time a note of real anger was heard in the streets and the shops, along the by-ways and in little taverns. The tragedy of Belgium had been told to the people, and its horror had begun to sink in. But all Belgium was enveloped in the fog of war, and there was still a feeling that the worst stories might be exaggerations, that German ruthlessness might have had some provocation, and that in many cases there was the excuse of the anger born of battle and danger. Here was a crime committed in the sight of all the world, upon the peaceful seas, against a helpless multitude in which were included many women and children. The feeling against Germany, which had been slowly growing, came out in a blaze.

Then followed quickly the unforgettable days of what d'Annunzio called " The Week of Passion." As it appears from the Austrian

Red Book, Baron Sonnino's denunciation of the alliance caused a rapid change in the attitude of Baron de Burian. Prince Bülow and the Austrian Ambassador, Baron von Macchio, were given full authority to conclude a new treaty on the basis of further concessions. Baron Sonnino was immovable, and Prince Bülow and Baron von Macchio decided on a last desperate throw. Baron von Macchio has explained exactly what was done. His words are enshrined in

GARIBALDI THE LIBERATOR.

the Austrian Red Book. He telegraphed to Vienna on May 10, accusing Baron Sonnino of having kept back information regarding the Austrian concessions, both from the King and the majority of the Cabinet. He explained that on these grounds " it seemed opportune to make known a list of the Austro-Hungarian concessions, authenticated by Prince Bülow and myself. By this means there was a chance of countermining the game of Salandra, Sonnino and Martini."

A list of the Austrian concessions was printed and circulated among people who were thought likely to be influenced against

GABRIELE D'ANNUNZIO
(In the car and on left of inset), the Italian Poet,
in the uniform of cavalry lieutenant.

Prince Bülow. On passing through Turin, the stronghold of neutralism, he was hissed On arriving in Rome he was the object of a very hostile demonstration. It was suspected by this time that Prince Bülow and Baron von Macchio had gone behind the backs of the Government and had appealed to the party of the man who had for so long been almost dictator in Italy. There were four days of rumour and tension. Some of Signor Giolitti's chief supporters said that he would do nothing to embarrass the Government, but others took a very different line. They hailed him as the coming saviour from a ruinous war. The supporters of Signor Giolitti were in a majority both in the Chamber of Deputies and in the Senate, and it was clear that if he chose he could overthrow the Government. Parliament was to meet on May 20, and it was altogether uncertain how the Salandra Ministry would fare. The excitement and anxiety were already intense when late in the evening of May 13 the announcement was made that Signor Salandra had resigned.

The news was the signal for a great burst of anger throughout the whole of Italy. Rome is not easily stirred, but Rome, already moved by the eloquence of D'Annunzio, who arrived the evening before Signor Salandra's resignation, became a burning protest. It was only

the Government. The German Catholic deputy, Herr Erzberger, was assiduous in spreading the new offers, but there were various channels of distribution. Signor Salandra has stated definitely that the concessions were made known to various "politicians and journalists " before they reached the hands of himself or the Foreign Minister. Unfortunately there were Italians who were ready to lend themselves to the German-Austrian game. Signor Giolitti had been at his country home in Piedmont all through the parliamentary vacation, but he arrived in Rome on May 9, summoned, it is said, by Prince Bülow, but more probably by an urgent call from his party henchmen, at the instance of for a day that the situation seemed really uncertain. The King summoned various politicians to his residence, and it was reported that Signor Marcora, the venerable President of the Chamber, was asked to form a Cabinet. On May 14 it was announced by the *Corriere della Sera* that the Triple Alliance had been denounced early in May, and the report spread that about the same time Italy had entered into engagements with the Triple Entente. It was clear that the die had been cast, and that Signor Salandra's foreign policy was bound to be continued, whatever the fate of himself and his Cabinet. But it was not this fact that roused the whole country to demand the recall

take part, either in the mile-long procession that marched from the Piazza del Popolo to the Quirinal, or in the vast crowds that lined the whole route.

Signor Giolitti had not been able to stir from his house during the three days of crisis, and on Monday, May 17, he left Rome. He could not face Parliament. It is said that he was ready to do so, but that the police authorities declined to guarantee his safety. What *rôle* Signor Giolitti had played or intended to play is not quite clear. It is maintained on the one hand that he meant to accept the Austrian offers and preserve Italian neutrality. On the other hand it is suggested that his aim,

GARIBALDIAN MARINE VOLUNTEERS
Marching to their quarters.

Inset : Peppina, Ezio and Ricciotti Garibaldi
about to start for the Front.

of Signor Salandra. It was the knowledge that the representatives of foreign Powers had dared to go behind the Government of Italy and treat with others, and that there were Italians who had lent themselves to such an intrigue. The demonstrations were extraordinary. Italy was aflame from north to south. By Saturday, May 15, it was evident that no Government could exist except that of Signor Salandra. When the announcement was made on the following afternoon that the King had declined to accept Signor Salandra's resignation, there was a great outburst of joy and triumph. In Rome an immense gathering which had been called to protest against the Bülow-Giolitti intrigues and demand the recall of Signor Salandra was turned into a demonstration of rejoicing. All Rome seemed to

and those of his adherents, was simply power and place ; that he would have assumed the reins of government only to find, after further negotiation, that war was inevitable, and then bow to the demands of that "historical necessity" which he had invoked as a reason for the Libyan expedition. Nor is it clear how far Signor Giolitti was responsible for the intrigues that ended so disastrously for himself and his followers. There is some reason to think that

SIGNOR MARCORA,
President of the Italian Chamber.

he was only brought in as the name to conjure with, that the conspiracy against the Government was not his doing so much as that of a small group near the throne of the ex-Dictator. Signor Giolitti's remarkable position in Italian politics had been won, to a very considerable extent, by his faculty of yielding to the desires of his supporters. The so-called Dictator had preserved his dictatorship by keeping an ear ever open to suggestion from those upon whom he relied. Perhaps it is true that on this fatal occasion he was manœuvred into a position which his own judgment would have refused.

On May 18 Herr von Bethmann-Hollweg disclosed to the Reichstag the offers which Austria-Hungary had finally made. These differed materially from the list of concessions circulated by Herr Erzberger and others, but they attracted little notice in Italy, which thought no more of concessions. The Giolittian party had crumpled. When Parliament met on May 20 Signor Salandra secured overwhelming majorities (367 to 54 and 407 to 74) on a Bill conferring extraordinary powers upon the Government in the event of war. General mobilization was ordered on May 22. On May 23 the Duke d'Avarna delivered the formal declaration of war against Austria-Hungary.

No one who lived through the days of crisis, when for a moment at least it seemed as though the intrigues of the foreigner might succeed, will ever forget the marvellous uprising of the Italian people. Never in history has a nation so strikingly proclaimed its will. Gabriele D'Annunzio spoke for the soul of Italy in the burning words with which he addressed a great crowd on the night of his arrival in Rome. " Could he, Garibaldi the Liberator, descend from the Faniculum, would he not brand as cowards and traitors, would he not set the seal of infamy, on all those who to-day in secret or openly work to disarm our Italy, to debauch the country, to thrust her again into servitude ? . . . Can we allow aliens, those in our midst and those without, enemies of our own race or intruders, to impose this kind of death on the nation ? " The spirit of the Garibaldian hymn awoke again throughout all Italy. " *Va fuori d'Italia, va fuori stranier.*"

IN THE COURTYARD OF THE STATION AT MILAN.
Workmen engaged in linking up the City tramway with the railway lines in order that trains
conveying the wounded may go direct to the hospitals.

CHAPTER LXXXI.

THE ITALIAN ARMY AND ITS TASK.

The Austro-Italian Frontier—Main Factors of the Strategical Problem—The Trentino, Cadore and Carnia Fronts—Italian Preparations, 1914–1915—Italian Military System and Conscription—The Permanent Army and its Distribution—The Artillery—Uniform —Italy's Record in Recent Wars—Bersaglieri and Alpini—Spirit of the Army.

ONE glance at a map shows the great inferiority of Italy's strategical position in relation to Austria-Hungary. The Trentino runs down like a wedge into Italian territory, a wedge that holds a wide gate open to attack. From the Lombardo-Venetian plain Italy looks up to Italian mountains that are held by another Power. An Austrian fortress frowns upon her richest provinces, and its outermost bastion, Monte Baldo, is plainly visible from Verona itself. Along the whole frontier, except for the short stretch in Friuli between Cividale and the sea, Italy has to fight uphill.

The eastern border from Pontebba to the Adriatic is the only sector of the front where an Italian offensive on a large scale is in any way feasible, but such an offensive is impossible unless the open gates on the north are closed. The detachment of large forces is necessary to secure the base of operations and the left of the attacking army. The Trentino presents the most serious problem, but the mountain valleys that converge from the Carnic Alps upon the valley of the Tagliamento give good opportunity for a flank attack, and this route is supposed to have been a main feature of the offensive planned against Italy some years before the war by General Conrad von Hötzendorf. In Cadore, between the Trentino and Carnia, the masses of the Dolomites are a protection to Italy as well as to Austria, and

no important offensive is possible for either side. Except for this limited tract, Austria holds the advantage all along the line, for even if the Italian base and flank be secured, the country to the east is very unfavourable to an Italian offensive. The plain of the Veneto continues eastwards through Frinti nearly as far as the lower Isonzo. But the upper and middle reaches of the Isonzo flow through mountainous and difficult country, and all along the left bank of the river the advantage is with the defending armies. North of Tolmino there are few gaps in the barrier of the Italian Alps, and nearer the sea the rough and broken plateau of the Carso presents great difficulties to an attacking force. In a general order issued to the Austro-Hungarian troops on the Isonzo line they were told that they were in the position of men in a six-story building whom the enemy had to attack from the level. Securely posted on their heights, they were to " decimate and destroy" the advancing Italians.

Reduced to its simplest terms Italy's strategical plan, imposed upon her by geographical conditions, must be to hold on the north, and push towards the east. This does not in any sense imply a passive defensive on the Trentino, Cadore and Carnia fronts. In each case a tempting objective presented itself for a limited offensive, though in the Trentino and Cadore the aim of such movement would primarily

31

be to strengthen the defensive position. In the Trentino particularly a quick though limited offensive would make all the difference to the Italian position. Although the Trentino threatens Italy, it is itself threatened from Italian soil. It has the weaknesses of a salient as well as its advantages. The Italians could do more than merely close the gates. They could make it dangerous for an enemy to come too near the gateway. It seemed unlikely that any offensive on a large scale would be undertaken against the Trentino, though the temptation to occupy the " unredeemed " lands must be very strong. The conquest of the Trentino would lead no further, for Northern Tyrol must be regarded as inexpugnable. But the Austrian position in the Trentino might quite well be rendered untenable by steady pressure on both sides of the salient, in the valleys that branch out from the Adige—the valleys that were to have been the routes for an Austrian offensive. The whole situation was changed by the fact that Austria-Hungary could not dispose of enough troops to receive full benefit from the overwhelming natural advantages of the ground. The forts that were to cover an Austrian advance could only be used to check the Italians. From Cadore also the Italians could threaten, indirectly, the Austrians in the Trentino. The Trentino depends upon the two railway lines that meet at Franzensfeste. The northern line from Innsbruck is safe from direct interference, but the Pusterthal line passes close to the Italian frontier, and a successful Italian offensive here would not only close one entrance, or exit, of the Trentino, but would threaten the other line from the east. From Carnia, again, or rather from the passes which cross the Carnic Alps to the Gailthal, though the main object of the troops must be to defend the valleys that run down to the Tagliamento, the Italians looked towards Hermagor and the strategic railway which connects it with Villach. The railway was built for an Austrian offensive. Now it could hardly serve this purpose, but the Gailthal was all-important to the defence of the Malborghetto - Tarvis - Villach line. Movements in the Alpine regions is difficult in the extreme, and operations on a large scale could not be expected. Communications were difficult for the Italians and easy for the Austrians, who could bring troops readily from the neighbouring valley of the Upper Drave, as well as by the Hermagor line, but the region was so important, and the number of Austrian troops available was relatively so small, that the Carnia front must give grave cause for anxiety to the Austrian General Staff.

It was clear that the Italian armies had a difficult task before them. The advantages that naturally lay with the Austrians were to a great extent nullified by the fact that Austria was short of troops. The position was changed to this extent that the Austrian General Staff was in no position to take the offensive. But the defensive lines upon which they must rely were very strong. The enormous difficulties that face the attack in modern warfare had been amply proved in Flanders and elsewhere, and these difficulties were of necessity greatly increased when the natural lie of the ground favoured the defending forces. The Austrians had had many months to prepare the lines they had chosen, and they had made good use of their time. Their trenches were constructed of metal and concrete. Their elaborate systems of wire entanglements were connected with electric power stations, and there was the further complication of mines. All along the eastern front there were rails on which to move their heavy guns, and the nature of the ground made it easy to conceal their artillery positions.

Italy had a hard task before her, but Italy had had time to prepare, and opportunity to learn from the lessons of the war. During the nine months that elapsed between the outbreak of war and the denunciation of the alliance with Austria, General Cadorna had practically re-made the Italian Army. It was necessary. In August, 1914, Italy had men and rifles and good field-guns, but she did not possess a modern army. There was a shortage in every kind of munitions, stores and equipment. The late Government had neglected to make good the expenditure in *matériel* caused by the Libyan War, and a great quantity of equipment had gone rotten in store. General Porro, at the outbreak of war sub-chief of the General Staff, had been offered the portfolio of War Minister in the spring, but he made his acceptance conditional upon the adoption of a programme of re-equipment which demanded large sums of money. This was refused, and the European War found Italy unprepared to an alarming degree. The situation was complicated by the fact that the field artillery was being re-armed with the Deport gun, a process which had little more than begun in August. There were a certain number of good medium-calibre guns, but there was no modern heavy artillery ready

GENERAL RUELLE

GENERAL GARIONI.

GENERAL MAMBRETTI.

GENERAL DI
ROBILANT.

GENERAL DRUETTI.

GENERAL ZOPPI.

GENERAL LEQUIO.

GENERAL BRICCOLA.   GENERAL CAMERANA.   GENERAL FRUGONI.

ITALIAN ARMY CORPS COMMANDERS.

to take the field. And Italy had a lower proportion of machine-guns than any of the Great Powers. All these deficiencies had been realized and pointed out. To make them good cost too much money.

Between August, 1914, and Italy's intervention all the gaps had been filled, and every additional weapon or item of equipment that experience had shown to be necessary had been supplied. In addition, there were a great number of new formations—the strength of the first line must have been increased by nearly 50 per cent. Details of the remarkable work that had been done cannot be given here. Only a few items of the completed programme could be made known, and it was laid down by the Italian Government that no further details were to be published. In what follows, therefore, we confine ourselves in the main to the information about the Italian Army that was available before the war, noting certain alterations and additions that had become public property.

Every Italian citizen fit to bear arms was liable to military service. Liability began in the year in which the recruits completed their twentieth year, when the levy of each class was held, but service began on the first of January of the following year. In the event of an emergency recruits could be called earlier, and a case in point occurred towards the end of 1914, when the 1895 class (of recruits born in that year) was called to the colours more than a year before its time. Volunteers were accepted who had completed their eighteenth, or exceptionally, their seventeenth year.

The annual contingent was divided into three categories. The first category consisted of the number of men required each year to fill the peace establishment of the Army. The second category consisted of those over and above this number who could claim no exemption from service. The third category consisted of those who were exempt by law from military service, such as only sons of widows. Various family reasons still allowed exemption, but the law had been narrowed of late years, and if the levy of 1911 were compared with that of 1900, it would be seen that the third category of the later year numbered only a little over 26 per cent. of that in the earlier levy.

The terms of service in the three categories were as follows :

First Category.—Two years with the colours ; six with the reserve ; four in the Mobile Militia ; seven in the Territorial Militia.

Second Category.—A period of training not to exceed six months with the colours ; seven and a half years or more with the reserve ; the rest as above.

Third Category.—Nineteen years in the Territorial Militia. Third category men as a rule receive no training, but are inscribed as belonging to the Territorial Militia, and are liable to service if required.

Men with a certain educational qualification were permitted to serve in the first category as "one-year volunteers," on payment of £64 in the cavalry and £48 in the other arms.

The 1911 census gave the population of Italy as 34,686,683 persons, and the levy lists for the year gave a total "class" of 487,570. Of these only 433,670 came up for medical inspection. A number were struck out for various reasons, and the others failed to present themselves, most of them, probably, having emigrated. Those who were examined were assigned as follows :

Put back to the next levy	118,073
Unfit for service (*riformati*)	98,138
First category	158,927
Second category	35,102
Third category	23,430
	433,670

The actual number of men joining the colours was considerably less than that assigned. A good number failed to present themselves, others were already in the Army or the Customs Guards, others obtained leave to put off their service. In all 122,852 men were actually posted to one or another branch of the Service.

Officers of the first line were recruited from the Military School at Modena (for infantry and cavalry), the Military Academy at Turin (for artillery and engineers), and from complement officers (*ufficiali di complemento*). Twenty-five per cent. of the commissions vacant each year were reserved for under-officers (sergeants and upwards) who had had at least four years' service, and had completed a prescribed course at the Military School.

Complement (or reserve) officers were recruited from under-officers, qualified one-year volunteers, and officers of the active army who had retired before the age of 40. Classes of instruction were formed for under-officers and one-year volunteers who wished to qualify for commissions.

Auxiliary officers were those who were unfit for active service, but were considered able to undertake certain special duties.

The permanent army of Italy was organized in 12 army corps, 25 divisions and 3 cavalry

TYPE OF ITALIAN ALPINE REGIMENT WITH FULL SERVICE KIT.

divisions, with a peace strength of some 14,000 officers and 250,000 men. The details were as follows:

12 legions of Carabinieri or Military Police ;

2 regiments of Grenadiers (24 companies and 2 depôts) ;

94 regiments of the line (1,225 companies, 94 depôts, and 85 " nuclei " of Mobile Militia) ;

12 regiments Bersaglieri (153 companies and 12 depôts) ;

8 regiments Alpini (78 companies, 8 depôts, and 25 " nuclei " of Mobile Militia) ;

88 recruiting districts (6 of them double) ;

29 regiments of cavalry (150 squadrons and 29 depôts) ;

36 regiments of field artillery (289 batteries, 36 companies of train and 36 depôts) ;

2 regiments of heavy field artillery (20 batteries, 2 depôts) ;

1 regiment of horse artillery (8 batteries, 4 train companies and 1 depôt) ;

3 regiments of mountain artillery (39 batteries and 3 depôts) ;

10 regiments of fortress artillery (110 companies and 10 depôts) ;

6 regiments of engineers (75 companies and 6 depôts) ;

10 companies of train troops ;

2 aviation " commands " (1 airship battalion, 1 aeroplane battalion, an unknown number of air squadrons, and an aviation school!) ;

12 companies medical corps ;

12 companies commissariat ;

Various special services.

The army corps and divisions had their headquarters as follows :

1st Army Corps, Turin.—1st Div., Turin ; 2nd, Novara.

2nd Army Corps, Alessandria.—3rd Div., Alessandria ; 4th, Coni.

3rd Army Corps, Milan.—5th Div., Milan ; 6th, Brescia.

4th Army Corps. Genoa.—7th Div., Piacenza ; 8th, Genoa.

5th Army Corps, Verona.—9th Div., Verona ; 10th, Padua.

6th Army Corps, Bologna.—11th Div., Bologna ; 12th, Ravenna.

7th Army Corps, Ancona.—13th Div., Ancona ; 14th, Chieti.

8th Army Corps, Florence.—15th Div., Florence ; 16th, Leghorn.

9th Army Corps, Rome.—17th Div., Rome ; 18th, Perugia.

10th Army Corps, Naples.—19th Div., Naples ; 20th, Salerno.

11th Army Corps, Bari.—21st Div., Bari ; 22nd, Catanzaro.

12th Army Corps, Palermo.—23rd Div., Palermo ; 24th, Messina.

The 25th Division, stationed at Cagliari, Sardinia formerly attached to the Rome Army Corps, had been attached to the 12th (Palermo) corps.

The army corps consisted of :

2 divisions of infantry (division = 2 brigades of 2 regiments, 6 battalions) ;

THE CHARGE OF THE FAMOUS BERSAGLIERI TROOPS.

36

1 regiment of Bersaglieri (3 battalions and a cyclist battalion);

1 regiment of cavalry;

1 section of carabinieri;

36 field guns (1 regiment of 8 batteries);

2 to 3 heavy howitzer batteries.

with ammunition column, telegraph and engineer parks, ambulance section, supply section, supply column, reserve supply park, reserve store, section of army cattle park, section of field bakery.

The division consisted of 12 battalions of infantry, 24 to 36 field guns, pontoon section, engineer company, divisional ammunition column, ambulance and supply sections, reserve store, section of carabinieri.

Comparing these figures with the totals given earlier, it will be seen that there was a considerable surplus of first line troops outside the corps organization. In 1912, in order to garrison Libya without weakening the permanent army at home, 24 line regiments were given a fourth battalion and 3 Bersaglieri regiments a fifth. There were in addition the Alpine troops and the mountain artillery, which were not within the organization of the 12 permanent army corps.

The Alpini consisted of 8 regiments in first line (26 battalions, 78 companies). Each Alpine battalion had a "nucleus" of Mobile Militia attached to serve as a centre of formation on mobilization. There were three regiments of mountain artillery, each containing four "groups" of three batteries. A thirteenth group of mountain artillery was attached to the Messina division, in lieu of a similar unit of field artillery.

Behind the formations of the active army and their reserves came the organized Mobile Militia, consisting of about 320,000 men. These were made up of four classes of 1st and 2nd category men—from 29 to 32 years of age. The Mobile Militia formations were as follows :

51 regiments of the line, of 3 battalions each. Three of these were detailed for service in Sardinia. The other 48 were attached to the 48 brigades of the first line army.

20 battalions of Bersaglieri, and

38 companies of Alpini.

    These were attached to the Bersaglieri and Alpini depôts.

31 squadrons of cavalry. These were not properly Mobile Militia, but were used to make new formations in time of war.

63 batteries of field artillery.

15 mountain batteries.

78 companies of coast and fortress artillery.

24 companies of artillery train.

    These were attached to the artillery regimental depôts.

54 companies of engineers and 4 companies of train, who were similarly attached to their depôts.

Commanding officers and squadron and company commanders were supplied from regimental officers on the active list. The rest came from reserve officers or officers on the auxiliary list.

The Alpini were used to swell the battalions or regiments of the first line. The rest of the Mobile Militia was organized for war in brigades or divisions. Certain army corps took in a division of Mobile Militia on mobilization. The brigades were attached to first line divisions in other cases.

Behind the Mobile Militia came the Territorial Militia, consisting of seven classes each of

AN ITALIAN SOLDIER

Wearing a respirator as a protection against poisonous gas.

1st and 2nd category men, and all the 19 classes of the 3rd category. The organization for war was as follows :

324 battalions of infantry of the line.

26 battalions of Alpini.

100 companies of fortress artillery.

30 companies of engineers.

The Territorial Militia was primarily designed for garrison duty, guarding railways, bridges, etc., but it was liable for any service. It was embodied in time of war, and new formations were made for training purposes. There was a certain proportion of active officers, but the greater number were reserve officers or new appointments.

ON THE WAY TO THE FRONT.
An Italian Artillery column takes a brief rest by the roadside.

Another military force was the Customs Guards. These consisted of some 400 officers and 17,000 men. They were employed with effect in the Libyan campaign, and four regiments of three battalions each had been organized for the present war. A large proportion of them were accustomed to work on the mountain frontiers, and they were expected to be very useful.

The normal war strength of Italian infantry units, with the exception of the Bersaglieri and Alpini, was as follows :

			Officers.	N.C.O.'s & Men.
Company	...	...	5	... 250
Battalion		...	24	... 1,019
Regiment	...	...	78	... 3,116

The organization of the Alpine regiments was rather different. Some battalions had three companies and some four, while the regiments had either three or four battalions. On mobilization each battalion was reinforced by one or more companies of Mobile Militia. On a war footing the company, the only constant unit, had 6 officers and 250 men. The battalion staff consisted of 2 officers and 10 men, and the regimental staff of 3 officers and 12 men.

The Bersaglieri numbers were practically the same as those of a line regiment, but a Ber-

saglieri regiment consisted of four 3-company battalions (one cyclist) instead of three 4-company battalions.

In war time each infantry regiment had 103 pioneers. They carried 48 spades, 18 saws, 12 sets of gimlets, 24 picks, 24 axes, 36 choppers, 6 mètre measures, rope, etc. An entrenching tool was also carried by the soldiers.

The Italian cavalry regiment used to have six squadrons, but when the number of regiments was increased the strength was reduced to five squadrons. In 1912 a sixth squadron was added to five regiments in order to provide for the Libyan garrison.

The war strength of a squadron was 5 officers and 137 men. In each regiment there were 55 pioneers, who carried saws, axes, choppers, pickaxes, spades, mètre measures, etc., while the regimental transport carried explosives and special instruments for the destruction of railways, etc.

The service weapon of the Italian infantry was a magazine rifle on the Männlicher system (Männlicher-Carcano), known as the 1891 pattern. It is of very small calibre—·253 in. ; the magazine holds six rounds and is loaded with a clip. The length without bayonet is

4 ft. 2¾ in., with bayonet 5 ft. 2½ in. It weighs without bayonet 8 lbs. 6 ozs. The muzzle velocity is 2,296 f.s., and it is sighted up to 2,200 yards. The cavalry carbine, which is also used by cyclists, is similar in construction, taking the same cartridge, but it is just under 3 ft. in length without bayonet and weighs a little under 7 lbs. The length with bayonet fixed is 4 ft. 2 in. It is sighted to 1,640 yards.

Active army and Mobile Militia were both armed with the 1891 pattern rifle, but the Territorial Militia, for the most part at least, had the old Vetterli-Vitali pattern, 1870–1887, which carries four rounds in a fixed magazine. This rifle has a calibre of ·407 in., and is sighted to 2,000 yards. It weighs 9½ lbs. The sword-bayonet is over 2 ft. in length.

It is difficult at present to write with any sort of accuracy about the Italian artillery. The outbreak of the Great War found a process of re-armament going on, but this process had come on the top of a previous process that had never been completed. Thirteen or fourteen years earlier it was decided to replace the old 7 cm. field-gun by an improved Krupp Q.F. 75 mm. gun, but 1914 saw this re-arma-

ment unfinished (there were only about 100 batteries armed with the quick-firer), and a new re-armament begun. The 75 mm. Deport gun, 1911 pattern, had been adopted. It is impossible to say how many batteries of this gun had been completed, but it was a very large number, and the artillery had been accustoming themselves to its use for many months.

The same may be said of heavy artillery, which the experience of the war had shown to

THE ITALIAN ARTILLERY.
A commander giving orders to his men by hand-signals. Inset: a heavy gun.

be so important. When the war broke out Italy had no adequate siege train (*parco d'assedio*). Her heaviest mobile weapons were 210 mm. howitzers (8·2 in.), and 149 mm. guns. All that can be said here is that the deficiencies were fully repaired, and that Italy was not likely to suffer from lack of medium or large calibre guns.

A word should be said about the mountain artillery, of which there were 39 batteries. The gun was an efficient weapon, but the men and the mules were remarkable. An Italian mountain battery could go anywhere.

All information regarding the latest types of aeroplane and dirigible being used or constructed for military purposes had been suppressed by the authorities. Airships (type P, gas capacity 4,500 m.c., speed 50 km. an hour) had been used by the Italian Army for a number of years. This type did good service in Tripoli. A larger model of similar design (type M, gas capacity 12,000 m.c., motors 400 h.p., speed over 70 km. an hour) had been employed with success in time of peace. The aeroplane service had already been well tested. Italy was the first country to use aeroplanes in war, and the experience gained in Tripoli gave a great impulse to military aviation. Unfortunately, lack of money prevented many of the developments that were studied and put forward by experts, but the winter of 1914 saw a great increase in the Italian Flying Corps. And Italians are notably quick and skilful at flying.

The uniform of the whole army was of a serviceable grey colour. The headgear formed the readiest means of distinction. Infantry of the line, artillery and engineers wore a soft *kepi*. The shiny black hat of the Bersaglieri, with its drooping cocks' feathers, is well known, but in war time the hat is covered with grey cloth. The Alpini wore a grey felt hat with a high crown, a small brim turned up at the back and down at the front, and a black eagle's feather at the side. The Customs Guards wore a similar hat. Of the cavalry, the first four regiments wore a helmet, the others a busby. In war time both helmet and busby were covered with grey cloth.

Not very much was known in England of the Italian Army. The picturesque figure of the Bersaglieri was familiar, and the illustrated papers soon made known the appearance of the Alpini. Italian cavalry officers had done great things at Olympia, and some people knew that the Italian cavalryman is very good across country. But the Army as a whole had been handicapped in people's estimation by the fatal memory of Adowa, where the Italian forces met with real disaster, and by the slowness of the Tripoli campaign, where the soldiers, for political reasons, were not allowed to do what they were able and anxious to do.

The Bersaglieri were known for their cocks' feathers. Their wonderful marching capacity was less familiar even to military men. They were all picked men, of splendid physique, though not big. Their ordinary marching rate is four miles an hour, with a pace of 34 in. They double at a rate which works out at about nine minutes to the mile, and they practise the double relentlessly. On manœuvres they sometimes cover 40 miles in a day, and in Tripolitania the 11th Bersaglieri accomplished two wonderful desert marches of 50 miles in 26 hours and 33 miles in 19 hours. The first march was made necessary owing to a well being found dry. The second was carried out, for the greater part of the distance, in a sandstorm.

The Alpini are perhaps the finest mountain troops in the world. Their physique is magnificent, and their skill and endurance in mountainous country marvellous.

These were picked troops, and in the end one must always come back to the infantry of the line. First it should be said that the physique of the Italian nation had improved out of all knowledge in the last twenty years. Perhaps military training had had a good deal to do with bringing about the change, though it was not the only factor. Increased national prosperity had meant more and better food and improved conditions all round. The material was far better than it used to be. As a result the Italian Army showed a very high level of physique. The Italian soldier is not big, but he is tough and sound and a hard worker. He is not smart, sometimes he seems even slack. But he is keen and cheerful and obedient to command. The officers do not seem to insist upon a rigid discipline, but they get out of their men what they want, and the relations between officers and men are excellent.

CHAPTER LXXXIII.

THE CAMPAIGN AGAINST THE BALTIC PROVINCES.

The German Advance into the Baltic Provinces—Its Aims—The Settlement of the German on the Baltic Shore—The Baltic Germans and Russia—The Past Mutual Relations of the Germans and the Letts—The Military Operations in Samogitia and Courland up to May 18.

ON April 30 official *communiqués* brought the news of the German raid in the direction of Libau and Shavle. By May 2 the Germanic offensive in the district of Gorlice in Western Galicia had developed into an action of almost unprecedented magnitude.

It was evident from the very beginning that the advance against Libau and Shavle was devoid of independent strategic importance. Even after having penetrated for about a hundred miles into Russian territory, the German forces were still further away from any point of immediate strategic importance than they were in any other part of the entire Eastern front. Naturally, therefore, much speculation arose concerning the real aim of that new enterprise.

Very few human actions in ordinary everyday life can be traced back to one single exclusive motive; both life and the human mind are too complex to admit of singleness of purpose. The same is true about strategies; different possibilities, some of them belonging to a distant future, are usually present in the thoughts of the directing mind. Such a multiplicity and variety of purposes is of positive advantage; should the wider hopes and expectations never be realized, it is desirable

that immediate advantages should be reaped, such as would justify the undertaking.

The explanation which seemed most natural was at first given for Hindenburg's new undertaking. It was said that he had chosen the line of least resistance, and had found in addition employment for his cavalry, which could not be used along the other parts of the front, where fighting had assumed the character of trench-warfare. Raids are naturally directed against unguarded points, and there is no reason to colour with a touch of reproach and contempt the statement that the enemy was moving along the line of least resistance. If the Germans found that the district between Libau, Shavle, and the Prussian frontier was left practically unguarded, it was sound generalship on their part to take advantage of that fact. The Russians had done the same in the case of Memel, towards the end of March. The lesson learned from that raid of our Allies constituted probably one of the motives for the German advance against Shavle. By pushing the front line away from their own territory the Germans secured its safety against hostile inroads; and it must be admitted that when economic attrition had come to play a prominent part in warfare, the German policy of attaching supreme

SOLDIERS OF THE TSAR.

importance to the security of their own territory found justification.

There are, however, two limitations to the usefulness of raids or advances such as are devoid of immediate strategic importance. First, care must be taken that the raiding force should not be exposed to dangers out of proportion to the results which may be obtained by means of the raid. In this respect the Germans were fairly well guarded. In view of their naval strength in the Baltic they could always retire to the shore, should a Russian advance from Kovno seriously threaten their right flank. The second restriction on the usefulness of raids is this, that they should not withdraw forces which might be of greater use in the decisive theatre of war. It would be difficult to estimate the effects which Hindenburg's advance on Shavle had on the general situation, and particularly on the offensive in West Galicia. Cavalry was, during April, of small use in other parts of the front, and most of the raiding force, as is shown by the very speed of its advance, consisted of cavalry. But the first week in May saw the Russians in full retreat in West Galicia. It is an open question whether the Germanic armies disposed anyhow of sufficient cavalry in Western Galicia, and could spare the divisions which the Baltic raid had withdrawn to the front in Lithuania and Courland, or whether the speed of the advance which followed on the breakdown

of the Russian line on the Dunajec and Biala came as a surprise to the German commanders themselves. On the other hand, the view has been put forward that the advance along the Baltic shore aimed at diverting the attention of our Allies from the Dunajec-Biala front. On careful consideration it seems, however, very doubtful whether the Baltic raid could, did, or was ever meant to affect the operations which a week later were opened in Western Galicia.

Another aim ascribed to the Baltic raid was that of foraging. Riga and Libau have been for centuries two of the great granaries of Eastern Europe ; moreover a rich potato crop, preserved from the autumn, and plenty of cattle, were to be found in Lithuania and Courland. The German raid, says the Russian official *communiqué* of May 1, " may be explained as an attempt to include for foraging purposes, within the sphere of operations, a section of frontier territory which had not yet been ruined by the war."

When the great French Revolution was losing its cosmopolitan ideals, and substituting for them, in so far as international affairs were concerned, that doubtful worldly wisdom which is now generally known by the name of *Realpolitik*, Danton, the incarnation of much that was best and of some that was worst in the Revolution, made the remark that " *Vaincre l'ennemi, et vivre à ses dépens, c'est le vaincre deux fois.*" During the Great War the Germans faithfully kept to that maxim. We know it for a fact that the Germans requisitioned great quantities of wheat at Libau, and robbed the peasant population throughout most parts of Courland and Lithuania of grain, potatoes, cattle, poultry, in short of anything they could lay hands on. Similarly they immediately requisitioned all metals which they could find in the invaded districts.

We shall not quote any of the many letters from Polish and Lithuanian peasants to relatives in America, which appeared in the American Polish and Lithuanian newspapers, and which tell the story of the depredations committed by " the cursed Swabians." We shall limit ourselves to one example coming from a German source and concerning Poland, which had suffered even more severely by the war than Belgium. The shortage of food in Poland was recognized by an official Austrian *communiqué* of April 8, which begins with the following phrase : " Considering that the question of food forms at present the most important and most urgent problem for the population of

GERMAN TRANSPORTS ON THE RIVER NIEMEN.
Schooners to convey barges of troops and ammunition about to start for Russian territory.

the occupied parts of Russian Poland. . . ." This, however, seems to have in no way concerned the Germans. The *Deutsche Tageszeitung* of March 27 announces to its readers the joyful news that the German military authorities had requisitioned in Poland 60 million hundredweight of potatoes, and that the Silesian Chamber of Agriculture had "succeeded" in buying in Poland 8,000 hundredweight of bran at 24 marks the hundred-weight. We are not told whether, and in what way, the German military authorities helped them in making that splendid bargain. If such methods were adopted in the devastated regions of Poland, little mercy could the peasant population of Lithuania, and least of all that of Courland, expect from the German invaders. For a hatred, which all the waters of the Baltic Sea could never extinguish, burns in the heart of every Lettish peasant against the Germans, and the Germans have always answered it with a hatred equally strong, and with persecutions and oppressions such as hardly any other nation in Europe has ever had to suffer.

Seven centuries ago the first German conquerors set foot on the coast of the Baltic Sea, in the land inhabited by different Letto-Lithuanian and Finnish tribes ; less than ten years before the war, during the revolution of 1906, Letts and Germans were once more hunting one another in the Baltic Provinces, as

the White men and the Redskins had done in the virgin forests of America. What the German " Baltic Barons," the *Herrenvolk* of Courland, would do when their kinsmen from across the Prussian border had come to their aid, anyone could guess who knew those distant districts stretching along the quiet backwaters of the Baltic Sea. There is a sinister political aspect to Hindenburg's raid.* In order to understand its full meaning it is necessary to review, if only briefly, the political condition and problems of those districts.

It ought to be marked first of all that we are dealing, in the case of the Baltic raid, with two different countries, with Samogitia,† which forms the western half of the government of Kovno, and with Courland. These two districts, although they had originally been parts of the same nation and political system, came subsequently to differ widely owing to their different historical developments. The entire Baltic shore, from the Finnish Gulf to the Lower Vistula, and its hinterland up to the Vilia and Dubissa, were inhabited in the twelfth century by different Lithuanian and Finnish tribes ; the border zone between them ran

---

* The Hindenburgs themselves were a family settled also in the Russian Baltic Provinces, and Hindenburg as a good *Junker* was certain to view the concerns of the German Baltic Barons as his own family affairs.|

† "Samogitia" means in Lithuanian the "Lowlands" ; its language differs slightly from the Lithuanian as spoken round Kovno and Vilna.

A RUSSIAN PATROL BOAT,
Fitted with machine guns.

RUSSIAN ARTILLERY IN ACTION.
Inset : Guns disguised by fir branches.

more or less through the middle of Livland. The Lithuanian tribes were known in various parts of the country by different names, and their dialects varied to some extent. Still, all of them were merely subdivisions of the same group : the Lithuanians proper, the Samogitians, the Letts, and finally the Prussians, who are now practically extinct in their nobler Lithuanian form ; there are only about two hundred Lithuanian Prussians left in East Prussia. The languages of these Letto-Lithuanian tribes were more closely allied to the Slav languages than to any other European speech, though it is a mistake to describe them as Slav. In the thirteenth century two German Knightly Orders settled on the shores of the Baltic, one at the mouth of the Vistula, the other round Riga. They pursued identical aims ; they were waging a war of extermination on the Letto-Lithuanian tribes. For the sake of strength and efficiency these two Orders amalgamated about the year 1225. Besides fighting the Letto-Lithuanians, the Northern branch, centring round Riga, had to carry on war against the Finnish Esthonians, the Danes, and the Russian town-republic of Novgorod ; the Southern branch of the Teutonic Knightly Order, which had its chief seat at Marienburg in West Prussia, was waging wars also against the Polish kingdoms of the Vistula basin. These were the first stages of the gigantic,

continually renewed struggle for the dominion over the Baltic Sea and its shores. In this struggle the two great warrior-kings of Sweden, Gustavus Adolphus and Charles XII., achieved world fame. This struggle formed the chief preoccupation of Peter the Great, during whose reign the Baltic Provinces passed under Russian rule ; it was in the wars for the dominion of the Baltic that Prussia achieved her silent rise, and Poland received her first crushing blow. The Great War witnessed only a further stage of the old contest for the Mediterranean of the North.

The foundation of the new Russian capital by Peter the Great on the eastern shore of the Baltic marked its final annexation by Russia, but the name of St. Petersburg gave expression to the accomplished fact of another conquest, which was to prove of even greater importance in the history of the world—namely, to the conquest of the Russian Government by the Baltic Germans and by other German immigrants, who now became the teachers and the tyrants of Russia.

Having passed through a longer period of political development, and having stood nearer to the centres of West-European culture, the Germans were naturally better fitted to be the servants of the modern State in Russia than were the native Russian boyars. They were especially well fitted for servants of an autocratic system ; devoid of any feeling for the country and its people, hated by it, they developed the art of government for government's sake. The offices of State became the fourth German province in Russia. "The highest posts in the Russian Army and the diplomatic service," wrote Count Vitzthum in 1853,* "were filled by Germans, and the numerous sons of the nobility of Courland and Livonia regarded the Russian Empire as an inexhaustible mine of offices and riches." Still, such was the hatred against them among the true

Russian people that at that time a Courlander occupying one of the highest posts in the Russian Foreign Office thought it necessary to warn the Emperor " of the arrogance of the Russian party." † " If your Majesty does not check this mischief," said he, " we shall live to see in your reign a St. Bartholomew's Night of all German officials." " The mischief " was " checked," and with the blood and tears of the best Russians and of the other nationalities inhabiting the Russian Empire, the Baltic Germans continued to write, throughout the nineteenth century, the blackest pages of Russia's internal history. The destruction which they wrought surpassed a hundredfold any good which they may have done. They never felt with the Russian people ; at the best they served the Government. But in most cases they worked only for the interests of their own tribe, and the spiritual home of that tribe was at Königsberg and Berlin.

It was but natural that the Baltic Germans should have used their power in the Russian Government for strengthening their own position in the home-provinces of Courland, Livonia, and Esthonia, and for maintaining their dominion over their Lettish and Esthonian peasant population. As a matter of fact, the Germans formed and form to the present day in those provinces merely a ludicrously small minority. Esthonia had in 1897 a population of 412,716 inhabitants ; of these 365,959 spoke the Esthonian language,‡

---

* *Memoirs*, Vol. I. Count Vitzthum was a German himself ; he was Saxon Minister to St. Petersburg.
† *Ibid.*
‡ Esthonian is a Finnish language, and in no way

allied to Lettish. The binding link between the Esthonians and the Letts is not language but common sufferings and a common hatred against the Germans.

RUSSIAN TROOPS DRAWN UP FOR INSPECTION.

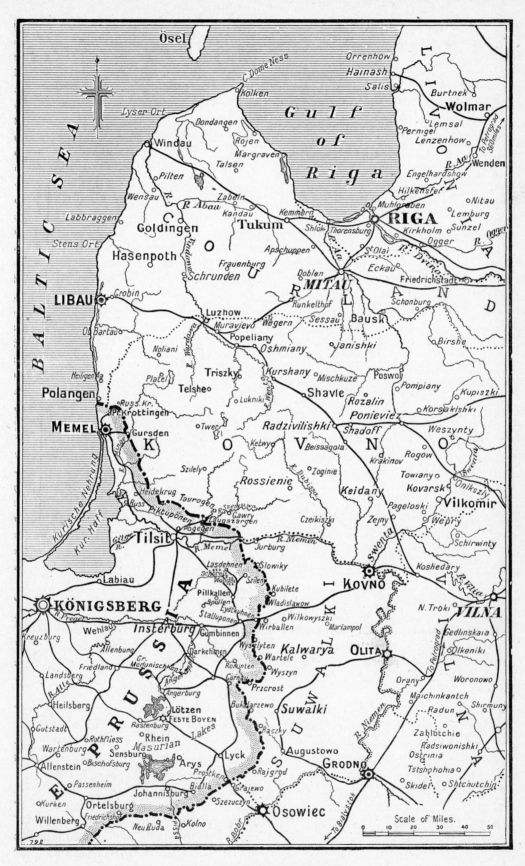

THE BALTIC PROVINCES.

16,037 German. The population of Livland was 1,299,365 inhabitants, including 510,523 Letts, 518,594 Esthonians, and 98,513 Germans. In Courland, of 674,034 inhabitants the Letts count 524,042, the Germans 51,017. Thus the total population of the three Baltic Provinces amounted in 1897 to 2,386,115; of these 165,627 were Germans, 884,553 Esthonians, and 1,094,565 Letts. But still the Germans own the greater part of the land, they were, and endeavour to remain, the "masterfolk" (das Herrenvolk) of these provinces, whilst the Letts and Esthonians are mostly farmers and labourers, the descendants of their serfs.

Towards the end of the eighteenth century Catherine II. tried to improve the condition of the peasantry in the Baltic Provinces, but failed. "The nobility . . . consisting largely of retired officers, in whom camp-life had developed that contempt for other men which the difference of nationality had by itself implanted in them . . . resented the demands of the Empress as an unjustified and ruinous intrusion into their private affairs." *

At last, in the course of the nineteenth century, under pressure from the Russian Government, the German masters consented to the abolition of serfdom in the Baltic Provinces; the emancipation of their peasants was, however, carried through in such a manner that the property of practically all the land was vested in the German aristocracy, and the economic condition of the peasantry changed for the worse rather than for the better. In Courland, even at the present day, although hundreds of thousands of acres have been redeemed by the Letts, a few hundred big landowners, almost all Germans, own more land than half a million Lettish peasants.

The war was likely also to settle the fate of the Lettish and Esthonian peasantry for generations to come. An able summary of their views and position was given in a letter written by a Lettish national revolutionary to the famous French writer, M. Romain Rolland.† The Letts had lived under the German yoke for centuries before the coming of the Russians, writes M. Rolland's correspondent. "Compared with the Germans the Russians appeared

to us as liberators. For centuries the Germans kept us by brute force in a state comparable to slavery. Only 50 years ago the Russian Government gave us our freedom (from serfdom), but at the same time committed the grave injustice of leaving all our land in the hands of German proprietors. In spite of all, we have managed in 20 or 30 years to redeem from the Germans a portion of our soil, and to attain a certain level of culture, thanks to which we are regarded, with the Finns and the Esthonians, as the most advanced nation of the Russian Empire." Germans call the Letts ungrateful, he goes on to say, but they have no right to do so. "We acquired our culture in spite of them, against their will."

In 1906 the Lettish revolution was directed mainly against the Germans. After it had broken down, "at the head of the majority of the military detachments sent to chastise the country were officers of German nationality who had asked for this employment." Having received the command, they displayed a simply uncanny zeal "in shooting down men and burning houses." The nation of masters carried out its vendetta.

Now, says M. Rolland's Lettish correspondent, "our soldiers have left for the front filled with enthusiasm . . . because the war is against Germany, and we are capable of any sacrifice to prevent the annexation of the Baltic Provinces." The German landowners and merchants in the Baltic Provinces, says he, though Russian subjects, will welcome the German armies with open arms. Not so the Letts or the Esthonians; in fact, these were, in August 1915, forming legions of volunteers for the defence of the Baltic Provinces against the Germans.

The delegate of the Estho-Lettish group had declared in the Duma on August 8, 1914: "We have many accounts to settle with the Germans of the Baltic Provinces, but we shall not choose this moment for settling them." Not so the Germans; in the last days of April the armies of Hindenburg were crossing Samogitia on their way to Courland, the land of blood and tears and German barons.

"German troops have again occupied an important part of the late Duchy of Courland," announced the semi-official Berliner Lokal Anzeiger on the occupation of Libau on May 8 1915. "Seven centuries ago German knights and merchants had entered that country in order to subdue it to German dominion

* This description of the relation of German masters and Lettish peasants does not come from the pen of a Lett. It is taken from Dr. Seraphim's Baltische Geschichte (1908). Dr. Seraphim is an ardent German patriot.

† This letter was published in the Journal de Genève on October 12, 1914. We quote the translation from Mr. Alexinsky's book on "Russia and the Great War."

and in order to lay in it the foundations of German culture, which rules there unchanged to the present day. German warriors under Knight Hindenburg follow now in their footsteps. May this be a lucky omen for the future. . . ."

Fighting on a small scale had been proceeding on the confines of East Prussia and Samogitia, round the town of Taurogen, ever since the time of the Russian raid on Memel (towards the end of March). During these battles Taurogen had to suffer severe German bombardments ; very little was left of that ancient seat of the Princes Radziwill. By some irony of fate, one of the few things which survived the German bombardment was the monument of the Russian General Dybitch, who concluded with the Prussian general York at Taurogen, in 1813, the famous convention against Napoleon which marked the beginning of the so-called Wars of Liberation.

In the last week of April the Germans concentrated considerable forces between Tilsit and Jurburg. Their strength was at first estimated at three brigades of cavalry and one brigade of infantry, and they were said to have been commanded by General von Lauenstein, who in March had been in command of the 39th German Reserve Corps. Subsequent estimates put the strength of the German forces in the Baltic Provinces at one and a half corps of infantry, and about the same number of cavalry. It is probable that the former figure renders more accurately the numbers engaged in the first advance, whilst the latter includes reinforcements which were sent during the following week to the support of the advanced bodies. Only small numbers of infantry could have taken part in the first raid. Almost a hundred miles seem to have been covered in two days. German military writers ascribe that fact to what they call the marvellous endurance of the German infantry. The truth of the matter is in all probability that the infantry made use for its advance of motor-transport, at least for part of the way. A first-class high road leads from Tilsit by Taurogen and Shavle to Mitau and Riga ; that road, being about 50 feet wide, provides sufficient space for three cars moving in one line. It was used by the infantry, artillery, and transport, while smaller side roads were probably followed by the main bodies of cavalry.

RUSSIAN CAVALRY ON THE MARCH.

The invading forces seem to have started on April 27, and moved in three columns. The main body moved along the Taurogen-Shavle road. On its left a considerable body of cavalry advanced by Telshe towards Mura-vievo, where the Riga-Mitau-Libau railway meets that coming from the direction of Shavle ; thus Libau was cut off straight away from all communication with Riga or with Kovno. A third body, also consisting chiefly of cavalry, crossed the Niemen over a bridge constructed by German engineers near Jurburg. These forces had a double task before them. They had to screen the lines of communication of the central column from possible Russian flank attacks from the south-east, from the direction of Kovno, whilst advancing further by Rossie-nie towards Radzivilishki, they had for their objective the junction of the railways from Vilna and from Ponieviez. By seizing the rail-way junction of Radzivilishki, and establishing themselves on the line Shadoff-Beissagola, they prevented a quick concentration of Russian troops on the flank of the main German group which was moving by Shavle against Mitau and Riga.

The first more serious encounter between the German and the Russian troops took place near Shavle,* on April 29. The Russians, being outnumbered by the Germans, withdrew

* Shavle is a picturesque old town of about 15,000 inhabitants. The upper classes are mainly Poles, the officials Russians, the peasants Lithuanians, the small shopkeepers and artisans are Jews. Shavle has acquired

RUSSIAN RETREAT FROM GALICIA.
Galician peasants watching the departing Cavalry.　Inset : A Russian priest on the field.

ON THE ROAD TO WARSAW.
German infantry passing through a village.

in the direction of Mitau.* On April 30 the Germans reached the railway stations of Muravievo and Radzivilishki. On May 1 German patrols appeared near Libau; on the same day a few German torpedo-boats visited the Gulf of Riga. Libau and Riga were their main strategic objectives. Their calculation was that should the Russians concentrate

recently a peculiar connexion with the British Empire. In the decade preceding the outbreak of the Boer War some 60,000 Jews emigrated to South Africa from Shavle and a dozen other small surrounding towns. It is difficult to explain the reasons of that emigration, but by far the greater part of the Jewish population of South Africa hails from that one small district. There are at present more Jews from Shavle in South Africa than in Shavle itself, and South Africa plays the same part in the life of its Jewish population as America does in that of most other towns of Poland, Lithuania, and the Ukraina.

* Louis XVIII. of France spent at Mitau many years of his exile. That small Courland town became at that time the centre of the French aristocratic émigrés.

considerable forces in the Baltic Provinces, Libau and Riga, if once occupied, could still be held under the protection of the fleet; a base would thus be gained on the Baltic shore for future operations.

Under date of May 3 we hear of fighting on the flanks, round Muravievo and Rossienie. On the 5th the Germans attempted an advance against Mitau, but were repulsed with considerable losses. On May 7 the Germans were compelled to retreat still further; on that day they had to evacuate their strongly fortified positions near Janishki, about thirty miles south of Mitau; they withdrew, leaving behind a great quantity of booty. Meantime further operations were developing on both flanks. A German column, which had not hitherto taken part in the advance, moved from Memel, along the sea, towards Libau; it was accompanied by

RAILS ON ROLLING STOCK.
Russian soldiers placing guns on trucks on the railway.

a flotilla composed of two cruisers, four torpedo boats, and several destroyers. On May 8 the Germans entered Libau, which the Russians had almost completely evacuated. One German destroyer, having struck a Russian mine, sank outside Libau.

About the same time a much more serious movement was undertaken by the Germans from the direction of Rossienie. Whilst one body of troops was detaining the Russians on the Beissagola-Shadoff front, to the east of Radzivilishki, a Bavarian cavalry division, supported by a regiment of Prussian Guards, was advancing along the northern bank of the Vilia. On May 8 the Bavarians reached the station Zejny on the Vilna-Shavle railway line. They thus threatened to outflank the Russian troops which were operating between Beissagola and Keidany, and, which was still by far more important, they threatened to attack from the north the railway between the important fortress of Kovno and the main Petrograd-Vilna-Warsaw railway line.

Our Allies were, of course, fully aware of the significance of the German move against Zejny; on the same day—i.e., on May 8—the Bavarians were attacked in the vicinity of the station of Zejny by Russian cavalry and completely routed. The pursuit was continued throughout the night, and on the fol-

lowing morning a second battle was fought, about thirty miles north of Zejny, near the river crossing of Krakinov. Its result was equally disastrous for the Germans as had been that of the previous engagement.

During the following day the German retreat extended to the entire line. On May 14 the Russian railway service was resumed between Riga, Mitau, and Muravievo. All the territory east of the rivers Vindava and Dubissa was free of the enemy. An official communiqué from Russian Main Headquarters on May 18 says: "In spite of the concentration in the Shavle district of large enemy forces of all arms, the German armies, after the complete repulse of the attacks delivered by two of their divisions on May 14, passed to purely defensive tactics."

Thus about the middle of May the first stage of the German invasion of the Baltic Provinces can be considered as closed. Their advance against Mitau and Riga and their attempt against Kovno had failed, but Libau and most of the territory to the west of the Vindava and the Dubissa remained in their possession. This advance brought them nearer to the Vilna-Petrograd line; from here they were going to threaten two months later a gigantic turning movement against the entire Niemen-Vistula line.

RUSSIAN TRANSPORTS.
Machines broken down from the wear and tear of the war.

CHAPTER LXXXIV.

THE AUSTRO-GERMAN VICTORY ON THE DUNAJEC.

The Dunajec-Biala-Ropa Line—The Composition and Distribution of the Austro-German and the Russian Forces in the Galician Theatre of War at the Commencement of the Austro-German Offensive—The Concentration of Austro-German Artillery—The Battle of Gorlice—The Fight for Hill 419—The Crossing of the Dunajec near Otfinow—The Further Advance of the Austro-German Forces on May 3-4—Fighting in the Eastern Carpathians.

THE Germanic offensive against the Dunajec line must rank as an operation surpassing in magnitude almost anything which had hitherto been experienced in the war.

The Germans once more showed their incomparable powers of organization. In matters which can be foreseen, calculated and prepared, hardly anyone can equal, and no one can surpass, the Germans. The human machine which they have created is as mighty in its strength as it is ghastly in its spirit. It marks the highest triumph of the reasoning mind and the closest welding of the modern mass-individuality. When watching the Germans at their destructive work, one's thoughts wander back to the tales of the eccentric, coldly calculating imagination of Jules Verne, especially to the story about the "Millions of the Begum." A German and a Frenchman inherit between them an immense fortune. The German uses his share for the construction of an enormous—shall we say—howitzer? The Frenchman builds a garden city. One shell fired from the giant gun is to wipe out the throbbing life of the Latin city. But the usual happy unravelling of the plot saves

its existence. The deadly shell rises too high, it leaves the spheres of life, and joins the dead stars in their regular, fantastic courses.

Against the German hurricane of steel and fire stood the patiently enduring nature of the Russian peasant. The artillery which was to equalize the conditions of battle, though splendidly staffed and managed, was unable to cope with the superiority in number, weight, and ammunition possessed by its Germanic opponents. The Russian peasant-soldier had to meet the storm in his own way. He stood at his post and perished. It is the resistance offered by the Russian infantry which imparts the heroic, tragic touch to the fighting on the Dunajec line. Some German military writers cannot abstain from expressing their admiration for that silent, unassuming heroism; they recall the words spoken by Frederick II. after the battle of Zorndorf in 1758, that if a Russian soldier is hit by three bullets one has still to push him before he falls. Other German writers simply foam with fury and annoyance; according to the ordinary calculations a wild panic ought to have gripped the Russians. Nothing but stupidity and total absence of nerves can, according to them, explain such

RUSSIA'S RULER AT THE FRONT.
The Tsar talking to Count Brobinsky, Governor of Galicia; the Grand Duke Nicholas,
and the Chief-of-Staff.

resistance; paraphrasing Schiller, they suggest that "against stupidity, gods and howitzers thunder in vain." Was it stupidity? Let those Germans answer the question who shrink with fear before the mighty, suffering spirit of a Dostojewski. The Russian Slav faith and the Russian religious feeling have arisen from the depths of the peasant heart and have grown up amidst the misery and endless pain of peasant life. It was not primarily against the upper classes of Petrograd, then St. Petersburg, but against the spirit of the Russian peasant nation that the Germanic States opened this war. With the peasant nation they had also to fight it out. The fight on the Dunajec was only the opening of a gigantic struggle between the souls of two nations.

In previous chapters we have referred to the western front in Galicia as the Dunajec-Biala-Ropa line. Up to the beginning of May 1915 it was, on the whole, of only secondary importance, and we therefore abstained from entering into detailed descriptions of that line, along which the Russian and the Austro-Hungarian armies had been facing one another since about the middle of December. The description of the front by the names of those three rivers was naturally never meant to imply that their course marked the actual dividing line between the

two armies. In a war for positions—and the fighting in West Galicia had assumed that character—rivers even bigger than the Dunajec hardly ever remain a barrier between the contending forces.

Several times previous to May 1915 offensive movements had been undertaken by one side or the other. Practically each movement left its mark on the configuration of the line. On some occasions the defending side was unable to recover all the ground from which it had been compelled to recede before the first impact of the attack; at other times and places the attempts ended in failures so serious that the aggressors were finally unable to stop their retreat along the previous lines. Thus almost each offensive movement left its salients. It would be both tiresome and futile to attempt a detailed description of the history and the gradual evolution of the West Galician front. We shall limit ourselves to a brief consideration of the main geographical features of the theatre of war in which the Germanic offensive started in the first days of May 1915, and of the relative positions which the two armies were then holding in that district.

In its upper reaches the Dunajec cuts its way between high, steep rocks. Along a considerable part of its course, from close to Novy Sacz to Zakliczyn, the main roads avoid the neighbourhood of the river. Several miles above the confluence of the Dunajec and the Biala their valleys widen out considerably, and numerous islands facilitate the crossing or bridging of the rivers. From the village of Biala, which lies near the confluence of the Dunajec and the River Biala, to the confluence of the Dunajec and the Vistula, on a stretch of almost twenty miles, the Dunajec can be forded at only very few places. Its valley is about five miles wide. On both sides of it hills rise to a height of between 200 and 300 feet above the level of the river. Both these ranges dominate the river valley; during April the Austrian positions followed, in the main, the western range of heights, the lines of our Allies stretched along the eastern hills. Further protection was derived by both sides from the woods which cover the slopes and tops of the hills. On the western side these woods form a belt between two and three miles deep. Little strategic interest attaches to the river valley itself. The dams which on both sides encompass the river are its main feature. At several points our Allies were holding practically the entire valley; at others the river formed the dividing line between the armies. Of all the Russian salients on the western bank of the Dunajec the most marked was that near Radlow. This entire village remained up to the beginning of May in the hands of our Allies.

Between the villages of Biala and Gromnik, for a distance of about fourteen miles, the two armies were facing one another on the western side of the river Biala; this sector of the front lay almost entirely within the triangle, of which the Dunajec and the Biala are the sides, their confluence the apex, and of which the Zakliczyn-Gromnik road is the basis. About two miles to the south of the river junction, between Bogumilovice and Tarnow, the double-tracked railway Cracow-Lwow crosses the Dunajec and the Biala. The big railway bridge across the Dunajec had been blown up by the Austrians during their second retreat in November 1914; the Russians replaced it by a wooden structure, but this in turn was destroyed by our Allies during their retreat from before Cracow about the middle of December. Since then the Dunajec had become at this point the unbridgable borderline between the armies, which slowly settled down to the routine of trench warfare. But as surprise attacks were in most parts impossible on account of the intervening river, sniping became the chief occupation of the troops in that sector. Behind the big eastern pillar of the broken bridge was the post of a Russian sniper, who by his exploits earned for himself among the enemy local fame and the nickname of "Ivan the Terrible"; he finished by becoming in turn the victim of a sniper.

THE RAILWAY BRIDGE ACROSS THE DUNAJEC.

There was only one period of " close season " observed by both sides in that sector ; during a certain hour either side was allowed to fetch water from the river without being molested by the enemy. The Russian trenches near the bridge had been dug in a field covered by beautiful winter rye. " The Russian moujiks," says the correspondent of a Viennese paper, who visited this locality after the retreat of our Allies, " in their superstitious reverence for crops, characteristic of peasants, have carefully respected the sown field and followed, in walking through it, only a few narrow paths." The civilized German correspondent, however, does not seem to feel the same respect for that reverence and love which, according to his own statement, the so-called barbarians were showing for the labour of another poor peasant and for the bread of his children.

Even here, where the broad river formed a fairly serious obstacle to communication between the two sides, it did not constitute an absolute barrier. At one place, to the north of the railway bridge, near the village of Ostrow, the Russians had gained a foothold on the western bank of the Dunajec, and the Austrians, notwithstanding the most desperate efforts, were unable to dislodge them. During the

night a small ferry used to carry food and munitions to the outpost beyond the river.

The main battle in that region consisted, however, of the artillery duel which Austrian batteries, from west of Bogumilovice, were carrying on with the Russian batteries posted above Tarnow. The first Austrian 42-cm. howitzer had been got into position as early as January 15, and was, from a distance of almost eight miles, directing its fire against the town of Tarnow. The Russians in return were bombarding most effectively the Austrian positions near the left bank of the Dunajec from 28 cm. howitzers.

South of the railway line two first-class high roads cross the Dunajec, one near Vojnicz, the other near Zakliczyn. About a mile to the east of the bridge by which the Vojnicz road crosses the river, lies the village of Zglobice ; the bridge and the village are both dominated by Hill 269,* which rises to the south of the road. The other road, having crossed the Dunajec near Zakliczyn, runs in a northerly direction past the western edge of the Mount Val, which is the highest point within the

* If a figure stands for the name of a height or mountain, that figure expresses its height in metres. A metre is equal to about 3·28 feet.

A MESSENGER OF THE AUSTRIAN GENERAL STAFF
Carrying dispatches across a river in Galicia.

THE AUSTRIANS IN GALICIA.
Officers of the Headquarters Staff studying a plan of campaign.

triangle (526 metres—*i.e.*, 1,725 ft.) ; on Height 402 the Zakliczyn road is met by a secondary road descending from that mountain.* The two roads meet opposite Tarnow, close to the western bank of the Biala.

To the north-west of the Val lies the second highest hill of the district, Hill 419 ; Hill 402 forms a bridge between them. Together these three heights encircle a valley traversed by a small, nameless stream. The heights are covered by fine dense forests of elms and beeches, and offer excellent strategic ground ; given an approximately equal strength of artillery they form practically impregnable positions. At the time when the great Germanic offensive opened in West Galicia Hills 269, 419, and 402 were held by the Russians, Mount Val by the Austrians.

On a front of about ten miles, between Gromnik and Bobova, the positions of the two armies extended close to the banks of the Biala. Further south the Austrian line crossed over to the eastern side of the river. The sector between Ciezkowice, Gorlice, and Mala-stow was the decisive district of the entire West Galician front. There are only two possible lines for an advance through Galicia, and they are marked by the two railway lines running east and west ; on the Dunajec-Biala-Ropa line the gate to the " Transversal

Valley " lies between Ciezkovice and Gorlice. Apart from tactical reasons, which it would take too long to discuss, on purely strategic grounds it paid the Germans better to direct their main attack along the southern line than to press it along the Tarnow-Rzeszow railway. The " Transversal Valley " runs along the northern slopes of the Carpathians ; just beyond the main crest, on the Hungarian side, stood Russian troops. A successful piercing of the Gorlice front carried the Germans at once on to the basic lines of communication of that army. Further, the Russians had better means for a quick concentration of forces along the northern than along the southern line. The former is a first-class double-tracked rail-way, the latter a rather poor single-track line. Moreover, the Russians had used the winter and spring for the construction of new lines, linking up from north to south their own railway system with that of Galicia. At the outbreak of the war not a single link existed between the two systems from Granica at the extreme western end of Galicia, to Brody in the furthest north-eastern corner of the country. By May 1915 our Allies had con-structed two links between the Vistula and the Bug, connecting the Cholm-Lublin-Warsaw railway with the Lwow-Rzeszow-Tarnow-Cra-cow line. One line had been built from Cholm by Zamosc and Tomaszow to Belzec, where it joins the Lwow-Rawa Ruska-Belzec railway.

---

* Val (in Polish spelling Wal) means " a rampart," the root of the word is the same as of our word " wall."

HEAVY AUSTRIAN ARTILLERY ON THE GALICIAN ROADS.

The other, which was of much greater importance for the Dunajec front, ran from Lublin
to Rozvadow (south-east of Sandomierz).
Moreover, the Austrian circular railway Dem-
bica-Rozvadow-Przeworsk had been enlarged
down to Dembica to the Russian broad gauge,
so that Russian trains could run straight
through from Lublin up to the main Cracow-
Lwow line. Neither of these new railways
could be of much immediate use in a quick
concentration of troops in the southern gate
round Gorlice.

In the most important district round Gorlice
the Russians had failed to secure a decisive
superiority of position. It is by no means
certain, we might perhaps venture to say that
it is improbable, whether even a marked
advantage in positions could have counter-
balanced the superiority in artillery of the
Germanic armies. Be that as it may, it is still
of importance to mark that even in that
respect our Allies possessed no advantage over
the enemy.

The Maslana Gora (it is 747 metres—i.e.,
2,450 feet high—and lies between the Grybow-
Biecz railway and the Grybow-Ropa-Gorlice-
Biecz road), together with the Magora of
Malastow, form the key-stone between the
Biala line and the Carpathian Mountains. The
Maslana Gora was held, towards the end
of April, by the Germanic forces, whilst the
Russians' hold on the Magora was, as we shall
see below, by no means complete or secure.
The front between Bobova and Gorlice had the
shape of a capital S, drawn from west-north-
west to east-south-east. Near Bobova and

Vola Luzanska were its furthest northerly
points; Luzna lay in the "no man's land"
between the lines. Beyond Vola Luzanska
the positions again extended almost due north
and south, crossing the Grybow-Gorlice road
between Szymbark* and Gorlice. South of it,
near Senkova, the Germanic positions approached very close to the Gorlice-Malastow-
Konieczna-Zboro-Bartfeld road. The Austrians
had gained ground at that place during an
earlier attempt which they had made at
crushing the Russian lines in the Carpathians
by a flank attack from the west. They
had tried it as a desperate means for the
relief of Przemysl. On March 8 they reached
the hills east of the Gorlice-Malastow road,
facing Senkova. Although the attempt at
piercing the western Russian line failed, they
remained in possession of that salient.

The Gorlice-Konieczna-Zboro road was of
considerable importance to the Russian troops
which had advanced into Hungary. It will
be remembered from Chapter LXXVI. that
on April 2 our Allies had reached the Hungarian village of Cigielka, which lies, as the
crow flies, six miles west of the road. In
order to secure completely their hold of that
road, the Russians would have needed to occupy
in strength the entire line of the Ropa to the
south of the village bearing the same name;

---

* In the region of Gorlice a considerable number of
place-names can be found which are corruptions of
German names; these are mostly townships which had
been founded by German colonists in the fourteenth
century. Thus Szymbark (pronounce: Shymbark) is
a corruption of Schoenberg; Rozenbark of Rosemberg;
Rychwald of Reichwald; Szymwald for Schoenwald, etc.

that village was, however, entirely within the Austrian lines. What the exact position of the two armies was towards the end of April in the region south of the Grybow-Szymbark-Gorlice road cannot as yet be ascertained with certainty. So much, however, appears from subsequent events, that the important secondary road from Uscie Ruskie to Gladyszow which, following a tributary of the Ropa, connects the valley of the Ropa with the Gorlice-Zboro high road, was neither held in force, nor even properly guarded by the Russians.

Thus in the decisive sector of the Dunajec-Biala-Ropa front, to the south of Ciezkovice, where the gate opens into the "Transversal Valley," and along the flank of the Russian armies which were facing Hungary, the position of our Allies was by no means one of strategic superiority. It may be that the failure of the offensive undertaken at that point by the Austrians in the beginning ot March misled them concerning the degree of danger which they had to expect from a frontal attack from the west. Anyhow, even the number of troops concentrated in that district failed in any way to counterbalance the other disadvantages of their position.

We have previously spoken of the great length and the complexity of the Eastern front. One of their military effects was the development of "group command" to an even greater extent than it was known in the West.

One commander cannot possibly direct the operations on the entire Eastern front, not even to that limited extent to which it is still possible to do it in the West. Therefore a system which one might call the group system of armies grew up. It was very marked in the case of the Austro-German drive in Galicia, though the apparent distinction between the Austro - Hungarian and the German Armies was apt to obscure to the superficial observer the real reason for the separate grouping of the northern and of the southern Germanic armies on the Russian front.

Nominally the chief Commander of the Austro-Hungarian Army, the Archduke Frederick, stood at the head of the forces operating on the Galician front. The real leader was undoubtedly the Prussian General von Mackensen, who had been Hindenburg's chief assistant during the second invasion of Poland in November 1914. The offensive and the necessary preparations were worked out by the general staffs of the two allied armies. Mackensen, who was sent to Galicia as Commander of the Eleventh German Army, directed the execution of the plan.

Since about the middle of December the region of the Pilica was the zone in which the Austrian and the German Armies met. During the following four and a half months German reinforcements were continually poured into the Austrian lines. At the end of April there was hardly an Austro-Hungarian Army com-

NAPHTHA MINES FIRED BY SHELLS.

A CONFERENCE OF AUSTRO-GERMAN
COMMANDERS.

General von Emmich (x). Inset: The General
with his staff at a railway station in Galicia.

posed exclusively of Austro-Hungarian troops.
Each of them included at least some auxiliary
German forces. Two armies standing on
Austro-Hungarian soil were predominantly
German.

In front of Warsaw, from the confluence of
the Bzura and the Vistula, down to the middle
course of the Pilica stood the Ninth German
Army, the extreme left wing of Hindenburg's
armies. A group of Transylvanian regiments
under General von Kövess formed the connecting link between these troops and the Army of
General Woyrsch, which was facing the district of Ivangorod. General Woyrsch's Army
consisted mainly of Silesian troops; the
Hungarian troops on his left flank were included in General Woyrsch's command. In
the course of the spring his Army seems to have
been depleted by drafts for other parts of the
front, and we can hardly suppose that it included about that time much more than two
army corps. South of it, along the Nida down
to the Vistula, stood the First Austrian Army
under General Dankl. This army also was
probably under strength at the time when the
Germanic offensive opened in Galicia. The
average estimate puts it at about two army
corps.

With the southern bank of the Vistula begins
the immediate theatre of the Germanic drive
of May 1915. The region between the Vistula
and the Carpathians was, towards the end of
April, that where the greatest concentration
of forces took place. This concentration was,
however, effected without any forces being
withdrawn from the Carpathians. In other
words, the concentration effected in North

Hungary during the four preceding months remained undisturbed, but additional troops were moved from the interior and from other fronts into the district from which the drive was to begin. From the confluence of the Dunajec and the Vistula down to the Zakliczyn-Gromnik road stood the Fourth Austro-Hungarian Army under Archduke Joseph Ferdinand. Its strength was estimated at about five army corps ; it included also a German Cavalry Division under General von Besser. On its right wing, to the south of Tarnow, stood the Ninth Army Corps, consisting mainly of Hungarians and the Fourteenth Austrian Army Corps. The hilly region of the Val was occupied by Tyrolese regiments. A considerable proportion of the Archduke's Army had only come to the Dunajec front during the great concentration towards the end of April. The entire district from the Vistula to the Carpathians had formerly been held by the Fourth Army, which then consisted of only three Austro-Hungarian army corps (those of Generals Arz, Roth and Kralicek) and the Prussian Division of General Besser. On its right wing round Grybow stood then the Sixth Austro-Hungarian Army Corps under General Arz von Straussenburg. This corps included the Galician 12th Division and the Hungarian 39th Division, besides Moravian and Silesian troops.

During the great concentration in the second half of April the Austro-Hungarian corps of General Arz von Straussenburg got embedded, and consequently included, in the Eleventh German Army, which remained under the direct command of Mackensen. On the left of the Sixth Austrian Army Corps now stood the *élite* of the Prussian Army, the Guards ; on its right, Bavarian troops under General von Emmich, the commander who, in August 1914, had opened the Western campaign by his costly attacks against Liège.

In the corner, south-west of the Magora of Malastow, the Eleventh German Army was joined up by the Third Austro-Hungarian Army under General Borojevic von Bojna.* On its extreme left wing near the Magora stood the 10th Army Corps under General Martiny. The 10th Army Corps is the " home force " of Przemysl, for it draws its recruits from the districts of Przemysl and Jaroslav.

* In Chapter LXXVI. General Borojevic was described as commander of the Second Austro-Hungarian Army, and General von Boehm-Ermolli as that of the Third. It ought to have been the other way round.

The important district of the Laborcza was held by the 7th Army Corps under Archduke Joseph, consisting almost entirely of Hungarians, and commanded by a member of what is considered to be the Hungarian branch of the Hapsburgs. On the extreme right wing of the Third Austrian Army stood the German corps under General von der Marwitz, generally known in Germany as " das deutsche Beskidencorps."* It was explained in Chapter LXXVI. that this Army was brought up to the Carpathian front during the last days of March when the Russian pressure in the district round the Lupkow Pass was threatening to break the Austro-Hungarian defences in the north of

* " The German Corps of the Beskid Mountains." " Beskid Mountains " is the name given to the western sectors of the Carpathians.

FIELD-MARSHAL VON HINDENBURG.

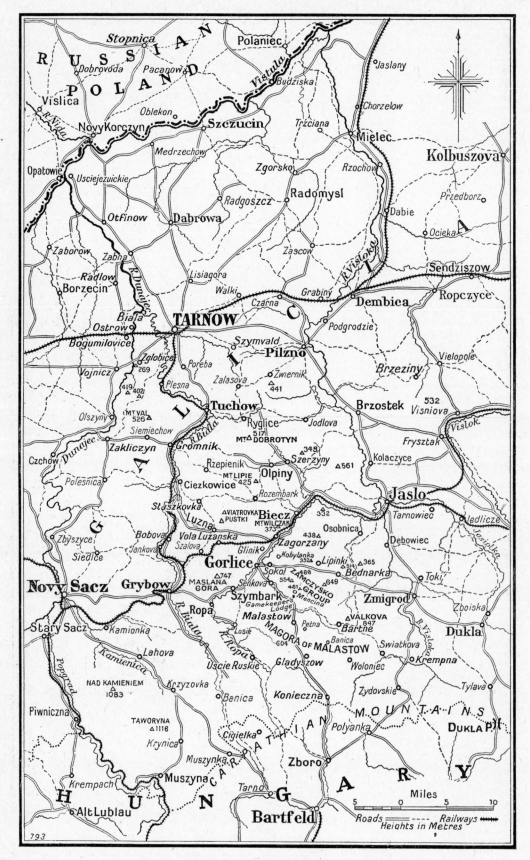

MAP TO ILLUSTRATE THE BATTLE OF GORLICE.

the Hungarian Plain. Between the 7th Hungarian Army Corps in the Laborcza Valley and the 10th Army Corps, north of Bartfeld, stood some additional Austrian forces, forming at least one army corps.

The region between the Lupkow and the Uzsok was held by the Second Austro-Hungarian Army under General von Boehm-Ermolli. It had taken up that position towards the end of February; from here the last desperate attempt at the direct relief of the fortress of Przemysl was undertaken in the first weeks of March. The army of General von Boehm-Ermolli had remained in this region ever since. It consisted almost entirely of Austro-Hungarian troops, and included among others, the *élite* of the Viennese regiments. On its extreme right wing stood the 5th Austro-Hungarian Army Corps under Field-Marshal-Lieutenant * von Goglia. The Uzsok Pass itself was held by the army-group of F.M.L. von Szurmay; the troops under his command were almost all Hungarians. This corps formed now, towards the end of April, the extreme left wing of the so-called German " Südarmee " (Army of the South). Its chief commander was General von Linsingen

In the entire theatre of war which was occupied by the mixed armies of Austro-Hungarian and German troops this was certainly the most composite of them all. There was hardly a corps in it which did not bear traces of a long and eventful development. East of F.M.L. von Szurmay's troops stood a Prussian corps, composed of a division of the Prussian Guard, and of Pomeranian and East Prussian regiments, under a Bavarian General, Count Bothmer. This corps included moreover the 38th Hungarian Honvéd division under F.M.L. Bartheldy. It was the corps of Count Bothmer which had been delivering desperate and unsuccessful attacks against the heights of Koziova ever since the Army of General von Linsingen had arrived at the Carpathian front, in the last days of January 1915. Next to it, in the region of the Ostry, the Makowka, and the Tatarowka mountains, stood the corps of General Hofmann, composed mainly of Austro-Hungarian troops. To his corps belonged the division under General Fleischman. There is

* A Field-Marshal-Lieutenant is, in the Austro-Hungarian Army, a much lower rank than the name would imply to the mind of the English reader. Practically every Austrian corps commander is a Field-Marshal-Lieutenant. In future we shall denote this rank by the initials " F.M.L."

hardly an Austrian nationality which was not represented in that division; it had a most varied history, and had come into existence during the fighting which took place in the Bukovina in the autumn of 1914. It included all kinds of irregular formations. Its history reminds one to some extent of the ethnical history of countries like the Caucasus or the Bukovina itself. Huge waves of stronger nations swept the

FIELD-MARSHAL VON MACKENSEN.

plains, and the remainders of the smaller nationalities were driven under the shelter of the forests and mountains. Thus also now, in the valleys intervening between the highest massifs of the Carpathians different regiments had found shelter; they were formed into a division and were now, entrenched in the mountain valleys, offering resistance to the further advance of the Russians. On the right of the corps of General Hofmann round the Wyszkow Pass, almost down to the valleys

GERMAN TRANSPORT CROSSING A RIVER IN GALICIA.

of the Bystrzycas, the ground was held again by German troops.

Along the northern edge of the Pruth Valley stood the army group of General von Pflanzer-Baltin. We do not know its exact strength, but judging from indications which can be gathered occasionally from German reports, it must have included something between two and three army corps; one of them was the Hungarian corps of the F.M.L. Czibulka, consisting very largely of Croats and Hungarians. F.M.L. Czibulka himself had taken part in the disastrous Austrian expedition into Serbia. He is said to have been more successful than most of his colleagues at extricating his own division (he then commanded only a division) from the catastrophe which befell his Army, and was transferred in January 1915, with some of his troops to the Bukovina front.

To sum up: At the end of April more than four Germanic army corps were holding the district between the middle Pilica and the confluence of the Nida and the Vistula—that is, the sector intervening between the Ninth German Army in front of Warsaw and the Galician border.

On the West Galician front, down to the south-western corner round the Magora of Malastrow, stood at least ten army corps, consisting of almost equal numbers of Austro-Hungarian and German troops. The Carpathian front was held by three distinct armies, each of which included about four army corps; of these altogether not more than four were German. Finally, the district between the Carpathians, the Dniester and the Russian frontier was held by two or three Austro-Hungarian army corps. Thus towards the end of April, on the Galician front alone, at least twenty-four army corps were concentrated, to say nothing about the reinforcements which continued to pour in later on, whilst these armies were advancing and suffering heavily during that advance.

What were the forces with which our Allies were opposing that extraordinary and unprecedented concentration?

We cannot speak about the Russian forces with the same freedom with which we were able to enumerate and name the Austro-Hungarian German corps and their commanders. We must limit ourselves to that which by now is common property among our enemies.

The Russian forces in Galicia, from the Vistula down to the farthest eastern corner between the Dniester and the Austro-Russian frontier, formed the group of armies commanded by General Ivanoff. The West Galician front, from the Vistula to the region of the Dukla, was held by the Third Russian Army under General Radko Dmitrieff. The Carpathian front was held by two armies; one of them was the Eighth Russian Army under General Brusiloff; the other, the Ninth Army, included large bodies of troops which had previously been in the siege army of Przemysl. On the extreme left wing, north of the Pruth Valley were concentrated about two corps of Russian cavalry. Among them were several famous "native divisions" and also the 12th Russian Division, which included some of the best

THE SOLDIERS' DINNER.
A Russian officer tasting a sample of the food before the men take away their supply.

Cossack regiments under General Mishtshenko; his name is well known to any student of the Russo-Japanese War.

Thus we find that our Allies, at the end of April, were facing a concentration of at least twenty-four Germanic corps with certainly not more than fourteen Russian corps. The disparity of forces was worst in the West, where the five army corps of General Radko Dmitrieff (according to German statements, these were the 9th, 10th, 12th and 24th Russian and the 3rd Caucasian Army Corps) had to face at least twelve Germanic corps of the armies of Archduke Joseph Ferdinand, of General von Mackensen, and, on the extreme left wing, part of the army of General Borojevic von Bojna, forces equipped with an infinitely stronger force of artillery and provided with an infinitely larger supply of ammunition.

Even more remarkable than the Austro-German concentration of men was, in the battle of Gorlice, the concentration of artillery, especially of heavy guns. Their exact numbers are not known as yet, but the best estimates put their total number at about 4,000, half of which are said to have been equal or exceeding the 8-inch types. They further state that the two Russian corps in the district of Gorlice were faced by a concentration of 1,500 guns, 500 of which are said to have been of heavy calibre. In four hours, on the morning of May 2, they fired about 700,000 shells against the Russian trenches. It has been calculated that 1,500 guns with their train would occupy a length of road amounting to over one hundred miles ; 700,000 shells are approximately equivalent to one thousand car-loads. A similar number of shells must have been, moreover, kept in reserve. Calculating on the basis of only one line, we find that against every Russian soldier in the firing line—i.e., against every one and a half step of front—10 shells were fired of the weight of about 14 pounds. These few figures give an approximate idea of

the enormous task of preparation which preceded the opening of the Germanic offensive in West Galicia.

For months Austrian aviators had been at work taking photographs of the Russian positions until they had completed an exact bird's-eye view survey of their lines. Then all the ranges were exactly calculated and the disposition of their own artillery mapped out and emplacements prepared. The broken, hilly character of the country is very well suited to a strong and masked concentration of howitzers within a comparatively narrow area. As howitzers, which formed the main strength of the Germanic artillery, admit of very considerable variations in the angle of firing, the possibilities for concentration are very great. The actual moving of troops to the front does not seem to have started on any large scale until in the second half of April. A glance at the map of railways and roads in West Galicia will explain how that enormous task could have been performed in such comparatively short time.*

In the net of communications along the

* Readers should refer to the map published in Vol. IV., chapter 76, p. 410.

AN AUSTRIAN BIG GUN.
The Skoda 30·5 cm. gun about to be fired.

AUSTRIA'S GIANT ARTILLERY IN GALICIA.
The Skoda 30·5 cm. guns in action.

Dunajec-Biala-Ropa line itself there is hardly any difference between the eastern and the western side. The area of exceptionally favourable conditions for quick concentration in West Galicia lies 40 miles to the west of the Dunajec, on the Cracow-Chabowka line. No less than five first-class railways reach that line from the north-west, the west, and the south-west, on a front of about thirty-five miles. In the north-west the Cracow-Chabowka area is connected with the railway system of Russian Poland; the Thorn-Kutno-Skiernievice-Piotrkow-Czestochova railways and the western sector of the Kielce-Miechow line had been in the hands of the Germanic armies ever since the beginning of December. Over these railways they could transfer reinforcements from the Vistula front to West Galicia. From the west the highly developed Silesian and West-Austrian railway net reaches the Cracow-Chabowka front by three main branches. From the south-west, a Hungarian railway leads by Novy Targ to Chabowka. Besides these lines, another important Hungarian railway runs from Kaschau by Eperies to Novy Sacz, and thus enters the " Transversal Valley " about twenty miles to the west of the battle front of Gorlice, whilst two other Hungarian railways approach the Carpathians from the south within what then was the Austrian area, though they do not cross the mountain range. From the Cracow-Chabowka-Novy Targ area two railways and four first-class high roads lead up to the Dunajec-Biala-Ropa front, besides two Hungarian high roads running from the south-west to Novy Sacz. It must further be remembered that towards the end of April (and also later on in May) the weather in West Galicia

was quite exceptionally fine and dry, so that also secondary roads could be used by the armies. Nevertheless the concentration accomplished by the German armies in West Galicia in the second half of April remains one of the most extraordinary feats of army organization which had been achieved in this war.

The Russian official *communiqué* of May 2 contains the following statement : " During the night of April 30-May 1 strong Austrian forces opened an offensive in the region of Ciezkovice. Our fire forced the enemy to entrench 600 paces in front of our trenches." Moreover, during the last few days of April and on May 1 artillery fire, sometimes followed by infantry attacks, was opened by the Germanic forces at different points on the Rava, Pilica, Nida and the Dunajec. These were movements really aiming at diversion, they were meant to mask the intentions of the Germanic armies and to mislead the Russians concerning the sector which had been chosen for the main attack.

During the last few nights preceding that of May 1–2 the Germanic forces in the district between Ciezkovice and Senkova had moved closer to the battle line. On the opposite slopes of the hills, to the east, the Russians were holding carefully constructed lines. The Russian front line extended from Ciezkovice in a south-eastern direction ; between Staszkovka and Zagorzany the heights of the Viatrovka and Pustki (1,475 feet) and the Kamieniec (1,384 feet) formed the main Russian *points d'appui*. Near the town of Gorlice itself their strongest strategic point was the mountain

AN ABANDONED RUSSIAN TRENCH.
German Red Cross workers searching for the wounded.

rising to the east of the town between the River Ropa and the Gorlice-Sokol-Zmigrod road (about 1,200 feet high). On its western end is the cemetery of Gorlice ; farther east extended a beautiful grove of oaks, almost a thousand years old. The square between the roads connecting Gorlice, Malastow, Bartne and Bednarka is filled by a mountain group which consists of about a dozen hills, varying in height from 1,500 to 2,200 feet. The most important among them, from the strategical point of view, was the Zamczysko height, after which the whole group is sometimes named. The strategic importance of this group can be easily seen on the map. An advance to Bednarka will carry the German troops on to the flank of the Jaslo line, the *third Russian line* of defence, and will also bring them dangerously near to the Jaslo-Zmigrod-Krempna road, which, after the loss of the Gorlice-Malastow-Zbow road, remained the only line of retreat for the Russian troops that were holding the Zboro district. South-west of the Zamczysko and south of Malastow the two mountains, of the Magora (2,778 feet), east of the Malastow-Gladyszow-Zboro road, and the Ostra Gora (about 2,400 feet), to the west of it, formed the chief Russian *points d'appui.*

Towards the evening of May 1 the Germanic batteries started " practice shooting " against the Russian positions. The fire was continued throughout the night with intervals during which the engineers attempted to destroy the first line of Russian wire-entanglements. The Austrians claim to have brought up during the same night several batteries of heavy howitzers, across the serpentine road from Gladyszow to Malastow, without the Russians noticing it. To Gladyszow they evidently must have been brought by the road from Uscie Ruskie. It is not easy to understand how all that could have been done without the Russians knowing about it, and it is hardly credible that this really occurred. The Austrian report which contains this account claims that the Austrian artillery after having passed between the Magora and the Ostra Gora during the night started in the morning the bombardment of the Russian positions on those heights from the direction of Malastow.

On May 2, between 6 and 7 a.m., an artillery fire was opened against the entire Russian line such as had never been witnessed before. In the following four hours 700,000 shells were fired. The first lines of Russian trenches were practically wiped out. As Prof. Pares, who was present in that battle, says about one part of line, " the whole area was covered with shells till trenches and men were levelled out of existence." The German and Austrian artillery continued that hurricane of shells for about four hours. After that they passed to the *tire de barage :* a curtain of fire is thereby placed *behind* the front line of the enemy trenches, thus isolating the area which had been previously bombarded ; the shells now pass over the heads of that front line, but establish behind it an area which no living being can pass. The men in the front trenches who have survived the previous shelling cannot receive any reinforcements from behind and the infantry of the attacking side advances against them. This stage was reached along the greater part of the Ciezkovice-Malastow line on May 2, about 10 a.m. " In this part of the front," says a German military writer, " infantry fighting has given place for the time being to the action of our heavy artillery, which is subjecting to a terrific fire the positions of the enemy. These positions had been carefully reconnoitred during the lull in the fighting which prevailed during the last few months. Only after all cover is destroyed, the enemy's infantry killed or forced to retire, we take up the attack against the positions ; the *élan* of our first attack now usually leads to a favourable result." One would not expect much *élan* to be required on the part of the infantry after the condition described above had once been reached ; but nowadays *élan* or " bravery " has become with German writers the necessary *epitheton ornans* due to the Germans, and like the classical *epitheta* it is used in season and out of season. As a matter of fact, the statement that the first attack *usually* sufficed for the conquest of the Russian trenches is incorrect ; even German and Austrian writers frequently mention attacks that failed, though the ground had been previously prepared by the most terrific bombardment ; we shall have to say more of that farther on.

At the extreme northern end of the sector which had been chosen for the main onslaught round Ciezkovice and Staszkovka the Prussian Guard and other Prussian troops under

General von François attacked the Russian positions. Our Allies had to retire by the end of the day to positions about half-way between the previous positions and the Olpiny-Biecz line. On the whole, Mackensen seems to have chosen for his Prussians the less difficult work, and comparatively least seems to have been achieved in that district ; the most arduous task was left to the Austro-Hungarian and the Bavarian troops. The Russian positions on Mount Viatrovka were attacked by the 39th Hungarian Division, those on Mount Pustki by the 12th Galician Division, both belonging to the 6th Austro-Hungarian Army Corps under F.M.L. Arz von Straussenberg. The ground had been prepared for them by heavy artillery, consisting of the 21-cm. Krupp howitzers and the terrific Austrian 30·5-cm. howitzers manufactured by the Skoda-Works at Pilsen. These guns, surpassing in mobility most of the German artillery of similar calibre, had been adopted by the Austro-Hungarian Army in 1912. Their shell weighs about sixty stone and has proved almost as effective as that of the 42-cm. giants. Its shot is said to throw up the earth about 100 ft. high.'

Farther south the town of Gorlice was subjected to a merciless bombardment. Whatever had remained of that unfortunate town was now destroyed ; about 300 of its remaining civilian population of about 1,300 perished whilst the Austrian and German batteries were throwing " from the south and the west

TRENCHES IN A GRAVEYARD.
Scene in the cemetery at Gorlice after the battle.

GERMAN ARTILLERY PASSING THROUGH A TOWN IN GALICIA.

fire and death into the town " (we quote that cheerful description from a German source). The horror of the situation was heightened by the conflagration of the oil-wells and oil-refineries. Gorlice is the centre of an important oil district. In the building of the town hall of Gorlice, some sixty years ago, the chemist Lukasiewicz conducted his researches which resulted in the discovery of the first process whereby lamp-oil was gained from raw petroleum ; it was he who constructed the first oil-lamp. Of that old town hall nothing survived the German bombardment. The fire spread also to the Gorlice factory of sulphuric acid and to the oil-wells which extend between Gorlice and Glinik. Yet our Allies were still hanging on to the town, which had been changed by noon into a living inferno. Step by step in hand-to-hand fighting the Silesian divisions had to conquer the town. In the afternoon the struggle was continued on the cemetery mountain and in the oak-grove of Sokol. A hail of shells soon changed the fine old oaks into matchwood. The position became untenable. By the end of the day our Allies had to withdraw to the Biecz-Lipinki-Bednarka front, their second line in that district. Of that line the heights of Kobylanka, Tatarowka, Lysa Gora and Rekaw were the most important supports.

South of Senkova, in the district of the Zamczysko, Bavarian regiments under General von Emmich had replaced the Austrian troops of General von Arz about April 26. At that time our Allies had still been in possession of the intervening valley through which flows the small river Senkova. These positions, to which little importance was attached at that time, were conquered by the Bavarians in the last days of April, in order to obtain a better starting point for the grand offensive. During the night of May 1-2 everything was prepared for the attack. At 7 a.m. the artillery, which included German 21 cm. howitzers, Austrian 15-cm. howitzers, Austrian mountain batteries and field artillery, commenced its work of destruction. By 10 a.m. it seemed that everyone within that area must have perished, and the *tire de barage* commenced. A few regiments of Bavarian infantry opened the attack, but were received by a most murderous Russian machine-gun and rifle fire. It is a proof of incomparable nerve and endurance on the part of the Russians that after three hours of such an inferno they could still offer effective

resistance. The first attack of the Bavarians broke down and their first lines perished, having achieved little more than to break at a few points a way through the wire entanglements. Only by costly, slow and cautious work were their successors able to approach the Russian positions. At one point a small ridge protrudes from the slope above the Senkova-Malastow road, offering a certain amount of dead ground ; it is grown all over with shrubs, which form fairly good cover. Across that ridge the Bavarians managed to reach the bat-

FIELD-MARSHAL
ARZ VON STRAUSSENBERG.

tered Russian trenches, which had been cut off from their supports by a screen of the enemy's artillery fire. Having conquered at a considerable cost the first heights, the Bavarian infantry reformed close to the forest which the artillery fire had rendered untenable. The Austrian 15 cm. howitzers and their mountain batteries at once moved on to their support. The Chief of the Austro-Hungarian General Staff, General Conrad von Hötzendorf, had for a long time taken a great interest in increasing the mobility of the heavy artillery. A few years before the outbreak of the war the

A SCENE OF SEVERE FIGHTING.
On the battlefield in Galicia.

Austrian 15-cm. and even the 24-cm. howitzers had been adapted to motor transport ; may be that also General Conrad " built better than he knew."

Whilst the Bavarians were advancing in the northern part of the sector, our Allies were counter-attacking from the south and disputing hard to the enemy every foot-breadth of ground. Only the combined attack of the Bavarians and of Austrian troops, which were fighting farther south in the Mencina district, finally dislodged the Russians from the positions round the " gamekeeper's lodge " ; this group of buildings lies at the foot of Hill 469, on its eastern side, between it and Heights 461, 501 and 598. From the " gamekeeper's lodge " access can be comparatively easily gained to these neighbouring hills. One by one the heights of the Zamczysko group were now falling. At last, towards nightfall, the fire of the heavy Austrian batteries was directed against the Zamczysko height itself ; it was finally abandoned by our Allies about 8 p.m., and the Bavarians now held this entire sector extending to the east beyond Height 649. They were now only a short distance outside the village of Bednarka.

To the south of the Zamczysko group the 10th Austrian Army Corps (of Przemysl and Jaroslav, under the command of FML. von Martiny) had conquered the Magora of Malastow and most of the Ostra Gora group.

The net result of the operations of May 2 round Gorlice was the breaking in of the Russian defences on a front of about ten miles and to an average depth of over two miles. The depth attained was, however, by no means even approximately uniform. It was worst in the centre round Gorlice and Senkova rather less marked on the flanks.

" The Germans had shot their first bolt," wrote the special correspondent of *The Times*, Mr. Stanley Washburn, " a bolt forged from every resource in men and munitions. that they could muster for months of preparation." The Russian Army " was outclassed in everything except bravery, and neither the Germans nor any other army can claim superiority in that respect." In the case of many an army a disaster such as that which overcame the Russian lines round Gorlice on May 2 might have changed into a catastrophe for the entire force. The Eighth Russian Army, no doubt, suffered severely. " With the centre literally cut away, the keystone of the Russian line had been pulled out, and nothing remained but to retire." Yet the spirit even of that Eighth Army, which had suffered worst, was in no way broken. Many of its units, though decimated, established on their retreat a record of which a victorious army could be proud.

The conquest of the triangle between the rivers and the Zakliczyn-Gromnik road, in other words, the taking of Heights 402, 419 and

269, was the first problem which confronted, in the region south of Tarnow, the Fourth Austro-Hungarian Army under Archduke Joseph-Ferdinand. Until that was done no direct advance against Tarnow could be undertaken. During the months of February and March the Austrian troops had delivered most desperate attacks against the positions of our Allies on those hills ; all of them failed. They returned to the work on May 2, supported by a concentration of artillery similar to that employed in the district of Gorlice

On the morning of May 2, at 6 a.m., the Austrian artillery opened fire from the Mount Val and from the western bank of the Dunajec against Hill 419. The bombardment was continued for more than three hours. Meantime a few regiments of the Tyrolese "Kaiserjäger" (Imperial Fusiliers), belonging to the 14th Austrian Army Corps crossed the forests which cover the northern slopes of the Mount Val, and the valley intervening between it and Hill 419, and took up positions in the forest at the southern foot of the latter, ready to attack the moment when the artillery fire

A YOUNG RUSSIAN VOLUNTEER.
He was aged 14, and was with his regiment at the front.

should stop. About 400 yards of an open, steep slope intervened between the positions now occupied by the Austrian Fusiliers and the Russian trenches. But a few hundred yards to the east, in the forest descending from Hill 412, was another Russian position, of which the Austrians seem to have had no knowledge. About 9.30 a.m. the Austrian artillery fire ceased and the Fusiliers proceeded to the attack. They came at once under a fierce rifle and machine-gun fire directed against them from Hill 419, and they had not yet proceeded much farther when they found themselves enfiladed from the right flank. A small cemetery on the slope now marks the spot at which perished the greater part of the 4th Regiment of the Austrian Imperial Fusiliers. The attack failed completely. The survivors escaped back under the shelter of the forest.

On May 3 the Austrian batteries reopened their fire against the Russian positions on Hill 419. Germans and Austrians who have subsequently visited those trenches express their unbounded admiration for the men who were able to endure such a trial without losing their nerve. From the first trench till about 100 steps in the rear, not a foot of ground was left untouched by shells. The whole hill looks now as if covered with volcanic craters, like a

IN A RUSSIAN TRENCH.
Looking through a periscope.

field ploughed by devils; all the woodwork of the trenches has been reduced to matchwood and the gruesome mixture of earth, wood, human limbs, torn clothes and fragments of shells testifies to the ghastliness of modern weapons.

But even after that second bombardment the Austrians did not repeat their attempt of the previous day at a direct attack against Hill 419. They prepared their way by first conquering step by step the Russian trenches on Hill 412. Its fall rendered the isolated positions on Hill 419 untenable. Still the resistance of our Allies was not broken even now. They withdrew on to Height 269, next to the Vojnicz-Tarnow road, and maintained themselves at that point until they had to

THE RUSSIAN RETREAT.
A gun which was rendered useless by the Russians before leaving Galicia.

evacuate it in consonance with the general retirement in other parts of the front. The defence of this district forms one of the most glorious episodes in the Russian retreat in West Galicia.

On the night of May 1–2, which marks the beginning of the Germanic offensive in West Galicia, Austrian troops effected a crossing of the Dunajec near Otfinow. Under cover of the forests which extend along the range of hills west of the river, the Austrians had concentrated considerable forces of men and artillery. On the night of May 1–2 their engineers, protected by powerful artillery fire, succeeded in constructing a pontoon bridge across the river. The small groups of Russians which were holding at a few points the western bank of the Dunajec, fought with extraordinary obstinacy.

Even German sources record different individual acts of bravery achieved by the Russian soldiers. At one spot a Russian soldier who had swam across the river, plunged back into it in order to rescue his officer; he succeeded in doing it, but on reaching the eastern bank of the Dunajec was killed by what the German prefers to describe as a "stray" bullet. At another point the commander of a Russian battery, having fired off his last shell, and seeing that nothing was left to him except surrender, is reported to have committed suicide.

By the evening of May 2 the Austrian troops had established themselves along a fairly wide front on the eastern bank of the Dunajec. The strategic importance of that move consisted in that it carried the Austrian forces on to the Tarnow-Szczucin railway; thus the connexion was broken between the West Galician Army of General Radko Dmitrieff and the neighbouring Russian Army on the Nida—i.e., the left wing of General Alexeieff's group of armies.

Yet the entire advance effected by the army of Archduke Joseph-Ferdinand, both north and south of Tarnow, would have remained without much consequence had it not been for the further developments which ensued along the Gorlice-Jaslo line.

The German scheme was simple, says a semi-official *communiqué* issued at Petrograd on May 13; it was all "based on lightning rapidity of movement." On May 2 the German forces had pierced the first line of Russian defences in the district of Gorlice, the following days were to decide the actual value of that initial success. On the Dunajec, south of Tarnow, the Russians were holding their own, and even the loss of Hills 402 and 419 on May 3 did not destroy their defence. Once before, in December 1914, after the battle of Limanova, the Austrian armies had broken through the gate of Gorlice and crossed the Western Carpathians from Hungary; they had advanced in the depression, which we call the "Transversal Valley," as far as Sanok. But that success had proved devoid of far-reaching consequences; the Russian armies stood firm round Tarnow and fresh reinforcements brought up from Russian Poland enabled them, in the second half of December, to drive back the Austrians beyond Gorlice and across the Carpathians. Thus experience had taught the Germanic armies to count, in their new offensive in May

"GASSED" RUSSIAN TROOPS.

Russian soldiers suffering from the effects of poisonous gas which was used by the Germans, waiting
for treatment at a Red Cross station. Inset: A little samaritan brings water to a "gassed" man.
This wounded man is holding in his right hand a piece of cotton wool which had been dipped in a
soothing chemical. He sniffed at it from time to time.

1915, with the strength of the Russian positions round Tarnow. The enormous concentration of forces in the district of Gorlice allowed them to adopt this time a peculiar plan of advance. Although Mackensen's army had pierced the first Russian lines near Gorlice by a frontal attack from west to east, its main forces did not continue their offensive in the same direction, but advanced to the north-east at an angle of about 45° to the original line. Only the extreme right wing of Mackensen's army continued its advance due east with extraordinary rapidity; its aim was to reach the Dukla Pass before the Russian troops from north-western Hungary could have effected their retreat across the mountains.

The movement, which we might best describe as a "left incline," presented evident advantages to the Germanic armies. It tended to widen the breach which had been effected in the Russian lines round Gorlice; it was bound to result in the abandonment of the Tarnow front by the Russians; and it rendered possible the unimpeded advance of armies which had been standing originally at right angles to one another, along the Dunajec-Biala front and along the southern foot of the Carpathians. Mackensen knew only too well the dangers of an advance through a narrow gap in the enemy's line; he had done it in the battle of

Lodz, and had it not been for the late arrival of two Russian generals, von Rennenkampf and von Scheidemann, he might by now have been a prisoner of war, together with about two or three entire corps of the Prussian Army. The advance of the left wing and centre of Mackensen's army from the Gromnik-Gorlice front in a north-easterly direction automatically carried them into the rear and on to the lines of communication of the Russian forces round Tarnow; at the same time it relieved the pressure which the Russians were bringing to bear on the Fourth Austrian Army. The army of Archduke Joseph-Ferdinand, though inferior in numbers to the Eleventh German Army under Mackensen, was holding a front of about thirty miles, whilst that of the latter did not exceed twenty. Moreover, for reasons given above, the Russian reinforcements could quickest reach Dembica; had not Mackensen moved his army from the Gromnik-Gorlice front against Dembica and Rzeszow, our Allies might have successfully checked his advance by a counter-offensive from the neighbouring sector extending between the Vistula and Tarnow. The swerving towards the north-east implied a redistribution of forces and a devolution of the extraordinary concentration of forces round Gorlice.

As we have previously stated, the extreme

NEAR PETRIKAU.
This is the place where the Germans met the Caucasian army.

RUINED POLISH VILLAGE.
A street scene in a town in Poland, showing the effect of a bombardment.

right wing of Mackensen's army continued a rapid advance due east, towards the Dukla. With that exception the triangle between Gorlice, the Uzsok and Radymno (half-way between Przemysl and Jaroslav), which was left free by the north-easterly swerve of Mackensen's army, was filled by the Third Austro-Hungarian army under General Borojevic von Bojna, and the Second Austro-Hungarian army under General von Boehm-Ermolli. Only a most magnificent army organization and a most careful preparation, extending to detail, could execute a plan of such magnitude at the speed at which it was done by the Austrian and German armies during the month of May 1915.

On May 2 our Allies had been dislodged from their first lines of defence on the Ciezkovice-Luzna-Gorlice-Malastow front. The attack against Hill 419, to the south-west of Tarnow, had failed. Even after the loss of that position, on May 3, the Tarnow-Tuchow front stood firm. The main thrust had been delivered in the direction of Gorlice and Biecz; soon, however, the entire line had to give way; it was not feasible much longer to pivot on Tuchow. The River Visloka, between Dembica, Pilzno, Brzostek, Jaslo and Zmigrod, offers positions parallel to the original Dunajec-Biala-Ropa front. The Visloka was the third Russian line of defence, and hopes were entertained that our Allies might be able to stop on it the Austro-German advance. It is difficult to give a precise description of the second Russian line. It did not follow any river, but extended across the hills which intervene between the

Biala in the west and the Visloka in the east. In fact, three lines could be traced in that district, but as the retreat did not proceed systematically from the one to the other, it is not necessary for our purpose to enter into the detail of these positions. Different groupings were possible, and the front was changing from hour to hour in accordance with the advance of the Austro-German offensive or of the Russian counter-attacks. Between Tuchow and Olpiny, the Mountain Dobrotyn formed, after the breakdown of the first Russian line, one of the chief Russian defensive positions. It is about 1,800 feet high, and is, like most mountains in that district, covered with thick woods. To the south of the Dobrotyn the Mountain Lipie (about 1,400 feet high) formed an important *point d'appui*. The Mountain Wilczak (1,225 feet), south-west of Biecz and close to the road and railway line which connect that town with Gorlice, forms the key to the valley of the lower Ropa. Between Biecz and Bednarka, the second Russian line followed the heights of the Kobylanka, Tatarowka, Lysa Gora and of the Rekaw; east of it, as the last defence of the Jaslo-Zmigrod road, extended the entrenched positions on the Ostra Gora. To the south of the Gorlice-Zmigrod line the mountain group of the Valkova (almost 2,800 feet high) constituted the last defence of the line of retreat of the Russian forces from Zboro.

During the two days of May 3 and 4 a desperate battle developed for the possession of the wooded hills between the Biala and the Visloka. On May 3 the Prussian Guard advanced to the foot of the Hill Lipie and late in the evening captured the hill itself. On the next

TO ASSIST THE AUSTRIANS.

One of the German Army Corps marching into Galicia to relieve the Austrians.

day it captured, after fierce hand-to-hand fighting in which the Germans vastly outnumbered the Russian forces, Olpiny, Szczerzyny and the hills which surround these townships from the east. Farther south, the 39th Hungarian division (Corps Arz) attacked on May 3 the Russian positions on the Mountain Wilczak, near Zagorzany, close to the junction of the Grybow-Biecz railway line with the branch line from Gorlice. Although effectively supported by a tremendous concentration of artillery, the Hungarians seemed at first incapable of making any impression on the Russian positions. It was only after having delivered six unsuccessful attacks that they were able to dislodge by a seventh attack our Allies from their trenches on the Wilczak. The taking of that mountain settled the fate of Biecz and practically opened to the Austrians the road along the lower Ropa towards Jaslo. That town can be considered the key to the Visloka line, just as the district of Gorlice was for that of the Biala and Upper Ropa. It is the most important railway junction in the district between Tarnow and Przemysl, and lies at the head of the main high roads entering Hungary, between Bartfeld and the Lupkow. Jaslo had been for the last four months the headquarters of General Radko Dmitrieff, the commander-in-chief of the Eighth Russian Army. By the night of May 4 it was evident that the fall of Jaslo itself had become unavoidable. South of it the Bavarians, under General von Emmich, and the 10th Austro-Hungarian Army Corps, under General Martiny, were hacking through their way, by weight of shells and numbers of men, along the Bednarka-Zmigrod road and the secondary road leading from Malastow, past the Valkova Mountain to Krempna. By the night of May 4 they had approached Zmigrod and Krempna; the last direct line of retreat of the Russian troops which had advanced into the region round Zboro was threatened. The evacuation of that district had begun on the same day. On May 4 opened also a more vigorous Austrian offensive round Tuchow, and the fate of Tarnow was by then practically decided, though our Allies still held the town with great skill and stubbornness.

The retreat had spread by the end of May 4 to the entire West Galician front and compelled the Russians to evacuate Northern Hungary west of the Lupkow; even in the Lupkow itself the retreat became more and more a mere question of time. Now that the Austro-German armies were approaching rapidly the Visloka, and that even Jaslo had become practically untenable, no hope was left of any effective resistance being offered to the German concentration of artillery and men before the San and the Dniester were reached. The history of the next three weeks is mainly marked by rearguard actions, interpolated only here and there by bigger battles, which were fought in defence of specially important junctions of roads or railways or in order to gain the necessary respite for the evacuation of some big military centre.

A sudden retreat of a big army cannot possibly be effected without serious losses in prisoners being suffered. Wounded have frequently to be left behind; stragglers, or even whole detached bodies, cannot rejoin the main forces. Finally, now that even rearguard actions are fought in trenches, their occupants, who cannot hope for any fresh supplies or reinforcements, naturally have to surrender as soon as their ammunition is exhausted or when the enemy reaches their positions with vastly superior forces. The German *communiqués* put the approximate figure of Russian prisoners taken during the three days of May 2–4 at about 30,000. The figure does not seem unlikely, especially as it is certain to include the majority of the Russian wounded. Further, we must remember that as the defeat was caused mainly by lack of guns and ammunition, the Russians were bound to harbour whatever artillery they possessed. When an army retires which is well equipped with artillery and ammunition, its guns cover the retreat; they hold the enemy at bay to the last and are sacrificed for the sake of the men. The Russians during their retreat from West Galicia were compelled many a time to sacrifice men in order to save their artillery and in order to preserve it for a coming greater battle at some more important strategic point.

The losses suffered by the Austro-German armies during their attack against the Dunajec-Biala-Ropa line have never been published; their casualty lists appear only some considerable time after the events, and it is difficult to form on that basis any, even approximate, idea about the losses suffered by them in particular battles. On the other hand, a retreating army enjoys even less than the usual facilities for forming an opinion about the casualties of the enemy. Still, it can be seen from the casualty lists of Austro-Hungarian officers that the losses which they suffered in the first three days of the West Galician offensive must have been enormous. Occasionally the date of death is put in the Austrian lists after the name of a killed officer. As late as August the days May 2–4 continue to occur in them ; and it ought to be remembered that during those early days the share which the Austro-Hungarian forces had in the fighting was smaller, in comparison with that of the Germans, than towards the middle of May, when the Carpathian armies, consisting mainly of Austro-Hungarian troops, were brought into the main battle line.

Hardly any fighting took place on the day of May 2 in the Carpathian Mountains, west of the Lupkow. During the preceding week the Russians seem to have withdrawn from that part some troops for the support of the western line, which was known to be threatened. All further offensive in the Western Carpathians had thus come to an end. The Austrians naturally abstained from a counter-offensive. Their forces were not sufficiently big for that purpose on the Hungarian front, and it paid them better to leave the Russians in their advanced southern positions ; Mackensen's offensive from the west, if successful, by cutting their lines of retreat, was bound to create a position of extreme difficulty for the

Russian troops round Zboro and to the south of the Dukla.

Only in the extreme east, where our Allies were facing the mixed Austro-German Army of General von Linsingen, do we hear of some serious fighting taking place in the first days of May. On May 2, says the Russian official *communiqué* published at Petrograd on the following day, "in the direction of Stryj and south-east of Holoviecko, we captured Mount Makovka and took 300 prisoners, including ten officers." On the following night the Austrians recaptured part of these positions, but were again dislodged by the Russians on the morning of May 3. On that day the captures rose to 1,200 prisoners, 30 officers, and three mitrailleuses. Some further fighting is reported on the same day in the region round the village of Osmoloda, near the sources of the Swica and on the Upper Lomnica.

In the region east of Verchovina and Bystra the 79th Austrian Regiment belonging to the 7th Division surrendered voluntarily on grounds of bad food and bad treatment. We are told that "Austrian prisoners complain of their cruel treatment by German officers, who for the slightest misdemeanour, especially on the part of the Rumanians, inflict on them corporal punishment."

EVENING.

CHAPTER LXXXV.

THE RECONQUEST OF PRZEMYSL AND LEMBERG.

The Main Outlines of the Austro-German Advance through Central Galicia—The Evacuation of Tarnow—The Russian Retreat from Hungary—The Evacuation of Central Galicia by the Russians—The Retreat from the Nida—The Battle of Opatow—The Russian Offensive in East Galicia and in the Bukovina—The Russian Retreat from the Eastern Carpathians—The Battle for Przemysl—The Russian Counter-Offensive—The Fall of Przemysl—The Austro-German Advance Against Lwow—Their Attempts to Cross the Dniester—The New Concentration on the San—The Fall of Lwow.

THE conquest of Central Galicia forms the first section of the history of the great Austro-German offensive which opened on the Eastern front in May, 1915. The drive began with the battle of Gorlice, on May 2. Its first stage closed about May 14; on that day the attacking forces reached the San, the frontier of East Galicia, and the natural southern extension of the strategical line of the middle Vistula.

On May 1 the Russian front in Western Galicia and Northern Hungary extended from the confluence of the Dunajec and the Vistula to Zboro; along the rivers Dunajec, Biala and Ropa, past the towns of Tarnow, Ciezkovice and Gorlice; from Zboro it ran on Hungarian soil, in the main in an easterly direction, past Sztropko, Krasnibrod, Virava, Nagy Polena to the Uzsok Pass. The length of that segment of the Eastern front, between the Upper Vistula and the Uzsok, amounted to about 120 miles. Along that line on May 1 at least 19 Austro-German corps, supported by an enormous concentration of heavy artillery, were facing some eight Russian army corps, poorly provided with guns and ammunition. The district between Gromnik and Malastow was occupied by what came to be known afterwards as the "phalanx." No less than six army corps (the

11th German Army under Mackensen, including the 6th Austro-Hungarian Corps under Arz von Straussenberg, and the 10th Austro-Hungarian Army Corps, belonging to the adjoining army of Borojevic) were here concentrated on a front of about 20 miles. On May 2 Mackensen's "battering-ram" broke the Russian line in front of Gorlice. By the night of May 4 the Austro-German troops reached a line extending from the Mountain Dobrotyn (south-east of Tuchow) across the heights on the eastern bank of the Visloka in front of Jaslo, to Zmigrod on the Jaslo-Zboro road. The right wing of the "phalanx" was advancing quickest; its aim was to cut off the Russian forces which had penetrated into Hungary across the Carpathian Mountains to the west of the Lupkow. On May 5 the Austro-German forces, which were standing south of the Carpathians between Bartfeld and the Uzsok, began to exert pressure against the Russian line in Northern Hungary. On the left of Mackensen's army the Austrian troops under Archduke Joseph-Ferdinand had by the night of May 4 occupied on the front between Tarnow and Tuchow most of the ground between the Dunajec and the Biala, and had established themselves on the right bank of the Dunajec, to the north of Tarnow, thus cutting the connexion between

THE TSARITZA DISTRIBUTING CIGARETTES TO HER TROOPS.
Convalescent members of the 15th Regiment of Dragoons about to return to the front.

the Third Russian Army and the Russian forces on the Nida.

We do not intend for the present to enter into the detail of the fighting which developed during the following days, but shall try to give merely the main strategic outlines of the Austro-German advance through Mid-Galicia. As was pointed out in the last chapter, Mackensen broke the Russian front round Gorlice by a frontal attack from west to east, but the further advance of his main forces did not continue in the same direction. They executed between the Biala and Visloka what we have previously described as a " left incline " ; they were now facing north-east and were advancing by echelons, which were, however, kept in close touch with each other. The swerve of Mackensen's army to the north-east threatened to outflank from the south the Russian forces which were offering in front of Tarnow stubborn resistance to the advance of the Fourth Austro-Hungarian Army under Archduke Joseph-Ferdinand. At the same time it made room for the Third and the

Second Austro-Hungarian Armies from across the Carpathians. We can best visualize their advance in the following way : the right end of the line—*i.e.,* the extreme right wing of Boehm-Ermolli's army—remained fixed to the west of the Uzsok, in the district of Volosate ; the left end of the line—*i.e.,* the extreme left wing of the army of General Borojevic (the 10th Austro-Hungarian army-corps under General Martiny)—advanced in close touch with the Bavarians under General von Emmich, who formed the right wing of Mackensen's army. In fact, that Austro-Hungarian corps must be included in his first " phalanx," as we have indicated above. Mackensen's advance to the north-east was gradually drawing the two Austro-Hungarian armies across the Carpathians.

Mackensen's " phalanx " has been occasionally talked of as if it had been a fixed formation. It was nothing of that kind. It was a concentration of troops along the lines on which the main resistance was expected or along which the quickest advance was intended. But there was no one special group of forces earmarked for that purpose. It was the most admirable part of the entire Austro-German plan of advance that there seems to have been very little horizontal shifting or regrouping within the line. The advance was laid out in such a way that the concentrations occurred, as it were, automatically at the points at which they were most needed.

There are four centres of pre-eminent strategic importance in Central Galicia. All the main roads and railways of the country between the Dunajec-Biala-Ropa line in the west, and the San in the east, focus in the districts of Jaslo, Dembica, Rzeszow and Sanok. The occupation of these four centres marks the conquest of Mid-Galicia. The Austro-German forces conquered the district of Jaslo by the *élan* of the first advance after the breakdown of the Gorlice front. The outflanking movement from the south compelled our Allies to evacuate the district of Tarnow and thus to relinquish the main defences in front of Dembica. The rapid advance of the Austro-German armies in the south and the fall of Jaslo rendered impossible any attempt to stop their

drive on the Visloka, *i.e.,* on a line parallel to the original West Galician front. The south-western angle had been knocked in by the first onslaught round Gorlice, and the following days marked a continuous advance in the process of the straightening out of the line between the Vistula and the Uzsok Pass. When on May 8 the Russian forces rallied for a renewed resistance, coupled with attempts at a counter-offensive, the two groups of armies most immediately concerned in the battle for Mid-Galicia were facing one another along a practically straight line, extending from the Vistula near Szczucin to the mountain group west of the Uzsok Pass.

In the corner between the Nida and the Vistula, and in the Uzsok Pass, the Russians were still holding on May 8 approximately the same positions which had been held by them for a period extending over four to six months ; but the intervening front, which on May 1 was about 160 miles long, measured now only about 120 miles. That shortening of the line was entirely accounted for by the change which had occurred on the front between the Vistula and the Sanok-Homonna railway. On May 1 the Austro-German forces had stood in that

AUSTRIAN TROOPS CLEARING AWAY WIRE ENTANGLEMENTS
ERECTED BY THE RUSSIANS.

A FIGHT ON A—

Germans cut off and annihilated after crossing the water on a temporary bridge which was des-
bayoneted, or drowned

sector along a line forming a concave curve, with its centre round the Magora of Malastow, and its arms extending to the north and east for about 60 miles each.   By May 8 the centre of the Austro-German front had advanced to Frysztak on the Vislok,* north-east of Jaslo. Thence it extended for 40 miles to the north-west, to the Vistula, along an almost straight line, running south-west of Dembica and Radomysl, to Szczucin.   To the south-east of Frysztak the front followed the extension of the former line through Krosno to Besko; from Besko it curved round the Bukovica mountain to Komancza; the Frysztak-Komancza line measured another 60 miles.   Between the

Lupkow and the Uzsok the battle-line had receded during the first week of May, but it had not changed either in length or direction.

The line along which our Allies were trying to stop the Austro-German advance between May 8-10 was neither strong by nature nor had its positions been carefully prepared beforehand.   In fact, it was a line which no one could have foreseen, and which no strategist would have chosen of his own free will for a line of defence.   It extended diagonally across Central Galicia, cutting its main rivers.   Across the railway lines and in front of the three main centres our Allies were holding short river-fronts: west of Dembica they were standing on the Visloka; near Strzyzow, south-west of Rzeszow, on the Brzezanka-Stobnica line; and to the west of Sanok, on the upper Vislok. There existed, however, no proper connexion between these main positions, and thus the front of May 8, taken as a whole, could not possibly have been changed into a fixed defensive line of the kind which had previously existed on the Dunajec and the Biala.   Each separate position could be, and in fact was, threatened

* The *Vislok* ought not to be confounded with the *Visloka*.   The names of the Vislok, Visloka, of the Vistula, and also the old name of the Nida, which was Vislica, are all of the same derivation.   We have drawn attention in a former chapter to the frequent occurrence of the river-names of Bystra and Bystryca in East Galicia, *bystry* meaning "quick, rapid."   The name *Visla* (the Polish for Vistula) is a transformation of *Bystra*.   The *t* has dropped out in these names of the Western Polish rivers, being preserved only in the French and English name for the "Visla"; the transition of *b* into *v* is most common in European languages, similarly that of *r* into *l*.

—BARREL BRIDGE.

troyed by the Russians, and the men of three German companies, thus cut off, were either shot, in attempting to retire.

from its southern flank. To an army equalling in strength that of the attacking side, the line of May 8 might have served as a basis for a counter-offensive which would have had the reconquest of the line of the Visloka for its first aim. Once before, in December 1914, the Austrians had advanced through the "Transversal Valley " * to Sanok without being able to make headway in the north, and were then driven back to the west beyond Gorlice by fresh Russian forces brought up from Poland. An army inferior in numbers to that of the attacking side could use the positions which our Allies held on May 8 merely to retard the advance of the enemy and to gain time for the organization of its retreat.

By May 10 our Allies had withdrawn from the Szczucin - Dembica - Strzyzow - Sanok line. Mid-Galicia was lost, and the San now offered

* We must remind our readers that what we call " Transversal Valley " is not the valley of one river, but consists of the upper valleys of a number of confluents of the Vistula. They form together an almost continuous depression on the northern side of the Carpathians. Through that depression runs the so-called " Transversal Railway."

the next possible line of resistance. The Russian retreat from Central Galicia, by uncovering the flanks of the adjoining forces, rendered necessary a withdrawal of the Russian front also from the Nida in the north, and from the Carpathian passes in the east. It seemed, however, at that time as if our Allies were going to stop the Austro-German drive on the line of the San and Dniester, on which they had once before, in October 1914, arrested the advance of the enemy.

On reaching the northern edge of the Mid-Galician hills on the Dembica-Rzeszow line, the Austro-German forces executed an enormous " right-wheel," which brought their armies against the San, facing east. This wheel was connected with a new concentration of forces. Again the left wing of the Austro-German battle-line assumed, on the whole, the part of a containing force. Its front was now even longer than it had been in the beginning of May, when its task included an offensive against Tarnow. The five army-corps of the Fourth Austro-Hungarian Army were now deployed on a front of about 50 miles, extending from

AN INCIDENT IN THE BRILLIANT RUSSIAN OFFENSIVE ON THE BESKO-JACMIERZ FRONT.

126

AUSTRIANS REPAIRING A DAMAGED BRIDGE ACROSS THE VISLOKA.

Tarnobrzeg on the Vistula to the confluence of the Vislok and the San, north of Sieniava. Towards the end of May we find near Piskorovice, on the San, the same Transylvanian regiments, belonging to the 9th Austro-Hungarian Army Corps, which in the first days of May had stood on the Biala, on the extreme right wing of the army of Archduke Joseph-Ferdinand. The fact that comparatively small forces were deemed and proved sufficient for the defence of the left flank of the main Austro-German armies proves that, at that time, our Allies could have had but very small reserves to spare from the battle-line in Russian Poland, and that this was known to the enemy ; it ought to be remembered that not far from the confluence of the Vistula and the San, at Rozvadow, the new Russian railway line from Lublin joins the Galician railway system, and therefore, had any reserves been available from Russian Poland, they could easily have been concentrated in the corner between the Vistula and the San against the left flank of the Galician armies of the enemy.

The district between Sieniava and Sambor became about May 14 the region of the greatest concentration of forces. The three armies which, in the beginning of May, had held the entire front from Gromnik to the Uzsok occupied about May 14 only the district between Sieniava and Sambor. The Eleventh German Army under Mackensen held a front of approximately the same length as it had occupied on May 1. Its left wing and centre,

consisting mainly of Prussian troops, had moved by Strzyzow, Rzeszow, Lancut and Przevorsk, against Sieniava and Jaroslau. The 6th Austro-Hungarian Corps had advanced from Luzna by Biecz, Szebnie, Lutcza and Dynow against Radymno. The Bavarians under General von Emmich, having first advanced due east, from the Senkova valley by Zmigrod, Dukla and Rymanow against Besko, swerved from there to the north-east and were approaching the northern sector of the ring of forts which surrounds Przemysl. The 10th Austro-Hungarian Army Corps, whose home is Przemysl, kept during the entire drive through Central Galicia on the right of the Bavarians, and reached about May 14 the western front of the fortress. The 7th Austro-Hungarian Army Corps under Archduke Joseph advanced from Mezo-Laborcz by Sanok and Bircza ; the rest of the army of General Borojevic von Bojna, including the German Corps of the " Beskids " under General von der Marwitz, enclosed the district of Przemysl from the south-east. It was joined on the Novemiasto-Dobromil line by the Second Austro-Hungarian Army under General von Boehm-Ermolli ; the positions of the latter extended to the east beyond Sambor. Thus the 13 army corps which on May 1 had held a front of about 130 miles were now gathered within about 55 miles. The degree of concentration was thus approximately the same as that of Mackensen's first " phalanx " round Gorlice. And indeed the task with which

IN THE RUSSIAN TRENCHES.

On the right is a Russian officer scanning the enemy's position through binoculars; while the men, with fixed bayonets, are waiting the word to charge. Inset: On the look-out.

they were faced was of a similar nature. They had again to tear out the keystone of the Russian front. To the Dunajec-Biala front of May 1 corresponded a fortnight later the line of the San; to the positions on the Carpathian flank those of the Russian armies retiring towards the Dniester; and the keystone of these new positions was the famous fortress of Przemysl.

Let us now consider in short the main incidents of the Austro-German advance through Central Galicia beginning with May 5.

By the night of May 4 our Allies were still holding the entire right bank of the Dunajec and Biala between Otfinow and Tuchow, although the advance of the enemy across the Mountain Dobrotyn was rendering more and more precarious the position of the Russian troops round Tarnow, whilst the crossing of the Dunajec near Otfinow by the Austrians on the night of May 1-2 had cut the connexion between the Russian forces on the Dunajec and those on the Nida.

On the night of May 4-5 two Transylvanian regiments belonging to the 9th Austro-Hungarian Army Corps (Army of the Archduke Joseph-

Ferdinand) crossed the Biala near Tuchow; they were the 62nd infantry regiment from Marosvasarhely and the 82nd, consisting mainly of Szeklers, a Magyar tribe which lives in the centre of the Roumanian district of Transylvania. These two regiments formed the vanguard of the 10th Austro-Hungarian Division under General von Mecenseffy. Their first objective was the road from Ryglice to Zalasova. A group of hills rising to a level of about 1,500 feet extends north of the Mountain Dobrotyn, between the river Biala, the Tarnow-Pilzno road and the river Visloka. A deep valley intervenes between the Dobrotyn and these hills; in that valley lies the town of Ryglice and through it runs the Tuchow-Brzesko road, the most important road connecting the valleys of the Biala and the Visloka.

between the Tarnow and the Gorlice lines. To the north of Ryglice, on a hill about 1,150 ft. high, lies the village of Zalasova ; from that hill flows to the north a stream called Szymvald towards a village bearing the same name ; towards Ryglice, to the south, flows another stream called Zalasova. A road, connecting that from Tuchow to Brzostek with a secondary road leading from Tarnow to Pilzno, follows the course of these two streams. The occupation of that road by the enemy threatened Tarnow as well as Pilzno. Still the hills along the Ryglice-Szymvald line could not be held long after the enemy had captured the positions on the Dobrotyn ; in fact, these hills are the northern continuation of the Dobrotyn-Valkova front which the Austro-Germans had conquered on May 3-4. The ground between the Biala and the Visloka was held by the Russian rearguards for two days after the abandonment of the Dobrotyn, thus giving the main forces round Tarnow sufficient time to fall back beyond the Visloka. Only the position on the hills west of Pilzno was kept by our Allies for one more day. Pilzno is the junction of four first-class high roads and four secondary roads, and had to be held till the evacuation of the entire district was complete. The positions on

the Hill Zdol (about 1,000 ft. high) which dominates the town and district of Pilzno were not abandoned by the Russians until on May 7.

By the morning of May 6 the Russian troops had withdrawn in perfect order from Tarnow, having first removed the great military stores which had been accumulated in the town ; Tarnow had been the base of the Russian troops operating on the Dunajec. Only a small detachment of cavalry was left behind, but even of this rearguard a considerable part succeeded in hacking its way through the lines of the enemy and in rejoining the main forces. At 10 a.m. the Austrians entered the town which their heaviest artillery had been ravaging for the last few months. The bombardment of the railway station, and possibly also that of the park of Prince Sanguszko, served a definite military purpose ; it is, however, difficult to see what excuse can be given for the partial destruction of the old town-hall and of the fine cathedral, which contains the marble-graves of the families of the Counts Tarnowski and the Princes Ostrogski. It rather seems to suggest the idea that the Austrians did not expect ever to re-enter the town. Tarnow was the first important centre in Galicia which the Germanic armies reconquered after it had remained

AUSTRIANS ENTERING A TRENCH VACATED BY THE RUSSIANS.

THE GERMANS PRESSING INTO POLAND.
Troops of the Death's Head Hussars resting after a march.

for a considerable time in the hands of our Allies. They set out at once to punish everyone who could be accused of having in any way rendered services to the Russians. A short time after Tarnow had been occupied by the Austro-German armies seven of its inhabitants were condemned to death for "high treason." Even from the semi-official account of their trial it can be seen that at least some of these accusations and convictions rested on an exceedingly slender basis and on very doubtful evidence.

On the night of May 6–7 the two Transylvanian regiments, Nos. 62 and 82, crossed the river Visloka both north and south of the town of Brzostek. Artillery posted on a hill near Przeczyca was supporting and covering the operations in that region ; that hill, on the left bank of the river, facing directly the low-lying right bank on which stands the town of Brzostek, rises about 400 feet above the level of the river and dominates the entire district. On the morning of May 7 Hungarian troops occupied Height 384 (*i.e.*, 1,260 feet high), north of Brzostek and the hills above Kamienica Dolna. Meantime their engineers constructed a bridge across the Visloka. The town of Brzostek itself was defended by the Russian rearguards with extreme tenacity. Bayonet fighting developed in its streets and was continued with the greatest violence on the cemetery hill. Our Allies did not evacuate the town until they were threatened by an outflanking movement from the south. They were greatly outnumbered by the Hungarian troops, which were now pouring in masses across the Visloka. Having withdrawn from Brzostek, the Russians took up fresh positions along the western and southern fringe of the forests which stretch between Height 320 and Januszkovice. During the night of May 7–8 our Allies continued their retreat to the strong positions in the Chelm Mountains (about 1,750 feet high), between Brzeziny and Frysztak.

Let us now turn to the south, where on the night of May 4 the troops of Mackensen were approaching the Visloka in the district of Jaslo. The main forces were advancing through the valley of the Ropa, along the high-road which leads from Biecz to Jaslo. On the left bank of the Visloka stretches a range of heights ; the Ropa, near its junction with the Visloka, breaks its way through a narrow gorge between these hills. East of that gate the Ropa enters a wide valley, turns to the north and joins the

Visloka, to the west of Jaslo. The road continues in its easterly direction, and crosses the rivers before their junction. On these hills, west of the Visloka, the Russian rearguards took up fortified positions and maintained them during the day of May 5. They retired at night on to the hills above Szebnie and round Tarnoviec.

Jaslo is the junction of the Transversal Railway and of a side line from Rzeszow, which connects it with the northern Cracow-Lwow line. Between Jaslo and Szebnie the two railways follow the valley of the river Jasliska, running on its opposite banks. The Russian positions near Szebnie dominated that important strategic district ; it was as

GERMAN SOLDIER FIXING UP WIRE-ENTANGLEMENTS.

important from the point of view of the attacking side that they should be taken, as it was difficult to effect their capture. Mackensen entrusted with that arduous task the Hungarian troops of the 39th Honvéd Division (Corps Arz) ; it is interesting to mark how he left the hardest work to Austro-Hungarian or Bavarian troops, but with what loving care he spared his Prussians, especially the Guards. Attack after attack broke down in the fire from the Russian positions above Szebnie ; had it not been for their heavy artillery, the Hungarians would probably never have succeeded in dislodging our Allies from their trenches. But the howitzers did their work, and by the night of May 6 the Russians had to withdraw to positions east of the Vislok. They were followed by the Austro-Hungarian corps of Mackensen's army, whilst the Guards advanced against Frysztak. From here onwards the Prussians kept to the valley of the Vislok and its road and railway-line, leaving to their Austro-Hungarian and

COSSACKS PICKING UP AND
An episode of the retirement of the rear-guard

Bavarian comrades the much less comfortable path across the hills. By the night of May 7 Mackensen's troops had crossed the Frysztak-Krosno line and were hammering against the Russian positions east of the Vislok ; especially near Odrzykon and Korczyna desperate fighting is reported to have taken place.

On the extreme right wing of Mackensen's army the Bavarians and the adjoining corps of the Third Austro-Hungarian Army, after having broken through the Russian positions in the mountains of the Zamczysko and the Magora of Malastow, had advanced to the east at top speed. They reached the Zmigrod-Krempna road on May 4, late at night on May 5 entered the towns of Dukla and Tylava, and reached Rymanow on May 6. The news of the defeat on the Dunajec on May 2 was so sudden and surprising that it sounded almost incredible. The commanders of the 12th Russian Army Corps, which stood south of the main Carpathian range in Northern Hungary, on the extreme right wing of the Third Russian Army, do not seem to have grasped in time the whole gravity of the situation. Whilst they were preparing to withdraw, the Austro-German forces on the northern side of the mountains were closing one

after the other the exits from the passes. When at last they realized the entire extent of the disaster, for some of them at least the roads were closed.

Some brigades, especially those farther east, were still able to cross the Dukla before the coming of the enemy. Others were left with the choice of surrendering or of hacking their way through the Austro-German lines which were barring their road to the north, whilst other enemy troops from the army of General von Borojevic were pursuing them from the south. The Second Austro-Hungarian Army, with the exception of the 10th Army Corps, had taken no part in the battle of May 2 ; it was against their interest to hurry up the retreat of the Russian troops from Hungary. By May 4 they were however, pressing forward with full strength along the entire line, so as to prevent the Russians from the Ondava valley from effecting a junction to the east with the troops of the Eighth Russian Army in the valley of the Laborcza. On May 7 the 48th Russian Division, under General Korniloff, found itself surrounded in the Dukla Pass by vastly superior enemy forces. Its commander did not, however, give up the game for lost, and succeeded with remarkable skill in breaking through the Austro-German ring and in rejoining the main

CARRYING THEIR WOUNDED COMRADES.
columns of the Russian army in Poland.

Russian forces which were falling back through the "Transversal Valley" towards the Brzo-zow-Besko-Ordzechova line. But not all the troops retreating across the Carpathians west of the Lupkow were equally enterprising and equally successful.

By May 6 the Russian troops in the entire district of the Lupkow were involved in the retreat. On May 7 our Allies had to evacuate the Virava-Telepovce-Zuella-Nagy Polena line which they had conquered in April as the prize of many hard-fought battles. Their retirement was covered mainly by the 49th Division, which was holding the main positions until the entire force had crossed the mountain-range, and then withdrew, after having first blown up the Lupkow tunnel. West of the Lupkow the 7th Austro-Hungarian Army Corps under Archduke Joseph and the Germans under General von der Marwitz were delivering desperate attacks against the retreating forces of our Allies. Severe fighting took place on the Varentyzow Mountain, but the Russians were practically taking their own time. The retreat of General Brussiloff's Army was a true military achievement and contributed much towards enabling the heroic, but badly mauled troops of the Third Russian Army to extricate themselves from Central Galicia. On May 8 the forces of

these two Armies were joining hand in the region of Sanok. East of the Uzsok Pass no marked changes had as yet occurred.

We have indicated the main outlines of the battle-front of May 8 in our strategic survey of the Austro-German advance through Mid-Galicia. We have also drawn attention to the most serious strategic weakness of the Russian positions, which was that the most important sectors, the Mielec-Dembica line, the Strzyzow-Lutcza front and even the Brzozow-Besko-Bukovisho position could be outflanked from the south. Another serious obstacle to effective defence seems to have been the uneven distribution of the Russian troops. The German drive had been planned for weeks ahead, and even comparative details of the direction of advance and the concentrations of troops must have been settled beforehand. The absence of properly prepared lines of defence behind the original positions in the west proves that the collapse of the Dunajec-Biala front and the subsequent retreat to the San must have come as a surprise to the Russian army-command. Under these circumstances the Russian retreat was no smaller feat of military skill than was the Austro-German advance. Our Allies never and nowhere were really routed and their troops did not dissolve in a panic. The mere

fact that the average advance of the enemy
did not exceed six miles a day bears witness
to the orderly character of the Russian retreat.
Yet a proper distribution of forces, making the
most of them, and securing the different points
of the line with due regard to their importance
can hardly be expected where the plans have
not been laid down beforehand. The continuous shortening of the line, which led to a
concentration of the forces of the enemy, was
liable to cause a conglomeration, rather than
concentration of the retreating army.

On the extreme right wing, on the lower
Visloka, the Russian troops had given least
ground to the enemy and were as yet most
effectively resisting his advance. South of
Strzyzow, the positions of our Allies followed
on May 8–9 in the main the course of the
stream Brzezanka till Lutcza, and then that
of the Stobnica almost till Brzozow. The hills
stretching along these valleys rise about 300
feet above their level and are covered with thick
woods. They offer fairly favourable positions
for defence. Unfortunately insufficient numbers of Russian troops seem to have been directed towards this line. The main forces retreated along the safest and most direct road—
i.e., through the " Transversal Valley " towards
Sanok. In front of that important town, which
had for many months served our Allies as a
base for their operations in the Carpathians,
strong defensive positions had been constructed.
They extended approximately along a semi-
circle. From Brzozow they ran for about
five miles to the south, passing west of the
village of Jacmierz ; that village lies where
the hills descend to the broad, completely
flat valley of the Vislok. Three miles south-
west of Jacmierz, at the other fringe of the
valley, where the high-road from Rymanow
to Sanok crosses the River Vislok, lies the
village of Besko, an important strategic point
on the line which our Allies defended between
May 8–10. For more than five miles to the
south-east of Besko stretches a mountain-group,
called Homondova Gora ; it rises about 650
feet above the valley of the Vislok and is
covered with big, dense forests. On its southern
slope lies the village of Odrzechova, and to the
west of the Homondova Gora the village of
Novotaniec. Through these two villages and
across the Bukovica towards the Sanok-
Homonna railway-line extended on May 8 the
main Russian positions south-west of Sanok.
In this region our Allies had gathered consider-

able forces and not merely offered a decided
resistance to the enemy, but even attempted
from here a counter-offensive to the west.

Between May 8–10 raged along the entire line
from Szczucin to the Uzsok what we may describe as the battle of Mid-Galicia. Having
occupied Pilzno on May 7, the Austrian troops
on the following day broke the Russian front
near Dembica, and our Allies had to retire on to
the Ropczyce-Vielopole line. The junction of
the Lublin-Rozvadow-Mielec line with the railway from Rzeszow was lost, and the Szczucin-
Mielec line and even that of the lower Visloka
became untenable. Meantime the main German offensive was developing in the central
sector south-east of Strzyzow, in which the
Russian forces were comparatively weakest and
which reinforcements could not reach in time
to stop the German advance. " In the evening
of the 9th," says the Russian official communiqué
of May 11, " a situation unfavourable to us was
created in the principal sector of the fighting—
namely, in the region of Strzyzow." The
situation was saved for the time being by a
brilliant Russian counter-offensive from the
Besko-Jacmierz front, and time was gained
for an orderly retreat of the main forces. There
was, however, no hope of arresting the Austro-
German advance for any longer period of
time until the San-Dniester line was reached.
On May 10 the Russian defence in the valley
of the Vislok broke down and the German
centre was quickly approaching the Dembica-
Rzeszow-Jaroslau railway-line. The troops
concentrated in Sanok were themselves hard
pressed from all sides. The district of Rymanow had been reached by the Bavarians
on May 6 ; during the following two days they
had brought up heavy artillery, including some
21-cm. howitzers, with which they were bombarding the Russian positions west of Sanok.
From the south-west the 10th Austro-Hungarian Army Corps was pressing against the
Russian positions in front of Odrzechova, the
7th Austro-Hungarian Army Corps and the
Germans under von der Marwitz were advancing
from the south. East of the Sanok-Homonna
railway-line the entire Second Austro-Hungarian Army, under General von Boehm-
Ermolli, was hammering against the Baligrod-
Lutoviska front ; they reached on May 9 the
same line along which they had stood two
months earlier, when trying desperately to
break through to the relief of Przemysl.

By the night of May 10 the battle of Central

GERMAN UHLANS CAUGHT IN A RUSSIAN BARBED WIRE ENTANGLEMENT.

Galicia was practically over. Across all the roads Austro-German troops were advancing like a gigantic flood against the line of the San ; the Russians were falling back on Przemysl. On May 11 the enemy occupied the districts of Sendziszow, Rzeszow, Dynow, Sanok and Lisko, on May 12 those of Lancut and Dubiecko. On May 13 our Allies evacuated Przevorsk ; among the last to leave was Captain Ratlow with the 7th Russian railway-battalion ; it had been their task, beginning with Rzeszow,

to destroy the railway-bridges, stations, plant, etc. During the following few days the outer ring of the fortress of Przemysl was reached by the enemy from the west. Then a lull set in in the fighting, in so far as the sector west of Przemysl was concerned. On their retreat the Russians had carefully destroyed all bridges, culverts, and tunnels, and torn up as much as they could of the roads and railways. Time was required for bringing the lines of communication into such a condition as would admit the transport of the heaviest siege artillery ; without at least 30·5 cm. howitzers an attack against Przemysl was unthinkable. Although the Austro-German engineers were working day and night, they were unable to reconstruct more than about four miles of railway a day, and as late as May 25 the trains from the west could not proceed beyond Lancut on the northern line, and not farther than half-way between Krosno and Sanok on the Transversal Railway. Moreover, fresh forces had to be brought up to fill the gaps which had been torn in the Austro-German lines in the many battles fought between May 2–12 ; the wounded, on the other hand, had to be sent back to the base hospitals. What exactly was the price in blood with which the Austro-German armies paid for their victory is not known, but the calculation which puts them at well over 120,000 certainly does not seem likely to prove an exaggeration. During the same period (May 2–12) the three armies of the Archduke Joseph-Ferdinand, Mackensen, and Borojevic claim to have captured 103,500 men, 69 guns, and 255 machine-guns. These figures do not seem unlikely. The toll in prisoners which has to be paid by a retreating army is always heavy ; it must further be remembered that the retreat of our Allies had led them through hilly or even mountainous country, where it is impossible for a retiring army to keep close together, and where detached bodies are in great danger of being captured by the enemy. Moreover, the figure of prisoners is certain to include many wounded, and that not only of battles fought during the advance itself ; Sanok and its surroundings, especially the watering-places of Rymanow and Ivonicz, contained some of the most important Russian base-hospitals. They were considered there as safe as a German hospital would have been at Brussels or Liège. It is certain that their complete evacuation was not possible in the short time at the disposal of the Russian authorities.

The number of guns captured by the Austro-German armies, even if exactly stated, is remarkably small. Four guns to a thousand men was the normal ratio laid down by Napoleon I., and it has certainly not been lowered since his days. Of the guns captured by the enemy a considerable proportion is known to have been taken from the Russian troops which had been cut off on their retreat from Northern Hungary. Otherwise the Russian commanders were specially careful to save their guns, and

hardly ever abandoned any, unless they were absolutely unfit for further use ; it was, after all, the weakness of their artillery and the lack of ammunition which had been the main cause of the defeat, and whatever artillery there was had to be preserved for the defence of the San line.

The breakdown of the front near Dembica was followed by a withdrawal of the Russian troops from the lower Visloka. On May 11 the Austrians crossed the river near Mielec, on May 12 they reached Kolbuszova. During the next few days our Allies continued their retreat to the north, towards the confluence of the Vistula and the San ; they retired, fighting continuous rearguard actions, on to the Tarnobrzeg-Rozvadow line, thus maintaining their hold on the two important bridge heads of Sandomierz and Rozvadow.

The Russian retreat from the Szczucin-Dembica line necessitated a rearrangement of positions in the adjoining sector on the left bank of the Vistula. The strongly fortified positions on the Nida, which our Allies had occupied since December, 1914, had to be abandoned, and the entire line south of the Pilica had to be withdrawn in conformity with the retreat in Galicia. The retreat pivotted on Inovlodz, the Bzura-Rawka-Inovlodz line in front of Warsaw remaining firm. The positions on the Nida were evacuated during the night of May 10-11, our Allies retiring slowly towards their new positions behind the Kamienna river. Mr. Stanley Washburn, the special correspondent of *The Times*, who inspected these positions, described them as even stronger than the Blonie line before Warsaw. On May 12 German troops of the Army Woyrsch occupied Kielce.

But it was not without striking a heavy blow at the pursuing forces of the enemy that the undefeated Russian Army withdrew on to the new lines, south of Ilza and Radom. "Regarding the movement as a whole," writes Mr. Washburn, "suffice it to say that in the two weeks following the change of line this one army inflicted upon the enemy a loss of nearly 30,000 in killed, wounded, and prisoners. The Russian losses were comparatively trifling." The Austro-German forces were following up leisurely the retreating Russian corps, not expecting any serious fighting to occur until the line behind the Kamienna were reached. Instead of that, on May 15 the Russian commander halted the main **body** of his troops in front of his fortified positions on a line extending from Brody by Opatow towards Klimontow. Between May 15-17 a battle developed on this front, which is the more interesting as it is one of the few in this war fought in the open without trenches. "In any other war," says Mr. Washburn, "it would have been called a good-sized action, as from first to last . . . more than 100,000 men and perhaps 350 to 400 guns were engaged." The enemy came on in four groups. The 3rd German Landwehr was moving from the south-west by Wierzbnik against Ilza, slightly to the north of Lubienia. Next to it, coming from the direction of Kielce, was the German Division of General Bredow, supported by the 84th Austrian Regiment. This body was advancing against Ostroviec, the terminus of a railway which runs from the district of Lodz to the south-east by Tomaszow and Opoczno, and crosses the Iwangorod-Olkusz line half-way between Kielce and Radom. Farther to the

south three Austro-Hungarian Divisions were advancing—namely, the 25th Austrian Division against Lagow, and the 4th Austrian Landwehr Division, supported by the 41st Honvéd Division, against Ivaniska ; they moved along roads converging on Opatow. The 25th Austrian Division, commanded by Archduke Peter Ferdinand, was composed of crack regiments, the 4th Hoch-and Deutschmeisters of Vienna, and the 25th, 17th and 10th Jäger Battalions.

"It is probable," says Mr. Washburn, "that the enemy outnumbered the Russians by at least 40 per cent. Certainly they never expected that any battle would be given by the supposedly demoralized Russians short of their fortified line, to which they were thought to be retiring in hot haste. General —— selected the Austrians for his first surprise, but began by making a feint against the German corps, driving in their advanced guards by vigorous attacks and causing the whole force to halt and begin deployment for an engagement. This took place on May 15. On the same day,

A RUSSIAN WOMAN DOCTOR,
Attached to the Siberian Regiment.

GENERAL VON EMMICH (X) AND HIS STAFF STUDYING PLANS.

with all his available strength, he swung furiously with Opatow as an axis, from both north and south, catching the 25th Division on the road between Lagow and Opatow with a bayonet charge delivered from the mountain over and around which his troops had been marching all night. Simultaneously another portion of his command swept up on the 4th Division coming from Ivaniska to Opatow. In the meantime a strong force of Cossacks had ridden round the Austrians and actually hit their line of communications at the exact time that the infantry fell on the main column with a bayonet charge, delivered with an impetuosity and fury that simpled crumpled up the entire Austrian formation. The 4th Division was meeting a similar fate farther south, and the two were thrown together in a helpless mass, losing between 3,000 and 4,000 in casualties and nearly 3,000 in prisoners, besides a large number of machine-guns and the bulk of their baggage. The remainder, supported by the 41st Honvéd Division, which had been hurried up, managed to squeeze themselves out of their predicament by falling back on Wszachow, and the whole retired to Lagow, beyond which the Russians were not permitted to pursue them, lest they should break the symmetry of their own line, ..."

The Austrians themselves admit that they suffered serious losses in that battle. Thus we derive from an Austrian source the information that on May 16 not a single officer and only twenty-six men were left of the entire 4th company, 1st battalion of the 10th Austrian Infantry Brigade. By May 17 the Austrians had withdrawn more than twelve miles to the south-west and south of Opatow.

A spur of the Lysa Gora, the highest mountain-group of Russian Poland, separates the Lagow-Opatow road, along which the 25th Austrian Division had been moving, from the line of advance of Bredow's troops. During the night following on the defeat of the Austrians the victorious Russians crossed the mountains by a forced march, and fell on the right flank of the German formation, whilst other troops opened a general frontal attack against it. General Bredow was forced to fall back in haste in the direction of Bodzentyn and to summon to his support the adjoining 4th German Landwehr Division. Its sudden withdrawal to the south weakened, however, considerably the German line south-west of Radom, near the crossing of the Radom-Kielce and the Konsk-Ostroviec railways. The Russians did not fail to profit from the thinning of the German line in that sector. "Near Gielniow, Ruski Brod and Suchedniov," says the Russian official *communiqué* of May 17, " our sudden counter-attacks inflicted severe losses on the enemy's advance guards."

Having thus checked the German advance the Russians stopped, awaiting the further development of the situation on the San.

"On the left bank of the upper Vistula, in the Opatow region," says the Petrograd *communiqué* of May 15, "fighting continues, the enemy here having apparently received a certain number of reinforcements. His attempts to take the offensive were repulsed with success by our counter-attacks, in the course of which the enemy suffered heavy losses."

In East Galicia and in the Bukovina, between the Carpathians and the Dniester, the Russian and the Austro-Hungarian armies were still facing each other on May 1 along approximately the same lines on which they had stopped about the middle of March. From the Szlis Mountain and the valley of the upper Lomnica the battle front extended to the north of Nadvorna and Kolomea, by Ottynia towards Niczviska on the Dniester ; east of Niczviska it followed approximately the course of the river down to the Bessarabian frontier.

The floods, which during spring had prevented military operations in the wide, flat valleys of the Bystrzycas, had receded by the beginning of May, and fighting was resumed. The Russians were certain to attempt the reconquest of the Pruth valley ; for the Austrians, especially in view of the successful advance through Central Galicia, it was a matter of supreme importance to gain a foothold on the northern bank of the Dniester. The district south of Stanislau was in itself a strategic backwater and would have been of no value to our Allies, had it not been for the Odessa-Stanislau railway line, which runs through the valley of the river Pruth, past Czernowitz and Kolomea.* About 60 miles of that line, between Bojan and Ottynia, were on May 1 in the hands of the Austrians, whilst the Russian troops were standing at a distance on the average of only about 20 miles to the north of the railway. Could they have carried it by a quick advance they would have gained an

* For a map of that district refer to p. 435, Chapter LXXVI.

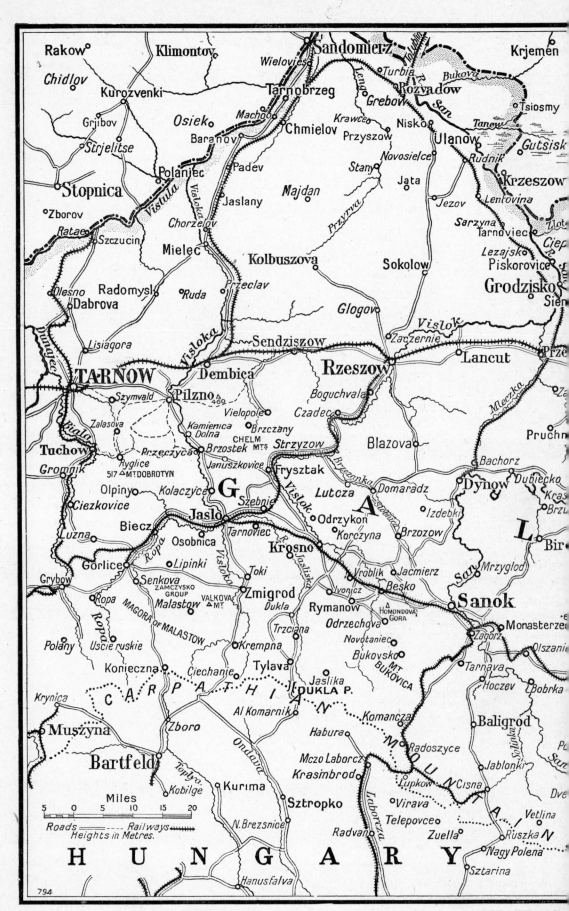

WESTERN

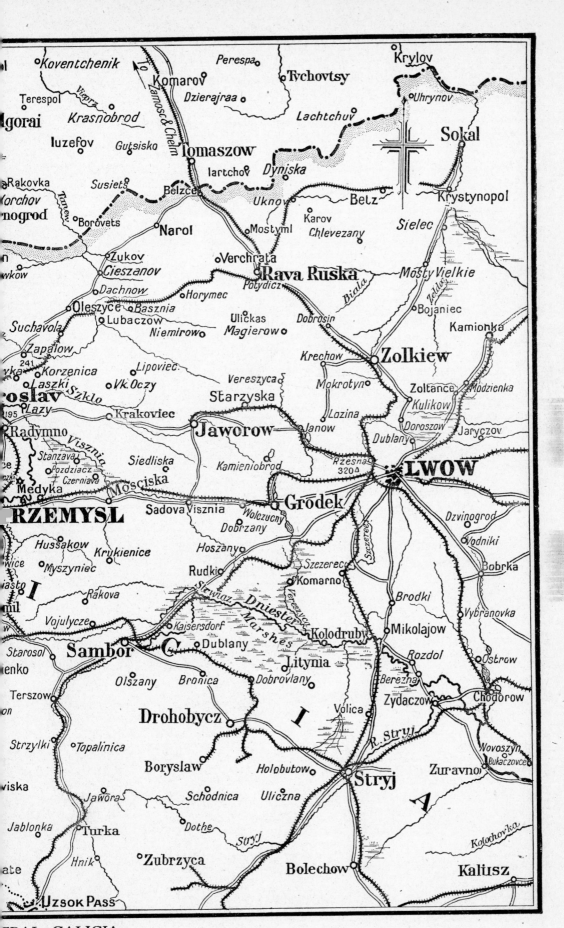

TRAL GALICIA.

important line for the transport of reinforcements and supplies from Southern Russia to the threatened Mid-Galician front. It must be remembered that Kiev and Sebastopol are military centres equal in importance to Brest-Litovski, Vilna or Petrograd. It is only by the occupation of the Czernowitz-Kolomea railway line that a Russian counter-offensive in East Galicia could have affected the course of the main operations in Mid-Galicia and on the San. Otherwise, however successful, it could not have exerted any immediate influence on its development. The eastern flank of the Austro-German armies was safe. The mountain range of the Transylvanian Carpathians, with its peaks approaching a level of 7,000 feet and its passes more than 3,000 feet high, formed an insuperable obstacle to rapid operations, and not even the conquest by the Russians of the entire region between the Dniester and the Carpathians would have stopped the Austro-German advance on Lwow.

For the enemy the breaking through of the Dniester line was of supreme strategic importance ; could his armies have crossed the "dead belt" of the Dniester on the Bukovinian frontier, and firmly established themselves on its left bank, the retreat of at least large portions of the Ninth Russian Army might have been cut, and even the other armies of General Ivanoff's group, which about the middle of May were holding the line of the San and of the marshes on the upper Dniester, might have been involved in the disaster. They would have lost the support which they were deriving during the following two months from the river cover on their southern flank, and which alone enabled them to carry out their retreat through East Galicia without ever suffering a crushing defeat.

As a movement forestalling the offensive of the enemy in that region, the Russian advance undertaken about the middle of May against the valley of the Pruth proved a complete success ; it was a success also as a military operation. Our Allies did not, however, succeed in capturing in time Kolomea, which was indispensable for the use of the southern railway line ; after the second fall of Przemysl the chief strategic aim of the advance was lost, and conforming to the retreating movement of the other armies, toward the middle of June, the two corps of cavalry, which formed the main body of the Russian Army in the valley of the Pruth, fell back beyond the Dniester.

The fighting on the Dniester front began on May 6. On May 8 the Russians attacked Ottynia, and on the same day the Austrians succeeded in capturing by a surprise attack the important bridge-head of Zaleszczyki. On the following day they were again driven out of Zaleszczyki by our Allies, losing 500 men in prisoners, three heavy guns, one field gun, and several machine guns. On May 10 the Russians opened their offensive along the entire Dniester line from west of Niczviska to Uscie Biskupie, on a front of about 40 miles ; they crossed at the same time the Bukovinian frontier from Novosielica on the Pruth and advanced to Mahala,* a village about five miles to the east of Czernowitz.

South-west of Uscie Biskupie a small stream called Onut joins the Dniester from the right bank, near a village bearing the same name. It is practically the only confluent which the Dniester receives from the Bukovina. Near its mouth the cañon of the Dniester widens out into a broad, flat valley, and the river itself is shallow ; a hill rising near the village of Onut bears the significant name "Kolo Bolota," which means in Ruthenian "next to the mud." This small valley was on May 10 the scene of a remarkable and almost unique feat in military history. The Don Cossacks, having cut a passage in the wire entanglements in front of the fortified positions held by the enemy's infantry, drove the Austrians in a hand-to-hand fight from three rows of trenches. Through the opening thus formed the Russian horse poured into the valley of the Onut and dashed into the enemy's rear. The Austrians were compelled to evacuate the entire district on the Onut. Charging into the masses of the retreating enemy the Cossacks sabred many and captured several thousand prisoners, a battery of machine guns, and several searchlights and caissons.

By the night of May 10 the Russians held the entire right bank of the Dniester. On May 11 the Austrians attempted counter-attacks, which, however, broke down completely. "In this operation," says the Russian official *communiqué* of May 13, "the Austrian units which led the offensive were repulsed near Chocimierz with heavy losses. Our artillery annihilated two entire battalions and a third surrendered. Near Horodenka the enemy gave way about

---

* The name of Mahala is an interesting reminiscence of Turkish rule over the Bukovina. "Mahala" means in Turkish simply "a place, a township."

AN AMBUSCADE IN POLAND.
A Party of Cossacks surprise German Cavalry.

7 o'clock in the evening of the same day and began a disorderly retreat. We again captured several thousand prisoners, guns, and some 50 ammunition caissons." Horodenka is the junction of six first-class high roads and a station on the Zaleszczyki-Kolomea railway ; it is, in fact, the most important strategic point between the Dniester and the Kolomea-Czernowitz front. On the same night the Austrians evacuated their entire line of positions from the river Bystrzyca to the Rumanian frontier, of a length of 88 miles, and on the following day retired south of the Pruth. On May 13 the

Cossacks under General Mishtchenko entered the town of Sniatyn on the Pruth, about half-way between Kolomea and Czernowitz, and occupied Gwozdziec, a place eight miles north-east of Kolomea. Farther west they captured, on May 14, after severe fighting, the town and district of Nadvorna and part of the railway line from Delatyn to Kolomea, cutting thereby the connexion between the group of corps under the command of General von Pflanzer-Baltin and the German Army " of the South " under General von Linsingen.

Meantime the Russians were also from the

RUSSIAN DUG-OUTS OCCUPIED BY THE AUSTRIANS.

north closing in on Kolomea. On May 13 a Russian reserve regiment under Colonel Asowsky carried the strongly fortified Austrian positions near the villages of Zukow and Jakobowka, about eight miles north of Kolomea. Only in front of the town the Austrians were able to maintain their positions with the assistance of reinforcements brought up by train and by bringing into action their last reserves, composed of sappers, and even of detachments still in course of formation. In the six days between May 9 and May 14 our Allies pressed back the enemy on a front of more than 60 miles for a distance amounting on the average to more than 20 miles, capturing about 20,000 prisoners and a rich booty in guns, machine guns and ammunition.

After May 15 a lull set in in the fighting on the Pruth. Only round Kolomea and Czernowitz violent artillery duels were continued. The decision had to fall in the west, and for that struggle all available forces were required. Events were moving at such a rate that even the acquisition of the entire Odessa-Stanislau-Lwow railway could not have any more seriously affected their development. In the first days of June, after the fall of the town of Stryj, our Allies had to abandon their advanced positions on the Pruth. On June 6 Pflanzer-Baltin re-established his connexion with Linsingen. On the next day our Allies evacuated

Kalusz and Nadvorna, and on June 9 they withdrew from Obertyn, Horodenka, Sniatyn and Kocman.

The retreat now extended also to the north-eastern corner of the Bukovina, between Zaleszczyki, Onut and Czernowitz. The Austrians were here moving in three groups, along the Dniester in the north, along the Pruth in the south, and across the hills in the middle against the village of Szubraniec. Near this village the Russian artillery inflicted very severe losses on the enemy, but finding themselves in danger of being outflanked by the 42nd Croatian infantry division, which was advancing through the forests on the Dniester, our Allies withdrew on June 12 from the Bukovina on to Russian territory.

Between the Uzsok and the upper Lomnica, in the district where the group of F.M.L. von Szurmay and the army of General von Linsingen were facing parts of the Ninth Russian Army, the first fortnight of May was comparatively uneventful. The main movements in that region were merely complementary to the changes of front which were developing to the west and east of it.

On May 12 the group of Szurmay opened its advance to the north of the Uzsok Pass; the fall of Sanok had compelled our Allies to evacuate their positions in the pass, as the

Austrian advance on Sambor was threatening to cut off their line of retreat. On May 16 the troops of General von Szurmay crossed the upper Stryj near Turka, and leaving the high road and railway which lead towards Sambor, advanced over secondary roads against the famous oil district of Schodnica, Boryslaw and Drohobycz. They occupied its most important centres on May 17–18.

The main forces of the army of General von Linsingen started their advance on the same day as those of General von Szurmay. The Russian troops which had during the last four months repelled round Koziova the most violent attacks of German crack regiments, had to retire in order to keep in touch with the entire line ; just as the Austrian advance on Sambor had necessitated the evacuation of the Uzsok, the advance on Drohobycz, rendered inevitable the retreat of our Allies from the passes of the Vereczke and the Beskid. Fighting stubborn rearguard actions, the Russian forces, which included in that district some of the best Finnish regiments, withdrew in the direction of the town of Stryj and of Bolechow. The German advance proceeded quickest along the main road and railway. On May 18 their vanguards reached the outskirts of the wide valley

in the centre of which lies the town of Stryj. Here they were stopped on a line of strongly fortified Russian positions, stretching in a concave semicircle from Uliczna and Holobutow in the west to the hills in front of Bolechow in the east. The position of the army corps of Count Bothmer, which was standing south of Stryj in the valley of the River Stryj, was thus by no means an easy one. On May 18 it was holding in the centre a salient about six miles long and only about three miles wide. On its right the army corps of General Hoffman was advancing slowly against the Bolechow-Dolina line ; in the narrow valleys and on the spurs of the mountain group of the Bukovinec it suffered more than one serious reverse or even defeat at the hands of the retreating Russians.

Meantime on the extreme right of General von Linsingen's army the brigade of General von Bluhm and other adjoining German troops were trying in vain to relieve, by means of an advance through the valleys of the Swica and Lomnica, the pressure which our Allies were exerting on the group of army corps under General von Pflanzer-Baltin. It was not until the beginning of June that the army of General von Linsingen succeeded in crossing the " Transversal Valley "

RUSSIAN REINFORCEMENTS LEAVING FOR THE FRONT.

F.M.L. VON SZURMAY
Being decorated with an Iron Cross by
General von Linsingen.

and thus in entering into close, direct touch and
cooperation with the adjoining armies in the
north-west and south-east.

The battle for Mid-Galicia closed on May 14
with the reaching of the line of the San by the
Austro-German armies. The fighting of the
next three weeks (May 14-June 3) can be
described as the battle for Przemysl. The direct
attack against its forts had to be postponed
until the arrival of the heavy Austrian siege
train, and the intervening time was taken up
by an enveloping movement against the
fortress on the part of the Austro-German armies.

On May 14 German troops of Mackensen's
army occupied Jaroslav, an important strategic
point on the left bank of the San, about 16 miles
north of Przemysl. On the same day the
Fourth Austro-Hungarian Army reached the
western side of the river on a broad front
between Rudnik and Lezajsk. By the night of
May 16 the Austro-German forces occupied
practically the entire left bank of the San from
Rudnik to Jaroslav for about 40 miles. " Near

Jaroslav," says the Russian official *communiqué* for May 17, " the Germans, heedless
of the countless losses inflicted on them by our
very severe artillery fire, are endeavouring to
establish themselves on the right bank of the
San." They succeeded on the same day in
effecting a crossing at several points. On
May 18 they enlarged their hold on the right
bank of the river between Jaroslav and Leza-
chow (at the junction of the San and the
Vislok). A German Division, consisting of
Oldenburg and Hanoverian troops, reached
Radava on the Lubaczowka; farther north
the enemy captured Sieniava. " South of
Jaroslav," says the Petrograd *communiqué*
for that day, " we maintain ourselves on both
sides of the river." Mackensen was planning an
advance in force from the Sieniava-Jaroslav
front to the south-east, against the Przemysl-
Lwow railway line ; its sector between Mosciska
and Sadova Visznia was the most vulnerable
point of the Russian line of retreat from
Przemysl ; it was most easily accessible from
the north. Between May 20-24 the Austro-
German engineers constructed 15 bridges across
the San between Jaroslav and Sieniava, thus
preparing the way for a new " phalanx " and
" battering ram " against the Russian lines.

To the south of Przemysl the weakest sector
of the Russian line extended between Nizan-
kovice and the big marshes of the Strwiaz and
the Dniester, north-east of Sambor. " South of
Przemysl," says the Russian *communiqué*
dealing with the fighting of May 14-15, " the
enemy has only established contact with our
cavalry by mounted patrols." The next few
days mark the beginning of one of the most
desperate battles of the war. About four
Austro-Hungarian and one German army corps
were massed between Dobromil and Sambor.
On May 15 the enemy occupied the Height of
the Magiera (about 1,050 feet high) and entered
the town of Sambor. During the next few days
the Austro-German troops attempted to hack
their way from the Novemiasto-Sambor front
against Hussakow and Krukienice. Their aim
was to reach from the south the sector of the
Przemysl-Lwow railway line against which
Mackensen was pressing from the north.
" Between Przemysl and the great marshes of
the Dniester," says the Petrograd *communiqué*
of May 18, " the masses of the enemy which
attacked us reached in many places the wire
entanglements of our defence, but were
scattered by our fire. Nevertheless, at the cost

of enormous sacrifices, the enemy succeeded in capturing the trenches of our two battalions." These trenches near Hussakow were recaptured by the Russians on the following day (May 17). The offensive was, however, resumed by the Austrians on the following day, and by May 19 they had crossed the line Lutkow-Jacwiengi-River Strwiaz and got within six miles of Mosciska. By May 21 the Austrian troops had conquered the main Russian defences in that region, and the Russian forces in Przemysl were seriously threatened with having their line of retreat to Grodek cut off by the concentric advance of the enemy against Mosciska from north and south.

A Russian counter-offensive along the entire line opened on May 21. Its aim was not to save Przemysl, but to render possible the evacuation of the place. Przemysl could not be held ; most of its forts had been destroyed by the Austrians before their surrender of May 21. Those which had survived were too well known to the enemy to be of much value to the defending force. The new works constructed by the Russians could not be compared in strength with those on which the Austrians had worked for many years. The most favourable line for the defence of Przemysl against the Austro-German advance would have been the outer ring, along part of which the original Russian siege army had met and withstood the Austrian attempts at relieving the fortress. That ring was not, however, sufficiently complete, and, moreover, the forces of our Allies seem to have been insufficient for holding that far-flung line.

Whatever there was of the fortress of Przemysl was bound to fall before the heavy Austro-German artillery. Its defence was merely meant to retard the advance of the enemy, but it would not have paid had that had to be done at the price of losing its garrison. It was not meant to shut itself up in the doomed fortress, and its line of retreat had to be preserved intact.

The Russian counter-offensive of May 21-25 was planned as an enveloping movement against the envelopers of Przemysl. They tried from the north and the north-east to sweep down on the lines of communication of the Austro-German forces which had crossed the San between the rivers Tanew and Szklo. In the extreme north, in the corner between the Vistula and the San, our Allies advanced from the Tarnobrzeg-Grebow-Rozvadow line in a southerly direction and captured the towns of Nisko and Ulanow and the villages of Krawce, Przyszow and Novosielce. They advanced simultaneously from the east against the San between Rudnik and Sieniava, and got within a mile of Radava. On almost the entire line of the San, to the north of its junction with the Lubraczowka, our Allies compelled the Austro-German forces to fall back on to the left bank of the river and captured many guns and prisoners. The culminating point of that advance was reached on May 27, when the 3rd Caucasian Corps, under General Irmanoff, captured Sieniava, taking about 7,000 prisoners, 6 heavy guns and 6 field guns ; that corps belonged to the Third Russian Army of General Radko Dmitrieff, had gone

A REST FROM THE TRENCHES.
Men of the Siberian Regiment marching from the trenches after several days' duty.

through the whole retreat from the Dunajec, and on several occasions previous to May 27 had been reported partly annihilated in German *communiqués*. Yet in face of the superior artillery of the enemy our Allies were unable to cross the San, and the advance of the enemy north of Przemysl was not delayed for long. On May 24 Mackensen resumed the offensive. Containing the Russians between Rudnik and Sieniava along the San and using the Lubaczowka as cover for his left flank, he opened a vigorous advance due east of Jaroslav. On the same day his troops captured Drohojow, Ostrow, Vysocko, Vietlin, Makovisko, and approached from the north-west the railway station of Bobrowka. The Austro-Hungarians under General Arz von Straussenberg occupied the town of Radymno and compelled the Russians to fall back beyond the San ; the Austro-German encircling movement against Przemysl was thus pressed even south of the Szklo. On May 25 the Austro-Hungarian troops crossed the San opposite Radymno and captured the bridge-head of Zagrody on its right bank ; on the following day they conquered the village of Nienovice, about four miles further east, and the Height of Horodysko, which rises between the valleys of the Visznia and the Szklo, halfway between Radymno and Krakoviec ; meantime, north of them Mackensen's troops reached between the Lubaczowka and the Szklo the line Zapalow-Korzenica-Laszki-Lazy, about 10 miles east of Jaroslav, and captured Height 241, the most important strategic point in that low-lying marshy plain. During the next few days stubborn fighting continued with varying results on the Tuchla-Kalnikow-Naklo-Barycz line. The village of Naklo lies between the San and the Visznia, only about five miles to the north of Medyka, a station on the main railway line, halfway between Przemysl and Mosciska. South of Naklo rises a hill about 650 feet high. Against this height the enemy was now directing his attacks. Its capture would have exposed to the fire of his artillery the only Russian line of retreat from Przemysl.

South of Przemysl the Russian counter-offensive attempted to outflank the Austrian troops which, near Hussakow, had drawn close to the fortress and to the Przemysl-Grodek-Lwow railway line. The arrival of considerable reinforcements enabled the Russians to check the Austrian advance almost in this whole region, except in the direct neighbourhood of Hussakow. "The offensive which we opened on the 22nd," says the Petrograd *communiqué* of May 24, "is being pursued along the left bank of the Dniester, and was developed yesterday with great success, notwithstanding the enemy's counter-attacks. We captured, after a fight, the new and old villages of Burczyce, as well as the villages of Iszechnikow and Holobova, and part of the village of Ostrow." In the course of the day our Allies took, moreover, 2,200 prisoners, several machine guns and a considerable amount of ammunition. During the following day slight progress was made from the direction of Burczyce ; by May 24 the advance of our Allies came to a stop. On the line Krukienice-Mosciska our Allies were offering effective resistance to the advance of the enemy on the heights on the little river Blozewka, but the Austrian attacks against the Russian positions round Hussakow were daily increasing in violence. The village of Hussakow lies in the valley of the small river Buchta, only about three to four miles east of the Fort Siedliska, which guards from the south the Przemysl-Mosciska-Lwow railway line. That fort forms part of the outer ring of Przemysl. The evacuation of Przemysl could not be delayed much longer, especially as also the direct attacks against its forts were opened from the west in the last days of May by the heaviest types of Austrian and German howitzers.

The successful Russian offensive against the San, north of the Lubaczowka, and along the left bank of the Dniester had exercised no direct effect on the position round Przemysl itself. By the end of May only a zone about 10 miles wide, running eastward from Przemysl past Mosciska towards Grodek, separated the 6th Austro-Hungarian Army Corps and the Prussian Guard which were standing between the San and the Visznia from the troops of General von der Marwitz and the Third Austro-Hungarian Army round Hussakow. Except for that opening to the east, the fortress was surrounded on all sides by the enemy, and on May 30 even the railway line Przemysl-Grodek came, near Medyka, under the fire of the heavy Austrian batteries.

As early as May 17 Przemysl had been invested from three sides. The Bavarians, under General Kneussl, who occupied the northern front, had managed to bring with them some of their 21 cm. Krupp howitzers, and were bombarding the Russian positions round Mackovice and Kozienice, and were

A FRONTIER SKIRMISH.
Russian Troops repulsing an advance guard of the enemy.

working their way towards the forts of Dunko-viczki that commands the road and railway from Przemysl to Radymno. The 10th Austro-Hungarian Army Corps which had approached Przemysl from Krasiczyn tried at first a *coup de main* against its outer works, but, repulsed with heavy losses, settled down in front of the forts and works of Pralkovicé, Lipnik, Helicha and Grochovce and those situated round the Mountain Tatarowka; its line joined to the north-east of Przemysl, near the blown-up fort of Lentovnia, the positions of the Bavarians. The Russian commander of Przemysl, General

Artamanoff, had reconstructed some of the old Austrian forts and equipped them with Russian 12 cm. howitzers; besides that, new works had been erected. The Austrians had brought with them only their 15 cm. howitzers, and had to wait for their 30·5 cm. batteries before they could open their attack against Przemysl, though it was now only a shadow of what it had been before the capture by our Allies on March 22, 1915.

The 30·5 cm. howitzers arrived about May 25, and the attack against Przemysl began on May 30; in many places the enemy was making

GERMAN TRANSPORT AND CAVALRY
On the way to Dukla Pass.

use of the earthworks which our Allies had constructed when they had been the besiegers, and which they had had no time to destroy on their retreat into the fortress. On May 30 the Bavarians captured the Russian positions near Orzechovce, which cover the northern sector of the outer ring of forts round Przemysl. On the same day a violent bombardment was opened and infantry attacks were delivered against the entire northern and north-western front of the fortress, which extends from the river San (above, *i.e.* west of Przemysl) to the Przemysl-Radymno road, that is from Lentovnia to Dunkoviczki ; or to put it in more technical language, the attacks of May 30 were directed mainly against the front defined by the line of forts from No. 7 to No. 11. Fort No. 7 lies within the big loop which the San forms to the east of Przemysl. South of it, on the bank of the river, lies the village of Ostrow, to the east extends the ridge of Height 241, closing off the neck of the river loop. Fort No. 7 forms in the outer ring of forts the key to the sector of the San valley occupied by Przemysl. Against this fort an attempt was made by Austrian troops, which seem to have got across the San from the west or south-west, having first concentrated behind the dense forests which cover that region. " During the night of May 30-31," says the Russian official *communiqué* of June 1, " the enemy succeeded in approaching within 200 paces, and at some points even in gaining a footing in the precincts

of Fort No. 7, around which raged an obstinate battle that lasted until two in the afternoon of the 31st, when he was repulsed after suffering enormous losses. The remnants of the enemy who had entered Fort No. 7, numbering 23 officers and 600 men, were taken prisoners."

On May 31 the Bavarians concentrated again the fire of their heaviest batteries against the forts round Dunkoviczki (Nos. 10a, 11a and 11). The bombardment was continued till 4 p.m., when the fire stopped, and the enemy's infantry, consisting of one Prussian, one Austrian and several Bavarian regiments, proceeded to storm the forts, which by that time had been changed into mere wreckage. Their garrison, decimated by the bombardment, could not resist much longer, and withdrew beyond the road which runs behind the outer ring of forts round Przemysl. On the same day the 10th Austro-Hungarian Army Corps opened its attack against the south-western forts of Pralkovice and Lipnik. On June 1 the German troops of Mackensen captured two trenches east of Fort No. 11 ; they had to pay a heavy price in blood for every yard of their advance. Meantime the heavy batteries directed their fire against Forts Nos. 10 and 12. The breach in the outer ring of forts had to be enlarged, and these two forts were chosen for the attacks of the following day.

At noon of June 2 the 22nd Bavarian infantry regiment captured Fort No. 10, and towards night the Prussian Grenadier Guards occupied

Fort No. 12. During the night of June 2–3 the enemy entered the village of Zuravica, which lies within the outer ring of forts. Meantime the Austrian troops had broken through from the south-west, and in the afternoon of June 2 occupied the Zasanie (literally "the part beyond the San"), on the left bank of the river.

For the last few days the Russians had been evacuating the fortress, and the only part of the fortress which they held with considerable forces was that which covered directly their line of retreat towards Grodek and Lwow. During the night of June 2–3 the last Russian forces were withdrawn to the east, and early in the morning of June 3 the Bavarians and Austrians entered the town of Przemysl. The semi-official account, sent out by the Wolff Bureau, emphasises the fact that the first to enter the town was a battalion of the 3rd Regiment of the Foot Guards, and that the Austro-Hungarian troops *followed* the Germans. It is not altogether clear why a small body of the Prussian Guard was detailed to assist the very much larger bodies of Austrians, Hungarians and Bavarians in the storming of Przemysl ; the description of the entry into the conquered fortress seems to suggest the underlying motive.

The fall of Przemysl had been unavoidable from the very moment when the immense superiority of the Austro-German artillery and the enormous concentration of their troops had broken the Russian defences on the Dunajec-Biala line. But in the fall of Przemysl were involved those not only of Lwow, but even of Warsaw and Ivangorod. A sweep through East Galicia to the line of the San had been in recent years as much part of the Russian strategic plan for the case of a war against the Central Powers, as was the abandonment of Western Poland. The Vistula-San-Dniester line from Thorn in the north to Chocim in the south-east is the one strong, continuous line stretching across the Polish and Galician plains, between the line of the Oder and the Carpathians to the west and south, and the line of the Niemen and Bug to the north-east of it. No stable balance can be attained with one side holding the line of the middle Vistula round Warsaw and the other commanding its natural southern extension, the San line round Przemysl.

The outbreak of the Austro-Italian war on May 23, was followed by a regrouping of the Austro-Hungarian armies in Galicia and by certain changes in the army commands. Generals Dankl and Borojevic von Bojna were transferred to the Italian frontier. General Dankl had been in any case in command of an army of only about half the normal size ; his troops were united with the German army of

AUSTRIANS FIRING FROM THEIR TRENCHES.

General Woyrsch, in conjunction with which they had been fighting for the last half year ; it will be remembered that in May also that army was considerably under strength. General Kövess von Kövesshasa, who before the war had commanded the 12th Austro-Hungarian Army Corps, and had stood during May at the head of certain Hungarian regiments included in General Woyrsch's army, seems to have been now put in command of all the Austro-Hungarian forces included in that army. General Borojevic von Bojna was transferred to the Italian front probably owing to the vast experience of mountain warfare which he had acquired during the half-year of fighting in the Carpathians. It is impossible to say as yet how much of his army he took with him to the south. One thing is fairly certain : that no extensive regrouping of forces was undertaken until after the fall of Przemysl. The Austro-Hungarian official report of May 25 speaks of an " Army Puhallo " ; it is evident from its position that this was the army of General Borojevic under a new commander. After the fall of Przemysl that army seems, however, to have undergone far-reaching changes. Part of it was probably transferred to the Italian front ; other parts were distributed among the other Austro-Hungarian and German armies, to replace regiments withdrawn to the southern front or to make up for the heavy losses suffered during the Galician campaign. Thus, e.g., we find that the 10th Austro-Hungarian Army Corps, which from Gorlice till Przemysl had always moved on the left wing of the Third Austro-Hungarian Army under Borojevic, next to the right wing of the Eleventh German Army of Mackensen, appears in the beginning of July near Krasnik, i.e., in conjunction with the Fourth Austro-Hungarian Army under Archduke Joseph-Ferdinand Some other parts of the Third Army seem to have been included in those of Mackensen and of Boehm-Ermolli, which from now onwards became direct neighbours ; thus, e.g., the German Corps under General von der Marwitz forms during the battle of Lwow part of the Second Austro-Hungarian Army. The status and composition of the surviving " Army Puhallo " is not clear.

About the same time, whilst in the north the reconstructed forts of Przemysl were being demolished by the heavy howitzers of the enemy, another important position, farther south, was crumbling down under their fire.

Since May 18 the German troops had been busy enlarging their narrow salient in the Stryj valley against Uliczno in the west and Bolechow in the east. At the same time they were getting their heavy mortars and howitzers into position in front of the Russian trenches between Holobutow and Stryj. On the morning of May 31 fire was opened against them, and after a few hours of bombardment little was left of the defences before which thousands of Austrians and Germans had died in vain in attempts to carry them by assault. The final conquest of the Russian positions near Holobutow was effected by the 38th Hungarian Honvéd Division under F.M.L. Bartheldy, to which the German corps-commander, Count Bothmer, left the most difficult part of the work. They were *followed* by the Germans, thus inverting the arrangement which had been adopted for the triumphal entry into Przemysl ; but this time the order of procedure did not appear in the report of the Wolff Bureau.

The fall of Stryj rendered inevitable the withdrawal of the entire Russian line towards the Dniester. Step by step our Allies retired to the north ; their retreat will remain memorable in military history, for, whilst falling back, they were capturing thousands of the " pursuing " enemy. They retired behind the Dniester, but preserved their hold on the main bridge-heads and on whatever important strategic points could be kept to the south of the river, without disturbing excessively the symmetry of the line.

With the fall of Przemysl and Stryj closed the second stage of the Austro-German offensive. The third we may call the battle for Lwow, and date it as extending from June 3 till June 22, the day of the recapture of the Galician capital by the Austrians.

The strategic plan underlying this third chapter of the Austro-German offensive can be explained in very few sentences. The most effective way of crushing the retreating Russian armies would have been a flank attack from the south. A successful crossing of the Dniester by the enemy would have had disastrous consequences for our Allies. Their armies would have been outflanked, some of their lines of retreat would have been cut, and a dissolution of a large portion of the retiring forces could hardly have been avoided. All the Austro-German attempts at breaking through the Russian armies holding the line of the

A RUSSIAN SUDDEN COUNTER-ATTACK.

Dniester ended, however, in failure. Our Allies gradually rolled up their line on the Dniester from west to east, keeping step with the retreat of the armies which were facing west. But nowhere did the enemy succeed in breaking effectively through the defences of their southern flank.

To the west of Lwow stretches a line which might almost be compared in strength with that of the Dniester. It is the line of the lakes and marshes which extend along the small river Vereszyca; those positions are best known as the Grodek line, by the name of the town guarding the most important passage across it.

The chief weakness of that line is that it reaches for only a very short distance to the north. In the north-west of Lwow, between the towns of Vereszyca and Rava Ruska opens a gap in its western defences. That gap lies east-north-east from Jaroslav. Against it was advancing the army of General von Mackensen.

After the fall of Przemysl the Fourth Austro-Hungarian Army attempted to effect a "left wheel" from the line of the San. Pivotting on its extreme left wing, it was trying to wheel its centre and right wing so as to get to face due north, and thus to cover the left flank of the forces which were advancing on Lwow.

It was supported by at least one army corps (the 10th Austro-Hungarian) from the late army of Borojevic. That corps moved from Przemysl due north against the line of the river Tanew, as an immediate cover for Mackensen, who was advancing from Jaroslav and Radymno against Rava Ruska and Zolkiew, and was thus turning from the north the defences of Lwow. The Second Austro-Hungarian Army under General von Boehm-Ermolli was moving on both sides of the Przemysl-Lwow railway line under a slight angle to the north-east. The armies of General von Linsingen and General von Pflanzer-Baltin were standing south of the Dniester; the advance of the Second Army was gradually drawing them to the north across the river, just as Mackensen's advance from Gorlice towards Rzeszow had drawn the armies of Borojevic and Boehm-Ermolli across the Carpathians.

During the 10 days which followed on the fall of Przemysl little progress was made in the centre, in front of the Jaroslav-Sambor line, by the armies of Mackensen and Boehm-Ermolli. Part of the time was probably required for the regrouping of the forces and for the concentration of fresh material with which to re-open the campaign. Moreover, the operations on the wings, *i.e.*, on the Lower San and on the Dniester, seem to have tied down for the time being a certain amount of reserves, and the result of those operations had to be awaited before any new move was undertaken from the centre.

In the north, between Krawce, Rozvadow and Rudnik, our Allies were vigorously pursuing their counter-offensive. On June 2 they pierced the enemy's lines and captured an important fortified position in the region of Rudnik, taking about 4,000 prisoners and many guns and machine-guns. "West of Rudnik," says the Russian *communiqué* of June 3, "we almost completely annihilated the 2nd, 3rd and 4th Tyrolese regiments." The success thus gained was followed up on the following day in the direction of the village of Novosielec, and the enemy was driven back in disorderly retreat. The 14th Austro-Hungarian army-corps fell back on fortified positions extending from Stany on the River Leng (a small tributary of the Vistula which joins it east of Sandomierz) by Jata to Lentovina, a station on the Rozvadow-Przevorsk railway line; from here his lines extended by Sarzyna towards the San. About 1,000 prisoners were taken in that region on June 4. The Russians had by now got over about one-third of the distance from Rozvadow to the Tarnow-Jaroslav railway, the most important line of communication of Mackensen's Army. In view of this advance of our Allies, German reinforcements were sent to the support of the retreating Austrians. On the night of June 3-4 they delivered from the left bank of the Leng three furious attacks against the Russian flank between Krawce and Burdzyn, but were repulsed with heavy losses. The advance of our Allies to the south was, however, arrested.

No important movements took place on the San between Lezajsk and the Lubaczowka during the week following on the fall of Przemysl. Between the Lubaczowka and the Szklo some fighting is reported to have occurred on the Zapalow-Korzenica line. Between the San and the Viszina in the direct neighbourhood of Przemysl the German troops were advancing from the Pozdziacz-Medyka towards the Starzava-Czerniava line. South of the Przemysl-

RUSSIAN TROOPS HAULING A HEAVY GUN
On to a Platform of a specially constructed line.

GENERAL ARTAMONOFF,
The Russian Governor of Przemysl, in his quarters during the Russian occupation.

Lwow railway the German troops under General von der Marwitz were approaching Mosciska from the south-west. How slow the movements were in that region and how obstinate was the resistance offered by our Allies can be recognized from the fact that the town of Mosciska, only about 11 miles east of Przemysl, was not reached by the Germans until May 14.

The main fighting during those days centred round the bridge-heads on the Dniester. On a front of about 20 miles, between the Sambor-Rudki railway and the Litynia-Kolodruby road, the marshes of the Upper Dniester form an absolutely impassable barrier to military operations. They are on the average about 8–10 miles wide, and not a single road or railway leads across them. Between Kolodruby and Zuravno, on a front of about 30 miles long, the marshes still cover a certain amount of ground on both sides of the river, which attains in that sector a width of about 100–150 feet and a depth of about 3–4 feet. At Mikolajow and Zydaczow* important roads and railways cross the river. Mikolajow, on the northern bank of the Dniester, due south of Lwow (about 20 miles), was strongly fortified; the district is by nature very well fitted for

* Zydaczow (pronounce Jidatchoff) had been in the Middle Ages a Roumanian settlement. Its name had been "Judatchu"; it was derived from the word "judex" (judge). Zyd (pronounce jid) means in Slav languages "a Jew"; by a process of assimilation, the foreign name, of which the meaning was obscure to the local population, was changed into one which they were able to understand.

ARRIVAL OF KING LUDWIG OF BAVARIA IN LEMBERG.

purposes of defence. Hills covered with dense woods rise between Mikolajow and the river to a height of about 1,250 feet; they dominate the valley of the Dniester and form a most formidable defensive position. Nor does the bridge-head of Zydaczow offer much better chances for an attack from the south. The Russian positions in that region lay in the midst of a maze of rivers and ponds. Covered from the south by the Lower Stryj, the Dniester and the marshes, which are especially broad in this district, the Russian positions on the hills north-east of Zydaczow, between the Dniester and the lakes of Chodorow, were equal in strength to any defences on the Dniester. Ten miles south-east of Zydaczow lies Zuravno; between Zuravno and Nizniow, on a front of over 40 miles, the Dniester presents the comparatively least serious natural obstacles to an army trying to force its line. Hardly any marshes encompass the river, though its banks are low; it is only east of Nizniow that begins the district of the deep cañons, of which a detailed account was given in Chapter LXXVI. Half-way between Zuravno and Nizniow lies Halicz,* one of the most important strategic centres of Galicia and the most important passage across the Dniester. The railway bridge, which the Austrians had blown up before their retreat in September 1914, had been reconstructed by the Russians, who in addition had built five wooden bridges across

* Halicz was once one of the chief capitals of Eastern Europe. The name Galicia is derived from it.

the river. Halicz itself had been originally fortified by the Austrians; our Allies had added three new lines to its defences. They stretched in a semicircle round it, at a radius of more than five miles.

Zuravno offered to the Germans comparatively the best chances of breaking through the Russian defences on the Dniester, and against it they directed their main forces. On May 31, after the fall of Stryj, the Germans pushed forward vigorously in the direction of Mikolajow and Zydaczow; their main aim probably was to establish themselves safely on the left bank of the Dniester between Kolodruby and Zydaczow, and thus to secure the left flank of the troops which were to attack Zuravno against the possibility of an attack from that direction. It seems less likely that they hoped to capture either of these bridge-heads. "Between the Tysmienica and the Stryj," says the Russian *communiqué* of June 2, "the enemy, who had concentrated there a considerable amount of heavy artillery and had brought up reinforcements, by stubborn attacks made with large forces, achieved some successes in the course of the night" (May 31-June 1). In the course of the following two days the Russians fell back on to the Dniester bridge-heads. The German attacks made against them on the night of June 2-3 were repulsed with very heavy losses and were followed by successful Russian counter-attacks.

"On June 3," says the Russian official *communiqué* of June 5, "the enemy continued his attacks against our bridge-heads over the Dniester between Tysmienica and the Stryj-Mikolajow railway. During the day we repulsed four desperate assaults on our positions near Ugartsberg (two miles south of the Dniester), using our bayonets and hand grenades. About midday, on the following day, on the whole of the above-mentioned front, the enemy was repulsed, and began to take up a position along a new front out of gun range. Our troops, assuming the offensive in their turn, attacked the enemy near Krynica (five miles south of the Dniester)." During the following three days no further attacks were undertaken by the enemy against the Dniester between the mouth of the Tysmienica and that of the Stryj; only Russian counter-attacks continued from the direction of Litynia. The Germans resumed their operations round Mikolajow and Zydaczow about June 7, but henceforth this sector is of only secondary importance.

On June 5 began the German attacks against the bridge-head of Zuravno; on that day the enemy occupied the town on the right bank of the river, and to the south of it the important Height 247, which dominates the valley. On the 6th Austro-German troops succeeded in forcing the passage of the river, and on the 7th they enlarged considerably their positions on the northern bank by capturing the hills near Novoszyn and by reaching the important

strategic point of Bukaczowce. "On the left of the Dniester, near Zuravno," says the Russian report, "the enemy's forces have been increased, invading the forest as far as the railway." It was evidently their intention to turn from the north the defences of the Martynow-Siwka bridge, on the high-road from Rohatyn to Kalusz. Had they succeeded, they might have firmly established themselves on the flank and in the immediate neighbourhood of Halicz. On June 6 the troops operating on their right wing had joined hands with those of Pflanzer-Baltin and occupied Kalusz. Paying an awful price in dead and wounded, they reached on June 7 south of Siwka the Myslow-Wojnilow-Kolodziejow line. Near Siwka alone about 2,000 of the enemy perished in an ambush; they were first mown down by machine-guns and then the survivors were finished off in a bayonet attack. It was the aim of the Austro-German commanders to reach from the east Halicz and Stanislau, whilst the forces which had crossed the Dniester at Zuravno were to turn the Russian positions along the river.

June 8 marks a turning-point in the battle. On the following day the German advance to the north of the Dniester was brought to a stop. After a fierce fight the enemy was driven back behind the Chodorow-Bukaczowce railway line, several villages, including Raczewko, were reconquered by the Russians and about 800

THE AUSTRO-GERMAN TROOPS ENTERING PRZEMYSL.

prisoners were taken. On June 10 the battle attained its climax. The Austro-German forces were driven back across the Dniester. On that day the Russian captures amounted to 17 guns, 49 machine-guns, 188 officers and about 6,500 men. Among the prisoners was an entire company of the Guard regiment of the Prussian Fusiliers ; the entire captures of the three days June 8–10 were 17 guns, 78 machine-guns, 348 officers and 15,431 men.

On June 11 the Germans renewed their attack on Zuravno, recaptured the town and on the following day advanced for a distance of about five miles to the north of it. On June 13 they reached Roguzna, a village about ten miles north of Zuravno. During the next few days, however, our Allies drove them again back towards the Dniester.

Meantime, farther east, the Austro-German armies had reached the river almost along the entire line between Jezupol and Zaleszczyki, forcing several passages across it below Nizniow. But these successes proved of no avail. As we have previously stated, below Nizniow it is not the river itself that matters, but its "dead belt," the belt of river-loops, cañons and forests. After having crossed the river itself, the enemy nowhere succeeded in emerging from that zone.

By June 16 it was fairly clear that the line of the Dniester could be nowhere forced to any considerable depth and on a front sufficient to

enable bigger bodies of troops to open an attack against the Russian flank ; hence the attack against Lwow, if it was to be taken, had to proceed from the west.

During the lull in the fighting on the Middle San Mackensen effected round Jaroslav a new concentration of artillery similar to that which had won the day round Gorlice. He seems also to have received fresh reinforcements in men. A new "phalanx" was gathered west of the San, mainly in the district between Piskorovice and Radymno.

On June 12 a violent bombardment was opened against the Russian positions. On the same day Austro-Hungarian troops crossed the San and occupied Piskorovice and Sieniava. On the 13th the advance extended to the entire line, from the River Zlota down to the Radymno-Javorow road ; it was continued on the 14th. The heavy Austrian batteries adapted to motor-transport were accompanying the advancing troops and breaking down the resistance of the Russian troops. By the night of June 14 the Ninth Austro-Hungarian Army Corps (Fourth Austro-Hungarian Army) stood before Cieplice, and the entire army of Archduke Joseph-Ferdinand was slowly wheeling from the San towards the River Tanew. On the same night Mackensen's troops reached a line extending from Oleszyce by Nova

INTERIOR OF THE FORTRESS OF PRZEMYSL.
After the German Occupation.

FORTS NUMBER 10 AND 11, PRZEMYSL,

**After the Bombardment by the Austrian
Heavy Artillery.**

Grobla and Vielkie Oczy * to Krakoviec.
Meantime General von der Marwitz reached
Mosciska. On June 15 Cieplice and Dachnow
were taken and the enemy's forces approached
Lubaczow, Niemirow, Javorow, and Sadova
Visznia. The report sent out by the Wolff
Bureau on June 16 says : " The Army of
Colonel-General von Mackensen has captured
since June 12 more than 40,000 men and 69
machine-guns." It is evident that this sentence
applies to the entire group of armies operating
in Galicia, not merely to the Eleventh German
Army. Thus by June 12, in the German
official and semi-official language, Mackensen
had replaced as commander of the Galician
armies the Austro-Hungarian Generalissimo,
Archduke Frederick.

On June 16 the Austrian troops of the Fourth
Army, continuing their " left-wheel," advanced
through Maydan and Cewkow and crossed the
Russian frontier, facing due north. Meantime
Mackensen's Army, advancing with its cha-
racteristic impetuosity, had passed Lubaczow,
Niemirow and Javorow, and was pressing
forward across the hills against the line of

---

* These names give an idea of the character of the
country. " Nova Grobla " means " The New Dam,"
" Vielkie Oczy " " The Big Eyes " : ponds and small
lakes are frequently called " eyes " in Slav countries.

Rava Ruska, Magierow and Janow. The
Army of General von Boehm-Ermolli was
moving along the high road towards Grodek.
Late in the afternoon of June 16 it came into
contact with the Russian rearguards near
Wolczuchy, about three miles west of Grodek,
by the night it reached the River Vereszyca
and occupied its western bank. About midnight it captured by assault the western part
of the town of Grodek.

On June 17 the advance of the Fourth
Austro-Hungarian Army to the north continued
between the Vistula to the Jaroslav-Oleszyce-
Belzec road. In the corner above the junction
of the Vistula and the San our Allies, conforming

to the retreat on the right bank of the San, fell back on to their old positions between Tarnobrzeg and Nisko. West of the San the Austrians occupied on that day Krzeszow, Tarnogrod, and Narol, thus establishing themselves on the entire line, along the Tanew front. During the fighting of the following week the valley of the Tanew served as an effective cover for the northern flank of the Austro-German Armies which were advancing against Lwow. The valley of the lower and middle Tanew is one huge marsh for about 35 miles to the east of its junction with the San ; that marsh is about 10 miles wide and covered with forests. Only very few roads lead through that region. Whoever would dare to leave the beaten track is lost ; he would perish in the bog. Even where the marsh ceases, the ground is still unfavourable to military operations ; it is soft sand in which men and horses sink deep and across which heavy transport is impracticable. Having reached that region, the Austrian troops could securely hold it with small forces.

From the junction of the San and the Tanew till Narol, for a distance of 45 miles, the Austro-German forces were facing due north ; between Narol, Rava Ruska and Magierow, on a line of about 15 miles, the front was turning toward the north-east ; south of Magierow " the other armies of General von Mackensen " * were holding the line of the Vereszyca down to its junction with the Dniester. The distance from Magierow to Lelechow on the Upper Vereszyca amounts to 10 miles, the line of the Vereszyca down to Kolodruby on the Dniester to 30 miles. The new line offered our Allies fairly good defensive positions. Several ranges of hills, rising to an average height of 1,200 ft., extend between Narol and Magierow. Similarly the line of the Vereszyca, which is covered against the west by the river, and by ponds and marshes, is reinforced by a chain of wooded hills which exceed in height by several hundred feet the level of those extending to the west of the line.

* Quoting that passage from the German official *communiqué* the Viennese *Neue Freie Presse* adds in brackets the following remark : " It is not known whether Mackensen commands several armies, or which armies are under his command." Thus notwithstanding its exceedingly, one might say excessively, close connexion with Berlin, the *Neue Freie Presse* seems to have had no " official knowledge " about the " supersession " of Archduke Frederick by Mackensen.

From Rava Ruska to Komarno, on a front of over 40 miles, a furious battle raged during June 18 and 19 and throughout the intervening night. The Austrians succeeded in capturing a few positions of our Allies in front of Grodek and Komarno, yet it was not on the Vereszyca that the decision was to fall. With the help of their heavy artillery the Germans had borne down the resistance of our Allies in the north, and on June 20 Mackensen's Army occupied the towns of Rava Ruska and Zolkiev. The line of the Vereszyca was turned and our Allies had to fall back on their lines in front of Lwow.

On June 21 our Allies rallied to resist the advance of the enemy in front of Lwow, the capital of Galicia, which had been in their possession ever since September 3, 1914. Eight miles to the north of the town they held against the troops of Mackensen a line extending from Zoltance past Kulikow towards the hills north of Brzuchovice. West and south-west of Lwow they were defending the line of the River Szczerec, against the army of Boehm-Ermolli ; its high eastern banks and its chalk-rocks were offering good positions for defence. The battle round Kulikow and on the Szczerec was fought on June 21. During the following night the Russians fell back on to their last positions round Lwow, the evacuation of which had by then been completed.

The fiercest fighting took place along the Janow-Lwow road. Here, on a narrow front between the village of Rzesna and Hill 320, across the high road, our Allies were offering a last resistance to the advance of the Austrians. Their flanks were covered by marshy streams, the positions themselves had been carefully built and fortified. Premature attacks delivered by the enemy ended in disaster for the attacking columns. Then followed the usual bombardment by the batteries of heavy howitzers. The Russian defences were smashed and across their wreckage the Austrian infantry was storming to the east, towards Lwow. About the same time the enemy was crossing from the north the hills on the Mlynowka and carrying the last Russian trenches on the Lysa Gora.

Lwow was entered by the enemy on Tuesday, June 22, at 4 p.m., after having remained for 293 days in the possession of our Allies.

CHAPTER LXXXVI.

GERMANY AT WAR.

German Opinion at the Outbreak of War—The "Wrong" Done to Belgium—Building up of German Legends—Political Unity Assured—Germany under Martial Law—Patient Acceptance of the Military Regime—Disappearance of the Personal Factor—Position of the Kaiser—The Public Propaganda and War Literature—Press Organization—Hatred of England—The Food Problem and Its Solution—Industry and Trade—The Control of Labour—Finance—The War Loans—Germanism Runs Riot—Internal Politics—Attitude of Socialists—German Aims and Ambitions Revealed—The Demand for Annexations—The Imperial Chancellor's Challenge to Europe.

WHEN the tension of the brief diplomatic crisis that followed the presentation of the Austrian ultimatum to Serbia was relieved by the declarations of war on Russia and on France, by the invasion of Belgium, and by the consequent intervention of Great Britain, the anxiety of the German people gave place to an outburst of jubilant patriotism and warlike enthusiasm. The first outburst of joy did not last long. The crowds in Berlin and other capitals might cheer, and the politicians and newspapers might rejoice, but the country as a whole was pretty well aware that the coming struggle was such as the world had never seen, and that Germany had assumed a task with which Bismarck's three wars provided no comparison.

Nevertheless, the common belief was that the war would be short. There was great anxiety about the possibly disastrous blows that might be expected from the British Navy, and the people vented all its wrath and sarcasm upon the failure of German diplomacy to divide Germany's enemies and to prevent the coincidence of naval war with the great trial of strength on land. But, apart from that peril, it was hoped that a smashing blow would be given to France in a very brief space of time, and that Germany could then feel secure

against invasion and continue offensive operations in the light of events and at greater leisure. The country rapidly settled down to the business of economic preparation for such emergencies as could then be foreseen, and if the wonderful resistance of Belgium was a bitter disappointment and sadly disturbed the dream of the early fall of Paris, Germans generally found relief in a passionate explosion of feeling against England. Meanwhile, the still, small voice of conscience, protesting against the wrong done to Belgium, was drowned by a hoarse chorus of calumny and vituperation. It took some months for the German Government to build up the lying tale—chiefly by absurd manipulation of such documents as were ultimately found discarded or forgotten in the Foreign Office at Brussels—that Belgium had long before the war abandoned her neutrality and thrown in her lot with France and England. The German public was fooled by coarser methods. While the German army tore its way, murdering and pillaging, through the little State whose neutrality Germany had guaranteed, the German public was fed on stories of Belgian cruelty and treachery and taught that the Belgians earned their fate by "pouring oil on German soldiers" or gouging out German eyes. They soon forgot the fatal words, which echoed and re-echoed through the whole

MAKING OUT CASUALTY LISTS IN BERLIN.

civilized world, of the Imperial Chancellor, in his speech in the Reichstag on August 4 :

The wrong—I speak openly—that we are committing we will endeavour to make good as soon as our military goal has been reached. Anybody who is threatened as we are threatened, and is fighting for his highest possessions, can have only one thought—how is he to hack his way through.

The Chancellor tried subsequently, especially in another speech in the Reichstag (December 2, 1914) to explain his words away. All the intellectuals of Germany toiled at the same task, like murderers striving to wash bloodstains from their garments. After a year of such efforts Professor Schoenborn, of Heidelberg, summed up the results in the following delightful formula :

These sentences can, of course, be rightly understood and appreciated only if regard is had to the whole situation in which they were spoken. They were uttered at an hour of fate of the German Empire, to a political gathering, and as part of a Government declaration of high policy. They were not intended, therefore, to constitute, and could not constitute, an impartial and considered theoretical judgment, from a legal standpoint, upon the merits of this German procedure. On the contrary, they are one section of a political action.*

If that was good enough for the professors, it is not surprising that for the public Belgian neutrality soon became " the English swindle."

———————
* From a large volume of German apologetics, called " Deutschland und der grosse Krieg " (page 566), published in July 1915.

Meanwhile the nation answered as one man to the call of the Emperor and the Government, and the whole country was inspired by the spirit of unity and determination. As every competent judge of German conditions had predicted, the great Socialist party, although it embraced one-third of the whole people—and probably at least one-half of the men who first took the field—offered no serious opposition whatever. After brief deliberation and an unimportant difference of opinion behind the scenes, the Socialists voted for the war credits that were immediately demanded by the Government. As the war progressed their attitude showed certain fluctuations, but it was never such as to give the Government the slightest anxiety. They were quite content, it seemed, with an empty phrase, such as that in which the Kaiser after his speech from the Throne on August 4 exclaimed : " I no longer recognize parties. I know only Germans." It is true that when the Kaiser followed up this demonstration by proposing to shake hands with the party leaders, the Socialist leaders did not accept the invitation, but they soon bowed to public opinion and did nothing to mar the increase of admiring loyalty which, as we shall see, the Emperor most adroitly used.

The more preposterous the abuse of all

Germany's enemies, but especially England, the more confident became the belief in Germany's " cause." Was she not fighting a " defensive war for her existence " against " a world of enemies " ? Had not perfidious England, after years of jealous efforts to " hem Germany in," fallen upon her in her hour of need ? Were not Germany's enemies striving to overrun her territories and destroy her industry and trade because they could not face the competition in the world's markets of her intelligent and industrious people ? It was a fit soil for national heroes and the creation of legends. Perhaps it is not inappropriate that the first hero the German nation took to its heart was not a man but a gun—the famous 17 in. howitzer which Krupps had built in secret and which battered down the forts at Liége. But then in rapid succession came others—"father Hindenburg," the " saviour of East Prussia from Cossack hordes," Captain von Müller of the Emden, which for so long raided commerce and defied British sea power, and Weddigen, the pioneer in the submarine war.

Before, however, we deal with the machinery and methods by which opinion was guided and controlled and the great German war legends were built up, let us briefly consider the internal position. Again and again in the years before the war German statesmen protested before God and man that the best proof of their good

intentions was that they had kept the peace for 40 years. In public and in private the Kaiser loved to claim this as his own personal achievement, and there were many who believed that his highest ambition was to go down in history as the *Friedenskaiser*, the great ruler who had controlled vast armies but never used them, who had increased the power and prestige of Germany without ever striking a blow. What this strange and unfamiliar theory of the virtue of keeping quiet really meant was that Germany regarded war as something normal and in the nature of things. Peace was rather the excessively virtuous interruption of war than war the rude interruption of peace. When at last the Great War came, it was hailed with something like relief. Prussia-Germany had been delivered from the perils of pacifism and internationalism, and was once more about to convince Europe that might is right. After a year of war the Imperial Chancellor, suspect of feebleness and international prejudices, could rally all German opinion with the cry, " We have got over our sentimentality (*Wir haben unsere Sentimentalität verlernt*)." After all, the State was founded upon force, and force should prevail.

It is difficult to describe in terms easily intelligible to an English reader the facility with which Germany threw off her whole civilian trappings and reverted to the pure type

IN THE STATE APARTMENTS OF THE KING OF BAVARIA'S PALACE, MUNICH.
Bavarian Court Ladies.

THE KAISER IN THE EASTERN THEATRE OF WAR.

of the military State. Within a few hours of the issue of the mobilization order the whole country was under military control. Government Departments, provincial administrations, municipal administrations, all lost the very show of independence, and became handmaids of the military rulers of the country. In Berlin, for instance, all power passed at once into the hands of the Military Governor. Throughout the Empire the real control of administration was vested in the generals in command of army-corps districts—that is to say, the generals left behind as deputies for the generals who took the field. It was they who guided and coaxed and threatened the public by constant proclamations. It was they and their subordinates who really managed everything, and saw to it that in every sphere the needs of the army and the prosecution of the war were held superior to any other consideration whatever. It was the military authorities who suppressed newspapers, exercised the censorship upon news and upon private communications, prevented the holding of public meetings which did not suit their view of the country's interests, and generally directed the whole course of civil life. They had ample powers to commandeer supplies and, as we shall see later, to control labour. The whole machinery of the State was at their disposal and subject to their will and pleasure.

It must not be supposed that this military regime was felt to be irksome or was accepted with reluctance. It was, rather, regarded as perfectly natural. Germany at war had no thought or care for anything but the successful prosecution of the war, and the people generally had no more eager desire than to play their part as willing members of the great machine. The more perfect the organization for war proved to be, the more enthusiastic did the country become. The people were willing to make any sacrifices, because they felt themselves to be integral parts of the whole complex scheme which contained the whole forces and resources of the Empire. Immediately war broke out, the country was given a great object-lesson in the perfect precision of the mobilization. The State railway system, which was at once taken over by the military authorities, moved the vast armies without any confusion or delay. The fighting forces were called out in accordance with arrangements of which every detail was fixed in advance. Knowing almost exactly what part every man would have to play as the war progressed and as reinforcements were needed, the public, inspired and encouraged by the feeling of a real equality in sacrifice, could adapt and readjust its whole life to meet the strain. There were no idle hands and shirkers were, necessarily, rare. Men who were left at their industrial or commercial work knew that they were left because, after consideration of each individual case, their work was considered to be necessary. And they also knew that they might at any time be called to the colours.

In contemplating the spirit of Germany, one must not forget the force of tradition. It was only 50 years before the war that the German Empire had been united by the sword. Very many of the most prominent men in Germany had themselves taken part in the war against France. Every family had its personal ties with the great time of Bismarck. Above all, the whole country knew how the German victories then had brought unimagined wealth and prosperity and prestige. It was easy to persuade such a people that it was fighting to hold and defend what its fathers had won, and to complete their work, and that defeat would mean relapse to the old conditions and the breaking up of the Empire into a number of small and impotent States. Moreover, the people upon which such arguments were employed was essentially bellicose, and in its heart welcomed a policy of aggression and of conquest by the sword.

The most remarkable immediate effect of the swallowing up of Germany in the military machine was the apparent disappearance of the personal element both in government and administration. Not only were the minor

CAPT. WEDDIGEN.

statesmen, from Herr von Bethmann-Hollweg, the Imperial Chancellor, downwards, whom a strange fate had placed in command at such a time, easily pushed into the background. No great soldier appeared to take their place. The Chief of the Great General Staff soon proved to be a Moltke only in name, and he was actually superseded after a few months of war. The whole machine, as it were, ran itself. There were very few ministerial or administrative changes. There was soon a new Imperial Finance Minister. Otherwise the men who were found in office remained in office. Delbrück, as Imperial Minister of the Interior, was responsible for control of food supply and industrial reorganization generally, Havenstein continued to perform his important functions as head of the Imperial Bank—and so on. From time to time questions of high policy involved personal conflict—especially, as the result of the dispute with the United States about submarine "piracy," the revival of the old feud between Grand Admiral von Tirpitz, Secretary of State for the Imperial Navy, and the Imperial Chancellor. But upon the whole there was less friction than in times of peace, and among the mediocre administrators there was seldom any marked assertion of personal ambition or of claims to predominance.

The most striking and important illustration of this state of things was the change in the position of the Emperor. The whole truth about

[*Swaine.*

CAPT. VON MÜLLER,
Of the "Emden."

his personal and direct responsibility for precipitating the war is still unknown, but it is beyond dispute that he directed the course of German action in the last days of crisis. When war had broken out he played his part with great caution and skill. On August 17 he left Berlin for the Western Front, and established himself at Luxemburg, where he was accompanied by most of the Ministers and an enormous retinue. From time to time he addressed some message to the troops or to the people at home, but such utterances were like reticence in him. He watched the most acute phase of the First Battle of Ypres in October, and made other spectacular appearances in the field, but the more marked became the failure to reach Paris (or even Warsaw), the more modest

DOCTOR DELBRÜCK,
Imperial Minister of the Interior.

became the Emperor's bearing towards his people. In December, 1914, he even returned to Berlin in the dead of night, in order to avoid all public demonstration. As the war progressed, the Emperor succeeded in forming something like a new Kaiser legend. He was more and more careful to avoid all appearance of interfering either in strategy or in policy, and he gradually became a sort of venerable father of his people, sharing their sacrifices and mourning their losses rather than calling upon them to do his Imperial will. The impression of venerability, which became so strong as to constitute almost an infringement of the monopoly so long enjoyed throughout Europe by the Emperor Francis Joseph, was strengthened by changes in the Kaiser's personal appearance. He aged visibly, and the Court photographers made no

secret of his grey hairs and diminished vivacity of bearing.

Apart from everything else, and from the undoubted fact that in his new guise the Emperor rapidly gained in the affections of his people, account had to be taken of the obvious failure of the Royal Family to win distinction in war. It was only for a short time that the German newspapers were instructed to insist upon the presence of all the Emperor's sons in the field. The name of the Emperor's brother, Grand Admiral Prince Henry of Prussia, soon disappeared altogether. Above all, the German Crown Prince not only failed notoriously as a commander, but by his personal habits acquired a reputation hardly more savoury than, say, that of the Turkish commander in Syria. He shocked even the German Army and the German people. Of all the German princes the only one who gained solid prestige in the first year of war was the Crown Prince Rupprecht of Bavaria, who had the popular task of opposing the hated British in the West.

In no previous war had there been anything to compare with the prodigious propaganda that began all over the world with the very beginning of hostilities. In no country was the campaign conducted so deliberately—and unscrupulously—as in Germany. It soon appeared that there was no service too mean and no intellectual prostitution too base for patriotic German pens. In the German view it was the duty and privilege of every citizen to promote the German cause in time of war by any method that seemed to offer itself. For the civil population no less than for the armed forces—to quote the Imperial Chancellor's phrase—"necessity knew no law." The whole intellectual forces of the nation and the whole spoon-fed Press were mobilized immediately, and the world was invited to watch the strangest war of words in history. The leading ideas were much the same as those of the generals. There must be great rapidity and no squeamishness. There must be plenty of heavy artillery. The main enemy must be attacked with peculiar violence. There must be no dissipation of forces. We have said that Germany expected a short war. The literary campaign was planned accordingly. It is inconceivable that, if they had had any conception of the probable duration of the war, the Germans would have conducted their propaganda on the same lines. They seem to have believed that they could drown the truth in a hurricane of high explosives, and so deafen the whole world with their shrieks and protestations that it would not recover consciousness and the power of criticism until the war was over. At the same time there was evidently more anxiety about opinion in Germany itself than the event justified. As a matter of fact, German opinion proved to be entirely docile and perfectly willing to be misled. It fed greedily upon the official version of the causes of the war, and responded instantly to every call.

There is no occasion to discuss here the ethical basis of this sort of patriotism or to examine closely the reasons which caused Germans generally to adopt a very bad case with very great unanimity. But there is no doubt that the rapid growth of material prosperity had for years before the war been undermining intellectual honesty and preparing the "learned classes" to play the part they did. The fact was evident, if only from the condition of the Press, which had grown steadily in influence and prosperity, especially in the last 10 years, without acquiring any shreds of decency or raising at all the low standards and evil repute of German journalism. Neverthe-

A CORNER OF KRUPP'S WORKS
Showing the Sheffield-made Machinery.

less, the results were astonishing even to those who were well acquainted with Germany, and they will stand to the credit of German civilization for all time.

There is no better illustration of the general character of the German propaganda than a manifesto which in October, 1914, when the German crimes in Belgium had moved universal horror, was published broadcast over the names of almost every German well known for scientific or artistic achievement. We will quote it in full :

We, as representatives of German Science and Art, raise before the whole civilized world our protest against

THE KAISER AND MARSHAL VON HINDENBURG.

Photographed by the German Empress. The proceeds from the sale of this picture were handed over to the German Red Cross Fund.

the lies and calumnies with which our enemies try to besmirch Germany's pure cause in the struggle for existence that has been forced upon her. The iron mouth of events has disposed of the carefully propagated fictions about German defeats. All the more eager now is the effort to pervert facts, and to sow suspicion. Against these efforts we raise our voice. This voice shall proclaim the truth.

It is not true that Germany was guilty of this war. Neither the people nor the Government nor the Kaiser wanted it. The utmost efforts were made on the German side to avert it. The documentary proofs are open to the world. Often enough did William II. in the twenty-six years of his reign prove himself the protector of the world's peace ; often enough have even our enemies recognized this fact. Yes, this very Kaiser whom they

now dare to call Attila has for a decade past been ridiculed by them for his unshakable love of peace. It was only when superior forces which had long been lying in wait on our frontiers fell upon our people from three sides that the people rose like one man.

It is not true that we criminally violated the neutrality of Belgium. It has been proved that France and England were determined to violate Belgium's neutrality. It has been proved that Belgium consented. It would have been suicide not to anticipate them.

It is not true that the life or property of a single Belgian citizen has been assailed by our soldiers without the compulsion of most bitter necessity. Again and again, in spite of all warnings, the population shot at our soldiers from ambushes, and mutilated wounded and murdered doctors engaged in their Samaritan work. More contemptible forgery is inconceivable than the keeping of silence about the crimes of these murderers, in order to make the just punishment which they suffered into a crime on the part of the Germans.

It is not true that our troops raged brutally against Louvain. With heavy hearts they were compelled to practise reprisals—by bombarding part of the city—on the mad populace, which treacherously fell upon them in their bivouacs. The greater part of Louvain has been preserved ; the famous Rathaus remains entirely unhurt, and our soldiers sacrificed themselves to preserve it from the flames. If works of art have been or shall be destroyed in this terrible war, every German would lament the fact. But just as we yield to nobody in the love of art, we decidedly refuse to pay by a German defeat for the maintenance of any work of art.

It is not true that our leaders have disregarded the provisions of international law. Unbridled brutality is unknown to them. But in the East the earth is drenched with the blood of women and children who have been butchered by the Russian hordes, while in the West dum-dum bullets have torn the breasts of our warriors. The right to pose as the defenders of civilization belongs least of all to those who have allied themselves with the Russians and Serbs, and provided the world with the horrible spectacle of Mongolians and niggers being spurred against the white race.

It is not true that the struggle against our so-called militarism is not a struggle against our *Kultur*, as is hypocritically asserted by our enemies. Without German militarism German *Kultur* would long ago have been swept off the face of the earth. It is for the protection of *Kultur*, and out of *Kultur*, that militarism has arisen in a country which for centuries has been tormented like no other country by robber raids. The German Army and the German people are one. The consciousness of this fact to-day makes brothers of seventy millions of Germans, without distinction of education, class, or party.

We cannot deprive our enemies of the poisoned weapons of lies. We can only cry out to all the world that the witness they bear against us is false. To you who know us, and who, together with us, have guarded the highest possessions of humanity, we cry aloud—believe us ! Believe that we shall fight this fight to the end as a *Kultur* people, for which the heritage of a Goethe, a Beethoven, and a Kant is as sacred as hearth and home. For this we pledge you our names and our honour.

The 93 signatories of this precious document included such historians, philosophers and political economists as Brentano, Brandl, Eucken, Häckel, Harnack, Laband, Lamprecht, Lenz, Schmoller, Wilamowitz and Wundt, writers like Hauptmann and Sudermann, men of science like Ehrlich and Wassermann, and representatives of all the arts.

Here, indeed, was the whole German legend—

THE WAR-WORN KAISER.

THE KAISER'S YOUNGEST SON.
Prince Joachim wearing his Iron Cross.

the undesired and uninvited " struggle for existence," the unprovoked assault by a coalition of treacherous neighbours, the evil intentions of France and England against Belgium which had to be " anticipated," the gentleness of the German soldiery, the need for reprisals, the treason committed by Germany's enemies against the white race, the defence of *Kultur,* and the sacredness of the struggle inspired by the purest German traditions. For all this these distinguished Germans " pledged their names and their honour."

The professors went on as they had begun. The student of the German history of this time will always find in their utterances and actions in the first three or four months of the war the most damning proof of Germany's ambitions and Germany's guilt. Their excesses did their country a good deal of harm, and before the end of 1914 the Government began to put a check upon them and recommended more cautious and considered behaviour. " The German intellectuals," said the *Berliner Tageblatt* in December, " have a preference for

kicking neutrals in the stomach, and it is evident that this practice does not lessen the enormous difficulties which Germany has at present to overcome. Anybody who knows something of contemporary history will refrain from singing the praises of the diplomatists. But the so-called intellectual leaders sometimes have less political insight than the youngest attaché."

The manifesto that we have quoted introduced the world at large to a little-known conception—German *Kultur.* Henceforward *Kultur* played a more prominent part in the war than any other word in the German vocabulary. The Germans distinguished between *Kultur* and civilization, but by the former they meant little else than civilization of the peculiarly German type. Its significance and meaning for other peoples they put in a popular couplet :

" Denn es muss am deutschen Wesen
Einmal noch die Welt genesen."

(For the world must one day find
Its healing in the German mind.)

The Germans, in fact, were the chosen people. The idea ran through the whole German war literature. It was Professor Adolf Lasson, of Berlin University, who expressed it most plainly. His utterances did more than anything else to bury the extreme propagandists in ridicule and to provoke the mingled amusement and resentment of the whole world at German pretensions. Professor Wilhelm Ostwald had already said : " Germany has reached a higher stage of civilization than the other peoples, and the result of the war will be the organization of Europe under German leadership." Professor Haeckel had demanded the conquest of London, the division of Belgium between Germany and Holland, and the annexation of the Congo State, a great part of the British colonies, the North-East of France, Poland, and the Russian Baltic provinces. Professor Lasson went further. " We are," he wrote, " morally and intellectually superior to all men. We are peerless. So, too, are our organizations and our institutions." Germany was " the most perfect political creation known to history," the Kaiser was " deliciæ humani generis," and the Imperial Chancellor, Herr von Bethmann-Hollweg, was " the most eminent of living men." The language was crude and ridiculous, but it was an expression of the ruling German idea— that the ties of common humanity had been destroyed, and that Germany now stood not merely alone but " peerless."

Germany set about the mobilization and manipulation of opinion with extraordinary zeal and energy. There was, as we have seen, rigid military control of the Press, which prevented all criticism of an undesired kind, while the newspapers were compelled to publish what the authorities wished to be published. The whole machinery of control of the Press, which was considerable in peace time, was reorganized and "speeded up." The Press Bureau of the Foreign Office, which was a survival from Bismarck's time and usually worked in the dark, was put upon a new basis, and became a full-fledged "department" of the Foreign Office, thus giving almost perfect independence to its notorious chief, Dr. Hammann. The military authorities organized intelligence bureaux, and editors and leader-writers were kept in the straight path by daily

"Press conferences" under the auspices of the Great General Staff. A number of trustworthy writers were directly employed by Government departments to prepare articles and descriptive reports. There was even a distinct "corruption bureau." The greatest attention was paid to the Press of all neutral countries. Wherever possible, the German Government bought outright or subsidized "neutral" newspapers, and it went to infinite pains to get the assistance, as correspondents in Germany or as organizers of "neutral news agencies," of pro-German writers whose names were well known abroad. The Swedish explorer, Sven Hedin, was a more than welcome guest, who described with much skill and infinite obsequiousness German life in the field and the virtues and heroism of the German Army. There was a host of satellites from other neutral countries,

THE GERMAN CROWN PRINCE AND HIS STAFF.
At his headquarters in the North of France.

and the Government was even able to secure the services of a few needy British renegades. One of the most scurrilous organs of the German Government was created out of a Berlin news sheet, published in English and called the *Continental Times*, which before the war had lived a precarious existence for the benefit of American and British tourists.

Immediately after the outbreak of war subsidized agencies were established—the most notorious was controlled by the Centre Party Deputy in the Reichstag, Herr Erzberger—to flood neutral newspapers with German news. Regardless of the cost, these agencies would telegraph many thousands of words a day to every important neutral newspaper, and be content if a few hundred words got into print. It must not be supposed that the German news was mainly false news. On the contrary, the German authorities were alive to the importance of establishing some reputation for veracity. They were utterly unscrupulous in case of need, but, as a rule, the German reports were not remarkably inaccurate. The successes of German arms were, indeed, sufficient to justify, at most times, the luxury of truthfulness. The German Navy was less fortunate, and the Naval Press Bureau almost invariably published false accounts of events at sea. Confidence was not increased abroad by boasted devotion to " truth." As early as September, 1914, an appeal for an intense " truth " campaign, promoted apparently by Herr Ballin and the

publicity department of the Hamburg-Amerika Line, had laid it down that the world must be taught unceasingly " that Germany was shamefully fallen upon, that the German cause is just, that Germany is united for victory or death, and that Germany's enemies are conducting the war with a shamelessness that cries to Heaven."

One curious method of the propaganda was the circulation on a vast scale of " private letters " addressed not only to neutral but even to belligerent countries. An office was established in Berlin at which suitable compositions were dictated and copied, and unsuspecting British families would suddenly receive an elaborate statement of " the German case " in the form of a letter from some long-forgotten German travelling acquaintance or old servant. They suddenly developed eloquence like the following :

> We fight for the existence of our country, which our enemies have long been trying to crush, for Western civilization, and for humanity, against the barbarism of the East and the sway of the knout.

Meanwhile German opinion was skilfully and successfully guided into what seemed to be the most profitable channels. A particular line of argument was maintained as long as its popularity lasted, and then there was an immediate diversion. At first there was a torrent of abuse of the " treacherous, worthless and murderous Belgians," who had " richly earned their fate." Then came a passionate

MEN OF A BAVARIAN REGIMENT
Parading before King Ludwig at Munich.

DR. HELFFERICH,
Secretary of State for the Imperial Treasury.

crusade against England. Partly because of the failure to carry through the original plan of campaign and reach Paris, partly because of the stubborn hope that France would weaken in her resolution and consent to make a separate peace, it soon became the fashion in Germany to regard France with an assumed pity and magnanimous toleration. There was a good deal of curious discussion as to whether Russia or England was the "chief enemy," and Russia's claims to the position remained fairly strong during the invasion of East Prussia and the menace to Posen and Silesia. But public opinion was too strong, and throughout the first year of war nine-tenths of the German effort was directed against the British Empire. In October the Munich illustrated paper *Jugend* published the following poem by a certain Herr Ernst Lissauer:*

French and Russian they matter not,
A blow for a blow and a shot for a shot:
We love them not, we hate them not.
We hold the Weichsel and Vosges-gate,
We have but one and only hate,
We love as one, we hate as one,
We have one foe and one alone.

He is known to you all, he is known to you all
He crouches behind the dark grey flood,
Full of envy, of rage, of craft, of gall.
Cut off by waves that are thicker than blood.
Come let us stand at the Judgment place.
An oath to swear to, face to face,
An oath of bronze no wind can shake,
An oath for our sons and their sons to take.
Come, hear the word, repeat the word,
Throughout the Fatherland make it heard.
We will never forgo our hate,
We have all but a single hate,

* This brilliant translation, by Barbara Henderson, first appeared in the *New York Times*.

We love as one, we hate as one,
We have one foe, and one alone—
ENGLAND !

In the Captain's Mess, in the banquet-hall,
Sat feasting the officers, one and all,
Like a sabre-blow, like the swing of a sail,
One seized his glass held high to hail ;
Sharp-snapped like the stroke of a rudder's play
Spoke three words only : "To the Day !"

Whose glass this fate ?
They had all but a single hate.
Who was thus known ?
They had one foe, and one alone—
ENGLAND !

Take you the folk of the Earth in pay,
With bars of gold your ramparts lay,
Bedeck the ocean with bow on bow,
Ye reckon well, but not well enough now.
French and Russian they matter not,
A blow for a blow, a shot for a shot,
We fight the battle with bronze and steel,
And the time that is coming Peace will seal.
You will we hate with a lasting hate,
We will never forgo our hate,
Hate by water and hate by land,
Hate of the head and hate of the hand,
Hate of the hammer and hate of the crown,
Hate of seventy millions, choking down.
We love as one, we hate as one,
We have one foe, and one alone—
ENGLAND !

These verses won immediate fame, and there is no doubt that they accurately represented German feeling. It was idle for the *Frankfurter Zeitung* to say : "The greatest mistake we could make would be to reply in kind to the impotent hatred which spits at us everywhere." Not until a year later was it recognized that there might be some truth in this view, and Herr Lissauer was induced to explain that his poem was an outburst of momentary passion and not intended to be "political." Hatred became intensely popular, and professors and journalists raised the new doctrine of "the right of hate" to the same level among Germany's national possessions as "the will to conquer." Somebody coined the expression "*Gott strafe*

PROF. LASSON,
Doctor of Philosophy
at Berlin University.

DR. KARL PETERS,
The German
Explorer.

57—3

RETURNING TO THE FRONT.
German troops who recovered from their wounds.
Inset: A Berlin Idyll.

a torrent of abuse of the "mercenaries" who were supposed to be recruited in the slums of England while all well-to-do people stayed at home. Before the war was six weeks old the *Hamburger Nachrichten* wrote :

> The sons of German mothers are fashioned in the image of God, who brought a sword into the world. But the sons of French, English, Russian. and Belgian mothers have shown themselves to be as beasts which shoot with horribly tearing bullets at German warriors, mutilate German wounded, and commit murder.

England ! " as a form of greeting for German patriots, and it was freely used as an inscription on notepaper and stamped on letters and parcels for foreign countries. An extraordinary feature of the campaign was the peculiar " hatred " of Sir Edward Grey. The British Foreign Minister was given a position all to himself as a callous, cruel and crafty schemer, the chief author of the war, and, indeed, the worst man living. This view was quite deliberately propagated by the German Foreign Office, and any sign of decreased passion was promptly remedied by a flaming attack in the *Cologne Gazette* or some other mouthpiece of the Government.

There was hardly any subject in connexion with the war which the Germans did not regard mainly in relation to England. They were well provided with a series of exciting topics. The appearance of the British Expeditionary Force in the field was the signal for

HERR BALLIN,
Of the Hamburg-Amerika Line.

Stories about the use of dum-dum bullets and about horrible mutilation of German wounded were for a long time deliberately encouraged by the military authorities, and were immensely popular. When, in the course of the autumn of 1914, it became necessary to deal seriously and systematically with the problem of food supplies, the Government described the British blockade as the British *Aushungerungsplan*, or scheme to starve Germany out. The phrase was almost as useful as what was called *Einkreisungspolitik*, or the British policy of trying "to hem Germany in." It was of no avail to quote German precedents or the utterances of German statesmen. The blockade was to be regarded as "war upon women and children." In March, 1915, after the slander had done its duty, the Socialist *Vorwärts* summoned up enough courage to say, "The truth is that starving out is the oldest method of war, and a method privileged by international law to the present day. Of course the object is not really that human beings should die of hunger. The purpose is only, by pressure upon the stomach, to compel people to make peace." The furious campaign against the sale of munitions of war by the United States to the Allies was conducted with equal indifference to German precedents and to the obvious facts of the case. Another extremely

PROF. ERNST HAECKEL.

popular subject was "reprisals." They were demanded against all and sundry, and the newspapers were perpetually discovering wrongs or indignities done to Germans which called aloud for vengeance. It was in this way that the Germans made themselves responsible for the general internment in the chief belligerent countries of "alien enemies." Two or three months after the outbreak of war, Dr. Karl Peters, the African explorer, who had for many years enjoyed British hospitality after disgracing himself by ill-treatment of African natives, published violent articles, declaring that "the best lot that befalls Germans in England is to rot like dogs." This was followed by numerous lying "interviews" with Germans who had been released from such internment camps as then existed in England and allowed to return home. The German Government was induced to demand the release of all German subjects, and, having failed to obtain this preposterous demand, proceeded to intern all male British subjects in Germany without distinction. With great difficulty arrangements were afterwards made for the exchange of certain classes of civilians.

The general temper of the country swayed, naturally, with the course of military events. But it found constant solace during the first

PROF. OSTWALD.

year of war in the achievements of the German submarines and the raids of Zeppelin airships on England. It was quite seriously believed that, when the "submarine blockade" began on February 18, 1915, England would be completely cut off. And little doubt was felt that the Zeppelins would rapidly produce panic and probably at the least reduce London to ashes.

Let us turn now to the economic situation, and deal first with the question of the food supply. In Germany, more than in any other of the belligerent countries, it dominated politics, and, partly of necessity, partly by choice, Germany pushed it into the forefront of international controversy and made it the basis of her most frantic appeals to neutral opinion, and also of her most violent accusations against Great Britain.

At the beginning of the war ridiculous stories were spread all over the world about the imminence of German starvation. Later on, when Germany, as we shall see, had solved her main problems, it became the fashion to say that the whole discussion of scarcity had been "bluff." The talk of "bluff" was nearly as ridiculous as the talk of "famine." The truth was that as soon as the British Navy

cut her off from the world's seas Germany was faced with the difficult and delicate problem of readjusting her system in such a way as to make good a diminution of her ordinary food supply which, as regarded bread stuffs at any rate, could be estimated at from 15 to 20 per cent. of her total consumption. The problem could be solved upon certain conditions, the chief of which were continued protection of German corn lands from invasion, administrative efficiency, and a general willingness among the people to practise economy and to bear any reasonable sacrifices. There can be no doubt that Germany had made less direct preparation in this than in any other sphere. The main reason was that the all-powerful Prussian agrarians would brook no interference. Eighteen months before the war the Kaiser, in one of his rash and ill-considered speeches, had said: "There is no longer any doubt that Germany not only can now supply, but also will be able for the future to supply, bread and meat for all her people." Although this Imperial utterance was hotly disputed, assumption of its truth was the only basis of calculation, and even after the war broke out very little was done until prices soared up and discontent became general. It was not until nearly six months after the outbreak of war

STUDY OF A PRUSSIAN HOUSEHOLD HAVING ITS MORNING HATE.

[*Barnett.*

SIR EDWARD GREY,
British Secretary of State for Foreign Affairs.

that the Government put into force a really comprehensive system of control.

The first action of the Government was to take a census of the actual supplies in the country. The results were not published, but in the month of November, when the scheme of *maximum* prices was introduced, an official statement said :

We have bread and corn enough to feed the Army and the people until the next harvest. We must be sparing with our supplies in order to start the next harvest year with the necessary reserves. We desire to be able to see the war through under all circumstances until we have won the certainty of a permanent peace. The Government knows that in this desire it is at one with the whole population, and it is convinced that the population will be ready to understand and to promote all measures which this aim requires.

At the same time the Government indicated that there was enough rye for all requirements up to the beginning of September, 1915, and enough meat for all requirements up to the beginning of August, 1915. These calculations took into account the serious damage done to the harvest in East Prussia by the Russians, and in Alsace-Lorraine by the French. They also took into account the very serious fact that the German farmers had wasted large quantities of corn as fodder, when the importation of fodder barley from Russia ceased. The total corn deficit as compared with normal years was probably about 16 per cent. The German harvest of 1914 had been, in spite of all official statements to the contrary, below the average. When, at the end of the year, the German Government desired for obvious reasons to give the other side of the picture, it published the following comparative statis-

tics (in tons) of the harvests of 1914 and 1913 :

		1914	1913
Wheat	...	3,971,995	4,655,956
Rye ...	...	10,426,718	12,222,394
Barley	...	3,137,983	3,673,254
Oats ...	...	9,038,185	9,713,965
Potatoes	...	45,569,559	54,121,146

Before the autumn of 1914 was far advanced the situation, as might have been expected, became intolerable. The farmers pursued a purely selfish policy, insisting upon maintaining their stocks of cattle at the expense of the bread supply, and encouraging the rise in price of bread corn. Prices not only rose, but varied enormously in different parts of the country. When the Government at last, and rather timidly, intervened, they had to deal with a situation infinitely worse than at the outbreak of war. What they did was to establish *maximum* prices in the markets, and to establish bakery regulations. This was the origin of the famous " war bread," which played almost as important a part in German propaganda abroad as in the sustenance of the German people at home. The basis of the scheme was a *maximum* price of £11 per ton of rye in Berlin. The prices then varied geographically, being lowest in the east, and highest in the west and south—that is, at the points most distant from the main sources of supply. For example, the *maximum* price of rye (which cost £11 in Berlin) was £10 9s. at Königsberg, and £11 17s. at Munich and Aix-la-Chapelle respectively. The *maximum* price of wheat

SIR EDWARD GREY
As he appeared in German War Cartoons.

were compelled to produce *minimum* percentages of flour from the grain.

The institution of "war bread" consisted in compulsion upon bakers to "mix" their bread. They were required to put at least 10 per cent. of rye into wheat bread, and at least 5 per cent. of potato into rye bread. They were allowed to put 20 per cent. or even more, of potato into their compositions without depriving them of the title of "bread." The next step was to popularize these new kinds of food. As in everything else, the Prussian Royal family was expected to lead the way,

"THE YEAR OF VICTORY."
German soldier passing the Pillar of Victory in Berlin and saying he must march further before receiving his wreath (*Lustige Blätter*, August, 1915).

was fixed uniformly at £2 more than the local *maximum* price for rye. The price of flour was not fixed, and the Government did not deal at all with the vital problem of potatoes. With certain exceptions, however, the use of rye and wheat as fodder was forbidden, and millers

"GOD PUNISHED ENGLAND."
(*Lustige Blätter* Cartoon after bombardment of Yarmouth.)

and the newspapers were soon full of descriptions of the consumption of "war bread" in the Palace at Potsdam, and by the Emperor and Crown Prince in the field. The "sacrifice" entailed does not seem to have been very great. Some towns distinguished themselves by the extreme nastiness of their "war bread," but travellers who tested it in various places came to the conclusion that its bitterness was in no proportion to the sweetness of the feeling that the British attempt "to starve Germany out" had been doomed to failure.

The new scheme came into force on November 4, 1914. It was all very well but for the fact that there was no compulsion on the

Victoria!!

THE KAISER EN ROUTE FOR PARIS.
(From *Lustige Blätter*, Jan. 27, 1915.)

"THE SPLENDID ISOLATION."
(*Simplicissimus* Cartoon in March 1915.)

farmers to keep the markets supplied. The
scarcity of corn became more acute than ever,
and the dealers promptly made use of the
differentiation in prices in different parts of the
country, which bore no true relation to the
cost of transport, in order to sell in the dearest
rather than in the nearest market. The
Government was profuse in its appeals to the
public to practise economy, but before the end
of the year it was compelled to revise the whole
system. It was announced that new measures
were required in order to insure Germany's
ability to survive a " critical " period, which
would begin about the middle of May, and
end only with the gathering in of the harvest
of 1915. As neither the Ministry of the Interior nor any other department was capable
of assuming control of the whole matter, it was
decided to form a limited liability company,
with powers of expropriation, and with the
duty of acquiring, conserving, and ultimately
distributing, corn supplies. The company,

which was given the name of War Corn Company (*Kriegsgetreidegesellschaft*), was composed of large industrialists, and of towns with a population of more than 100,000. The directors were representatives of the State and industrial magnates. The profits were limited to 5 per cent. of the capital. At the same time the bakery regulations were stiffened, and the proportion of potato to be mixed with rye was increased.

All this was preliminary to the final plunge. Towards the end of January it was announced that the Government had decided to seize all supplies of corn as a monopoly of the Empire, and to establish a new system of distribution and restriction of consumption. Holders of stocks of corn were required to declare them by a fixed date, and the stocks passed into the possession either of the War Corn Company or of local municipal organizations. These bodies dealt with the supply of corn to the mills, and an Imperial administration was set up to deal with the distribution of supplies to the local authorities, which in turn had to regulate the distribution to the public. The essence of the scheme was the establishment of an uniform bread ration. It was originally intended to leave the local authorities free to deal with the distribution of the *quantum* of bread and flour allotted to them, but after a period of uncertainty a system of " bread tickets " was adopted all over the country. The basis of the system was a ration of slightly more than 7 ounces of flour per head per day. The ration was subsequently increased, and exceptions were made for classes of persons engaged in heavy manual work.

When the " bread tickets " were introduced, the Prussian Government issued an explanatory statement, which included the following :

There can be no doubt that this measure goes far deeper into the economic life of our people than all other measures taken during the war. It is, however, necessary, in order to assure a sufficient and regular supply of our people with bread until the next harvest, and it is therefore a vital necessity for the State and for the nation. The measures taken hitherto have not proved sufficient to guarantee an economic use of our supplies of corn, which are indeed in themselves thoroughly sufficient, but are nevertheless limited. In particular, the previous measures did not effectively prevent the use of corn as fodder. There are only two ways open for the attainment of our purpose. Either there must be a quite extraordinary rise in corn prices, which would limit consumption and make the use of corn as fodder impossible, or all corn supplies must be confiscated and distributed to local authorities in proportion to the number of people to be fed. The Federal Governments have decided upon the second

course, in order to spare the German people during the period of war a great increase in the price of bread.

The measure that has been taken gives us the certainty that the scheme of our enemies to starve Germany out has been brought to nothing. It assures us a sufficient supply of bread until the next harvest. It makes our country, in this economic war also, invincible. We are confident that the authorities in all branches and every single official, even though they are not officially bound to co-operate, will work with all their strength for the carrying out of this great task, and will assist the population by their advice and by their actions. We are sure of the willing cooperation of all circles of our people and its economic organizations. Every individual will remember that conscientious obedience to the regulations is a grave and sacred duty to the Fatherland.

The patriotic spirit and the firm will for victory, which in this great time manifest themselves so splendidly in our people, give us the certainty that every man and every woman will do their duty gladly and with joy in making sacrifices. As our heroic troops out there on the ramparts, so we, who stay at home, will and shall for our part hold out victoriously in the great battle for the existence and the honour of the Empire.

The initiation of this scheme necessarily caused a good deal of anxiety, and a certain amount of local disturbance, but as soon as the public discovered that these extraordinary measures did not conceal any real peril of " starvation," they rapidly adapted themselves to circumstances, and the " bread ticket " became as natural a feature of daily life as the " insurance card " and other similar German institutions.

The war pressed heavily upon the German people as a whole, and the longer it continued the more serious became the increase in prices —especially of meat—while the British blockade involved the complete disappearance of many ordinary articles of food. The situation was made good by extraordinary and very well organized economy, and by a general willingness, at any rate among the poorer classes, to make sacrifices " for the Fatherland." All over the country there was systematic instruction in the art of war cookery, and the public took readily to the most extraordinary food substitutes—for example, substitutes for coffee, eggs, butter, and oil. Every inconvenience and hardship was accepted almost as evidence of Germany's " power to hold out." Germany, indeed, earned the compliment paid by Mr. Lloyd George in his tribute to the " potato bread spirit."

As the first year of war drew to a close, the Government was able to announce that there was a surplus in hand of 70,000 tons of wheat and rye remaining from the 1914 harvest, and that the outlook for the coming year was satisfactory. Enormous efforts had been made to increase the crop area, and care had been taken that there should be no repetition of the

MARSHAL VON HINDENBURG.
" May the Spirit of 1914-15 remain with us—Von Hindenburg," is the translation of the autograph
inscription above.

scarcity of potatoes. Corn was grown wherever corn could be grown, and imagination was stimulated by the putting under cultivation of open spaces in and about large cities. Towards the end of July, 1915, details were published of a revised scheme of organization. The main features of the scheme which we have described remained unchanged, and as regards prices the basis was as before, £11 per ton of rye in Berlin ; but the organization was simplified and brought more effectively under Government control.

It must not be forgotten that the most important condition of success was the security of German territory against invasion. At the end of the first year of war the German Armies, both east and west, were occupying large areas of enemy territory, and, so far from being

SEEKING NEWS OF THE MISSING
Relatives of Germans in the field at the Casualty Information Bureau, Leipzig.

exposed to the menace of invasion, Prussia was steadily engaged in the "restoration" of her eastern Provinces.

If Germany had made little preparation before the war for the solution of the food supply problem, she had also made comparatively little special preparation for the adaptation of her industry and trade to war conditions. As regards industry, however, her system of organization for the capture of the world's markets had been such that it was comparatively easy for her to concentrate her whole effort upon the purposes of war. The intervention of Great Britain made it obvious that she would sooner or later be cut off from the seas, and lose, at any rate temporarily, the bulk of her foreign trade, which in the year before the war had, according to German statistics, amounted to considerably more than £1,000,000,000. Germany was importing every year raw materials to the value of about £250,000,000, and foodstuffs to the value of about £150,000,000, and she was exporting manufactures worth some £375,000,000. While her oversea trade was in great part doomed to destruction, she could go on trading with the small neutral States that were her neighbours —but even this only so long as these neutrals could resist British and other belligerent

pressure, to which they were naturally subject in view of the necessity for them to maintain their own foreign trade. As we have seen, one of the main objects of German propaganda in neutral countries was to stir up hostility to all British measures which affected neutral trading.

It is not surprising that this state of affairs pressed with special severity upon Hamburg and Bremen, and that these cities developed a quite peculiarly venomous hatred of England. Lübeck, which was open to the Baltic, enjoyed an artificial revival, but Hamburg became almost as dead as Bruges. Herr Ballin, the head of the great Hamburg-Amerika Line, was put out of work, and had to devote himself to new duties of organization in Germany. He and other shipping magnates endeavoured for a time to pretend that nothing was wrong, and two months after the outbreak of war the Director-General of the North German Lloyd, Herr Heineken, was blandly asserting that German shipping had nothing to fear except "a temporary reduction of dividends." But such pretences were soon abandoned. It was much the same with the export trade. At the end of August, 1914, it was triumphantly calculated that during that month the falling off in German exports had been only 44·8 per cent., as compared with the falling off in British exports of 45·1 per cent. It was, however, very soon decided to publish no export or trade figures at all, and at the end of the year Chambers of Commerce and similar institutions were positively forbidden to issue reports.

Meanwhile Germany set about the task of revising her whole industrial and commercial system, in order to make the most of the home market, and to meet every requirement of war. The history of the first year of war in Germany is the history of an intense and concentrated effort directed solely to the purposes of war, and regarding such possibilities of foreign trade as remained as secondary windfalls. Customs duties on imports were, of course, abandoned, and a veto was put upon the export of everything which Germany required. The first and most important matter to take in hand was the problem of raw materials. It was treated, like everything else, from the point of view that the needs of the military forces must be superior to every other consideration. The Prussian Ministry of War opened a Raw Materials Department under the direction of Herr Walter Rathenau, of the *Allgemeine*

DISTRIBUTING CLOTHING
to the East Prussian refugees in Berlin.

Elektrizitäts-Gesellschaft. This Department obtained a census of all important materials in the country, and kept a tight hand upon them. Care was taken that only what the forces did not need could be used in ordinary trade, and by its hold upon the various industrial organizations the Department stimulated all efforts to use up old material and to provide substitutes.

25 Gramm 1. Woche	25 Gramm 1. Woche	250 Gramm 1. Woche	250 Gramm 1. Woche	50 Gramm 1. Woche	50 Gramm 1. Woche
25 Gramm 1. Woche	25 Gramm 1. Woche	Nicht übertragbar — Berlin und Nachbarorte. — Ausweis für die Entnahme von Brot und Getreidemehl. — Gilt nur für die 1. Woche vom 22. bis 28. Februar 1915. Rückseite beachten! — I — 000000		50 Gramm 1. Woche	50 Gramm 1. Woche
25 Gramm 1. Woche	25 Gramm 1. Woche			50 Gramm 1. Woche	50 Gramm 1. Woche
25 Gramm 1. Woche	25 Gramm 1. Woche			50 Gramm 1. Woche	50 Gramm 1. Woche
100 Gramm 1. Woche	100 Gramm 1. Woche	250 Gramm 1. Woche	250 Gramm 1. Woche	100 Gramm 1. Woche	100 Gramm 1. Woche

THE GERMAN BREAD TICKET.
As issued to the people of Berlin in February, 1915.

BRITISH PRISONERS IN GERMANY.
Serving out War Bread.

At the same time, by the cooperation of the rival industrial associations, a joint industrial committee was formed for the whole Empire. Under its auspices special committees were constituted for the special industries. These schemes did not work without considerable friction and difficulty, but their main purpose was successfully achieved. Scarcity did not, of course, show itself in all directions at the same time. At one moment the main difficulty was rubber, at another moment it was petrol, at another moment copper. Cotton was the last problem of all, and the Germans succeeded in hiding this great difficulty until almost the end of the first year of war. It was not until abundant evidence showed the seriousness of the cotton situation that the British Government was induced to change its policy, and to declare cotton absolute contraband of war. By that time the Germans had reorganized their cotton trade, and stopped the manufacture for civilian use of all cotton goods that were not absolutely necessary.

The point upon which the Germans insisted with the greatest pride was the rapid and skilful adaptation of their factories and workshops to new purposes. Great electrical works were soon turned into munition factories; firms which made machinery before the war made shells instead; boiler makers produced field kitchens; umbrella manufacturers produced waterproof clothing, and so on.

This process of adaptation stimulated the imagination of the country, and the newspapers were never tired of explaining that it was a most wonderful exhibition of German genius. This feeling was so strong that people hardly stopped to inquire why the German Navy fulfilled none of the functions—especially the protection of trade—for which it was supposed to have been built. Isolation became a virtue, and a whole literature sprang up, reviving the doctrines of Fichte, and glorifying the "self-contained commercial State" as an ideal. Public interest was also encouraged by appeals for the systematic collection of all unused materials which might help to make good the deficiency in imports. Thus there was an Imperial metal week, and an Imperial wool week, during which German patriots brought the contents of their cupboards and lumber rooms to collecting centres, and offered them up on the altar of German sacrifice. A copper collecting scheme achieved special popularity, and the women and children produced a wonderful assortment of pots and pans to be made into ammunition for the destruction of Germany's enemies.

For the reasons already explained, it is impossible to gauge the real extent to which industry and trade were maintained. German writers confined their attention almost entirely to the iron and coal industries. There is no reason to doubt the assertion that in the course of 1915 the production of coal was brought up to about 70 per cent., and the production of iron and steel up to about 60 per cent. of the peace figures. Germany took away, of course, all the raw materials that could be found in France and Belgium, and seized large quantities of machinery.

The most serious question of all was perhaps the supply of labour. As to this, the main point to observe is that Germany was enabled to economize and to use to the last ounce all the labour that was available. Side by side with the control of industry and the adaptation which we have described went a highly developed system of control and distribution of labour. Of course the distribution could not be quite uniform, and the trades which could not adapt themselves to war purposes had to suffer immediately, in addition to all their other troubles, by the withdrawal of men. As in England, great changes were effected in regard to women's work, and there was so much of it in the market that unemployment among women continued to be serious. A neutral correspondent of *The Times*, describing the situation in June, 1915, said that 40 per cent. of the workers engaged in the manufacture of high explosives and shells and in the packing of cartridges were women. They formed 15 per cent. of the " hands " occupied in the making of harness, saddles, bridles, and other leather goods used for military purposes ; 50 per cent. of the makers of tents, shelters, haversacks, and other equipment ; 33 per cent. of the workers in pharmaceutical industries ; 15 per cent. of the surgical instrument makers ; and 20 per cent. of the field-glass producers ; 75 per cent. of all the employees in the tinned meat and conserve factories working exclusively on Army contracts were women ; a

BRITISH PRISONERS IN GERMANY.
Dinner time.

A GERMAN FIRST-AID AND "REFRESHMENT" STATION IN EAST PRUSSIA.

similar number were engaged in textile mills providing the clothing for the soldiers ; and 70 per cent. of the tobacco workers were women. But it does not seem that the most important industries were ever in serious danger. This was due in part to the efficient working of the Labour Exchanges, but above all to the character of the German military system. Every German of military age was a potential soldier, liable at any time to be called to the colours. Moreover, the country was and remained under martial law, and the local military authorities kept just as sharp an eye to problems of industry and labour as to their purely military business. Strikes were impossible. "Pilfering " of labour was impossible. Whenever difficulties of any sort seemed likely to arise, military intervention was certain. Another

called to the colours, and the proportion of unemployment at different periods :

Date.	Membership.	On Active Service.	Unemployed.
August 1, 1914 ...	533,814	Nil.	13,132
August 29, 1914 ...	377,756	143,343	73,895
October 31, 1914 ...	348,271	172,202	27,727
January 30, 1915 ...	316,822	199,760	8,318
May 1, 1915 ...	291,526	228,594	4,593
July 31, 1915 ...	264,677	259,529	3,414

Regarding the industrial and commercial situation as a whole, it must be said that the upheaval caused by the war was less intolerable than might have been expected. So-called " luxury " industries, which could command a supply neither of raw materials nor of labour, and could not be converted into " war " industries, were squeezed out of existence. There was great suffering in the distributing trades, although the vast proportion of the

TRANSPORTING GERMAN HIGH-EXPLOSIVE SHELLS IN WICKER BASKETS.

and not unimportant factor was the systematic use that the Germans made of the labour of prisoners of war. It was especially valuable to the farmers, but large numbers of prisoners were also employed in the mines, and in various forms of skilled work.

The immediate consequence of the outbreak of war was a considerable increase in unemployment. Before the end of August, 1914, unemployment in skilled trades was more than 22 per cent. But the figures fell very rapidly, and in the spring of 1915 they were at or below the ordinary peace level. The whole movement of the labour market is well shown by the following returns published at the end of a year of war by the largest labour organization in Germany—the Metal Workers' Union. It illustrates the fluctuations in trade union membership, the rate at which men were

men normally employed in them were in the field. On the other hand all the " war " industries were not only very busy but immensely prosperous. The great syndicates and combines reaped a large harvest, and the war profits soon became a public scandal, so that the Government was compelled to promise a scheme of special taxation—after the war. Almost the most serious anxiety was the question whether the industries and trades that had so successfully been turned to the purposes of war could with equal facility be turned back again to the purposes of peace. What, in particular, was the prospect of the recovery of foreign markets by a people whose methods of warfare had not only horrified the whole world, but warned every nation of the consequences which followed close upon the heels of " peaceful penetration " by Germans ?

We have already described (Vol. I., pp. 196 *et seq.*) the main features of the financial situation in Germany at the outbreak of war and the special machinery which was then set up. On August 4, 1914, the Reichstag had voted war credits to the amount of £250,000,000. One year later the total amount of war credits voted was brought up to £1,500,000,000. In December there was a vote of £250,000,000; in March 1915 came the third vote of £500,000,000; and in August 1915 came the fourth vote, also of £500,000,000.

One of the special measures taken at the outbreak of war was to authorize the Empire to discount three-month Imperial Bills instead of Treasury Bills. The result was that the stock of Bills in the Imperial Bank, which a week before the war was only £37,500,000, increased by the end of August to £237,500,000. At the end of March 1915 the amount of Bills was not less than £343,000,000. Similarly, the amount of notes in circulation rose from about £95,000,000 at the end of July 1914 to nearly £212,000,000 at the end of August, to more than £280,000,000 at the end of March, and to more than £290,000,000 at the end of June 1915. In other words, the mobilization of the German armies was financed by the creation of paper, and the pressure on the

Imperial Bank, which throughout was very heavy, became most severe immediately before the issue of War Loans.

Early in September the Government made the first War Loan issue. It took the form of £50,000,000 of 5 per cent. Treasury Bonds with a five years' currency, and a 5 per cent. Loan of undefined amount, irredeemable until 1924. The price of both the Treasury Bills and the Loan was 97½. During the ten days in which the lists remained open, a tremendous propaganda was carried on in the Press. Savings Banks were mobilized and every sort of appeal was made to the public. The following quotation from an official newspaper article is typical:

The victories which our glorious Army has already won in the west and east justify the hope that now, as in 1870, the expenses and burdens of the war will fall ultimately upon those who have disturbed the peace of the German Empire. But first we must help ourselves. Great interests are at stake. The enemy still expects salvation from our supposed financial weakness. The success of the Loan must baffle this hope.

German capitalists, show that you are inspired by the same spirit as our heroes, who shed their hearts' blood in the fight. Germans who have saved money, show that you have saved, not only for yourselves, but also for the Fatherland. German corporations, companies, savings banks, and all institutions which have blossomed and grown up under the powerful protection of the Empire, repay the Empire with your gratitude in this hour of fate. German banks and bankers, show what your brilliant organization and your influence on your customers are able to produce.

BISMARCK'S BIRTHDAY: CELEBRATIONS IN BERLIN, APRIL 1, 1915.
A group of distinguished personages led by Herr von Bethmann-Hollweg, the German Chancellor, Bismarck's grandson, and Herr Kämpf, President of the Reichstag, proceeding to the memorial service.

The results were satisfactory. The total amount of subscriptions was £223,000,000, and a remarkable feature was the large number of small subscriptions. There were, for example, 231,000 subscriptions of from £5 to £10, 241,000 subscriptions of from £15 to £25, 453,000 subscriptions of from £30 to £100, and 157,000 subscriptions between £100 and £250. Probably about £40,000,000 came from the Savings Banks. A considerable sum came from the pledging of securities with the special War Banks, which were set up for this very purpose, but it must be admitted that the use made of these institutions was not so great as had been expected. The war lending institutions, established in connexion with the Imperial Bank, were authorized to issue their special paper up to a total amount of £150,000,000, but according to the published statistics the amount of paper actually issued never exceeded £79,000,000. This total was reached in April 1915 in connexion with subscriptions to the second War Loan.

It was soon recognized that the control of the Treasury in war time was too much for the commonplace official Herr Kühn, who had been in office since the beginning of 1912. Herr Kühn succumbed to his chronic gout, and a young and able director of the Deutsche Bank, Dr. Helfferich, was appointed to succeed him. He was a man of large ideas, who regarded the affairs of State from a purely businesslike point of view. He was by no means above methods of advertisement, and after the success of the first War Loan he had produced a bombastic pamphlet for neutral countries, in which he said that the German Loan "overshadowed in importance the largest financial operations yet known in history," and that Germany had performed " a feat unique in the history of finance." He had also qualified for Ministerial office by the publication of an extremely misleading analysis of the causes of the war.

In March 1915 the second War Loan issue was made—this time an unlimited amount both of Treasury Bonds and Imperial Loan, with interest as before at 5 per cent., but with the price raised from 97½ to 98½. The second loan, like the first, was irredeemable until 1924. The issue was hailed as a great success, and produced no less than £450,000,000, the number of subscriptions being officially stated to be nearly 1,700,000. No accurate information was forthcoming regarding the various sources of these subscriptions, and an official announce-

BISMARCK CELEBRATION IN BERLIN.
A parade of students in front of the Bismarck statue on April 1, 1915.

ment that the Savings Banks provided only about £98,000,000 was soon proved to be far below the mark. The result was a triumph of organization and of public propaganda, and the Government no doubt succeeded in raking in a great part of the " war savings " which had been made by the profitable business of supplying the forces, and in the country districts by the high prices obtained for the harvest. At the time of the second War Loan issue Dr. Helfferich made his first appearance in the Reichstag and loudly proclaimed the doctrine that Germany had only to " carry on " to victory, and then recoup herself at the enemy's expense. He said :

The future development of the Imperial Debt depends upon the result of the war. We shall not be able to refrain, and we do not think of refraining, from making our enemies pay for the material loss which falls upon us on account of the war begun by them.

He described the British method of increasing taxation in war time as " useless adhesion to tradition." He estimated the total cost of the war to all the belligerents to be at that time £75,000,000 a week.

The success of the second War Loan was regarded as an immense victory. In a message

THE KAISER AND HIS ADVISERS,

1st (back) Row: Von Mackensen, Von Moltke, Crown Prince, Von Francois, Von Ludendorff, Von Falkenhayn, Von Einem, Von Beseler, Von Bethmann-Hollweg, Von Heeringen.
2nd Row: Von Bülow, Crown Prince of Bavaria, Duke of Wurtemburg, Von Kluck, Von Emmich, Von Haeseler, Von Hindenburg, Von Tirpitz, Kaiser.

of congratulation the Kaiser declared that it was " a manifestation of the will to conquer and of the confidence in victory of the German people, relying in God."

Although the proceeds of the second War Loan were exhausted, and the Government was again financing the war by Treasury Bills, the third War Loan was not issued until September 1915. It was again a 5 per cent. issue, but included this time no Treasury Bonds. The price of issue was raised to 99—chiefly for purposes of demonstration. It was admitted that war loan enthusiasm had diminished, but success was confidently awaited, especially on the ground that the position of the banks was again strong, and that the Savings Banks deposit now amounted to more than £1,000,000,000. Dr. Helfferich now estimated Germany's war expenditure at about £100,000,000 a month. He again sought to inspire confidence by insisting on the prospect of a large war indemnity, saying :

If we desire the possibility of shaping a peace in accordance with our needs and our vital requirements, we must not forget the question of cost. We must see to it that the whole future livelihood of our people shall, so far as is in any way possible, be relieved of the burden. The leaden weight of thousands of millions is due to the people who got up this war. They, not we, shall drag it along with them. Of course, we know that this is a matter of peculiar difficulty, but everything that can be done in this direction shall be done.

In addition to the increased insistence on indemnity prospects, the Germans at this time were becoming more and more enamoured of the doctrine that they were " self-contained and self-supporting," carrying on the war by exploitation of their own internal resources while other peoples piled up debt, and making " finance " consist in payments from one pocket to the other. It was almost seriously maintained that this process could be continued indefinitely. This comfortable doctrine was also used to allay anxiety at the fact that foreign exchanges remained entirely unsatisfactory, the value of the mark falling 12, 14, or even 16 per cent. in every neutral country, from Sweden to Brazil. The German public was urgently implored to sell foreign, and especially American, securities in order to invest the proceeds in the German War Loan, thereby " taking advantage " of the " temporary " depreciation in German currency.

Meanwhile the Germans kept a discreet veil over the affairs of their Allies. In Austria-Hungary there was no attempt to publish a Bank Return or to give any other clue to the deplorable state of finance and trade. Turkey was soon living on paper money with no better backing than imaginary hoards of gold " for Turkish account " in Berlin banks. Even in Germany the situation was carefully concealed by a permanent veto upon publication of stock exchange prices. There was a good deal of speculation in the shares of industrial concerns which profited, or were likely to profit, by the war, but the transactions were secret, and great pressure was employed by the Government to check speculation which was supposed to endanger the prospects of the War Loans.

After the first few months of the war the German States—and the municipalities—sup-

GERMANY'S SHORTAGE OF COPPER.
Owing to the shortage of copper, teachers were instructed to request their scholars to collect and bring copper articles to school.

pressed all information about their finances, and it was merely announced that they were in entire agreement with the Imperial Government. The *Frankfurter Zeitung* admitted in February 1915 that all the State budgets had been thrown into confusion. They seem, indeed, to have contented themselves with periodical issues of Treasury Bills as and when need arose.

During the first year of war the pride and joy of the Imperial Bank and of the whole people consisted in the accumulation of gold. Before and on the eve of war Germany had obtained all the imports of gold that were possible, and much annoyance was caused by

" POUR LE MÉRITE."
The Archduke Frederic of Austria obtains the Order from the Kaiser.

the increase of the Bank Rate in London, four days before the war, to 10 per cent. The stock of gold in the Imperial Bank on July 30. 1914, was returned at something over £62,000,000. Little by little and by intense effort, it was increased to £120,000,000, and the amount was only slightly below that figure at the end of the first year of war. The total was increased by December 1914 to £100,000,000, chiefly by the total suspension of specie payments, and there was then an immense campaign of collection. The public were told that it was an imperative duty to let " patriotism become the key to the most carefully guarded money chest." An " Imperial gold week " was organized, and school children were rewarded if they brought gold coins to school to be exchanged for paper. Women were urged, and to a considerable extent induced. to offer up rings and ornaments " for the Fatherland." The sum obtained was large, but it was not nearly so large as had been expected.

In one way and another, then, Germany succeeded in creating and maintaining a tolerable financial situation. Above all, and thanks to successes in the field, the public was satisfied.

There was no apparent disposition to enquire too closely into the real situation, and the steady flow of money into the Savings Banks was a fair proof of the general sense of confidence and security.

We have said that the first outburst of jubilation about the war did not last long, and it will appear obvious that the economic conditions which we have just described were not calculated to promote enthusiasm, especially when it was proved again and again that the Allies could not be separated by diplomatic intrigues, and when it was seen that German successes did not frighten Italy, Germany's own ally, nor produce among neutral states generally the effects which according to all German theory ought to have been produced. As the struggle progressed there was increasing gloom among the people at home. This was proved by the calm with which news even of the greatest victories in the East was received, and by the constant complaints about difficulties and privations. Letters from home that were found on German prisoners amply illustrated the last point, and it was found necessary to publish repeated appeals to German women not to distress the men at the front by gloomy descriptions, but to write cheerfully and bear privations patiently. Both public speeches and newspaper articles during the greater part of the first year of war insisted less upon the prospects of positive victory than upon Germany's " ability to hold out." *Wir werden durchhalten* was the constant refrain, and it was usually added, " We shall win because we have got to win."

The enormous casualties of the German armies had a very depressing effect from an early stage of the war, and it was found desirable to start a movement against the wearing of mourning in public. After the appearance of the first few casualty lists the newspapers were forbidden to publish any but local casualties, together with the names of officers killed, and the public had either to purchase the lists as issued by the military authorities or to visit the military buildings or municipal offices where they were displayed.

The whole matter of " celebration " of victories was, like everything else, organized by the Government. When it was decided that a celebration was desirable, orders were given that the bells should be rung, and flags were hoisted on public buildings as a signal to the people to display flags on all the houses. At the same time the schools were closed for a day, after the teachers had delivered appropriate patriotic addresses. The best organization sometimes breaks down, and there was a ridiculous exposure of the defects of the system at the time of the great Austro-German drive in Galicia at the beginning of May, 1915. This was the most critical stage of the negotiations with Italy, and in his haste to create the desired impression the Kaiser sent orders to Berlin for celebration of a triumph, unfortunately without supplying any information about what had happened. Some people said that "the great battle in the North Sea" had at last taken place, others that "20,000 French had been taken prisoners," others that the Russians had lost 180,000 men. In Munich crowds filled the streets all day, quarrelling as to whether the victory had been won by Hindenburg or by an Austrian. The *Tägliche Rundschau* boldly complained of the failure of the authorities "to spare the nerves of the people," and said :

Were we in any way impatient ? There was not a trace of the public hysteria which prevails in France. We lived in the calmest confidence, and Herr Hindenburg had unlimited credit upon which he could have fed for weeks and months. And now this obscure sensation is officially thrown to the public. When the flags have been flying for half a day on every official building we should like to know why and for what reason. Has anybody considered what foreign countries will say when they are told that the whole capital of the German Empire is floating in flags without any human being having half an idea of the reason ?

The effect of the official blunder was all the more bitter because there had after all been a real and important victory, and public confidence in the authorities had received a quite unnecessary shock. Even the German public was capable of understanding that German strategy was not infallible. They had been promised in vain during the first months of the war, first Paris, then Warsaw, and then again Dunkirk and Calais.

Another unfortunate mistake on the part of the authorities was the too liberal distribution of military awards. From the very beginning there was a wholesale distribution of Iron Crosses. Before the war the possession of an Iron Cross was a rare distinction and a cherished memory of the war of 1870. Iron Crosses soon became as plentiful as blackberries. According to official statistics there had up to the end of March, 1915, been distributed five Grand Crosses, 6,488 Iron Crosses of the First Class, and 338,261 Iron Crosses of the Second Class.

TO HONOUR THE IRON CROSS.
A parade of German troops.

IN A GERMAN HOSPITAL AT BERLIN.
Princess August Wilhelm visits the wounded soldiers.

During the whole of the war of 1870 only 1,304 Iron Crosses of the First Class and 45,791 Iron Crosses of the Second Class had been distributed. At the end of the first year the Kaiser began profuse distribution even of the famous Prussian Order *Pour le Mérite*. It was conferred upon all the commanders in the East, and even upon the German Crown Prince and the other commanders in the West. At the same time the Iron Cross, with a white instead of a black ribbon, was conferred upon all sorts of civilians for their services in administration and organization. Matters were made worse by favouritism. When it became almost a disgrace for officers not to wear the Iron Cross it will be understood that the claims of the private soldier were apt to be neglected.

A Germany thrown upon her own internal resources and shut in, and at the same time taught to believe that Zeppelins and big guns were the unparalleled expressions of German genius and that submarines were really almost a German monopoly, not unnaturally gave way to strange excesses of "national" sentiment. Pan-Germanism took new shapes and directions. Great efforts were made to rid the German vocabulary of all foreign words. The police conducted systematic raids upon signs and advertisements containing foreign expressions of any sort. German women were even required to make the patriotic sacrifice of

submission to German fashions, and eager societies were formed for the promotion of Germanism in hats. It was also seriously maintained that the German Universities—not content with the abandonment by German Professors of their foreign degrees and academic distinctions—should close their doors entirely both to foreign students and foreign influences. The main argument was that German science was so infinitely superior that its fruits must be retained for German use and for the domination of the world. In a word, Germanism ran riot through all classes of society.

The circumstances in which Germany had provoked the war, and the very nature of the war and of her internal problems, made it necessary for the German leaders to concentrate their attention on the maintenance of domestic unity and on the preservation for as long a time as possible of the fiction that Germany had been " fallen upon " and had to defend her existence. Hence, while the sessions of the Reichstag and of the various State Diets were restricted as much as possible, and public meetings were rare, all official utterances in the greater part of the first year of war which were not concerned with technical details or economic problems returned invariably to the German doctrine of the origins of the war and attempted to confirm its defensive character. It is, indeed, hardly worth while to waste more words on such gatherings as those of the Reichstag in December 1914 and January 1915. As regards political unity, it has already been said that the Socialists gave no trouble. From time to time they discussed in secret their favourite academic question—whether they ought to vote supplies in a non-Socialist State. They decided the question three times in the affirmative sense, although there was a fairly large minority. Their Press in great part remained sober and moderate in its language, although some of the provincial Socialist organs, especially at Hamburg and in parts of Saxony, became violently chauvinist and peculiarly Anglophobe, and attacked the attitude of the official Socialist organ, *Vorwärts*. In June 1915 the Socialist party summoned up its courage to produce a manifesto containing the following passage :

We utter afresh the sharpest protest against all efforts and proclamations in favour of annexing foreign territory and of doing violence to the territory of others, such as have been made public by the demands of great economic associations and the speeches of leading non-Socialist politicians. The mere fact that such efforts are made postpones yet further the peace for which the whole people so ardently yearns. The people desire no annexations. The people desire peace.

If the war, which daily demands fresh sacrifices, is not to be indefinitely prolonged and to last until all nations are utterly exhausted, one of the belligerent Powers must extend the hand of peace. Germany, who, attacked by greatly superior forces, has hitherto victoriously kept her enemies at bay, brought to naught the scheme of starvation, and proved herself invincible, ought to take the first step towards the attainment of peace.

PROF. ISRAEL, THE FAMOUS BERLIN SURGEON.
In the Empress's Hospital train.

In the name of humanity and *Kultur*, and strengthened by the favourable military situation created by the valour of our comrades in arms, we call upon the Government to declare itself ready to enter into peace negotiations, in order to bring the bloody struggle to an end.

This manifesto was a mere flash in the pan, and had no other result than the very temporary suspension of the newspapers which published it. It was really only part of a controversy about the right to discuss Germany's aggressive intentions at all, and when, as we shall see, after the successes against Russia in May, June, July and August, the Government thought fit to lift a little of the veil, the Socialists made not the slightest effort to stem the tide.

GERMAN WOUNDED IN A CONVALESCENT HOME.
Passing away the time making paper chess-boards.

MODEL TRENCHES IN BERLIN.
To view these trenches visitors paid entrance fees, which were given to Red Cross Societies.

Apart from the Socialists, there was no material whatever which could have made an Opposition. We need not consider the tendencies of the various parties, little divergent as they were. The only point that needs to be observed is that the war had put an end for the time to the old antagonism between economic interests—between the agrarians and the industrialists. When Germany was thrown on her own resources they entered into a natural alliance. The agrarians in particular could claim that they had not only maintained the strength of the military forces, but that every German owed to them his daily bread. As for the Roman Catholic Centre Party— really the strongest effective force of all—it need only be said that after the intervention of Italy it conceived that it had a double stake set upon the success of the Central Powers.*

In putting, as it did at a very early stage, an absolute veto upon the discussion of German aims (*Kriegsziele*), the Government may have considered the inadvisability of raising hopes which might be too rudely disturbed by military failure. But the main consideration was the need to maintain the pretence that Germany had no "aims." During the month of February the Imperial Chancellor went so far as to rebuke in his official organ, the *North German Gazette*, those who wanted to discuss "romantic schemes of conquest." The veto upon discussion was described as the "well-weighed decision of the political and military leaders." There was no "desire to exclude the cooperation of the German people," and "when the time came" the Government would be "grateful for the support of a strong public will." As a matter of fact, the rule against discussion had on several occasions been broken—notably in a demand for the annexation of Belgium which was contained in a speech by the National Liberal Leader, Herr Bassermann, and in a "New Year message" in which Herr Ballin had said:

The mischievous interference which is bringing our oversea trade almost to a standstill is possible for the English Navy only because the North Sea area proved liable to easy blockade. . . . We must out and away beyond the North Sea area, and seek a naval base which in future, at any rate in this part of the world, will

* The strength of the principal parties in the Reichstag was on Nov. 1, 1914, Socialists, 110; Centre Party, 91; Conservatives, 53; Radicals, 45; and National Liberals, 44.

assure to us the same possibilities that England enjoys and ruthlessly exploits.

There was not really any doubt about German appetites. In March a joint petition in favour of free discussion was addressed to the Imperial Chancellor by all the important industrial and agricultural organizations of the Empire. It declared that the whole German people was inspired by a single powerful will —that Germany should emerge from the war "greater and stronger, with secured frontiers in west and east, and with the European and Colonial extensions of territory which are necessary for the security of Germany's sea power, as well as for military and economic reasons." The Imperial Chancellor replied with fresh admonitions, saying that these "polemics against a decision of the highest military and civil authorities" were untimely, and "would not accelerate victory in the field." In June—this was the occasion of the Socialist manifesto to which we have referred —the King of Bavaria blurted out the admission that he had rejoiced at the intervention of Great Britain in the war, because he saw the hope of an extension of German frontiers in south and west, and the fulfilment of his dreams of better connexion of South Germany with the sea.

So matters went on through the summer. The attitude of the Imperial Chancellor exposed him to attack, and there was a more or less determined attempt to get rid of him when the conflict with the United States arose out of the sinking of the *Lusitania*, and Grand Admiral von Tirpitz, who had staked his reputation on the success of the "submarine blockade" of Great Britain, resisted all idea of concessions to American demands. In August, before the meeting of the Reichstag, the National Liberals, after their leader, Herr Bassermann, had had a personal dispute with the Imperial Chancellor, adopted, and published, a resolution demanding outright "extension of the German frontiers in east and west and over seas."

By this time, however, little attempt was still made to conceal at any rate the general character of Germany's ambitions. Upon the anniversary of the outbreak of war the Kaiser issued a long and jubilant manifesto, with the following very significant conclusion :

In heroic action we suffer and work without wavering until peace comes, a peace which offers us the necessary military, political, and economic guarantees (*Sicherheiten*

GETTING FIT TO RETURN TO THE TRENCHES.
German wounded undergoing scientific treatment in a Berlin hospital.

for the future, and which fulfils the conditions necessary for the unhindered development of our producing energy at home and on the free seas.

In the political slang of the time the expressions "the necessary military, political and economic guarantees" and "the free seas" meant everything that the "annexationists" could ask. They were well satisfied.

Soon afterwards the Paris *Temps* was able to publish the text of a second petition which had been submitted to the Government in May by the representative industrial and economic organizations—the Agrarian League, the two Peasant ' Leagues, the Central Union of German Industrialists, the League of Industrialists, and the Union of the Middle Classes. This very important document removed a great deal of what *The Times* called "the drapery with which Germany has sought to hide from innocent neutrals the true scope of her ambitions." We will give the main passages in full.

After asserting that the war must produce "an extension of German power," the signatories said :

Together with a colonial Empire which will fully satisfy the numerous economic interests of Germany, together with guarantees for the future of our trade and our fiscal system, and together with an indemnity both sufficient and of an appropriate kind, we regard the principal aim of the struggle which has been put upon us as consisting in a guarantee and an improvement of the European basis of the German Empire.

The chief direct claims against the British Empire were contained in this comprehensive formula. About the Continent of Europe the

petition was more precise. It dealt first with Belgium :

Because it is necessary to assure our credit at sea and our military and economic situation for the future *vis-à-vis* England, and because the territory of Belgium, which is of such great economic importance, is closely linked with our principal industrial territory, Belgium must be placed under the legislation of the German Empire as regards monetary, financial, and postal questions. The Belgian railways and waterways must be closely linked up with our communications. By constituting a Walloon area and a preponderant Flemish area, and by placing in German hands the economic enterprises and properties so important for the domination of the country, we shall organize government and administration in such a way that the inhabitants will not be able to acquire any influence upon the political destinies of the German Empire.

The writers then turned to France :

As regards France, and always bearing in mind our situation *vis-à-vis* the English, it is a vital interest for us, with a view to our future at sea, that we should hold the coastal region bordering on Belgium up to about the Somme This will give us an outlet on the Atlantic Ocean. The hinterland which must be acquired at the same time must be of such extent that, both economically and strategically, the ports at which the canals terminate can assume their full importance. It is necessary to annex the mine basins of Briey, but no further territorial conquests ought to be made in France except in consequence of considerations of military strategy. As regards this matter, it is very natural, after the experiences of this war, that we should not expose our frontiers to fresh invasions by leaving to our enemy the fortresses which threaten us, especially Verdun and Belfort, and the western spurs of the Vosges situated between these two fortresses.

By the conquest of the line of the Meuse and of the French coast, with the outlets of the canals, we should acquire, in addition to the iron districts of Briey already indicated, the coal areas in the Departments of the Nord and the Pas-de-Calais. These territorial increases —as is a matter of course after our experiences in Alsace-Lorraine—assume that the population of the annexed territories will not be able to obtain a political influence upon the destinies of the German Empire, and that all

WOMEN TRAM CONDUCTORS IN BERLIN.
Taking lessons in the mechanism of electric trams.

the sources of economic power in these territories, including properties large and small, will pass into German hands. France will indemnify the proprietors and absorb them.

Having thus disposed of the west, the petitioners explained that the industrial gains there must be balanced by an increase of agricultural territory at the expense of Russia. They said :

It is necessary to strengthen the agrarian foundation of our economic system. We must make possible a German agrarian colonization on a large scale, and the repatriation upon German territory of German peasants living abroad, and especially in Russia. We must also largely augment the number of our nationals capable of bearing arms. All this demands a considerable extension of the Eastern frontiers of our Empire and of Prussia by the annexation at least of certain parts of the Baltic Provinces and of the territories to the south of them, without losing sight of the necessity for making possible the military defence of the Eastern frontier.

In order to reconstitute Eastern Prussia, it is absolutely necessary to protect the frontiers by including certain strips of territory. East Prussia, Posen, and Silesia must no longer remain our outer marches, exposed as they are at present.

The memorandum said that what had been stated about the population of the areas annexed in the west held good in the east also, and remarked that the war indemnity to be demanded of Russia should consist in great part of cessions of territory.

Finally there was an elaborate explanation of the economic reasons for seizure of the French coal districts by Germany. It was argued, in particular, that if Germany's enemies were to hold the chief of the world's sources of mineral oil, Germany must secure all her requirements of gas coal and soft coal.

The evidence was already overwhelming, but the last touch was added on August 19, 1915, when the Imperial Chancellor delivered a speech in the Reichstag which confessed Germany's ambitions before all the world. Once more, but with unwonted violence of language and with much deliberate perversion of the truth, Herr von Bethmann-Hollweg protested Germany's innocence and love of peace, proclaimed the " blood-guilt " of her enemies, and charged England in particular with the responsibility for the failure of diplomatic efforts to procure an arrangement between England and Germany in the years before the war, and to avert war when the great crisis came. But the real significance of the speech, which was hailed with enormous satisfaction throughout the Empire and brought the Imperial Chancellor public orations and an unexpected popularity, was that it marked the abandonment of the fiction of " Germany's defensive war." The

A HUGE WOODEN STATUE OF FIELD-MARSHAL VON HINDENBURG,

Which was erected in the Siegesallee in Berlin. The public hammered nails into the statue on payment of a certain sum to war charities.

fall of Warsaw, Ivangorod and Kovno and the conquest of Galicia and Poland were the signal for German diplomacy also to take the offensive. The vital passages of the speech ran as follows :

The world which arises out of this war shall and will not wear the aspect of which our enemies dream. They strive for the restoration of the old Europe, with a powerless Germany in the midst of it as the playground for foreign intrigues and covetousness, and if possible as the battlefield of Europe—a Germany in which impotent little States shall be at foreign beck and call, a Germany with her industries shattered and carrying on only petty trading in her home markets, without a navy, a Germany the vassal of the gigantic Russian Empire.

No, this tremendous world-war will not restore the old conditions. A new system will arise. If Europe ever comes to peace, it can be only by the establishment of an inviolable and strong Germany. The English policy of the balance of power must disappear. . . .

Germany must so build up, fortify and strengthen her position that the other Powers shall never again think of a policy of hemming Germany in. For the protection and welfare of ourselves and of all peoples, we must win the liberation of the world seas—not as England desires to do, in order to rule them alone, but in order that they may be at the service of all peoples in equal degree. . . .

This war has shown of what greatness we are capable, when we rely on our own moral strength. We do not hate the peoples that have been driven into war against us by their Governments. But we have got over our sentimentality. We shall see the fight through, until those peoples demand peace from the really guilty, until the road becomes free for a new Europe, liberated from French intrigues, Muscovite passion of conquest, and English guardianship.

To this insolent challenge to Europe Sir Edward Grey promptly published a scathing reply. What was the German programme? Germany to control the destiny of all other nations—Germany to be supreme and alone to be free—" free to break international treaties; free to crush when it pleased her; free to refuse all mediation; free to go to war when it suited her; free, when she did go to war, to break again all rules of civilization and humanity on land and at sea; and, while she may act thus, all her commerce at sea is to remain as free in time of war as all commerce is in time of peace. . . . Not on such terms can peace be concluded or the life of other nations than Germany be free or even tolerable."

At the same time Herr von Bethmann-Hollweg's speech led to overwhelming disclosures concerning the efforts of Germany to assure herself of the neutrality of Great Britain before she proceeded to attack Russia and France. In view of grossly misleading statements by the German Chancellor, directed to show that England had prevented the peaceful settlement of differences with Germany and had refused benevolent offers made in the interests of peace, the British Government was forced to publish a full account of the unfortunate negotiations which Lord Haldane, then a member of the Government, had been permitted to conduct in Berlin in 1912. Germany had, under the cloak of willingness to abandon some part of a measure then being prepared for the increase of the German navy, demanded a neutrality treaty which would have prevented Great Britain from giving assistance in war to Russia or France, while Germany remained free to participate in a war against those Powers in fulfilment of the terms of the Triple Alliance. This disclosure confirmed the opinion which had become general in England regarding the dangerous influence exerted by Lord Haldane in the years before the war. What was more important, it disposed for ever of the excuses and prevarications of Germany, and stripped bare her persistent and determined scheme for the domination of Europe.

In a year of war Germany had given a remarkable demonstration of her military power, of the patriotism of her people, of the great strength and resources of the country, and of her unsurpassed efficiency in organization and administration. She had shown little sign either of war weariness or of political, moral or economic exhaustion. But she stood alone. She held the reins at Vienna and Budapest, and her puppets governed Turkey. Her strength and her violence had made a certain impression. But, just as she had been abandoned, in spite of all material temptations, by her ally Italy, she had won neither friends nor sympathy nor approval. She had only hardened with all her blows the courage and resolution of all the nations whom she had driven to war, and wherever in all the wide world men believed in human ideals and cherished national independence and liberty, it was realized that no peace could be tolerable but a peace that put an end to Germany's arrogant ambitions and lust of conquest.

CHAPTER LXXXVII.

THE WORK OF THE CANADIAN CONTINGENT.

CANADA AND THE SECOND BATTLE OF YPRES—STRENGTHENING THE IMPERIAL TIE—THE MEMORIAL SERVICE AT ST. PAUL'S CATHEDRAL—THE FULL COST OF WAR—ANGER OVER THE USE OF POISONOUS GAS—ARMY OF 150,000 MEN PLANNED—THE PRINCESS PATRICIA'S REGIMENT —FIRST DAYS IN FRANCE—WINTER LIFE IN THE TRENCHES—FIGHTING AT ST. ELOI—OFFICERS KILLED—THE GREAT FIGHT OF MAY 8—THE FIRST CONTINGENT LEAVES FOR FRANCE— FIGHTING QUALITIES OF THE CANADIANS—THE ROSS RIFLE—SOME MISCONCEPTIONS IN FRANCE— M. MAURICE BARRES ON THE CANADIANS—MORAL AND PHYSIQUE OF THE MEN—CANADIANS AND THE BRITISH SOLDIER—SIR JOHN FRENCH'S OPINION—RELATIONS BETWEEN OFFICERS AND MEN—DISCIPLINE—RESOURCE—BACKWOOD WILE—GENERAL ALDERSON—TAKING OVER TRENCHES —THE CONTINGENT IN ACTION—THE FOUR CHIEF FIGHTS—THE CANADIAN CAVALRY—SECOND CONTINGENT ARRIVES—SIR ROBERT BORDEN VISITS ENGLAND—THE SPIRIT OF CANADA.

THE story of the great fight of the Canadian Division at St. Julien sent a thrill of pride through the Empire. The Canadian people themselves would be the first to disclaim and to protest against any attempt to picture the gallantry, the dash, and the stubborn valour of their men as something overshadowing that of other British troops. "We will be proud," wrote one young Canadian corporal, "if we may prove ourselves worthy to stand side by side with the Regular Army of England." But men realized that in the final and most severe test Canada had proved herself a nation. It was felt, and with reason, that things could never be the same again between England and Canada. The tie between them, strong before, had been deepened and strengthened by the ultimate sacrifice offered by the Dominion. "It is the supreme consecration of Canada to the Empire," wrote Lord Rosebery. A memorial service to the Canadian fallen was held in St. Paul's Cathedral, and hours before the service commenced not only were the great aisles of the cathedral itself thronged, but thousands waited outside, anxious to show by their presence their sympathy and admiration.

In Canada the long casualty lists that quickly arrived brought grief, but no repining. In cities like Toronto and Montreal, Winnipeg and Vancouver, there was scarce a family of note but had its honoured dead. In Toronto, for example, regiments such as the 48th High- landers and the Queen's Own Rifles had been recruited in the years of peace from the great financial, professional and commercial families of the city. The University, the clubs, the exchanges and the banks were all strongly represented in the lists. When the regiments first set out for the Front it was difficult for the cheering crowds watching them to realize the gravity of their mission. Now, however, Canada learned to the full what the war meant and what it must cost.

There was passionate pride from one end of the Dominion to the other. East and West, the French of Quebec, the Scottish of Nova Scotia, the English of Toronto, and the Ameri- cans of Southern Alberta were united in common grief and common glory. The univer- sal emotion found its expression not alone in glowing speeches in Parliament and in im- passioned editorials in the great Canadian newspapers, but also in the quick response of the nation. If there was pride there was also anger, anger at what the Canadian people felt to be the illegitimate methods of war the enemy employed. The story of the use of poisonous gas by the Germans deepened the resentment. Canada felt that there could only

FIELD-MARSHAL H.R.H. THE DUKE OF CONNAUGHT
With officers of the Royal Canadian Horse Artillery at Montreal.   On the left of His Royal Highness
is Major Eaton, in command of the B Battery; on the right is Colonel Panet, commander of the
Regiment.

be one response to warfare such as this.   The
Minister of Militia, General (afterwards Sir)
Sam Hughes, led the movement for a great
increase in the forces.   Canada had started at
the beginning of the war to raise 30,000 men ;
now she placed the figure at 150,000, with as
many more afterwards as might be necessary.
There had been 6,000 Canadian casualties in
the fighting.   For every Canadian who had
fallen ten came forward.   From all parts of
the Dominion recruiting officers reported that
they were overwhelmed with offers of service.
The question before the Dominion Government was not how many men it could raise,
but how many it could equip, drill, and maintain of the men who offered themselves.

The story of what Canada did in the first
days of the war is told in an earlier chapter.*   In
the autumn of 1914 the first Canadian contingent arrived at Salisbury Plain accompanied by
the Princess Patricia's Light Infantry—a
special corps raised at the cost of Mr. Hamilton
Gault, a wealthy Montreal citizen, and named
after the daughter of the Duke of Connaught,

* Vol. II., page 237, et seq.

the Governor-General.   The contingent, placed
under the command of Lieutenant-General
E. A. H. Alderson, spent an exceedingly trying
winter on the Wiltshire downs.   The season
was one of the wettest on record.   The men
were for most of the time under canvas.   The
roads around the camp sites, ill-fitted for
heavy traffic, became mere quagmires.   The
troops were many miles from a town, and considerable distances even from small Wiltshire
villages.

The Princess Patricia's, largely composed of
old soldiers who had seen service in war, were
the first to go to the Front.   They arrived in
France in December, and were at once hurried
north and given a heavy spell of trench digging
in the rear lines.   From there, early in the New
Year, they were moved into the fighting
trenches.

Two days of heavy marching, sixteen miles
each day, brought them close to the front firing
lines.   After a brief pause at a ruined village,
they moved quietly along sheltered roadways
into the communicating trenches, and then to
the front, where they relieved French troops.

LIEUT.-GENERAL EDWIN HERVEY ALDERSON, C.B.,
Commander of the Canadian Division of the British Expeditionary Force.

203

The night was pitch dark; it was raining heavily, and everywhere the countryside was deep in mud. No light could be struck, and commands had to be whispered along the ranks. The slightest sign of life brought an instant bullet from a German sniper. Star shells fired from the German lines at frequent intervals sent a sudden hard blue light on the muddy fields, the broken wire entanglements, and the barely visible earthworks. The men could hear the Germans opposite to them, scarce a stone's throw away, baling the water out of their trenches. The Patricia's settled down at once, with the remainder of the allied forces, to the

the subject of a great deal of adulation, through no desire of its own. Its nickname—" Pat's Pets "—was the subject of much good-humoured banter. The men protested vigorously. They begged their admirers in Canada to stop talking about them. "Do us the credit of believing that we are neither boasters nor idiots," said one of them at the time, "but just soldiers who are trying to do our soldier's work at the Front as every other regiment in the British Army is. We know that our experience is trivial compared with other regiments, but we try to do as well as we can, like everybody else."

CANADIAN TROOPS READY TO LEAVE CANADA FOR ENGLAND.
Sir R. L. Borden, Premier; Hon. G. E. Foster, Minister of Commerce; Hon. Robert Rogers, Minister of Public Works; and Major-General Sir Sam Hughes bidding good-bye to the officers of the Canadian Expeditionary Force.

dull and exacting winter routine work. Bitter cold, constant rain, and omnipresent mud were their chief trials. They soon learned that for the moment at least there was nothing to do but to wait, to watch, and to guard themselves from the German fire, keeping under cover. Scouts and sharpshooters were present on either side. It was scarce possible for a man to raise his hand above the trenches without drawing a quick bullet. It seemed as though the Germans knew the position of every dugout in the Princess Patricia lines. They had rifles so fixed as to cover them exactly, enabling the trigger to be pulled without the necessity of aiming.

Princess Patricia's Regiment had been made

Within a month of its arrival at the Front the Princess Patricia's Light Infantry had won the good-will and admiration of every regiment which saw its men and knew its record.

One of the first actions by which the Patricia's drew special attention to themselves was around St. Eloi, where they were holding a line of trenches. Some Germans completed a sap from which they were able to cause the British at this point much trouble. The Patricia's were ordered to sweep them back. Two officers, Lieutenant Crabbe and Lieut. Colquhoun, went to have a look over the ground at midnight, and never returned. The advance was covered by a party of snipers, and they were followed by a group of bomb throwers commanded by Lieut. Papineau. They crept up to

THE NURSING STAFF OF THE McGILL HOSPITAL.

Waiting inspection of H.R.H. the Duchess of Connaught, April 22, 1915.   The McGill Hospital Corps was organized by Dr. (Colonel) Birkett, Dean of Faculty of Medicine at McGill University, and was recruited among the Faculty, Graduates, and Undergraduates, with staff of nurses from two leading hospitals at Montreal.

within twenty yards of the enemy's trenches, and then leapt right into the German lines. Lieut. Papineau behaved in a way that won him special distinction. To every Canadian there seemed something strangely dramatic in the fact that a Papineau, a lineal descendant of a great rebel of 1837, should thus in one of the earliest engagements of Canadians in France

stand out as a hero among heroes in the defence of the Empire.

The work of the Princess Patricia's during the next few weeks was prosaic, monotonous, and costly. Several officers were disabled, picked off by snipers, wounded by hand grenades or shot in attacks on the trenches opposite. Captain Newton, who had come

H.R.H. THE DUCHESS OF CONNAUGHT INSPECTS THE McGILL HOSPITAL CORPS.

THE SECOND CANADIAN CONTINGENT IN TRAINING AT TORONTO.
Men of the 4th Battery bringing a gun into position.

from the Duke of Connaught's personal staff, was one of the first to be killed. He was followed by Captain Fitzgerald, an officer who had won in a few weeks the enthusiastic love and admiration of his men. Fitzgerald gave his live in attempting to bring back from the open the body of one of his own soldiers lying in front of our trenches, although he knew that the venture would mean almost certain death. "He was a hero, and he met a hero's end." his soldiers declared. Colonel Farquhar, the commander of the regiment, was killed by a stray bullet. Major Hamilton Gault, the founder of the Patricia's, was wounded, had to return to England, recovered, and went to the Front again, only once more to be severely hurt, all within a very few weeks. In this time of constant trench fighting the strength of the regiment, which probably with the fresh drafts sent out, had totalled 1,500, was reduced to less than one half.

On April 18 the Patricia's were in barracks in Ypres when the Germans began reshelling the town with very heavy guns. The men had quickly to clear out of their barracks into the fields. The bombardment continued day by day, but did not reach its full strength until the 22nd, when the town was largely destroyed by shell fire. The regiment moved to a wood

some distance south and west of the trenches then occupied by the Canadian Division. The Germans endeavoured at this point to cut them off from the Canadian front. The commander who had succeeded Colonel Farquhar, Lieut.-Colonel Buller, was wounded on May 5, and Major Gault, who arrived that day, having just recovered from a former wound, took command. On May 6 and 7 the German bombardment of the lines became much more intense. On the night of May 7 the roll-call showed that the strength of the regiment was then 635 men. At half-past four on the following morning the Germans fired some ranging shells into the lines, and not long afterwards an almost overwhelming bombardment began. Between seventy and eighty heavy German guns concentrated a heavy fire of high-explosive shells and gas shells upon the section held by this regiment. By six in the morning every telephone wire to the brigade headquarters and to the trenches had been cut, and heavy bodies of German troops could be seen pausing, waiting for their opportunity to rush on our front. An advance at this point would have enabled the Germans to execute a forward movement, dangerous to the line the British held.

The German artillery fired upon the regiment

from three different sides. Trenches were useless as protection. The British artillery was inadequate to reply to such a tornado. There was nothing for the Patricia's to do but to lie low in their lines, to wait, and to endure. All available men, orderlies and scullions, scouts and signallers, were called into the trenches. The Germans, thinking that their bombardment had surely effected its purpose, came on at the double. Those of the Canadians who were left stood up to them and drove them back. The Germans, however, succeeded in getting some machine guns into position.

An orderly was sent back to the Brigade headquarters telling of the desperate position. Major Gault, while encouraging his men and sustaining them by his courage and coolness, was struck by a shell and severely wounded in the left arm and thigh. He had many companions lying wounded or dying in the trenches by now. The command was taken over by Lieut. Niven. The German fire grew even more intense than before. Heavy howitzers supported the field guns. It seemed as though the whole line must be wiped out. At nine o'clock the German shelling decreased, and the German infantry again attempted to storm the position. The remnants of the Patricia's met them once more with such a fierce fire from rifles and machine guns that the attack utterly failed. Thereupon the bombardment was renewed;

KEY MAP OF THE BRITISH POSITION.

soon every British machine gun was buried by heavy shell fire. In two instances the unwounded men dug the guns out again and mounted them afresh. The official description of the battle told that one gun was actually disinterred three times and kept in action, until a shell annihilated the whole section.

MAJOR-GENERAL SIR SAM HUGHES AND HIS SON, MAJOR GARNET HUGHES, OF BRITISH COLUMBIA, AT A REVIEW.

PRINCESS PATRICIA'S LIGHT INFANTRY BEATING OFF A GERMAN ATTACK, MAY 8, 1915.

The fight continued hour after hour from dawn until noon and then until late in the day. Soon only four officers were left—all of them lieutenants. By noon the supply of small arms ammunition was running low. By half-past one, when the men were still holding on desperately a detachment of the Rifle Brigade reached them as reinforcements. They brought a machine-gun section with them, and the two regiments joined forces on the one front. Later in the afternoon a detachment of the King's Shropshire Light Infantry arrived and brought them twenty boxes of small-arms ammunition. The Patricia's had already used up nearly all of their own cartridges and the cartridges of those who had fallen. The fresh supply was quickly handed round.

Barely had the scattered lines again got in place before the Germans launched their third attack. This was the most desperate of all. Some of the Germans actually got into the far trenches at the right at a point where every one of the Princess Patricia's had been killed. They were few in numbers, and were hunted out. The great body of the Germans were driven back by the steady fire from the British troops.

At ten o'clock that night the two officers who were left, Lieut. Niven and Lieut. Papineau, took the roll-call. Only one hundred and fifty fighting men and a few stretcher-bearers were left to answer. Late that night the battalion was relieved by the King's Royal Rifles. Before retiring the Patricia's, helped by the others, gathered together, as far as they could, the bodies of their dead. "Behind the damaged trenches," wrote the Canadian Eye-Witness, Sir Max Aitken, in a moving and eloquent dispatch, "by the light of the German flares and amid the unceasing rattle of musketry, relievers and relieved combined in the last service which one soldier can render another.

"Beside the open graves, with heads uncovered, all that was left of the regiment stood while Lieut. Niven, holding the colours of the Princess Patricia's, battered, bloody, but still intact, tightly in his hand, recalled all that he could remember of the Church of England service for the dead.

"Long after the service was over the remnant of the battalion stood in solemn reverie, unable, it seemed, to leave their comrades, until the colonel of the 3rd King's Royal Rifle Corps gave them positive orders to retire. Then, led by Lieut. Papineau, they marched back 150 strong to reserve trenches."

[Lafayette

LIEUT.-COLONEL H. C. BULLER,
Of the London Rifle Brigade, who succeeded Colonel Farquhar, Commander of Princess Patricia's Light Infantry, killed in action at Neuve Chapelle.

The first Canadian Contingent remained in England until February, 1915. Elaborate precautions were taken to ensure the safety of its voyage to France.

The Germans were known to be preparing special efforts to torpedo the transports. The Canadian rank and file anticipated that they would first be sent to the big military camp outside Rouen, and after a further spell of training would be moved to the front.

The regiments marched out from Salisbury Plain one night as though on a route march. But in place of returning they were taken straight to a port on the west coast. The transports made an immense detour, and while

NEWFOUNDLANDERS FOR THE FRONT
On parade, and troops wearing sun-helmets leaving
Britain's oldest colony.

German submarines, waiting stealthily around Havre, were watching for their prey, the ships containing the troops, now well out into the Atlantic, turned and made for port on the coast of the Bay of Biscay. Many of the transports for safety sake took four or five days for a crossing that could have been made by a direct route in as many hours. The entire Contingent arrived in safety.

Landed in France, the Canadians were agreeably surprised. There was to be no waiting in base camps. Enormous piles of trench clothing had been accumulated in sheds near the quays. As each company stepped ashore its men were served out with wolfskin coats, mittens and trench socks. They were then led straight to trains drawn up in the siding and taken across France to Flanders.

In England there had been much speculation about the fighting qualities of the Canadians. There had been many complaints concerning their alleged lack of discipline. It was common knowledge that a small proportion of them had by no means appreciated the loneliness, the mud, and the harsh conditions of life on Salisbury Plain. How would they take to the still harder life at the Front ? Military experts, those familiar with fighting armies, never had a doubt what the answer would be, and their confidence was immediately justified. The physique, equipment, bearing and discipline of the Canadians as they reached the British lines in Flanders aroused general admiration. Their fine motor transport services, the perfection of the minute details of their outfit, their horses and their medical and commissariat arrangements were all in keeping. The one part of their equipment about which there was some criticism was the rifle. They were armed with the Ross rifle, a weapon made in Canada. There had been considerable controversy concerning the Ross rifle in former years between the British and Canadian authorities, and there was a feeling in Canada that England had attempted to discriminate against this weapon because it was manufactured outside the United Kingdom. Old soldiers who examined the Canadians expressed their fears that the Ross rifle, while possibly one of the best for competition firing in peace times, was too fine an instrument for the rough-and-tumble work of the fighting field. It was soon to be given a very exacting test, and the British authorities eventually re-armed the Canadians with the regulation British Army rifle.

Many people in France expected the Canadian

FIRST CANADIAN ACTIVE SERVICE CONTINGENT.
Colonel V. A. S. Williams inspecting the rifle ranges at Valcartier.

CANADIAN MEDICAL STAFF IN FRANCE.
Front row—left to right: Capt. Bentley, Major Elliott, Lieut.-Col. Shillington, Major Bell, Capt. Walker. Second row: Capt. Penticost, Capt. Fisher, Capt. Doe. Back row: Capt. C. A. Walker, Capt. Wood, Capt. Jowen, Capt. Young, Capt. Moffat.

CANADIANS' NIGHT ATTACK AT YPRES: RETAKING OF THE GUNS

The fight in the wood: Canadian Scottish and the 10th Battalion Canadian Infantry recapture their 4·7's at the point of the bayonet.

Contingent to be largely composed of Red Indians, trappers and cowboys. This was amusingly illustrated by some of the articles by famous French writers after visits to the Canadian lines. M. Maurice Barrès, for ex-ample, wrote a charming description of them that was largely taken up with accounts of a Red Indian soldier who had just died, like the last of the Mohicans, for the honour of his people, with the ingenious devices, the tricks and the wiles of the trappers and hunters; and with the Canadian-built huts in Flanders, which brought to his mind the huts of villages of the American Indians of olden days. Actually the larger proportion of the members of the first Canadian Contingent were English-born young men who had lived for some time in Canada; there were only a very few of American-Indian descent, and these were men who had been brought up under European conditions. Most of the soldiers were drawn from the cities: bank clerks, railway men, estate agents, business leaders and the like. Nearly all the officers had been active imme-diately before the war broke out in commerce, in finance, or in the learned professions. The old Militia force had proved merely a skeleton, an invaluable skeleton, which had been clothed with flesh and blood, drawn from all ranks of the Canadian people.

There were a certain proportion of trappers, hunters and mining men in the ranks. Their knowledge proved invaluable, and the trappers were quick to use the same guile that they had employed in catching the fur-bearing animals of the north in now deceiving the Germans. It was soon found that the average young man from Canada, British-born or Canadian-born, of French descent from Quebec, or prairie farmer of the Mid-West, had a vigour and an abundance of resource all his own. The people of Canada live an open-air life. In most places there is hunting of some kind within reach of even the young man of very modest means. The forests of Eastern Canada and of the Rockies give one and all opportunities of hardy outdoor life impossible to most men in Europe. The stimulating air of the northern lands makes for real vitality. The Canadians are a well-fed and a sober race; they drink less alcohol than any other division of the British people, with the possible exception of the New Zealanders; poverty as known in the slums of Europe is very rare, and the children of the labourer have an abundance of wholesome food. The life of

the people is singularly sound. In the great cities, notably in Toronto, there is a high standard of personal conduct which enlists a powerful current of public sentiment against the low, the base and the unworthy.

When the Canadian Contingent reached the British lines it was found that these factors told. The physique of the men was a topic of general comment. Equally remarkable was their resourcefulness. The Canadians were given a time for preparation, being sent to the trenches with British companies to learn the

[*Elliott & Fry.*

LIEUT.-COL. F. D. FARQUHAR, D.S.O.,
Princess Patricia's Light Infantry (killed).

ways of trench war. A real comradeship was quickly formed between them and the English regiments, a comradeship which endured. The English Regular soldier had heard with some suspicion of the privates in the ranks from the Dominion who were paid nearly five shillings a day, as against his one and twopence. The Canadians had expected to find the average British soldier something of an automaton. They discovered one another as they really were. " I think a hundred times more of the British Tommy than I ever did before," wrote one Canadian. " These few days in the

CANADIANS IN TRAINING AT CANTERBURY.
Riding practice at the Cavalry Depôt.

trenches with a British regiment have been a revelation to me," another young fellow wrote to his parents in Toronto. "The British Tommy is splendid. He is alive to his finger-tips. He is full of devices to deceive the enemy ; he knows all kinds of tricks ; he hasn't a mean

SIR ROBERT BORDEN.
The Canadian Premier meets in London Lieut. Horsey of the 48th Canadian Highlanders who was twice wounded. On Sir Robert's left is Mr. R. D. Bennet, M.P. for Calgary, Canada.

streak in him, and he's a first-class fighting man. He uses his brains. It has been a revelation to me to find him as he really is." From this it may be fairly deduced that if the British troops had been inclined to regard the Canadian as somewhat untrained, the latter had been inclined to consider the former as wooden in their methods. Closer contact enabled both to found saner judgments.

"The Canadian troops having arrived at the Front," Sir John French wrote to the Duke of Connaught on March 3, "I am anxious to tell your Royal Highness that they have made the highest impression on us all. I made a careful inspection a week after they came to the country, and was very much struck by the excellent physique which was apparent through-out the ranks. The soldierly bearing and steadi-ness with which the men stop in the ranks on a bleak, cold and snowy day are most remark-able. After two or three weeks' preliminary education in the tenches, they have now taken over their own line, and I have the utmost confidence in their capability to do valuable and efficient service." This favourable impres-sion of the men was echoed by all military observers. The Canadian soldiers were marked from the beginning for their high spirits, their enthusiastic energy, and their determination. They were full of jokes, even when fighting was hottest. "Say, boys," one Canadian remarked to his comrades during the heavy fighting at St. Julien, when a particularly heavy blast of fire struck them, "say, there seems to be some kind of a war on here !" The relations between the Canadian officers and the men doubtless seemed surprisingly free and easy to those accustomed to the stricter outward forms of the European armies. Officers and men in the ranks often enough shared in social intercourse and mixed freely outside the hours of duty. The private in the regiment is often of as good position in civil life as his captain. Those who noted the Canadians carefully, however, observed that, if there was free intercourse when off duty, there was ready obedience and willing discipline, One point of difference sometimes arose between the officers and the men on the field of battle— a difference that would be impossible in Continental armies—emulation as to which should take the more dangerous part. "Our officers always lead the way," the Canadian soldiers said. They would relate how one colonel advanced in front of his men armed only with a cane in one of the most desperate charges of the war ; l ow another paused for a second when it seemed as though the fire of the enemy must annihilate them all to light a cigarette and to exchange a jest with a soldier near him ; and many mo e tales of the same kind. At Festubert a captain was leading his men in a desperate venture where they all had to go single file.

As they neared the most perilous point the non-commissioned officer in charge of the bomb-throwers stepped up hastily. "I beg your pardon, sir," he said gruffly, "but bomb-throwers always go first." And before the officer could have ordered him back, he had run ahead. That was typical of the Canadian spirit. When the Canadians found a chance to charge the enemy they went ahead uttering all manner of cries, unless the order was given for silence. "As we charged up the hill on to the wood held by the Germans outside St. Julien," one man related, "some yelled, some shouted, and we made a row that you could have heard half a dozen miles off. It seemed to drown for a moment even the roar of the guns."

Another quality of the Canadians which attracted much attention was their resource. Many of the men had experienced spells of rough work in mining camps or on pioneer work in the West. Some were familiar with every trick of the woodman. They were fertile in disguises, keen to develop fresh enterprises, and eager to trick the enemy in front of them. The Canadian bomb-throwers and snipers soon developed a reputation of their own among the Allied forces.

OFF TO THE FRONT.

H.R.H. The Duke of Connaught bids good-bye to the officers of the 42nd battalion Canadian Expeditionary Force, after the inspection, May, 1915.

LORD KITCHENER (on right).

THE KING INSPECTS THE CANADIAN
March past of the 7th

Before the First Contingent left England fears were expressed in some quarters lest it should be split up among different British Divisions and so lose its distinctive characteristics. Happily the British military authorities did not attempt this. The Division remained united, and General Alderson continued in command in Flanders as on Salisbury Plain. The aim of the Canadian Government was to have at the earliest possible moment a Canadian Army Corps at the Front with adequate reserves in England. General Alderson succeeded almost on the first day of his arrival at Salisbury Plain in winning the confidence and respect of the Canadians. He more than retained it in Flanders. "Alderson is a human being, not a military ramrod," wrote one young Canadian observer to his friends at home. General Alderson did not attempt to eliminate the somewhat free-and-easy style of the Canadian rank and file. He saw that, utilised properly, it could be made into a source of fighting strength. He talked to the soldiers under him as man to man. Before they went for the first time into the trenches, he told them how his old regiment —the Royal West Kent, which had been in France since the beginning of the war—had never yet lost a trench. "The Army says, 'The West Kents have never budged.' I am proud of the great record of my old regiment. And I think it is a good omen. I now belong to you and you belong to me, and before long the Army will say, 'The Canadians never budged.' Lads, it can be left there, and there I leave it. The Germans will never turn you out." A General who could strike this note in addressing the men of the West was sure of their enthusiastic support.

General Alderson's advice to the troops under

TROOPS ON SALISBURY PLAIN, 1915.

Battalion British Columbia Infantry.

him before they entered the trenches was full of practical wisdom.

We are about to occupy and maintain a line of trenches. I have some things to say to you at this moment which it is well that you should consider. You are taking over good and, on the whole, dry trenches. I have visited some myself. They are intact, and the parapets are good. Let me warn you first that we have already had several casualties while you have been attached to other divisions. Some of these casualties were unavoidable,

and that is war. But I suspect that some—at least a few—could have been avoided. I have heard of cases in which men have exposed themselves with no military object, and perhaps only to gratify curiosity. We cannot lose good men like this. We shall want them all if we advance, and we shall want them all if the Germans advance.

Do not expose your heads, and do not look round corners, unless for a purpose which is necessary at the moment you do it. It will not often be necessary. You are provided with means of observing the enemy without

THE KING INSPECTS THE CANADIANS AT SALISBURY PLAIN,

Previous to their departure for the Front. His Majesty, Lord Kitchener (on left), and Commanding Officers leaving the parade ground after the inspection.

THE CANADIANS AT YPRES.

An exchange of patriotic enthusiasm as British reinforcements advanced through the Canadian lines. The Dominion troops answering the cheers of their commander's (General Alderson) old regiment, the West Kents, who are shown in the background of the picture.

e xposing your heads. To lose your life without military necessity is to deprive the State of good soldiers. Young and brave men enjoy taking risks. But a soldier who takes unnecessary risks through levity is not playing the game, and the man who does so is stupid, for whatever be the average practice of the German army, the individual shots whom they employ as snipers shoot straight, and, screened from observation behind the lines, they are always watching. If you put your head over the parapet without orders they will hit that head. There is another thing. Troops new to the trenches always shoot at nothing the first night. You will not do it. It wastes ammunition, and it hurts no one. And the enemy says, "These are new and nervous troops." No German is going to say that of the Canadian troops.

You will be shelled in the trenches. When you are shelled, sit low and sit tight. This is easy advice, for there is nothing else to do. If you get out you will only get it worse. And if you go out the Germans will go in. And if the Germans go in we shall counter-attack and put them out; and that will cost us hundreds of men instead of the few whom shells may injure. The Germans do not like the bayonet, nor do they support bayonet attacks. If they get up to you, or if you get up to them, go right in with the bayonet. You have the physique to drive it home. That you will do it I am sure, and I do not envy the Germans if you get among them with the bayonet.

On March 1 the Canadian Division took over some 6,500 to 7,000 yards of trenches. The work of the Division during the next few weeks was one mainly of endurance. The Germans did not attack, but continued sniping and shell-fire was kept up between the two sides.

The First Canadian Division was engaged in four principal fights during the spring and summer of 1915. The first of these was the advance on Neuve Chapelle. Following this came the second battle of Ypres, when the Division saved the line on the retirement of the Algerians and Turcos after being gassed, and resisted the desperate and almost continuous attacks of the German troops for almost three weeks. The Canadians took a prominent part in the fighting at Festubert in May, making a brilliant advance on May 20–21, and seizing several of the enemy's trenches. They also took a large part in the action of June 15 at Givenchy. All of these actions are fully described in the sections dealing with the general campaigns in Flanders. After mid-June the Canadians were mainly engaged until the autumn in holding a section of the trenches.

It might well seem invidious to pick out any for special mention among troops all of whom did so well. The 8th Battalion the Winnipeg Rifles won special distinction at the second battle of Ypres for being the one regiment able to hold its trenches firmly although heavily gassed. Our troops at that time had no respirators or anti-gas helmets. With quick ingenuity the Winnipeg troops transformed their handkerchiefs into respirators and stood their

ground. The 2nd Infantry Brigade, the Western Canadians, under Brigadier-General Currie, did magnificently at Ypres. It was placed in a desperately dangerous salient. It held its ground until the trenches were wiped out by German gun fire, and then its remnants retired in good order. The Highland regiments more than maintained the ancient Scottish reputation. Among the many great deeds of the Highlanders one must be mentioned—the charge of the Canadian Scottish under Lieut.-Colonel Leckie and the 10th Battalion under Lieut.-Colonel Boyle at Ypres, when they went

[*Elliott & Fry.*

LIEUT.-COL. H. C. BECHER,
1st Battalion West Ontario Regiment (killed).

through the German lines, recovered the big guns that had been lost, and held them long enough to remove their breech blocks and render them useless. The character of the fighting in which the Canadians were engaged can best be judged by the casualties. One typical case can be named, the British Columbia Regiment. Every officer in this regiment who came out with the first troops from Canada was killed or wounded before the autumn of 1915, and only two of the wounded were able by that time to return to their regiment.

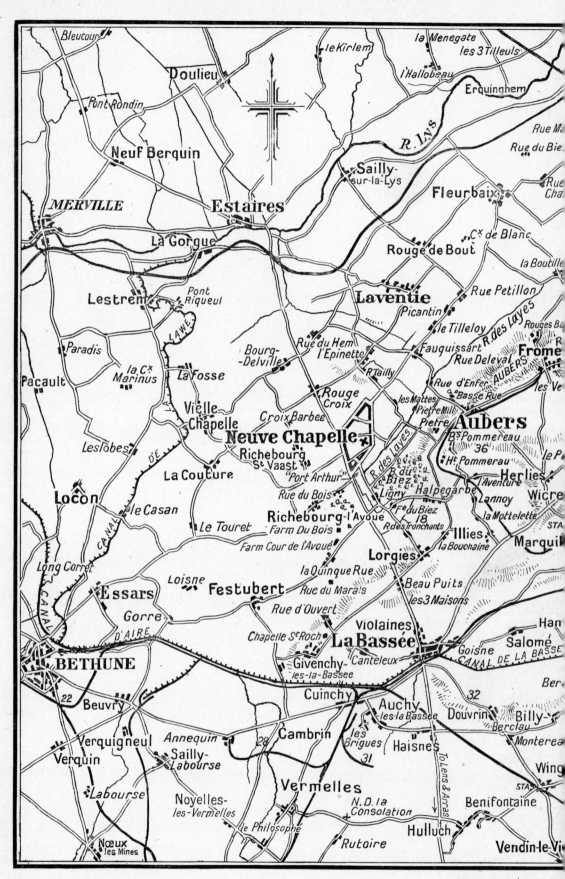

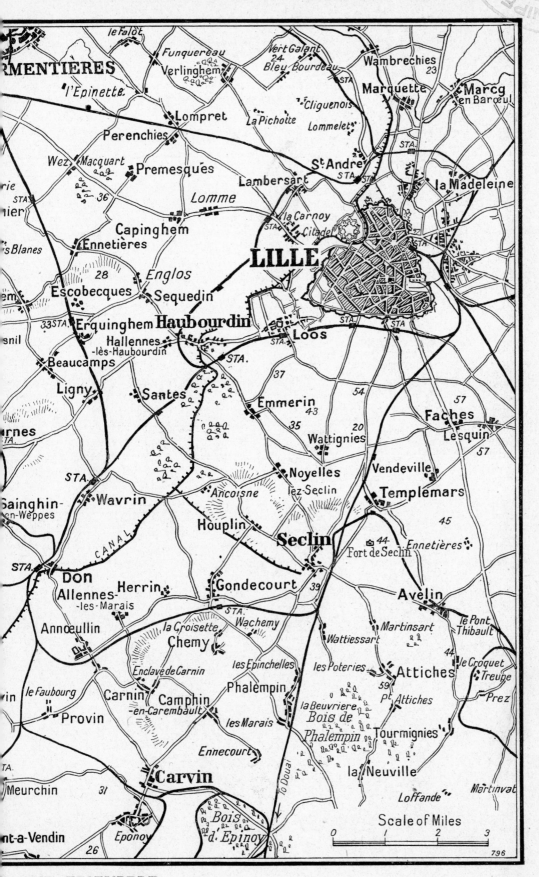

AND FESTUBERT.

The Canadian Cavalry (the Royal Canadian Dragoons, Lord Strathcona's Horse, and the 2nd King Edward's Horse) were made into a Cavalry Brigade before the First Division left England and were placed under the command of General Seely, formerly British Secretary of State for War. The scope for cavalry in the first year of the war was necessarily limited. The best tribute to this Brigade was paid by Sir John French, in an address to the troops :

I am very glad to have this opportunity of coming here to tell you how very highly I appreciate all the services you have rendered. The eagerness with which you came forward to place your services at the disposal of the Empire, and the great part you are playing in this war, have served to strengthen the bonds that bind our great Empire together—bonds that will never now be severed. I wish to express my appreciation to you for the splendid manner in which early in the year, when the Canadian Infantry Division had suffered great losses, you volunteered to leave your horses and to come out here. At the commencement you took a very prominent part in the battle of Festubert, where we not only gained a considerable amount of ground, but inflicted great losses on the enemy, and captured a large quantity of material. Then afterwards at Givenchy you kept up the same fighting record, and since that up till a few days ago you have been doing very hard work in other trenches.

I am quite confident that whatever you are called upon to do in the future will be nobly carried out. Your record will go down to history as one of the most splendid in British history.

Almost immediately after the first Canadian contingent left Salisbury Plain for the Front the second Canadian contingent began to arrive. The command of this division while it remained in England was given to a distinguished Canadian soldier—General Sam Steele—a soldier whose active military record went back to the days of the Red River Expedition, and who had long been a familiar figure in Canadian life. There had been more time to organize this contingent, and it was in some ways even more distinctly Canadian than its predecessor. The great Canadian Universities were notably represented, in some

instances by separate units. The Eaton Machine Gun Brigade, named after Sir John Eaton, of Toronto, who contributed 100,000 dollars towards its organization and equipment, was efficient and valuable. There had been splendid competition, not only among the different Provinces but among the great cities, to see which should be best represented, and the result was one worthy of Canada.

In the latter part of the summer of 1915 Sir Robert Borden, the Canadian Premier, and General Hughes, the Minister of Militia and Head of the War Department, visited Europe. They were given a splendid reception. Sir Robert Borden was presented with the Freedom of the City of London, the highest civic honour England can bestow, and General Hughes was knighted before his departure home. The visit of these two Canadian leaders was almost wholly concerned with detail questions of administration, and in discovering how Canada could co-operate most effectively in the war.

The spirit of Canada at the end of the first year was the same as it had been at the beginning. Partisan quarrels had been largely wiped out. The leader of Liberalism, Sir Wilfrid Laurier, worked in accord with his old political opponent the Premier for the common end. From Halifax to Prince Rupert the Canadian people knew only one thing, and that was that this was their fight, and that they would see it through, if needs be, to the last man and to the last dollar. Politicians recognized that the war must necessarily be followed by a great development in Imperial relations, particularly by a unity of Empire forces for purposes of defence : but they were prepared to leave the discussion of such developments until afterwards. For the moment their single purpose was to aid in bringing the war to a successful conclusion.

CHAPTER LXXXVIII.

THE BATTLES OF AUBERS AND FESTUBERT.

IMPORTANCE OF THE BATTLE OF AUBERS—"THE TIMES" CORRESPONDENT'S TELEGRAM— NECESSITY FOR INCREASED SUPPLIES OF HIGH EXPLOSIVE SHELLS—DESCRIPTION OF THE BATTLE—NEW PLAN OF SIR DOUGLAS HAIG—BATTLE OF FESTUBERT—VICTORY OF THE BRITISH.

ON the early morning of Sunday, May 9, the British troops defending Ypres from the onslaughts of the Germans, were aroused by the sound of a terrific cannonade south of the Lys. This marked the opening of the fight for the Aubers ridge, part of a great Franco-British offensive extending from the south of Armentières to the north of Arras. On May 14 appeared the report of the Military Correspondent of *The Times*, who had been staying at British Head-quarters, that the want of an unlimited supply of high-explosive shells had been a fatal bar to the success of the British attempt to storm the heights commanding Lille, which, if taken by the Allies, would render the German salient at La Bassée untenable. Five days later Mr. Asquith announced the coming formation of the Coalition Ministry, and on May 25 the list of the members of the new Cabinet was published. On June 16 Mr. Lloyd George became Minister of Munitions.

The Battle of Aubers, therefore, marks an important point in the history of the war, and deserves for this reason, as well as on its own merits, treatment in considerable detail. Although complete success did not crown the efforts of our troops, yet the losses incurred on the Aubers ridge were by no means wasted. The assaults directed by Sir Douglas Haig forced

the Crown Prince of Bavaria to concentrate a large portion of his available troops and artillery to the north of the La Bassée salient, and the consequence was that the Germans were not in sufficient strength to resist Joffre's thrust from the Arras region towards Lens.

La Bassée, the point of the salient, was surrounded by a network of brickfields, mine works and other enclosures skilfully fortified by the Germans. A direct attack on it could not be entertained for one moment by com-manders who did not regard their infantry as mere food for cannon. But an advance from the Lys to the ridge which, starting near Fort Englos, four miles or so west of Lille, runs in a south-westerly direction to Aubers, two miles east of Neuve Chapelle, and termi-nates abruptly on the hill called Haut Pom-mereau, an advance across this ridge and then over a narrow strip of low-lying land to the second ridge which follows the road from Lille through Fournes to La Bassée would, if successful, turn the position of the Germans and oblige them to evacuate La Bassée and its environs.

Such an advance had been almost success-fully made by the British in the first three weeks of October 1914. They had carried Neuve Chapelle, crossed the first ridge and the low ground and occupied Le Pilly, a mile from Fournes, at the edge of the second ridge. But the German counter-attack, backed by enormous numbers and a gigantic artillery, had driven them from Le Pilly, dislodged them from the Aubers-Fromelles-Radinghem ridge, and flung them out of Neuve Chapelle. The Battle of Neuve Chapelle in March 1915 had, however, enabled Sir John French to start his second offensive to secure the ridges.

Since October the Germans had been en-trenching their lines from Lille to La Bassée. They were now rabbit-warrens bristling with machine-guns and protected by barbed wire, some of extra stoutness, which could not be cut by ordinary clippers or broken by shrapnel. The lessons learnt from the bombardment to which the enemy had been subjected at the Battle of Neuve Chapelle had been turned by him to good account. Deep trenches, reinforced with concrete, and underground galleries had been constructed to shelter the garrisons defending them. Heavy guns posted on the hills south-east, near Pont-à-Vendin, could deluge with shell the British if they stormed the heights.

Ypres was protected by the Second Army, under Sir Herbert Plumer, the III. Corps holding Armentières. It was the task of Sir Douglas Haig with the First Army to carry the entrenchments and redoubts on the right wing of the Crown Prince Rupprecht's Army. The IV. Corps, according to Sir John French's plan, was to attack the German trenches and redoubts in the neighbourhood of Rouges-Bancs, north-west of Fromelles, the Indian Corps and the I. Corps were to carry those in the plain at the foot of the Aubers ridge between Neuve Chapelle and Givenchy and afterwards to storm the heights.

At midnight on May 8–9. the streets of Béthune, behind the extreme right of the First Army, were crowded with reserve troops. From Béthune round to Armentières the roads and lanes leading to the British trenches were filled with marching men and the material of war. The soldiers knew that they were about to engage in one of those encounters which in Napoleonic times would have been reckoned a pitched battle, but in 1915 were held to be mere incidents. It was understood that, as at Neuve Chapelle, the action would be opened by a bombardment of the hostile lines.

At 3.30 a.m. there was sufficient light for the gunners to find their targets. Sighting shots were fired by the field guns and howitzers.

The artillerymen were feeling for the parapets of the German trenches. About 4.30 the firing died away. Save for the humming, throbbing aeroplanes overhead or the passage of a motor ambulance, there was nothing to rouse the attention of the waiting soldiers. The aeroplanes were engaged in giving information to the gunners and, as at the battle of Neuve Chapelle, in bombing, during the day, stations and bridges (for example, the canal bridge near Don) through or over which the German reinforcements were moving or likely to be moved.

The morning was bright and clear. To the right were Cuinchy, with its brickfields, and the ruins of what had once been Givenchy. Trees and hedgerows obscured the view of the trenches on the low ground, but against the sky rose the Aubers ridge and the silhouettes of the villages crowning it. The firing round Ypres had temporarily subsided. Here and there an officer took out his watch and looked at it impatiently. Suddenly at 5 a.m. the guns spoke out, at first singly, but shortly the individual reports developed into one long roar. The air quivered as the huge shells swished through it, the earth shook as they struck their targets. On the horizon a cloud of smoke and dust speedily formed. It was as if one long street of houses in the distance had been bombarded and set on fire.

Shortly before six o'clock the order was given to the British troops to advance. North of Fromelles battalions of the IV. Corps dashed for the German advanced trenches. Firing their rifles, they approached the first line, then flinging their hand grenades they poured into the enemy's position, thrusting back the defenders with the bayonet, and carrying everything before them.

At 6.17, from the south, beyond the ridges, a thunderous sound told that the French had also begun their advance from the south of La Bassée.

Elated by their success, the men of the IV. Corps pressed on. They saw Lille before them. The prize missed at Neuve Chapelle seemed within their grasp. They were close to Haubourdin, a suburb of the city. But at this moment masses of Germans debouched from Lille and counter-attacked, and, as the German centre was still practically intact, the order was given to retire. Sullenly the troops withdrew, turning from time to time to fire or charging to stop the pursuing foe.

THE CANADIANS ON THE WEST FRONT.
Private Smith carrying bombs to his comrades in the trenches.

Meanwhile the Indians and I. Corps, moving forward from the line Neuve Chapelle-Festubert had at the outset been successful. The Pathans and Gurkhas had occupied the wood in front of Fromelles; the villages of Fromelles and Aubers and the first-line German trenches on the Aubers ridge, which had been pounded to a shapeless mass, had been seized. But the second-line trenches had not received sufficient treatment from the artillery, and, when the victorious troops moved on against them, the Germans issued from their hiding places, and with rifles and batteries of machine guns mowed down the attacking forces. The machine-guns were, as usual, the most formidable obstacle in the British path. The fire from these skimmed the ground, inflicting wounds on the lower parts of the body. Yet, still undaunted, both the Indians and British endeavoured again and again to close with the enemy.

If individual courage and initiative could have gained the day, Lille would that evening have been cleared of the enemy. At both ends of the battlefield British soldiers were winning names for themselves in history. Near Rouges Bancs Lieut. O. K. Parker, of the 2nd Battalion Northampton Regiment, who during the fighting exhibited extraordinary courage and resolution, before the attack was delivered made a daring reconnaissance along the German front. Under a terrific fire Second-Lieutenant H. M. Stanford, Royal Field Artillery, imperturbably mended telephone wires. Acting-Sergeant F. W. Shepherd, of the 1/13th (Kensington) London Regiment (T.F.), advanced 400 yards from the firing line to the enemy's breastwork with a telephone iine. It was cut, and he started laying a second. Subsequently he carried two wounded men out of the line of fire. From an isolated tree close behind the trenches, Major J. R. Colville, of the 55th battery of the Royal Field Artillery, amidst bursting shells, observed the havoc wrought by the battery which he was directing.

In the foreground of the fight Acting-Corporal Charles Sharpe headed a bombing party and cleared 50 yards of trench. His companions were killed or wounded, but with four other men he attacked and captured a further trench,

[Swaine.

LIEUT.-COL. C. B. LECKIE,
Commander of the Canadian Scottish.

250 yards long. He had secured the V.C. So had Corporal James Upton, of the 1st Battalion Sherwood Foresters, who displayed amazing courage when rescuing the wounded.

At one point the line ceased to advance. Second-Lieutenant Nevile West, of the 2/ Royal Berks Regiment—the sole surviving officer—placed himself at its head and the attack was resumed. West was shot and fell to the ground. Pulling himself together, he got up and ran forward, only to be wounded a second time.

South of Neuve Chapelle similar heroic actions had been or were being performed. On the night of the 8th, in the Rue du Bois region, Second-Lieutenant John Millar, of the 1/ Black Watch, had reconnoitred a German trench, and loosened or cut the wire in front of it. The next day, under intense fire, he established flag communication with our signallers who had reached the German parapet. A non-commissioned officer of the same battalion, Corporal John Ripley, who subsequently received the V.C., was the first to ascend the enemy's parapet. Standing on it, he directed those following him to the gaps in the German wire entanglements. Then, leading his section to the second-line trench of the enemy, with seven or eight men he blocked both flanks and arranged a fire position, defending it until he was badly wounded in the head and all his comrades had fallen. Lance-Corporal David Finlay, of the 1/ Black Watch, led a bombing party of twelve. Ten of them fell. Finlay ordered the two survivors to return, but himself, regardless of his own

[Elliott & Fry

MAJOR G. W. BENNETT,
2nd Batt. (killed).

CAPTAIN G. J. L. SMITH,
1st Batt. West Ontario Regiment (killed).

personal safety, went to the assistance of a wounded man and carried him over a distance of a hundred yards of fire-swept ground. He, like Ripley, was awarded the V.C.

Near Richebourg Lance-Corporal W. Stuart, of the 1/ Royal Highlanders, started playing the pipes as he left the trench, and, though grievously injured, never ceased playing them until the German line was reached. Private G. Anderson, also of the 1st Battalion Royal Highlanders, in broad daylight went out and warned several wounded men lying in front of the trench that a bombardment was about to commence. He then crawled back in full view of the enemy, dragging with him an officer badly wounded. Before sunset he saved three more severely wounded men, and during the night brought in eight more. These exploits were performed under heavy rifle, machine gun and shell fire.

Two more of the innumerable heroic episodes on that day may be recorded. Near Fromelles a British soldier found himself the sole survivor of the party with which he had advanced. He was surrounded, but managed to crawl into a deep shell crater. The Germans knew where he was, and with their usual chivalry wished to kill him. Unable to hit him with their rifles, unwilling to risk being shot by the British in the background if they went for him with the bayonet, they contented themselves with lobbing hand-grenades into the hole. By some miracle the British soldier escaped, and, all day long, lay there flinging back such of the grenades as did not explode. At night he crawled back in safety to his comrades.

The second incident was of a more tragic nature. Hard by, the men of a machine-gun detachment took two German machine-guns and turned them against the enemy. For some time they continued alone in a trench fighting the captured guns to the last. They were overpowered by numbers and killed.

We have seen what one or a few individuals did, let us observe the movements of the 5/ (Cinque Ports) Territorial Battalion of the Royal Sussex Regiment as they are recorded by Lieut.-Colonel F. G. Langham, who commanded the battalion and was himself wounded:

We had to attack. The assaulting line—2/ Sussex on the left, and the 2/ Northamptons on the right—both over establishment. Second line—ourselves on the left, and the 2/ King's Royal Rifles on the right. Third line—1/ Loyal North Lancashires on the left, and the 9/ King's Liverpools (T.F.) on the right. Our job was to "mop up" the trenches after the assaulting line had taken them and support our 2nd Battalion and the Northants. The 60th had to go on behind the latter and work along the right to a point forming a sort of bastion in the German second line, and if they got there to go further on to a point still further to the right. We had, therefore, to "mop up" on the front of the two assaulting battalions, and it meant sending up a third company to follow the King's Royal Rifles to " mop up " behind the Northants.

LIEUT.-COL. HART McHARG.
7th Vancouver Batt. (killed).

After a bombardment of forty minutes the advance began. Three companies of the 2/ Sussex and the Northants went out over our parapets and got to from forty to eighty yards from the German lines. From us "C" Company, less one platoon, "A" Company, less one platoon, and the whole of "B" Company went out in the second line, with two companies of the King's Royal Rifles. Then the most murderous rifle and machine gun and shrapnel fire opened. and no one could get on or get back. People say the fire at Mons and Ypres was nothing to it. No end of brave things were done, and our men were splendid but helpless. After some considerable time we got orders to retire, but this was easier said than done. Some men were 300 yards out from our parapet, many dead, and some even on fire. Every now and again you would see the men roll over on the ground. The men began to crawl in, most of them wounded.

After getting in all we could, we were ordered to go back to a supporting trench. We were then told we should assault again at 12.30, it being then about 9.30 a.m. These orders were varied from time to time, and at last we moved up to another trench, and were told to act if necessary in support of troops who would assault at 4.45. All the time a tremendous artillery fire was on, and we were being shelled by howitzers. The Black Watch and 1/ Cameronians then assaulted, and got it just as badly as we did; a few got in only to be bayoneted. Several of our men, still alive, got up and joined them in their charge, after lying out there twelve hours. Unfortunately I cannot find out that any of these brave fellows got back safely, though there may be some among the wounded. If I can trace any as having survived I shall certainly recommend them for some reward. It was getting cold when, about 6 p.m., we received orders to retire to billets.

Besides the regiments mentioned in the above letter, the Munster Fusiliers distinguished themselves by their desperate efforts to break into the enemy's trenches. The nature of the obstacles in the way of the Munsters and other battalions of the I. Corps will be seen when we describe the Battle of Festubert. The ordeal which they and other regiments underwent may be surmised from an extract from the letter of an officer who took part in the battle :

The orders said that the guns would bombard the trenches for ten minutes, the entanglements for ten minutes, and then the trenches again for ten minutes. During the shelling of the last ten minutes, and under its cover, we were to advance to within fifty yards or so of the German trenches, and the instant it ceased to rush them and proceed on to the reserves. Well, almost as soon as our shelling proper started at five o'clock, the enemy replied, and with some effect, too, a big lyddite landing in the traverses on either side of the one I was in—in one case killing four and wounding three. All this time there was no sign that the hostile trenches were even manned, except for one poor fellow that got blown up some dozen feet by one of our high-explosive shells.

I suppose we all looked pretty awe-inspiring, as we all had on muslin masks dipped in hypo as a counter-actant for asphyxiating gases. Ten minutes or so after the commencement of the bombardment we were all down at the bottom of the trench, for the enemy's shells were bursting in front, behind, and in our lines. By this time you can imagine we were fairly excited, but we still believed that we would do our job

without much opposition from the Germans. who were mostly dead—perhaps ! Of course, in the row it was impossible to hear orders shouted from traverse to traverse. so one of our men dashed round. A lyddite shell choked the air with yellow fumes just by : that was the end of him. Another went round : "C Company advance : pass it on ! " he yelled. "C" got up, scrambled—with the aid of many hands—from the trenches, and flung themselves over the parapet. Immediately an absolute hail of bullets met them even before they were through our own entanglements, and the hostile shelling was terrific.

After a short interval—"G to advance ! " comes the shout. Up we get : machine-guns sweep the parapet up and down, backwards and forwards, and many fall back into the trench dead or mortally wounded. Once on the level again down we go flat. The number of dead and wounded lying about is awful—and the shells !

Inch by inch, foot by foot, yard by yard we work ourselves forward, through the grass, in many places even then soaking with blood. . . . .

Our artillery has slackened fire, almost stopped. in fact—thinks we are almost at the enemy. The place is an inferno—a red hell, and oh ! those frightful lyddites : blow the place to bits, and rip, and slash, and tear to pieces those puny things lying in the grass—so still.*

Any real progress was impossible.

Behind the British lines were massed the reserves waiting eagerly to join in the fight. But Sir Douglas Haig, informed of the strength of the German second line, decided to break off the combat.

The news of the French victory at Carency, where, with an expenditure of 276 rounds per gun, the German defences had been demolished and their positions taken, had reached him. By obliging the enemy to keep such large bodies on the north of the La Bassée salient he had materially contributed to the French success, and, with the Second Battle of Ypres still undecided, it would have been foolhardy to take unnecessary risks. Orders were, therefore, given to the troops to cease their advance. All night wounded men were limping or being carried back from the Aubers ridge. The unburied dead lay on it in thousands.

The moral of the day's fighting was drawn by the Military Correspondent of *The Times* in these words : " If," he wrote, " we can break through the hard outer crust of the German defences, we believe that we can scatter the German armies, whose offensive causes us no concern at all. But to break this hard crust we need more high explosive, more heavy howitzers, and more men. This special form of warfare has no precedent in history. It is certain that we can smash the German crust if we have the means. So the means we must have, and as quickly as possible."

By the morning of May 10 the IV. and I. Corps and the Indian Corps were back in their

---

* From a letter published by the *Morning Post.*

FRANK DADD
1915.

THE CANADIANS IN A HOT CORNER.

Lieutenant F. W. Campbell and a handful of men with a machine gun gained the enemy's front trench, and advanced along it under heavy fire until a barricade stopped them. When the little band was reduced to two—Lieutenant Campbell and Private Vincent—and in default of a tripod, the lieutenant set up the machine gun on Vincent's back and fired continuously. Afterwards the German bombers entered the trench and Lieutenant Campbell fell wounded. Eventually he crawled away in a dying condition, while Vincent succeeded in dragging the gun to safety.

old positions and Sir Douglas Haig had decided that the better course would be to approach the Aubers ridge from the Neuve Chapelle-Givenchy front alone. Sir John French sanc-

tioned this proposal, directing that the fresh assault, however, should not be made without a powerful and deliberate artillery preparation. The 7th Division, part of the IV. Corps, was to be moved round to support the offensive, which was to begin on the night of May 12. The very dull and misty weather, however, so interfered with the observation of the gunners that the advance was postponed till the 15th. During the interval the artillery on both sides played on each other's trenches. To ensure Sir Douglas Haig's success, on the day chosen for the assault Sir John French placed the Canadian Division under his orders. The Canadians had recovered from the effects of the German asphyxiating gas and from their exertions at the Second Battle of Ypres which was just finishing. They were inflamed with righteous fury against their dastardly opponents, and were anxious to mete out further punishment to them. They did not accompany the first advance; but they were destined to render later most valuable assistance to their British comrades.

Saturday, May 15, dawned, and all were in a state of expectancy, because it was known that a further attack was to take place after sunset. The Military Correspondent of *The Times* has left us his impressions on that day:

On Saturday morning I visited the Ypres district, and found that all was reasonably quiet after the furious bombardments of the previous days. Our troops there had suffered much from their inability to silence the German guns, of every calibre up to 12 in. But our

INDIAN TROOPS ERECTING TELEGRAPH WIRES.

troops were still in good heart; the German infantry would not stand up to them. and, in spite of our losses there seemed to be no immediately serious danger on this side.

A look along the rest of the line down to the region of Laventie gave an impression that no hostile action was impending. and I passed on—fairly confident that we should not be disturbed that night by a German offensive—down to the village of La Couture, whence a good view was to be gained of the bombardment against that part of the German front selected for the night attack.

This village had suffered much. Most of the inhabitants, except a most gallant *curé*, had fled. The church and churchyard, as well as the village, showed signs of devastation. But the havoc wrought by our own shells on the German lines was greater still. From our guns and howitzers a well-aimed, deliberate, and fairly heavy fire was in progress all the afternoon and well into the night. This fire struck the German trenches and fortified posts. It wrecked the barbed wire in parts, and every now and then a heavy explosion, or the outbreak of a fire, showed where our shells had told.

I noticed that the heavy battery, which was to the right rear of my observation post, was firing with great precision, and, in general, the effect of the fire appeared to be good, although it could not be described as overwhelming, or as likely to drive good troops out of their works.

In the late afternoon Sir John French rode out amongst the troops and was received with enthusiastic acclamation. He wished them good luck, and addressed to all a few warm and inspiring words. No one knows better than he how to strike the right note in an appeal to soldiers, and he had the pleasure of observing how keen the men were for a dash at the enemy, how confident they were in his leadership, and how delighted they were that the hour had come at last for the attack.

The Staff arrangements for the attack were well done. All column roads were marked by signboards, and every attention paid to the perfect ordering of the troops. Every movement took place after dusk, and it was in complete silence that the various units drew out of their billets and bivouacs, and gradually took their place at the appointed spots.

The night was dark, but not very dark, though there was no moon. The wind was scarcely perceptible, and the weather was warm.

All was ready. The Royal Engineers at great risk had been cutting the barbed wire in front of our own trenches, and bridging two ditches which would have to be crossed. They had made scaling ladders for the men, and, in a dozen other ways, sought to render easier the very difficult task in front of their comrades. Officers had maps revised from the photographs taken by aeroplanes. The negatives, procured under such hazardous circumstances by the aerial operators, revealed to the military cartographers the German position as seen from above. These photographs somewhat resembled those taken through telescopes of the surface of the moon. Features which escaped the eyes of officers stationed on the ground were indeed revealed, but the heights of obstacles, the depths of trenches and ditches could only be guessed. The men were cleaning their rifles and sharpening their bayonets.

"Behind the lines," writes an eye-witness. "I saw a chaplain prepare his fighting men for the great assault." It was in an orchard carpeted with blossoms shaken off by the concussion of the guns. "He stood at a small table," continues the narrator, "with the pure white linen and glistening silver. Kneeling on the grass was one of the best-known fighting battalions in the British Army, and I saw officers and men step out and kneel before the Holy Table with hands stretched out to receive the Blessed Emblems of the Body Broken and the Blood Shed."

The trenches were filling up. The Indians were on the left, the 2nd Division of the I. Corps in the centre, and, on the right, the 7th Division of the IV. Corps. The attack was to be delivered from that section of our front which from Richebourg St. Vaast followed the road known as the Rue du Bois and then ran south of the road until it reached the turning to the hamlet of La Quinque Rue. Thence the line proceeded southward, passing in front of the ruins of Festubert, which has given its name to the battle.

The Indians and the 2nd Division were to assault the German trenches under cover of the night : the 7th Division was to advance at dawn.

On the extreme right, south of the hill, crowned by the battered church and houses of La Bassée, stretched a plain, the monotony of which was broken by the factory chimneys and spoil heaps of a mining district. The trenches, connecting the French army which had won Carency with the British First Army, could be discerned in the distance. To the left of La Bassée a little knoll and a pile of crushed masonry indicated Festubert. Thence to Neuve Chapelle was a fenny country, intersected by broad ditches filled with mud and slimy water and hidden by tall, coarse grass. At least two of these had to be crossed by the British.

Some clumps of poplars and willows afforded a little natural cover to the enemy. Among them and in groups of cottages, in farms, and isolated houses were hidden many of their deadly machine-guns. The main strength of the defence, however, lay in three lines of trenches drawn by the Germans across the fields and meadows which, in places, were water-logged and thus added to the difficulties of the assaulting troops. Low redoubts and breastworks running from the front to rear, divided the

INDIAN TROOPS IN THE TRENCHES.

German lines into sectors each capable of independent defence, and no pains had been spared to make their works an impregnable barrier. Formidable, indeed, was the long serpentine obstacle which lay between the British and their objective, the Aubers ridge.

The sun had sunk to rest and the men waited calmly for the signal. Neither moon nor stars lit up the sky. Facing the British and Indians was the 7th Prussian Corps, recruited from the industrial and mining districts of Westphalia. The 57th, 56th, and 54th Infantry Regiments and the 24th Pioneers were in the trenches. Of these the 57th Regiment alone was destined to lose in two days 2,400 out of 3,000 men.

The Germans were on the alert. Shouts of "Come on, we are ready," had been heard during the afternoon.

At 11.30 p.m. the order to assault was given. As our men left the trenches, the sky was illuminated with flares shedding downwards a bright white glare. German searchlights swung round to meet the advancing tide of British Imperial troops. The rattle of the rifle and the rat-tat-tat of the machine-guns were both heard in their highest intensity. Men fell as they clambered over the parapets, fell in increasing numbers as they pushed gallantly forward. The Indians making for Richebourg l'Avoué were held up.

South of the Indians advanced the 2nd Division. Its left captured the first line of trenches, but halted in order to keep touch with the Indians. The centre and right broke into the German second line of trenches, gaining 800 yards in frontage and about 600 yards in depth at the furthest part. An officer who was present in this sector of the battle-field relates some incidents of the fighting :

In our immediate vicinity the attack was to take place on a front of about half a mile, while away to right and left other divisions were attacking. Here the regiments attacking were the Worcesters, Royal Innis-killing Fusiliers, 60th King's Royal Rifles, and the King's Liverpool Regiment. Soon after ten o'clock along this front there were four lines of men lying in the open in front of the breastwork, with more behind waiting to support. At 11.30, in pitch darkness, they rose with one accord to the attack. In perfect quietness they went forward at a walk. They had hardly started when a flare rose from the German trenches ; on they went, still walking. The flare had apparently discovered them, for other flares went up ; then a hail of lead was poured into the advancing troops, who then started to charge. The sharp bark of the machine guns and the crackling of " rapid fire " of the rifles, was deafening.

For some reason most opposition was met on the left of our line by the Worcesters and Inniskillings. The King's Royal Rifles and the King's on the right soon obtained their trench and went on to their second. On the left, nothing daunted by the sheet of lead that they had to penetrate, the Worcesters and Inniskillings went on bravely. Numbers fell, and the Worcesters found their task impossible ; but the Irishmen, pushed on, line after line, and after terrible losses in officers and men obtained their section of trench and immediately made for the second line. A rush through another hail of lead, and the second line fell to them. At dawn the successful regiments joined up, and five or six hundred yards of the first two lines of German trenches were held by our brave men. Many heroes from our front trenches during the day shouldering bandoliers of ammunition—or carrying boxes of bombs—attempted the 300 yards dash across the open to the captured German trenches. Some got across, but many fell. There is no recognition for these—they were brave men doing their duty. They knew the risk and took it gladly, willing to do their share for the honour of their country and regiment. During the day our trenches, supporting trenches and communication trenches were subjected to a terrific bombardment. The wounded suffered most by this, for although the stretcher-bearers took all risk, it was quite impossible to remove many of them. It was not until dark that any real attempt to clear off the wounded, who had been lying in the trenches all day, could be made. On Monday the Oxford and Bucks and the Highland Light Infantry pushed on from the captured trenches and won more ground.*

Captain C. L. Armitage, of the 6th Battalion of the Worcestershire Regiment, had been among the leaders in this attack. After his men had failed to gain their objective, he skil-fully withdrew and reorganized them behind our breastwork. After sunset he rescued many wounded men.

The King's Liverpool Regiment referred to above attacked two farms. A company reached the outbuildings of one of these, but eventually had to withdraw. Lance-Corporal Tombs of

* This narrative was published in *The Daily Chronicle*.

this regiment crawled on his knees no less than five times to bring in wounded. Lieutenants Hutchinson and Fulton, with a bombing party, advanced down a trench, captured many Germans and put to flight others, who were promptly fired upon by their own men. In response to calls for ammunition, Hutchin-son the next day led up a party through machine gun fire, the last part of the journey being per-formed on hands and knees. Later, on May 18, this officer conducted some bombers who forced 200 Germans to surrender and as many to retreat.

The Inniskillings advanced up both sides of a road called " the cinder track." Their left, owing to the delay in bringing up a supporting regiment, was exposed to the concentrated fire of machine guns and had to halt. The two companies on the right, however, reached the enemy's trenches. Second-Lieutenant J. L. Morgan, who had repeatedly returned to hurry up reinforcements, was mortally wounded.

It was now that a surprise was sprung on the enemy, who may not have suspected the presence of the 7th Division round Festubert. At 3 a.m. on Sunday, the 16th, the Division was launched at the very intricate entrench-ments in that quarter. We will follow the progress of some of the regiments engaged in the attack.

The Welsh Fusiliers had arrived on the evening of the 15th. During the small hours of the night Royal Engineers had been out in front cutting passages through our own wire entanglements and bridging a wide ditch which separated our lines from the enemy's. In the dull light preceding the dawn, our artillery at 3 a.m. began to hurl shells at the parapets of the German entrenchments. Sud-denly the curtain of shell fire receded east of the enemy's line. The moment had come for the assault. Up the ladders provided to scale our own parapets the men clambered ; they dropped down on the further side, and under a terrific fire streamed off to the openings in the wire entanglements. Lieutenant-Colonel Gabbet, their commander, fell riddled with bullets. Major Dixon, shot through the legs, lay at the edge of our own trench. Passing beyond and thinning visibly, the Fusiliers sprinted for the bridges over the ditch a hundred yards away. The cheery shouts of the Celts mingled with the hoarse, guttural cries of the Westphalians. Had the artillery breached the German parapets ? A wild yell of joy

HIGHLAND PIPERS PLAYING THE CANADIAN SCOTTISH INTO YPRES.
Canadians honoured by their British comrades on their return from the battle at Langemarck.

told the Warwicks in reserve that the gunners had done their work. Into two smoke-obscured trenches the wave of excited Welshmen poured. There was a short, hand-to-hand encounter. Then the Teutons fled down a long communication trench leading to an orchard. Careless whether they hit their own men or not, the German gunners opened on what a minute before had been the Westphalian trench. While Sergeant Butler, badly

wounded, was firing the only machine gun which had not been knocked out, Captain Stockwell led his men up the communication trench. He had been joined by thirty-five men of the Scots Guards, which regiment was abreast of the Welshmen. A hundred yards on they met a barrage of British shells. Our gunners had expected the Westphalians to put up a better fight.

The news that the Welsh Fusiliers had reached this point, was conveyed to our artillery which then turned its attention to the trenches and redoubts beyond.

The shelling ceased, and Captain Stockwell was about to lead his men to the orchard when a German officer and two men appeared in the communication trench with a machine gun. The Fusiliers and Scots Guardsmen fired a volley and, over the corpses of the three Germans, they rushed to the orchard. There —1,200 yards from the British lines—they were brought to a standstill by machine gun fire from six ruined cottages. The four bomb-throwers with the party made an entrance into the first cottage, and throughout Sunday Captain Stockwell and his little band maintained themselves in it. Only one of seven orderlies sent for reinforcements got back. At night he received orders to retire to the second line of German trenches, which had been meanwhile occupied by us and put in a state of defence.

The clearance of these trenches had been chiefly due to the bombers, each of which carried half a dozen grenades. Among them Company-Sergeant-Major Barter with seven men had bombed 500 yards of trench, cut the wires of eleven mines, and captured three officers and 102 prisoners. He was awarded the V.C. " I had only just arrived at the front," a German officer, who belonged to the 57th Regiment, afterwards explained, " I was in Lille for three days, and was then sent to the trenches. The first day I was shelled ; the next day a British soldier threw a bomb at me. I thought I had had enough, so I surrendered." Some of the prisoners were Polish miners, who were rejoiced to escape from German tyranny.

Similar scenes had occurred in the neighbouring area attacked by the Scots Guards and Scottish Borderers. The Borderers met with a mishap. Colonel Wood was wounded and fell into a stream and would have been drowned but for Sergeant Burman and Corporal Coleman, who jumped in and pulled him out. Caught by a torrent of machine gun fire, the Borderers came to a halt.

The Scots Guards, headed by Sir Frederick Fitzwygram, went on alone. Sergeant Heyes joined a bombing party of the Borderers and, when the officers were killed, with typical British initiative he took command. He succeeded in capturing some 250 yards of German trenches.

Sir Frederick Fitzwygram and a company, borne away by their eagerness, outdistanced the rest of the regiment. Near the Rue du Bois they were surrounded and killed. A few days later their bodies were found in the midst of a circle of German dead, empty cartridge cases, twisted bayonets and broken rifles.

On the other flank of the Welsh Fusiliers the West Surreys (the Queen's), a regiment largely composed of Londoners, were fully equal to their great reputation. The two leading companies had been almost wiped out in the first few minutes of the charge ; Major Bottomley was mortally wounded. The other companies, however, stormed the first-line trenches of the enemy and stuck to them all Sunday. For tactical reasons they were then withdrawn. One of their number, Private Hardy, had joined Sergeant-Major Barter's bombing party, whose exploits have been already described. Wounded in the right arm, Hardy fell fainting to the ground. The wound was dressed and he recovered. No sooner was he on his legs than he cried, " Luckily I'm left-handed," and ran off to rejoin Barter. With his uninjured hand he flung grenades until a shot laid him low.

Hardy's heroic death was the culmination of one of the most curious incidents in the war. Some time after the outbreak of hostilities a certain Captain Smart, of the 53rd Sikhs, who had been in England on furlough, absented himself without leave and joined the Expeditionary Force as a private. The " Hardy " whose dauntless action we have described was Captain Smart ! He had told Barter what he had done, explaining that he had deserted in order to get into action as soon as possible. " Luckily I'm left-handed," is a phrase that should live from its association with this gallant officer, who, after his death, was reinstated in his former rank.

The answer of another man of the Queen's, Private Williamson, deserves to be recorded. He had been bringing in wounded men through storms of bullets. The Adjutant of the South Staffords, seeing that he was exhausted, told him to take cover ; " No, sir," he said, " my place is in the firing line with my regiment, and I must go back to it."

No less meritorious was the conduct of the South Staffordshires. The men from Walsall and Wolverhampton had been taunted by the Germans the night before. But the enemy proved more valiant with their mouths than with their hands. Charged by the South Staffords, they bolted down the communication trench, and several hundred yards of the

German line were won. Second-Lieutenant Hassall, a reserve officer, when bombing, exhibited personal courage of no ordinary kind. Under heavy fire he also returned to fetch grenades. Captain Singleton Bonner also distinguished himself, and Captain A. B. Beauman handled his company with great skill and, after reaching the line allotted to the battalion, entrenched himself and during that and the next two days held on under heavy artillery fire.

As the battle proceeded, fresh troops were thrown in to increase the momentum of the British attack. Late on Sunday evening the Grenadier Guards advanced, and joined in hunting the Germans from their lairs. One Grenadier was seen methodically bombing a large body of Germans huddled together in a trench. A machine gun was brought up and laid through a hole in the parapet. As the Germans scuttled away from the exploding grenades, they were torn down by its fire.

The Gordons, too, did yeoman's service. Lieut.-Col. A. Gordon, shot through the knee, refused to be taken to a dressing station, and remained until the parapet of the captured trench had been reversed, and faced the enemy.

The Warwicks, behind the Welsh Fusiliers, who had been the recipients of special attention from the German artillery, went forward and explained to the Germans with their bayonets that Birmingham exports men as well as arms and ammunition. Second-Lieutenant Chavasse, bearing a name well-known in Birmingham, and a nephew of the Bishop of Liverpool, led the leading company in the attack. The young officers in this battalion showed great courage and skill.

Turning from the deeds of individual regiments, officers and men, let us consider the results of the fighting on May 15 and 16 from a wider standpoint. By 7 a.m. on May 16 the 7th Division had entrenched itself on a line running nearly north and south, half-way between their original trenches and La Quinque Rue. Dividing it from the 2nd Division were, however, two breastwork entrenchments running back from the front of the enemy's first-line trenches, and so constructed as to give fire laterally in both directions; also a series of redoubts. The entrenchments were armed with machine guns behind steel shields, and high explosive shells were required to render them untenable. At 10.30 a.m. of the same day an attempt had been made from La Quinque Rue against the communications of the enemy, but it ended in failure. On the extreme left the attack of the Indians had been

INDIAN TROOPS IN NORTHERN FRANCE.

"SHABASH! KUCH DAR NAHIN HAI!—"BRAVO! THERE IS NO FEAR!"
The Charge of the 40th Pathans near Ypres.

suspended, and the rest of the day had been spent in endeavouring to unite the inner flanks of the 2nd and 7th Divisions. At nightfall the Germans had counter-attacked, and the furthest point occupied by the 7th Division—the cottage taken by Captain Stockwell of the Welsh Fusiliers—had had to be abandoned.

By the morning of Monday, May 17, the British had driven two salients into the German lines—one north of Festubert, the other south of it. At about 9.30 a.m. the operation of connecting the salients recommenced. Rain was falling.

Pressed from three sides, subjected to a cross fire from several directions and to continuous bombing and shelling, the resistance of the enemy gradually weakened, and many prisoners were captured. In front of the farm Cour de l'Avoué, between La Quinque Rue and Richebourg l'Avoué, a horrible scene, already referred to at page 80, was witnessed. The remains of a battalion of Saxons hastily brought up to reinforce the Westphalians had proposed to surrender. They advanced towards our line and were at first greeted by a hail of bullets. Immediately they threw down their rifles, and one of them waved a white flag tied to a stick. At that moment the Westphalians north of them poured volley after volley into their Saxon comrades, while the German artillery behind opened on them. In a few seconds all that was left of the band were a few wounded men writhing on the ground.

Meanwhile the 7th Division in front of Festubert pressed southwards along the German trenches, bombing and bayoneting everyone in their path. Their task was to push on in the direction of Rue d'Ouvert, Chapelle St. Roch and Canteleux, while the 2nd Division on their left was directed on Rue du Marais and Violaines. The Indian Corps was ordered to keep in touch with the 2nd Division and the 51st (Highland) Division was directed to Estaires to support the First Army. By nightfall the whole of the German first-line trenches from the south of Festubert to Richebourg l'Avoué were in our possession. In places the second and third lines had been captured, and beyond them many important tactical points were also held. The men, some of them wet through and covered from head to foot with mud, were eager to continue the fight. The news of the gassing at Ypres and of the torpedoing of the Lusitania had infuriated them, and their

tempers had not been softened by such incidents as that about to be recounted.

A party of sixty Germans, dressed in khaki, advanced towards a British trench. One of the treacherous scoundrels called out in excellent English : " Don't shoot, we are the Grenadier Guards." A British officer climbed out and walked forward. Immediately he was fired upon, though not hit. His men, full of a righteous indignation, rushed from their trench and slew them to a man.

That night a Territorial Battalion, the 4th Cameron Highlanders—men from Skye and the Outer Islands and Inverness-shire, many of them gillies or gamekeepers, had an experience which the survivors will not soon forget. At 7.30 p.m. they received orders to attack some cottages. In the dark they stumbled on a deep and wide ditch. Some swam it ; others found planks left by the Germans and so crossed over. All the while they were being shelled and also fired at from some houses on their left. One company completely missed its way ; another was virtually wiped out. A third company reached the back end of a German communication trench. By 9 p.m. this company was in desperate straits. No bombs and few cartridges were left. About midnight two platoons managed to reach it, but they had no machine guns with them. It would have been folly to remain any longer in such an exposed position. The survivors made their way back as best they could. Their commander, Lieut.-Col. Fraser, and twelve other officers were killed, and half the battalion killed, wounded or missing. In this retirement Sergeant-Major Ross, a veteran, was noticed as behaving with remarkable coolness and courage.

Tuesday, May 18, was the birthday of Prince Rupprecht of Bavaria, the author of the order not to take prisoners. In *The Lille War News*—a paper published for the consumption of the credulous German soldiers—there appeared this crazy exhortation :

Comrades, if the enemy were to invade our land, do you think he would leave one stone upon another of our fathers' houses, our churches, and all the works of a thousand years of love and toil ? . . . and if your strong arms did not hold back the English (God damn them !) and the French (God annihilate them !), do you think they would spare your homes and your loved ones ? What would these pirates from the Isles do to you if they were to set foot on German soil ?

In spite of this frenzied appeal the " strong arms " of the Germans were unable to prevent the British making further progress, although the weather was cold and rainy, which interfered with artillery preparation. Our troops advanced from the Festubert-La Quinque Rue road to a point about 1,200 yards north of it, and they seized a post 300 yards south-east of the hamlet. The enemy, however, still retained two large farms south of Richebourg l'Avoué and west of the Festubert-La Quinque Rue road—viz., the farm of the Cour de l'Avoué, before which the unfortunate Saxons had been butchered, and the farm du Bois. These farms were very strongly defended ; they bristled with machine guns. But still our men would not be denied, and by Tuesday night success crowned their efforts, the total number of prisoners taken had reached 608, and several machine guns had been captured.

That day Lieutenant J. G. Smyth, of the 15th Ludhiana Sikhs, near Richebourg l'Avoué—after two attempts had failed—with a party of ten men conveyed 96 bombs to a point within a few yards of the enemy. To do this he had to swim a stream, and all the time he was under the fire of howitzers, machine guns and rifles. The V.C. was his reward.

Lieutenant A. V. L. Corry, of the 2/ Grenadier Guards, had also distinguished himself. At Rue du Bois, when his commander was killed and all the other officers wounded, he had reorganized the company and handled it with great coolness.

The next day Sir Douglas Haig withdrew the 7th and 2nd Divisions. The former was relieved by the Canadians, the latter by the 51st (Highland) Division. Both divisions were, with the artillery of the 2nd and 7th Divisions, placed under the command of Lieut.-General Alderson. The 7th Division remained in Army Reserve. The weather continued wet and cold. There was little to be recorded, though during the night of the 19th–20th a small post in front of La Quinque Rue was captured, and Corporal T. G. Earl, of the 2/ Welsh Fusiliers, distinguished himself at Richebourg l'Avoué by bringing in wounded men on five separate occasions, eventually being himself struck down.

On Thursday, May 20, the rain ceased, but the day was dull and cloudy. Between 7 and 8 p.m. the Canadians brilliantly seized certain points to the north-east of the Festubert-La Quinque road, including an orchard. Some prisoners and machine guns were captured. The 21st, apart from an artillery duel, was uneventful, though some slight progress was made

near Festubert. The next day the 51st (Highland) Division was attached to the Indian Corps, and the Canadians repulsed three very severe hostile counter-attacks from the direction of Chapelle St. Roch, the enemy suffering heavy loss.

But the Germans were still capable of further effort. The 7th Prussian Army Corps, now strongly reinforced, made on Sunday, May 23, another effort to break through the Canadian line near Festubert. They advanced in masses, and, as usual, were mowed down by shrapnel, machine-gun and rifle fire. Many of their batteries had been silenced during the day. On the 24th and 25th the 47th Division (2nd London Territorials) carried some of the enemy's trenches, and in the centre on the 24th near Bois Grenier, between Armentières and Neuve Chapelle, a slight success was gained. During the night several attacks made by the Germans near Festubert were repulsed.

" I had now reasons to consider," says Sir John French, " that the battle which was commenced by the 1st Army on May 9 and renewed on the 16th, having attained for the moment the immediate object I had in view, should not be further actively proceeded with. . . . In the battle of Festubert the enemy was driven from a position which was strongly entrenched and fortified, and ground was won on a front of four miles to an average depth of 600 yards.'

The advantage gained was, in space, perhaps small, but measured by moral standards great. Immediately after the failure of the Germans to gas and blast their way through to Ypres, British troops, fighting as ever with clean hands and without the assistance of an overwhelming artillery, had broken through an elaborately fortified German position. In bayoneting, bombing, and whatever requires personal courage in the individual, they had again displayed a marked superiority over those opposed to them.

We have already given some examples of the daring and noble courage exhibited by certain regiments, officers and men during the desperate fighting from Saturday, May 15, to Tuesday, May 18. Those examples were not exceptional. A few more instances of British heroism may fittingly conclude this chapter.

Private J. Jones, of the Scots Fusiliers, repeatedly carried messages over dangerous ground. He was mortally wounded on the last of his important errands. Summoning up his

READY TO START FOR THE TRENCHES.

An evening scene near the battle-line. British troops about to start for the trenches carrying sacks of coke, planks of wood and broken up packing cases for making fires, and, in addition to full pack and rifle, the men carry parcels of food.

last strength he waved the paper he was carrying to attract the notice of his comrades. The message was taken by one of them from his dead body. Lieut. A. T. Quinlan, R.A.M.C., attached to the same regiment, was dangerously wounded while tending a wounded man in the open. Shells were bursting around him. He forbade two stretcher-bearers in a neighbouring trench to come to his assistance.

Lieutenant Graham, of the Essex Regiment, who accompanied the Fusiliers, was a man of exceptional height, and therefore an easy mark for the enemy. The Colonel of the Fusiliers advised him to keep at the rear of the attacking party. When the charge began, he rushed ahead and was almost immediately shot down. Lance-Corporal J. Lonigan, of the 60th Rifles, a stretcher-bearer, was buried by the explosion of a shell. No sooner was he dug out than he resumed his duties as if nothing out of the way had happened to him. Second-Lieutenant Lloyd Jones, of the Yorkshires, was bombing a trench. A German sniper from behind a hedge killed a non-commissioned officer by his side. The Lieutenant, creeping forward, flung his grenade with such excellent aim that two German soldiers were blown up and the sniper's hand was smashed to pieces. The 8th Royal Scots, a Territorial Battalion brought into the front line, remained through the thickest of the fighting and proved itself worthy of those it joined. Its gallant commander, Lieut.-Colonel Brook, was killed by a shell on the third day.

Of the work of the Royal Engineers and the Royal Army Medical Corps it is superfluous to speak. One section of the Engineers from late in the afternoon of Sunday to 3 a.m. on Monday under constant shell and rifle fire constructed two trenches, one nearly two hundred yards long and six feet deep. The stretcher-bearers and orderlies of the R.A.M.C. moved in the deadliest areas as unconcernedly as if they were in a hospital ward. Both the artillery observers and the signallers who were responsible for the telephone communication between the fighting line and the batteries and head-quarters also displayed the utmost gallantry.

Modern war is shorn of much if not all its ancient pageantry, but for practical fighting our men still possess the heroic qualities of the race.

The Canadians rendered invaluable assist-ance in the last phase of the battle of Festubert, as they had previously done in the fighting round Ypres when the Germans first opened their gas retorts. Collectively they lived or died up to the reputation which they had gained in the St. Julien trenches. Of the acts of gallantry performed by individuals the following may be mentioned :

Private H. T. Cameron, attached to the Field Ambulance of the 1st Canadian Division, volunteered on the night of May 20–1 to assist in collecting the wounded in an orchard cap-tured from the enemy. Of the seven men who accompanied him four fell. He was awarded the Medal for Distinguished Conduct. On May 23 Colour-Sergeant J. Hay, of the 8th Canadian Infantry Battalion, after all the officers had been killed or wounded, took com-mand of his company, and by his coolness and gallantry rallied them and kept them steady throughout the day. Private E. H. Hester, of the 5th Canadian Infantry Battalion, who had already distinguished himself on the 20th, 21st and 22nd, on the 24th led an attack-ing party, and with it entered a bomb-proof shelter, cutting the wires of a number of mines, and thus saving the lives of many of his com-rades.

BRITISH ARTILLERY GOING INTO ACTION.

CHAPTER LXXXIX.

AMERICAN OPINION AND THE FIRST YEAR OF WAR.

GERMAN POPULATION IN THE UNITED STATES—OPINION IN AMERICA—RESPONSIBILITY FOR THE WAR—GERMAN PROPAGANDA—EDUCATIONAL CAMPAIGN—COUNT BERNSTORFF—HERR DERNBURG DISMISSED—*The New York World's* EXPOSURES—THE FATHERLAND—AMERICAN NEUTRALITY—EXPORT OF MUNITIONS—THE ARCHIBALD EXPOSURES—DR. DUMBA RECALLED—MR. ROOSEVELT, COLONEL WATTERSON, AND OTHER PRO-ALLIES' OPINION—GERMAN SUBMARINE " BLOCKADE "—AMERICAN SHIPS SUNK—THE LUSITANIA—UNITED STATES NOTES TO GERMANY—RESIGNATION OF MR. BRYAN—SINKING OF THE ARABIC.

NOTWITHSTANDING the large proportion of people of German birth in America, the cause for which the Allies were fighting was sure from the first of a large measure of American sympathy. The United States Government, of course, at once proclaimed an official neutrality. Indeed it was the only first-class Power of the Western world that could maintain an attitude of even comparative detachment towards the combatants. During the first year of the war this attitude was maintained in spite of the utterly lawless and abominably inhuman acts perpetrated by the German Government against innocent American citizens : acts which severely tried the President's patience. But the formal attitude of the Government is one thing : that of the American masses another.

The relative importance of the German population is usually greatly exaggerated in discussing the activities of the German-Americans. It is true that of the total foreign-born population 25 per cent. were of German birth, but on the other hand 24 per cent. were born in the British Empire. To carry the comparison a point further, it will be found that whilst Germany and her Allies represent

33 per cent. of the total foreign-born population, as reported by the last United States Census (1910), Great Britain and her Allies represent 54 per cent. It is evident that the German-Americans in the United States from the outbreak of the war created a noise out of proportion to their numerical importance. Had the British Canadian, Italian, Russian, and other nationalities identified with the Allies conducted themselves in a similar manner, an intolerable condition of affairs would have resulted, which might have ended in civil riots. Happily this was not the case. Whilst Germans and Austro-Hungarians, backed by their Embassies, used the neutral territory of the United States to disseminate the most shameless propaganda and encourage deeds of violence, representatives of the Allied nations retained a dignified and law-abiding attitude towards the Republic that had offered them hospitality and broader opportunities. For these and other reasons the sentiments of the American people were overwhelmingly on our side. They were not slow to see, in spite of German propaganda to the contrary, that this was a war fastened upon Europe by the arrogant ambition of one Power, that Great Britain

went to the uttermost lengths of persuasion in order to avert it, and that in entering upon it she acted under compulsion of irresistible obligations of honour and duty as well as of self-interest.

The relations of the United States with Germany, it should be borne in mind, were, and had been for a generation or more, of a close and cordial character. It is true that of late years German emigration had declined, but this was, in part at least, made up by the increase of travel and commerce, and by the extension of financial connexions between the

DR. WALTER H. PAGE,
American Ambassador in London.

two countries. It was further helped by the establishment of splendidly equipped German steamship lines plying between New York and Hamburg and Bremen ; by the interchange of American University professors with those from German Universities ; and by the broadened relations resulting from common studies in science, literature and music. In all these departments of knowledge Germany exercised a distinct influence on the people of the United States. Throughout the United States there existed a deep feeling of friendship for the German people, and an equal admiration for what were supposed to be their ideals and matchless progress. Many Germans fought on the side of the North in the Civil War. Next to the British, German emigration to the United States had always been the most satisfactory in every respect. The Germans were law-abiding, industrious, thrifty, and, until the war brought about the awakening,

were regarded as sound and loyal citizens of the country of their adoption. Certainly no prejudice existed in any quarter against Germans, therefore to their own acts alone must be attributed the stupendous change of sentiment which took place during the first year of the war. The wanton and barbarous destruction of Belgium, the murder of innocent non-combatants and women and children on the high seas and in undefended towns and watering places, caused a powerful revulsion of sentiment against the Germans. The friends of Germany, both in the Universities, where exchanges of professorships had introduced new and intimate ties between the Republic and the Empire, and in the scientific institutions, as well as those engaged in trade, commerce and finance, were amazed to find men they had hitherto regarded as civilized advocating and defending the most barbarous acts of war. It took some time for men who had enjoyed intimate relations with Germany and the Germans to identify their late friends and colleagues after they had thrown aside their masks. The amiable, engaging Dr. Jekylls became distorted into bloodthirsty Mr. Hydes, and it was not surprising that their American friends failed to recognize them.

One of the earliest and most striking illustrations of this awakening occurred before the destruction of the Lusitania sent a wave of unspeakable horror throughout the length and breadth of the United States. In October, 1914, a manifesto, signed by 93 of the most prominent men of Germany, distinguished in various branches of science, art, education and literature, was circulated broadcast throughout America. It was entitled "An Appeal to the Civilized World" * and in it an attempt was made to change public opinion in the United States on the subject of the war. Judged by the weight and importance of the names attached to it, this document should have served the purpose intended, but unhappily for the enemy the American public were not to be influenced by mere assertions, even when promulgated by men of great distinction. That public decided to go deeper than the surface in its search for truth. The most comprehensive reply to the manifesto of the German professors was that made by Samuel Harden Church, President Carnegie Institute, Pittsburg.† After assuring the pro-

---

* This document is printed in full in Vol. V., page 168
†Published in full by *The Times* in pamphlet form.

DR. WOODROW WILSON,
President of the United States of America.

(From a portrait painted specially for " The Times History of the War.")

243

PROFESSOR SAMUEL HARDEN CHURCH,
Of the Carnegie Institute, Pittsburg.

fessors of the esteem in which many of them were held in America, of the appreciation of their eminent services to humanity, and reminding them that their names were as well known in America as in Germany, Mr. Church proceeded to say that it would be impossible for America to take sides against Germany unjustly or from prejudice. Whilst earnestly striving to maintain an impartial neutrality, Americans would at the same time earnestly strive to find the right and condemn the wrong, because neutrality can never mean indifference. In short, the American people, having divested themselves of prejudice, proceeded to study the evidence in order that public opinion might conform to the facts. After remarking that it was pathetic to note the importunity with which the people of Germany were seeking the good opinion of America in this strife, Mr. Church said :

Your letter speaks of Germany as being in a struggle " which has been forced upon her." That is the whole question ; all others are subsidiary. If this struggle was forced upon Germany, then indeed she stands in a position of mighty dignity and honour, and the whole world should acclaim her and succour her, to the utter confusion and punishment of the foes who have attacked her. But if this outrageous war was not forced upon her, would it not follow in the course of reason that her position is without dignity and honour, and that it is her foes who should be acclaimed and supported to the extreme limit of human sympathy ?

I believe that the judgment on this paramount question has been formed. That judgment is not based upon the lies and calumnies of the enemies of Germany, nor upon the careless publications contained in the newspapers, but upon a profound study of the official correspondence in the case. This correspondence has been published and disseminated by the respective Governments concerned in the war ; it has been reprinted in full in our leading newspapers, and with substantial fullness in our magazines, and has been republished in a complete pamphlet form in one huge edition after another by the *New York Times,* and again by the American Association for International Conciliation ; and the public demand for this indisputable evidence has not yet been satisfied, although many millions of our people have read it. These documents are known officially as (1) The Austro-Hungarian Note to Serbia. (2) The Serbian Reply. (3) The British White Paper. (4) The German White Book. (5) The Russian Yellow Book. (6) The Belgian Grey Book. They contain all the letters and dispatches which each government desired to publish to the world as its own justification for being at war. And, by the way, every man who studies these papers will regret two things ; first, that Germany has not dared to publish her correspondence with Austria, and, second, that Austria has not dared to publish her correspondence with Germany. If the world were in possession of this suppressed evidence, its judgment on the question of guilt would doubtless be greatly facilitated. But, in so far as they have been printed, all of these documents are before me as I write this letter ; I cannot help wondering whether they have been circulated in Germany ; I cannot help wishing that the German people might have the opportunity which my countrymen have had of reading these State papers in their fullness.

In concluding his spirited indictment of German methods and of the German professors, Mr. Church said :

And so, at last, we find ourselves shocked, ashamed and outraged that a Christian nation should be guilty of this criminal war. There was no justification for it. Armed and defended as you were, the whole world could never have broken into your borders. And while German culture still has something to gain from her neighbours, yet the intellectual progress which Germany was making seemed to be lifting up her own people to better things for themselves and to an altruistic service to mankind. Your great nation floated its ships in every ocean, sold its wares in the uttermost parts of the earth, and enjoyed the good favour of humanity, because it was trusted as a humane State. But now all this achievement has

DR. CHARLES W. ELIOT,
President Emeritus of Harvard.

WATCHING THE WAR BULLETINS IN NEW YORK.

Crowds coming out of the down-town offices in the evening watching the war bulletins outside the "World," "Sun" and "Tribune" offices. The skyscraper on the right is the Woolworth building.

vanished, all this good opinion has been destroyed. You cannot in half a century regain the spiritual and material benefits which you have lost. Oh, that we might have again a Germany that we could respect, a Germany of true peace, of true progress, of true culture, modest and not boastful, for ever rid of her war lords and her armed hosts, and turning once more to the uplifting influence of such leaders as Luther, Goethe, Beethoven, and Kant ! But Germany, whether you win or lose in this war, has fallen, and the once glorious nation must continue to pursue its course in darkness and murder until conscience at last bids it withdraw its armies back to its own

boundaries, there to hope for the world's pardon upon this inexpiable damnation.

Mr. Oswald Garrison Villard,* writing some months after Mr. Church, apparently came to precisely the same conclusions. Mr. Villard said :

So far as has been ascertained, no German publication of the complete English and French documents has been

---

* *Germany Embattled, an American Interpretation.*
By Oswald Garrison Villard.

59—2

attempted ; the public has learned of them almost wholly through partisan comments by their own editors. Thus the writer has been unable to discover in the German papers to which he has had access any fair discussion or publication of Belgium's official statement of her side of the case, and the documents bearing thereon. Of all the literature of the war, nothing is more impressive and convincing than this. But the *New Yorker Staats-Zeitung,* for one, made haste to abridge and bury it in an inconspicuous place.

Dr. Charles W. Eliot, President Emeritus of Harvard, in a letter to the *New York Times** touched on the same point in these words :

The pamphlets by German publicists and men of letters which are now coming to this country, and the various similar publications written here, seem to indicate that the German public is still kept by its Government in ignorance about the real antecedents of the war, and about many incidents and aspects of the portentous combat. These documents seem to Americans to contain a large amount of misinformation about the attack of Austria-Hungary on Serbia, the diplomatic negotiations and the correspondence between sovereigns. which immediately preceded the war, and the state of mind of the Belgian and English peoples.

Space must be found for one other opinion on the responsibility for the war, because the basis of all the German propaganda in America was that the war had been forced upon Germany. In October, 1914, the *New York Times* submitted the White, Orange, and Grey Books of Great Britain, Germany, Russia and Belgium to Mr. James M. Beck, formerly Assistant Attorney-General of the United States, and one of the leaders of the New York Bar, and asked him to consider the evidence submitted to determine the legal responsibility for the war. Mr. Beck's brief occupied two pages in the *New York Times,* and is a close analysis of the testimony presented. His full arguments will be found in the pages of a pamphlet printed by *The Times,* from which is reproduced here only the " judgment," which in Mr. Beck's opinion " an impartial court would not hesitate to pass " :

1. That Germany and Austria in a time of profound peace secretly concerted together to impose their will upon Europe and upon Serbia in a manner affecting the balance of power in Europe. Whether in so doing they intended to precipitate a European war to determine the mastery of Europe is not satisfactorily established, although their whole course of conduct suggests this as a possibility. They made war almost inevitable by (a) issuing an ultimatum that was grossly unreasonable and disproportionate to any grievance that Austria had, and (b) in giving to Serbia, and Europe, insufficient time to consider the rights and obligations of all interested nations.

2. That Germany had at all times the power to compel Austria to preserve a reasonable and conciliatory course, but at no time effectively exerted that influence. On the contrary, she certainly abetted and possibly instigated, Austria in its unreasonable course.

3. That England, France, Italy, and Russia at all times sincerely worked for peace, and for this purpose

* Published October 2, 1914.

not only overlooked the original misconduct of Austria but made every reasonable concession in the hope of preserving peace.

4. That Austria having mobilized its army, Russia was reasonably justified in mobilizing its forces. Such act of mobilization was the right of any sovereign State, and as long as the Russian armies did not cross the border or take any aggressive action no other nation had any just right to complain, each having the same right to make similar preparations.

5. That Germany, in abruptly declaring war against Russia for failure to demobilize when the other Powers had offered to make any reasonable concession and peace parleys were still in progress, precipitated the war.

This impartial and neutral American jurist declared that in his judgment Germany and Austria were responsible for the war ; that Germany had it in her power to compel Austria to preserve a reasonable course, but did not exert that influence ; that England, France, Italy and Russia sincerely worked for peace, and that Germany in abruptly declaring war against Russia precipitated the war. Mr. Beck adds that he reached these conclusions with reluctance, as he had a feeling of deep affection and admiration for the German people. But " the German nation has been plunged into this abyss by scheming statesmen and its self-centred and highly neurotic Kaiser, who in the twentieth century sincerely believes he is the proxy of Almighty God on earth, and therefore infallible."

It will be seen that the very foundation of the German propaganda in America had been undermined. After failure in the endeavour to convince America that the Allies were the aggressors, there remained only the more difficult task of trying to demonstrate that it is right for a great nation to trample under foot another people because in her judgment her welfare demands that the weaker shall pay the price, to hide, distort, and travesty the facts, and to carry out an organized campaign against the truth. Great Britain, Russia, France and Italy did not find it necessary to initiate a propaganda abroad on behalf of their soldiers, their motives, or their policies. The Allies bore themselves with rare dignity and restraint, and their qualities of self-control contrasted favourably with the German propagandists, who sought to conquer hostile American opinion by the lowest and most disreputable methods.

The attitude of Great Britain in all this sordid business was simply one of anxiety, just anxiety, to have the moral support of the American people in this war for liberty and right. But we knew that it was behind

Left : At home in New Jersey.
Right : With his Secretary.

At a Naval Review.

A DAY WITH DR. WOODROW WILSON, PRESIDENT OF THE UNITED STATES.

us, and it was hardly becoming in us, while it might be disagreeable to the American Government, that we should openly solicit the good opinion that was already given us so freely. We were conscious of our own good right. The facts were before America as they were before the rest of the world. We were content that she should form her own judgment upon them.

The "German educational campaign" in the United States was undertaken by Herr Dernburg, who arrived in America on August 25, 1914, accompanying the German Ambassador, Count Bernstorff, who, at the outbreak of war, was at home on leave of absence. He euphemistically described his mission as "the enlisting of American support for the German Red Cross." The real purpose of this German emissary, however, was not long in developing, and under the direction of Count Bernstorff, the German Ambassador, a gigantic campaign was organized to feed the American public with German news and views, and to deflect their sympathies, if possible, from Great Britain to the side of Germany. The choice of Dernburg was characteristic of German methods. Twenty-five years before the war this son of a Berlin Jewish journalist had been a

MR. HERMAN RIDDER,
Editor of the *New Yorker Staats-Zeitung.*

volunteer bank clerk in Wall Street, and his methods were always regarded in Germany as "American." After a fairly successful business career he was "invented" by Prince Bülow at the end of 1906 to become Colonial Secretary, and to run the "national" elections to the Reichstag on a colonial issue which Bülow had forced for his own ends. The election campaign, which was managed on lines new in Germany, was successful, and Dernburg increased his reputation. It was, however, quickly discovered that a Jewish Minister was impossible in Prussia as soon as he had ceased to be actually necessary to his masters, and during a political crisis in 1910 Dernburg, anticipating his certain fate, took refuge in resignation. In the years before the war he had lost all influence in Germany, and to those who knew his situation it seemed something like an insult to the United States that he should suddenly be brought out of his retirement "to bamboozle the Americans." Dernburg had no lack of assistants. The American Embassy alone provided him with people like the naval attaché, Captain Boy-Ed, better known for his work in the Tirpitz press bureau than for his knowledge of the sea.

There were other lesser lights, and strong banking and other friends in America who volunteered to help in moulding public opinion. The Kaiser apparently felt sure of the support of the German-American population, but it was noted soon after the destruction of Belgium that the Kaiser's popularity with at least four-fifths of the American people was decidedly on the wane. The principal newspaper organs of these worthies were Mr. Herman Ridder's *New Yorker Staats-Zeitung*, once, but no longer, a paper of considerable influence, and Mr. Hearst's *New Yorker Morgen Journal.* There were many less important journals printed in German and perhaps others in English that were brought into line. New German organs were founded for the special purposes of German war propaganda. Most notorious among these latter journals was the *Fatherland*, edited by Herr Viereck, who claimed that he was "America's foremost living poet." From the headquarters in New York emanated a continuous stream of "statements" by the Ambassador, "letters to the public" from Dr. Dernburg, "addresses" and magazine articles by Dr. Hugo Muensterberg, who occupied the Chair of Psychology at Harvard. In short, the "news syndicate"

(From the " New York Tribune.")
DR. DERNBURG.
Will he take his dog with him?

statements received publicity in the leading journals of the country, reaching all the way from New York to the Golden Gate.

The movement was conducted with characteristic thoroughness and characteristic want of scruple. The Consular Service was mobilized, the German societies, which seek to preserve a separate German *Stimmung* amongst the German citizens of the United States, were marshalled and set to work; even German firms were employed to bring pressure on the American Press by furtive menaces of withdrawing support unless news and comments on the war were manipulated in German interests. Newspapers, as we have said, were purchased, and German newspapers published

methods so well known in America were worked for "all they were worth," and the "big drum" was beaten so loudly from Maine to California that at first it seemed likely that the purpose in view would at least partially be accomplished.

Such, then, were the *personnel* and their methods widely developed by the German Government for the purpose of working up public sentiment in the United States. An American correspondent in *The Times*, in commenting on the campaign said :

The general assault on American public opinion began with the moment of Count Bernstorff's arrival. He ceased to be an Ambassador and became a Press Agent Extraordinary and Publicity Promoter Plenipotentiary. The German Embassy in Washington put up its shutters as a diplomatic establishment and was converted into a news agency. The American newspapers were drenched with Ambassadorial communicativeness. The New York journals which had reporters to whom Count Bernstorff could pour out his heart got interviews measurable only in columns. To the great Press outside New York Count Bernstorff spoke through the medium of "statements" to the New York offices of the two leading American news agencies. For a week or ten days not a morning or evening journal of consequence in the United States went to press without some fresh effusion from Bernstorff. Now it was an "official denial" of the latest act of German brutality. Then there would be some new braggart prognostication of Germany's "absolute invincibility." To vary the monotony of Bernstorff's *pronunciamentos*, Captain Boy-Ed was now impressed into service, and he began feeding the Press with "interviews" and "statements." Then Dr. Dernburg was "put on the job." His *début* consisted of a long, carefully-prepared brief arguing the German case with the finesse of a shrewd counsel for the defence, for the Kaiser's cause in America was now at a point where it urgently required rehabilitation. By "news syndicate" methods widely developed in the United States, Dr. Dernburg's

DR. DERNBURG
Of the German Press Bureau in America.

COUNT VON BERNSTORFF,
German Ambassador at Washington, with his
American wife and daughter.

in the United States subsidized. Publicity
agencies of all kinds were employed for the
dissemination of news and articles favourable
to Germany, and correspondents in the pay of
the German Government were sent abroad for
the purpose of extolling German methods and
German arms, describing German " victories,"
and " interviewing " the military and political
leaders.* There never had been such a satur-
nalia of falsehood, calumny, and clumsy fictions
as this revelry of corruption, inaugurated and
carried out in the United States by Count
Bernstorff and his satellites. The sum of
money expended must have been enormous,

* See, for instance, the White Paper *re* Mr. James
F. J. Archibald referred to below. Thus Count Bernstorff writes to Mr. Archibald :—" I have heard with
pleasure that you wish once more to return to Germany
and Austria, after having promoted our interests out
here in such a zealous and successful manner," while he
notifies the German Frontier Customs Authorities that
Mr. Archibald " is proceeding to Germany with photographic apparatus, etc., in order there to collect material
for lectures in the United States of America in the
interests of the German cause."

some estimates giving the amount at £400,000 per week. But, as we shall presently see, when the sinking of the Lusitania caused the exit of Herr Dernburg, a series of damaging exposures, and the publication referred to below of Austrian and German papers found in possession of Mr. James F. J. Archibald, shed new light on these pitiful conspiracies to delude the American public, and it was found that these dishonest wares were not suited for the American market.

In spite of some vicissitudes and several exposures as to methods employed, Herr Dernburg's work continued until in May, 1915, he began a campaign the purpose of which was to justify the crime of the sinking of the Lusitania and the murder by Germans of innocent women and children. His defence of this was so callous and brutal that it sent a thrill of disgust throughout the country, and American newspapers began an agitation for his expulsion. As a first step to that end it was reported that the American Government had asked Count Bernstorff to explain the precise nature of Herr Dernburg's mission, and at the same time had suggested that Count Bernstorff's legitimate duties would be facilitated by Dernburg's elimination. Realizing

that his usefulness was at an end, the German Government granted the informal request, and Dernburg having obtained through the American Government a safe conduct from the British Government, left for Germany June 13, 1915, on board a Norwegian ship. It was generally conceded by the American Press that any Englishman who had taken the liberties Dernburg had taken with American hospitality would have been ejected much sooner. Thus the principal advocate of German barbarity and the nominal head of the missionary work ignominiously disappeared.

However much the loss of Herr Dernburg may have affected the character of the work done by the German Embassy Press Bureau, it did not curtail in any way its activities. From influencing the public Press and individuals it spent money lavishly in the promotion of strikes and the employment of spies, and engaged in every sort of intrigue to poison public opinion and cripple the legitimate industries of the United States. In August, 1915, a crushing exposure of these German plots was published in the *New York World*, and German treachery in America was brought to light. The exposure began by the publication of a series of secret Government docu-

COMMANDERS OF GERMAN WAR VESSELS.

Captain Thiedfelder of the "Kronprinz Wilhelm" on left, and Captain Thierichens of "Prinz Eitel Friedrich" on right. Both these vessels were interned in America in April, 1915.

(From the "Cape Times.")

LEAVING THE DOOR OPEN.

Hans—"Call off that dog: my Franz wants a
  drink."
Jonathan—"'Taint MY dog.   The water's fer all
  of 'em (AS CAN GET IT)."

ments which were lost by, or according to the
German version, stolen from Privy Councillor
Dr. Albert in the Elevated Railway, New York.
This exposure, in the words of that journal,
"raises for the first time the curtain that has
hitherto concealed the activities and purposes of
the official German propaganda in the United
States."   The documents suggested that Count
Bernstorff had at his command a revenue of
about £400,000 weekly.   This money was
used not only for the suborning of American
public opinion, but for the purposes of promoting strikes in munition factories, for
agitation against, and for an embargo on the
exportation of munitions.   Perhaps the most
damning document from the *World's* portfolio
of secret German papers was a report made to
the German Chancellor by one Waetzoldt, who
signed himself "Commercial Expert," and
wrote on the Consul General's notepaper, suggesting the best means to foment American
trade irritation against Great Britain.   After
expressing hopes that the cotton question
would soon become acute, the Chancellor's
Consular Agent observed :

From the German standpoint, pressure on the American Government can be strengthened by the interruption
of deliveries from Germany, even if the British Government should permit exceptions.   Those shipments
especially should be interrupted which American industries so badly require, especially chemical and dye
stuffs, as also goods which are used in the realm of fine
arts.   Withholding of goods is the surest means of

occasioning the representation to the Administration in
Washington of American interests.   Those protests
have most weight which come from American industries
which employ many workers.   The complaint of one of
the great American dye factories, which declared that
the continued withholding of dye stuffs would make
necessary the dismissal of 4,000 workmen, has done more
than the protest of importers.   A copy of this report is
being forwarded to the Imperial German Embassy.

The document was signed "Waetzoldt, Trade
Expert to his Excellency the Imperial Chancellor von Bethmann-Hollweg," and was
headed : "Regarding protests of American
importers of German and Austrian goods
against the British Order in Council."   Money,
it was shown by these letters, had been freely
expended for the purpose of fomenting strikes,
with the connivance of disloyal trade union
leaders.   An official in the office of the Military
Attaché of the German Embassy in Washington
was shown to have been in communication
with certain labour leaders for the purpose of
bringing about strikes in ammunition and
motor-car factories.   Conferences were actually
held, it appears, between agents of the German
Government and these labour leaders just
before the strikes at the Remington and other
works.

An important feature of the campaign was
an elaborate scheme to control the Press of the
United States—mainly through the American
Press Association—to establish newspapers

(From "Collier's Weekly.")

ANOTHER VICTORY.

And another Iron Cross for von Tirpitz.

THE DICTATOR. *From a German Cartoon.*

and news services, finance lecturers and film
exhibitions, and publish pamphlets and books
—all for the purpose of dividing the American
people to the advantage of the German Empire.
In furtherance of this aim the German Government was clearly shown to be a financial
backer of the *Fatherland* and similar pro-
German apologists. The correspondence as
published consisted mainly of facsimile letters
from Herr von Stumm, the head of the Political
Department of the German Foreign Office,
from Count Bernstorff, and from Dr. Hein-
rich Albert, chief financial agent of the German Government. George Sylvester Viereck,
editor of the *Fatherland*, appeared in the correspondence as an applicant for £300 sterling a
month. He acknowledged the receipt of £50,
and announced that he would send to the secretary to obtain the rest. In reply Dr. Albert
promised payment, but demanded the control
of the *Fatherland* counting house and an
agreement regarding the policy to be pursued

MR. ROBERT LANSING,
American Secretary of State.

by that journal.* Herr von Stumm wrote on behalf of Herr von Bethmann-Hollweg to Count Bernstorff, recommending that the expenses of the second visit to Germany of Mr. Edward Lyell Fox, an American journalist "who on the occasion of his last visit was most useful to us by reason of his good reports," be paid out of the funds of a German information service. Count Bernstorff approved the recommendation of the Chancellor, and wrote to Captain von Papen, the Military Attaché, instructing him to get in touch with Mr. Fox. The most interesting feature of the *World's* disclosures, however, was the reproduction of an ambitious scheme forwarded to the German Foreign Office for the inauguration of a news agency to supply American newspapers with German "information." The author of this scheme said :

In order to carry through our aim it is necessary to begin to carry through a Press agitation which is adapted

* Count Bernstorff's story is that Mr. Viereck refused to carry out the necessary conditions :—" Mr. Albert made it clear to him [Viereck] that we are not in agreement with his attacks on the Administration, and especially on the President, and that we could not give him any extensive support, however justifiable his claims might be in view of his friendly attitude towards Germany, unless he would grant us a sufficient control of the editing of the paper to enable us to prevent such attacks."

to the character, wishes, and way of thinking of the American public. Everything must be communicated to them in the form of news, as they have been accustomed to this, and only understand this kind of propaganda. For the distribution of news we have in view it will be absolutely necessary to found a new American news syndicate with German money. This has been accomplished by the United States Corporation, without them letting it become known that German money is behind it.

An elaborate scheme for the establishment of this bogus news association was worked out, the aim being to give American newspapers and magazines news and pictures. These articles were to be so subtly manipulated that the fact of their being pro-German was to be disguised from the guileless American editor, who was to be " spoon-fed " daily with this valuable " news " to the extent of from 3,000 to 4,000 words by wireless. This was to be sent with suitable pictures from Germany, Austria-Hungary, Turkey, and the Balkan States. On the eastern and western fronts " well-known popular American correspondents " were to be stationed, " who shall have access to all the material they absolutely require." A special Chinese service was even planned to counter-weigh " against the Japanese propaganda." A list of topics not to be dealt with by this precious news association was supplied as a guidance for German official propagandists. The list included :

1. The Belgian neutrality question as well as the question of Belgian atrocities should not be mentioned any more.

2. It should not be tried any more to put the blame for the world war and its consequences on England alone, as a considerable English element exists in America and the American people hold to the view that all parties are partly guilty for the war.

3. The pride and imagination of Americans and the regard for their culture should not be continually offended by the assertion that German culture is the only real culture and surpasses everything else.

In this way, and by methods that came close to being criminal, was the American public to be gulled. The exposures of the *World* connected not only the German Embassy in America and its principal officials, but the Foreign Office in Berlin itself with these scurvy tricks to mould public opinion, and if possible embroil the American Government with that of Great Britain. The *World's* exposure of the plot was opportune, and had the effect of curbing the activities of the German Government in the more hazardous enterprises. In short, the first year of this so-called campaign for moral support in America was a failure. The Germans had utterly failed to understand the American temperament. Bad as their case was they actually made it worse by their clumsy methods, which included, as we have seen, plots to destroy life and property, the forging of passports, the making of false affidavits, and the promotion of strikes. Though the Germans might pride themselves on their scientific method of getting to the root of a subject, with all their knowledge of America and Americans, they never got to the root of the American mind. The attempts during the first year of the war, both individually and collectively, to mould the public opinion of the United States were alike dismal failures. The American mind, perhaps more given to generalizing than to analysing, was at first slow to see what this " propaganda " work really was, but in the end it appeared that they saw both the men and the deeds they accomplished in their proper proportions. In all this work the Germans left out of account the fact that Americans, like Englishmen, are accustomed to form their own judgment in politics as in other matters. American opinion not only refused to be deluded by the shallow tricks of the German Embassy and propagandists, but it went straight ahead to the deeper issues of the war. It noted with Dr. Eliot and others that German militarism and all which it implied were the root causes of the conflict. It plainly discerned that " the fingerprint of the militarist " was stamped upon Louvain as it was upon Zabern. It realized that this militarist code was the direct negative of all civilization, all progress, and all morality, as the world had hitherto understood them. Only by their extermination could the ideals and principles which the democracy of the United States, like the democracy of England, loved and reverenced with their whole strength, be preserved to them and to mankind. The German propaganda did far more to awaken the American people to that truth, and to their own immense moral interests in the results of the war.

It is not possible in the space allotted to discuss the question of American neutrality in all its varied phases. As we have seen, the Government at the outbreak of the war declared itself absolutely neutral—as one eminent writer expressed it, " neutral in letter and in spirit." This was the Government attitude, and President Wilson's most inveterate enemy would hardly accuse him of not having lived up to his declaration. It has been said that the best proof of impartiality is that both sides are dissatisfied, and to a certain extent this may be said to be true. The " fierce neutrality " of ex-President Roosevelt would have favoured a declaration of war upon Germany ; whilst the friends of Germany would have liked the United States Government to have stopped the exports of munitions of war, and to have bought up the many interned German vessels, in order that the proceeds of the sale might have gone to Germany. The German-Americans, ignoring the fact that the German Government had always maintained and, wherever possible, exercised the right to sell munitions of war to belligerents, incessantly clamoured for the prohibition of the sale of munitions of war to England and France. When Mr. Bryan, American Secretary of State, in his letter to Senator Stone,* in a remarkably clear and cogent statement ruled in favour of the Allies, the pro-German press loudly complained of it as far too friendly to Great Britain. With characteristic mendacity the subsidized German Press of America, and the Governmentally controlled Press organs of Germany,

* Letter from the Secretary of State, Mr. Bryan, to Mr. Stone, Chairman of the Senate Foreign Relations Committee, defending the neutrality of the United States in the European War, January 24, 1915.

MR. JAMES WATSON GERARD,
United States Ambassador at Berlin.

proceeded to accuse Mr. Bryan of "flunkeyism towards England," and President Wilson of allowing England to dictate his Notes (see the cartoon taken from a German paper, printed on p. 253). The *Cologne Gazette* of February 8, 1915, concluded three columns of abusive criticism with the following outburst :

> It is the brutal British standard of might which finds expression in this American utterance. England is supreme at sea, therefore neither right nor reason, neither international agreements nor any other principles of universal law, can have sway. This is the language of the same man, Mr. Bryan, who formerly and with such self-complacence played the part of an apostle of universal peace. We are certain that the German-Americans and those who think with them will not fail to give his epistle the answer it deserves.

A few months later, as we shall see, when Mr. Bryan resigned office because he did not

Stone, the Senator from Missouri, where the German-Americans were strong, for information with which he might answer the complaints of his constituents. This it did so comprehensively, categorically, and authoritatively—the President is said to have taken a hand in its preparation—as to elicit the praise, irrespective of party, of nearly all the responsible newspapers of the country. We cannot follow Mr. Bryan through all the twenty specific points with which he dealt in this document. It is enough to say that he showed that the action of the Washington Government was based upon legal principle, and proved that in no instance had that Government exhibited the slightest bias in favour of either party. He swept away, once for all, a whole mass of

MR. WILLIAM J. BRYAN.
Ex-American Secretary of State.

MR. THEODORE ROOSEVELT.
Ex-President of the United States.

agree with President Wilson's attitude in relation to the sinking of the Lusitania, these same organs of the German Government, both at home and in America, were as freely beslavering Mr. Bryan with their nauseous flattery as they were in February bespattering him with their malignant abuse. In his letter to Mr. Stone, the Secretary of State, Mr. Bryan, refuted at length the charges persistently made by the pro-Germans that the United States Government had "shown partiality" to the Allies at the expense of Germany and Austria-Hungary. The letter, which at the time of its publication was regarded as the most remarkable document which the war had produced in America, was written in response to a request by Mr.

German and pro-German fictions, and placed the American people in the position in which Great Britain had particularly wished them to be—the position to know and to judge the facts for themselves. There are, we need hardly remark, certain points in international law as it affects neutral rights, and in the application of that law to particular circumstances, on which the English and the American view differed. But, subject to this reserve, it may be said, broadly speaking, that the doctrine laid down by Mr. Bryan was the doctrine of our own Courts. Perhaps the most important of Mr. Bryan's replies to the broader of the pro-German arguments was that in which he refuted the charge of general unfriendliness towards Germany and her ally. He pointed out with unanswerable truth that any suspicion on this head which the friends of Germany and Austria might have felt arose from the undeniable fact that " on the high seas German and Austro-Hungarian naval power is, thus far, inferior to the British." It followed, he showed them, that Great Britain could prevent contraband from reaching Germany and Austria, but that Germany and Austria could not prevent contraband from reaching us. It was not the duty of the United States or of other neutrals to do for them what they were powerless to do for themselves. The friends of Germany had assumed that it was America's business to prevent all trade in contraband and " thus to equalize the difference due to the relative naval strength of the belligerents. No such obligation," Mr. Bryan instructed them, " existed." The fact that Germany and Austria-Hungary could not draw upon the American markets in the face of our naval superiority did not make it the duty of America to close her markets to us. They were open upon equal terms to everybody who was strong enough at sea to get access to them. As Uncle Sam remarks in a cartoon on page 252, " 'Taint MY dog. The water's fer all of 'em (as can get it)." In commenting on the letter, *The Times* of January 26, 1915, said :

Mr. Bryan's defence of American neutrality, taken as a whole, can be unpalatable only to those who wish to see that neutrality surreptitiously infringed. There are, as we have said, points on which we do not see eye to eye with him. But as we and our Allies share the desire of the American people that their neutrality should be real and not a sham, and as we recognize and follow the general doctrines upon which it is founded, Mr. Bryan's letter commends itself to us as an admirable exposition of the policy which becomes the greatest of neutral peoples.

It must not for a moment be supposed that this trenchant declaration, showing that the sale of ammunition by the United States to the Allies was a well-established usage of nations and that Germany herself had furnished enormous quantities of arms and ammunition to belligerents in the Russo-Japanese War and in the Balkan Wars, satisfied the German-Americans. Failing to gain their point by fair means, the Kaiser's spies and agents in the United States tried foul methods, and began a campaign of intimidation and, on a small scale, one of " frightfulness." Allies' war material was burnt, and mysterious fires broke out in various parts of the United States, generally in factories manufacturing war material. One large establishment engaged on munitions of war was burnt down. German agents crossed the frontier to Canada perpetrating dynamite outrages, and breaches of neutrality were committed in the most reckless manner. Appeals, signed by hundreds of the publishers and editors of the subsidized foreign press in America, were sent to factories where foreign-born citizens were engaged in making munitions, calling upon them to desist from the work. When this failed, more drastic methods were attempted. Strikes were organized and engineered by the use of German money and the employment of German agents, and foreign-born workmen were denounced as traitors to their countries, and threatened by the German and Austro-Hungarian Ambassadors with severe punishment if they continued to labour in what President Wilson had called the " legitimate industries of the country "—the manufacture of munitions of war. While engaged in this propaganda and intimidation Count Bernstorff, three months after (April, 1915) Mr. Bryan had so fully disposed of the question of the trade in arms, had the impertinence to address another Note, in which he formally charged the United States with departing from her neutrality in favour of Great Britain. To this, however, he received from Mr. Bryan the following courteous but sharp rebuke :

I note with sincere regret that, in discussing the sale and exportation of arms to the enemies of Germany, your Excellency seems under the impression that it was within the choice of the Government of the United States to inhibit this trade, and that its failure manifested an unfair attitude towards Germany. This Government holds that any changes in its own laws of neutrality during the progress of the war which would affect unequally the relations of the United States with the nations at war would be an unjustifiable departure from the principle of strict neutrality by which it has consistently sought to direct its actions. I respectfully submit that none of the circumstances urged alters the principle involved. The placing of an embargo on the trade in arms at the present time would constitute such a change and would be a direct violation of the neutrality of the United States. It will be clear that, holding this view, and considering itself in honour bound thereby, it is out of the question for this Government to consider such a course.

The question of justifying exports of munitions was also brought up by the Austro-Hungarian Government in a protest addressed to the American Ambassador in Vienna, on June 29, to the effect that a neutral Government could not be allowed to trade in contraband unhindered if the trade took the form and dimensions whereby the neutrality of the country would be endangered. This peril the

THE SINKING OF THE LUSITANIA.
The Liner after being torpedoed by a German Submarine, May 7, 1915.

United States incurred, Austria-Hungary contended, by exporting war material for the use of the Allies. In one of the most pointed documents yet written Austria-Hungary was informed, in the words of Secretary Lansing's Note, that :

Manifestly the idea of strict neutrality now advanced by the Imperial and Royal Government would involve a neutral nation in a mass of perplexities which would obscure the whole field of international obligation, produce economic confusion, and deprive all commerce and industry of legitimate fields of enterprise, already heavily burdened by the unavoidable restrictions of war.

In this connexion it is pertinent to direct the attention of the Imperial and Royal Government to the fact that Austria-Hungary and Germany, particularly the latter, have during the years preceding the present European War produced a great surplus of arms and ammunition, which they sold throughout the world, and especially to belligerents. Never during that period did either of them suggest or apply the principle now advocated by the Imperial and Royal Government.

During the Boer War between Great Britain and the South African Republics the patrol of the coast of neighbouring neutral colonies by British naval vessels prevented arms and ammunition reaching the Transvaal or the Orange Free State. The allied Republics were in a situation almost identical in that respect with that in which Austria-Hungary and Germany find themselves at the present time. Yet in spite of the commercial isolation of one belligerent, Germany sold to Great Britain and the other belligerent hundreds of thousands of kilos of explosives, gunpowder, cartridges, shot, and weapons ; and it is known that Austria-Hungary also sold similar munitions to the same purchaser, though in small quantities.

As usual, the opinion of the pro-German editors was that the Note would prove a great satisfaction to Great Britain. To impartial observers, however, the position taken by

Secretary Lansing was unassailable. If Austria-Hungary and her present Ally had acted otherwise in these circumstances, the Imperial and Royal Government might with greater consistency and greater force have urged its contention. In giving the practical reason why America had advocated and practised trade in munitions of war, the Note wished it to be distinctly understood as speaking with no thought of expressing or implying any judgment with regard to the circumstances of the war, but as merely putting very frankly the argument which was conclusive in determining the policy of the United States. In conclusion Mr. Lansing said :

The principles of international law, the practice of nations, the national safety of the United States and other nations without great military and naval establishments, the prevention of increased armies and navies, the adoption of peaceful methods for the adjustment of international differences, and finally, neutrality itself, are opposed to the prohibition by a neutral nation of the exportation of arms, ammunition, or other munitions of war to belligerent Powers during the progress of the war.

Thus the American Government for a third time announced its determination not to yield to German agitation for stopping the export of munitions of war. This very able Note left no single loophole for further legitimate agitation for an embargo on munitions of war. It should have put an end to the insincere propaganda on this subject both in Austria and in America, which, however. had in reality been inspired from Berlin. It did not, however ; because the Austro-Hungarian Ambassador, as we shall show later, having been defeated in argument, entered into a conspiracy to accomplish by chicanery and even violence what he had failed to secure by proper diplomatic methods. The double-faced treachery of the crusade engineered by German agents (hiding behind American dupes) for the excitement of public opinion, demanded an embargo against Great Britain and France, while Germany herself planned enormous exports of war material through several agencies. Sufficient has been said to demonstrate that President Wilson had shown both patience and tolerance of the Austro-German propaganda as persistently carried on for the first year of the war. It had been of a character that might well have moved a more excitable ruler not merely to anger but to action. When it was deliberately aimed at the segregation of German-Americans from the main body of American citizens, and their enrolment for political purposes in the interests of Germany rather than of the United States, the President adopted an attitude of detachment.

We have shown how he allowed Herr Dernburg all the rope that he could possibly have desired, and how he maintained an attitude of the strictest official unconsciousness in the presence of the variegated campaign of commercial, social, financial, and political terrorism which the Austro-German agents waged. Early in September, 1915, however, a case arose which rightly aroused the President's indignation, and resulted in a request (September 10) for the recall of Dr. Dumba, the Austro-Hungarian Minister at Washington. Dr. Dumba was convicted on evidence which he was unable to deny of conspiring with Captain von Papen, the German Military Attaché, to disorganize American factories engaged in supplying the Allies with munitions. His scheme was to stir up strikes and discontent among the Austro-Hungarian employees in these works, and to bring home to them a sense of their " guilt " and disloyalty in furnishing war material for the enemies of the Dual Monarchy. The appearance of an Ambassador, who had been completely demolished in argument, as a fomenter of strikes in the country to which he is accredited is, to say the least, unusual ; but Dr. Dumba found in it nothing but what was perfectly proper. President Wilson, however, took a different view, and the Austrian

Foreign Office was requested to recall Dr. Dumba. The diplomatic career of Dr. Dumba had been somewhat unfortunate. Of Macedonian origin, he acquired his first experience in that tortuous school of diplomacy the Austro-Hungarian Legation at Belgrade. The sort of work that the Ballplatz used to demand of its representatives in the Serbian capital has been made sufficiently known to the world in a series of unsavoury trials and scandals. There was no reason for thinking that Dr. Dumba was anything but an efficient pupil in the arts that earned for Count Forgach a

CAPTAIN TURNER,
Passing through a street in Queenstown after the " Lusitania " outrage.

AFTER THE SINKING OF THE "LUSITAN[

"We find that this appalling crime was contrary to international law and the conventions of all civilized nations, and we
crime of wilful and wholesale murder before the tribunal of the civilized world. We desire to express our sincere condole
in this murderous attack on an unarmed liner."—The un

VORS CLINGING TO THE BOATS.

he officers of the said submarine, and the Emperor and Government of Germany, under whose orders they acted, with the
with the relatives of deceased ; the Cunard Company ; and the United States of America, so many of whose citizens perished
f the Irish jury at the inquest on the " Lusitania" victims.

European disrepute. But before he could fully prove his worth his career was cut short by domestic difficulties that led to his temporary retirement from active service. Eventually, however, he was reinstated, and the completeness of his restoration to official favour was shown when he was appointed to succeed Baron von Hengelmüller as Ambassador to Washington. In the American capital his peculiar training and talents found little scope until the outbreak of the war. But the revelations which ended in his recall proved that he had not been idle, and that his energies were marked with the unscrupulous obtuseness characteristic of Austro-Hungarian diplomacy.

GUSTAV STAHL,
A German Reservist, who confessed to perjury in "falsely swearing" he saw four guns mounted on the Lusitania. He was sentenced to eighteen months' imprisonment.

Here his blundering got him into trouble, and the American people and the American Government dealt with him as he deserved.

The immediate cause of Dr. Dumba's misfortune was the discovery of a letter from him to Baron von Burian, Foreign Minister at Vienna, on the person of one James Archibald,* who, while claiming to be an American war

* Published as a Parliamentary White Paper (Misc. Cd. 8012). "Austrian and German Papers found in possession of Mr. James F. J. Archibald, Falmouth, August 30, 1915."

correspondent, was in fact acting as dispatch-carrier to the Austrian and German Governments. The letter, of which the following is a textual translation, was found by the British authorities with other papers hidden in Mr. Archibald's cabin on his arrival at Falmouth :

NEW YORK,
August 20, 1915.
Yesterday evening Consul-General von Nuber received the enclosed *aide memoire* from the chief editor of the locally-known paper *Szabadsag* after a previous conference with him and in pursuance of his proposals to arrange for strikes in the Bethlehem-Schwab steel and munitions war factory, and also in the Middle West.

Dr. Archibald, who is well known to your lordship, leaves to-day at 12 o'clock on board the Rotterdam for Berlin and Vienna. I take this rare and safe opportunity to warmly recommend the proposal to your lordship's favourable consideration. It is my impression that we can disorganise and hold up for months, if not entirely prevent, the manufacture of munitions in Bethlehem and the Middle West which, in the opinion of the German Military Attaché, is of great importance and amply outweighs the expenditure of money involved. But even if the strikes do not come off, it is probable we should extort, under pressure of the crisis, more favourable conditions of labour for our poor downtrodden fellow-countrymen. In Bethlehem these white slaves are now working for twelve hours a day and seven days a week. All weak persons succumb and become consumptive. So far as the German workmen found among the skilled hands are concerned means of living will be provided for them. Besides this a private German registry office has been established which provides employment for persons who have voluntarily given up their places, and it is already working well.

I beg your Excellency to be so good as to inform me with reference to this letter by wireless telegraphy, replying whether you agree.   DUMBA.

In an excellently worded telegram to its Ambassador in Vienna the United States Government declared Dr. Dumba to be no longer acceptable as the representative of the Dual Monarchy. His offences were declared to have been twofold. In the first place he had conspired to " cripple the legitimate industries " of the American people, and in the second place he had been found guilty of a " flagrant violation of diplomatic propriety by employing an American citizen, protected by an American passport, as the secret bearer of official dispatches through the lines of the enemy to Austria-Hungary." His career, therefore, as a strike organizer and dispatch smuggler came to an end.

Some extracts from the other papers found on Mr. Archibald have been given above. The following characteristic extract from a letter, dated August 20, 1915, of Captain von Papen, German Military Attaché, to Frau von Papen, aroused a good deal of indignation in the United States :

We have great need of being " bucked up," as they say here. Since Sunday a new storm has been raging

THE SINKING OF THE LUSITANIA.
Saving the women and children.
263

One of the children rescued.　　A survivor wrapped up in a blanket.

SURVIVORS FROM THE

against us—and because of what ? I'm sending you a few cuttings from the newspapers that will amuse you. Unfortunately they stole a fat portfolio from our good Albert in the Elevated (English Secret Service, of course), of which the principal contents have been published. You can imagine the sensation among the Americans ! Unfortunately there were some very important things from my report among them, such as the buying up of liquid chlorine and about the Bridgeport Projectile Company, as well as documents regarding the buying up of phenol (from which explosives are made) and the acquisition of the Wright's aeroplane patent.

But things like that must occur. I send you Albert's reply for you to see how we protect ourselves. We composed the document together yesterday.

It seems quite likely that we shall meet again *soon*. The sinking of the Adriatic (sic) may well be the last straw. I hope in our interest that the danger will blow over

　．　　　．　　　．　　　．　　　．

How splendid on the Eastern front. I always say to these idiotic Yankees they had better hold their tongues—it's better to look at all this heroism full of admiration. My friends in the army are quite different in this way.

Whilst the country was being deluged with manufactured news and one-sided comment, the American people, who, as we have shown, were in no way deceived as to who began the war, were beginning to ask themselves :

" What is likely to happen to us if the Germans have their way in this struggle ? " To this Professor George T. Ladd, of Yale University, replied :

The Government at present, and the great body of the people at all times, have no desire to extend the possessions of the United States by conquest. But, on the other hand, they do not desire that the Governments of Europe should by violence extend their possessions on this continent. What, however, will ultimately happen in South America, Central America, and Mexico if Germany wins in this war and then takes another quarter of a century for recuperation without a change in its present policy of extending Germanic control and Germanic culture by superiority of numbers and modern " scientific " armament ? This is the question which many are seriously asking at the present time.

Professor Usher, author of "Pan-Germanism," in an article also warned Americans that unexpectedly unpleasant things might follow a German victory. He pointed out that it might cost Americans South American trade. England largely controlled the world's commerce. She could, if she wished, cripple American trade, but Americans had become so accustomed to a friendly understanding with England and the generosity of England's

The Cuban Consul-General at Liverpool.
LUSITANIA IN ENGLAND.

A cripple who was saved after being in the water
for four hours.

marine policy that they had lost sight of that fact. With England as the naval power American trade was safe ; but what would happen if Germany ousted England ?

From the first ex-President Roosevelt became an outspoken and consistent friend of the Allies. He did not hesitate to denounce the Government policy of strict neutrality as " supinely immoral," because it took no steps to redress the wrongs of the Belgians, a duty which Mr. Roosevelt contended was plainly imposed upon his country by the obligations of The Hague Convention. There never was, in his opinion, in any war a clearer breach of international morality than that committed by Germany in the invasion and subjugation of Belgium. How far Mr. Roosevelt would have gone towards armed participation in what he called an " international *posse comitatus* " is not quite clear. It is difficult to see how the United States could have vindicated The Hague Convention unless ready to fight. Upon another occasion Mr. Roosevelt said that, having informed itself of the facts, the Govern-

ment should " at least have put itself on record in reference thereto." On this point Mr. Robert Bacon, former United States Ambassador in Paris, was equally outspoken, and called attention (November 4, 1914) to the fact that German violation of Belgian neutrality constituted an open breach of The Hague Convention. Mr. Bacon asked :

Are we to suffer a nation to break a treaty with us on whatever pretext without entering at least a formal protest ? If the treaties we made at The Hague are to be so lightly treated, why not all other treaties ? It is our solemn duty to protest. We assume a heavy responsibility by remaining silent. To justify a policy of silence by the assertion that " we are fortunate in being safely removed from this danger that threatens Europe," and to urge that as a reason for us to sit still with hands folded, is as weak as it is unwise.

This utterance may be fairly taken as one of the strongest indications of the general disgust at Germany's treatment of her little neighbour—a disgust that was not modified by the strenuous efforts of the German press agency during the first twelve months of the war.

Later, in discussing the periodical peace

DR. DUMBA,
Austro-Hungarian Ambassador at Washington.

proposals emanating from the German propagandist bureau, Mr. Roosevelt said:

Of course, peace is worthless unless it serves the cause of righteousness. A peace which consecrates militarism will be of small service. A peace obtained by crushing the liberty and life of unoffending peoples is as cruel as the most cruel war. . . . A peace which left Belgium's wrongs unavenged, and which did not provide against the recurrence of such wrongs as those from which she has suffered, would not be a real peace.

Mr. Roosevelt analysed the causes of the conflict. There was room, he thought, for sincere differences of opinion about the initial positions of Austria, Serbia, Russia, Germany, and France. As for England, "when once Belgium was invaded, every circumstance of national honour and interest forced England to act precisely as she did act. She could not hold up her head among the nations had she acted otherwise."

About Belgium his contention was that only one view was possible. He said:

I admire and respect the German people. I am proud of the German blood in my veins, but it is impossible not to face the danger of a transatlantic application of all that Bernhardism implies. The United States must be prepared. Arbitration treaties, The Hague Court, and all the rest of the pacificist stock-in-trade are useless unless backed by force. No abundance of the milder

virtue will save the nation that has lost its virile qualities. On the other hand, no admiration of strength must make us deviate from the laws of righteousness. What has occurred to Belgium is precisely what would occur, under similar conditions, to us unless we were able to show that the action would be dangerous. If any Old World military Power, European or Asiatic, were at war and deemed such action necessary and safe it would at once seize the Panama Canal or the Danish West Indies or Magdalena Bay exactly as Belgium and Luxemburg have been overrun by Germany or as Korea has been seized by Japan

This was certainly disconcerting talk from the man for whose good will the Kaiser had for years assiduously angled. So strongly and so insistently had Mr. Roosevelt advocated the cause of the Allies that his attitude drew forth the following sonnet by William Watson, which was published in the *New York Herald* of March 14, 1915:

Hadst thou been sitting yet in Lincoln's chair,
A different voice had pealed across the sea,
Another hand had struck a deeper key,
A larger note had pulsed upon the air.
Thou, in whose blood our Scotland hath a share—
As once on thine own soil august and free
Thyself didst not unproudly tell to me
'Mid talk of statecraft wise and songcraft fair—
Thou hadst not watched our throes with breast supine,
Nor dost thou now, nor doth thy mighty land.
Something of her vast soul we understand,
And well we know that, in this hour malign,
Not human heart she lacks, but tongue divine,
To rouse the thunders lulled in her great hand.

Another well-known American writer, Colonel Henry Watterson, the veteran and eloquent editor of the *Louisville Courier Journal,* had from the beginning of the war used his powerful pen for the cause of the Allies. Extracts from the picturesque articles of Colonel Watterson have appeared from time to time in British journals, and many of our readers are possibly familiar with the "fierce neutrality" articles from the pen of this valiant champion of our cause, who, as will be seen from the following extract from the *Louisville Courier Journal* of August 25, 1915, favoured more drastic measures than President Wilson had up to that time professed. Colonel Watterson said:

The President should call Congress together and Congress should make a flat Declaration of War. No thoughtful American can say that the provocation is not more than sufficient. Nor will anything less meet the requirement. Nothing less indeed will reach the savages who murder our women and children. When we have seized millions of German property—especially German ships—and sent a fleet to help clean up the war zone—Berlin will understand. When we have established camps of detention and corralled the leaders among the Kaiser reservists, and suppressed the treasonable society called the German-American Alliance and the treasonable newspapers published in the German language, we shall know who is who, and the traitors in our midst will learn what is what. . . . So we have little, if anything, to lose by hoisting the flag and holding it high and standing by our honour and the courage of our convictions, whilst we have everything to gain by asserting our prowess, our rights, our manhood and our integrity as a nation and a people, marching to battle as one man crying " To Hell with the Hapsburg and the Hohenzollern—with autocracy, despotism and brutality —long life to freedom, to democracy and to civilization equally in Germany and the rest of the world ! "

With equal vigour Colonel Watterson denounced what he termed " those Kaiser American traitors." He said (*Louisville Courier Journal*, August 24, 1915) :

If anyone has doubted the treasonable character of the American newspapers printed in the German language, he need only read their comments upon the sinking of the Arabic to have his doubts set wholly at rest. As after the sinking of the Lusitania they take the anti-American, pro-Teuton view. Each and every one of them being subsidized by the Imperial Treasury it could not be otherwise. The time has come to put a quietus upon these jackals of the Kaiser. They are by no means beyond the reach of the civil law. Let us hope that the Department of Justice will not prove derelict in its duty to move against these traitors. Surely such sedition by citizens of the United States should be stopped. Each and every one of these American newspapers printed in the German language is a traitor and should be indicted, prosecuted and suppressed.

An appeal of a less picturesque character was made to German-Americans, who were by no means all in favour of Germany, by Dr. Newell Dwight Hillis, who occupied the pulpit of Plymouth Church, Brooklyn—formerly Henry Ward Beecher's Church. Dr. Hillis said :

And do they (German-Americans) not owe something to this Republic ? Having come to the kingdom for such a crisis as this, should they not use their influence with the Fatherland ? Having escaped conscription and years of military service, with heavy taxation, and enjoyed the liberty of the Press ; having become convinced that militarism does not promote the prosperity and manhood of the people, why should they not as one man ask the Fatherland now to present their cause to arbitrators ? To no body of American citizens has there ever come a more strategic opportunity, or a responsibility so heavy.

It may be safely asserted that no Englishman of distinction was more familiar with economic and political movements in the United States than Lord Bryce, ex-British Ambassador to America. In an article published in the *Daily Telegraph*, February 27, 1915, Lord Bryce estimated that not more than 10 per cent. of the population supported the German cause, and nearly all were men of German birth, who had naturally retained their attachment to their Mother Country. Very few Germans of the second generation took this view. Lord Bryce said :

Anyhow, it is a complete error to assume that the bulk of those who bear German names and own to German blood belong to the pro-German party. The children of Europeans who are born in America grow up normal American citizens for all practical purposes. Their loyalty is to the Stars and Stripes, and their feeling for the land of their parents is comparatively weak. What is called the German vote is in some few cities a force to be reckoned with. But when those who lead it try to use it

as a means of applying political pressure in such a case as this, native Americans resent such an attempt, for with them it is a fundamental principle that a citizen must have no loyalty save to the United States, and the great bulk even of the " hyphenated " German-Americans would refuse to respond.

Mr. Joseph H. Choate, the former Ambassador of the United States in London, and one of the most prominent public men of America, in the introduction to Professor Cramb's work on Germany, referred to Germany's " gross and admitted violation of all treaties in its hostile entrance upon Belgian soil," and added " there is no disguising the fact that the sympathies and hopes of the great mass of English-speaking people everywhere are with England and her Allies now." Of Germany's great illusion about the British Empire Mr. Choate said :

The actual conflict has gone far enough, one would think, to disabuse Germany of some of its ideas about England. Instead of her Empire being ready to fall to pieces by the dropping off of her Colonies, armies are marching to her aid from all her dominions beyond the seas, apparently ready to fight for her life with as ardent patriotism as the regular British soldier ; and instead of any flinching or holding back on the part of the individual Englishman, they are all, to a man, rushing to the support

CAPTAIN VON PAPEN,
German Military Attaché at Washington.

of the colours, or already engaged in the terrible conflict on the Aisne and the Marne with a courage worthy of the field of Agincourt.

A scathing letter from Mr. George Haven Putnam, the well-known publicist, giving an American view of German barbarity, was published in the *New York Times* of January 21, 1915. Mr. Putnam had been invited to join a newly formed " University League " of German-American students, and the letter was his reply. " Under the conditions now obtaining," he wrote, " I find myself unwilling to meet Germans, whether friends, acquaintances, or strangers. We Americans have," he said, " with but few exceptions, convinced ourselves that the responsibility for beginning the war rests with Germany and with Austria, and primarily with Germany, which not only influenced, but controlled the action of Austria." Continuing he said :

The destruction, by order, of Belgian cities, the taking of hostages, and the making of these hostages responsible for the actions of individuals whom they were not in a position to control ; the shooting of many of these hostages ; the appropriation for the use of the armies of the food which had been stored in Antwerp and elsewhere, so that the people in Belgium now officially classed as " subjects of Germany " are dependent upon American charity to save them from starvation ; the imposition upon these starving and ruined communities of crushing indemnities—all these things impress Americans as contrary to the standards of modern civilization. We find ground also for indignation at the use of vessels of war and of Zeppelins for the killing of women and children and other unarmed citizens in undefended places. Such killing, which has nothing whatsoever to do with the work of campaigns, can only be classed as murder. With these views I cannot, therefore—not at this time, at least—accept the companionship of German-Americans who are prepared to approve, defend, or excuse these actions.

Colonel George Harvey, editor of the *North American Review*, in a letter to *The Times*, took the ground that the United States was not with Great Britain simply because of ties of kinship. He said :

Why, then, are we for you and your Allies ? For no other reason in the world except that you are continuing the great battle for government of, for, and by the people which we began when at Lexington we fired the shot that was heard around the world, for the glorious cause that Franklin, and Jefferson, and Madison wrote for, that Patrick Henry spoke for, that Washington and Jackson fought for, that Lincoln died for, that McKinley suffered for, that every American statesman worthy of the title now lives for. To our minds the real issue is not, as your people seem to think, mere militarism ; it is the hideous conception of which militarism is but one of many manifestations ; it is despotism itself ; the despotism which united our people originally in armed resistance, and which is no less hateful to us now than it was then. Neutral ? Yes, in the name of the nation, but not in our heart of hearts. We are for the England which has been gradually freeing the world while Germany has been planning to enslave it. No one of the great colonies which owe her so much and are responding so nobly to her call is more true to the glorious aspiration for

which now she is giving her life-blood than these United States.

From all these utterances and from what may be gathered from leading American journals it is clear that the vast majority of the people of the United States condemned the German Government, laying the blame for the outbreak of strife upon it and Austria. This, as Colonel Harvey remarked, they did not do from racial sympathy with Great Britain, nor from traditional friendship with France, but because the public documents published by the respective countries convinced them that Germany was the aggressor, and, as nearly all these American authorities pointed out, had put herself utterly in the wrong by her invasion of Belgium. To this conviction they adhered, despite the unremitting efforts of the insidious German propaganda which we have fully described. This propaganda was conducted on a scale and at a cost hitherto unknown, even in a country like America, where millions sterling have been expended on the propaganda of a single Presidential Election. The authorities quoted above were men of distinction and weight in America, who were familiar with the views of their countrymen, and may be regarded as dispassionate observers of current events. With the average *unhyphenated* American the question at issue was freedom. Attached as Americans are to their democratic institutions, they were suspicious of Germany because they knew that the ruling powers of that country hated democracy as much as they hated England. In nearly all these quotations from American authorities we find the same refrain. Germany is opposed to freedom ; England and France represent it. Victory for Germany would be to side-track human progress.

It is not possible in the limits of this chapter to discuss the many important and perplexing questions that arose between the United States and Great Britain in relation to the carrying on of commerce in time of war. These included rules of international law, the use of the neutral flag, questions relating to contraband, blockades (not maritime lynch law), Prize Court adjudication, and many other interesting maritime problems that are bound to arise in a conflict between great commercial nations, and affect alike neutrals and belligerents. Dealing, as we are doing, with the attitude of the people and the Government of the United States towards

[From the "New York Sun," April 13, 1915.

THE AMERICAN NOTE.

the belligerents, we must next point out how Germany's uncivilized methods of warfare, both on the sea and in the air, were received in America. The ruin of Belgium, the unnecessary destruction of life, and other atrocities left the people of the United States shocked, ashamed, and outraged that a Christian nation should be guilty of such a criminal war. These horrors were quickly followed by other inhuman crimes, such as the dropping of bombs on Antwerp and Paris, one of which nearly killed the American Ambassador. Thus to travel far out of the sphere of military activity and kill unarmed people in some distant city was against all American ideas of civilized combat, and the Press of the United States vigorously denounced these "outrages on humanity." In doing so, the newspapers excoriated Professor

Muensterberg and other German apologists who rushed to the defence of Germany. The aerial raids of September were followed by the naval raid on undefended Yorkshire towns in December, 1914.* The enthusiasm which the murder of several scores of non-combatants evoked in Berlin did not assist the German cause in America, but on the contrary added depth to the conviction that a victory for the Kaiser would be a victory of scientific barbarism over civilization. Thus the first five months of the war had produced a wave of bitter resentment in America against the Germans for restoring barbarities which the world had hoped to see eliminated from the practices of war.

Disturbing and discouraging as these factors were, the New Year brought evidence that the German Government contemplated further deeds of so desperate and abominable a character as to involve the lives of innocent neutrals, the sanctity of the American flag, and the safety of American shipping. By the rules of international law, the customs of war, and the dictates of humanity, it is obligatory upon a belligerent to ascertain the character of a merchant vessel and of her cargo before capture. Germany had no right to disregard this

* See Vol. II., Chapter XLIII.

obligation. To destroy ship, non-combatant crew, and cargo, as Germany declared her intention of doing, was nothing less than a proposed act of piracy on the high seas, and the new German policy met with vigorous American comment and protest. Early in February, 1915, the German Admiralty announced * that on and after February 18 all the waters round the British Isles would be treated as a war-zone, and that all British merchant ships therein would be destroyed, even though it was impossible to warn the crews and passengers of their peril. At first

* The text of the German proclamation, dated February 5, 1915, was :

All the waters surrounding Great Britain and Ireland and all English seas are hereby declared to be a war area.

From February 18 all ships of the enemy mercantile marine in these waters will be destroyed, and it will not always be possible to avoid danger to the crews and passengers thereon.

The shipping route round the north of the Shetlands, in the east of the North Sea, and over a distance of thirty miles (nautical) along the coast of the Netherlands will not be dangerous.

These measures by the German Government are worthy of note by neutral countries as counter measures against England's methods, which are contrary to international law, and they will help to bring neutral shipping into closer touch with Germany.

The German Government announces its intentions in good time, so that both neutral and enemy shipping can take the necessary steps accordingly.

STRIKERS ATTACKING THE STANDARD OIL WORKS, NEW JERSEY.

BRITISH AMBASSADOR TO WASHINGTON.
Sir Cecil Spring-Rice and Lady Spring-Rice, with their children.
On the right is Viscount Campden, an Attaché at the British Embassy.

it was thought in America that Germany had engaged in a campaign of bluff and intimidation calculated to raise insurance rates and instil fear in shipping circles, thereby crippling so far as possible the transatlantic trade. Her declaration was regarded in other quarters as something between a hint and a threat, and in either light constituting an extraordinary international claim and a vicious invitation to international embroilment. The proclamation of this blockade of "the waters surrounding Great Britain and Ireland" met with comments by the American Press outspoken enough to penetrate even Teutonic imperviousness. But in so far as it was intended to frighten American shippers, and

VISCOUNT BRYCE,
Ex-British Ambassador at Washington.

of friendly Powers. While occasional use of the flag of a neutral or an enemy under stress of immediate pursuit, and to deceive an approaching enemy, the American Government admitted, was justified, the explicit sanction by a belligerent Government for its merchant ships generally to fly the flag of a neutral Power within certain portions of the high seas frequented by hostile warships could not be practised without a serious menace to the lives and vessels of American citizens. *The Times* (February 15, 1915), in commenting on this Note, said :

> The validity of this doctrine is a matter for international lawyers to consider. Without admitting its soundness, or that of the contentions urged to support it, it is enough for us, in the conditions which actually exist, to know that the American Government would view such general use of their flag "with anxious solicitude," and that they trust we will endeavour to restrain it. We shall certainly do all that is judged consistent with our military safety to meet their wishes, and to assuage their uneasiness for American ships and lives, in the piratical warfare which Germany intends to wage against all shipping near our shores.

The language of the American Note to Germany (February 12, 1915) was friendly but decidedly firm. It warned the German Government that the destruction of neutral vessels without first determining their nationality and the contraband character of their cargo would be an indefensible violation of

coerce American opinion into subscribing to the view that Germany was too "terrible" to be resisted, it failed to gauge the character of the American people. Before the Imperial Government put this threat into execution the Secretary of State issued a Note of warning, clearly defining the attitude of the Government on Germany's attempt to destroy the freedom of the seas. About the same time a controversy had arisen between the United States and Great Britain on the subject of the use of the neutral flag, and Germany, by the circulation of false reports from Berlin, tried to make this controversy one of the excuses for her proposed act of piracy on the high seas. The American Note to the British Government was conceived throughout in a friendly spirit. The British Government was asked to do all in its power to restrain vessels of British nationality from the deceptive use of the American flag in the sea area defined in the German declaration. The German Government had used the incident of the captain of the Lusitania raising the American flag as the vessel approached the British coast as an excuse for its intention of attacking vessels

MR. JOSEPH H. CHOATE,
Former American Ambassador in London.

neutral rights, which would be very hard to reconcile with the friendly relations between the two countries. The United States Government would be constrained "to hold the Imperial Government to strict accountability," and to "take any steps which might be necessary to safeguard American lives and property. Accordingly they express their confident hope and expectation that the Imperial Government can, and will, give an assurance to American citizens that their vessels will not be molested, otherwise than by visit and search." In this Note President Wilson laid down very clearly the elementary rule of war—namely, that visit and search must precede attack in all cases where effective blockade is in force. The destruction of a ship on the high seas in other circumstances, without first determining with absolute certainty her belligerent nationality and the contraband character of her cargo, was an act without precedent in naval warfare. It was so novel, and we may add so inhuman, that the American Government were, at the beginning of the controversy, reluctant to believe that the German Government contemplated it. They brushed aside the pretence that a suspicion that enemy ships might use a neutral flag could justify it. The right of visit and search is admitted by international law expressly to determine the character of suspected vessels. These fundamental doctrines were iterated and reiterated in subsequent Notes to the German Government, not only after American life had been endangered and American property destroyed, but after many American lives had been lost. The tone and substance of what may be termed the first Note to Germany was fully approved by the people and the Press of the United States. As already remarked, at first, and until American and other neutral vessels were actually sunk, Americans were inclined to look upon the German threat of sinking everything within the paper "war area" as bluff, with a proviso that, should it prove to be serious and lead to the loss of "a single American ship or a single American life," the State Department would do their duty and compel Germany to respect the flag of the Republic and the elementary rights of her citizens. The above, in brief, indicates how matters stood just previous to what became known as "Pirate Day," February 18, 1915, when Germany began to carry out the terms of the decree to sink all

merchant vessels found in the waters around Great Britain, without warning crew or passengers of the threatened danger.

It is a notable fact that the underlying principle, as brought out in the first Note in relation to American lives and property and respect for the American flag, was calmly and firmly insisted on by President Wilson in each of his subsequent Notes. The German Govern-

CAPTAIN BOY-ED,
German Naval Attaché at Washington.

ment for a long time in the rejoinders as persistently insisted on making a bargain with the American Government, or as it has been more aptly termed, insisted on "diplomatic blackmail," the demand being that, in return for assurance as to the safety of American vessels in the war zone, the United States should insist upon Great Britain allowing free importation of American food supplies to Germany. The reply to this impudent demand was simply that the United States Government were dealing directly with the German Government, and insisting that the rights of neutrals should be respected by Germany, and that such demand had nothing to do with Germany's relations with Great Britain, and further that the German Government would be held to "strict accountability" for the loss of American vessels and American lives. The German Government's answer to this showed its utter contempt alike for President Wilson and the American people, as the following incidents show :

The American ship W. P. Frye was sunk by the Prinz Eitel Friedrich.

The American steamer Carib was blown up by a mine in the North Sea.

Theodore Roosevelt

EX-PRESIDENT ROOSEVELT.
(From a painting by Sargent.)

The American steamer Evelyn was sunk by a mine near Borkum.

The American steamer Gulflight was sunk by a torpedo without notice near the Scilly Islands, and three American citizens were drowned.

The American steamer Cushing was attacked by aeroplane in the North Sea.

The British steamer Falaba was torpedoed, and Mr. Leon Thrasher, an American citizen, was drowned.

The Falaba and Gulflight came within the scope of "strict accountability." There was

no difference in principle in the sinking of these vessels and in the sinking of the Lusitania, except in the number murdered. It was during the interval between Germany's declaration of her intention to torpedo merchant ships without warning and the sinking of the Lusitania that the insulting Press propaganda described above reached its maximum point, and when every kind of trick was employed to create ill-feeling between America and Great Britain on contraband and other questions. Space will not permit the discussion of the details of these crimes, which were soon to be overshadowed by the culminating atrocity of the Lusitania. There was " a passionate ring of abhorrence," we were told, throughout America of these deliberate and cold-blooded murders on the high seas. Heading its leading article " If not Murder, What Is It ? " the *New York Sun* recounted the outrages of which Germany had been guilty up to the end of March, 1915— the invasion of Belgium, the destruction of Louvain, the attack on the cathedral of Reims, the bombardment of unprotected sea-coast towns—" events which have counted incalculably in the formation of neutral opinion adverse to the German cause," it said, and now " the murder of probably more than one hundred men and women non-combatants, the passengers and crews of the Falaba and the Aguila, peacefully and inoffensively navigating the high seas." " This is not war, it is murder ! " exclaimed the *New York Times*. " It has not even the palliation of piracy, for the pirate, like the highwayman, kills for gain and not because he delights in slaughter." Continuing, the *New York Times* said :

The sinking of the Falaba is perhaps the most shocking crime of the war. It is a crime directly chargeable against Germany, a crime for which Germany will be held responsible in the judgment of civilization. The sinking of a peaceful merchant ship, even though she belongs to the enemy, and the killing and drowning of her officers, crew, and passengers, are no part of the operations of war.

But this crime, with its wanton destruction of human lives, was soon to be outdone by the wholesale slaughter of innocent men, women, and children on a great Atlantic liner, an act which in the light of common humanity was wickedness such as the history of war will find it difficult to match.

The news of the sinking of the Lusitania, May 7, 1915, was received throughout the United States with a hush of horror, broken only, said *The Times* New York Correspondent,

by "the sniggers of German-Americans." *
An eye-witness wrote that outside the newspaper offices dense crowds assembled and
watched in breathless silence the successive
bulletins telling of this latest outrage. Sand-
wiched in between them were Germans, who
were saying: " We warned them ; our Embassy
advertised the warning ; we were within our
rights." One of these Huns was pummelled
into insensibility by the indignant crowds near
the *Tribune* office, but others were allowed to
continue their remarks unmolested.

Before referring to the exchange of Notes
which took place between the United States and
the German Governments in relation to this
ghastly crime, the reader's attention is called to
the words of Colonel Harvey, editor of the *North
American Review*, who opened the June, 1915,
number of his Review with words so scathing
and yet so calm, dispassionate, penetrating, and
comprehensive that it is doubtful if this
inhuman crime will ever be more adequately
and concisely visualized. "Because," said
Colonel Harvey, "Great Britain refused to
permit the United States to supply the German
army with foodstuffs, Germany officially assas-
sinated more than a hundred American citizens.
That is the naked fact from which escape is
impossible. Explanations cannot explain ; excuses cannot palliate ; the monstrous crime
was premeditated, was threatened, and was
perpetrated. The whole story of the sinking
of the Lusitania is contained in those few words.
Nothing need be added, and nothing can be
taken away. Whatever course future events
may take, whatever settlement of the great war
may finally be effected, whatever attitude our
own or any other country may assume, the
debasement of Germany as a civilized nation
is writ upon the pages of history by her own
hand ; her reversion to barbarism is established
at the bar of humanity, there to remain throughout the lives of this and succeeding generations ;
the stain upon her honour is indelible. This
nation is confronted by no necessity of inflicting
punishment upon Germany. The reprobation
of all mankind, whose effect will continue for
years to come, is a fully adequate penalty
which, unfortunately but inevitably, the innocent German people, in common with the guilty
German Government, must prepare to suffer."

Unhappily the "stain upon her honour "
and the "reprobation of all mankind " were

* The account of the torpedoing of the Lusitania will
be found in Vol. IV., pages 85 and 86.

COL. GEORGE HARVEY.
Editor of the *North American Review.*

sentiments that were not likely to disturb or
even penetrate the opaque Teutonic conscience.
President Wilson in his first Note (May 14,
1915) failed to recognize any necessity of
inflicting punishment upon Germany, and
rested his case upon the following points :

1. The German methods of retaliation for loss of
commerce are again declared to be inadmissible as in-
compatible with the freedom of the seas, and the Government must be held to "strict accountability " for all
infringements of American rights.

2. The "practical impossibility " of employing submarines to destroy commerce without an infringement of
the accepted rules of justice and humanity is insisted
upon.

3. The indisputable right of American citizens to sail
in ships travelling wherever legitimate business calls
them upon the high seas, and that with confidence that
their lives will not be illegally endangered, is firmly
maintained.

4. Having regard to the character of the German
Government, the Government of the United States
assumes that the guilty naval commanders acted under a
misapprehension, that their acts will be disavowed, that
reparation will be made, and that steps will be taken to
prevent the recurrence of such deeds.

5. Expressions of regret and offers of reparation cannot excuse a practice the "natural necessary effect of
which is to subject neutral nations or neutral persons to
new and immeasurable risks."

6. The German Government must not expect the
United States Government to "omit any word or act "
necessary to preserve the rights of American citizens.

We were told that this Note was received in
America with a unanimity which had rarely,
if ever, been accorded to any other State
document, and the reply of Germany was
awaited with calm restraint. There was no

MR. J. PIERPONT MORGAN.
Head of the firm of J. P. Morgan and Co., the British Government's Agents in the United States.

disposition either towards " swashbuckling " or towards undue optimism, and the fact was recognized that the future rested with Germany.

In commenting on this Note *The Times* said :

It is a Note that both in substance and expression recalls the best traditions of American diplomacy. Courteous and even considerate in form, it can leave the Wilhelmstrasse under no illusions as to the state of American feeling or the determination of the United States Government. It reminds the directors of German policy that the sinking of the Lusitania is an incident that does not stand alone. There have been other occurrences that have shown an equal disregard of the lives and properties of neutral American citizens, occurrences observed by the Government of the United States "with growing concern, distress, and amazement." An American life was lost when the Falaba was sunk ; the American steamship Cushing was attacked by German airmen ; and the Gulflight, flying the Stars and Stripes, was torpedoed without warning. The Note politely assumes that these acts " so absolutely contrary to the rules, practice, and spirit of modern warfare " have not the countenance and sanction of the German Government. It points out, however, that the events of the past few weeks have proved the practical impossibility of employing submarines against hostile commerce "without inevitable violation of many sacred principles of justice and humanity." It claims as "indisputable" the right of American citizens to take ships and travel wherever their legitimate business may call them without having their lives endangered "by acts in clear violation of universally acknowledged international obligations." It dismisses with stern contempt the preposterous plea that a notification of the intention to commit "an unlawful, inhuman act " can be accepted as an excuse or palliation for its commission.

The "notification" of the intention to commit this infamous crime was first published on May 3, 1915, as an advertisement in American newspapers, and was as follows :

TRAVELLERS intending to embark for an Atlantic voyage are reminded that a state of war exists between Germany and her Allies and Great Britain and her Allies ; that the zone of war includes the waters adjacent to the British Isles ; that, in accordance with the formal notice given by the Imperial German Government vessels flying the flag of Great Britain or any of her

Allies are liable to destruction in those waters ; and that travellers sailing in the war zone in ships of Great Britain or her Allies do so at their own risk.
IMPERIAL GERMAN EMBASSY, WASHINGTON, APRIL 22.

The German reply to the United States Note on the sinking of the Lusitania was generally regarded as unsatisfactory. Not one representative newspaper had anything but the hardest words for it. It was excoriated as a mass of quibbles and untruths, insulting to the United States, and unworthy of a civilized Power. It had four main objects :

1. To smother the Lusitania incident in a long diplomatic and legal controversy.
2. To further the chronic German campaign to prevent the export of munitions of war to the Allies.
3. To aggravate the current of American discontent with our blockade policy by inculcating the idea that this policy is responsible not only for the troubles of meat and cotton exporters, but for the danger of the submarine blockade.
4. By insisting upon the obstinacy of German maritime frightfulness to drive neutral shipping from British trade.

Among other assertions was that the Lusitania had cannons on board, which were mounted and concealed under the deck. This contention was supported by the affidavit of one Gustav Stahl, which affidavit was submitted to the State Department by Count Bernstorff. Four months later this man Stahl, who had been arrested by the United States authorities, pleaded guilty to the charge of perjury, and was sentenced by a United States Court to eighteen months' imprisonment.

The second Note (issued June 11, 1915) discussed the cases of the Cushing, the Gulflight, and the Falaba, as well as that of the

COL. HENRY WATTERSON.
Editor of *The Louisville Courier Journal.*

BY WAY OF A CHANGE.

Uncle Sam: "Guess I'm about through with letter-writing."

Lusitania, and brushed away the various contentions of the German Government, advanced as excuses for sinking the Lusitania, as irrelevant to the real question, which was the legality or the lawlessness of the way in which the Germans destroyed the ship. Upon that point Mr. Wilson expressed no doubt. "Whatever may be the other facts," he observed with unanswerable force, "the principal fact is that a great steamer, primarily and chiefly for the conveyance of passengers, carrying more than 1,000 souls who had no part or lot in the war, was torpedoed and sunk without so much as a challenge or warning, and that men, women, and children were sent to their death in circumstances unparalleled in modern warfare." That was the fact upon which America based her demand for assurances.

A sensation was caused during the preparation of this Note by the resignation (June 8, 1915) of Mr. Bryan, Secretary of State. It appears that Mr. Bryan was opposed to sending anything in the nature of an ultimatum to Germany, because he believed such an act would constitute a violation of the peace principles which he had for many years advocated, and that in leaving the Cabinet he would not embarrass the President should he feel it necessary to adopt a more drastic policy. The resignation of Mr. Bryan was regarded in the United States as much more a personal than a political event. It was aptly described as a dramatic incident in a highly dramatic career, but not a turning point or even a milestone in national policy. It may be truthfully said that, apart from the pro-German Press, the comments of American newspapers were nearly all condemnatory of his action. The German Press was somewhat dazzled by the new recruit, and with characteristic disregard of former attacks proceeded to describe the "sycophant of Great Britain" as "a patriot who has come into this German atmosphere."

The German reply (July 8, 1915) to the second American Note relating to the sinking of the Lusitania may be said to have reached the climax of effrontery, such as only Teutonic diplomacy could have evolved. Of the assurances twice demanded by the United States Government after the sinking of the Lusitania not one was granted. Not one, indeed, was even mentioned. The Imperial Government approved by implication and alleged justification for the acts of its naval commanders. It neither promised nor refused financial reparation for the American lives that had been lost. It neither agreed nor declined to furnish assurances that similar outrages would not be perpetrated in the future. The solemn representations of the United States Government were treated with the silence of disdain. To talk of neutral rights, of "fairness, reason, justice, and humanity," the Wilhelmstrasse preferred to return no answer at all. Instead it merely outlined various proposals for safeguarding American ships and citizens against submarine attack. The Note said :

In order to furnish adequate facilities for travel across the Atlantic for American citizens, the German Government submits for consideration a proposal to increase the number of available steamers by the installing in the passenger service of a reasonable number of neutral steamers under the American flag, the exact number to be agreed upon under the same conditions as above mentioned. The Imperial Government believes it can assume that in this manner adequate facilities for travel across the Atlantic Ocean can be afforded to American citizens. There would, therefore, appear to be no com-

pelling necessity for American citizens to travel to Europe in time of war in ships carrying an enemy flag.

In other words the citizens of the United States were coolly invited to become the accomplices of Germany's violations of the rules of warfare. If they would agree to sail only under their own flag and in vessels guaranteed by the American Government to be carrying no contraband goods, their lives would be graciously spared. Unless they were willing to submit to these restrictions on their personal liberty, and to this absolute surrender of the right of neutrals to supply belligerents with the materials of war, they would continue to be blown out of the water whenever a German submarine could get at them. They were asked, in brief, to connive at the illegal and inhuman practices of the German Admiralty. The unscrupulous agitation in America of Germans against the Allies resulted in an explosion at the Capitol, and in a severe attack (July 3, 1915) by a weak-minded creature of German sympathies on Mr. J. Pierpont Morgan, the head of the firm of J. P. Morgan & Co., who in January had been appointed commercial agents to the British Government to superintend any purchases which Government Departments might have to make in America. This crime, which happily did not prove fatal to the victim, was admittedly the direct result of the sentimental Teutonic propaganda against the part that the United States was alleged to be playing towards the prolongation of the war. Fortunately Mr. Morgan recovered from his wounds, but his assailant committed suicide in gaol.

The third Note of the United States, dated Washington, July 28, characterized the German Note containing the above impudent proposals as most "unsatisfactory." "Repetitions," it said, "by the commanders of German naval vessels of acts of contravention of those rights must be regarded by the Government of the United States when they affect American citizens as deliberately unfriendly." This advanced the controversy to a definite and critical point. It is true this was not an ultimatum, but it was nevertheless an exceedingly strong and definite warning. It took nearly three months for the deed which sent a thrill of horror throughout the United States to reach this stage. No one could accuse President Wilson of being very precipitate. He offered Germany every chance to re-establish herself in the judgment of civilization. Nevertheless her

THE LAST MOMENTS OF THE ARABIC,

Which was torpedoed by a German submarine on August 18, 1915. The above illustration, from a photograph taken by Professor Still, of Purdue University, who was saved in one of the ship's boats, shows the vessel at the moment of her going under, stern first.

efforts to penetrate the conscience of the German Government had up to this time gone unrewarded. Referring to the situation at the close of July, *The Times* said :

The responsibilities of an American President in such an emergency as this are very great. We do not know when they have been discharged with more skill or dignity or self-restraint than by Mr. Wilson. His diplomacy has precisely interpreted the national wish to avoid a conflict and the national resolution not to shirk it if Germany forces it on. That is why the President has carried with him during the past few anxious months the great mass of American opinion. It is with him now when the gravity of the situation can no longer be concealed. We are confident it will stay with him in whatever further decisions or action, however serious, that German barbarities on the high seas may compel him to take. He has placed the responsibility for all future developments squarely upon the shoulders of Germany. Americans will await the upshot with a clear conscience and a united front.

It was not to be expected that President Wilson, who had shown such miraculous patience and self-command in dealing with the perplexing relations of the United States with Germany, would be likely to act hastily. It must be admitted that as outrage succeeded outrage, and insults, in the way of contemptuous Notes, succeeded insults, Englishmen were somewhat amazed at American patience, and surprised that no hasty word escaped the President's lips or fell from his pen. It was said of Mr. Wilson that he was himself so reasonable and impartial that he wanted to make all the people of the United States equally open-minded and patient.* When at last it dawned upon the German Government that even President Wilson's patience was exhausted, and that Uncle Sam (see cartoon from *Punch*, page 277), tired of letter-writing, possibly preparing for action, Count Bernstorff was instructed to promise the Washington Government that no more passenger ships would be torpedoed by German submarines without warning unless they tried to escape when summoned to stop, or offered resistance. Count Bernstorff's promise, however, proved but a " scrap of paper," for on August 19 the White Star liner Arabic was torpedoed without warning and sunk by a German submarine. There were twenty-six Americans on board, and some of them lost their lives. This brought about another " crisis " in America, and the Press was almost unanimous in proclaiming

* " The Neutrality of the United States in Relation to the British and German Empires," by Professor Shield Nicholson.

that Germany's action, if the Arabic gave no provocation, was " deliberately unfriendly," and that more words were useless. Of course, Count Bernstorff played for delay, and after it had been granted a story was telegraphed from Berlin that the submarine commander who sank the Arabic declared the liner turned towards him ; he naturally supposed he was going to be rammed, so fired a torpedo. This story, arrayed in official attire, was subsequently submitted by the German Ambassador, with a further insulting statement that as the Arabic had been sunk in self-defence, the German Government declined to admit liability for Americans killed. Count Bernstorff was confronted by Secretary Lansing with affidavits made by American survivors of the Arabic, showing that the ship did not attempt to ram the submarine, and that therefore its commander was not acting in self-defence. This the Count declared made a further explanation necessary. In the case of the Allan liner Hesperian, which was torpedoed and sunk September 6, 1915, with loss of life, the Germans claimed that the vessel was sunk by a mine and not a submarine. Of Bernstorff's promise the *New York Herald* said :

Apparently the German Ambassador meant not one word of the written memorandum, and the conclusion is irresistible that Germany has been continually trifling with the United States.

Of the Hesperian assassins the same journal remarked :

In attacking the Hesperian the German submarine commander was absolutely ruthless. He could not tell whether he was attacking a liner or a cargo boat. The boat might just as well have been the St. Paul or the Philadelphia of the American Line.

The President demanded a copy of the orders issued to submarine commanders as a proof of good faith. This request the German Government showed no desire to grant.

CHAPTER XC.

POLITICAL CHANGES AT HOME: A COALITION GOVERNMENT

POLITICAL SITUATION PRECEDING THE OUTBREAK OF WAR: THE HOME RULE BILL—THE PARTY TRUCE—LORD KITCHENER AS MINISTER OF WAR—EMERGENCY MEASURES—THE VEIL OF SECRECY —RECRUITING—PENSIONS AND ALLOWANCES—ENEMY ALIENS—TRADING WITH THE ENEMY— LABOUR TROUBLES—MUNITIONS—DRINK—SPORT—UNREST AT THE ADMIRALTY—THE COALITION GOVERNMENT—THE MUNITIONS OF WAR ACT—THRIFT CAMPAIGN AND WAR LOAN—NATIONAL REGISTRATION BILL—BOARDS AND COMMITTEES OF EXPERTS—THE GOVERNMENT AND THE SOUTH WALES COAL STRIKES.

THE announcement on Friday, July 24, of the Austrian ultimatum to Serbia coincided to a day with one of the most dramatic moments of the Parliamentary Session of 1914. The Irish Question, that malignant problem which for a generation past had, more than any other influence, tended to corrupt political life, was reaching its climax. In order to realize the situation with which the gathering of the coming storm found the Parliament and people of England preoccupied it is necessary to recall briefly the phases of the Home Rule controversy immediately preceding the outbreak of war.

In spite of a wholly unprecedented passage in the King's Speech at the opening of the Session, in which His Majesty had expressed his most earnest wish that the goodwill and cooperation of men of all parties and creeds might heal dissension and lay the foundations of a lasting settlement, the future position of Ulster had once more proved the apparently insuperable obstacle to agreement. Violent altercations in the House of Commons, the incendiary attitude adopted by Mr. Winston Churchill, First Lord of the Admiralty, in a speech at Bradford on March 4, the " precautionary " movements of troops and warships, which convinced the Ulster Unionists that a deliberate

campaign to overawe them had been set on foot, the alarming culmination of the crisis in the resignation of the Brigadier-General and 57 officers of the Cavalry at the Curragh on March 20—all these deplorable incidents had raised public excitement to a pitch which is almost inconceivable to-day. No one who recalls the black week-end of the " Curragh crisis " will forget the common feeling that the whole foundations of our society were rocking ; and the general sense of bewilderment threatened to turn into an appalling national schism when certain Radicals and Nationalists thought fit to raise the cry of " the Army against the People." So far had party passion obliterated all sense of decency that the Army, which was so soon to cover itself with imperishable glory, was represented as threatening the authority of Parliament by the very men whose blind ambitions had long since reduced that authority to a mere figure of speech. The situation became momentarily calmer with the judicious assumption by the Prime Minister on March 30 of the post of Secretary of State for War.*

---

* Colonel Seely, Secretary of State for War, together with Sir John French, Chief of the Imperial General Staff, and Sir Spencer Ewart, Adjutant-General of the Forces, had resigned in the midst of the chaos.

THE ULSTER VOLUNTEERS.

Sir Edward Carson inspecting the Guard of Honour.

Inset : Sir Edward holding up the name sheet with "Mountjoy" painted on it.

A month later the landing by the Ulster Volunteer Force of a large store of rifles and ammunition caused a profound sensation. The Home Rule Bill passed through its second and third readings (April 6 and May 25) on the understanding that the question of the exclusion of Ulster would be further raised by an Amending Bill. Meanwhile, the recognition by Mr. Redmond of the National Volunteers, which had been formed as a response to the Ulster Volun-

teer Force, brought a new and disturbing factor into play. When, at length, on June 23, Lord Crewe introduced the Amending Bill in the House of Lords it was found to contain no more than had been offered by the Prime Minister early in March—the exclusion for six years of such Ulster counties as voted themselves out of the Home Rule scheme. The Lords, in Committee, quickly transformed the measure into one which, permanently excluding the whole of Ulster, could obviously not expect acceptance by the Government. Matters were fast reaching a deadlock when on July 20 *The Times* startled the political world by announcing that the King had summoned a conference of two representatives of each of the four parties to the controversy, under the chairmanship of the Speaker, to meet at Buckingham Palace. During the days which followed there was a breathless lull in hostilities. His Majesty opened the Conference with a gravely worded speech, in which he spoke of the cry of civil war being on the lips of the most responsible and sober-minded of the people. The Conference held four meetings. On

July 24 the Speaker briefly reported its failure to the House as follows :—" The possibility of defining an area to be excluded from the Government of Ireland Bill was considered. The Conference, being unable to agree, either in principle or in detail, upon such an area brought its meetings to a conclusion."

Such was the pass to which the " obtuse blindness," as Mr. Balfour called it, of the Government had brought the country at the moment when the mists of war which had long been hanging on the European horizon condensed into the definite menace of the Austrian Note. The bursting of the storm found England apparently impotent to prevent a domestic tragedy which would shake the British Empire to its foundations. Parliamentary government had become an empty farce. All sense of leadership had been lost in a turmoil of talk ; all sense of realities had vanished in the struggle of conflicting party interests. The ship of State had become a raft, drifting no one knew whither amid the wrangling of the crew. No wonder that foreign observers, ignorant of the greater character of the nation, attributed to it as a whole the unworthy qualities of its least representative politicians.

It is impossible yet to determine how far the divisions of parties on the Irish question were a factor in the hope of Germany that England would keep out of the war. It may well be that, seeing the Government under the lash of their Nationalist supporters, sinking daily deeper and deeper into the morass, unconscious of any but their

RECRUITING IN LONDON.
Outside the Central Recruiting Office.

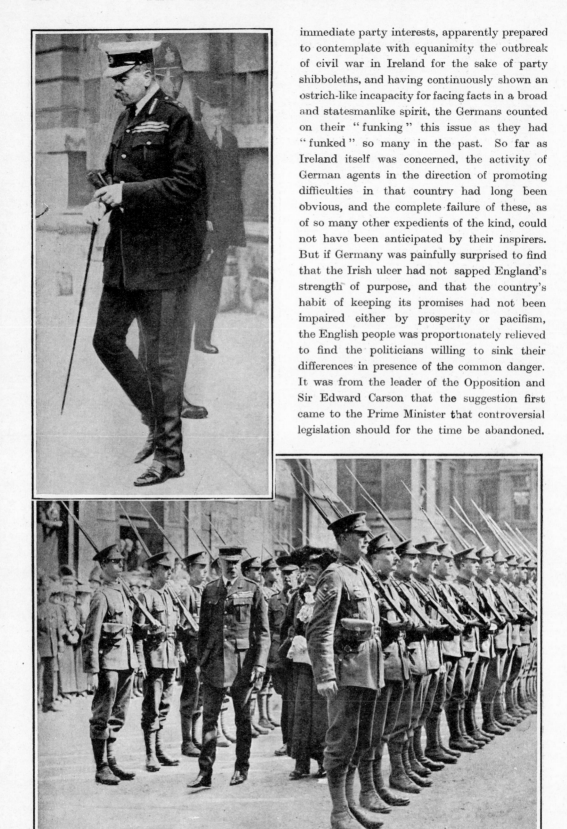

immediate party interests, apparently prepared to contemplate with equanimity the outbreak of civil war in Ireland for the sake of party shibboleths, and having continuously shown an ostrich-like incapacity for facing facts in a broad and statesmanlike spirit, the Germans counted on their "funking" this issue as they had "funked" so many in the past. So far as Ireland itself was concerned, the activity of German agents in the direction of promoting difficulties in that country had long been obvious, and the complete failure of these, as of so many other expedients of the kind, could not have been anticipated by their inspirers. But if Germany was painfully surprised to find that the Irish ulcer had not sapped England's strength of purpose, and that the country's habit of keeping its promises had not been impaired either by prosperity or pacifism, the English people was proportionately relieved to find the politicians willing to sink their differences in presence of the common danger. It was from the leader of the Opposition and Sir Edward Carson that the suggestion first came to the Prime Minister that controversial legislation should for the time be abandoned.

LORD KITCHENER'S VISIT TO THE CITY.
The War Minister inspecting the Guard of Honour outside the Guildhall.
Inset : Lord Kitchener leaving the War Office.

LORD KITCHENER IN THE CITY.

The War Secretary receives a great ovation from the crowd outside the Guildhall after his recruiting speech.

In announcing on July 30 the postponement, without prejudice, of the Amending Bill, Mr. Asquith gave his reasons in language which struck the keynote of the momentous debates which were to follow :

We meet to-day, he said, under conditions of gravity which are almost unparalleled in the experience of every one of us. The issues of peace and war are hanging in the balance, and with them the risk of a catastrophe of which it is impossible to measure either the dimensions or the effects. In these circumstances it is of vital importance in the interests of the whole world that this country, which has no interests of its own directly at stake*, should present a united front, and be able to speak and act with the authority of an undivided nation.

With the agreement of the House to confine itself to non-controversial business, a party truce was declared for the period of the national peril, and was only broken, as the Opposition considered, by Mr. Asquith's insisting on placing the Home Rule Bill and the Welsh Church Bill on the Statute-book about six weeks later (September 18).

Meanwhile the country went through another of those anxious week-ends (August 1–3) when

* This speech was made at a moment when it was still assumed to be possible that the neutrality of Belgium might be respected.

the crisis abroad became momentarily over-shadowed by doubts at home. The Government—in the persons of Mr. Churchill and Prince Louis of Battenberg, his First Sea Lord—had already taken the prompt and invaluable step of keeping the Fleet in a state of mobilization after its summer exercises. What would they do further ? Would they recognize obligations which, though never specified or disclosed, were tacitly endorsed by everyone who understood the situation ? Would the people on the other hand consent to shoulder a burden which had been so studiously kept from their sight ? The Cabinet was in session almost without intermission throughout that fateful Sunday (August 2), and by the evening the stern logic of events had to all intents and purposes swung the country into war. The German hosts were already across the border.

The closing of the political ranks which accompanied the actual bursting of the storm was a magnificent demonstration of patriotism. On the same Sunday morning, as was after-wards revealed, Mr. Bonar Law had addressed the following letter to Mr. Asquith :

Lord Lansdowne and I feel it our duty to inform you that, in our opinion, as well as in that of all the colleagues whom we have been able to consult, it would be fatal to

60—2

RIGHT HON. H. H. ASQUITH,   [*Walton Adams & Sons.*

Prime Minister and First Lord of the Treasury.

the honour and security of the United Kingdom to hesitate in supporting France and Russia at the present juncture ; and we offer our unhesitating support to the Government in any measures they may consider necessary for that object.

Next day, a memorable Bank Holiday, Sir Edward Grey made his historic statement. He began by recalling to the House the way in which during the last years, and notably throughout the Balkan crisis, " we have consistently worked with a single mind, with all the earnestness in our power, to preserve peace."

In the present crisis it has not been possible to secure the peace of Europe, because there has been little time, and there has been a disposition—at any rate in some quarters, on which I will not dwell—to force things rapidly to an issue, at any rate, to the great risk of peace, and as we now know, the result of that is that the policy of peace, as far as the Great Powers generally are concerned, is in danger. I do not want to dwell on that, and to comment on it, and to say where the blame seems to us to lie, which Powers were most in favour of peace, which were most disposed to risk or endanger peace

RIGHT HON. DAVID LLOYD GEORGE. [*Walton Adams & Sons.*
Minister of Munitions.

because I would like the House to approach this crisis in which we are now from the point of view of British interests, British honour, and British obligations, free from all passion as to why peace has not been preserved.

After tracing the course of diplomatic conversations at the time of the Algeciras Conference and during the Agadir crisis, in order to show that nothing which had previously taken place in the Government's diplomatic relations with other Powers restricted the free-

dom of the Government and House to decide what their present attitude should be, Sir Edward Grey pointed out that the present crisis, unlike the previous ones, had not originated with anything which primarily concerned France.

I can say this with the most absolute confidence—no Government and no country has less desire to be involved in war over a dispute with Austria and Serbia than the Government and the country of France. They are involved in it because of their obligation of honour under

SPECIAL CONSTABLES IN THE CITY.

Inset: Receiving instructions at Scotland Yard.

I gave to the French Ambassador the following statement :

"I am authorised to give an assurance that if the German Fleet comes into the Channel or through the North Sea to undertake hostile operations against the French coasts or shipping, the British Fleet will give all the protection in its power. This assurance is, of course, subject to the policy of His Majesty's Government receiving the support of Parliament, and must not be taken as binding His Majesty's Government to take any action until the above contingency of action by the German fleet takes place."

Sir Edward Grey went on to describe the treaty obligations of Great Britain towards Belgium, and added :

We were sounded in the course of last week as to whether if a guarantee were given that, after the war, Belgian integrity would be preserved that would content us. We replied that we could not bargain away whatever interests or obligations we had in Belgian neutrality.

Meanwhile the King of the Belgians had appealed to King George for the diplomatic intervention of the British Government to safeguard the integrity of Belgium. Now England, in the words of Mr. Gladstone, had

a definite alliance with Russia. Well, it is only fair to say to the House that the obligation of honour cannot apply in the same way to us. We are not parties to the Franco-Russian Alliance. We do not even know the terms of that Alliance.

But for many years England had had a long-standing friendship with France.

The French fleet is in the Mediterranean, and has for some years been concentrated there because of the feeling of confidence and friendship which has existed between the two countries. My own feeling is that if a foreign fleet engaged in a war which France had not sought, and in which she had not been the aggressor, came down the English Channel and bombarded and battered the undefended coasts of France, we could not stand aside and see this going on practically within sight of our eyes, with our arms folded, looking on dispassionately, doing nothing ! I believe that would be the feeling of this country. . . . We feel strongly that France was entitled to know—and to know at once !— whether or not in the event of attack upon her unprotected Northern and Western coasts she could depend upon British support. In that emergency, and in these compelling circumstances, yesterday afternoon

an interest in the independence of Belgium which is wider than that which we may have in the literal operation of the guarantee. It is found in the answer to the question whether, under the circumstances of the case, this country, endowed as it is with influence and power, would quietly stand by and witness the perpetration of the direst crime that ever stained the pages of history, and thus become participators in the sin.

If in a crisis like this (said Sir Edward Grey) we run away from those obligations of honour and interest as regards the Belgian Treaty, I doubt whether, whatever material force we might have at the end, it would be of very much value in face of the respect that we should have lost. . . .

The one bright spot in the whole of this terrible situation is Ireland.

Mr. Bonar Law briefly assured the Government of his support, concluding with the words :

> The Government already know, but I give them now the assurance on behalf of the party of which I am Leader in this House, that in whatever steps they think it necessary to take for the honour and security of this country they can rely on the unhesitating support of the Opposition.

Then Mr. Redmond, after admitting that in past moments of stress the sympathy of the Nationalists of Ireland, for reasons to be found deep down in the centuries of history, had been estranged from England, declared :

> To-day I honestly believe that the democracy of Ireland will turn with the utmost anxiety and sympathy to this country in every trial and every danger that may overtake it. . . . I say to the Government that they may to-morrow withdraw every one of their troops from Ireland. I say that the coast of Ireland will be defended from foreign invasion by her armed sons, and for this purpose armed Nationalist Catholics in the South will be only too glad to join arms with the armed Protestant Ulstermen in the North.

These several declarations left the House united as it had seldom been in its history. From this moment the Government, enjoying an immunity from criticism almost complete and altogether unprecedented, settled down to the work in hand.

The action of Germany in invading Belgium overcame the doubts of those members of the

THE "SCRAP OF PAPER."
A Recruiting poster, showing a reproduction of the treaty signed in 1839 guaranteeing the independence and neutrality of Belgium. Palmerston signed for Britain, Bülow for Prussia.

Government who were still unconvinced of England's duty to her Allies, and thus saved the country from a Cabinet crisis at a moment when, before all things, unity was essential. It is, therefore, unnecessary to consider what would have happened if a change of Government had taken place, though it seems improbable that a Unionist Cabinet could have counted on the same immunity from criticism as that enjoyed, all too long, by the Ministers who continued in power. Even before the declaration of war the possibility of a Coalition had been discussed. But at that moment the obvious difficulties seemed insuperable. How, it was asked, could Unionists produce effective cooperation by becoming a minority in a Government which remained a party Government ? Would they not merely be surrendering their powers and responsibilities without the certainty of thereby adding to the common advantage ? Was the country ripe for so great an experiment ? These questions were to await an answer until circumstances stronger than party considerations arose to make a Coalition inevitable. It remained to

A WAR LOAN POSTER.

INTERCESSION DAY AT ST. PAUL'S, AUGUST 4, 1915.

"We commend to thy Fatherly goodness the men who, through perils of war, are serving the nation"; the scene in St. Paul's Cathedral on the day which began the second year of the war.

be seen how far the arrangement would justify the original anxiety as to its success.

On August 6 Mr. Asquith announced that he had relinquished the post of Secretary of State for War and that it had been accepted by Lord Kitchener. The appointment was received by the nation with the utmost satisfaction and relief. There had, as we saw in an earlier chapter,* been a moment of intense anxiety lest the Lord Chancellor, Lord Haldane, should be invited to return to his former position at the War Office. It was felt that the occasion called, not for a man skilled in the subtleties of debate, but for a soldier of proved experience in the organization of warfare. It was freely admitted that during his tenure of office as Minister of War Lord Haldane had done much to improve the efficiency of the Army. If, for the sake of the cheap applause with which his party was ever ready to welcome any apparent economy in military expenditure, he reduced the Artillery, he was to be credited with the foundation of the Territorial Force, and for this, as also for his being one of the first to realize the potentialities of military aeronautics, the country had abundant reason to be grateful. But his well-known predilections for Germany rendered the prospect of his appointment to the War Office liable to arouse misapprehension in France. Above all, his inherent desire to avoid unpopularity at all costs disqualified him for a post in which many unpopular actions might become necessary. Nor had the public forgotten that during the Army crisis Lord Haldane, by the insertion of the word "immediate" in the official report of a speech on the coercion of Ulster, had, as it seemed, sought to qualify in a highly important manner the sense of his utterances in the House itself. At this distance the incident, however unfortunate, appears trivial, but it was not so at the time, and it undoubtedly injured Lord Haldane's reputation for straightforwardness to a very serious degree.

For the first time, therefore, a soldier with no Cabinet experience became Secretary of State for War. Other Cabinet changes had already been announced. During the week preceding the Government's momentous decision and while Germany's intentions were still undeclared, the Prime Minister, in view of the importance of standing before the world with the support of an absolutely united Cabinet, had been engaged in his familiar struggle to keep

his colleagues together. But in the case both of Lord Morley, Lord-President of the Council, and of Mr. Burns, President of the Board of Trade, the moment seemed opportune for retirement. Neither the advanced age of the former nor the personal sympathies of the latter justified them any longer in forming part of a Cabinet from which, before all things, strenuous labour and unanimity with regard to the policy to be pursued were to be expected, and on August 4 the two Ministers resigned, to be succeeded respectively by Lord Beauchamp and Mr. Runciman. At the same time Mr. C. P. Trevelyan resigned the Parliamentary Under-Secretaryship of the Board of Education, and Mr. Ramsay MacDonald, who had been an outspoken critic of Sir Edward Grey's diplomacy, resigned the Chairmanship of the Parliamentary Labour Party.

The die once cast by England's declaration of war, the House of Commons, awaking as from an evil dream, set to work with a zeal and unanimity which have never been surpassed in its long, eventful history. The first war vote of credit for £100,000,000 and the increases of the Army and Navy by 500,000 and 67,000 men respectively were agreed to on Report without debate. Before the House was prorogued on September 18 no fewer than 37 Emergency Bills of various kinds had been passed—for the most part without any close examination. Among the more important measures were those dealing with the Defence of the Realm and those necessitated by the financial crisis. The former, while avoiding the appearance of imposing martial law, did in fact place remarkably extensive powers in the hands of the military authorities. The latter, of which the first was passed (on August 3) before war was actually declared, authorized the proclamation of a moratorium on certain payments. Confidence that the Government had the situation well in hand grew rapidly, largely owing to the patriotic action of the Press, which, while abstaining from criticism, encouraged the people to adapt themselves willingly to the unaccustomed interference with their liberty and comfort involved by this mass of legislation. Meanwhile, industrial disputes fell into abeyance, the trade union leaders showing themselves conspicuously public-spirited and the men forgetting for the time their grievances in the general enthusiasm for the country's cause. After lasting more than six months the strike in the building trade in London was concluded

* See Vol. I., p. 280.

BRITAIN'S NEW ARMY: LORD KITCHENER
Inset: Mr. Bonar Law and the

anxiety to Ministers during the preceding months.

The period of acquiescence in the desirability of avoiding controversy, so far as matters relating to the war were concerned, lasted longer than could have been expected, and certainly longer than, as appeared later, was conducive to the welfare of the State. The chief source of constructive criticism in the first few months of the war was the House of Lords, which set a good example to the House of Commons by curtailing its Christmas holiday. The tendency of Ministers, which had grown, as it always grows, with the prolongation of their tenure of office, to live exclusively in that politician's heaven which ignores the existence of the real world without, was too deeply rooted to be disturbed even by a European war. No sooner had the first wave of excitement and the glamour of the great speeches died away than the natural desire of the public for information began to express itself. An official Press Bureau was established on August 8, with the promise that all information which could be given without

by mutual consent at a moment when a national lock-out was threatened. Other disputes which in the aggregate represented a serious amount of industrial unrest were laid aside. Equally remarkable and significant was the entire abandonment of the campaign in favour of woman suffrage, which, with the concomitant outrages on public property committed by the militant section, had caused additional

REVIEWING THE "SERVICE" BATTALIONS.
Hon. Sam Hughes at Shorncliffe.

prejudice to the public interest "should be given fully and given at once." This is not the place to consider how far the Press Bureau carried out its duty efficiently. Opinions differ as to whether its activities were, as many considered, the worst managed of all branches of the Government's operations during the war. What is certain is that, sheltering itself behind the alleged wishes, now of our French Allies and now of our naval and military authorities, the Government adopted an attitude of reticence which, at a moment of intense general anxiety, was only prevented from producing a disastrous effect by the hitherto unimpaired confidence of the public in its leaders. Coupled with this reticence and intended, doubtless, to allay the suspicions engendered by it, came a series of soothing speeches, emphasizing the valour of the British troops and the greatness of the response to Lord Kitchener's appeal for men, and of the support forthcoming from the Empire. All was for the best. If new recruits were lodged in scandalous conditions, that was inevitable in the circumstances. If there were

complaints about the insufficiency or non-payment of separation allowances, they were exaggerated. The truth about the Antwerp expedition could not expediently be revealed, but the Government could do no wrong.

There can be no doubt that the policy of impenetrable secrecy with which the Government veiled their operations was injurious to the common cause. It may have been based on the practice of countries in which, owing to the existence of universal military service, the conditions were altogether different from those prevailing in England. It was more probably due to the ingrained habit of Liberal Ministers of despising the intelligence of their supporters. It certainly indicated the completeness with which, in the past Parliamentary generation, the politicians had divorced themselves from the opinion of those whose votes had put them in power. It showed to what extent the old party cry of "Trust the People" had given place to the insidious substitute of "Trust the Government." No member of the Opposition, which had so patriotically abandoned its right of criticism, dreamed of embarrassing the Government by extracting from them information which could possibly be of service to the enemy. What the Government failed to realize was, first, that the enemy, and through the enemy the whole outer world, was perfectly well aware of the facts which were concealed from the public at home, and, secondly, that the country was composed, not of excitable children, but of serious men and women, prepared to make any sacrifices the moment the necessity for those sacrifices was explained to them. In the early days of the war there was no "pessimism" to be overcome by cheerful assurances. Perhaps, if the country had been aware of the magnitude of its task there might have been a stricter enquiry into the steps which the Government were taking to fulfil their responsibilities. But the country had been lulled to sleep by false prophets, and when the time came to arouse it, those same false prophets proved themselves incapable of shaking off the habits of a political lifetime

In the midst of the prevailing ignorance, which the occasional sketches of past naval and military operations vouchsafed by the First Lord of the Admiralty and the Secretary for War only served to deepen, and in spite of the general obscurantism of the Government, several unpleasant truths were brought home to the public by the efforts of a few private members and of the Press. The first was that the military authorities were largely unable to cope with the flood of recruits which poured into the enlistment offices in response to Lord Kitchener's appeal for men. Not only was accommodation, and, still more, equipment lacking for those accepted, but the mere process of enrolment was beset with difficulties which could not fail to have a discouraging effect. Nothing having been foreseen, the recruiting officers had to "muddle through" as best they could, and although in many cases goodwill performed miracles, in others lack of guidance and of adaptability to new ideas effectively chilled the ardour of those wishing to volunteer. Nevertheless, the first 100,000 men between the ages of 19 and 30 demanded by Lord Kitchener were quickly forthcoming, under the impulse of a campaign of advertisement which was later to assume the most humiliating forms.

Before a month had elapsed Lord Kitchener appealed for another 100,000, the age limit being raised to 35. At this period the average enlistments from the whole country were stated to be 30,000 a week. On September 10 Mr. Asquith announced that 438,000 had already been recruited. The establishment of the Army was raised by a further 500,000. By the end of October, in spite of strenuous appeals to the patriotism of employers, who in many cases had placed obstacles in the way of their men, there was a great falling off in the daily average of enlistments. Men were, it is true, freely joining specialized corps, the Territorials, and various unofficial bodies which were being raised throughout the country. But the recruiting for what was popularly known

TRENCH-DIGGERS—MEMBERS OF THE NATIONAL GUARD.

as "Kitchener's Army" showed a serious decline. For this the Government had only themselves to thank. The habitual failure to tell the truth on the part of the only people who were in a position to know it, the altogether false view of the situation produced by the absence of news, the very raising of the height standard for recruits, which, however necessary as a momentary expedient for checking the first overwhelming rush, undoubtedly produced the impression that more men were not needed, all these combined with stories of improper treatment of the enlisted and uncertainty as to the Government's intentions with regard to separation allowances and pensions to damp the ardour to enlist.

Under the instigation of that portion of the Press which had refused to be hoodwinked by official complacency, and which realized that until the need for an unlimited supply of men had been properly explained to the country its response would continue to be inadequate, a variety of new methods were set on foot. An appeal to householders to state the names of members of their households who were willing to enlist was signed by Mr. Asquith, Mr. Bonar Law, and Mr. Henderson, the new Chairman of the Parliamentary Labour Party, and issued from November 12 onward by the Parliamentary Recruiting Committee. The filling up of the form was purely voluntary, and its issue, which had been postponed at the wish of the War Office, was at first confined to the rural districts of the Eastern Command. The response was so satisfactory that in November the War Office requested that the form should be sent to the Northern, Southern and Western Commands, large cities and towns being excluded. By the middle of December 4,400,000 householders had been circularized, and by December 22 2,500,000 replies had been received, of which 225,000 were promises to enlist. Lord Kitchener, at a Guildhall meeting on November 9, asked for "men and still more men." Recruiting speeches filled the air, while every conceivable form of advertisement appealed to the eye, if not to the taste, of the beholder. These advertisements, ranging from the simple "Join the Army Now" of the taxicabs to the highly coloured pictures of the hoardings, in which every sentiment from shame to anger was adduced as a motive for enlistment, were, in spite of their undoubted cleverness, a humiliating confession of the Government's reluctance

to face the facts. It was a new experience for a generation of citizens which had been brought up to concentrate its attention solely on its "rights" to be reminded that there was such a thing as "duty" too. Very surprising and shocking also to our Allies, accustomed to universal service, was the discovery that the idea of serving the country had to be conveyed, as it were, for the first time to the people of this country by methods of this kind. An extraordinarily high percentage of the new recruits were married men. The disastrous effects of this indiscriminate recruiting, both on the cost of separation allowances and in the robbing of war industries of many of their best and most patriotic men, were frequently pointed out to the Government in vain. Lord Kitchener had been entrusted with the task of raising armies on the voluntary system, which had existed, and more or less sufficed, to meet altogether different conditions. To all enquiries in Parliament and arguments in the Press the Government were impervious. But still the cry went up for "men and still more men."

Appeals for a relaxation of the censorship restrictions, which would have enabled the country to learn "the truth about the war," were treated with high-handed contempt. Instead, an active process of individual canvassing was set on foot. While "international" football matches were abandoned, partly from the belief that, in default of them, spectators would join the colours, though partly, no doubt, for fear lest their continuance should be misunderstood abroad, numerous proposals for improving the comfort of recruits was brought to the attention of the Government and largely adopted. The result of all these measures was to revive recruiting, and when on November 16 an increase of another 1,000,000 men was asked and granted the House sat back on its benches and once more "trusted the Government." On November 17 Mr. Lloyd George informed the House that there were at the moment "at least 2,000,000 serving the country under arms," and a few days later Lord Kitchener, in the House of Lords, described the rate of recruiting as approximately 30,000 a week, in addition to regiments raised by particular localities.

The difficult question of pensions and allowances to the dependants of soldiers next occupied the House. The numerous hardships and incongruities of the existing arrangements were pointed out, and on the proposal

THE ROYAL NAVAL VOLUNTEER RESERVE.
Men of the Glasgow and Clyde Divisions marching in the grounds of the Crystal Palace.

of Mr. Bonar Law the matter was referred to a small Committee. Ultimately, extensive changes were made in the Government's already amended scale. Much debate took place as to the proper machinery for the administration of the allowances, but as regards the financial aspect there was no disagreement as to the need of combining generosity with justice. As for the alleged grievances in the matter of delayed payment, they were attributable to the complete inadequacy of existing machinery for its enormously increased work.

The minimum weekly scale of pensions issued in November, 1914, while still open to amendment, was much more liberal than that previously in force. It failed to cope satisfactorily with the fact that the circumstances of the material composing the huge new Army were not only superior to but far less uniform than those of the smaller Army of the past. The widow of a private received a pension ranging from 7s. 6d. a week in the absence of children to £1 a week in the case of four children, with 2s. additional for each child in excess of four. Additional allowances were given in necessitous cases. The minimum total disablement allowance for unmarried men of the lowest grades without children was 14s. a week, which might be increased at the discretion of the authorities up to 23s. The

allowances for partial disablement in the lowest grades ranged from 3s. 6d. to 17s. 6d. a week. The separation allowance in the case of soldiers making the usual allotment of 6d. a day from their pay (and including that allotment) ranged from 12s. 6d. a week, and was irrespective of whether or not the wife was " on the strength." On the whole, the Government were less open to criticism in this particular matter than in almost any of their proceedings.

It was the policy of Ministers—or, rather, the absence of any consistent policy—with regard to alien enemies in the United Kingdom that at this period chiefly strained the confidence of the country. By the Aliens Restriction and Defence of the Realm Acts of August the Government had taken extensive powers for dealing both with the movements of aliens and with espionage. The Prime Minister claimed that, " at once, or as soon as might be after the outbreak of war all those persons who, after many years of careful and continuous observation," there was reason to suspect of being spies had been arrested or interned. The Home Office was optimistic and did in fact lay hands on a number of obvious undesirables. But it was long before public opinion, expressing itself in a few cases by the breaking of windows, induced the authorities to realize that more comprehensive measures were required. Not until the beginning of October were instructions given for the internment of all unnaturalized male enemy aliens of military age. The question of accommodation at once arose. Certain accommodation was forthcoming, notably at Olympia, in the neighbourhood of Aldershot, and in the Isle of Man. Then the internment instructions were countermanded, reissued, and again countermanded within a few days. From October to May, except in a few special cases, enemy aliens were left undisturbed. In the following September the work of internment was still incomplete.

In comparison with other countries there was a praiseworthy absence of " spy mania." But plenty of evidence was forthcoming that the danger of espionage was not confined to unnaturalized enemies. The Home Secretary, in face of an anxious House, exhibited the inveterate desire of the politician to disclaim responsibility, while magnifying the work actually accomplished by his Department. Meanwhile, it was obvious that the lack of co-ordination between the naval and military authorities on the one hand and the police authorities on the other produced the most

RECRUITING IN REGENT STREET, LONDON.
Miss Alice Lakin singing outside the Polytechnic Institute.   Inset : Recruits for the Black Watch
in Edinburgh.

unfortunate incoherence in practice. In reply to suggestions that the whole matter should be in the hands of a single responsible Minister, Mr. McKenna announced in March that there was no single Department of State, except the military authority, which could undertake the work. The sole responsibility for the internment of aliens and their release from internment had rested, except for an inter-regnum of two or three weeks, with Lord Kitchener, who was unwilling to relinquish that responsibility. In reply Mr. Bonar Law pointed out with crushing force that the Government, as a whole, were responsible for their policy. The debate, otherwise inconclusive, left a painful impression of leaderless Ministers working without co-ordination.

In May public opinion on the subject became too strong. The English race is slow to wrath. The country, while resenting the freedom enjoyed by alien enemies as compared with the treatment of British subjects in Germany, had not yet lost confidence that, after all, "the Government probably knew best." Even the shameful bombardment of defenceless coast towns had aroused little active resentment. But, stirred by the wholesale murders of those on board the Lusitania and the shock to civilized ideas caused by the use of poisonous gases at the Front, the wrath of the nation, at home and throughout the Empire, was no longer to be restrained. It became obvious that, if only for their own protection, Germans and Austrians must be segregated on a comprehensive scale. On May 13, more than nine months after the outbreak of war, Mr. Asquith announced that all male enemy aliens of military age would be interned. Males above military age would be deported "unless grounds were shown for exceptional treatment." Women and children "in suitable cases" would be repatriated. Naturalized persons "of hostile origin" would be interned in cases of proved necessity or danger. An advisory body of a judicial character was to be set up to consider claims for exemption from the general rule. The Home Secretary would be responsible for ascertaining who were the persons to whom the new policy applied. Mr. Bonar Law, in expressing his approval, took occasion to point out that, just as the Government had lagged behind the House of Commons in the matter, so the House of Commons had lagged behind the general

feeling of the public outside. Two curious phenomena which followed the Government's decision were the embarrassing rush of enemy aliens to surrender to the police and the haste of naturalized members of City institutions to declare their loyalty.

A proclamation prohibiting trading with the enemy was issued on August 5, the day after the declaration of war, and was extended to Austria-Hungary a week later. It was obscure in many points, and an explanation of it was published on August 22. By a second proclamation of September 9 the various prohibitions were restated and extended. Further extensions were published on September 30 and October 8, 1914, and January 7, 1915. Under these regulations, which proved exceedingly necessary, a number of prosecutions took place. Among them was one which resulted in the conviction of a firm of Glasgow merchants for being instrumental in supplying part of a cargo of iron ore to Messrs. Krupps and other German firms.

One of the first and most widely felt consequences of the outbreak of war was a rise in the cost of living. This natural phenomenon was to have far-reaching effects. It was, indeed, to cause the first rift in the unity with which all classes of the population had embarked upon the war. Nothing had been more remarkable than the way in which, in the face of the common danger, employers and employed alike had called a truce in the stubborn conflicts which had been raging for the past four years. Prompt steps were taken to minimize distress resulting from the dislocation of industry. The absorption into the Army of many men thrown out of work during the first days of shock, and the foundation of Queen Mary's and other funds for finding re-employment for women, gave time for the working population to adjust itself to the new conditions. Before the end of September the Local Government Board was able to report that, with an abundance of relief schemes, there was no abnormal distress. Money, in this respect as in all others, flowed like water. Much of it, doubtless, was ill-spent.

It was not until the war was five months old that industrial difficulties first threatened to impair the harmony of the country. But already the congested state of the ports and railways had raised the price of foodstuffs and some other commodities to an unusual pitch. The people murmured, being convinced that

"NOSING" A SHELL.

The metal cylinder is being heated in a furnace by the man seen in the foreground, who passes it on to his mate, who puts the glowing end beneath a press which gives the cylinder the conical head on which the percussion or fuse cap is eventually fixed. Walls of shell are banked up behind the long lines of workers.

better organization on the part of the Government would have obviated many of these difficulties, and being naturally incapable of appreciating the equally responsible effect of the rise in freights and the interference with normal trade routes. Added to this there gradually grew up a belief in the minds even of men who were receiving better wages for more regular work than they had ever known before that the employers were making large fortunes at their expense. In the middle of January a dispute arose in the West Yorkshire coalfield concerning the interpretation of an award given under the Minimum Wage Act in the previous July. A strike was only averted by the concession by the coalowners of the men's demands "during the continuance of the war." Simultaneously, the railwaymen, who had agreed at the outbreak of war to postpone the negotiation of a new scheme for improving their condition

THE COALITION CABI

1. Mr. Arthur Henderson, President
(L.); 4. Mr. Winston Churchill, Chance
(Non-party); 7. Mr. H. H. Asquith,
(L.); 10. Mr. Lewis Harcourt, First C
Sir Edward Grey, Secretary of State for F
16. Mr. Augustine Birrell, Chief Secrete
ture (U); 19. Sir Edward Carson, Att
Lansdowne, No Portfo'io (U.).

THE GREAT WAR.

Education (Lab.) ; 2. Mr. Austen Chamberlain, Secretary of State for India (U.) ; 3. Mr. T. McKinnon Wood, Secretary for Scotland
y of Lancaster (L.) ; 5. Mr. Bonar Law, Secretary of State for the Colonies (U.) ; 6. Lord Kitchener, Secretary of State for War
and First Lord of the Treasury (L.) ; 8. Lord Crewe, Lord President of the Council (L.) ; 9. Mr. Lloyd George, Minister of Munitions
Works (L.) ; 11. Mr. Reginald McKenna, Chancellor of the Exchequer (L.) ; 12. Sir Stanley Buckmaster, Lord Chancellor (L.) ; 13.
.) ; 14. Sir John Simon, Secretary of State for Home Affairs (L.) ; 15. Mr. Walter Runciman, President of the Board of Trade (L.) ;
..) ; 17. Mr. Walter Long, President of the Local Government Board (U.) ; 18. Lord Selborne, President of the Board of Agricul-
(U.) ; 20. Lord Curzon of Kedleston, Lord Privy Seal (U.) ; 21. Mr. A. J. Balfour, First Lord of the Admiralty (U.) ; 22. Lord

MUNITION WORKERS.

Recruits enrolling in London.   Centre: Stamping
out a section for ammunition
pouches.

which had been maturing for some time past,
came forward with demands which were temporarily satisfied by the usual compromise.
The men asked for a war bonus of 5s. a week
all round ; they received 3s. a week in the
case of those earning less than 30s. a week and
2s. in the case of those earning 30s. or more.
Henceforward for months the history of labour
presents a painful spectacle to the historian—
painful not because the men's demands for
higher wages to meet the increased cost of
living were unpatriotic or unreasonable, but
because of the failure of the Government to
handle the question on any carefully thought-
out lines.   The hearts of the wage-earning class,
as a whole, were not less earnestly engaged in
the war than those of other classes.   But, failing
any endeavour on the part of the Government
to render the true seriousness of the situation
clear to them, the trade unions instinctively
reverted to their time-honoured practices.
Disputes were settled on the old lines by bargain-
ing, in which, after a grievous waste of time, the
men generally received all, or most, of what
they claimed.   Meanwhile, in the midst of a
sea of demands, concessions, reprisals, conferences, negotiations, strikes and resumptions
of work, the war tended to sink out of sight.

A strike of engineers on the Clyde brought
matters to a climax.   The Government intervened, calling upon the men to resume work

AN ETON BOY OPERATING A DRILL.

MUNITION WORKERS.

Clerks at work at a London Factory. They gave two hours each evening and Saturday afternoons to the work.

immediately. Mr. Lloyd George, in a notable speech at Bangor on February 28, at length showed that he had the courage and imagination to take the nation into his confidence. "We are conducting a war as if there was no war," he said, pointing out that it was intolerable that the life of Britain should be imperilled for the matter of a farthing an hour.

We have raised the largest voluntary Army that has been enrolled in any country or any century—the largest voluntary Army, and it is going to be larger. I saw a very fine example of that Army this morning at Llandudno. I attended a service there, and I think it was about the most thrilling religious service I have ever been privileged to attend. There were men there of every class, every position, every calling, every condition of life. The peasant had left his plough, the workman had left his lathe and his loom, the clerk had left his desk, the trader and the business man had left their counting-houses, the shepherd had left his sunlit hills and the miner the darkness of the earth, the rich proprietor had left his palace and the man earning his daily bread had quitted his humble cottage.

In contrast with this picture of unanimity, Mr. Lloyd George described in vivid words the manner in which a fortnight of work absolutely necessary for the defences of the country had been set aside by the dispute between masters and men upon the Clyde. How, he asked, was it to be stopped ?

Employers will say, "Are we always to give way ? " Workmen say, "Employers are making their fortunes out of an emergency of the country, why are we not to have a share of the plunder ? " "We work harder than ever," say the workmen. All I can say is, if they do, they are entitled to their share. But that is not the

MORE ETON BOYS AT WORK.

point—Who is right? Who is wrong? They are both wrong. There is a good deal to be said for and there is a vast amount to be said against compulsory arbitration, but during the war the Government ought to have power to settle all these differences, and the work should go on. The workman ought to get more. Very well, let the Government find it out and give it to him. If he ought not, then he ought not to throw up his tools. The country cannot afford it. It is disaster, and I do not believe the moment this comes home to workmen and employers they will refuse to comply with the urgent demand of the Government. There must be no delay. . . . This war is not going to be fought mainly on the battlefields of Belgium and Poland. It is going to be fought in the workshops of France and Great Britain.

The men, who had thrown over their responsible leaders for an executive committee of extremists, were very little moved by his exhortations. But after remaining out for a few days longer, in order to show their independence, they gradually returned to work. Strikes, however, continued in other parts of the country.

On March 9 Mr. Lloyd George took the House of Commons by surprise by producing a new Defence of the Realm Bill, the most far-reaching of the series. In introducing the measure, the Chancellor of the Exchequer insisted on the vital importance to the country of an increased output of munitions of war. The Government had already obtained power to take over any works in which war material was being produced. Power was now sought to take over in addition works which might be adapted for that purpose. There was no opposition to the proposal, the only feeling being one of surprise that the Government should not have made it half a year before. It is probable that few members of the House, and certain that few people in the country, realized the new cause of anxiety with which Mr. Lloyd George's Bill was concerned, and which, together with its own internal differences of opinion, were to lead to a reconstitution of the Government. The House had been recently agitating itself about such questions as inoculation, the employment of child-labour on farms, the censorship, a demand by the Labour Party that the Government should "prevent the continuance of the rise in the necessities of life," and an alleged unbusinesslike arrangement in connexion with the purchase of timber. On February 8 Mr. Tennant, Under-Secretary of State for War, had assured the House that "recruiting had been very satisfactory." "Of course," he added, "it varied from week to week, and possibly at the present moment if a little more energy were to be put into recruiting it would not be out of place." On the whole there had been no cause for discontent,

still less for disquiet. "But we want more men." He went on to invite the trade unions to help the Government "to organize the forces of labour." By this he meant not only the relaxation of restrictions for the period of the war and for Government contracts, but the releasing of men for the Army by the substitution, wherever possible, of women. "I do not say," he mildly observed, "that it is a possible thing to do. I only throw it out tentatively in the hope that something may occur to hon. gentlemen, and that they may be able to assist us in that matter." Appeals for men and tentative suggestions to trade unions— these were the preoccupations of the Government at this period of the war. But the real need of the moment, as the House was soon to discover, was not men but munitions.

On February 4 a Committee on Production had been appointed to report on the best way to get a full output from the engineering and shipbuilding establishments working for the Government. On February 20 the Committee reported that it had been represented to them very strongly by both the Admiralty and the War Office that there was "a present and continuously increasing need for shells and fuses." It was Mr. Bonar Law who was the first to express, on March 1, a doubt whether in the matter of munitions the Government was doing everything it could to end the war. A few days later, when Mr. Lloyd George introduced his Bill, Mr. Bonar Law returned to the point. The Committee on Production had in the interval found it "necessary to emphasize very strongly the need of a rapid and continuous increase" in the output of all munitions of war. But neither the House nor the country had any evidence as to the exact position of affairs. It had trusted the Government, and the Government had concealed the truth.

On March 15 Lord Kitchener made his first appearance in the House of Lords since Parliament had reassembled, and delivered a grave and important speech. For the first time in his public utterances since the war began he showed that the supply of men was not in itself sufficient for victory. He dealt almost entirely with the output of war material and the necessity of making the best possible use of the available machinery. He pointed out that unless the whole nation cooperated "not only in supplying the manhood of the country to serve in our ranks, but also in supplying the necessary arms, ammunition, and equipment, successful operations in the various parts of the world in which we are engaged will be very seriously hampered and delayed." Notwithstanding the efforts made to meet requirements, he said,

We have unfortunately found that the output is not only not equal to our necessities, but does not fulfil our expectations. . . . I can only say that the supply of war material at the present moment and for the next two or three months is causing me very serious anxiety, and I wish all those engaged in the manufacture and supply of these stores to realize that it is absolutely essential not only that the arrears in the deliveries of our munitions of war should be wiped off, but that the output of every round of ammunition is of the utmost importance and has a large influence on our operations in the field.

He laid stress on the various causes which had contributed to the shortcomings—absence, irregular time-keeping, slack work, " in some cases the temptations of drink," " on more than one occasion the restrictions of trade unions." But there was no suggestion that these defects had been accompanied by failure on the part of the Government to make the best use of the material which lay ready to their hands. As a matter of fact, the Government had hitherto sought to meet the demand merely by giving huge orders to the great armament firms and leaving them to make what arrangements they could with sub-contractors, as they had been accustomed to do in peace-time. Consequently many firms were trying to do work for which they were very imperfectly equipped, and delays in delivery were inevitable. Meanwhile the columns of the Press teemed with the complaints of manufacturers who, filled with a patriotic desire to help to the best of their ability, were discouraged by months of red tape correspondence, fruitless journeys, and failure to get either instructions or orders. No wonder that the impression had got about among the men that there could not, after all, be any particular urgency.

Mr. Lloyd George's reply to the criticism that the Government should have brought in the Bill before was that he did not think it would have been justified " unless they felt that they could not get on very much farther without it." To this Mr. Bonar Law, with a far truer sense of the feeling of the country, retorted that the powers sought under the Bill could have been obtained just as readily six months previously as now. Mr. Lloyd George told the House, as he had told the workmen, that " we could not conduct war and still allow business to be conducted as usual." It is certain, on the other hand, that the tendency to conduct " business as usual " might have been counteracted from

A STOCK OF SHELLS READY FOR DISPATCH.

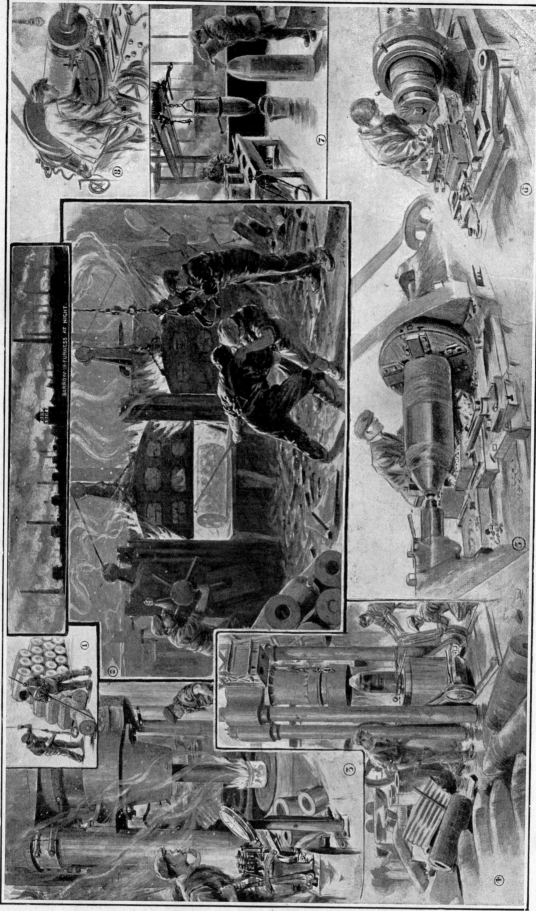

STAGES IN MANUFACTURING 12-IN. HIGH-EXPLOSIVE SHELLS IN THE VICKERS' WORKS.

1. Billets ready for the furnace. 2. Taking a billet from the furnace in which it has been heated for forging. 3. Forging a 12-in. shell in a hydraulic press.
4. Withdrawing a shell from the heading press, that makes the "nose" conical. 5. Turning the radius head and body of shell. 6. Placing the base of a shell in position. 7. Varnishing the inside of a shell. 8. Turning a copper driving band

the first if the Government had been open with the manufacturers.

From this moment, however, Mr. Lloyd George decided to take the business men into his confidence, and announced that the idea was to get a business man—" a good strong business man with some push and go in him " —at the head of the organization. The first step was the appointment, announced on April 7, of a War Office Committee " to take the necessary steps to provide such additional labour as may be required to secure that the supply of munitions of war shall be sufficient to meet all requirements." The announcement, after nearly a month's delay, caused a lively disappointment, not because the energetic shipowner, Mr. G. M. Booth, whose name was most prominently associated with the Committee, was not a highly efficient man, but because it was clear that the coach had not yet been lifted out of the old rut. But there was little pretence that the appointment of the Booth Committee had solved the problem. It appeared that all that had happened was the creation of a recruiting agency for the armament works to compete for men with Lord Kitchener's recruiting agents.

Parliament took its Easter holiday, and the interval was filled by a new campaign, which, without seriously affecting matters, for the moment distracted public attention. At a conference with representatives of trade unions on March 17 Mr. Lloyd George announced his intention to impose a limitation of profits on works controlled by the Government, and requested that, in return, the workmen should abandon stoppages of work (pending the reference of disputes to an arbitration tribunal) and should suspend, where necessary, all rules and regulations tending to restrict output. But he went on to lay stress on reports which he had received from the Admiralty and War Office to the effect that excessive drinking on the part of the workmen (admittedly a minority) in some districts was gravely interfering with the work. The latter idea was taken up throughout the country, and for a time it seemed, to judge from reported utterances, that drink was really at the bottom of all the labour troubles. Mr. Lloyd George himself went so far as to say : " Drink is doing us more damage in the war than all the German submarines put together," and again, " We are fighting Germany, Austria,

and Drink ; and, as far as I can see, the greatest of these three deadly foes is Drink." Ever anxious to sacrifice himself even in minor matters, for the common good, the King on March 30 wrote to the Chancellor of the Exchequer that " if it were deemed advisable he would be prepared to set the example by giving up all alcoholic liquor himself and issuing orders against its consumption in the Royal Household." His Majesty's letter, which was followed on April 6 by the issue of the orders in question, received an immediate voluntary response from the country and Empire. For a while it looked as if the Government contemplated drastic legislation in the direction of prohibition.

But, as *The Times* insisted, the drink question had been allowed to overshadow the real problem—that of producing war material. Not compulsory self-denial but an entire reorganization of war work was needed. No attempt had been made to utilize to the full the national resources. Factories employed on Government work had been over-driven, while others which might have been brought into use had been neglected. The loss of time and slackness might in some degree be attributable to drink ; they were far more certainly due to overwork and fatigue. The primary reason why the country was short of munitions was not drink at all. The real remedy was to deal with the muddle at the War Office and to put an end to the tradition that only soldiers could control war manufactures. It was not surprising that the net result of the drink campaign, in spite of an explanatory letter from Mr. Lloyd George, was to annoy the sober workmen (the vast majority), who had been doing their best from the beginning, by confusing them with the weaker brethren for whom unusually high wages had facilitated existing habits of intemperance.

On April 10 the formation of the North-East Coast Armaments Committee, on which the men, the employers, and the Government Departments were represented, was hailed with public relief. It was heartily welcomed at a meeting of 21 engineering and shipbuilding societies at Newcastle, which sent a resolution to the Prime Minister containing the bluff assertion : " We do not want any more speeches about the failings of the workers, the employers or the Government ; we want to pull together and get on with it. You may tell Lord Kitchener that we shall deliver the goods."

BARBED WIRE
These obstacles have to be

A few days later a great step in advance was made. A new committee was appointed, presided over by the Chancellor of the Exchequer himself and including representatives of the Admiralty, the War Office, the Treasury, the Board of Trade, and others. The first task of the committee was to ascertain the full extent of the problem, the second to map out the whole country and draw every available factory and workshop into the scheme. The great merit of the scheme was that it left the War Office free to concentrate upon the sufficiently overwhelming task of organizing and training the new armies. There was danger, on the other hand, lest the Government should imagine that by the mere appointment of committees it had done all that was needed. What was at least equally essential was that the country should be told the truth about the war.

The truth was, though it was not fully revealed until May 14, when the Military Correspondent of The Times explained the failure of the British attacks in the districts of Fromelles and Richebourg, that "the want of an unlimited supply of high explosives was a fatal bar to our success." Public opinion at length awoke to the fact that the shell problem was far more vital than all the rest put together. Not only was the Army provided with insufficient shells of any kind, but it especially lacked the kind best suited to the character of the work in hand. It needed the man-killing shrapnel, indeed, but far more did it need the trench-battering high explosive. The Government had had plenty of warning. As long before as September 18 a well-informed correspondent, in a letter to The Times, had pointed out the absence of any systematic attempt to secure a maximum production of

ENTANGLEMENTS.

swept away by shell fire.

the various commodities, including arms and
ammunition, required by the new armies. As
already mentioned, the Committee on Production had urged the need of an increased
output of shells. Sir John French was reported
on March 22 as saying that the problem of the
war was a comparatively simple one—" munitions, more munitions, always more munitions.
That is the essential question, the governing
condition of all progress, of every leap forward."
Similarly he told Lord Durham, in a conversation published on April 13, " I know when the
time comes for us to make our great move we
can break through the Germans. But I know
what we want and must have, and that is
more and more munitions." In his dispatch
on the battle of Neuve Chapelle, dated April 5,
the Field-Marshal wrote : " An almost unlimited
supply of ammunition is necessary and a most
liberal discretionary power as to its use must

be given to the artillery commanders. I am
confident that this is the only means by which
great results can be obtained with a minimum
of loss." But three days after the publication
of the dispatch of *The Times* Military Correspondent, machines and men were reported to
be standing idle on the Clyde simply on account
of trade union restrictions which were supposed
to have been relaxed.

The appointment of the Munitions of War
Committee and a number of local committees
was followed by some remarkable inconsis-
tencies of statement on the part of Ministers.
On April 20 Mr. Asquith went to Newcastle
to appeal to the munition workers to increase
their output. His speech was full of soothing
and comforting assurances ; there was no
reference whatever to drink. He defended
the Government against charges of remissness,
and, apparently forgetting Lord Kitchener's

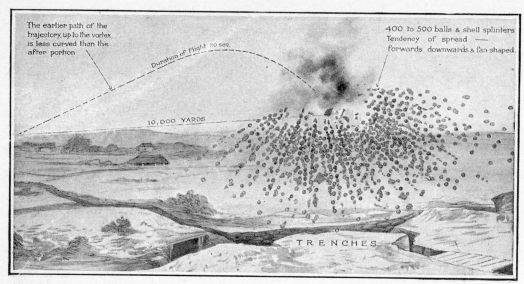

THE POWER OF THE FIELD ARTILLERY SHELLS.
Shrapnel shell breaking over enemy communication trenches and scattering 400 balls.

own statement in the House of Lords on March 15, deliberately affirmed that there was not a word of truth in the statement "that the operations not only of our Army but of our Allies were being crippled, or at any rate hampered, by our failure to provide the necessary ammunition." Nor, he added, was there any more truth in the suggestion that the Government had only recently become alive to the importance and urgency of these matters. What he omitted to indicate was why, if the Cabinet Committee appointed in September had not failed, it was now necessary to appoint two new committees and take additional powers for the purpose. Mr. Lloyd George, however, in the House of Commons, while equally extolling the great work already accomplished by the Government, admitted frankly that the War Office had realized neither how great would be the expenditure of ammunition nor that high-explosive shell would "turn out" to be the right thing.

THE POWER OF THE FIELD ARTILLERY SHELLS.
High-Explosive shell breaking fortified enemy entrenchments.

While the public were still wondering what to make of it, Mr. Lloyd George came out with a series of proposals for remedying the evils caused by drinking on the part of munitions workers. The duty on spirits was to be doubled. There was to be a graded surtax on the heavier kinds of beer. The duty on wines was to be quadrupled, not because the consumption of wine had anything directly to do with the output of munitions, but as a sop to the beer and spirit drinking classes. Power was sought to close or control for the period of the war public-houses in any particular area. The proposals, which were apparently framed without consultation with any of the political parties, were received with general protests, except from the usual temperance advocates. It was felt that the Chancellor of the Exchequer was trying to smuggle through a temperance or a Budget measure under cover of munitions of war, and that the evils of drinking, especially noticeable, not in the ammunition business but in the shipbuilding trade and the transport service, might have been attacked without interference with the mass of the temperate population. As matters turned out, the tax proposals were withdrawn after a few days, and a compromise was arrived at on the basis of the entire prohibition of the sale of immature spirits. The only part of the scheme to pass into law was that concerning the control of the sale of intoxicating liquor in munitions, transport and camp areas.

The question of the propriety of continuing "Sport as usual" had been raised from an early period in the war. International football matches had been abandoned on December 4, but it was not until May 19 that the Government conveyed to the Jockey Club its decision that all race meetings in Great Britain, with the exception of those at Newmarket, should be suspended from May 24. This action, apparently the result of the strongly expressed views in a remarkable series of letters to *The Times*, was at once accepted by the Jockey Club. The correspondence was remarkable not only for the interest which it aroused, but for the eminence of many of those who took part in it, on one side or the other. Among them were Lady Roberts, the Dukes of Rutland and Portland, Lord Rosebery, Lord Dunraven, Lord Curzon, Lord Newton, Lord Winchilsea, Lord Heneage, Lord Hamilton of Dalzell, Sir R. Lethbridge, Mr. H. Chaplin, Mr. Frederic Harrison, and the Stewards of the

LORD FISHER.
Head of the Central Committee of the Inventions Board.

Jockey Club. Nor did the Universities need any persuasion to abandon the Boat-race. From the first moment of the war they had realized intensely the seriousness of the task before the nation, and already at least two-thirds of the undergraduates of Oxford and Cambridge were under arms, including every member of the previous year's crews. Similarly from the outset the more modern Universities vied with each other not only in supplying officers to the forces, but in working at munitions and in prosecuting valuable technical researches. As for cricket, all first-class matches were abandoned, and Lord's Cricket Ground became a place of military training.

By the middle of May the public had begun to realize that something was seriously amiss with the Government's handling of the various problems of the war. The discrepancies and contradictions between the utterances of Lord Kitchener, Mr. Asquith, and Mr. Lloyd George on the subject of munitions, the chaotic treatment of the internment question, which culminated in assaults by the mob on enemy aliens, the growing tendency of the Cabinet

MR. BALFOUR,
First Lord of the Admiralty.

prepared to welcome the infusion of new blood into the Government were still doubtful whether a Coalition, in the absence of any official Opposition, might not lack the stimulus to energetic action which even the restrained criticism prevailing during the war had tended to supply.

But events were moving rapidly. In the House of Commons on May 12 Mr. F. H. Booth, a Liberal Member, asked the Prime Minister " whether, in view of the war and in view of the steps necessary to be taken in order to grapple with the rearrangement of industry and social life consequent upon a prolonged struggle, he would consider the desirability of admitting into the ranks of Ministers leading members of the various political parties in the House." Mr. Asquith replied that, while the Government was greatly indebted to the leading members of all parties for suggestions and assistance on certain specific subjects, the step suggested was " not in contemplation," and he was not aware that it would meet with general assent.

But two days later was published the dispatch of the Military Correspondent of *The Times.* The public at last began to realize that something was seriously amiss with the supply of munitions. The Opposition leaders saw that the well-meant policy of " Trust the Government " had run its course. Anxious discussions led to more general conferences. There was talk of an " ultimatum " to the Prime Minister, and something of the kind was almost launched when matters were suddenly precipitated by another and quite independent crisis inside the Government. During the week-end of May 15–17 it became known that Lord Fisher had resigned his office as First Sea Lord of the Admiralty.

This untoward occurrence, the details of which were naturally largely matter of conjecture, was attributed to disagreement, partly temperamental, partly due to fundamental divergence in vital matters of policy, between the two men in chief control of the British Navy. The tendency of the First Lord, Mr. Winston Churchill, to assume responsibilities and override his expert advisers on questions of the gravest import was well known. He had been conspicuous during the war for his personal appearances at the Front in circumstances which harmonized ill with the proper functions of a civilian Minister. He had a large share, though by no means the sole share,

to resent as attacks on individual Ministers even the rare and moderate criticism to which the Opposition had confined itself—all these considerations suggested the necessity of comprehensive changes. Additional dissatisfaction with the Government's handling of affairs was caused by the belief that the invasion of Gallipoli, with its rumoured enormous casualty list, had been mismanaged, as a policy, from the beginning. Nor did the progress of our arms in the Western theatre of war appear to be justifying the losses incurred. There was something amiss, not only with the national organization of the country, but with the internal condition of the Cabinet itself. Not only among the Opposition but also among political supporters of the Cabinet there was a growing feeling that the time had come for the constitution of a Government of Public Safety which should combine the best brains of both political parties. On the other hand, the idea of a Coalition was naturally distasteful to those who had not yet succeeded in emancipating themselves from the political ideas of peace-time, while many who were

LORD LANSDOWNE,
Minister without Portfolio.

MR. LLOYD GEORGE,
Minister of Munitions.

MR. WINSTON CHURCHILL,
Chancellor of the Duchy of Lancaster.

MR. R. McKENNA,
The Chancellor of the Exchequer, and Mrs. McKenna.

SIR F. E. SMITH, Solicitor-General, and
SIR EDWARD CARSON, the Attorney-General.

PROMINENT MEMBERS OF THE COALITION CABINET.

313

MR. AUSTEN CHAMBERLAIN,
Secretary of State for India.

in the series of decisions which led to the original attempts to make the forcing of the Dardanelles a purely naval operation. It was believed that Mr. Asquith had supported the First Sea Lord in his efforts to restrain the rashness of the Cabinet Minister, but Lord Fisher's own continued abstention from office became inevitable when, rightly or wrongly, he refused to serve under a Government of which Mr. Winston Churchill remained a member.

The situation had become chaotic, and the prospect of a discussion in the House of Commons on the shells question, which the Government could hardly hope to survive, determined Mr. Asquith to take the initiative and invite the Opposition leaders to come to his aid. Exactly a week after his reply to Mr. Booth the Prime Minister announced in the House that "steps were in contemplation which involved the reconstruction of the Government on a broader personal and political basis." He added that there was absolutely no change of any kind in contemplation in the policy of the country in regard to the continued prosecution of the war with all possible energy and by every available resource. Further he reassured his supporters by emphasizing the fact that any reconstruction was for the purposes of the war alone and was not to be taken in any quarter as indicating anything in the nature of a sur-

render or compromise on the part of any person or body of persons of their several political purposes and ideals. Thus came to an end a Liberal Government which had been in power for nine and a half years.

The process of making the new Cabinet proved slow. The first decision, namely, that the Prime Minister and Sir Edward Grey were to remain at their posts, was generally welcomed by the country as an indication to the world that the broad lines of British policy remained fixed and unalterable. But with regard to the filling of other important posts there were many party and personal considerations to be taken into account. The method adopted appeared to be the allocation of certain offices to the various party leaders, who were practically free to fill them as they would. Certain names, no doubt, were eliminated by agreement; but the general result turned out to be rather a combination of Front Bench politicians than a National Cabinet in the wider sense. As ultimately constituted the Ministry consisted of twelve Liberals, eight Unionists, one Labour member and Lord Kitchener. The total of twenty-two, an increase of two on the old Cabinet, was made up by the inclusion of Lord Lansdowne as Minister without portfolio, and the creation of the new and important post of Minister of Munitions, which was taken by Mr. Lloyd George. Mr. Balfour became First Lord of the Admiralty, Mr. Winston Churchill receiving the Chancellorship of the Duchy of Lancaster. Mr. Bonar Law and Mr. Chamberlain—both of them men already devoted by birth and tradition to the problems of Empire—became respectively Secretaries of State for the Colonies and for India. Sir John Simon, refusing the great but final office of Lord Chancellor, became Home Secretary, while Mr. McKenna left the Home Office to take Mr. Lloyd George's place at the Exchequer. The way to the Woolsack was thus left open to Sir Stanley Buckmaster, who had been Solicitor-General in the late Administration. Lord Crewe became Lord President and Lord Curzon became Lord Privy Seal, while Mr. Long came into the Local Government Board and Lord Selborne into the Board of Agriculture. Both Sir Edward Carson and Mr. Redmond were invited to join the Government, and the former became Attorney-General to the great strengthening of the Cabinet. Mr. Redmond, never a free agent, refused Mr. Asquith's offer.

The Education Office, an ancient stronghold of Toryism, passed into the democratic hands of Mr. Arthur Henderson, the Leader of the Labour Party, whose inclusion in the Cabinet was also destined to strengthen the Government in dealing with industrial disputes. It should be added that five Cabinet Ministers— Lord Haldane, Lord Beauchamp, Lord Emmott, Mr. Hobhouse, and Mr. Pease—left the Government altogether, while two—Mr. Montagu and Mr. Herbert Samuel—were satisfied to take minor office outside the Cabinet.

The completion of the new Ministry was announced on June 11 in the following form:

Office.	The Late Ministry.	THE NEW MINISTRY.
Prime Minister	} Mr. ASQUITH	Mr. ASQUITH (L)
First Lord of the Treasury		
Minister without portfolio	—	LORD LANSDOWNE (U)
Lord Chancellor	LORD HALDANE	SIR S. BUCKMASTER (L)
Lord President of the Council	LORD BEAUCHAMP	LORD CREWE (L)
Lord Privy Seal	LORD CREWE	LORD CURZON (U)
Chancellor of the Exchequer	Mr. LLOYD GEORGE	Mr. McKENNA (L)
Secretaries of State:		
Home Affairs	Mr. McKENNA	SIR J. SIMON (L)
Foreign Affairs	SIR E. GREY	SIR E. GREY (L)
Colonies	Mr. HARCOURT	Mr. BONAR LAW (U)
India	LORD CREWE	Mr. CHAMBERLAIN (U)
War	LORD KITCHENER	LORD KITCHENER
Minister of Munitions	—	Mr. LLOYD GEORGE (L)
First Lord of the Admiralty	Mr. CHURCHILL	Mr. BALFOUR (U)
President of the Board of Trade	Mr. RUNCIMAN	Mr. RUNCIMAN (L)
President of the Local Government Board	Mr. H. SAMUEL	Mr. LONG (U)
Chancellor of the Duchy of Lancaster	Mr. MONTAGU	Mr. CHURCHILL (L)
Chief Secretary for Ireland	Mr. BIRRELL	Mr. BIRRELL (L)
Secretary for Scotland	Mr. McKINNON WOOD	Mr. McKINNON WOOD (L)
President of the Board of Agriculture	LORD LUCAS	LORD SELBORNE (U)
First Commissioner of Works	LORD EMMOTT	Mr. HARCOURT (L)
President of the Board of Education	Mr. PEASE	Mr. HENDERSON (Lab.)
Attorney-General	SIR J. SIMON	SIR E. CARSON (U)

THE ABOVE FORMED THE CABINET.

Postmaster-General	Mr. Hobhouse (in the Cabinet)	Mr. H. Samuel (L) (not in the
Solicitor-General	Sir S. Buckmaster	Sir F. E. Smith (U) Cabinet)
Parliamentary Under-Secretaries—		
Home Affairs	Mr. Harmsworth	Mr. Brace (Lab.)
Foreign Affairs	Mr. Primrose	Lord Robert Cecil (U)
Colonies	Lord Islington	Mr. Steel Maitland (U)
India	Mr. C. H. Roberts	Lord Islington (L)
War	Mr. Tennant	Mr. Tennant (L)
Financial Secretaries :—		
To the Treasury	Mr. Acland	Mr. Montagu (L)
To the War Office	Mr. Baker	Mr. H. W. Forster (U)
To the Admiralty	Dr. Macnamara	Dr. Macnamara (L)
Civil Lord of the Admiralty	Mr. Lambert	The Duke of Devonshire (U)
Parliamentary Secretaries :—		
Board of Trade	Mr. J. M. Robertson	Captain Pretyman (U)
Local Government Board	Mr. J. H. Lewis	Mr. Hayes Fisher (U)
Board of Agriculture	Sir H. Verney	Mr. Acland (L)
Board of Education	Dr. Addison	Mr. Herbert Lewis (L)
Munitions	—	Dr. Addison (L)
Paymaster-General	Lord Strachie	Lord Newton (U)
Assistant Postmaster-General	Captain Norton	Mr. Pike Pease (U)
Parliamentary Secretary to the Treasury	Mr. Gulland	Joint { Mr. Gulland (L) / Lord Edmund Talbot (U)
Lords Commissioner of the Treasury :—		
	Mr. Wedgwood Benn	Mr. G. H. Roberts (Lab.)
	Mr. Beck	Mr. Howard (L)
	Mr. Webb (unpaid)	Mr. Bridgeman (U)
	Mr. Walter Rea (unpaid)	Mr. Walter Rea (unpaid) (L)

SCOTLAND

Lord Advocate	Mr. Munro	Mr. Munro (L)
Solicitor-General	Mr. Morison	Mr. Morison (L)

IRELAND

Lord Lieutenant	Lord Wimborne	Lord Wimborne (L)
Lord Chancellor	Mr. I. O'Brien	Mr. I. O'Brien (L)
Attorney-General	Mr. J. Pim	Mr. John Gordon (U)
Solicitor-General	Mr. J. O'Connor	Mr. J. O'Connor (L)
Vice-President of Department of Agriculture	Mr. T. W. Russell	Mr. T. W. Russell (L)

(L. Liberal, U. Unionist, Lab. Labour)

A number of changes were also made in the appointments to the Royal Household.

[*Swaine.*

MR. WALTER LONG,
President of the Local Government Board.

This remarkable combination was admittedly a great experiment, involving a complete rearrangement of political ideas.

"The transformation," wrote Mr. Asquith to the Liberal Chief Whip, "implies a temporary abandonment of the system of Party Government which has ever since 1832 dominated our political arrangements and which I hold to be, under normal conditions, the best adapted to our national requirements. . . . There is one reason, and one only, which could justify or explain such a new departure—a clear and urgent case of national necessity."

Supported by a fresh flood of public hope, the Coalition began its work with laudable activity. For a moment, indeed, the country was disgusted to find precious time wasted over a party vendetta of the type which it had trusted had been abandoned. The proposed appointment of Mr. J. H. Campbell, an ardent Unionist, as Lord Chancellor of Ireland aroused a violent controversy in the party newspapers. Although, on the ground that Home Rule was not yet an accomplished fact, the Nationalists had deliberately excluded themselves from any responsibility for the task of beating the common enemy, they still exercised their old control over the Government in matters relating to Ireland. Their objection to Mr. Campbell's appointment had nothing to do with his personal qualities or legal attainments : it depended entirely on his attitude towards Home Rule. Seeing that one of the

original intentions in the reconstruction of the Cabinet had been to give proportional representation to all the parties in Parliament—an intention which was not successful owing to the abstention of the Nationalists—and in view of the fact that the other great Irish offices had remained in the hands of their former Liberal holders, the Unionists sought to fill the Lord Chancellorship with a member of their own party. In this they were unsuccessful. A Unionist, indeed, was appointed Attorney-General, but the offer made to Mr. Campbell by the Prime Minister was withdrawn.

With the formal creation of the Ministry of Munitions, however, a better spirit prevailed, except among such as saw "Prussianization" in the new powers sought under the Munitions of War Act. The appointment of Mr. Lloyd George to the new post was generally applauded, for the country was aware of his quick perception of the national short-comings, his energy, his infectious enthusiasm, and his hold on the working classes. It was felt that, if anybody in the world could make up for lost time in the matter of munitions, Mr. Lloyd George was the man. After negotiations with the trade unions, he introduced a Bill which provided, among other things, for compulsory arbitration of disputes, the return of as many skilled men as possible from the ranks, the immediate voluntary enrolment of skilled men in a mobile munition corps, the institution of a Munitions Court to enforce contracts entered into by these volunteers, and Government control of workshops. On the other hand, trade union regulations restricting output were to be suspended and employers' profits to be limited.

Meanwhile, as the result of sustained external pressure, of which the most cogent example was a masterly letter from "A Banker" in *The Times* of June 9, the Government were induced to set on foot a long delayed campaign in favour of public thrift. This coincided fortunately with the issue at par of a second War Loan,* which, introduced without warning on June 21, and backed by a colossal campaign of advertisement and a great deal of public spirit, had by July 10, when the lists

* The first War Loan, for £350,000,000, had been issued on November 17, the price of issue being 95 and the interest 3½ per cent. It took the form of inscribed stock and bonds to bearer, in amounts of £100, £200, £500 and £1,000, repayable at par on March 1, 1928, but redeemable at par at any time on or after March 1 1925.

closed, succeeded in replenishing the National war chest by something approaching £600,000,000. Its special feature was the encouragement of small investors to contribute through the Post Office sums ranging from five shillings upwards. The rate of interest was 4½ per cent., and the loan was repayable in or after 1925 or in any event in 1945. It was followed by the appointment on July 20 of a Retrenchment Committee to inquire into and report upon possible savings of public expenditure.

The National Registration Bill, which was introduced by Mr. Long, the new President of the Local Government Board, on June 29, excited more attention than any other of the early measures of the Coalition. It had long been recognized that, so long as the Government abstained from a serious stock-taking of its available resources in the shape of labour, no complete mobilization of the country's industry was attainable. The effects of its inevitable groping in the dark were notorious. Men had been recruited for the Army who should never have left the work-shops, while many others who were well capable of serving the country in some efficient way were contributing nothing to the national effort, or were doing work which could equally well be done by women. At the same time many were offering themselves as workers, of whom, in the absence of any machinery for recording and acting upon their offers, no use could be made. The objects of the Bill were to discover what everybody in the country between the ages of sixteen and sixty-five (with certain exceptions) was already doing and whether he or she was skilled in and able and willing to perform any other than the work (if any) at which he or she was at the time employed, and, if so, the nature thereof. The Bill was not carried without opposition on the part of those who saw in it the thin end of the wedge of "conscription," although, as Mr. Long explained, "it left the question of compulsory service exactly where it was; it did not affect it one way or the other."

Incidentally, indeed, its operation rendered needless the haphazard harrying of men of military age, which had amounted, in practice, to compulsion in a particularly unfair and offensive form, while the ascertainment of the names of those doing no useful work enabled a methodical appeal for recruits to be made

COMPILING THE NATIONAL REGISTER.
Inside the Addressograph room.

LORD KITCHENER AT THE FRONT.
The War Minister's visit to the trenches in France.

on "voluntary" lines. On the whole the Bill so far as it went, was a useful preliminary to national organization which might have been carried with advantage many months before.

Among the miscellaneous signs of tardy recognition of the necessity of enlisting in the public service, irrespective of party or other grounds, the best available ability in the matter of expert advice, were the appointment of a number of Boards and Committees.

Of these perhaps the most important was the Committee on Food Production, appointed on June 17, which combined an exceptionally strong body of experts under the presidency of Lord Milner. Similar committees were appointed for Scotland and Ireland. An Inventions Board which was established in July to assist the Admiralty in co-ordinating and encouraging scientific effort in its relation to the requirements of the Naval Service comprised a central committee under Lord Fisher and a consulting panel composed of a dozen eminent members of the Royal Society. This was followed by a comprehensive scheme for the permanent organization and development of scientific and industrial research throughout the whole of the United Kingdom.

While these various plans for the better exploitation of the scientific resources of the nation were maturing, and while it seemed as if at last some real progress might be made to recover lost ground, the country was shocked by one of the ugliest of the many labour troubles which had occurred during the war. The South Wales coal miners had on April 1 given three months' notice to terminate the existing wage agreement. The employers refused to contemplate the making of any new agreement until the end of the war. Weeks of negotiation on the old-fashioned Board of Trade lines resulted in an ultimatum from the men threatening a strike in three days' time if their original proposals were not accepted. The Government, which had hitherto left Mr. Runciman ("alone," as he pathetically explained later) to deal with the men, now applied by proclamation to the South Wales coalfield that section of the brand-new Munitions of War Act which made it an offence to strike without invoking the machinery of the Act. But Welsh miners are not easily alarmed by proclamations. Convinced that the employers, while refusing to make a new wages agreement, were making enormous profits, and failing to recognize the change effected by the Munitions Act itself in the relations of employers and employed, they simply ignored the proclamation, and the Government were impotent to enforce it. Finally, Mr. Lloyd George was dispatched posthaste to the scene of inaction, and succeeded at length, by a combination of exhortation and concessions, in inducing the men to return to work. No wonder he described himself as "sick at heart." It was a discreditable business all round. More discreditable still was the dispute which arose a little more than a month later over the terms of Mr. Runciman's award upon the points referred to him for settlement in connection with the new agreement. Again, after prolonged conferences, the men got their way, but the loss of hundreds of thousands of tons of coal at a time when every ounce of coal was of vital importance was sufficiently painful evidence of the want of organization of the country for war. Public opinion was far more inclined on the merits of the dispute to sympathize with the men, however misguided and irreconcilable might be the small section to which the disputes were primarily due, than with the Government who had failed in their duty to bring home to them the seriousness of the war.

The chief lesson suggested by this survey of the political history of England during the first year of the war is the failure of the party politician to change his outlook and to rise to the greatness of the occasion. One cannot imagine a nobler opportunity for a statesman than to find, for the first time, an entire people united in a patriotic desire to sink domestic differences and work disinterestedly for the common good. Where the people looked for leadership they found the old inclination to "wait and see." While they offered themselves freely, willing for any sacrifice if only they might be told how best to sacrifice themselves, the Government showed neither vigour nor courage in accepting their offers. It was the people, not the Government, which provided the motive power in nearly every display of energy —the supply of munitions, the imposition of fresh taxes, the inculcation of thrift, the "mobilization of science." Whenever the Government, after much hesitation and pressure, took a decided line they invariably met with unlimited public support. Every fresh demand for money, every new form of interference with the normal habits of the people, was not only met without a murmur, but criticized, if at all, for not going far enough.

MR. ASQUITH INSPECTING MEMBERS OF THE ROYAL FLYING CORPS.

The fact that the country was slow in realizing the seriousness of its task was the fault, not of the people, but of the Government which never realized their duty, and which had too long been accustomed to regard ingenious oratory as an adequate substitute for simple if unpleasant truths. The new Cabinet was undoubtedly stronger than the old, but it was perhaps too much to expect that it would show itself permanently more efficient than its predecessor. For though some weak Ministers were dropped and some dangerous ones displaced, the type was limited to the politicians, and party considerations were still the basis of its composition. It was likely to suffer, even more than its predecessor, from its own unwieldy bulk, which necessarily hampered the swift decisions required of a Cabinet in time of war. But it rapidly proved itself completely free from differences due merely to the mixture of parties. If it was not (as the enthusiasts claimed) a true "National Cabinet" but a Front-Bench combination, it none the less marked a definite and most necessary stage in the process of replacing Party Government by a Government for War.

MINERS' STRIKE IN SOUTH WALES.
Men leaving their work. Inset: A Welsh miner.

CHAPTER XCI.

THE FALL OF WARSAW.

Strategical Considerations in Poland—Effects of the Reconquest of Lwow by the Austro-Germans—Offensive Against the Dniester—The Zlota Lipa Line—German Dispositions at the Beginning of July—Russian Lack of Ammunition—Fighting on the Dniester—Fall of Halicz—Battle of Krasnik—German Offensive in the Baltic Provinces—Germans Cross the Vindava—Shavle Captured—Fighting at Krasnostaw—The Bzura-Rawka Line Evacuated—The Vistula Crossed—Germans Enter Warsaw—German Promises in Poland—Polish Opinion.

FORTY-TWO days intervened between the reconquest of Lwow by the Austro-German armies on June 22 and the fall of Warsaw on August 5. The fall of Warsaw practically concludes the Austro-German offensive in ethnical Poland; the following advance from the Vistula to the Bug is a mere epilogue of the preceding drama.

On August 6 closed the first year of the war between Russia and Germany; on the Eastern front it can be best described as the fight for the line of rivers of which Warsaw is the centre and the Vistula the main component part. For one short month, following on the first fall of Przemysl, this contest seemed to have been definitely settled in favour of our Allies; relying on the defensive power of their front facing west, they undertook an offensive across the Carpathians against the plains of Hungary. On May 2 opened the Austro-German counter-offensive against the Dunajec-Biala line. However remarkable were their achievements during the first month of the Galician drive, they did not succeed during that period of their offensive in inflicting more than what we might call a flesh-wound on the body of the Russian positions. The districts between the San and Dniester in the north-east, and the Dunajec and

the Carpathian Mountains in the south-west, were the necessary basis for a Russian offensive against Cracow and Silesia or against Hungary; they formed, however, by no means an indispensable part or cover of the main defensive line, which stretched along the Vistula, the San and the Dniester. The Austro-German advance from the Dunajec to the San did not affect the Russian line north of the Pilica. This remained unchanged even after the fall of Przemysl and Lwow; yet from the moment when the Austro-German forces pierced the southern flank of the Russian system of defence it was certain that the outlying positions in Poland would have to be abandoned, as soon as any direct pressure was brought to bear against them. By June 22 the Austro-German armies had crossed the San-Dniester line on a broad front of more than 100 miles, extending from the junction of the Tanev and the San to Mikolajow on the Dniester. The holding of the line of the San and the Dniester was, from the point of view of the Russian defence, indispensable for the safety of Warsaw. All Russian plans for the defence of Warsaw had, therefore, necessarily implied from the very outset the conquest and holding of East Galicia. Lwow had not yet passed back into the hands of the enemy when our Allies began

THE TSAR.

their preparations for the evacuation of Warsaw.

German writers are now fond of describing Poland as a Russian *place d'armes*, which threatens the safety of the German Empire. The absence of Russian strategic railways to the west of the Vistula is in itself a sufficient proof of the patent untruth of that contention. It becomes simply ludicrous if one considers the distribution of the Russian garrisons in Poland before the outbreak of the war. The average aggregate strength of the Russian army west of the Vistula, between 1910 and 1914, was only about 30,000 men. Considering that the population of that district amounted to more than 6 millions and that certain sections of it did not invariably show a peaceful disposition, the Russian garrisons in Western Poland could hardly be considered anything more than the natural reinforcement and reserve for the local police and constabulary. In the much less populous part of Poland east of the Vistula, the strength of the Russian garrisons was five times that of the forces posted to the west of the river. The country between the Bug and the Vistula, and that lying between the Pripet and Dnieper and the Austrian frontier was, especially since 1910, the main Russian *place d'armes* in the west. The grouping of garrisons, the plans of mobilization, finally the most palpable of all military preparations, the distribution of strategic railways, pointed to an offensive against East Galicia. But the preparations for such an offensive do not yet by themselves prove in any way the existence, on the part of Russia, of aggressive intentions against Austria. The conquest of East Galicia formed, in case of war with the Central Powers, a necessary measure for the safeguarding of Warsaw. The Austro-Russian frontier between the Vistula and the Bug is practically open; a broad avenue leads past Zamosc and Lublin into the interior of Eastern Poland. By following it an army advancing from East Galicia to the north can turn the positions of which the Vistula, between its junction with the San and that with the Bug, forms the front, and of which, between Novo-Georgievsk and Grodno, the Narev and Bobr constitute the northern flank. An army advancing to the north between the Vistula and the Bug can easily protect itself against attacks from the east by taking the marshy valley of the Bug as cover for its right flank; moreover, on the line facing Cholm and Brest-Litovsk that cover is reinforced by the morasses of the Pripet. From the very outset it was clear that our Allies had either to take Przemysl, the key of the San-Dniester line, and thus acquire the natural protection for the southern flank of the positions along the Vistula, or that they would have to abandon Poland and retire on Brest-Litovsk and the Bug. The position as we had known it in August, 1914, repeated itself in its main outlines in June, 1915, but the superiority in numbers and armament which the Central Powers had gained by the summer of 1915 left hardly any doubt concerning the immediate issue of the struggle for the Vistula line. Still, certain factors which had weighed heavily at the outset of the war were certain to make themselves felt once more in the fighting which was now imminent in the border district between south-eastern Poland

and East Galicia. Russia had provided her open frontier between the Vistula and the Bug* with the same kind of defence as Prussia employed, with such marked success, along her eastern borders. Of the entire Russian Empire the district between Grodno, Warsaw, Ivangorod and Rovno, and especially its southern part, possesses probably the most highly developed railway net. Between Ivangorod and Kovel the Warsaw-Kieff railway is met from the north by four first-class railway lines. The average distance between them amounts to about 40 miles. Before the war that railway system was not linked up with that of Galicia.† At no point between the Vistula and the Bug did the Russian railways get nearer than within 40 miles of the Austrian territory. Even farther east, between the Bug and the Styr, they did not touch the frontier; the main line runs at an average distance of 40 miles from it, the branch

* Speaking of the "open frontier between the Vistula and the Bug," we do not in any way overlook the difficulties which confront an invading army in the Tanev region. But it is the weakest link which determines the strength of a chain, and there are so many of these weak links between the Vistula and the Bug as to justify our description.

† In the winter 1914–15 the Russians constructed a railway line from Lublin to Rozwadow and another from Cholm to Belzec, thus linking up the railway-net of Eastern Poland with that of Galicia (cf. Chapter LXXXIV. pp. 97-8).

THE GERMAN ADVANCE ON WARSAW.
General von Mackensen (on white horse), Commander of the Eleventh Army.

line from Kovel stops at Vladimir Volynski, 15 miles from the border. It is only across the eastern frontier, at Radzivilow-Brody, at Volotchyska, and near Novosielitsa, that the Russian lines link up with the Austrian railway net.

The reason which originally had made the Russians leave a wide gap between the Austrian frontier and their own railways is self-evident. They had to count with the slowness of their own mobilization and with the probability of the Austrians crossing the frontier between the Vistula and the Bug before their own preparations were complete. They calculated that they would be able to check that advance in front of the Lublin-Cholm line. The numerous lines from the north and east were to provide for a quick concentration of forces for a counter-offensive against East Galicia. In the case of the eastern frontier of Galicia, between the Styr and the Dniester, they did not need to entertain any fears of an early invasion, nor did they therefore need to take similar precautions. An Austrian offensive to the east could not have been undertaken as the opening move of the war. No vulnerable points are to be found near the frontier, and the Volhynian fortresses and the marshes of the Pripet separate almost completely that region from the adjoining strategically important districts in the north. Meantime a diversion of the Austrian forces to the east would have uncovered their northern flank ; the frontier between the Vistula and the Bug is open in either direction. The Russian calculations proved true. We have recounted them, as in June, 1915, when the fighting again reached those districts, many of the original strategic problems of the war reappeared in a form very similar to that in which they had presented themselves at the outbreak of the war.

Before Lwow was reached, no question could arise concerning the direction which had to be followed by the Austro-German advance in Galicia. The question came, however, to be discussed as soon as that important centre of roads and railways passed into the hands of the enemy ; a junction of roads marks for an advancing army also a parting of roads. As a matter of fact, the dilemma existed only in the imaginations of those who are, or at least in the past were, in the habit of imputing to the supreme German army command undue regard for political considerations. An advance to the

east would have secured the political and sentimental purpose of completing the reconquest of Galicia, but it would not have served in any way the main strategical aims of the Austro-German armies.

The main Russian forces were concentrated in Poland. An Austro-German advance to the east would have left open to them the northern flank of the armies, protected neither by natural nor by any powerful artificial defences. A counter-offensive similar to that of August 1914 might have swept down on East Galicia, had the Austro-German armies north of Lwow been weakened to any considerable extent. The same reasons which at the outset of the war had precluded an Austrian advance to the east held good also in the summer of 1915. Moreover, it ought to be remembered that the forces which had carried out the Galician drive of May and June were not an independent army. It is true more than two-thirds of their effectives were composed of Austro-Hungarian troops, and they stood, at least nominally, under the command of the Austrian Generalissimo, Archduke Frederick. Yet they were primarily working *pour le roi de Prusse*, and for his generals and armies. In August, 1914, the Austrians had been ordered to advance between the Vistula and Bug against the line Warsaw-Brest Litovsk. Had they succeeded, the whole of Poland, severed from Russia by their advance along its eastern border, would have fallen into the grip of the Germans without any effort on the part of the latter. The Austrians were now to carry out that which they had failed to achieve during the preceding summer. Moreover, a successful Austrian advance from Galicia against Brest-Litovsk would have relieved the German armies north of the Pilica from the necessity of attempting to break through the Russian lines, which they had previously attacked on repeated occasions with heavy casualties but with no success. The deadlock on the Niemen, the Bobr, the Narev, and the Vistula would have been broken through without the Germans having to pay for it by any serious losses. One would have naturally expected an offensive against the northern flank of the Russian armies in Poland to accompany from the very beginning the Austro-German advance against the Lublin-Cholm line. But Hindenburg seems to have spared his own men, waiting to see whether the Austrians could not do the work with only that help which they were receiving

Waiting for food. On right: A Russian peasant giving a wounded Austrian a drink of milk.

Families with their belongings who had to leave the town of Lublin on its occupation by the Austrians. Circle picture: Austrian troops searching a cart of a refugee.

THE GERMAN ADVANCE: REFUGEES LEAVING POLAND.

from the Germans, included in the southern armies, mainly in the army of Mackensen, and the army of Linsingen.

The Germans were to meet once more with disappointment. An isolated advance between the Vistula and the Bug could not break through the Russian lines in front of Lublin and Cholm. A second time the Austrians suffered defeat in front of Krasnik—*i.e.*, in the same district in which their first offensive had broken down in the summer of 1914. The second battle of Krasnik, in the first days of July, 1915, marks the end of the Galician campaign which started round Tarnow and Gorlice on May 2. When fighting on the Eastern front is resumed, in the middle of July, it proceeds along the entire line from Libau on the Baltic coast, to Zaleszczyki on the Dniester, near the Roumanian frontier.

Although Lublin and Cholm, and ultimately Warsaw were the main objectives of the Austro-German armies in East Galicia, the securing of their hold on Lwow was bound to be their first preoccupation. A centre of the strategical importance of Lwow cannot be allowed to remain within striking distance of the enemy's forces.

The first move against the Russian armies east and south of Lwow consisted of a new attempt to break through the "dead belt" of the Dniester. In the immediate neighbourhood of the Galician capital, and in the districts of Rava Ruska and Zolkiew, hardly any fighting took place during the first days following on the occupation of Lwow. It is possible that Mackensen's advance to the north was delayed in expectation of the development of the fighting on the Dniester. Had Linsingen and Pflanzer-Baltin succeeded in breaking through the Russian flank on the Dniester and thus in getting into the rear of the Russian armies, Mackensen would probably have tried to complete their defeat by enveloping from the north their other flank and by cutting off their connexion with their centre in Volhynia. The considerations which stood in the way of an original Austrian offensive in an easterly direction would hardly have prevented Mackensen from postponing his offensive to the north, if at that price he could have definitely broken the left wing of General Ivanoff's armies.

The attempts at piercing the Russian line on the Dniester failed, just as they had after the fall of Przemysl. The Austro-German armies

were able to gain just as much of the Dniester region as the Russians had to abandon in consonance with their retreat to the east. That retreat had to continue, and could not be reversed even after the second victory of Krasnik. The forces at the disposal of our Allies were not sufficient for a new advance from East Galicia similar to that of General Brusiloff in August, 1914; the main Russian armies had to be concentrated and kept in Poland, which was the decisive theatre of war. In East Galicia a line of compromise had to be found along which both armies could settle down for that " treuga Dei " (now called trench warfare), which in this war bore out the well-known contention of Clausewitz, that inaction and not action is the normal condition of armies in the field. That line was found along the upper Bug and the Zlota Lipa; it extended from Krylow and Sokal in the north, past Krasne, Gologory and Brzezany, to Nizniow on the Dniester.

It was for both sides the most natural line beyond which neither of them had any desire to advance, at least not for the time being. It forms an effective and continuous barrier, though neither of the two rivers is of a size which would by itself present serious obstacles to an army attempting to cross it. But then the real significance of rivers as defensive positions lies in most cases, not so much in the size of the river itself, as in the configuration of its banks. In the present war rivers and even small streams attained to an unprecedented importance. That rise in their defensive value was largely due to the most significant new factor in warfare: the continuity of the battle-line. The best strategic position is now of small value if isolated. Along rivers certain features of the ground are apt to repeat themselves along continuous lines. It is the river banks that matter, rather than the rivers.

The banks of the Bug and the Zlota Lipa were well suited to form a barrier between armies. Along the greater part of the line these rivers are lined with marshes and encompassed by hills. The marshes along the Zlota Lipa stop only where it enters the typical Dniester country. For the last 15 miles before its junction with the Dniester, the Zlota Lipa flows through a cañon as favourable for purposes of defence as any in that region. Finally, it ought to be remembered that it is below its junction with the Zlota Lipa at

THE RUSSIANS ON THE VISTULA FRONT.
Charging the German trenches.

Nizniow that the cañon of the Dniester forms the most formidable barrier.*

The defensive value of the line of the Bug and the Zlota Lipa is still heightened by the fact that they form a well-nigh continuous line; in the hilly district of Gologory,† the

---

* For a description of the cañons of the Dniester region, *cf.* Chapter LXXVI., Vol. IV., pp. 428-9.
† "Gologory" means in Polish "naked mountains."

distance intervening between them amounts to less than a mile. It was of importance for our Allies to retain their hold on the railway junction of Krasne which lies east of the upper Bug. Near that town the railway line from Rovno meets that running from Volotchyska by Tarnopol and Zloczow to Lwow. There was another reason which pointed at the Bug and Krasne as the natural boundary, the line of equal balance between the two armies. During the winter of 1914–15 our Allies had reconstructed the railway up to Krasne, enlarging its track to the broad Russian gauge. Thus Krasne had become the border between the two types of railway track. Finally, for the enemy the reaching of the line of the upper Bug in Galicia was a necessary preliminary of his advance into Russian Poland, as the middle Bug formed the natural cover for the right flank of the advancing armies.

The Austro-German advance in East Galicia was arrested on July 4 on the line of the upper Bug and the Zlota Lipa ; apart from a few local changes, the line remained untouched until August 27. There is one fairly safe test for judging as to which side was the deciding factor in the closing of a strategic advance ; it can be deduced from considering in whose hands remained the dominant positions. The dominant positions along a river line consist usually of its most convenient crossings ; the so-called bridgeheads are the gates of the fortified lines of rivers. All the dominant positions on the Bug remained on July 4 in the hands of our Allies. At Sokal and Dobrotwor the Russians retained a hold on both sides of the river. This was the more important considering the proximity of the Volhynian fortresses, which formed the centre of General Ivanoff's armies. We hear comparatively little of General von Mackensen's army during the first stage of the advance from Lwow to Warsaw ; at this stage it showed hardly any of its usual impetuosity. It can hardly be supposed that the Wolff Bureau failed in its function of Mackensen's advertising agency and omitted to record any of the achievements of that undoubtedly efficient army. Towards the end of June and in the beginning of July the advance against Southern Poland was conducted mainly by the left wing under Archduke Joseph-Ferdinand ; the most probable reason for the comparative inactivity of Mackensen's army must have been that large portions of it were tied down to the region between Grubieszow and Kamionka Strumilova, where, together with some of Boehm-Ermolli's troops, they formed an army of observation against Ivanoff's centre. They were guarding against a counter-offensive from Volhynia the right flank of the forces which were advancing to the north. When, after the second defeat of Krasnik, a new and more general advance was undertaken against Warsaw, the more complete securing of the line of the Bug by the capture of Sokal formed one of the first tasks undertaken by the Austro-German armies.

The Austro-German advance to the north of the San, the Tanew, and the district of Narol and Rava Ruska began on June 28. On July 1 the Fourth Austro-Hungarian Army reached the district of Krasnik, the Eleventh German Army the region of the Rivers Por and Volica. In four days they had covered distances varying from 30 to 40 miles. Between July 1 and 7 the Austrian forces attempted a further advance from Krasnik against Lublin, but suffered a severe defeat and were obliged to fall back on to the lines which they had previously held round Krasnik. The positions of the enemy armies east of the Vistula were now almost exactly the same as they had been in August, 1914. The armies of Generals Boehm-Ermolli and Linsingen stood along the line of the Bug and the Zlota Lipa, which had then been assigned to the Austrian troops under General Brudermann. The armies under Mackensen and Archduke Joseph-Ferdinand were occupying positions almost identical with those which had been held by the armies of Auffenberg and Dankl. From the west the armies under Generals Woyrsch and Kövess were now operating against that same sector of the Vistula, between the mouth of the San and that of the Pilica, which was in August, 1914, the objective of the armies of Woyrsch and Kummer. But north of the Pilica, where a year earlier the German forces were not sufficiently strong to defend even East Prussia against the Russian troops under Rennenkampf, now stood a most powerful group of armies under Field-Marshal von Hindenburg.

The line between the middle Pilica and the junction of the Bzura and the Vistula was held by the Fifth German Army. It had occupied those positions since the middle of December, and, notwithstanding the most desperate efforts, had been unable to make any impression even on the outer line of the Russian positions. On August 4, when that army, following up the retreating forces of our Allies, was approaching Warsaw, we suddenly learned from the German official *communiqué* that its commander was Prince Leopold of Bavaria. He appeared like a " *deus ex machina* " to solve the problems of ritual which arose between the Germanic Allies in connexion with the entry into Warsaw. As a son-in-law of the Austrian Emperor he

HINDERING THE GERMAN ADVANCE ON WARSAW,
Russians preparing to blow up a bridge : Wreathing strings of dynamite cartridges about the girders.

stood for a compromise between the two German Courts. The fact that he was a member of the ruling house of the most clerical Roman Catholic State of Germany was expected to appeal to the feelings of the Poles. But with the attitude of the Poles we propose to deal later at greater length.

Among the commanders of the German Armies north of the Vistula and Narev we find three generals who had risen into prominence as Hindenburg's assistants in the second battle in the Masurian Lakes in February, 1915— von Gallwitz, von Below, and von Eichhorn. The army in the district of Mlava had remained since then under the command of General von Gallwitz ; next to it, facing the Narev and the Bobr, stood the army of General von Scholtz. The Tenth German Army, operating against the Niemen, was commanded by General von Eichhorn. On his left stood the army of General von Falkenhausen. The troops which had held since the middle of May the line of the Vindava and the Dubissa in Courland and Samogitia, and which had been originally commanded by General von Lauenstein, as their operations grew in importance, received for their chief commander General von Below.*

About the middle of July began the new Austro-German attack against the Russian salient in Poland. The Vistula line was now to be forced and Warsaw taken by a concentric attack ; the main pressure was brought to bear from the north against the line of the Narev, and from the south against the Lublin-Cholm front. Yet none of the other parts of the Eastern front were left untouched. The armies standing west of the Vistula were pressing towards the river. The most serious attacks in that region were, however, directed against the two angles where the northern and southern flanks join with the line of the Vistula. The Austrian forces under General von Pflanzer-Baltin attempted once more, at the extreme south-eastern end of the line, to force the line of the Dniester ; in case of success, his move threatened to inflict a crushing defeat on the left wing of General Ivanoff's armies, should they have been unduly weakened by drafts for Russian Poland. The troops under Baron von Kirchbach (Army Boehm-Ermolli) were meantime attacking in the district of Sokal. At the extreme northern end von Below resumed the offensive against Courland and Lithuania, which had stopped about the middle of May, and was since then only once repeated for a short while in rather half-hearted manner. The advance in the north was more than a mere attempt at preventing the withdrawal of Russian troops from that region. It implied a serious threat against one of the most important railway lines feeding the armies in Russian Poland—namely, the Petrograd-Vilna-Warsaw line. Had the attacks against the immediate flanks of the Vistula line ended in failure, an enveloping movement on a stupendous scale might have been attempted from the north, consisting mainly in a thrust directed from east of Shavle against Kovno and Vilna.

* His name is occasionally given erroneously as von Buelow. General von Buelow held from the very beginning the command of an army at the Western front and was never moved to the East.

Meantime a simultaneous converging attack was calculated to prevent the Russian armies in Poland from making full use of their "interior lines." They were standing in the centre ; the southern Austro-German armies which up to Lwow had had to deal only with the armies of General Ivanoff, had by July come into striking distance of all the forces gathered within the quadrilateral between the Narev, Vistula, the Ivangorod-Cholm line and the middle Bug. If pressed from all sides simultaneously they could derive hardly any advantage from their central position. An army which is well equipped with heavy artillery and machine guns can hold for some time a strong line with comparatively weak detachments, whilst it concentrates its main force in one single direction. This was, on an enormous scale, the way in which the Germans profited from their central position between Russia and her Western Allies. But the Russians lacked the necessary amount of artillery, machine guns, and ammunition. Even had they pierced in any place the ring of their enemies, they could hardly have followed up their success. In the course of the Galician campaign they had several times broken through the Austro-German lines, but being short of guns and ammunition had been unable to develop an effective counter-offensive. It will be sufficient to remind the reader of the successful recrossing of the San by the Russian army north of Sieniava towards the end of May, of the almost contemporary breakdown of Linsingen's line at Bolechow, finally of the second battle of Krasnik in the beginning of July. Each of these victories, if gained by an army equal to its opponents in equipment and ammunition, might easily have resulted in a second Marne, and even in greater successes ; for, after all, it was again the German superiority in heavy artillery which rendered possible their rally on the Aisne.

To sum up : in July, 1915, our Russian Allies did not possess sufficient artillery and ammunition to enable them to hold lightly some parts of the line and to concentrate their forces for a decisive blow in one direction. Even had they done it, incurring thereby considerable risks, it is unlikely that their success could have been followed out to a decisive conclusion. Hence the advantages which the inner lines in Poland seemed to offer them were of a rather illusory character.

The dangers of their position were on the other

THE FALL OF WARSAW.

Russian Artillery on the road during the retreat. Centre and bottom: Russian troops removing church bells, copper and metal, which were likely to prove of military value to the enemy.

hand very real. The armies on the Vistula were dependent for supplies and reinforcements on four railway lines. The most northern of them leads from Petrograd by Vilna, Grodno and Bialystok to Warsaw ; it was covered from the enemy mainly by the defences on the line of the Niemen and the Narev, but could have been reached by the Germans also to the north of that line. The two central lines run by Siedlce and Brest-Litovsk to Warsaw and Ivangorod, and hardly any natural defences cover them from the enemy, besides those which protect also the outer railways. The fourth and most southern railway line runs by Kovel, Cholm and Lublin to Ivangorod. These four railways are inter-connected, between the Vistula and Brest-Litovsk, by three lines running north and south.

About the middle of July Hindenburg opened his attack against the defences of the Warsaw-Vilna line and against the northern corner-stone of the Polish salient, Novo-Georgievsk, Mackensen against the Kovel-Ivangorod railway, and the southern corner-stone, Ivangorod. It is evident that it would have been sheer folly on the part of the supreme Russian army command to delay the withdrawal of the armies from the Vistula line for long after the outer two railways were threatened by the enemy. The position in the Polish salient did not offer the Russians any special advantages, as they

NIGHT FIGHTING ON THE ROAD TO WARSAW.

could not profit from their central position. On the contrary, it compelled them to maintain a longer front, which is always a serious disadvantage for an army inferior in numbers and less well provided with artillery and ammunition.

We shall not enter now into the detail of the campaign. We propose to deal with it when describing at a greater length the military operations which intervened between the fall of Lwow and that of Warsaw. We merely wish to indicate at present the main stages of the new offensive against the salient of the Vistula. It opened about the middle of July. During the first week the northern and southern armies were advancing gradually towards their main objectives, the outer railway lines. On July 23-24 the armies of von Gallwitz and von Scholtz forced the Narev between Pultusk and Ostrolenka, threatening thereby the Vilna-Warsaw railway. On July 19 our Allies had withdrawn practically without fighting from the Bzura line, which they had held with so much valour for seven months. On July 29 German troops crossed the Vistula north of Ivangorod. On August 4 the Austrians entered Ivangorod. On August 5 came the fall of Warsaw.

The struggle for the Vistula line was settled for the time being in favour of the Central Powers. One of the most magnificent armies which had ever taken the field had to retreat from position to position on account of lack of guns and ammunition. German writers were given a chance of spinning by the yard tirades about "unsere herrlichen Armeen," "unsere tapferen Truppen," or, when waxing more sentimental, about "unsere braven Jungens." * Many of them also thought fit to speak contemptuously about the quality of the Russian armies. No one, however, has done so who has ever actually seen them fighting.

"If I am to sum up my impressions and observations of the Russians," writes a Styrian workman, who served with a battery of heavy Austrian howitzers, "I must state, against the opinions of the patriots at home and of the newspaper strategists, . . . that the Russians are a brave, well-trained and well-disciplined army, which can be beaten only by far better generalship and superior artillery. The fact that we are taking so many prisoners is due to the Russian tactics; disposing of big numbers

of men they calculate on mass-effects which naturally entails frequently the loss of many prisoners. But, indeed, the Russians are not cowards. In the building of earthworks and trenches their work may serve as a classical model. . . . We shall never be able to equal them in that respect." * The one remark in this letter which cannot be said to be based on immediate experience is that instituting a comparison between the generalship of the two armies. Could the writer survey the whole of the operations, he would see that it was not the faults of the Russian generals in the field which led to defeat.

We shall quote only one other appreciation of the Russian armies by a German eye-witness; this one occurs in a newspaper correspondence written towards the end of July, from the headquarters of General von Emmich (Eleventh German Army under Mackensen): "We have before us . . . still always a d——d vigorous and tough enemy," writes Herr Zimmermann, in the *Schwäbischer Merkur*, of July 28, "however much he may have been beaten in Galicia and elsewhere. . . . That his reinforcements are no good one learns every time when someone arrives from home; at the front, I have never heard it or marked it myself."

It is not for us to judge with whom lay the fault for the serious set-back which our Allies suffered in the spring and summer of 1915. The Russian nation and its Tsar are the only competent judges. They have expressed their judgment in the changes which were made in the Russian administration; those changes were not, however, really directed at individual persons. Their aim was a change of system. The meeting of the Duma about the anniversary of the outbreak of the war, which coincided with the time of the worst reverses, was symbolic of the mobilization of the entire national strength. At its first meeting it passed an order of the day affirming the unshakable and unanimous resolution of the entire population of the Russian Empire "to continue the struggle with our faithful Allies until the final success

---

* "Our magnificent army," "our brave troops," "our good boys."

* This letter was printed in the Viennese *Arbeiter-Zeitung* of July 23. It contains also an explanation of the real use served by the oaken clubs, with which some Russian troops were said to have been armed. These clubs serve for the driving of the poles for wire entanglements. "Some time ago," says the writer, "I have read in newspapers that being short of weapons the Russians were armed with oaken clubs. Evidently one of the much-honoured war-correspondents was taken in. I myself have found such clubs near Bolechow, but guessed at once for what purpose they are used."

is attained and not to conclude peace before victory is complete."

During the week preceding the fall of Lwow, little fighting occurred on the Dniester. It recommenced with violence as soon as the retreat of our Allies beyond the line of the Szczerec became inevitable. At first the most intense fighting developed in the big loops of the Dniester, below Nizniow. Here the Austrians attempted to establish themselves on the northern bank of the river, and thus to gain a firm base for an offensive against the Russian lines of retreat. Had they succeeded, our Allies could not have stopped on the line of the Zlota Lipa the advance of the troops which were pressing on from the west (Nizniow lies close below the junction of the Zlota Lipa and the Dniester) ; with luck and unavoidably heavy losses they might have, in that case, extricated their forces from Galicia. In a previous chapter we have drawn attention to the peculiar tactical conditions which the ground presents in the region of the big river-loops of the Dniester.* Hardly anywhere are they more marked than in the sector below Nizniow. The distance from that town to the mouth of the Strypa amounts to less than twenty miles ; the course of the river between these two towns extends, however, for more than three times the distance. For reasons which we

* Cf. Chapter LXXVI., p. 429.

explained in Chapter LXXVI., the mere crossing of the river in either direction can hardly be prevented ; it is the configuration of the country round the river that offers the splendid opportunities for defence which enabled our Allies to withstand all flank attacks from across the Dniester. It is difficult to overestimate the importance which that resistance had in shaping the course of the Eastern campaign.

We cannot enter into the detail of the fighting which was proceeding in that region about the time of the fall of Lwow. Let us, however, by explaining a short paragraph in a Petrograd dispatch, try to give a general idea of the conditions under which the battle was fought and won by our Allies. " On the Dniester," said the Russian official communiqué of June 23, " the battle continued south of the village of Kosmierjine, where the enemy is holding his ground on the left bank of the river. In the bends of the Dniester we drove back the enemy from the village of Unijh towards the village of Luka." With the help of the map given in Chapter LXXVI., on page 435, the reader will be able to trace the main outlines of the course of the Dniester. Below Nizniow the Dniester forms a big bend ; at its northern end it is met from the left bank by a small stream called Kovopiec, which flows past Podhajce and Monasterzyska. After having followed for about one and a

DIFFICULTIES OF TRANSPORT IN RUSSIA.
German troops pulling a transport car along a worn-out road.

THE GERMANS OCCUPY WARSAW.

General von Scheffer-Boyadel (×), the Governor of Warsaw, awaiting the arrival of Prince Leopold of Bavaria. Inset: General von Scheffer-Boyadel and members of his staff at Fort No. 6.

half mile an easterly course, the Dniester turns due south and continues in that direction for more than five miles. In the middle of that sector, on the eastern side of the cañon, which is there about 500 feet deep, lies the village of Kosmierjine. At the extreme end of that sector the Dniester, turning to the north, forms again a small loop. The inside of it—i.e., the left bank—is low (its highest point rises only about 150 feet above the level of the river); it consists of open plough-land and can be easily swept from west, south, and east by the fire of artillery posted on the higher right bank of the river. Our Allies could not possibly have prevented the Austrians from crossing at that point and from estab-lishing themselves south of Kosmierjine. But what then ? The open field east of the sector of the Dniester round Kosmierjine is like a narrow island. Straight parallel to that sector, at a distance of about a mile to the east, through a cañon between 200 and 300 feet deep, winds a small tributary of the Dniester. Its cañon is covered with thick wood and big forests extend for miles to the east of it; the gate which opens at the place where the cañon of the Dniester recedes from that of the parallel stream is closed by a group of wooded hills, on the average about 1,200 feet high. The

Austrians were able to cross the Dniester south of Kosmierjine, and to hold the ground on its left bank, but were unable to advance any farther. Only at one point they succeeded in penetrating into the belt of hills and forests behind Kosmierjine ; the Russian official com-muniqué of June 24 gives the history of that adventure.

"In the region of Kosmierjine . . ." says the report, " our troops taking the offensive on the 22nd approached Mount Bezimianna, which was occupied and strongly fortified by the enemy. After digging themselves in, our troops at dawn yesterday advanced impetuously to the assault of the mountain, and the enemy, not daring to face a bayonet attack, fell back in

disorder to the second line of his works. Pressing close on his heels, our troops entered the works and put to the bayonet almost the whole garrison holding the hill. The remnants, consisting of two officers and 210 of the rank and file, were made prisoners."

The village of Luka can be easily located on the map; it lies on the left bank of the Dniester, straight opposite Niezviska, at the bottom of an almost circular loop, which is about eleven miles long, but has a neck only about 800 yards wide. It stands to reason that an army holding the southern bank of the river commands also by its fire the inside of that loop. From here the Austrians attempted to advance to the north, but were driven back; the statement in the *communiqué* which we quoted above refers to the bottling up of their forces within the loop.

After these failures the Austrians seem to have abandoned for some time all attempts at breaking through below Nizniow. The main attack on the Dniester was now

THE ENTRY OF THE
Prince Leopold of Bavaria (×) and Staff outside the
as they entered the city.

developing in the district between Zuravno and Halicz.

In consonance with the retreat from Lwow our Allies had to abandon the part of the Dniester round the bridgeheads of Mikolajow and Zydaczow, which the Germans had tried in vain to conquer by frontal attacks. From there the Germans advanced to the railway junction of Chodorow, which, since the fall of Lwow, had lost all its importance for our Allies. About the same time considerable bodies of troops, belonging to the army of von Linsingen, crossed the Dniester between Zuravno and Halicz; the German centre of the army (probably the army corps of Count Bothmer) was operating near the village of Kozary, near Martynow, half-way between Zuravno and Halicz, Austrian troops were attempting to break through the belt of the Dniester; the hardest task, the attack against the bridgehead of Halicz, was left, as usual, to an Austro-Hungarian army corps—namely, to that of General Hoffmann.

On June 22 the enemy forces which had advanced on the northern bank were driven back towards the river, suffering enormous losses.

The battle continued during the night of June 23–24, and the remaining detachments of the Austro-German troops which had crossed the river were thrown back to its right bank. Similar ill-luck accompanied the Austrian operations.

On June 24 our Allies effected new successes and new captures in the Dniester region. Yet the sector of the Dniester between Zuravno and Halicz had finally to be abandoned in accordance with the retreat of the Russian armies farther north. By June 26 our Allies had fallen back on to the line of the Gnila Lipa (Halicz lies near its junction with the Dniester).

During the first three days following on the fall of Lwow no fighting of any importance occurred in its immediate neighbourhood. Our

GERMANS INTO WARSAW.
Alexander-Nevsky Cathedral reviewing the troops
Inset: Prince Leopold of Bavaria.

ADVANCING ON RAFTS ON THE VISTULA: RUSSIAN
A feature of the war on the Eastern front was the enormous use that was made of the rivers as lines
thus afforded them by the wide and sluggish rivers which

Allies took up fortified positions east and south-east of the town, at distances varying from six to ten miles ; their line ran approximately from Jaryczow, past Davidowka and Dmytrovice, to Bobrka. On June 25 the Austrian troops of General Boehm-Ermolli's army resumed their offensive ; it followed, in the main, the roads and railway-lines leading from Lwow by Bobrka to Chodorow, and by Przemyslany to Brzezany on the Zlota Lipa. After a day and a night of severe fighting our Allies resumed their retreat, withdrawing to the Gnila Lipa. Mr. Stanley Washburn, the special correspondent of *The Times*, who was with the Russian troops on the Zlota Lipa in the beginning of July, describes as follows their " retreat " from the Lwow-Mikolajow line. " A number of streams running almost due north and south flow into the Dniester, and as each of these rivulets runs between more or less pretentious bluffs, it is a very simple matter to hold them with very few field works. What the Russians are doing is this. They take up one of these natural lines of defence and throw up temporary works on the bluffs and wait for the Austrians. When the latter come up they find the Russians too strong to be turned out with anything short of the full

enemy strength." Then some time passes before the Austro-German forces come up and get their guns into position. " The Russians in the meantime sit on their hills taking all the losses that they can get and repel the Austrian preliminary attacks as long as they can do so without risking too much." During these operations they frequently carry out successful counter-attacks and capture considerable numbers of prisoners, largely owing to the inexperience of the young Austrian officers, and also because many of the Austrian troops have no heart in the fight. " By the time that enemy operations have reached a really serious stage and an attack in force is made," says Mr. Washburn, " it is discovered that the main forces of the Russians have departed, and when the positions are finally carried only a rearguard of cavalry is discovered holding the trenches, and the bulk of these usually get away on their horses, leaving the exhausted Austrians sitting in a hard-won line with the knowledge that the Russians are already miles away waiting for them to repeat the operation all over again."

On July 26 the Russians settled down on the line of the Gnila Lipa, and on the next day the Austrians began their offensive against it. Most desperate were, however, the attacks

REINFORCEMENTS BEING TRANSPORTED TO THE FRONT.
of supply and communication for the armies in the field. Both Germans and Russians took advantage seam the face of the country with a network of waterways.

directed to the north of it, in the region and against the town of Gliniany. "Here, in the course of our counter-attacks," says the Russian official *communiqué* of June 28, "we took prisoners belonging to all the regiments of the Austrian Fourth Division. Thrown back to his point of departure, the enemy remained entirely passive next day."

Between June 26 and 30 fighting proceeded almost along the entire line of the Gnila Lipa, round Bursztyn, Rohatyn, Firlejow, and Przemyslany, and also farther north, west of the upper Bug, near Kamionka, Mosty Wielkie and Krystynopol. It was not until the last day of the month that the enemy had gathered sufficient forces to effect a crossing of the river near Rohatyn. On the day of that "defeat" our Allies were, however, able to report the capture of over 2,000 prisoners and of several machine guns. The Russians now continued their retreat to the Narajowka. But it was not their intention to hold that line. The retirement to the Zlota Lipa had been foreseen and planned for a considerable time beforehand. As early as June 28 *The Times* correspondent reported from Petrograd that "a withdrawal to the Zlota Lipa, which is far better adapted for defence than the Gnila Lipa, is foreseen

in military circles." The line was reached on July 4; and, indeed, it was splendidly adapted for purposes of defence. The marshes in the valley * and the hills and forests beyond it, and farther south the cañon, offered unusually good opportunities for establishing there the front-line of the new Russian positions; its left flank rested on the famous Dniester belt between Nizniow and Zaleszczyki. The general commanding a division of Cossack cavalry from the Caucasus, which was defending part of that line, assured Mr. Washburn again and again that those positions could, as far as he was concerned, be retained indefinitely. His words proved true. We shall not hear again of that region until towards the end of August.

The fortress of Halicz, which was all-important for our Allies whilst their troops were still standing in positions far advanced to the west, was losing its significance with their retirement towards the Zlota Lipa. The

* South of Brzezany the different sectors of the valley of the Zlota Lipa bear the significant names of " old pond," " wet meadows," " big mud," etc. The hills on both sides rise several hundred feet above the level of the valley. The forests are very extensive. Whilst farther east between the Strypa and Seret seldom more than 20 per cent. of the land is covered with wood, on the Zlota Lipa the proportion frequently rises far above 50 per cent.

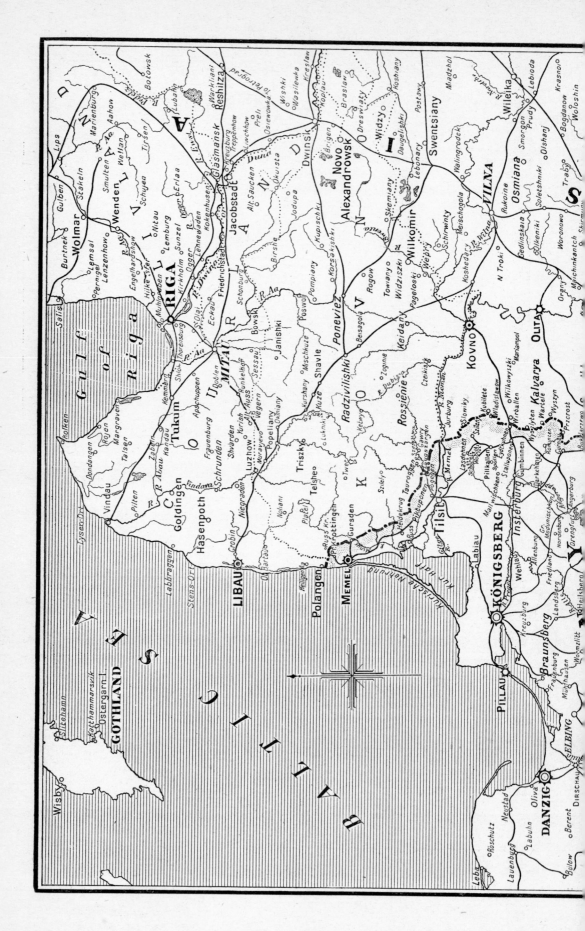

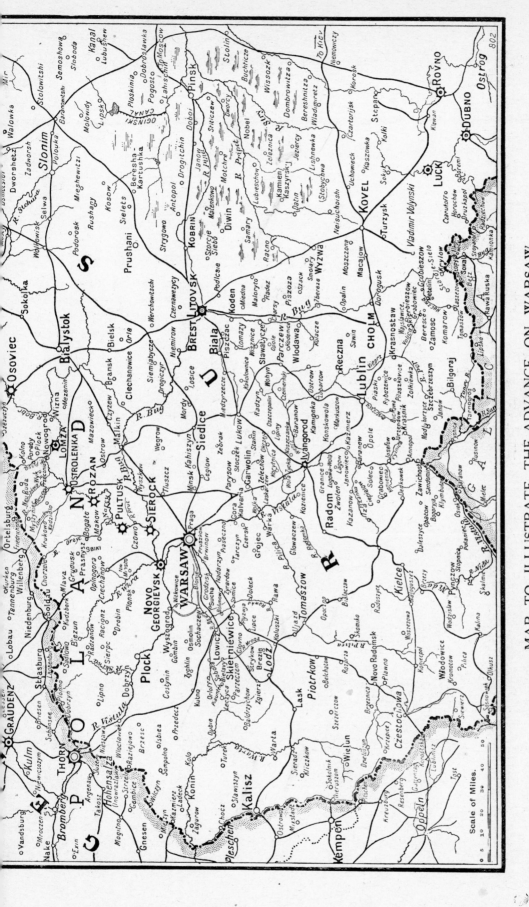

MAP TO ILLUSTRATE THE ADVANCE ON WARSAW.

EVERY MAN ACROSS; AND THE

The blowing up of a pontoon bridge on the Vistula by the retiring Russian rearguard.   On the right
with the pontoons, these having been

River Narajowka was the last line in connexion with Halicz could still be held. With the abandonment of those positions a continued defence of the fortress would have merely exposed its garrison to the danger of capture.

Halicz was the most powerful bridgehead on the Dniester. Lying in the midst of a maze of streams, it is, moreover, protected from the south by extensive forests. It had been originally fortified by the Austrians ; our Allies added three new lines of works. The diameter of its fortifications amounted to ten miles. One railway bridge and five wooden bridges span the river within the lines of Halicz. The Austrians arrived in its neighbourhood in the first week of June. Practically the entire army corps of General Hoffmann was detailed for the siege of its bridgehead. Eleven heavy Austrian batteries, including one of 30·5 cm. howitzers, were brought up against its fortifications. As the result of a whole fortnight of hard and expensive labour the enemy succeeded in taking the two outer

lines of the fortress. Then the Austrians sent floating mines down-stream against the wooden bridges and thus succeeded in destroying several of them. Large forces could no longer be kept on the right—*i.e.*, southern—bank of the Dniester, and preparations had to be made for the evacuation of Halicz. The retreat of the troops in the district farther north rendered it certain that this Dniester stronghold also would soon have to be abandoned. On June 27 the part of Halicz which lies south of the river passed into the hands of the Austrians ; on their retreat our Allies blew up the remaining bridges, including the big railway bridge.

But luck favoured the enemy ; during the night a very heavy river-fog rose over the Dniester. Under cover of that fog the Austrian engineers were able to replace the blown-up part of the railway bridge by a wooden structure. During the night of June 28–29 an entire Austrian division, under General Fleischman, succeeded in crossing the river and in conquering the northern part of Halicz. The fall of that

ENEMY PREVENTED FROM FOLLOWING.

of the picture the Engineer-officer and men are seen with their apparatus, connected by cable previously prepared with explosives.

part of the fortress came too early for our Allies. Had the Austrians maintained and enlarged their positions in that district, they would have been able to carry out a dangerous attack against the flank of the Russian armies which were retreating towards the Zlota Lipa. In a pitched battle fought on June 30 our Allies drove back the enemy to the very riverside. Then, during the first days of July, they retired from Halicz, following up the general movement of the left flank of General Ivanoff's armies.

On the fall of Halicz the last troops belonging to the army of von Linsingen crossed the Dniester. After July 1 only the army of Baron von Pflanzer-Baltin remained south of the Dniester, whilst that of von Linsingen held the line of the Zlota Lipa between Nizniow and Gologory. The Second Austro-Hungarian Army, under von Boehm-Ermolli, had meantime reached the upper Bug; the meeting ground between it and the adjoining Eleventh German Army, which stood under the immediate command of Field-Marshal von Mackensen, seems to have been the district north of Sokal.

Between June 22 and 28 hardly any progress to the north was made by the Austro-German troops between the Vistula and Bug. Only in the corner, between the Vistula and the San, and to the west of the Vistula, in the region of Opatow, the enemy continued to press his advance. By June 25 our Allies had withdrawn from their last positions south of the San, and given up also Sandomierz and Opatow. When the new Austro-German offensive began to the east of the Vistula, the front between the Vistula and the Pilica extended from Zavichost by Ozarow and Sienno to Novemiasto.

The new offensive started in a lightning fashion. For several days it seemed that the Austro-German armies would have their way, that they would break through the Russian lines, seize the Lublin-Cholm railway, and possibly advance by Vlodava, along the Bug, with a speed which might have forced the Russian armies in the Vistula district to surrender *en masse*. In one day the Austrians negotiated the difficult region of the Tanev. As a matter of fact, the nature of that

HOW THE GERMANS CONQUERED THE MARSHES.
A special railway constructed by German pioneers over the marshes in Russian Poland.

country of forests and marshes is such as to hamper even the defending side to a very serious extent. Both armies have to keep to the few tracks which lead through the morasses. Along these roads the superior Austrian artillery could have swept away easily, and with serious loss to the defending side, any resistance which our Allies might have tried to offer to their advance. Therefore no serious attempt was made at preventing their crossing. The Tenth Austro-Hungarian army corps, which had previously belonged to the Third Army under General Borojevic von Bojna, and since the fall of Przemysl had been included in the army of Archduke Joseph-Ferdinand, advanced along the road leading from Krzeszow to Bilgoraj. Having crossed the Tanev near Harasiaki, it turned to the north, and by way of Janow reached Modliborzyce on the Sanna. From here began, on June 30, their advance against Krasnik.

Meantime the other parts of the Fourth Austro-Hungarian Army and the left wing and centre of the Eleventh German Army had kept pace with it in the advance to the north. They crossed the Russian frontier, to the north of Cieszanow and Rava Ruska, and occupied Tomaszow on June 28. On the next day they

reached Zaklikow, 10 miles west of Modliborzyce, and Frampol, about 18 miles west of that village. On the same day the troops under General von Woyrsch resumed from the west their advance against the Vistula; on June 30 they had reached the heights south of Tarlow, a village situated in the corner between the Kamienna and the Vistula. East of the Vistula the Austro-German troops had meantime occupied Turczyn on the Por and Zamosc on the Volica. Zamosc lies exactly half-way between the positions which the enemy occupied on June 28 round Cieszanow and Plazow, and the Lublin-Cholm railway line, which was his immediate objective.

On July 1 the Austro-German forces crossed the Por; farther west the Austrians reached the River Vyznica and occupied Krasnik. On the same day, about 5 p.m., they succeeded in capturing the bridgehead of Jozefow, near the mouth of the Vyznica; they enlarged their hold on that district in the course of the following night. This was, however, to be the end of their rapid advance. They had reached the line along which our Allies had decided to offer vigorous resistance to their offensive. On the Jozefow-Krasnik-Plonka line, along which the battle developed on July 2, our Allies had the advantage of communications. It is true, there is no great difference in the distances which separate it from the Ivangorod-Lublin-Cholm line, and from the Galician railways, but the former is much superior in structure (the Galician railways near the northern border are single track branch-lines); moreover, the intervening ground is open and traversed by several excellent roads, whilst the lines of communication to the south, especially in the western sector, are seriously restricted by marshes and sand. The line south of the Lublin-Cholm railway was now held by two Russian armies. The army of General Loesche, bearing the number of that which had originally stood along the line of the Dunajec, was holding the positions north of Krasnik; on its left stood the army of General Everts. "Excellent field works had been prepared," wrote Mr. Washburn, who had visited the positions of General Loesche's army, " . . . and I felt sure that whatever the outcome of the German move against him would be, it would not result in anything like the Dunajec enterprise, nor would the enemy be able to drive through to Brest with sufficient rapidity to cut off the retreat of the Warsaw Army or those lying south of it."

On July 2 the Austrians were forced to evacuate Krasnik; the Austro-German advance was arrested almost along the entire line. Apart from an insignificant advance at one single point near Studzianki (east of Krasnik), no further progress was reported by the enemy on July 3. On the next day the Austrians re-entered Krasnik, our Allies retaining their positions in the forest north-east of the town and round the village of Budzyn. On July 5, suffering terrific losses from the Russian machine guns, the Austrians succeeded in occupying the village, and also in gaining considerable ground north of Krasnik. The success of that day was, however, destined to remain for some time the high-water mark of their advance.

The fighting of July 5–6 marked the turning of the tide. On the line of the Rivers Lower Vyznica, Urzendowka and of the upper Bystrzyca, our Allies commenced their counter-offensive. An Austro-German army of certainly no fewer than five army corps was gathered in that region under the command of Archduke Joseph-Ferdinand. North of Krasnik alone were massed three Austro-Hungarian army corps. On the left flank the Archduke's army stood in contact with the army of General Woyrsch; on its right, it joined up with the forces of Mackensen. On Monday, July 5, the same day on which he advanced to the north of Krasnik, the enemy experienced a serious check on his eastern flank. "On the front between the Vistula and the Bug," says the Russian official *communiqué* of July 6, "most desperate fighting took place Sunday evening and Monday morning in the sector Urzedow-Bychawa. The hostile offensive east of Krasnik was stopped by a blow which we delivered on the enemy's flank on the heights north-west of Vilkolaz, where we inflicted serious losses on the enemy, capturing during Monday morning more than 2,000 prisoners and 29 officers, while about 2,000 enemy corpses lay before our front."

During the following day, our Allies continued to press their offensive. Along the Krasnik-Vilkolaz-Lublin road and along the Rivers Bystrzyca and Kosarzewka, where the Austrian positions formed a salient, the Russians successfully continued to develop the counter-attack of the previous day. "The enemy," says the Petrograd *communiqué* of July 7, "was compelled to pass to the defensive. In the course of the day we took on this front no fewer than 2,000 prisoners and we captured several machine guns." To parry the blow and prevent a farther advance of the Russians, the Archduke seems now to have directed his main forces towards the valley of the Bystrzyca, on the eastern fringe of the Krasnik woods. This, however, resulted in a very considerable weakening of his left wing, and enabled the Russians to break through his positions near Urzendow, north-east of Krasnik. By the afternoon of July 9, our Allies were threatening to turn the western flank of the forces engaged near Vilkolaz and on the Bystrzyca. It was mainly the stubborn resistance offered by the troops which managed to maintain themselves on Height 118, south of Vilkolaz Gorny, that saved the Austrians from further disaster. Even so, their losses were very serious, in prisoners alone they lost more than 15,000 men. Still, in the absence of adequate artillery support, our Allies were unable to follow up their successes, or even to reduce the garrison which was holding the entrenched positions on Hill 118. They had to settle down on the line of the Urzendowka, and satisfy themselves with having stopped, for the time being, the advance of the enemy. With July 9 ends the first stage of the Austro-German advance from Lwow to Warsaw. A complete lull of almost a week followed the battle of Krasnik. When the new offensive commences about the middle of July, its first moves transfer us to the Baltic provinces and to the Narev front; about the latter we have had little to say during the entire spring of 1915.

The days after the second battle of Krasnik were like the silence before the storm. It was certain that the time of the final struggle for Warsaw and the Vistula line was approaching. Between July 12–14 a campaign began as it had never yet been witnessed, not even in this, the greatest of all wars. The new Germanic offensive extended over practically the entire Eastern front. An army composed of at least 45 army corps opened an offensive along a front stretching over about 1,000 miles. In the extreme north a group of six army corps commenced on July 13 the second offensive against the Baltic Provinces. On its southern flank an army composed of four army corps advanced against the line of the Niemen; the operations west of the Kovno-Grodno line were, however, in July 1915, of only secondary importance. Certainly not less than about nine army corps were facing, about the middle of July, the Bobr-Narev-Bug line, between Grodno and Novo-Georgievsk; they included three army corps composed of new formations from Schleswig-Holstein, Pomerania and Brandenburg. At least three army corps stood in front of Warsaw, between the Vistula and the Pilica; towards the end of the month they were reinforced by three more German and three Austro-Hungarian divisions (these six divisions are not included in our estimate of 45 army corps). Between the Pilica and the Roumanian frontier stood the

A RUSSIAN OUTPOST.
Inset : Field telegraphists at work in the trenches.

THE GERMAN ADVANCE.
Troops building a pontoon bridge between Warsaw and Praga.

" southern armies " which had borne the whole brunt of the fighting between May 2 and July 9. The strength of these six armies (von Woyrsch including the group of Kövess, Archduke Joseph-Ferdinand, von Mackensen, von Linsingen and the group of Count Bothmer, von Boehm-Ermolli and Baron von Pflanzer-Baltin) we can hardly put at less than 24 army corps.

About the middle of July the eastern front presented a curious succession of " flanks " extending east and west, and of " fronts " running north and south. The weight of the new Germanic offensive was directed mainly against the " flanks " ; the fighting along the three " fronts," *i.e.*, the lines of the Niemen, of the Vistula, and of the Bug and Zlota Lipa, was mainly of a supplementary nature (the southern end of the Vistula line near Ivangorod forms an exception). The most important of all were, of course, the two flank lines on both sides of the Warsaw and Ivangorod positions ; we may call them for short the line of the Narev and the Lublin-Cholm line. The importance of the " flank " north of Shavle, which was created by the first moves of the new offensive in the Baltic Provinces, did not come to be felt until much later. In the following account of the fighting which ensued during the second half of July we propose to deal first of all with the German advance in the Baltic Provinces. It forms, as it were, a separate chapter of the great offensive ; it has

to be treated apart from the main operations. In the extreme south, on the short Dniester flank, between Nizniow and Uscie Biskupie, Baron von Pflanzer-Baltin renewed, about the middle of July, his attempts to emerge from the river-loops ; they ended in the usual failure. As fighting in that region did not present any new features of special interest, and was not of any pre-eminent importance, we shall content ourselves with this mere registration of its occurrence.

Little fighting occurred in the Baltic Provinces between the middle of May and July 13. The two armies were facing one another between Libau and Kovno, on a front of 150 miles ; the rivers Vindava, Venta and Dubissa formed on the whole the dividing line between them. Most of the ground was held by comparatively small forces, and a considerable proportion of the troops consisted of cavalry. The district of Shavle, situated about half-way between Libau and Kovno, formed the centre of the Baltic theatre of war. About the middle of June the Germans attempted an offensive against it. They succeeded in advancing as far as Kuze, which is within artillery range of Shavle, but were unable to break through the Russian lines in front of the town. Thereupon a lull set in again in the fighting, which lasted till the great Germanic offensive against Warsaw reached its culminating stage in a simultaneous advance along the entire Eastern front.

RUSSIAN PIONEERS REPAIRING THE VISTULA BRIDGE BETWEEN PRAGA AND WARSAW.

The new German offensive against Shavle began with a flank attack, proceeding across the Vindava from the direction of Libau, and ended in a concentric movement which was meant to encircle and capture the main body of the Fifth Russian Army. The Vindava was first crossed by the Germans in the neighbourhood of Niegraden, about halfway between Schrunden and Muravievo, and then at a few more points between Muravievo and Kurshany. The crossing of the river in that district does not present any serious difficulties; it is hardly more than 50 yards wide and its banks are covered with big forests which shield it from observation. Moreover the district seems to have been only very lightly held by the Russians; after having crossed the river, some of the German cavalry was able to advance 50 miles in three days without meeting with any serious resistance. Beyond the Vindava the German forces spread to the north and to the east. Their left wing had Mitau for its objective; it was supported from the west by another body of troops which was advancing on the left bank of the Vindava and along the sea against Goldingen and Windau. The centre and right wing of the forces had for their immediate objective the railway from Mitau to Muravievo; having crossed it, they were to advance at full speed against Janishki and the river Musha so as to outflank the Russian forces round Shavle, and, if possible, to cut their only line of retreat, which led to the east.

The offensive against Mitau did not meet at first with any serious resistance. On July 15 the Germans occupied Frauenburg; two days later a battle was fought round Doblen. By noon of July 18 the enemy was within six miles of Mitau. Meantime, on the left of this group, the forces from Libau had occupied Goldingen and Windau, crossed the Vindava and reached the Windau-Tukum-Mitau railway. A few days later the Germans, on reaching the River Aa, east of Mitau, near the town of Bowsk, completed the semicircle by which they closed in from the south the district of Mitau. But the town could not be taken by a *coup de main*. It lies in a strong defensive position, near the confluence of several rivers, and is moreover covered from the south by a belt of forests, several miles wide. Moreover, its most important strategic line of communication, the railway to Riga, lay out of reach of the German forces. It was only on August 1 that the Germans were able to capture the town. But,

as a matter of fact, the immediate aim of the German advance against Mitau was not the capture of the town, but the cutting off of all direct communication between Riga and Shavle. In that way the containing force which surrounded Mitau from the south protected the flank of the forces which advanced in an easterly direction by way of Alt-Auss against Janishki.

The Russian troops between Mitau and Shavle were falling back before the German forces, which outnumbered them very considerably. Their retreat was covered by a series of brilliant rearguard actions, fought, with the support of a number of machine guns, by a brigade of Ussurian cavalry. Making the most of the natural advantages which a region of forest and marshes offers for that type of fighting, those Siberian horsemen succeeded in delaying the German advance until practically the entire Russian army had withdrawn from the danger zone. On July 20 a new body of German troops crossed the Dubissa in the Rossienie district, south of Shavle. A concentric attack from the south, the west, the north, and even north-east was directed against the Russian troops in the district of Shavle and Shadoff. No one can deny the strategic excellence of the German offensive; yet they failed in their main object of encircling the Fifth Russian Army, which was holding the provinces of Courland and Samogitia. By July 23 it had effected its retreat beyond Shadoff. In the course of the operations of those ten days the Germans claim to have captured 27,000 prisoners, 25 guns, and 40 machine guns. Even if these figures are correct the Russian losses can hardly be described as surprisingly large. In a retreat through wooded, marshy country, in which small groups get easily detached, losses in prisoners are unavoidable. The Russian reports do not name the aggregate figure of prisoners taken by them during the fighting in the Baltic provinces between July 13-23; yet, although they were the retreating side, the number must have undoubtedly risen into many thousands; thus, to take but one example, the Russian official *communiqué* of July 18 reports the capture of " 500 German prisoners, with 9 officers and 7 machine guns."

After the capture of Shavle and Shadoff, the German advance continued to the east in the direction of Posvol and Ponieviesh; both these districts were reached by July 25. Then

REFUGEES FLEEING BEFORE THE ADVANCING GERMAN ARMIES.

the advance became much slower ; on August 2 the German forces passed the Vobolniki-Subotch road, which crosses the Ponieviesh-Dvinsk railway about 15 miles to the east of Ponieviesh. By the end of the month, the Germans were still standing in that region practically along that same line.

As we have previously stated, the German advance in the Baltic provinces, which took place in the second half of July, had for its aim to tie up Russian forces in that region and to prepare the ground for an enveloping movement from the north against the line of the Niemen. Had the direct attack against the salient on the Vistula failed to achieve its object the Germans might have compelled the Russians to retire from Poland by cutting, or even merely by seriously threatening, their lines of communication with the north, in the districts of Vilna and Molodetchna. Meantime, however, the course which events assumed in the south deprived the operations in Lithuania of their immediate importance.

Hardly any fighting transgressing the limits of what might be described as the routine of trench warfare had taken place on the Narev front between the middle of March and July 12. In the district of Prasnysz, which the proximity of the Mlava-Novo-Georgievsk railway and the nature of the ground rendered the decisive region for a German offensive, no changes whatsoever had occurred since about the end of May in the main positions. The Germans were occupying a line stretching south of Mlava and Chorzele, with its centre on the hills near the hamlet of Granaty. Half a mile of ground intervened between them and the Russian trenches. When the failure of the first attack against the Lublin-Cholm line was realized, preparations for an offensive from the north were pushed forward with great speed. Artillery of all kinds and calibres was brought up ; saps were dug until their heads got within 200 yards of the Russian positions. Between July 9–12 the excavations were carried on not only by night, but even in day-time ; only for a few hours in the day, says the diary of a German soldier who took part in the work, it was allowed to rest altogether. During the night of July 12–13 the German artillery opened fire against the positions of our Allies. At 4 a.m. on July 13 all batteries started the bombardment of the Russian trenches ; at 7.30 a.m. it changed into quick fire. It stopped half an hour later, and the German infantry

commenced its advance. " I am told," wrote Mr. Washburn from the Headquarters on the Bzura front, under date of July 17, " that the Russians knew that the Germans had planned their advance against the old positions for 3 o'clock * in the morning, and they withdrew when darkness fell, leaving the Germans to fire 80,000 shells at the abandoned positions before they realized that the main Russian force was already sitting in its trenches in the new line." " The enemy has assumed the offensive on the Narev front," says the Russian official *communiqué* of July 14. " Great enemy forces are advancing between the rivers Orzec and Lidynia (*i.e.*, in the district of Prasnysz). Our troops, without accepting a conclusive battle, retired . . . on their second line of positions."

During the morning of July 13 the German forces continued their attack. Their right wing captured Hill 164, to the west of the Mlava-Ciechanow railway, their left wing occupied the village of Grudnsk. One Russian army corps was fighting against three German corps, which were reported to have been the 11th, 13th, and 17th Bavarians. From east and west the German troops were closing in on Prasnysz. The town, of which, according to an eye-witness, only four houses were left, was abandoned by our Allies on July 14. They retired on to the line Bogate-Sbiki-Opinagora-Ciechanow. On July 15 a brilliant charge was executed by the 14th Russian cavalry brigade with the purpose of delaying the German advance. But it could not be arrested altogether.

In the early morning of July 16 Ciechanow passed into the hands of the enemy. On the morning of the following day our Allies evacuated the town of Plonsk, west of the Wkra. A last stand was made by the Russians on the height near the railway station of Gorne ; their positions commanded from that hill the flat surrounding country, and the enemy had to pay a heavy toll of lives before he was able to gain that point. The Russian retreat continued. " West of the Omulev," says the Russian official *communiqué* of July 19, " our troops withdrew progressively towards the Narev bridgehead, and fought an obstinate

* To forestall the captious critic, we state that we are aware of the divergence in the hour named by Mr. Washburn and that given in the previous statement, where we follow the account given by the diary of a German soldier. We leave it to the critic to choose his own explanation of that divergence.

rearguard action near the town of Makow on the evening of July 17." On July 18 the heads of some German columns had got within the range of the artillery of Novo-Georgievsk. The entire army of General von Gallwitz stood now along the northern bank of the Narev from Novo-Georgievsk * past Pultusk, Rozan, till the district of Ostrolenka. Its advance was accompanied and supported from the east by the army of General von Scholtz. After prolonged and heavy fighting on the Omulev, Szkwa and Pissa, it reached the line of the Bobr and Narev between Osowiec and Ostrolenka. By the night of July 18 the northern ends of some of the bridgeheads on the Narev line were seriously threatened by the enemy.

The resumption of the Austro-German offensive between the Vistula and the Bug was preceded by an attack against the Russian positions round Sokal. The flank on the Bug had to be firmly secured, whilst the main forces were directed to the north. On July 15 our Allies were in that region in possession even of some parts of the western bank of the river. On July 19, under the pressure of much superior Austrian forces, our Allies withdrew from Sokal towards Tartakow, only to return on the following day. It was only with great difficulty that the Austrians maintained themselves in Sokal during the remaining part of the month.

The Austro-German offensive against the Lublin-Cholm line recommenced about the middle of July. The chief attack was not, however, delivered by the defeated Fourth Austro-Hungarian Army under Archduke Joseph-Ferdinand, but by a new force gathered north of Zamosc and remaining under the direct command of Field-Marshal von Mackensen. "From the time I left the Bukovina front," wrote Mr. Washburn under date of July 14, " I received reports at practically every front I visited that the hostile forces were disappearing piecemeal, and they were believed to be headed against the army which is protecting Cholm. . . ." It seems that it was at that time that the army of Linsingen was split up into two groups ; one

under Count Bothmer remained on the Zlota Lipa, the other under von Linsingen himself, joined Mackensen's armies. North of the Rivers Por and Volica stood against them the Russian army of General Loesche, " the best that Russia has ever placed in the field in this war," under the command of a general whom a war-correspondent of Mr. Washburn's experience describes as " one of the most remarkable individuals I have met in this or any other war."

The Austro-Germans employed their usual tactics ; they massed their heavy batteries against one section of the Russian line and gathered their best troops to follow up the bombardment, just as they had done in the days of Gorlice and Tarnow. Of the battle which developed on July 17 in the region of Krasnostaw we cannot give a better description than by quoting a letter that reached us from *The Times* correspondent, Mr. Washburn, who has enjoyed quite exceptional opportunities for watching the development of the campaign and for gathering first-hand information concerning its incidents. " The best trenches that I have seen," writes he concerning the Russian positions near Krasnostaw, " were washed away in a day by a torrent of big shells. The Russians did not retreat. They remained and died and the Germans simply marched through the hole in the line, rendering a change of front necessary. But this time there was no disorganization of the line as a whole. The moment the Germans were beyond their supporting artillery, the Russian infantry were at their throats with the bayonet and drove them back." For more than ten days after the piercing of the Russian line south of Krasnostaw no marked progress was made by the Austro-German forces between the Vistula and the Bug. Attacks were followed by counter-attacks ; here and there the Austro-Germans were gaining ground ; it was evident that they were bound sooner or later to attain their immediate objective, the Lublin-Cholm line, but it was equally certain that they would fail in their main aim ; they could not crush the Russian forces in Poland. Only a rapid advance of the enemy similar to that which had followed on the battle on the Dunajec could have spelled disaster to the armies which were holding the salient east of the Bug and Niemen. In the steady fighting that followed on the battle of Krasnostaw ground was lost by our Allies, time by the enemy. The German *communiqués* themselves clearly illustrate the

---

* The Bug and the Narev meet at Sierock ; they join the Vistula at Novo-Georgievsk. The correct name of the stretch of river between these two towns is Bug and not Narev. But having to deal along the northern flank with more than 90 miles of the Narev line and only with 15 miles of the Bug below Sierock, military writers have got into the habit of calling it all Narev, a mistake which may be condoned and continued.

nature of these battles. Almost every day they find some success with which to embellish their accounts (and some reverse which they prefer to pass over in silence, as is done by most official *communiqués*), but on the whole they sound by no means triumphant. They tell the tale of small gains achieved as the result of unproportionately hard fighting. " Between the upper Vistula and the Bug we follow up the retreating enemy " (July 20 ; no further details given) ; " . . . the enemy has offered fresh resistance to the armies of Field-Marshal v. Mackensen. . . ." (July 21) ; " . . . the battle . . . continues . . . " (July 22) ; " . . . the allied armies succeeded in breaking at different points the stubborn resistance of the enemy . . ." (July 23) ; " A stubborn battle continues between the Vistula and the Bug " (July 24) ; " No change " (July 25), etc., etc. Such was their daily story ; it was not until July 30 that the Germanic armies which on the 16th had started their advance from a line about 15 miles south of the Lublin-Cholm railway reached the town of Lublin. It was evident that the decision of the battle for Warsaw could not come from that quarter. Generals Loesche and Everts and their armies had saved the southern flank for Warsaw, an achievement which has had an incalculable influence on the development of the entire Eastern campaign, and thereby of the whole war.

Meantime the German offensive against the northern line was continuing with its previous intensity. On July 20 German troops captured the outworks of Rozan on the northern bank of the Narev. On July 23 the Army of General von Gallwitz forced the bridgeheads of Rozan and Pultusk ; between the 23rd and 25th ten divisions of picked German troops were able to cross the Narev on a broad front between Pultusk and Ostrolenka. Yet again they met with disappointment. They broke through the main line, as they had near Krasnostaw, but the stubborn resistance of the Russian troops prevented their further progress. A battle now developed between the Narev and the Bug

SCENES BY THE WAYSIDE.
Russian troops retreating from Poland. Inset : Honouring the graves of the fallen.

similar to that which was being fought in front of the Lublin-Cholm line. It had seemed at first that the passage of the Narev by the Germans would settle the fate of the Vilna-Warsaw line, and necessitate an immediate evacuation of Warsaw by the Russians. Their drive against Wyszkow and Ostrow soon proved a failure. The advance of one day was followed on the next by reverses, accompanied with heavy losses in casualties and prisoners. If anything, the position in the north offered the Germans even smaller chances of reaching a decision than did that in the south. The German official *communiqué* of August 5 announces that "fighting heavily, the Armies of Generals von Scholtz and von Gallwitz continue their advance against the Lomza-Ostrow-Wyszkow road." That road itself runs only about 10–12 miles to the south-east of the Narev line which the Germans had forced almost a fortnight before.

In the last days of July a wave of hope came over those who for the last few weeks had lost all hope of saving Warsaw. The splendid resistance of the Russian troops both in the south and in the north had put fresh courage into their hearts. Then suddenly came the dramatic end in a way in which it had least been expected.

The Vistula seemed to offer sufficient protection against the west and, with the exception of the districts round the bridgeheads of Warsaw and Ivangorod, was held by comparatively weak forces. Not a single permanent bridge spans it between those two towns ; the river, which is unregulated, is between 600 and 1,200 yards wide and 10 to 15 feet deep. Its ban's are fairly high, the eastern higher than the western. The valley is only a few miles wide, and the wooded hills approach in many places close to the river. Roads and the railway line which connects Warsaw and Ivangorod avoid its immediate neighbourhood ; very few villages and hardly any towns lie on its eastern bank, on that stretch of about 50 miles which formed between Warsaw and Ivangorod the western front of the Russian salient in Poland. In the district west of the Vistula our Allies followed during the second half of July the same tactics which they had adopted in October, 1914. They were falling back towards the river closing in on the fortified lines round the bridge-heads at the two ends of the front. On July 17 they had withdrawn beyond the Ilzanka, on the 20th they evacuated

Radom ; by July 22 the troops of General von Woyrsch had reached Kozienice, at the northern end of the lines which surround Ivangorod ; a few days later the fortress was completely invested from the west. A similar retreat was effected in the north ; on July 19 our Allies evacuated, practically without fighting, the Bzura-Rawka line, which they had held for more than seven months, and retired on to the so-called Blonie lines ; these extended in a radius of about twelve miles in front of Warsaw, and had been prepared as a second line ever since December, 1914. German attacks against that line delivered on July 25–26 ended in complete failure.

Then came the unforeseen. The Germans succeeded in crossing the Vistula about twenty miles north of Ivangorod. " On the Vistula, on both banks of the tributary Radomka," says the Russian official *communiqué* of July 30, " the enemy at some points sent his advanced guards across to the right bank of the river on pontoons, and attempted to throw bridges across the river. Our troops are attacking the enemy detachments which crossed. Our heavy artillery demolished an enemy bridge near the village of Kobylnica." The Germans were driven back towards the Vistula, but yet managed to maintain themselves on its eastern bank. A corps belonging to the army holding the Blonie lines, crossed the river to oppose the advance of the Germans east of the Vistula. But enemy reinforcements were pouring in from the west in great numbers. By August 1 two entire German army corps had reached the right bank of the Vistula, whilst three Austrian divisions, said to have come from the Serbian front, were available in immediate support. There were no sufficient Russian forces which could have been spared from other fronts to constitute a new rampart, as they had done after the battles of Krasnostaw and Rozan. The crossing of the Vistula by the Germans was the last straw which settled the fate of Warsaw.

The immediate objective of the Army Woyrsch and of the group of General von Kövess was Ivangorod. Threatened from all directions it could not be held much longer by our Allies. On the right bank of the Vistula a ring of fortified positions had been recently constructed as a cover for the inner forts, which had by now become obsolete and could not have withstood the fire of modern artillery even for a day. From the west and the south

CAUGHT BETWEEN TWO FIRES.
Cossacks clearing Austrians out of a village.

the Vistula and the Wieprz form a cover for the fortress, but it can hardly have been held against attacks from the north. As soon as the Germans had acquired a definite hold on the eastern bank of the Vistula, the position of the fortress became hopeless. In the morning of August 1 the Austrian artillery, ranging from field guns to 30·5 cm. howitzers, opened

a violent bombardment against the forts and on the same day the enemy entered some of them. The fall of the fortress was imminent; it followed on August 4. The fall of Ivangorod would have uncovered the western flank of the Russian southern army. Its retreat could not be delayed any longer. Eastern Poland had to be evacuated, and the Russian armies had

RUSSIAN AVIATORS.
At work on the field.

to be withdrawn to the lines of Brest-Litovsk and the Bug.

The evacuation of the city of Warsaw had been practically completed for some time ; it was now merely a question of withdrawing the army from the Blonie lines. That final retreat proved a masterpiece in strategy, for which the credit is mainly due to the chief commander of the armies in Poland, Alexeieff, and to his Chief of Staff, Goulevitch. The retreat began during the night of August 3–4 ; at the northern end of the Blonie lines the Russian forces crossed the Vistula on pontoons and went to the support of the defenders of the Narev line, thus rendering impossible the immediate breaking of the line. At the southern end, near Gora Kalvaria, our Allies similarly crossed the river during the night over pontoon bridges and joined the army corps which was screening Warsaw from the south ; together these forces were now forming a strong defence for the line of retreat towards Brest-Litovsk. "On August 4 by noon there was probably not over one corps on the west side of the Vistula," writes Mr. Washburn, who remained in Warsaw almost to the very end. "Half of that crossed south of Warsaw before 6 p.m., and probably the last division left about midnight, and at 3 a.m. on August 5 the bridges were blown up." The Germans arrived at 6 a.m. ; they were not even in touch with the Russian rearguards,

and their tales about the last battle for Warsaw must be treated as the due embroidery of an undoubtedly great event.

A well-known Polish writer, discussing the name which history would give to the war, suggested that it might best be called the War of the Great Disappointments. Hardly ever did that name seem more appropriate than at the time of the German entry into Warsaw. Our Allies had held for months, against the most desperate German onslaughts, the comparatively weak line of small streams, the Bzura, Rawka, Pilica and Nida. The line of the Vistula, one of the strongest defensive positions in Europe, and its centre, Warsaw, had now to be abandoned, practically without a struggle. To the German soldiers Warsaw had been represented as the Paris of the East—not in that sense in which it used to glory in that name in the eighteenth century, but in the sinister meaning of 1871. The capture of Warsaw was to form the triumphant close of the Eastern campaign. Instead of that it became for the German soldier only another short station on his endless, bloody pilgrimage. He now had the prospect of exchanging the quarters on the Bzura of the preceding winter for some still more desolate place in the plains, forests or marshes of Russia proper.

For those Poles who saw the future of their nation in union under Russia the fall of Warsaw meant a most severe blow. Many of them became refugees, and bitter is the path of the refugee, whatever consolation and help his friends may try to administer to him. The political life of the Poles who sided with Russia lost, with the fall of Warsaw, the natural contact with realities. The physical struggle against the invader is the one natural form of the life of the refugees who keep flying the flag of their nation. Those who remain behind, under a foreign yoke, and cannot take part in that struggle, become mute witnesses of the tragedy of their own lives. It was an irony of fate that Warsaw should have fallen at the time when an official Polish-Russian Committee had gathered at Petrograd to work out the material expression of those promises and hopes which the Manifesto of the Grand Duke had opened up to the Poles almost a year previously.

Worst of all was at the fall of Warsaw the disappointment of the Poles who, heedless of the proverb about the "Undank vom Hause

Oesterreich,"* had thrown in their lot with the Hapsburg Monarchy and were hoping for a reunion of Austrian and Russian Poland under the auspices of Austria-Hungary. Only a negligible number of Russian Poles declared in favour of this so-called "Austrian solution" of the Polish question. The few who did so were mostly old revolutionaries who had fought for years against the Russian government before the day had come of the reconciliation of the two great Slav nations. The overwhelming majority of the adherents of the "Austrian solution" were Galician Poles. In August, 1914, the official leaders of the Galician political parties decided to stand by Austria, and most of them stuck to their decision, especially if they remained in the part of the country which was not reached by the Russian armies. The capture of Lwow brought to light an amount of pro-Russian feeling among the Galician Poles which even men well acquainted with the country would hardly have expected. The leaders of the pro-Austrian Polish parties in Vienna constituted themselves, indeed, into a "Supreme Polish National Committee." It had, however, at

* "Ingratitude of the House of Austria."

first the prudence and decency not to claim to represent anyone except the Austrian Poles. It proceeded to form military organizations which were to serve in connexion with the Austrian Army and which assumed the name of "Polish Legions," in memory of the famous Polish volunteer regiments that had fought under Napoleon I.

Austria had conceded since 1860, and still more since 1867, a considerable measure of freedom to the Galician Poles ; it had endowed them practically with a monopoly of the government of Galicia, although the Ruthenians and Jews form together more than half of its population. This—the concession of freedom to the Poles—was not due to any enthusiasm for the principle of liberty, but to the fact that the Germans, being a small minority within the Hapsburg Monarchy, could not keep to themselves all the power in the State. If there is too much of dependent provinces, wrote in 1768 an English statesman who favoured union with Ireland as a means for the coercion of America, the head grows too heavy for the body. To prevent that the Austrian Germans concluded in 1867 a partnership with the Magyars and the Poles. In

THE GERMANS IN POLAND.
Troops resting after a long march.

the present war some Galician politicians put forward a programme of enlarging that combination. The Dual Monarchy was to be changed into a Tripartite State consisting of Austria, Hungary and Poland. The new Poland was to consist of Russian Poland and Galicia. The principle of nationality was to be applied to the Poles, that of the *status possidendi* to the Ruthenians of East Galicia, and to the small Slav nations which were to be left to the tender mercies of the Austrian Germans. The new Poland was to be proclaimed on the entry of the Germanic armies into Warsaw. Prussia seems to have been assigned in that scheme the part of a charitable midwife. The taking of Warsaw was to be the Pentecost at which the pro-Austrian Poles expected the ghost of the many-tongued Monarchy to speak the Polish language. But Prince Leopold of Bavaria talked only the thick Munich variation of German, and in general had not much to say, which may have been an additional reason for his being chosen to be the figure-head at the entry into Warsaw. On the other hand, Herr von Cleinow, who was sent from Berlin to direct the Warsaw Press, talked like one truly "full of young wine."*

If it were merely for the fantastic politicians who had been spinning in Viennese coffee-houses political schemes of a type not unknown in Oriental bazaars, we might pass over lightly their disappointments. But there can be no doubt that much honest, warm, sincere feeling was to be found in the camp of the pro-Austrian Poles, just as there had been among those who, ranging themselves on the side of Napoleon I., opposed more than a century before Prince Adam Czartoryski's " Russian solution " of the Polish question. In recognition of their sincere Polish patriotism, many of them, after 1815, were received into the service of Tsar Alexander I., and were given commissions in the army of the Kingdom of Poland which was then formed in connexion with Russia. Most of the Galician Poles who fought willingly against Slav Russia were brought up in Austrian schools, were saturated with the idea of the Austrian State, were fed since they were children

on the memories of 1830 and 1863, and filled with the fear of Russia. The sudden outbreak of the war had left them no time to reconsider their traditional position.

The period of Austrian reverses was comparatively uneventful and unimportant from the point of view of Austro-Polish relations. Promises were to be had for the asking, as they could not be put to the test of actions. Rumours were stimulated to the effect that Archduke Stephen, who owned estates in Galicia, spoke Polish, and had two Polish magnates for sons-in-law, was to be proclaimed King of Poland ; no such rumours were heard after the battles of Tarnow and Gorlice. When the luck of war turned in the East in favour of the Central Powers, the pro-Austrian Poles expected to see their hopes realized. But none of them materialized ; no beginning was made of the reconstruction of Poland. In the first days of June a conference of the pro-Austrian Poles met at Piotrkow ; it demanded that the Polish Legions, part of which had been sent to fight on the Bessarabian frontier, be united on Polish soil as the nucleus of a Polish army* ; that a Polish administration be built up in the occupied provinces of Russian Poland ; and that the union of the whole of Russian Poland with Galicia under Austria be officially proclaimed. Their wishes might have been fulfilled had it depended on the Viennese Court ; but how could the Austrian Government dare to assume an initiative concerning provinces that remained under German occupation when even at home it had to obey the commands of Berlin ? For almost two months no official reply was received from Vienna. Finally, on July 20, Baron Burian answered the memorandum of the Piotrkow Conference in a letter which contained a more or less polite refusal of all their demands. It ended with an unctuous appeal to the Poles to "look with confidence into the future " and the vague promise that " the great sacrifice which the Poles have brought in this war in blood and property for the Fatherland will certainly bear its fruits." Only this colourless ending was allowed to appear in the Austrian Press ; the part that mattered was carefully suppressed.

Meantime, parts of the Polish Legions were

---

* The speeches which Herr von Cleinow delivered to the Warsaw journalists in August, 1915, will go down to history. He instructed and he prophesied. He expounded the principles of the future : benign, but firm Prussian rule in Poland. Insensibly he encroached on the domain " des Allerhöchsten Herrn " (of the Supreme Master). A sudden dismissal from office cut short a promising career.

* There is some grim humour in the sending of the Polish Legions to Bessarabia. Their spiritual ancestors had been sent in 1803 by Napoleon I. to conquer the freedom of their country by fighting . . . mutinous negroes in the island of San Domingo, where a large number of them perished of yellow fever.

THE GERMANS IN POLAND.
A German prisoner interrogated by Cossack officers.

still left, *super flumina Babylonis*, far away
from the land for the " rescue " of which they
had joined the Austrian army. An Austrian
German, Baron von Diller, was appointed
governor of the part of Russian Poland which
remained under Austrian occupation. Even
more : for the first time, after more than fifty
years, a German was appointed governor of

Galicia. As soon as the Austrian governorship
of that country became again a reality, a
German, General von Collard, took the place
of the Pole, M. de Korytowski ; a promise was,
however, given that this would not be made a
precedent for future appointments. Shortly
afterwards the German language was introduced into the service on the Galician railways

and Germans took the place of Poles whose knowledge of the official language proved insufficient ; this time no promise was even given concerning the future.

The Germanic Powers had, in the opinion of the pro-Austrian Poles, one more chance of regaining the shaken confidence of their Polish adherents. Hitherto, they said to the Viennese Government, the Austrian authorities, military as well as civil, seem to have been doing all they could to uproot the friendship for Austria among the anti-Russian parties, and to discredit those parties in the eyes of the Polish public opinion. But the taking of Warsaw will be the decisive moment for the attitude of the Poles. On the way in which the occupation of Warsaw will be made, and on that which will then be said, will depend the attitude of the capital and of the entire country. Let delegates from the Polish Committee precede the Germanic armies in their entry into Warsaw, and let the Polish Legions march at the head of the troops entering the city. Unless that is done, people will look back with sadness after the retreating Russians, and regard the orders of the armies of occupation in an indifferent spirit. Let also this be the moment for the proclamation of the union of Galicia and Russian Poland into a Polish kingdom under Austrian suzerainty.

"To-day the German troops of the Army of Prince Leopold of Bavaria," says the Austrian official *communiqué* of August 5, "entered the capital of Russian Poland." *Pas de rêveries, messieurs !* The pro-Austrian Polish Committee thereupon published a manifesto in which laughter mingled with tears.

"Warsaw is liberated from the Russian chains ! . . . The fact, however, that the entry into the capital of Poland did not take place in the way in which we would have wished it makes it necessary to examine and explain the fact from the political point of view." Ironical comments in the German Press thanked the Austrian Poles for that frank expression of their displeasure.

Thus the Polish Legions never held their triumphal entry into Warsaw. But the semi-official German *Neue Warschauer Zeitung* says that the German troops on entering the city were received with joy by the inhabitants, and adds the naïve remark : " as if we were really fighting for their freedom."

At first the Citizens' Committees which had been formed under the Russian administration were left the work of relief and even entrusted by the Germans with all matters relating to education. They decided to retain the teaching of the Russian language in the Polish schools, thereby signifying to the Germans their hopes for the future. Such things could not be tolerated by German administrators of the " Vistula District " (" *Ne parlez pas de la Pologne*," wrote once Napoleon I. to Talleyrand asking him to delete an article on Poland from the official almanack ; " historical reminiscences are out of place "). The Poles were soon to feel the hand of the German administrator.

Several leaders of the Poles who favoured complete national independence, and had hitherto been bitterly opposed to *Russia*, were arrested by the Germans and sent to Küstrin, though they had enjoyed personal freedom under the government of our Allies. Finally, on September 12, the Polish Citizens' Committees were dissolved on a trumped-up charge of meddling with politics. Their main functions were " transferred " to the German military authorities. A few days later M. de Bilinski resigned the presidency of the Polish Club in the Viennese Parliament. He had sat in many Austrian Cabinets ; at the outbreak of the war he was joint Austro-Hungarian Minister of Finance ; since February, 1915, he directed the foreign policy both of the Polish Parliamentary Club in Vienna and of the pro-Austrian Polish National Committee. He had been the link between the Central Powers and the anti-Russian Poles. About the middle of September, 1915, he seems to have recognized that there was nothing left to him but to withdraw.

CHAPTER XCII.

THE DARDANELLES CAMPAIGN (I.).

Origin of the Dardanelles Campaign—First Operations—Policy and Strategy—Who was Responsible ?—Mr. Churchill's Part—Lord Fisher—Foreign Office and War Office—Russia's Appeal for Help—History and Topography—The Turkish Defences—Naval Preparations and Reconnaissances—The Naval Attack on February 19—The Attack on March 5—Bombardment of Smyrna—Attitude of Greece—First Resignation of M. Venezelos—Land Operations Prepared—Sir Ian Hamilton's Command—War Council at Tenedos—Transport Blunders Cause Postponement of Landing—Great Naval Attack of March 18—Its Failure—Loss of Bouvet, Irresistible and Ocean—Eve of the First Great Landing.

WHEN war broke out between the Allies and Turkey in the autumn of 1914, a joint Franco-British squadron at once established an effective blockade of the Dardanelles. On November 3, 1914, the squadron bombarded at long range the forts at the entrance to the Dardanelles, in order to ascertain the range and to test their defences. The reconnaissance was inconclusive, and was not pressed. On December 13 Lieutenant Holbrook navigated a British submarine beneath the mine-field in the Straits. He succeeded in torpedoing the old but still useful Turkish battleship, the Messudiyeh, and for this heroic feat received the Victoria Cross.* During January, 1915, a decision was reached by the Allies to attack the Dardanelles in real earnest. The watching warships were increased in numbers, and by February a powerful fleet had been assembled. It included the then newest British super-Dreadnought, the Queen Elizabeth. The islands of Tenedos and Lemnos, near the entrance to the Dardanelles, were occupied, and the bay of Mudros, in the latter island, became the principal base for the operations which followed.

The original attempt to force a passage of the Dardanelles was made in exclusive reliance upon sea power. On February 19 the forts at the entrance to the Straits were bombarded, but not permanently silenced. Bad weather prevented a resumption of the attack until February 25, on which day the forts of Sedd-el-Bahr and Cape Helles, at the tip of the Gallipoli Peninsula, were temporarily overcome. The forts on the Asiatic side of the entrance were also bombarded. During the night British trawlers from the North Sea swept the Straits clear of mines for a distance of four miles, and next morning several British battleships entered and bombarded Fort Dardanos, which lay far within the Straits on the Asiatic side. Landing parties attempted to complete the destruction of the works on both sides of the entrance.

Rough weather again interrupted the attack until March 1, when it was once more resumed. On March 5 and on subsequent days several battleships steamed far up the Straits towards the Narrows, while others, including the Queen Elizabeth, sought to assist them by firing from the Gulf of Xeros clean over the Gallipoli Peninsula at the formidable forts of Kilid Bahr and Chanak. The results were not substantial. By this time a joint naval and military operation had been decided upon, and the transports

* See Vol. III., p. 148.

VIEW OF TENEDOS, SHOWING THE CASTLE.

containing French and British units were already concentrated near the Dardanelles when General Sir Ian Hamilton, who had left England with his Staff a few days before, arrived at Tenedos on March 17 to take supreme command of the land forces. General Hamilton expected to begin at once, but he found that the transports had been wrongly loaded. They had to go to Alexandria to be loaded afresh, and the land attack was postponed, much precious time being thereby lost. Admiral de Robeck, who had taken command of the Allied squadrons, thereupon decided to deliver another unsupported naval attack. Shortly before noon on the following day, March 18, three successive squadrons entered the Straits and steamed towards the Narrows, bombarding vigorously. By the evening two British battleships, the Irresistible and the Ocean, and one French battleship, the Bouvet, had been sunk by drifting mines, the last-named losing most of her crew. Two others, the Gaulois and the Inflexible, had been seriously damaged, the first by gun-fire, and the second by a mine. The attempt to force a passage by warships alone had signally failed, and was never afterwards seriously resumed.

The first joint land and sea attack was delivered on April 29. More than five weeks had been lost, and the Turks and their German advisers had vigorously employed the interval in strengthening the defences of the Straits. The Land Expeditionary Force consisted of three army corps, numbering in all about 120,000 men, though only portions of these were present at the first landing. It included the Australian and New Zealand Divisions, the Royal Naval Division, a Division of British Territorials, a considerable number of Indian troops, and a French Division largely composed of the French Colonial Army and of marines. Sir Ian Hamilton attacked at dawn at several points on the Gallipoli Peninsula, while the French made a feint on the Asiatic side. By nightfall a foothold had been gained on most of the selected beaches, after deeds of the most desperate valour. But the attack had not produced the expected results. The dominating height of Achi Baba, which was to be stormed at the outset, had not been won or even approached. The Turks proved to be in much greater strength than was anticipated, and they resisted valiantly. The Fleet bombarded constantly, but could only render limited aid. The attacking force employed in the first day's operations numbered about 60,000 men. The troops performed a feat which many experts had considered impossible. In defiance of all the accepted rules of war, they had made their landing good, and had won ground which they ever afterwards retained. They could do no more. The Turks held the heights and refused to be dislodged.

The bold attack on the Gallipoli Peninsula was soon transformed into the trench warfare with which the Allies in France had become monotonously familiar. For the next six months the story of the Dardanelles was one of heavy strain, of constant conflict, of exhausting losses, of occasional bold attacks, of counter-attacks by the Turks, but of very little substantial progress towards the goal in view, which was the conquest and domination of the passage to Constantinople.

The attack upon the Dardanelles was at once the most daring and the most questionable of the many enterprises hitherto undertaken by the Allies. For the inception of the operations Great Britain was mainly responsible, and though the French rendered gallant and loyal help, the bulk of the work fell to the lot of the British naval and military forces. The idea which lay at the back of the undertaking was attractive enough. It was thought that if the Dardanelles could be forced, Constantinople would fall, the Turks would be swiftly ejected from Europe, and their subsequent opportunities of military activity would be to a great extent paralyzed. A clear way of access to Russia would be opened up through the Black Sea, which would enable her to obtain with ease the munitions and other warlike stores she so greatly needed, and to export in turn the vast quantities of surplus corn which lay mouldering in her warehouses. Above all, a successful blow at the heart of Turkey would probably settle the course to be followed by the still wavering Balkan kingdoms. It would, indeed, go far to decide the struggle for domination in South-Eastern Europe, and to solve, in a sense fatal to German ambition, the whole problem of Constantinople. No one can deny that the

VICE-ADMIRAL DE ROBECK,
Who succeeded Vice-Admiral Carden as commander of the Allied Fleet in the Dardanelles.

stakes were immense and vital, and that an incalculable effect upon the fortunes of the war would have followed an early victory. No one can deny that at the outset, and before the Turks had begun to pay much attention to the defences of the Gallipoli Peninsula, quick success might have attended a well-planned assault delivered in sufficient strength by a combined naval and military force.

The earlier attacks, although they produced much brilliant heroism, only achieved limited results because the difficulties were underestimated, the operations were begun too hastily, the scheme lacked forethought, and the fatal mistake was made of relying at the outset upon ships alone. An exaggerated conception of the power of modern naval guns against well-concealed land defences brought unfortunate consequences. The first naval operations gave the Turks ample warning of the dangers which lay ahead, and they had time to convert the principal positions in the Gallipoli Peninsula into improvised fortresses. When at length the belated decision was reached to rely in the main upon an army, and to use the Fleet in support, five precious weeks were lost after the troops were brought to the scene of the attack because of the mistake in loading the transports. A further error was that the

[Lafayette.

VICE-ADMIRAL CARDEN.

CREW OF A BRITISH WARSHIP CHEERING THE SUBMARINE "E11"
As she came out from the Dardanelles after her exploits in the Sea of Marmora in May.

original land attacks were delivered in insufficient strength, with insufficient supplies of munitions, and without a sufficient body of fresh troops in immediate reserve. There was much difference of opinion as to whether the right spot was chosen for the principal assaults. Those best acquainted with the Gallipoli Peninsula contended that the tongue of the peninsula should not have been assailed at all, but that the first great landing should have been either at Suvla Bay or at some quite different point. Others, again, argued that the chief advance should have been attempted on the Asiatic side of the Straits; but though a considerable body of French opinion supported this view, it was urged against it, doubtless with reason, that the force required would have been in excess of the utmost strength then available. The original errors of the Dardanelles Expedition were long wrapped in contentious obscurity. Authoritative information came slowly, and the materials on which to form an adequate judgment were lacking. The public assessment of relative personal responsibility for the initial mistakes of the Dardanelles Expedition, and for the subsequent errors from which it was certainly not free, had perforce to be postponed; but from an early stage there was a deep although smouldering conviction in Great Britain that the whole question required thorough investigation, and that at some future period the degree of responsibility resting upon the various Ministers and experts concerned would have to be clearly determined.

For a long time a widespread disposition prevailed to cast the blame, if blame there was, chiefly upon Mr. Winston Churchill, who was First Lord of the Admiralty when the Dardanelles operations began. The conspicuous part Mr. Churchill had played in the unsuccessful attempt to save Antwerp had involved him in much unfavourable criticism, and the tendency to criticize him revived in many quarters when the failure of the Dardanelles Expedition to make much progress became common knowledge. Riper judgment and fuller information eventually made it plain that Mr. Churchill could not thus be singled out for solitary condemnation. In the first place, it was manifest that the momentous decisions required could not by any conceivable chance have been reached on the responsibility of a single Minister. The Cabinet as a whole were responsible, and any invidious distinctions would have been fatal to the theory of collective Cabinet control. Moreover, in regard to the purely naval side of the operations, it was presumed that the First Lord's expert advisers, and especially Lord Fisher, the First Sea Lord, were to some extent involved. Either they approved of such departmental directions as were transmitted by Mr. Churchill or they did not. Their continuance in office suggested approval, and therefore implied on the surface a share of responsibility. Beyond that point discussion was impossible during the period in which the documentary evidence necessarily remained secret.

There were further factors which must be noted in connexion with the disposition to place the burden of the Dardanelles Campaign solely upon Mr. Churchill's shoulders. Apart from the general responsibility of the Cabinet, other Departments in addition to the Admiralty were very specially concerned. It was understood, and must in any case be obvious, that the War

Office did not remain entirely silent while this tremendous operation was being planned. The experts of the War Office, including in this instance the expert Secretary of State, occupied a position at least analogous to that of Mr. Churchill's own expert advisers. Even if the initial attacks were to be delivered by ships alone, it must have been manifest from the very beginning that at some stage of the enterprise military assistance would be required. Ships might have forced the Straits, but they could not occupy Constantinople. The inference was that the necessity for military aid was always foreseen, though perhaps not adequately; that provision of some sort was made from the outset for the supply of troops; and that to that extent the share taken by Mr. Churchill could not be dissevered from the responsibility also incurred by the War Office. Indeed, at Dundee

THE CREW OF THE BRITISH SUBMARINE "E11" AT THE DARDANELLES.
Commanded by Lieut.-Commander Martin E. Nasmith, V.C., in centre of the three officers on top of the conning-tower.

62—2

ONE OF THE CREW OF THE "E14"
standing outside as the submarine runs awash.

on June 5, 1915, Mr. Churchill pointedly stated that Lord Kitchener had not embarked upon the military operations at the Dardanelles " without narrowly and carefully considering their requirements in relation to all other needs, and in relation to the paramount need of our Army in France and Flanders." Again, the Foreign Office was believed to have given its very special benedictions to the undertaking. Though not directly associated with the planning of military operations, the Foreign Office was very eagerly interested in the political results of such operations in this particular region. It had also received urgent appeals from Russia. Specifically, it produced a promise of help from Greece, though the failure of that help was due to circumstances over which it had no possible control.

It will be gathered that there could never have been any ground for the light assumption that the attack on the Dardanelles was an operation exclusively or substantially originated and directed by Mr. Churchill. Moreover, some of the most costly errors were not naval, but military. It was impossible to conceive that Mr. Churchill had a deciding voice, or any very definite voice at all, in such matters as the strength allotted to the Dardanelles Expeditionary Force, or the points selected for the land attacks, or the manner in which those attacks were planned. It was not his province to say

that the height of Achi Baba should be attacked first, or that a specified number of troops ought to suffice to carry it. Yet upon these decisions, which had little or no connexion with the Admiralty, the early fate of the land operations largely turned. They produced the great list of casualties, they first aroused intense anxiety in England, and they were the cause of much of the bitter criticism which subsequently became rife.

But although technically Mr. Winston Churchill bore far less direct and undivided responsibility for the Dardanelles Expedition than was popularly assigned to him, it is also true that during the first few months of 1915 he exercised much more influence upon the project than any other single individual. Far from drawing a veil over the part he had played in its organization, he was for some time almost inclined to exaggerate his personal share in it. After he left the Admiralty in May, 1915, he referred publicly more than once to his strong belief both in the vastness of the results which would follow success, and in the certainty of ultimate victory. At Dundee, in the speech already mentioned, he declared that " through the Narrows of the Dardanelles and across the ridges of the Gallipoli Peninsula lie some of the shortest paths to a triumphant peace." The bold and dramatic character of the original project captivated his ardent imagination. He threw himself into the scheme with boisterous energy, and paid the closest attention to the problem of supplying the requirements of the naval forces. At his instance the naval requirements of the Expedition were so fully satisfied that the Royal Navy was for a time considerably hampered in some of its secondary tasks elsewhere ; but it must be recognized that while no provision could have been too lavish for the task at the Dardanelles, not even that huge enterprise was ever allowed for a moment to impede the imperative demands of the Grand Fleet, upon which the safety of England primarily depended. The question of Mr. Churchill's association with the Dardanelles Expedition has been considered here at some length because it was a constant subject of public discussion. It may be compendiously said that in his Ministerial capacity, both while he was First Lord and afterwards, his mind was far more engrossed with the undoubted magnitude of the results to be attained than with the practicability of the means by which the desired end was sought.

The world will probably never know who it was in the councils of Great Britain who first said the word " Dardanelles." It will not know because there is reason to suppose that several people whose words carried weight were simultaneously thinking about the Dardanelles, though from entirely different angles. Their views gradually united and crystallized, and the Dardanelles Expedition was the result.

There was, for example, the Foreign Office view, and it was perhaps in the Foreign Office that the Dardanelles first came fully into the picture of the war. The Foreign Office was naturally concerned about the situation in the Balkans. Its avowed desire was to resuscitate the Balkan League, and the idea gained currency that the passage of the Dardanelles would impress the hesitating kingdoms, and do what diplomacy had failed to accomplish. The Balkan kingdoms were quarrelling among themselves, but it was thought they all shared in the desire to see the last of the Turk in Europe. The appearance of a Fleet before Constantinople would undoubtedly have caused the hurried flight of the Ottoman Government to Asia Minor ; the Balkan States would have almost tumbled over each other in their anxiety to be in at the death ; so the alluring argument ran. Given the forcing of the Dardanelles, it was a sound argument, and there is nothing more to be said about it, except that, as things turned out, the Dardanelles Expedition had the worst possible effect upon the attitude of the Balkan kingdoms. The original view was, as has been said, subsequently reinforced by inquiries in Greece, where M. Venezelos, then the head of the Greek Government, tentatively agreed to join in operations against Turkey by supplying a Greek division.

While the Foreign Office was thus examining the Balkan situation, it was stimulated into quickened activity by a request from Russia. In an interview published in the Russian Press in August, 1915, Sir George Buchanan, the British Ambassador at Petrograd, made the following statement :

When Turkey declared war Russia turned to Great Britain with a request that she would divert a portion of the Turkish troops from the Caucasus by means of a counter-demonstration at some other point. The operations at the Dardanelles were undertaken with a double object—on the one hand, of reducing the pressure of the Turks in the Caucasus, and, on the other, of opening the Straits and so making it possible for Russia to export her grain and receive foreign products of which she stands in need.

The Turkish offensive in the Caucasus began in the middle of December, 1914, and reached

THE DAMAGED PERISCOPE OF THE SUBMARINE " E11."

its farthest point towards the end of the same month. Although it was brilliantly broken by

BRITISH DESTROYER

On patrol duty opposite Sedd-el-Bahr after the bombardment by the Franco-British warships.

Russia, its renewal was expected when the weather became more favourable. That it was not renewed during the summer of 1915, and that Tiflis was therefore relieved from all menace, was due to the great British attack upon the Dardanelles. The publication of Sir George Buchanan's statement in Russia at a time when the Russian armies in Poland and Galicia were being driven back instantly checked the tendency in Russia to inquire what was the precise degree of help which Great Britain was giving to the cause of the Allies. The " counter-demonstration " at the Dardanelles had meanwhile grown into a huge and costly operation. Sir George Buchanan's disclosure further enabled the people of Great Britain to grasp more clearly the true origin of the Dardanelles Expedition, though surprise was expressed that the British Government had not thought it worth while to make to the puzzled British nation a somewhat similar statement.

A request from Russia was, then, the predominating actual cause of the beginning of the attack on the Dardanelles. The request from Russia was apparently received by the British Foreign Office about the end of 1914. It was at this point that Sir Edward Grey turned to the Admiralty and the War Office. The British Government had already in their possession detailed plans for an attack on the Dardanelles. These plans, which represented a specimen of the elaborate strategical exercises conducted in time of peace by the General Staffs of all countries, were very carefully worked out, and undoubtedly provided for a joint naval and military attack. The plans were ignored in the earlier operations, for reasons which were not made public.

The British naval view, which must have carried great weight, related chiefly to the feasibility of a naval attack upon the Dardanelles. It was presumed that such naval authorities as were consulted reported that a successful naval attack was possible, because otherwise it would not have been attempted ; but it was understood that the probability of heavy losses was not disguised. The naval view was influenced by the fact that the Admiralty had at their disposal a considerable number of well-armoured ships which, by reason of their inferior speed and armament, were not fit to lie in the line of battle in a modern fleet action. The French Admiralty were similarly placed ; but after several of these older ships had been lost, many naval authorities began to urge that the Allies could not afford to denude themselves too rapidly of their old battleships. There were other uses to which such ships could well be put in waters nearer home.

Certain other views also affected the decision to attack the Dardanelles. One was that Great Britain was accumulating a powerful force in Egypt, which had repelled with ease an attack on the Suez Canal, and was becoming stale through inaction. The question was asked, " Why not send it to the Dardanelles ? " Again, in some responsible quarters there was a tendency to complain that the British operations on land were incommensurate with the magnitude of the national effort. At the end of 1914 the British forces in France and Flanders were holding rather more than thirty miles of front, and were making no progress. Why not try a diversion elsewhere, asked some speculative strategists ? Various points of possible attack were indicated, but the Dardanelles seemed the most accessible of all. It is reasonably certain that this somewhat vague desire to see Great Britain striking a great blow on her own account in a theatre chosen by herself was at the back of some, at least, of the support which the Dardanelles project received.

If there were any who counselled caution their opinions were either quickly silenced or they were placidly ignored. One or two writers in the Press sought to dwell upon the unwisdom of undertaking too many subsidiary operations. They recalled the early dispersed activities of Pitt, who frittered away much strength in minor campaigns all over the world. Their mild protests were in vain. In some cases they passed unheeded, in others they were told that the Dardanelles enterprise was not really subsidiary. Mr. Winston Churchill afterwards defined the accepted view in these words : " There never was a great subsidiary operation of war in which a more complete harmony of strategic, political, and economic advantages has combined, or which stood in truer relation to the main decision, which is in the central theatre." The statement correctly set forth the theory on which the attack was based, but it bore no resemblance to the faulty and inadequate means employed to carry the theory into effect. The cardinal defect of the whole Dardanelles enterprise was that while everybody was thinking about the end in view, nobody

ADMIRAL GUÊPRATTE.

thought sufficiently about the method to be adopted, and the precise strength required.

It must, in addition, be remembered that the Dardanelles attack was decided upon at a period when the British Ministry were collectively unaware of the grave shortage of munitions of war which the country was presently to discover. Both the country and the Cabinet had been soothed by assurances regarding the supplies of shells and guns which were afterwards found to be lacking in substantial foundation. There were periods after the Expedition had landed in the Gallipoli Peninsula when its reserves of gun ammunition reached a distinctly narrow margin. It was further obvious, even to the layman, that the reserves of ammunition available in France would have been much more plentiful had it not been for the constant drain caused by the Dardanelles. A very great amount of ammunition was blazed away on the peninsula in the first weeks after the landing. Had the Ministry known anything at all definite about the munitions question, its decision to go to the Dardanelles at all might conceivably have been affected, though this must always remain a matter of somewhat doubtful speculation. A cognate question of equal importance was that of the supplies of men. The Dardanelles decision was reached at a time when Great Britain had not faced in a careful and scientific fashion the question of the precise number of men required to enable her to join in bringing the war to a successful conclusion. The popular belief, avowedly shared by many Ministers, was that the late spring of 1915 would probably see the shattering of the German lines in the West, and the beginning of the downfall of the German Empire. Hand-to-mouth methods of recruiting were still in vogue. Few had any glimmering of the truth, which was that the attainment of victory would probably require the enlistment of every able-bodied man of military age not needed for war industries or the more essential public services. The number of men required for land operations at the Dardanelles was, moreover, grievously miscalculated. Neither the Ministry nor the public ever dreamed that the Gallipoli Peninsula would eventually absorb so large and valuable a force. It has been said that the problem of the supplies of men had never been properly investigated when the Expedition was planned. It cannot be said that, if the problem had been duly weighed, any other decision would have been reached ; but such might possibly have been the case.

To sum up, the Dardanelles Expedition was not the plan of any one man, but was the outcome of many contributory influences. It suffered because the requisite element of secrecy was quickly lost, and because the first attack was not made in overwhelming combined military and naval force, which alone would have rendered rapid success possible. It revealed in its earliest stages insufficient thought about the best methods to be pursued. It was begun before Great Britain had taken that careful stock of her supplies of men and munitions which should have been an imperative prelude to a definite decision. The naval operations were marred by preconceived beliefs about the utility of warships in such an attack which proved to be erroneous. The land operations were marred by attacking in insufficient strength and probably at the wrong points. The early months of the operations nevertheless furnished imperishable pages in the story of the British Empire, by reason of the amazing heroism of the soldiers and sailors, who won undying fame among their countrymen and even extorted the reluctant admiration of their foes.

KUM-KALE FORT

This photograph was taken while one of the British landing-parties was under the glacis of the Turkish
the remains of two windmills from which the Turks had fired on to the jetty and which were

The Dardanelles, whose ancient name was the Hellespont, was the long, winding channel giving access from the Aegean Sea to the Sea of Marmora, and thus to the Turkish capital. Since 1841, when a treaty was signed by all the Great Powers, the Dardanelles could not be passed by any ship of war without Turkish permission. From the geological point of view the channel was, like the Straits of the Bosphorus (between Constantinople and the Black Sea), the bed of a submerged river. Both the Dardanelles and the Bosphorus were originally river gorges into which the salt sea obtained access. The shores of the Dardanelles were formed, on the European side, by the long and hilly peninsula of Gallipoli, and on the Asiatic side by the coast of Asia Minor. The full length of the Dardanelles was reckoned at 47 miles, but the really narrow portion, extending from the town of Gallipoli to the Aegean, represented a sea passage of about 33 miles. This passage was at no point wider than 7,000 yards, and at one spot, known as the Narrows, it contracted to 1,400 yards. There was no more formidable channel for defensive purposes in the world. The depth in mid-channel varied from 25 to 55 fathoms. There were shallows in some of the bays. The surface current in the Dardanelles flowed westward into the Aegean at an average speed of 1½ knots, which sometimes was trebled in the Narrows, especially after strong northerly winds. There was an undercurrent flowing from the Aegean into the Sea of Marmora, due to the higher salinity of the water of the Mediterranean as compared with the outflow from the Black Sea. The outward current greatly favoured the Turks when they used drifting mines against the Allied warships. The inward current probably gave some assistance to the British submarines in their adventurous incursions into the Sea of Marmora. The whole passage was complicated for submarines, and also to some extent for ships not steaming at full speed, by the eddies set up in certain of the bays, which produced occasional cross-currents. The prevailing winds for nine months of the year were north-easterly, but their intensity was very variable, and they were wont to reach their greatest force about noon. It has been noted that unfavourable weather, and the frequent haze and mists, greatly impeded the earlier stages of the purely naval operations.

It is a mistake to suppose that both shores of the Dardanelles were of uniform character. There were very marked differences between the bare, rocky heights of the Gallipoli Peninsula and the low, wooded hills on the Asiatic

[*"Times" Photograph.*

ON FIRE.

stronghold. On the left is the jetty where a number of the British were killed. Beyond the jetty are afterwards destroyed by H.M.S. "Cornwallis." Inset : A Turkish shell exploding in the sea.

FRENCH TROOPS ON THE WAY TO THE DARDANELLES.

The Times
HISTORY OF THE WAR

Map of the
GALLIPOLI PENINSULA
AND
THE DARDANELLES

Scale of English Miles

0 1 2 4 6

Main Roads — Other Roads and Tracks

Telegraphs

★ Fortified Towns ⚓ Forts and Batteries

N

G

Boz Burnu
Ejelmer B.
(Aja Liman)

Mill

Karakol Dagh .446

KIZLAR DAGH

Mt Turchenkeui .882

Tombs

Turchen Keu

Mills

Suvla Burnu

Beach A

Lit Anafarta or Suvla Bay

Beaches B & C

Niebruniessi Pt.

Salt L.

Kuchuk Anafarta

Lala Baba .115

Burnt Hill .230

ANAFARTA HILLS .485

Yilghin Burnu (Chocolate Hill) .584

Well

Inam Ch. (Kasa D.)

Tekke

Æ G E A N

Chailak Dere

Biyuk Anafarta

Kirsilar Dagh .820

Uz

K

Fisherman's Hut

Walker's Ridge

KOJA CHEMEN .971

SARI BAIR

Baghchekeui

Ari Burnu

Beach Z

Dead Man's

Anzac Cove

R. Bloody Angle

Yal

Hell Spit

Quinn's Post .482

Shrapnel Valley

Courtney's Pt

Lonesome Pine

Kojadere

Brighton Beach

S E A

Damler

Koja Tepe .680

Gaba Tepe

Boghali

Mal Tepe .534

Ak Tepe

Asmak (Hazmak) D.

.114

Kibia Ovasi

Eski Keui

Kilia D.

Kilia Liman

Boghali Kalessi

.452

Kum Dere

Kum Tepe

Peren Ovasi

Smerli

Asmak

.706

Nagara Kalessi

Nagara Liman

Abydos

Ibrahim Agha Fm.

Saida

Chana Ovasi

Caramassal Farms

PASHA DAGH

Maidos

Cham Kalessi

Cham Burnu

Kosse Kale

Medjidieh Ba

Yazy Tepe .172

Aguil

Jisoi

Dermaburnu Ft.

Alexi

Maghram

Kilid Bahr

D

CHANAK

Beach Y

Saghir D. Bairamar

Eryeden

Soghan

.610

Hamidieh Ft.

Gurkha Bluff

Boomerang Fort

Kanli D.

Krithia

"The Nullah"

Gully Beach

.709

Hälar

Ziblik

Jambez D.

THE NARROWS

R

Sari Siglar Bay

Implacable Landing

Sotiri Fm.

Aptella

ACHI BABA

Meluk Hanum Fm.

Kephez Pt.

Beach X

Quadrilateral

Maltepe D.

Suleiman Bey Farm

Tekke Burnu

.114

Keteves D.

Domuz .344

Karakol Burnu

A

Dardanus Kephez Bay

.138

141

Haricot Redoubt

Kreostemu

Kephez

Lancashire Landing

Beach W

.236

Helles Burnu

Beach V

De Tott's Batty. (Ruined)

Kalabakli

Sedd-el-Bahr

Camber Beach

Morto Bay

Beach S

Eski Hissarlik Pt.

D

White Cliffs

Kum Kale

In Tepe Asmak

Erenkeui Bay

Kusukeui

Okjiler

Yeni Shehr

Ud Tepe

Erenkeui

.1106

GEORGE PHILIP & SON, LTD.

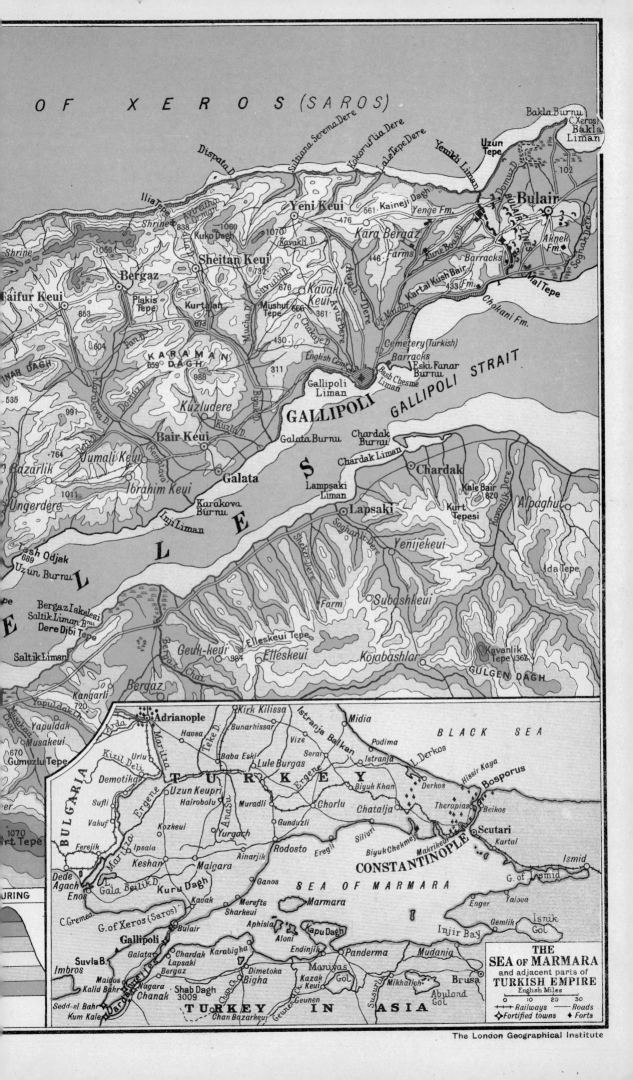

O F   X E R O S   (SAROS)

Bakla Burnu
C. Xeros
Bakla
Liman

Uzun
Tepe

Yemikli Liman

102

Dispata D.

Sultona Serema Dere

Kokoruflia Dere

Lale Tepe Dere

Domuz D.

Bulain

THE DARDANELLES

Ilia Te.

Shrine

Ayvailitin Orman

Yeni Keui

661 Kaineji Dagh

Yenge Fm.

Aknek
Fm.

838

1060

Kuko Dagh

1070

-476

Kara Bergaz

446

Farms

Kartal Kush Bair

Rune Bogazu

Barracks

Soghak Dere

Mal Tepe

1066

Sheitan Keui

732

Kavak D.

676

Kavakli
Keui

361

433 Fm.

Bergaz

Plakis
Tepe

Kurtalan

673

Mushuf
Tepe

666

Ok Maidan

Chokani Fm.

aifur Keui

853

604

KARAMAN
659 DAGH

988

430

Chataje D.

English Cemt.

311

Cemetery (Turkish)

Barracks

Eski Fanar
Burnu

GALLIPOLI STRAIT

991

Kuzludere

Kuzld D.

Gallipoli
Liman

Bash Chesme
Liman

535

Domuz D.

Navaron D.

Renaltava

764

Bair Keui

GALLIPOLI

Bazarlik

Jumali Keui

1011

Ibrahim Keui

Galata Burnu

Chardak
Burnu

Chardak

Kale Bair
820

Ungerdere

Galata

Inji Liman

Karakova
Burnu

Chardak Liman

S

Kurt
Tepesi

Alpaghut

Lampsaki
Liman

Yash Odjak
689

Uzun Burnu

L

Lapsaki

Shekertava

E

Yenijekeui

Ida Tepe

E

Bergaz Iskelesi

Saltik Liman Bu

Dere Dibi Tepe

L

Soghanli Dere

Farm

Subashkeui

Saltik Liman

E

Bergaz Chai

Geuk-keui

984

Elleskeui Tepe

Elleskeui

Kojabashlar

Kavanlik
Tepe 1362

GULGEN DAGH

Bergaz

Kangarli
720

Yapuldak Ch.

Adrianople

Kirk Kilissa

Istranja Balkan

Midia

BLACK   SEA

Yapuldak

Arda

Hausa

Bunarhissar

Podima

670

Musakeui

Maritza

Vize

Serai

Istranja

L. Derkos

Hissir Kaya

Gumuzlu Tepe

Kizil Deli

Urlu

T U R K E Y

Baba Eski

Lule Burgas

Ergene

Derkos

Bosporus

Demotika

Uzun Keupri

Muradli

Biyuk Khan

Therapias

Beikos

1070

Art Tepe

BULGARIA

Sufli

Hairobolu

Kozkeui

Chorlu

Chatalja

Scutari

Ferejik

Ipsala

Yurgach

Gunduzli

Siliuri

Biyuk Chekmeji

Makrikeui

Kartal

Dede
Agach

Enos

Keshan

Malgara

Ainarjik

Rodosto

Eregli

CONSTANTINOPLE

Ismid

Gala Beilik D.

Ganos

G. of
Ismid

C. Gremea

Kuru Dagh

Kavak

Merefte

Sharkeui

SEA   OF   MARMARA

Enger

Yalova

G. of Xeros (Saros)

Bulair

Marmara

Gemlik

Isnik
Gol

Gallipoli

Galata

Aphisla

Aloni

Kapu Dagh

Injir Bay

Mudania

Suvla B.

Chardak

Karabigha

Endinjik

Panderma

Imbros

Maidos

Lapsaki

Bergaz

Dimetoka

Manyas

Brusa

Kalid Bahr

Nagara

Bigha

Kazak
Keui

Gol

Mikhalich

Abulond
Gol

Sedd-el Bahr

Chanak

Shab Dagh
3009

Geunen

Susurlu

Kum Kale

Dardanelles

T U R K E Y   I N   A S I A

Chan Bazarkeui

Chan Ch.

URING

THE
SEA of **MARMARA**
and adjacent parts of
TURKISH EMPIRE
English Miles
0   10   20   30
+++ Railways ––– Roads
◆ Fortified towns ♦ Forts

The London Geographical Institute

side. Both shores possessed eminences which gave an enormous advantage to defensive artillery ; at the Narrows both sides towered above approaching ships ; but there was little resemblance between the steep and rugged cliffs of Gallipoli and the gentler altitudes of Asia Minor. The difference extended even to external vegetation and colouring, for on the Asiatic side woods were plentiful and the general character of the landscape was verdant, whereas on the European side the rough, yellow hills were clad in low scrub, and woods clung to the hollows alone. The Asiatic side began with the marshy plains of Troy, intersected by low ridges stretching to Mount Ida, thirty miles away. Thereafter came pleasant valleys, breezy pastures, and villages set in the midst of orchards. Small wonder that some ardent soldiers with an eye for country were in favour of initiating a campaign amid the agreeable environment of Asia Minor and of leaving the arid steeps of the Gallipoli Peninsula severely alone.

The peninsula was very like a compact and miniature replica of a section of the tribal country on the North-West Frontier of India. It was a mass of diversified heights, difficult enough to traverse in time of peace and for- midable obstacles in war when courageously held. Except in a few valleys there was little cultivation, though a cypress grove, or occasion- ally an olive grove, sometimes broke the mono- tony near one or other of the small and in- frequent hamlets. Roads were even fewer, and the scanty inhabitants of the peninsula generally preferred to make their journeys from place to place by boat. Water was scarce, and none at all was found at most of the points selected for the land attacks. The disheartening nature of the Gallipoli operations, in the form in which they were undertaken, was that each successive height surmounted seemed only to reveal further ridges beyond. Thus at Cape Helles, at the extreme point of the peninsula, the ground immediately rose from the sandy beaches to a height of 140 feet. A couple of miles inland were ridges 300 feet high. Beyond, at a distance of another mile and a half, was the peak of Achi Baba, 600 feet high, and the first great goal of the Allied Forces. In order really to command the Narrows, yet another height, the Kilid Bahr plateau (or Pasha Dagh), had to be won. At its highest point Kilid Bahr reached an altitude of 700 feet, and it lay six miles beyond Achi Baba, though only five

miles from Gaba Tepe, where the Australians and New Zealanders first landed. Farther on again, north-west of the Narrows, was the broad and precipitous knoll of Sari Bair, 971 feet high, and covered with ravines and dense thickets. All the way onwards to the town of Gallipoli there were hills, several of which rose above 1,000 feet, while others were 800 and 900 feet. The whole contour of the peninsula was scored with gullies and ravines, and the hills were intersected by watercourses. The shallow streams near the end of the peninsula mostly ran into the Straits, and few brooks found their way into the Aegean. The greatest breadth of the Gallipoli Peninsula was at a spot just past the Narrows, where it was a little under twelve miles wide. A roughly-paved road ran from the town of Gallipoli along the central ridges to the village of Maidos, near the Narrows. A con- tinuation of this road, little more than a track, passed from Maidos and skirted the slopes of the Kilid Bahr plateau to the village of Krithia, which lay under the western slopes of Achi Baba. Beyond the town of Gallipoli the penin- sula narrowed gradually until the isthmus of Bulair was reached. At Bulair the distance across the isthmus from beach to beach was exactly three miles, but the isthmus by no means amounted to a depression. In its centre was a hill 489 feet high. The shores of Bulair on the Aegean side, in the Gulf of Xeros, rose almost immediately to a height of 300 feet. The isthmus was further flanked by marshes. From Bulair to Cape Helles, at the entrance to the Dardanelles, the distance was 52 miles. Such, in brief, was the Gallipoli Peninsula, a most unattractive scene for major military opera- tions, especially as it offered very little room for extended movements by attacking forces. Nature seemed to have specially designed it to protect the most coveted of waterways, for the possession of which great armies and fleets had striven at intervals all through the history of the Western world.

The Turks called the Dardanelles "Bahr- Sefed Boghazi "—the Mouth of the White Sea. The Straits first figure in the story of mankind at the siege of Troy, but they must have been the scene of great conflicts in far earlier eras before written history began. Mr. Walter Leaf wrote in 1915 :

Even Priam's Troy was not the first. Below the feet of Priam and Hector there lay yet older Troys, of which they knew nothing ; many centuries must have passed since the days of the " Second City," where Schliemann found the great treasure of gold and silver, jade and amber, proving that even at that remote date the holding of the Straits was the source of wealth and power. And below the "Second City," again, lie the rude and humble walls of the first—how many centuries older still, who can say? Of those ancient cities no other record has come down to us; but in their remains forty centuries look down on the present battlefields as surely as they did from the Pyramids on the armies of Napoleon.

The Trojan War was fought, not for the fair face of Helen, but for the right to control trade. King Priam of Troy sought to levy imposts on the Greek galleys passing up and down the Straits to the Black Sea. He insisted that the ships should unload their goods upon his shores and that the merchandise should be carried overland to the Sea of Marmora, where it was to be once more put upon shipboard. The Greeks fought him until his capital was razed to the ground. That was in 1200 B.C., as the remains of pottery found in the excavations at Troy sufficiently attested. After more than three thousand years the issue fought out at the Dardanelles remained in one primary essential precisely the same. Australians and British and French shed their blood at the Dardanelles that corn from the fruitful lands bordering on the Black Sea should have free and unrestricted access to the Mediterranean.

Throughout the long pageant of history the issue remained unaltered. Greece rose to greatness, and Athens flourished, because the Black Sea trade was in Greek hands; and when, with the fall of Sestos, the Greek seaport on the Gallipoli Peninsula near the Narrows, Greece lost control of the Straits, she lost her proud position also. The two most famous military passages of the Straits in early times were those of Xerxes in 480 B.C. from Asia to Europe, and of Alexander the Great in 334 B.C. from Europe to Asia. Both crossed upon bridges of boats, and Herodotus says that Xerxes and his Persians took "seven days and seven nights, going continuously without any pause." From the earliest days the swimming of the Straits had been counted something of a feat, though indeed it is no very remarkable performance. What Leander did at Abydos, Lord Byron repeated, and it is recorded that certain officers of H.M.S. Shearwater, whose names are not preserved, performed the same exploit towards the end of last century.

When the Emperor Constantine decided to build his eastern capital on the Golden Horn the passage of the Straits was not vigorously guarded. The knights of the Fourth Crusade held Abydos in 1204, and some roving adventurers seized Gallipoli in 1306, but exactly 50 years later the Turks crossed from Asia, and thenceforth the story of the Dardanelles becomes part of the story of the Ottoman Empire. Constantinople did not pass into the hands of the Turks for nearly a hundred years afterwards; but when Mohammed the Conqueror entered the capital and slew the last of the Byzantine emperors in 1453 he quickly realized that he must guard his western gates. One of his first acts after conquering Constantinople was to fortify the Dardanelles. Abydos and Sestos were abandoned, and Mohammed chose the very narrowest portion of the Straits for his new structures. On the slope of a projecting hill on the European side he built Kilid Bahr, "the Key of the Sea," more generally known as the "Castle of Europe." On the Asiatic side he built Sultaniyeh Kalesi, "the Castle of Asia," beside which grew up the town sometimes called Dardanelles, known to the Turks as Chanak Kalesi, and figuring in the records of the war as Chanak. The castles of Mohammed were strongly made, and their tall keeps continued to dominate the Narrows through all the vicissitudes of Turkey's later history. The castellated towers of Chanak formed, with the aid of aeroplanes, a guide for the guns of the Queen Elizabeth when she bombarded the Narrows from the Gulf of Xeros. In recent decades Chanak became a pleasant marine resort, and it was the point at which all vessels traversing the Straits were compelled to stop and produce their papers. Passage was only permitted in daylight. Chanak and Kilid Bahr were the "Old Castles," and when they were built the outer entrance of the Dardanelles was undefended. By the middle of the seventeenth century ordnance had improved, and it was thought worth while to build fresh castles at the outer entrance. Kum Kale was therefore built on the Asiatic side and Sedd-el-Bahr on the Gallipoli side, on the western extremity of Morto Bay. They were called "the New Castles of Europe and Asia," and were separated by a channel about 4,000 yards wide.

A British fleet had twice traversed the Dardanelles during war, once by force, and once under menace. In 1807 Admiral Sir J. Duckworth was sent to Turkish waters with a squadron of line-of-battle ships and frigates, with the object of compelling the then Sultan to break his alliance with France. He passed the Narrows under fire, destroyed some Turkish ships near Gallipoli, and anchored before

H.M.S. "QUEEN ELIZABETH."
Inset : Captain G. P. W. Hope.

Constantinople. The enterprise called chiefly for skilful seamanship, and to sail a whole squadron through the tortuous Straits and against the swift currents was a brilliant achievement even in the face of guns for which our seamen felt contempt. But having forced the Dardanelles, Duckworth found himself in precisely the position in which, in the opinion of many experts, the British Fleet would have found itself if in 1915 it had effected the perilous passage. He lay in sight of Constantinople but he could not take the city. For that task an army was needed, and he had no troops. Finding himself short of supplies, he returned through the Dardanelles with his mission unfulfilled. He ran past the shore defences with wind and tide, was again bombarded, and suffered considerable damage.

MEN OF THE AUSTRALIAN ARTILLERY
Being landed at Gallipoli.

Yet the guns levelled against him chiefly fired stone cannon-balls ! The inference was that the difficulties of seizing the Dardanelles had not lessened with the flight of centuries.

The next time British forces entered the Dardanelles was in 1854, at the time of the Crimean War. As Great Britain and France were in alliance with Turkey, there was no opposition. British and French forces landed at Gallipoli, and afterwards fortified the isthmus of Bulair. The object was to secure the lines of communication with the Crimea, and the episode does not call for extended explanation.

In 1878 Admiral Hornby and a British Fleet traversed the Dardanelles and anchored before Constantinople as a naval demonstration. The moment was critical. Russia was at war with Turkey, and her army had reached the Sea of Marmora. The Russian troops were within sight of the dome of Santa Sophia. A popular song of the day compendiously epitomized British policy. Its refrain ran : " The Russians shall not take Constantinople." It was thought that the appearance of a British Fleet would deter the somewhat exhausted Russians from entering the city, and the demonstration effected its purpose. The danger lay in the

possibility that the Russians might make terms with the Turks, and induce them to resist Admiral Hornby in the Dardanelles. He ran through the Straits in a blinding snowstorm, with his ships cleared for action. His flagship, H.M.S. Alexandra, grounded for four hours near Chanak. But the Turks did not fire, and the situation was saved. Admiral Hornby was always convinced that he could have got through in any case, for the Turkish defences were not then powerful. Yet he was not blind to the difficulties, as the following extract from a dispatch written six months earlier clearly shows :

If you will send for the chart of the Dardanelles, you will see that from three and a half miles below Kilid Bahar to Ak Bashi Imian, six and a half miles above it, an almost continuous cliff overhangs the shore line, while the Straits close to half a mile in one part [this should have been three-quarters] and are never more than two miles wide. An enemy in possession of the peninsula would be sure to put guns on commanding points of those cliffs, all the more if the present batteries, which are *à fleur d'eau*, were destroyed. Such guns could not fail to stop transports and colliers, and would be most difficult for men-of-war to silence. We should have to fire at them with considerable elevation. Shots which were a trifle low would lodge harmlessly in the sandstone cliffs ; those a trifle high would fly into the country without the slightest effect on the gunners, except amusement.

Many of the shells fired during the naval bombardments in 1915 met with the fate herein predicted. The limited efficacy of naval fire under such conditions was repeatedly demonstrated, for not even the great progress made in naval armaments during the early part of the twentieth century had materially altered the limitations imposed upon warships firing at concealed and often invisible land batteries.

After the Russo-Turkish War the gorge of the Dardanelles was not seriously disturbed by any form of conflict, either actual or threatened, for nearly forty years. In the war between Turkey and Italy in 1911–12 the Italians made elaborate plans for a combined naval and military expedition against the Dardanelles; but the attempt was never made, in consequence of the understanding with the Powers that hostilities were not to be extended to the mainland of Europe. The Balkan War of 1912–13 did not affect the Straits to any marked degree. The Greek Fleet for the most part kept at a respectful distance. A Bulgarian force threatened the lines of Bulair, and Enver Pasha hurriedly embarked a motley expedition on the Bosphorus steamers and took it down to the isthmus; but the Bulgarian attack was never pressed. It remains to consider the condition of the Turkish defences at the time that Great Britain and her Allies came to the decision which, in the words of Sir Ian Hamilton, led to such "stupendous events." The influence of Germany upon Turkey's preparedness for war had begun to be felt even so long ago as the 'seventies of the nineteenth century. After peace was signed at San Stefano in 1878, Blum Pasha, a German officer, designed new fortifications for the Dardanelles, which were carried out. As Germany grew in grace in Constantinople, so did she pay increasing attention to the Straits. Many of the heavy Krupp cannon sold to the Turkish Government in the decade before the great war found their way to Chanak and Kilid Bahr. The batteries increased in number, and those at the outer entrance to the Straits were improved and modernized. It is impossible to attempt to describe the precise armament of the different positions, because even before the outbreak of the war with Turkey the defences of the Dardanelles were constantly undergoing change and development under German supervision. Certain illustrative facts can, however, be specified. The forts on both sides of the entrance to the Straits mounted at the begin-

ning of 1915 some 10·2 and 9·2 guns, and several 10-inch guns. They were flanked by concealed field batteries. The armament of the more powerful forts at the Narrows included a number of 14-inch Krupp guns, as well as some of 11-inch calibre. Lighter guns and field howitzers were plentifully planted on the shores of the Straits, and there were a few heavier howitzers moving on lines of railway. There was believed to be a powerful battery on Nagara Point, where the Straits make a great bend and open out into the Sea of Marmora. The Dardanus Fort, overlooking Kephez Bay, was less formidable. After Nagara Point was passed there were no important defences except at the lines of Bulair, where the batteries were not likely greatly to incommode an advancing squadron. The chief strength of the defences against a naval attack was concentrated at the Narrows, but it was further known that the defenders depended very largely upon their mine-fields and upon floating mines drifting with the current. They were also understood to have fixed in position some land torpedo-tubes. The chief defences of the

GERMAN COMMANDERS.
Marshal von der Goltz and Adjutant Haupmann von Raftdorff in the Dardanelles.

TRANSPORTS DISEMBARKING TROOPS UNDER COVER OF FIRE FROM WARSHIPS.

Dardanelles were under the direct control of the German Admiral Usedom, who was assisted by many German officers. General Liman von Sanders directed the disposition of the Turkish troops in the Gallipoli Peninsula.

Owing to German aid the Turks had accumulated very great supplies of ammunition, both at the Dardanelles and at Constantinople, and in the earlier stages of the operations they never revealed any pronounced shortage of shells. A cargo steamer which accompanied the Goeben had brought them in August, 1914, large quantities of mines. It may be asked why, if the armament of the Dardanelles defences was so efficient before any serious attack was made, it is held that the premature and unsupported naval attacks so greatly impaired the chances of success in the subsequent operations. The answer is that, stated broadly, the Straits had long been reasonably well armed against a prospective bombardment by a fleet. On the other hand, the Gallipoli Peninsula had not been fully prepared against offensive operations by an army attempting to land. Lines of trenches had been dug before Achi Baba, but the field works had not reached their subsequent elaborate condition. The Turks and their German advisers did not expect a land attack, and were understood to cherish the belief that a military enterprise against the Gallipoli Peninsula was not possible. Even after full although involuntary warning had been given, landings were made by the British troops at points which the Turks never foresaw, and therefore failed to defend. Had the original attack been delivered by combined land and sea forces, it was probable that the assailants on land would have found Achi Baba and the road leading from Gaba Tepe to the Kilid Bahr plateau, and thus to Maidos and the Narrows, not very strongly held. In the weeks which elapsed between the great naval attack on March 18 and the first great landing on April 25 field works were prepared by the Turks with feverish haste at many fresh points on the peninsula. The British troops, when they effected their lodgment, expected open fighting. They believed they would carry Achi Baba by nightfall on the first day. They actually found themselves in contact with a tremendous fortress, in which all the natural advantages possessed by the defenders were utilized to the utmost. The Turks held the heights, and the British were on the lower ridges. It was like the position at the Shipka Pass, where, in 1877,

the Russians held the summit for six months and were never dislodged.

The Turks had the further advantage of a supply of men which for the time being was almost inexhaustible. In February and March the number of troops stationed on the Gallipoli Peninsula was believed to have been comparatively small, apart from the gunners in the forts. The Athens correspondent of *The Times*, in a dispatch dated March 23, stated that, according to information from Tenedos, the Turks had concentrated 48,000 troops on the Asiatic side of the Dardanelles, where they feared a land attack. They had only collected 10,000 men on the Gallipoli Peninsula. The parties of British marines landed on February 26 and again on March 4 had found the enemy in no great strength at the entrance to the Straits, though they met with sufficiently stiff opposition. When the Turks discovered that land operations were contemplated they poured troops into the peninsula. They had always kept about 200,000 men in and around Constantinople from the outbreak of the war. The attack on the Dardanelles was initiated when the Turkish Army had no heavy demands elsewhere. Their attack on the Suez Canal had failed. Their offensive against the Russians in Transcaucasia had been broken and was abandoned. No very large numbers had been sent overland through Asia Minor to meet the British advance in Mesopotamia. The Turks, therefore, had their hands comparatively free. It might almost be said that there was no limit to the numbers they had available for the Gallipoli Peninsula. Nearly 800,000 men had been mobilized at the outbreak of war, and of these 600,000 had been armed. For all practical purposes, at the time the Allies landed on the peninsula at the end of April they were potentially in contact with the bulk of the strength of the Turkish Army. The Turkish troops were not all there, but they were "within call." The Allies were matching 120,000 men against a military reservoir containing perhaps half a million. But, despite the claims of the Dardanelles, the Turkish authorities never failed, during the summer, to keep a strong army between Constantinople and Adrianople. At that time they feared Bulgaria.

The motives which led, in the first instance, to an unsupported naval attack on the Dardanelles were not explained at the time. To the onlooker they, therefore, remained inexplicable. Possibly either the appeals of Russia, or the

H.M.S. "IMPLACABLE" COVERING THE LANDING OF TROOPS AT "X" BEACH.

A heavy fire was opened on the cliffs on both sides. The "Implacable" approached the beach, and the troops were ordered to land, fire being continued until the boats were close in to the beach. The troops were landed without any casualties.

supposed need for impressing the Balkan kingdoms without delay, led to the first naval bombardments. Perhaps both these causes were operative, but there was a third which doubtless carried weight. Great Britain was not in any case ready to concentrate a sufficiently strong military expedition at the Dardanelles by the first weeks in February. The British shortage in munitions and equipment, although still undisclosed, was the reason for delay with the land forces. On the other hand, those sections of British naval opinion which favoured the Dardanelles attack evidently believed that it was possible to carry the Straits by naval power alone. Great stress was laid on the armament of the Queen Elizabeth. She carried eight 15-inch guns, of a range and power surpassing any weapons ever seen afloat. The sanguine view was that after the forts at the entrance had been silenced, and the lower portion of the Straits swept clear of mines, the combined fire of battleships entering the Straits, and of the Queen Elizabeth and Inflexible firing over the peninsula under the guidance of aeroplanes, would suffice to settle the defences of the Narrows. It was a sad and costly mis-calculation, only equalled by the probable miscalculation of the power to be exercised by the Fleet after it had, as was hoped, forced its way into the Sea of Marmora. What would the Fleet have done if it had appeared before Constantinople ? The supposition appeared to be that Turkey would have instantly collapsed and made peace. Such an assumption had very doubtful foundations. The Turks had five army corps in the vicinity of their capital. The civil population might have fallen into a wild panic, the Government might have fled, the fleet might have laid half Constantinople in ruins, but nothing was more unlikely than that the Turkish Army would have surrendered, or that its leaders would have agreed upon peace terms. To subjugate Constantinople and to reduce the Turkish military forces to submission a powerful army was required. Until that army had appeared upon the scene the unaided attacks of the Fleet must be pronounced premature and inadvisable. Despite the reasons suggested, they seemed to reveal a lack of co-ordination among those responsible for the planning of British strategy.

The naval reconnaissance of November, and Lieutenant Holbrook's submarine exploit on December 13, have been already mentioned. At daybreak on November 3, 1914. a combined French and British squadron, composed of battleships and battle-cruisers, opened fire on the forts at the entrance to the Dardanelles at a range of six miles. Each vessel fired about 20 rounds. The forts replied, but no ships were hit. Most of the enemy's shells fell short, though one passed over the In-domitable. A spectator wrote that a heavy haze of smoke hung over the forts, and great columns of dust were thrown high into the air when the shells from the ships burst. The sole object of the bombardment was to ascer-tain the range.

Lieutenant Holbrook started on his perilous voyage at 3 a.m. on the morning of December 13. He was in charge of B11, one of the earliest of the British submarines. The B11 was launched in 1906, had a displacement of only 316 tons, and carried a complement of two offi-cers and 14 men. The passage of the Straits was made against the strong current at an average depth of 60 feet, and the submarine passed under five rows of Turkish mines. She came to the surface on the inner side of the mine-field within striking distance of the old Turkish battleship Messudiyeh, launched in 1874, and reconstructed and rearmed in 1901. The Messudiyeh was acting as guardship, and was anchored beyond the Narrows in the roadstead of Nagara. Submerging once more, and then slowly rising until his vessel neared the surface, Lieutenant Holbrook successfully torpedoed the battleship, which soon sank with a heavy loss of life. Diving once again, B11 found the bottom at 30 feet, and scraped her way into deeper water. She rose to the surface once to observe the fate of the Messudiyeh, but took nine and a half hours under water on the return voyage. For this daring exploit the second-in-command, Lieutenant Sydney T. Winn, received the Distinguished Service Order, and all the crew were granted the Distinguished Service Medal, while Lieutenant Holbrook himself received the Victoria Cross. Another British submarine, B9, entered the Straits next day, but was detected before she had gone very far, and observation mines were exploded all round her. She made good her escape, but a month later, on January 15, 1915, the French sub-marine Saphir was less fortunate. While traversing the Straits she struck the bottom near Nagara Point, came to the surface in a disabled condition, and was destroyed by the shore batteries.

By the middle of February, 1915, the naval

forces concentrated near the Dardanelles had considerably increased. The Queen Elizabeth had arrived, though her presence remained a profound secret from the outside world. The battle-cruiser Inflexible, fresh from the victory of the Falkland Islands, was another recent arrival. With these exceptions, all the British armoured ships were pre-Dreadnoughts. There was also a French squadron, commanded by Rear-Admiral Guépratte. The whole naval force was commanded by Vice-Admiral Sackville Carden, who had Rear-Admiral John de Robeck as his second-in-command. At 8 a.m. on February 19 the first real naval attack on the Dardanelles began with a bombardment, as before, of the forts and batteries at the entrance. At Cape Helles, the extremity of the Gallipoli Peninsula, there were two 9·2 guns, which were known to the Turks as the Ertoghrul Battery. At Sedd-el-Bahr, at the castle, was a fort armed with six 10-inch and two 5·9 inch guns. Between the two main positions a field gun battery had been established to repel a possible landing. On the Asiatic side there were two main batteries. One, near Cape Yeni Shehr, was armed with two 9·2 inch guns, and was named the Orkhanie battery. The other, at the " New Castle of Asia," near the pier at Kum Kale, was known as the Kum Kale Fort, and contained four 10·2 inch guns. There was also a field battery near the windmills on Cape Yeni Shehr. The bombardment began out of range of the enemy, who therefore made no attempt to reply. It was plainly seen that the Kum Kale and Sedd-el-Bahr Forts were considerably damaged, but the Ertoghrul and Orkhanie batteries were behind open earthworks, and the effect of the bombardment upon them was not easily estimated. In the afternoon, at 2.45 p.m., the British battleships Vengeance, Cornwallis, and Triumph and the French battleships Suffren, Gaulois, and Bouvet, steamed in closer and engaged the forts with their secondary armament. The Inflexible and the Agamemnon, the latter a powerful pre-Dreadnought battleship, supported with a long-range bombardment from their 12-inch guns. By dusk all the enemy batteries were apparently silenced, save one on the Asiatic side, which continued to fire fitfully. No ships of the Allied Fleet were hit, which indicated bad Turkish gunnery at the shorter ranges of the afternoon.

Next morning the seaplanes and aeroplanes of the Naval Wing made a reconnaissance from the Ark Royal, the new mother-ship for naval aircraft, named after Howard's flagship in the days of the Spanish Armada. The action was afterwards briefly resumed, but little more could be attempted for a week, owing to unfavourable weather. On February 25 the attack was reopened at long range at 10 a.m. by the Queen Elizabeth, Agamemnon, Irresistible (an old pre-Dreadnought battleship), and Gaulois. A shell from the Cape Helles battery soon struck the Agamemnon, which was 11,000 yards away, killing 8 men and seriously wounding 5 ; but within an hour and a half the two 9·2 guns on Cape Helles had been put out of action by the Queen Elizabeth, and the Vengeance and Cornwallis, steaming closer in under the protection of the super-Dreadnought's fire, completed the destruction of the position. The Irresistible and the Gaulois had meanwhile severely hammered the Kum Kale and Orkhanie batteries, which were afterwards pounded by the Suffren and the Charlemagne at the short range of 2,000 yards. The Vengeance, the Triumph, and the Albion completed the task, and by 5.15 p.m. all the forts had been silenced. The Turkish gunners had been under a terrific fire for seven hours, and their suppression brought them no discredit.

After nightfall mine-sweeping operations were begun under cover of a division of battleships and destroyers. The night was quiet and dark, but the scene was lit by flames from the villages at the entrance, which the Turks had fired. The mine-sweepers were trawlers from the North Sea, under the direction of Captain Johnson, R.N., and the courage with which their task was performed on this and subsequent occasions, generally under heavy fire, won the warmest praise from the whole Fleet. Several of the masters and men were afterwards decorated, and no war honours at the Dardanelles were more fully earned. By the early morning of February 26 the Straits had been swept clear of mines " up to four miles from the entrance." The Albion and the Majestic (battleships), supported by the Vengeance, thereupon entered the Straits for the first time, steamed to the limit of the swept area, and bombarded the battery of four 5·9 inch guns in Fort Dardanus, as well as some new batteries which had been concealed on the Asiatic side. The enemy's reply was weak. As working parties were noticed on the forts at the outer entrance, these were also successfully shelled from within the Straits. Forces of

H.M. SHIPS "OCEAN" AND "IRRESISTIBLE" IN ACTION

marines and bluejackets were landed at Kum Kale and Sedd-ul-Bahr, and completed the work of demolition, except at Fort Kum Kale, where they were interrupted by the enemy. Two new 4-inch guns were found concealed near Tombachilles, and were duly destroyed, and it was for gallantry displayed in this connexion that Lieut.-Commander (afterwards Commander) Eric Gascoigne Robinson, R.N., was decorated with the Victoria Cross. The act which won him this distinction was thus officially described :

Lieutenant-Commander Robinson on the 26th February advanced alone, under heavy fire, into an enemy's gun position, which might well have been occupied, and, destroying a 4-inch gun, returned to his party for another charge with which the second gun was destroyed. Lieutenant-Commander Robinson would not allow members of his demolition party to accompany him, as their white uniforms rendered them very conspicuous. Lieutenant-Commander Robinson took part in four attacks on the mine fields—always under heavy fire.

THE HEIGHTS

The success of the opening attacks raised expectations in Great Britain and France to the highest pitch, which the bulletins of the British Admiralty did nothing to diminish. For a time it was seriously thought that the channel to Constantinople would soon be open ; but, though the civil population at Constantinople was reported to be much alarmed, the Turkish and German Staffs preserved their confidence. A bitterly cold north-easterly gale again interrupted the operations, but on March 1 the Triumph, the Ocean, and the Albion once more entered the Straits and bombarded Fort Dardanus and the adjacent concealed batteries. That night the mine-sweepers, again covered by destroyers, completed their sweeping for about another five miles, up to within 1½ miles of Kephez Point, near the beginning of the Narrows. On the same day four French battleships entered the Gulf of Xeros and heavily bombarded the isthmus of Bulair. On March 2 the Canopus, Swiftsure, and Cornwallis, taking advantage of the clearance of mines, drew nearer to Fort Dardanus and bombarded it again. The three battleships came for the first time under the fire of the Yildiz or Tekke battery above the pine woods on the Gallipoli Peninsula, just below the Kilid Bahr plateau. All three ships were hit, but the only casualty was one man slightly wounded. At this period the Russian cruiser Askold, which had figured so prominently in the Russo-Japanese War, reached the Dardanelles. Her five long and slender funnels earned for her the name of " the Packet of

Woodbines." The French squadron was again busy in the Gulf of Xeros on March 2, and wrought great destruction in the lines of Bulair. The Suffren bombarded Fort Sultan, on the hill in the centre of the isthmus. The Gaulois tackled Fort Napoleon, on the western side, and her shells set fire to the barracks, which were burned down. The Bouvet went to the very head of the Gulf, and damaged the bridge over the River Cavack, thus impeding the principal road by which supplies and reinforcements were reaching the peninsula.

On March 3 several battleships again ascended the Straits and resumed the bombardment of Fort Dardanus. H.M.S. Dublin, a light cruiser, demolished an observation station on the Gallipoli Peninsula, and H.M.S. Sapphire (another light cruiser) created a diversion by bombarding guns and troops in the Gulf of Adramyti, far away down the coast of Asia Minor. On this day Admiral Carden reported that the field battery near Sedd-el-Bahr Fort had been destroyed, thus bringing the number of guns of all calibres demolished at the entrance to 40.

On March 4 fine weather greatly assisted the bombardment and the mine-sweeping work within the Straits. On the afternoon of that day demolition parties, covered by detachments of the Marine Brigade of the Royal Naval Division, were landed at Kum Kale and Sedd-el-Bahr " to continue the clearance of the ground at the entrance to the Straits." Both parties had a lively time, for the Turkish soldiery was drifting back to the ruins of the

OF ACHI BABA.

villages on either side of the entrance. A naval officer wrote that "although we have completely destroyed the three towns of Sedd-el-Bahr, Kum Kale and Yeni Shehr, so that not one intact house stands, yet among the wreckage there is any amount of cover for the Turks." The enemy, he added, were quite reckless, and dodged about picking off the men of the landing parties. As a matter of fact, a hot and steady rifle fire was maintained, and the Turkish numbers proved to be considerable. The Sedd-el-Bahr party managed to find and destroy four Nordenfeldts, and made good their withdrawal. The party across the Straits, at Kum Kale, were practically driven back to their boats. The casualties among the landing parties were stated to be 19 killed, 25 wounded, and 3 missing, which shows that the reception was warm. Apparently it was on this day that an incident occurred which was afterwards described thus by a midshipman on the Ocean :

Whilst our marine covering party was landed at Kum Kale a sergeant was wounded and left in a safe place under a wall. When they came back he had 14 bullet wounds in him. They searched round until they at last found a German in a wood exactly opposite the sergeant. He was put up against a tree and shot without a word.

On the same day, March 4, the Sapphire discovered and silenced a battery of field guns at Dikeli, on the channel between the island of Mitylene and the mainland of Asia Minor. The Prince George, a battleship of the Majestic class, which had not previously figured in the Dardanelles dispatches, shelled Besika, the town which gave its name to the bay in which Admiral Hornby's fleet had sheltered before

entering the Straits in 1878. That night Gunner William Walter Thorrowgood took an armed whaler twice to the beach on the Asiatic side of the entrance to the Straits, and brought off two officers and five men, two of them wounded. He was much exposed to rifle fire on both occasions, and received the Distinguished Service Cross for his bravery.

On March 5 the preliminary operations were considered complete, and the great attack upon the heart of the defences at the Narrows was begun. The bombardment was concentrated upon three of the Turkish batteries. The first was the Rumeli Medjidieh battery, armed with two 11-inch, four 9·4-inch, and five 3·4-inch guns. The second was the Hamidieh II. battery, consisting of two of the Krupp 14-inch guns. The third was the Namazieh battery, containing one 11-inch, one 10·2-inch, eleven 9·4-inch, three 8·2-inch, and three 5·9-inch guns. These three batteries were all established on the seaward side of Kilid Bahr, on the slopes of the peninsula, and close to the actual Narrows. The tremendous Namazieh battery dominated the very narrowest portion of the Straits. This was the first occasion on which the experiment was tried of bombarding by indirect fire right across the Gallipoli Peninsula. The Queen Elizabeth, accompanied by the Inflexible and Prince George, went into the Gulf of Xeros. The great 15-inch guns of "Lizzie," as the bluejackets affectionately called the mighty battleship, were said to be capable of "slicing off a hill-top." She fired 29 rounds, under the direction of aeroplanes. One of her shells

THE SINKING OF H.M.S. "IRRESISTIBLE" DURING AN ATTACK ON THE NARROWS OF THE DARDANELLES, MARCH 18, 1915.

struck the magazine in the Hamidieh battery, which blew up. All three batteries were considerably damaged, but the precise amount of destruction accomplished could not be ascertained. The Inflexible and Prince George, searched for the hidden howitzers, their fire being directed by wireless from within the Straits by a squadron consisting of the Irresistible, the Canopus, the Cornwallis, and the Albion. The Admiralty report stated that, "although these vessels were much fired at by concealed guns, they were not hit." On this day the forts on the Asiatic side of the Narrows were not bombarded at all.

The seaplanes were very busy during this bombardment on March 5. In order to discern the effect of the indirect fire over the peninsula, and to locate concealed positions, they had often to fly very low, and were consequently in great danger. The work was carried out with the utmost daring. Seaplane No. 172 (pilot Flight-Lieutenant Bromet, with Lieutenant Brown as observer) was hit no fewer than 28 times ; and seaplane No. 7 (pilot Flight-Lieutenant Kershaw, with Petty Officer Merchant) eight times. On the previous day a seaplane (pilot Flight-Commander Garnett, observer Lieutenant-Commander Williamson) became unstable and dived nose forwards into the sea. Both officers were injured. Flight-Lieutenant Douglas, reconnoitring at close quarters in another seaplane, was wounded, but managed to return safely.

New naval operations were also developed on March 5 on the coast of Asia Minor. To the general surprise, Vice-Admiral Sir Richard Peirse, Naval Commander-in-Chief in the East Indies, appeared in the Gulf of Smyrna with a squadron of battleships and cruisers. The precise composition of the squadron was not disclosed, but it was understood to include units hitherto stationed in the Indian Ocean and in the Pacific. The destruction of Admiral von Spee's squadron at the Falkland Islands, and the squaring of accounts with the Emden, had released a good many warships. It was said at the time that never before had such an enormous and diversified assemblage of ships of all kinds been seen in the Aegean and the Levant. Fresh units continually arrived, some of them from the ends of the earth.

Smyrna was the chief city of Asia Minor, and one of the greatest ports of the Turkish Empire. Of its population of a quarter of a million, half was Greek, and these included at least 45,000 subjects of King Constantine of Greece. To Greek industry and enterprise modern Smyrna chiefly owed its extreme prosperity, and it was to Smyrna and the highlands of Anatolia that the Greek nation looked in the hope of obtaining those further accessions of territory which were denied it in Europe. The principal defences of Smyrna were situated on the southern shore of the gulf. Admiral Peirse bombarded Yeni Kale, the chief port, for two hours during the afternoon of March 5 under very favourable conditions. The official account said that 32 hits were registered, and that there were two heavy explosions, apparently of magazines. The shooting of the after 9·2-inch guns of H.M.S. Euryalus, the cruiser which carried the Admiral's flag, was stated to have been remarkably accurate. The Turks did not return the fire, and it was afterwards said that they had been much perturbed by the attack. The Admiralty narrative declared that "the reduction of the Smyrna defences is a necessary incident in the main operation," but the justification for this assertion was not very obvious. No doubt it was important to harry the enemy wherever possible, but Smyrna did not lie on the main railway route to Syria. The weakness of the bombardment was that no attempt was made to seize the seaport, which remained in possession of the Turkish forces. On this day H.M.S. Sapphire continued her operations in the Gulf of Adramyti, firing on troops on the shore, and destroying a military station at Tuz Burnu.

Having bombarded the great batteries at Kilid Bahr, the Allies on March 6 turned their attention to the forts at and near Chanak, on the Asiatic side of the Narrows. The new attack was delivered against Hamidieh I. battery, south of Chanak, and just before the approach to the Narrows, and Hamidieh III., in front of the town of Chanak and on the very edge of the Narrows. The armament of Hamidieh I. was two 14-inch and seven 9·4 guns ; Hamidieh III. comprised two 14-inch, one 9·4, one 8·2, and four 5·9 guns. The Queen Elizabeth conducted the bombardment from outside the Gallipoli Peninsula, assisted by the Agamemnon and the Ocean. The range was officially given as 21,000 yards (about 12 miles), but no results were stated, and probably they could not be ascertained. The Turks had profited by their experience on the previous day. They got some field guns and howitzers on the heights of the peninsula, and

A corner in the Fort.

One of the heavy guns used in defence of the Fort.

Part of the Massiwa wall.

A dismantled gun in the sea.
THE FORT AT SEDD-EL-BAHR.

started shooting at the Queen Elizabeth. Their attempt was like firing with pea-shooters at the Matterhorn. Three shells from field-guns struck the huge battleship, but did no damage whatever. Meanwhile the Vengeance, the Albion, the Majestic, the Prince George, and the French battleship Suffren had entered the Straits and again engaged Fort Dardanus, as well as the Suandere battery, which was a new gun position near the shore, about equi-distant from Achi Baba and the Kilid Bahr heights. A number of concealed guns replied, and the ships were frequently struck, but there were no casualties. While this action was in progress, Fort Rumeli Medjidieh, near Kilid Bahr and the Narrows, suddenly opened fire. The warships replied with 12-inch shells, and several hits were scored. The episode showed that if Fort Rumeli had been damaged, its guns had not been put out of action by the indirect bombardment over the peninsula the day before. The German newspapers afterwards published reports which suggested that the defenders of the forts were chiefly troubled by the dense fumes from the naval shells. The gunners had at times to abandon their guns for this reason, and so the supposition arose that various forts had been silenced. There was also a Turkish order to economise ammunition in view of the expected grand attack within the Straits.

Next day, March 7, the Allies tried a change of tactics. The indirect bombardment was abandoned, and the Agamemnon and the Lord Nelson steamed into the Straits to engage at long range by direct fire the forts at the Narrows near Kilid Bahr. They bombarded the three forts which had been battered by shells flung over the peninsula on the 5th. The range was from 14,000 to 12,000 yards. The batteries at Fort Rumeli Medjidieh and Hamidieh I. replied for a time, but after explosions within the defences both became silent. The great 14-inch Krupps in Hamidieh II. never replied at all; clearly the explosion in the magazine on the 5th had brought about good results. In this action the two English ships were covered by four French battleships, the Gaulois, the Charlemagne, the Bouvet, and the Suffren, which went farther within the Straits and previously engaged Fort Dardanus and various concealed batteries. The Gaulois, the Agamemnon and the Lord Nelson were struck three times each, but in no case was the damage serious, though

H.M.S. "VENGEANCE" IN ACTION.

the Lord Nelson had three of her crew slightly wounded. Admiral Guépratte was on the Suffren, which penetrated to the extreme limit of the mine field. Several shells struck his ship, and a splinter from one fell at the admiral's feet. On this day the cruiser Dublin was hit three or four times by the 4-inch guns at Bulair, while she was watching the isthmus.

On March 8 the stately Queen Elizabeth entered the Straits, supported by four other battleships, and shelled at long range the irrepressible guns of Fort Rumeli Medjidieh. The weather was not good, and the British Admiralty issued no report of the action. Thereafter, for some days, the operations languished, although mine sweeping was vigorously pursued.

It will be gathered that on the whole the attempts at long-range bombardment had not greatly prospered. The majority of the batteries at the Narrows were still effective. Neither indirect nor direct fire from the biggest guns afloat had really put them out of action for any length of time. The high hopes created by the initiation of the naval operations had greatly diminished. Even the destruction of the batteries at Kum Kale and Sedd-el-Bahr, the two points forming the outer entrance, had not achieved the full purpose of the assailants. Turkish troops had crept forward and entrenched themselves near the ruins, and they had to be shelled once more on March 10

and 11. A special target was the field battery which had been brought to Morto Bay, near the end of the peninsula. It was evident that the Dardanelles would never be forced by long-range fire. It was still more evident that an army was needed to carry through the operation. The hope still cherished by the sailors was that a determined attempt to force their way through at close quarters might produce better results.

Every night the mine sweepers pushed their way nearer to the Narrows. They were guarded by light cruisers and destroyers, all of which, as well as the trawlers, were constantly under heavy fire and subjected to great danger. The big defending batteries rarely spoke during these nocturnal encounters. The defence against the flotillas was entrusted to smaller guns concealed in special places, and to motor-batteries. On one occasion at least the enemy did grave damage. On the night of March 13 the small light cruiser Amethyst was in Sari Siglar Bay, very near the Narrows, when she came under the plunging fire of a concealed battery of howitzers. She was struck several times at close range, was badly knocked about, and suffered over 50 casualties, many being among the engine-room complement. The episode gave rise to ridiculous rumours, and the statement that an unarmoured cruiser of only 3,000 tons had passed the Narrows was gravely circulated. There were other remarkable episodes that night, for the mine-sweepers were getting very near the batteries at the Narrows. Gunner John William Alexander Chubb, R.N., who was a volunteer on trawler No. 488, brought the vessel out in a sinking condition, his commanding officer and three of the crew having been killed. He received the Distinguished Service Cross, as did also Sub-Lieutenant Stephen Augustus Bayford, R.N.R., and Midshipman James Charles Woolmer Price, for gallantry while in charge of picket-boats. Commander John Rickards Middleton and Lieutenant Francis Hugh Sandford were given the Distinguished Service Order for the bravery they showed in the mine-sweeping operations on this and other nights. On March 16 a trawler was blown up in the Straits.

The subsidiary operations associated with the attack on the Dardanelles were continued during the lull. Thus French warships again bombarded the lines of Bulair on March 11. The Russian Black Sea Fleet, encouraged by the absence of the Goeben, which was undergoing repair, came near the Bosphorus on several occasions, and raised beliefs in the public mind which were not destined to be realized. The Russian warships sank a number of Turkish steamers, and also bombarded various small ports in Asia Minor. Their most useful work was the bombardment of the port buildings at Zunguldak, on the Bithynian coast, which interrupted the scanty coal supply of Constantinople. Admiral Peirse was still hammering at the defences of Smyrna. On the morning of March 6, the second day of his bombardment, he had swept his way through the mine fields and drawn near to the narrow entrance of the harbour of Smyrna. Various batteries had fired upon his ships. One near Paleo Tabia Point contained four 6-inch guns; another, containing five 4·7 guns, was in position 150 feet up the hillside; and there were many field guns scattered about in concealed positions. The squadron replied at ranges of from 7,000 to 8,000 yards, and continued for an hour, after which the Turkish fire ceased. In the afternoon the action was continued at closer range, and H.M.S. Euryalus and a battleship were each hit by 6-inch shells, though the casualties were slight. The bombardment was resumed on later days, but the general results appear to have been inconclusive, and Smyrna gradually disappeared from the records of the operations. It was supposed that the attack

was chiefly a demonstration to distract the attention of the enemy.

While the main attack on the Dardanelles was suspended, Vice-Admiral Carden relinquished the command of the Allied Fleet on March 16 owing to ill-health, and his place was taken by Rear-Admiral John M. de Robeck, who was promoted to the rank of Vice-Admiral.

The proceedings of the warships at the Straits had been followed with the closest interest and with the most intense excitement by the peoples of the various Balkan kingdoms. The expectation of the Entente Powers that Greece would participate in the later operations was, however, rudely shaken on March 6 by the announcement of the resignation of M. Venezelos, the Greek Premier. M. Venezelos was by far the ablest statesman in the Balkans. He had composed the internal dissensions in Greece caused by the activities of the Military League. He was the originator of the famous Balkan League, which led to the Balkan War and to the expulsion of Turkey from the greater part of her European provinces. He held very strongly that the future of Greece required that she should take an active part in the attempt of the Allies to expel the Turks from Europe for ever. He had led the Allies to understand that they would have the assistance of the Greek Navy, and that a division of the Greek Army would, at a suitable moment, join in the land operations which by this time were in full contemplation. Unfortunately his policy was not favoured by King Constantine, the ruler of Greece, who desired to maintain an attitude of neutrality. M. Venezelos, finding himself at issue with the King, resigned. In a letter to King Constantine, dated January 11, 1915, he had outlined the policy which he considered the Greek Government ought to adopt, in order to save "the greater part of Hellenism in Turkey," and to create "a great and powerful Greece." He foreshadowed the possible consequences of an Austro-German invasion of Serbia, and said that the destruction of Serbia would not only destroy the moral standing of Greece as a State, but would endanger the life of Greece as a nation. The document did not allude to the question of active co-operation with the Entente Powers, but that issue lay at its back. The whole subject of the successive political crises in Greece, and their ultimate effect upon the situation in the Near East, must be reserved for subsequent discussion. It is sufficient to note here that the temporary with-

TOWING BIG GUNS ASHORE.

Method of transporting the Allies' big guns at the Dardanelles. A capacious raft was specially constructed and ballasted with sandbags to prevent the gun rolling when aboard. The whole arrangement was then towed to the point of landing.

drawal of M. Venezelos from public life deprived the Allies of useful military help in their attack upon the Dardanelles. They saw that whatever they proposed to do must be done alone.

The first public intimation that land operations were to be undertaken at the Dardanelles was contained in an official Note issued by the French Government in Paris on March 11. It stated that an Expeditionary Force had been concentrated in North Africa, that General d'Amade had been appointed to the command, and that part of the corps was already on its

way to the Levant. The French had concentrated at Bizerta, and were all in the Ægean by March 15. Similar steps, although on a much larger scale, had also been taken by the British Government. The 29th Division and the Royal Naval Division had been designated for service at the Dardanelles. The Australian and New Zealand Divisions, a Territorial Division, and some Indian units had been summoned from Egypt. The bulk of these forces, of which further details will be given later, had been hurriedly placed on transports, which were assembled in the harbour of Mudros, at the island of Lemnos, by the third week in March. Lemnos was an island about 50 miles from the entrance to the Straits. It was nominally in the possession of Greece, but had not been formally occupied by her, and the Allies used it as an advanced base with her tacit consent. The smaller Turkish island of Tenedos, much nearer the Straits, became the headquarters of the operations.

The officer selected by the British Government to direct the land attack upon the Dardanelles was General Sir Ian Standish Monteith Hamilton, G.C.B., D.S.O., who at the outbreak of the war was General Officer Commanding-in-Chief in the Mediterranean and Inspector-General of the Oversea Forces. Sir Ian Hamilton was posted to the command of one of the New Armies some time after they were formed, and until he left for Gallipoli he also held a highly responsible post in connection with the internal defences of the British Islands. He left London on March 13 with his General Staff, and travelled by special train to Marseilles. There he embarked on H.M.S. Phaeton, one of the newer 30-knot light cruisers, and he was at Tenedos on March 17. It was a very rapid journey, even in answer to a summons of war.

General Hamilton was then just over 62 years old and had been soldiering all his life. Curiously enough, he was born in the Mediterranean, in the island of Corfu, within a short voyage of the scene of the greatest and most desperate undertaking he had ever been called upon to face. His father was Colonel Christian Monteith Hamilton, and his mother was a daughter of the third Viscount Gort. He was married to the eldest daughter of Sir John Muir in 1887.

He entered the Army in 1873, and had served in many campaigns. He had fought under Lord Roberts in Afghanistan in 1878–80. He had been in the Boer War in 1881, and was on the hill of Majuba on the fatal morning when Sir George Colley was killed. He had joined Lord Wolseley's expedition up the River Nile for the relief of General Gordon in 1884–85. He had gone up the River Irrawaddy to Mandalay in the Burmah War of 1886–87, and had emerged with the brevet rank of lieutenant-colonel, having previously won a brevet majority on the Nile. He had become a full colonel in 1891, and had marched to the relief of Chitral in 1895, receiving the C.B. for his work. He had commanded a brigade in the rough and harassing

Tirah War in 1897–98. Musketry having always attracted him, he found himself next year commandant at Hythe, but the troubles in South Africa took him to Natal in time to participate in the early action of Elandslaagte. He went through the siege of Ladysmith and was promoted to the rank of Major-General. Afterwards he commanded a column, whose exploits Mr. Winston Churchill admiringly recorded in a volume entitled " Ian Hamilton's March." Lord Kitchener chose him as his Chief-of-Staff in the later stages of the South African War, and on the conclusion of peace he became Quartermaster-General to the Forces. He represented the Army of India on the Japanese side during the great Russo-Japanese War, and witnessed most of the battles save the last desperate encounter of Mukden. His experiences were set forth in two vivacious volumes entitled " A Staff Officer's Scrap Book," the cream of diaries laboriously kept. He then commanded on Salisbury Plain for four years, until he succeeded Lord Kitchener in the Mediterranean command, and became also a peripatetic inspector of the troops of the Dominions. He had been mentioned in dispatches innumerable times, and his many decorations included the Prussian Orders of the Red Eagle and of the Crown of Prussia. He was a man of great personal charm, and in his leisure moments he had been wont to beguile himself with literary pursuits. Mr. Churchill wrote of him that he had once very nearly deserted the profession of arms for journalism, and a slim and forgotten book of verse, possessed by few, attested his love of poetry. In his military career he had been by no means a favourite of fortune. All his earlier advancement had been arduously won in the field, and there had been moments, of the kind known to most soldiers, when he feared that promotion had passed him by for ever. No soldier of high rank in the British Army had seen so many varieties of warfare, or had enjoyed so many opportunities of studying at first hand operations on the grand scale.

On his arrival at Tenedos on March 17 Sir Ian Hamilton found awaiting him Vice-Admiral de Robeck, General d'Amade, and Admiral Guépratte. The French corps had been concentrated at Bizerta, and had reached Mudros on March 15. General d'Amade had been selected by the French Government for the command of the French corps " owing to

NEAR CAPE HELLES.
British ships bombarding the Turkish position. A Captive Balloon is attached to the centre ship.

his experience of expeditions in distant lands."
His campaign in Morocco had won him European fame, and he was no stranger to the
British Army, for he had been an eye-witness
of the South African War. The two generals
and two admirals immediately held a conference. There can be no doubt that when
Sir Ian Hamilton left England' the prevalent
assumption was that a combined land and sea
attack would be made as soon as he reached
the scene of action. The transports and the
troops were there; yet it became his painful
duty to inform the conference that he could
not then make an attack. The cause was one
for which he was in no sense responsible. He
was expected to deliver an assault in the face
of difficulties for which, in his own words, "no
precedent was forthcoming in military history
except possibly in the sinister legends of
Xerxes." He knew that "nothing but a
thorough and systematic scheme for flinging
the whole of the troops under my command
very rapidly ashore could be expected to meet
with success." A "tentative or piecemeal
programme" would produce disaster. In
order to make a landing successfully the transports had to be so loaded that the operation
would go like clockwork. The respective troops

AFTER THE BOMBARDMENT.
Effect of the gun-fire from H.M.S. Queen Elizabeth.

had to be carefully allotted. The holds of the ships had to be so filled that the weapons, the equipment, the munitions first required were at the top and ready to hand. In the great flotilla of transports assembled at Mudros these imperative conditions were conspicuously lacking. The ships had been hurriedly filled without regard to subsequent necessities. Men and material alike had been swept out to the Aegean pell-mell. In English seaports and at Alexandria the same mistakes had been made. The Power with an unexampled experience of oversea expeditions had suffered the most elementary blunders to be committed. It was said that once before in his wide experience Sir Ian Hamilton had encountered a similar series of mistakes, and that he was instantly able to lay his finger on the insuperable defects. There was no help for it. He had to tell his colleagues that the military expedition must return to Egypt, in order that the transports might be re-loaded. The one exception was that of the vessels containing the Australian Infantry Brigade, which were permitted to remain. The one advantage gained was that the delay would bring more settled weather. The disadvantages were even graver than was then supposed.

The soldiers were thus for a time eliminated.

The word then lay with the seamen. Admiral de Robeck announced his intention of making on the morrow a general naval attack upon the Straits with the whole of the battleships at his disposal. The ultimate responsibility for this decision was not disclosed. It was an attempt to force the Narrows by sea power alone, to repeat the exploit which Admiral Duckworth had only accomplished with great risk against no more formidable missiles than stone cannon-balls. It was a naval adaptation of the onslaught of the Light Brigade. It was the tactics of the cavalry charge applied to battleships and big guns ; and when it failed, the leaders of the expedition knew that the Narrows would never be passed without military aid. It must be remarked that heavy losses had been so far foreseen that the battleships Queen and Implacable had already been dispatched from England in order, in the words of the Admiralty announcement, "to replace ships' casualties in anticipation of this operation." The anticipation proved to be justified.

The morning of the great adventure (March 18) was bright and clear, and the sea was smooth. At a quarter to eleven the battleships Queen Elizabeth, Inflexible, Agamemnon and Lord Nelson, supported by the Triumph and Swiftsure, entered the first reach of the

Straits, which, to an observer on a hillside at Tenedos, looked like a bright blue lake. The four most powerful ships took up a position about 3½ miles within the Straits, roughly between the Gallipoli village of Krithia and the village of Erenkeui, on the Asiatic side. The Queen Elizabeth was nearest the Gallipoli Peninsula. They opened a long-range fire on the principal batteries on both sides of the Narrows. The two smaller warships in support advanced farther in and dealt with the batteries at Fort Dardanus, at Kephez Point, and at Suandere, on the opposite side of the Straits. The howitzers and field batteries concealed on shore responded vigorously. The bombardment was by far the most terrific

to which the Narrows had been subjected. The town of Chanak, sadly battered on the 7th, was soon ablaze, and the dense clouds of smoke could be plainly seen by the watchers on distant Tenedos. At 12.22 Rear-Admiral Guépratte led his main squadron, consisting of the Suffren, the Gaulois, the Charlemagne, and the Bouvet, past the British ships and engaged the forts at close range, taking up his station near Kephez Point. Admiral de Robeck afterwards telegraphed his warm admiration of his French colleague's skill and bravery. There were now ten battleships in the Straits, and an hour later all the shore forts had ceased firing. It seemed as though the time had come to press forward the attack. Many thought

A TURKISH SNIPER

Being brought in under guard. The Turk was ingeniously screened by foliage attached to his clothing.

THE BRITISH COMMANDER-IN-CHIEF,
General Sir Ian Hamilton (centre), with General Braithwaite, being rowed ashore.

from the silence of the forts that the day was won.

A fresh British squadron came steaming into the Straits. It consisted of the Vengeance, the Irresistible, the Albion, the Ocean, the Swiftsure and the Majestic. As the new squadron approached Kephez Point all the other battleships turned to withdraw, save only the Queen Elizabeth, the Inflexible, the Agamemnon, and the Lord Nelson, which remained moving slowly to and fro in the first reach.

It was at this moment that tragedy began. The Bouvet was taking a course inside Erenkeui Bay, and out of the main current of the Straits, no doubt to avoid drifting mines. The eddies and cross-currents wrought her undoing, for the supposed course of safety brought her into contact with danger. An officer on a British destroyer saw her struck by three shells, and another officer on the Prince George saw two shells strike her on the starboard side; but the real cause of the disaster was almost simultaneous contact with a drifting mine. The explosion is believed to have fired her magazine. In three minutes she had heeled over and disappeared, and the Charlemagne, hurrying to the rescue, found only bubbles rising to the surface, and a pall of black smoke

slowly lifting. She sank in 36 fathoms at a point north of the village of Erenkeui. The Bouvet carried a crew of 630, and of these only 64 were saved. *The Times* afterwards thus described the nature of the drifting mines used by the enemy in these operations :

The form of drifting mine used by the Turks is believed to be the Leon torpedo, which resembles a short Whitehead torpedo, and is designed to be, if desired, discharged through a torpedo-tube, though it can equally well be merely dropped overboard from above water. The size and general arrangement of the mine are shown on pages 317 and 318 of the " Naval Annual " for 1914.

It is not an automobile torpedo, but merely a freely-floating mine, which can be set to oscillate between any depths below the surface that may be desired ; on becoming water-borne it assumes an approximately vertical position, and, having a certain negative buoyancy, it sinks until automatically the propeller is brought into use and drives it upwards again. As prearranged, the action of the propeller ceases and commences at any depth selected for use. There is a time arrangement embodied by which the duration of its floating can be regulated ; after such time the mine is flooded and sinks, or, if desired, can rise to the surface. It can also be so arranged that when first discharged it sinks to the bottom, and after a prearranged time rises and commences to oscillate.

The mine can be dropped from ships in the open sea, and was used in the raids on Yarmouth and Scarborough. In the case of tidal harbours it can be discharged from a vessel outside at such time as to find its own way into the harbour and possibly create destruction therein.

The swift disaster to the Bouvet was not allowed to check the attack. The new British squadron reached the narrowing portion of the Straits opposite Kephez Point, and resumed the bombardment at 2.36 p.m. It was plain that the forts had not been silenced, for the batteries at Dardanus and Suandere, and one each near Chanak and Kilid Bahr, reopened their fire. Yet much damage had been wrought. A German officer in one of the Hamidieh batteries afterwards wrote that the barracks and other buildings were reduced to heaps of ruins, and he acknowledged that one gun was completely destroyed. Under the cover of the British fire the mine-sweepers continued their perilous work. They were in charge of Commander William Mellor, R.N., of whom the Admiralty afterwards wrote that " he displayed conspicuous gallantry, always being to the fore in a picket-boat in the most exposed positions, encouraging his sweepers and setting a fine example." It was still hoped that the passage might be won.

But the Turks had not failed to draw conclusions from the loss of the Bouvet. They were dropping more Leon torpedoes into the swift current, and at 4.5 one of these struck the Irresistible, a battleship of the Formidable class, thirteen years old, with a displacement of 15,000 tons and a principal armament of four 12-inch guns. She quitted the line, listing heavily, and slowly dragged her way towards the entrance to the Straits. She did not sink until 5.50 p.m., and meanwhile practically all her crew had been rescued. Captain Christopher Powell Metcalfe, R.N., was the chief instrument in saving life on this occasion. He skilfully brought the destroyer Wear alongside the Irresistible under a heavy fire, and saved most of the crew. He had over 600 rescued men on board when he left the Straits. He received the Distinguished Service Order. Upon Midshipman Hugh Dixon, who saved several officers and men in the Queen Elizabeth's picket-boat while shells were falling all around, the Distinguished Service Cross was bestowed.

At 6.5 p.m. the Ocean, a battleship fifteen years old, with a displacement of 12,950 tons

THE FRENCH COMMANDER IN THE DARDANELLES.
General Gouraud (X) and his Staff at Sedd-ul-Bahr.

(On August 6th, 1915, General Sarrail was appointed to command the French Expeditionary Force at the Dardanelles in place of General Gouraud, who was wounded there in July.)

COMMANDER EDWARD UNWIN, R.N.

MIDSHIPMAN GEORGE EDWARD
DREWRY, R.N.R. (on right).

THE IMMORTAL LANDINGS ON THE GALLIPOLI PENINSULA,

and a principal armament of four 12-inch guns, also sank in deep water, having been struck in similar fashion by a mine. The Ocean went to the bottom very quickly, but nearly all the crew were fortunately saved.

Nor was this the sum of the damage. The Gaulois had been badly hit by the Turkish guns, and her bows were torn open. The Inflexible was hit in her fore-top by a shell which killed or wounded several men. At a later hour she was also struck by a mine, though this fact was not made public for many weeks. She made her way with great difficulty to Tenedos, and it was feared that she would sink. The episode produced many remarkable deeds of gallantry on the part of her officers and crew, which were fittingly described by the Admiralty as follows :—

Lieutenant-Commander Acheson, with Acting Sub-Lieutenant Alfred E. B. Giles, Chief E.R.A. 2nd Class Robert Snowdon, and Stoker 1st Class Thomas Davidson, went down into the fore magazine and shell room of H.M.S. Inflexible when the parties working in these places had been driven out by fumes, caused by the explosion of a mine under the ship ; they closed valves and water-tight doors, lights being out, the shell room having two feet of water in it, rising quickly, and the magazine flooding slowly.

The fumes were beginning to take effect on Acting Sub-Lieutenant Giles, but neither he nor the others left until

ordered to do so by Lieutenant-Commander Acheson, who was the last to leave the shell room.

During the time H.M.S. Inflexible was steaming to Tenedos, the engine-room being in semi-darkness and great heat, the ship in possible danger of sinking on passage, a high standard of discipline was called for in the Engineer Department, a call which was more than met. Engineer-Commander Harry Lashmore, C.B. responsible for the discipline of the engine-room department, was in the starboard engine-room throughout the passage, and set a fine example to his men.

Engineer-Lieutenant-Commander Lester was in the port engine-room carrying out the same duties as Engineer-Commander Lashmore did in the starboard engine-room.

Engineer-Lieutenant Parry went twice through the thick fumes to the refrigerator flat to see if the doors and valves were closed ; he also closed the escape hatch from the submerged flat, fumes and vapour coming up the trunk at the time.

Surgeon Langford brought up the wounded from the fore distributing station in the dark. Fumes permeated the place, rendering five men unconscious. Surgeon Langford, though partially overcome by the fumes, continued his work.

Able Seaman Smedley, though wounded himself, carried a wounded Petty Officer down from the fore top after it had been struck by a shell ; he subsequently went aloft twice more, and started for a third attempt.

Engine Room Artificer Runalls escaped up the trunk from the fore air compressor room with difficulty, helped up his stoker, and closed the W.T. door of the trunk before he fell insensible.

Chief Sick Berth Steward Hamlin, though partially overcome by fumes, assisted Surgeon Langford while the Inflexible was proceeding to Tenedos.

MIDSHIPMAN W. ST. AUBYN MALLESON, R.N.

SEAMAN G. McKENZIE SAMSON.

APRIL 25th, 1915: HEROES WHO WERE AWARDED THE VICTORIA CROSS.

All the officers named received the Distinguished Service Order, and the men were given the Conspicuous Gallantry Medal. Acting Sub-Lieutenant George Tothill Philip received the Distinguished Service Cross for his work on the same day in the Inflexible's picket-boat. He was out watching for floating mines when his boat was struck by a heavy shell, which injured his knee. He managed to get the boat back to the Inflexible, ordered the crew aboard, and, despite his injuries, got into the engine-room, shut off steam and closed the scuttle to stokehold before leaving the boat.

The bombardment died away when darkness fell, and the squadrons withdrew. The British casualties in *personnel* were only 61 killed, wounded, and missing. The naval authorities had then to consider their position. The great attack had ended with a loss of three battle-ships and with two others practically put out of action. Three days afterwards the British Admiralty issued an official statement which contained the following singular remark: "The power of the Fleet to dominate the fortresses by superiority of fire seems to be established." If the supposed power was established in the view of the Admiralty, there

were few other people who shared the conviction thus expressed. The general conclusion, which was undoubtedly accurate, was that the attack had been badly repulsed. Although the chief losses were caused by mines, the power of well-armed forts over ships had received a further signal demonstration. That this conclusion was eventually forced upon the reluctant British Government was proved by the fact that the naval attack was never afterwards seriously reopened.

In any case, bad weather set in on March 19, and for some days even sea-plane reconnaissance was impossible. There was meanwhile a great deal of desultory and mostly subsidiary naval work. The positions at the entrance to the Straits were frequently bombarded, in order to deter the Turks from repairing them. There were many signs that the enemy were actively preparing to resist a land attack, the imminence of which was no longer a secret. The Russian Black Sea Fleet again appeared off the Bosphorus on March 28 and bombarded the outer forts and batteries. The fire of the Russian ships was directed by sea-planes. The Turkish batteries replied, and a flotilla of Turkish torpedo-boats tried to come out into the Black Sea, but was repelled. A large Turkish four-masted sailing ship, which was vainly trying to seek refuge within the Bosphorus, was destroyed. On April 15 the Majestic and Swiftsure bombarded an observation post at Gaba Tepe, on the Gallipoli Peninsula, afterwards one of the landing places of the Australians and New Zealanders. Various warships crossed the Gulf of Xeros, and harried the Turkish camp at Enos, near the new Bulgarian frontier. Repeated visits were paid to Enos, with the object of conveying the impression that the port might be selected as the principal landing place of the Expeditionary Force.

One night the incredible happened. A little improvised Turkish torpedo-boat of 97 tons, named the Dhair Hissar, slipped out of Smyrna and got loose in the Aegean. She carried a crew of 34, of whom seven were Germans, men from the Goeben. For a whole month this tiny craft lurked in odd corners of the coast of Asia Minor and escaped detection. On April 16 she thought her chance had come when she saw a British transport, the Manitou, and tried to torpedo her. The attempt failed, but the Manitou had lowered boats, two of which capsized, as a result of which 51 men were drowned. One of the boats came to grief through the breaking of a davit, and the other was overturned through overcrowding. The Manitou signalled for help, and light cruisers and destroyers swarmed forth in search of the Dhair Hissar. She was seen near the Gulf of Smyrna, and instantly chased until she beached herself in the Bay of Kalamuti, on the Island of Chios, on April 18.

British submarines were constantly at work in the Straits, and on April 17 E 15 grounded near Kephez Point. The officers and crew, numbering 20, were taken prisoners, for it was impossible either to fight the vessel or to get her off. She was not much injured, however,

and it was feared that she might be salved by the Turks. Lieutenant MacArthur, R.N., conducted two very daring reconnaissances in submarine B 6, both being made under heavy fire. For this action he was rewarded with the Distinguished Service Cross. As a result of his report, it was decided to attempt to destroy E 15. During the night of April 18 Commander Eric Robinson, who had already won the V.C. for his valour near Kum Kale, took into the Straits the picket-boats of the Majestic and the Triumph. The party approached the stranded submarine, and at short range fired torpedoes. The torpedo actually successful was fired by Lieutenant Claud Herbert Godwin, R.N., who was in charge of the Majestic's picket-boat. He was afterwards decorated with the D.S.O. The exploit was performed within 200 yards of the forts, which had discovered the presence of the little expedition, and poured in a tremendous fire. The Majestic's picket-boat was sunk, but the other boat rescued all the crew. This brilliant feat was accomplished with the loss of one man, who was fatally wounded. The unlucky submarine was rendered useless by the torpedo. Other officers who received the Distinguished Service Cross for their courageous work that night were Lieutenant Arthur Cyril Brooke-Webb, R.N.R., and Midshipman John Blaxland Woolley, R.N.

Such is a broad chronicle of the unsupported naval attack upon the Dardanelles. Sir Ian Hamilton, after a hurried visit to Egypt to supervise the fresh loading of the transports, had returned to Lemnos on April 7, bringing with him the remainder of his staff, who had followed from London. The next act of the immense and tragic drama of the Dardanelles began on April 25, when in the still mists of dawn flotillas packed with troops moved silently towards the desolate beaches of the Gallipoli Peninsula.

CHAPTER XCIII.

AMMUNITION: SUPPLY AND MANUFACTURE.

Magnitude of the Requirements—Failure of Sub-Contracting—Local Committees— French Methods—Mr. Lloyd George as Minister of Munitions—Labour Difficulties— Munitions Act—Volunteer Workers' Enrolment—Pledge of Trade Unions—New National Factories—M. Albert Thomas—Russia—The Dominions—Armour-Piercing, High Explosive and Shrapnel Shells—Aircraft Bombs—The Making of Shells, Cartridge Cases and Bullets—Propellants and High Explosives—Cordite—Nitro-glycerine—Gun Cotton —Picric Acid—Trinitrotoluene—Supply of Nitric Acid—Asphyxiating Gases.

WHEN a country is suddenly plunged into war it does not require much foresight to perceive that an enhanced supply of ammunition will be one of the most important requirements, and the most obvious way of obtaining it is to increase the output of the State arsenals and place large orders with the private firms that make shells and explosives. This, the course adopted by the British Government, would probably have sufficed for a war of moderate dimensions, or even, with good fortune, for a great one conducted on the old lines, but it proved inadequate for a widespread conflict in which the expenditure of ammunition surpassed all the anticipations of the closest students of warfare. It may, indeed, be said that none of the armies that took the field fully expected such a prodigal outpouring of shells as actually occurred. Even the Germans, if the testimony of Field-Marshal von Moltke and Herr Dernburg is to be accepted, found themselves short of munitions in the early stages of the fighting, though, of course, they claimed that matters were readily put right by means of their wonderful industrial organization. The Boer War, the last important campaign of which our War Office had practical ex-

perience, afforded no guidance, for during the whole of the two and three-quarters years for which it lasted the amount of ammunition used was not much more than was spent by our artillery alone in a fortnight in and around Neuve Chapelle ; and if at the beginning of the war anyone had dared to prophesy in Whitehall that within a year one combatant in the assault of a single fortress would, as did the Germans at Przemysl, fire 700,000 shells in four hours—a quantity which, according to the standards of previous wars, might have been thought adequate for a siege of six months—his imagination would have been admired more highly than his intelligence. But even this record was surpassed at the beginning of the great offensive in Champagne in September, for if the German papers can be believed, one portion of the front there received in three days over 50,000,000 shots from the guns of the Allies.

We have described in an earlier chapter of this volume (pp. 308-312) how the supply of ammunition, and especially of high explosives, became in the spring of 1915 the most urgent British problem of the war. A series of disturbing indications culminated in May in the revelation by the military correspondent of

The Times that " the want of an unlimited supply of high explosives " caused the failure of British attacks. We have seen how it became impossible for Ministers any longer to satisfy the country with vague, and often contradictory speeches, how a Coalition Government was formed, and how the Ministry of Munitions came into existence. War Office control had been proved, and was now admitted, to have failed, and no demands for confidence in the Secretary of State for War could alter the fact that the War Office had neither grasped the magnitude of the effort required nor guided such efforts as were made in the right direction.

We need sketch but briefly the general course of action in the earlier period of the war. When, in the autumn of 1914, the immensity of the task began to dawn upon the War Office, the great armament firms, which were pressing their existing resources to the uttermost, and in many cases had made or were making large extensions to their works, were called into consultation, and largely on their advice it was decided to inaugurate a great extension of the system of sub-contracting. It was argued that, much of the work being of a highly technical character, the best plan was to parcel out such parts of it as could be done by inexperienced firms, while leaving in the hands of the armament firms with their skilled staffs the supervision, the production of the more difficult and delicate parts, and the work of assembling. This policy involved the employment of 2,500 to 3,000 firms in the production of munitions, either directly or as sub-contractors, and it would, according to Mr. Lloyd George, have secured an adequate output had the promised deliveries been made to time. But it was discovered in December that they would be late, and that the supplies would, in consequence, be inadequate. Even in that month, however, some progress had been made, for, again according to Mr. George, if the production in September was represented by the figure 20, in October it was 90 and in December 156. These figures, he explained, were " purely artillery."

The difficulties that interfered with the due performance of the contracts were to some extent problems of labour. Though in the early stage of the war there were fears of unemployment, an actual shortage soon declared

IN A FOUNDRY: MOLTEN METAL BEING POURED INTO MOULDS.

THE MUNITION WORKS.

[From a photographic study by Alvin Langdon Coburn, F.R.P.S.]

itself, at least in the skilled branches. Further, the production of the men who were available for engineering work was curtailed not only by actual strikes, but also by lost time and the restrictive rules and customs fostered by the trade unions. This question was touched upon in the House of Commons at the beginning of February. About the same time a Board of Trade Committee, consisting of Sir George Askwith, Sir Francis Hopwood, and Sir George Gibb, was appointed to inquire into the question of production in engineering and shipbuilding establishments. Reporting towards the end of the month, this committee expressed the opinion that the production would be considerably accelerated if there

THE KING'S VISIT TO BIRMINGHAM.
His Majesty in one of the Munition Factories.
Inset : Inspecting the interior of a case for an
18-pounder shell.

whether by lock-out or by strike, should take place on work for Government purposes, all disputes being referred to a Government tribunal for investigation and settlement.

It is, however, one thing for a Government Committee to report and another to bring its recommendations into force, and a long and weary series of appeals and negotiations was required to secure a reasonable degree of compliance with them. To meet the difficulties due to shortage of labour an endeavour was made in the first instance to fill up the deficiencies which were hampering the armament firms, the Labour Exchanges being utilized for the purpose. The earlier results were very promising, but afterwards they fell away, and by March, 1915, it had to be recognized that the object in view could not be attained by attempts to transfer men from the districts in which they were living to others where their services were wanted.

In these circumstances, the policy of working through the armament firms having been exhausted, other expedients were felt to be necessary if sufficient ammunition was to be obtained not merely for immediate purposes, but for larger and more aggressive operations in the future. Accordingly, steps were taken in the direction of bringing the manufacture more fully under Government control and of broadening its basis. An Amending Bill to the Defence of the Realm Consolidation Act,

were a relaxation of the practice of workmen confining their earnings, on the basis of existing piece rates, to " time and a half," or whatever the local standard might be, and that the piece rates, which this practice was designed to protect, could be adequately protected by other means than the restriction of earnings and output. To this end the recommendation was made that firms engaged in making shells and fuses should give an undertaking to the committee, on behalf of the Government, to the effect that in fixing piece-work prices the earnings of the men during the period of the war should not be considered as a factor in the matter, and that no reduction in those rates should be made unless warranted by a change in the manufacture—e.g., the introduction of a new type of machine. The committee further recommended that under proper conditions there should be an extension of the employment of female labour, which it was satisfied was suitable for many of the operations required, and that no stoppage, introduced on March 9, extended the powers which the Government already possessed over firms and factories engaged in munitions manufacture to others which were not being used for that purpose but which it was hoped to use very soon, and in bringing it forward Mr. Lloyd George explained that the proposal was to organize the whole of the engineering community to assist in increasing the output, but not without full consultation with all the manufacturers concerned. The regulations made by an Order in Council under this Act and published on March 24 empowered the Admiralty or Army Council to take possession of any unoccupied premises for the purpose of housing workmen engaged in the production, storage or transport of war material; to requisition particulars of the output of factories; to take possession of any factory or of the plant it contained; and to regulate or restrict the work carried on in any one factory, or remove the plant contained in it, with the object of improving the production in another.

In explaining the objects of this amending Bill to the House of Commons Mr. George stated that he was "on the look-out for a good strong business man with some go in him who will push the thing through and be at the head of the Central Committee." This announcement brought in thousands of applications from all sorts and conditions of men who in their own estimation at least merited the epithet "push and go." Apparently, indeed, the riches were so embarrassing that no choice could be made, and the only visible outcome was the appointment by Lord Kitchener, a month later, of a committee, communications in respect of which were to be addressed to Mr. G. M. Booth, a well-known member of the shipping industry, who, however, disclaimed being the "man of push and go." Later it appeared that this committee was a Departmental executive committee of the War Office for carrying out matters of policy determined, largely under the supervision of Lord Kitchener, by an Administrative

MAKING SHELLS AT SHEFFIELD.
Stack of shells ready for dispatch.   Inset: A pile of shell noses.

Committee representative of all the chief Government Departments. Mr. Booth was a member of this latter committee also.

In making these arrangements the first object in view was to ascertain the exact extent of the problem, the manner in which it was being met, and the plant and labour available or capable of being diverted to its purposes ; and the second to map out the whole country in order to secure larger, more rapid and better co-ordinated production. It was decided to work largely through local munitions committees, a plan which took an important place in the scheme developed later under the Ministry of Munitions ; the first of these was formed at Newcastle, and others followed at Leeds, Sheffield, Birmingham, Glasgow, Dublin and elsewhere.

In connexion with these efforts to organize the industrial resources of Great Britain for the production of munitions it may be interesting to refer to the measures which France had taken for the same end, at an earlier

HEADING 18-POUNDER Q.F. CARTRIDGE CASES.

date. In order to simplify control and obtain the fullest results, the whole country was divided into eight or ten districts, and here it must be remembered that France suffered under the disadvantage that some of her provinces that are richest in coal and minerals were in the hands of the enemy. The districts each contained one or more groups of industrials, and at the head of each of these was placed the chief metallurgist of the district, who was required to furnish the military authorities with an estimate of the number of shells his district could produce daily, and was held personally responsible for the due delivery of his daily quota. Sub-contracts were allotted to the various factories after conference with the manufacturers of the district concerned. On making known their requirements in coal and iron, the manufacturers received Government supplies, and they were furnished with special labels which gave their goods priority of conveyance on the railways. To begin with, the mistake was made of drafting skilled mechanics from the State arsenals and other factories for service at the front, and in this way some establishments lost a third of their staff. This mistake, however, was soon rectified by bringing such men back from the firing line, and manufacturers were empowered to requisition them from the depôts for work in the factories. It was found under this system that men who were not skilled mechanics occasionally made their way into the workshops, but this abuse was remedied by watching their work and returning them when it did not come up to the required standard ; later, however, a method was adopted of drafting suitable men in the ordinary regimental depôts into special industrial depôts, from which they were requisitioned by manufacturers. In the large towns workmen who were over military age, and men out of employment, were registered by the local municipalities and sent to the shell factories as required. The factories were under military control only to the extent that their activities were regulated by frequent conferences between their owners and the Ministry of War, that in each district a highly trained engineer officer travelled from factory to factory, giving the owners the benefit of his advice, and that the shells were subject to military inspection on delivery.

Pending the passage of the Act constituting the new Ministry of Munitions, Mr. George visited

SOLDIERS FROM THE TRENCHES IN A MACHINE SHOP.

Manchester, Liverpool, South Wales, and other industrial centres in the early part of June and delivered a series of stirring speeches to the local engineers and manufacturers, with the purpose of promoting the mobilization of the resources of each district. At Manchester he declared that we were the worst organized nation in the world for the war when it broke out, and that we had not so far concentrated half of our industrial strength on the problem of carrying through the conflict. The war, he impressed on his hearers over and over again, was a war of munitions, and for success all our available resources in men and machinery must be employed for turning out ammuni-

tion and equipment. A few days later, at Cardiff, he sketched the various methods of local organization that might be adopted. One was to set up one, two, or three national factories in the area to do nothing but turn out shot and shell. For this purpose either existing works might be utilized or un-occupied factories taken over. The latter alternative involved the installation of new machinery, and therefore presented the difficulty that, as the makers of machine tools were so busy that they could not give delivery for weeks or months, the factories had to be equipped by requisitioning plant from other works. This plan was, however, followed in

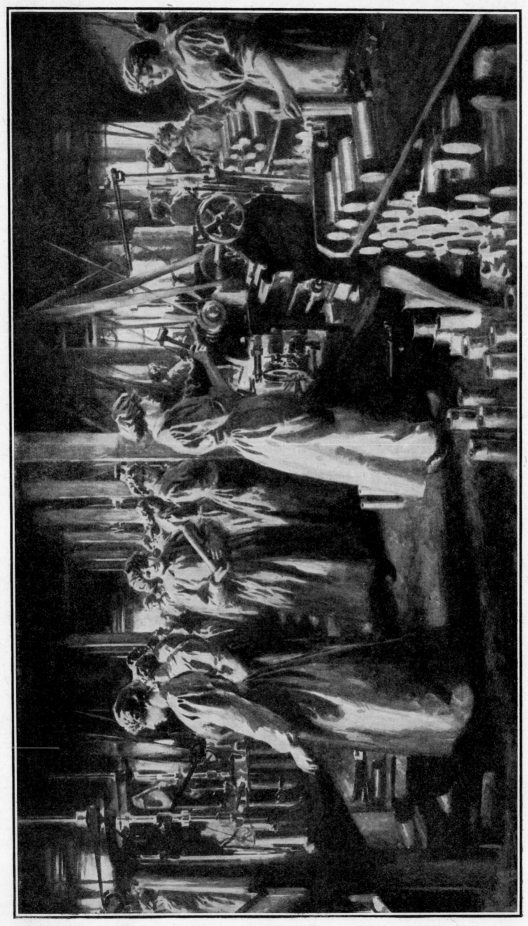

SCOTTISH GIRLS AT WORK IN A MUNITION FACTORY.

Leeds and other centres in Yorkshire. In Lancashire another method, similar to that which France had adopted with success, was preferred—the utilization of such factories and tools as were in existence, perhaps supplementing the equipment with some new machines but certainly with the indispensable gauges. A third plan, which combined the other two, was to select a few existing works and convert them into a kind of national arsenal with the aid of machinery obtained from other works, either voluntarily or under the Defence of the Realm Act, at the same time using other shops for parts of the work for which they were adapted. Whether or not the former works were able to carry out the manufacture of shells from the beginning, they would be designed to finish work sent them from the other factories, the equipment of which permitted only some of the necessary operations to be performed.

In the course of these speeches Mr. George laid stress on several other interesting and important matters. One was that there must be equality of sacrifice and contribution, so that one firm by concentrating its energies on its ordinary work might not be able to take advantage of another engaged in making shells and get the latter's custom and trade. Another was that the pilfering of men by one manufacturer from another must be stopped. The need for the trade unions to relax their regulations and to permit women and unskilled men to fill positions previously reserved to skilled men was, on the understanding that the safeguards established by trade union action before the war would be restored to their former position after the war so far as the Government was concerned, also insisted on, and the reservation was made with equal emphasis that the State control of labour must be for the benefit of the State and not for increasing the profits of any private organization.

These principles were embodied in the Munitions of War Act, the introduction of which was the first business of the Minister of Munitions after the scope of his office had been defined by an Order in Council published on June 18. In asking leave on June 23 to bring in the Bill he stated the problem as being to equal, and surpass, the tremendous production of 250,000 shells a day, which he was informed on good authority was being achieved by the Central Powers, and he enunciated the principles followed in organizing the new Munitions

Department. The first was that the help of some of the best business brains in the country must be called in to cope with the difficulties of establishing in a few weeks an organization which ordinarily would take years to build up. The second was that the different functions of the expert and the organizer must be recognized, the business of the latter being to make the best use of the brains of the former. Thirdly, the first-class business men having been secured, full scope must be given for their energies and they must be trusted. The services of the business men were to be utilized in

MACHINING A SHELL.

three ways—to organize the Central Office, to organize the resources of manufacturing areas locally, and on a Central Advisory Committee to secure dealing on right lines with the business community. Each man was allotted his own sphere—one to look after metals, another explosives, another machinery, another local organization, and so on.

Mr. George went on to explain the system of decentralization, which he had adopted because there was no time to organize a central department sufficiently strong and well-equipped to make the most of the resources of each district. His plan was to divide the country into munitions areas, each placed under a committee of management of local business men with local knowledge, and to establish in them offices attached to the headquarters of the

Ministry, where manufacturers could inspect specifications and samples. They were further helped by an expert engineer in each of the centres, with which also were associated representatives of the Admiralty and War Office.

The early operations of the Ministry of Munitions revealed a variety of difficulties. As regards materials, it was found that although some of them were abundant enough, others had to be husbanded carefully, while in the case of others, again, considerable expenditure was required in order to develop the supply at a later stage. It was necessary for the Ministry to be informed regularly and accurately of the stocks of raw and semi-manufactured metal in the country, and to that end monthly returns were required from all those concerned. Indications were noticed of supplies being held up in certain quarters, some contractors showing a tendency to delay the delivery of old and running contracts, apparently with the object of obtaining better prices at a later date. The adequate supply of high explosives involved the establishment of new factories, and as the raw material from which they are made is obtained from the distillation of coal, the supreme importance was recognized not merely of maintaining but of considerably increasing the output of the particular variety of coal required.

In regard to machinery, information had to be obtained regarding the amount and character of the plant in the country, so that it might be classified according to the kind of work for which it was suited. The Home Office at an earlier date had secured returns from most of the engineering firms showing what plant they had in their workshops and yards, but valuable as these were they did not give all the information needed, since they had not been compiled with a view to shell-making. More details were therefore asked for and were given with surprising celerity; indeed Mr. Lloyd George said he had never seen returns crowd in in such a way before.

The third, and perhaps the most serious, group of difficulties related to men. In the first place there was the old trouble of a shortage of skilled men, which was still accounting for many delays in delivery. It operated in two ways—partly by preventing existing machinery from being worked to its full capacity, and partly by delaying the erection of new machinery which was lying ready to be put

together. The second trouble, according to Mr. Lloyd George, was slacking and irregularity, which, although confined to a small minority of the men, often dislocated the work of a whole shop; its seriousness was abundantly demonstrated in a White Paper which was issued at the beginning of May. Thirdly, there was the existence of trade union rules and regulations which hampered the employment of women and the substitution, possible in many cases, of unskilled or partially trained men for skilled men, and which, in other ways, restricted the possible output, sometimes even to the extent of halving it. Some of these rules are written, but the "most devastating," to use Mr. George's phrase, were those which are unwritten and which limit the production by making it impossible for a man to put forth the whole of his strength without incurring the displeasure of his fellows.

Mr. Lloyd George recognized that it was vain to attempt to suspend these unwritten rules and practices by Act of Parliament, and that in regard to them the nation must rely upon the honour of the workmen; but provisions for removing or palliating others of his difficulties were inserted in the Munitions Act, which became law at the beginning of July. The first part was concerned with the settlement of labour disputes. Both strikes and lock-outs were declared to be offences punishable under the Act unless the difference over which they arose had been submitted to arbitration. This provision applied only to munitions workers; after many conferences Mr. Lloyd George had gained the assent of the engineers to it, but had not been able to persuade the miners to accept it. Power was, however, taken to extend it to any other work of any description by Royal Proclamation, if the existence or continuance of a difference was directly or indirectly prejudicial to the manufacture, transport, or supply of munitions of war.

The second part of the Act contained provisions designed to give the Government greater control, on the one hand, over the labour in establishments where munitions work was carried on, and, on the other hand, over the profits of their owners. Powers were given the Minister of Munitions to make an order declaring any munitions factory to be a "controlled establishment." In that case the owners had to pay over to the Exchequer

CUTTING A STEEL BAR INTO LENGTHS FOR SHELLS.

any excess of net profit over the amount divisible under the Act, which was fixed at an amount exceeding by one-fifth the standard amount of profit, the latter being the average profit made for the two financial years immediately preceding the outbreak of war ; and, subject to arbitration and with certain exceptions, they were forbidden to change the rate of remuneration of their employees except with the consent of the Minister. Rules, practices, and customs not having the force of law, which tended to restrict production or employment, were to be suspended, and any attempt to induce compliance with these was declared an offence ; but, on the other hand, the owner was deemed to have undertaken to carry out a series of provisions set out in a schedule to the Act, the purpose of which may be generally described as to secure after the war a return to the *status quo* as regards trade union rules.

Succeeding sections were designed to prevent employers from retaining workmen who had undertaken to work in controlled factories, and to stop the pilfering of men from one employer by another.

In the third and last part of the Act obligations were imposed on owners of factories to give any information the Minister might require about the number and character of their workmen and machines, and the nature of the work being carried out. The composition of the Munitions Tribunals, before whom any fine imposed for offences under the Act was recoverable, was also described. These tribunals were to consist of a person appointed by the Minister, sitting with two or some even number of assessors, of whom half were to be selected from a panel composed of representatives of employers and half from a panel composed of representatives of workmen, the Minister both choosing the assessors and constituting the panels. The tribunals were to be constituted by the Minister or the Admiralty as occasion might require.

Just about the time that the Munitions Act made its first appearance in Parliament a determined effort was made to remedy the shortage of men for munitions work by recruiting an army of volunteer skilled workers. A special department of the Ministry of Munitions, called the Munition Workers Enrolment Department, was constituted for the purpose, and the trade union leaders actively cooperated. The object was to get in a week 100,000 skilled men who were engaged on commercial work, not war contracts ; amateurs were not wanted. Offices were opened in hundreds all over the country, posters were displayed, handbills distributed, and large advertisements inserted in the newspapers. On the whole, employers, especially some of the largest, showed themselves favourable to the scheme, and did their best to promote it, but a certain number endeavoured to prevent their men from leaving them. To begin with, the response was declared to be up to official expectations, but at the end of the first week less than half the desired number had been obtained. The offices were, therefore, kept open for over a fortnight, and the final total when they were closed was 89,266. Unfortunately, however, investigation revealed that the larger proportion of the men were not available, some of them being, unknown to themselves, already employed on Government work, while many others

could not be moved without doing irreparable harm to the industrial system of the country. Arrangements were made for continuing the enrolment of these volunteers at the Labour Exchanges.

Another expedient adopted to swell the amount of labour in the factories consisted in bringing back skilled men from the Army. At first such men were invited to offer themselves, but many made no response, while others who were not in fact skilled engineers seized the opportunity of escaping from military life. The plan was therefore adopted of asking the engineering firms to furnish the names of their men who had enlisted, and inducing the War Office to bring such men back to the shops, when they had not gone abroad. When they were already at the front, or were on the point of leaving, their return was a matter of much greater difficulty.

The statement which Mr. Lloyd George made at the end of July in the House of Commons before it adjourned for its autumn holiday showed that his efforts were being rewarded with substantial progress, although motives of prudence restrained him from giving figures by which its amount could be definitely gauged. As regards the shortage of labour that was hindering the execution of contracts, he had the satisfaction of being able to state that he had provided the works engaged on munitions with 40,000 fresh workers, nearly half being skilled men, and that he was still pouring in labour supplies for the purpose not merely of utilizing machinery that had been lying idle, but also of increasing the number of night shifts worked. The effect was to expedite the fulfilment of contracts to an important extent—though the " yawning chasm between promise and performance " was not entirely bridged, the number of arches was considerably increased. But the tale he had to tell about trade union restrictions was far less satisfactory, for according to his information the output could be increased at least 25 per cent. if the men, as they had agreed to do, abandoned the rules and practices that throttled production. This statement was, of course, found very unpalatable in trade-union circles, but its justice was virtually admitted when seven weeks later a conference of the executives of unions concerned in munitions work agreed under his persuasion to pledge themselves to secure the suspension of the practices complained of, to assist in carrying

MUNITION WORKERS.
Steel ingot under a steam hammer.

out an investigation designed to ascertain the least possible amount of skilled labour needed to keep the machinery in the factories running for twenty-four hours each day, to promote the more extensive employment of semi-skilled and unskilled male and female labour in Government arsenals and controlled establish-

ments, and to help in the enrolment of men under the Munitions Volunteer Scheme and their transfer to any district where they were required.

At the end of July, 1915, in addition to the extension of existing factories for the manufacture of shells, sixteen national factories had been erected and were being provided with machinery and men. Further, an important new scheme was announced. As a result of conferences with the French authorities it was decided to set up ten more large national establishments, the labour for which was to be obtained partly by drawing on the new army of volunteer workers and partly by employing women. The experience of the armament firms was to be used in managing and equipping these new establishments and in providing them with staffs, but they were to belong to and be controlled by the Government. In organizing these new sources of supply it became apparent that there was an alarming shortage of machine tools. While the census, to which about 40,000 replies were received, proved that there was much machinery in the country which was not being used for Government work, it also revealed that the amount was quite inadequate for the programme adopted. In these circumstances it was decided to put all the great machine tool makers of the country under direct Government control, so that they might be able to concentrate their attention on increasing the amount of machinery available for munitions production, and a strong committee of the makers was constituted to direct their operations. In this connexion it may be recorded that the number of controlled establishments, which was 345 on August 6, and rose to 715 at the beginning of September, exceeded 1,000 in October, when the number of workpeople engaged on munitions production in such works and in Government establishments approached 1,000,000. At that time there were 18 cooperative areas, 20 national factories had been established, and steps were being taken to establish 11 others.

The fact that the decision to build the ten new factories just mentioned was preceded by consultation with France did not imply the initiation of any new policy so far as the relations between her and the United Kingdom were concerned. Immediately after the outbreak of war a Commission Internationale de Revitaillement was established by agreement with the French Government, with the objects of co-ordinating the purchase of munitions and other supplies by the two Governments, and of preventing harmful competition in the same markets and consequent inflation of prices; and subsequently the two Allies kept in touch with each other in matters that related to the production of munitions, Mr. Lloyd George, for example, having frequent conferences with his French counterpart, M. Albert Thomas. The latter, a prominent Socialist Deputy, became Minister of Munitions in France about the same time that Mr. Lloyd George was appointed to that position in England, and he had much to do with the measures taken by France in the early stages of the war to organize her industrial resources for the production of munitions. The success of those measures, to which reference has already been made, was undoubted—in April it was stated that the production of shells was 600 per cent. greater than had been thought necessary at the beginning of the war—but they did not suffice to meet all difficulties, and in time fresh efforts became necessary. The appointment of M. Thomas marked a new stage of advance, and from it dated a marked increase of output, through the mobilization of larger numbers of workmen and the erection and utilization of additional factories. The trade unions cooperated thoroughly, and strikes were unknown.

As regards Russia, her engineering and chemical industries, being less developed than those of France and England, she had to rely largely on outside supplies, yet she succeeded in increasing her internal production sevenfold in the first six months of the war. Some observers considered that there were no grounds for the apprehension of a shortage of shells which was felt in some quarters outside Russia, but they proved to be wrong, perhaps because they failed to take account of the possibility of incompetence, corruption and even treachery. The fall of Przemysl emphasized the necessity for a greater supply of munitions and spurred the country on to fresh efforts. A consultative Board, including representatives of the manufacturers and of the two Legislative Chambers, was created to stimulate and co-ordinate the participation of industries in war supply, and the manufacturers of Moscow led the way in mobilizing their resources for the production of munitions. In the latter part of the following August, when the output was stated to be twice as great as it was at the beginning of June, a decree was published reorganizing the administration of the War Office, General Bieliaeff, an Assistant Minister, becoming responsible for all preparatory work connected with orders and the actual supply of munitions to the Army in the field, and another Assistant

Tempering shells.
On right : Putting a shell into a lathe.

A view of a workshop where 305 mm. shells are made.
THE MANUFACTURE OF MUNITIONS IN FRANCE.

M. ALBERT THOMAS,
French Minister of Munitions.

Minister, General Lukumsky, for the actual carrying out of the orders by the Russian works, while M. Alexander Guchkoff, the " Russian Lloyd George," who was originally selected for the latter post, became head of the extra-Departmental Technical and Revision Committees.

Finally, before turning to a short description of the different kinds of ammunition, we may make a brief reference to the part taken by the Dominions in helping to meet the Empire's need for munitions. At the beginning of the war arrangements were made to take supplies from Canada, and a large number of factories in the Dominion were adapted for the purpose. At one time Canadian manufacturers seemed to think that insufficient demand was being made upon them, and that in placing orders preference was being given to the United States, where also many factories were busy and where Messrs. J. P. Morgan & Co. acted as the commercial agents of the British Government. It was explained, however, that no Canadian contracts were placed through Messrs. Morgan, and that practically all were arranged through the Shell Committee appointed by the Canadian Government. One of Mr. Lloyd George's first acts as Minister of Munitions was to ask Mr. D. A. Thomas, the Welsh coalowner, to represent and exercise the functions of the Munitions Department in both Canada and the United States. Mr. Thomas, of course, had to work in conjunction with Messrs. Morgan, but he was in a position to deal independently of them. In Australia great enthusiasm was shown in June for the proposal that the Commonwealth should manufacture munitions on a large scale, and, later, plans were initiated for the production of shrapnel by the State. India, too, joined in, and appointed a Superintendent of Munitions, who received many offers of help from the railways, private engineering firms and jute mills.

All ammunition used in firearms, whether for a rifle with a bore of less than one-third of an inch, or for the big 42 cm. (16·5 in.) gun which was one of Germany's surprise contributions to the war, consists of two parts—the projectile and the charge of powder which propels it from the barrel. For rifles and the smaller guns up to about 3-inch bore these two parts are commonly combined in one piece, which is loaded into the weapon at a single operation, but for larger sizes they are stored and transported separately, and are put into the gun one after the other. Ammunition of the first kind is known as " fixed " or "simultaneous loading," and that of the second as " separate loading."

The charge, which in modern military firearms consists of some variety of smokeless powder—in this country cordite—is contained in a cartridge, which may be of metal or of some woven fabric. Metal cartridges of brass are employed in British practice for rifles and for the smaller quick-firing guns. The objection to them in the larger sizes is that they become difficult to handle, and so lose their advantage of adding to the convenience and rapidity of loading ; moreover, they are expensive, although, especially with small guns, they can be used a considerable number of times, perhaps ten or twenty, if they are re-formed after each round. But they possess an important advantage in regard to " obturation " —that is, under the gas pressure developed by the burning of the charge they expand, and render the breech end of the gun gas-tight. This accounts for their employment by Krupp for big guns, even up to 12 inches, his wedge breech action presenting difficulties in the employment of other methods of obturation. Many arrangements have been devised to prevent the escape of gas at the breech. One of these that is largely used is the De Bange obturator, which consists of a ring-shaped canvas bag containing a mass of asbestos fibre and mutton suet strongly compressed by hydraulic power : this is inserted in the breech, and when the charge is fired the pressure of the gas forces it firmly against its seating, so that the passage of gas is prevented.

Non-metallic cartridge cases must not be made of material that is liable to smoulder, on account of the danger of premature ignition of the new charge when it is inserted. Hence materials like paper and canvas are avoided, and recourse is had to fabrics such as shalloon (made of long wool) and silk cloth (made of the refuse silk from the outside of the cocoons), which are free from this liability. In the case of cordite, which, as its name implies, is made up in the form of cord, a bundle of the required weight is taken, tied tightly together with silk, and placed in a bag of the selected material, which is then taped with silk braid. For large guns the charges are divided into fractions and made up into several cartridges, the purpose being not merely to facilitate handling but also to permit the use of reduced charges when required. The range of howitzers is some-

times altered by varying the amount of powder employed, and in this case what may be called the foundation of the charge consists of a bundle of cordite on one end of which is placed a ring of the same smokeless powder, the whole forming a mushroom-like object. Additional rings of cordite are then slipped over the stalk as may be necessary to make up the required weight.

Smokeless powder in a cartridge being rather difficult to ignite, a primer or igniter is inserted in the end of the cartridge to convey the flash from the " tube " or device employed

MAKING BASKET SHELL COVERS.
Inset : Russian shell of large calibre in case.

AFTER THE FRENCH 75 mm. GUNS HAD BEEN IN ACTION.
A collection of empty shell cases.

to fire the charge. In the case of large guns this " tube," which may be worked electrically or by means of a percussion cap, is inserted through the vent, and strictly forms part of the firing gear of the gun, not of the ammunition. In the larger Q.F. guns, for which a metal cartridge case is employed, an electric primer is screwed into the base of the case ; a percussion tube in an adapter can be similarly screwed in, should electrical firing be unavailable from any cause. In the fixed ammunition employed for the smaller guns and for rifles a percussion primer containing a chlorate mixture forms an integral part of the cartridge. There are two forms of electric tube, one with two long wires which can be joined up to the electric circuit, and the other or " wireless " form, in which the lock of the gun makes contact with an insulated disc in the head, the circuit being completed through the body of the tube and the metal of the gun and its mounting. The operation of the two is similar ; by the passage of the current a wire " bridge " of high resistance is heated to incandescence and fires the priming composition by which it is surrounded, the powder which fills the remainder of the tube being ignited in turn. The electric primer used for the larger Q.F. guns resembles the wireless tube. In percussion tubes the powder is fired by a percussion cap, which is struck by a brass striker. Another form of firing device is the friction tube, the powder in which is ignited by a roughened piece of copper wire being drawn sharply through the friction composition

in which it is embedded. This also is inserted in the vent, and the escape of gas is prevented by a small ball which is blown back and blocks the coned passage leading to the friction bar.

To leave the charge and come to the second component of ammunition, the projectile, the form of rifle bullet that remained orthodox for many years had a somewhat blunt, rounded nose, but later there was a growing realization of the advantages of a pointed nose, which offers less resistance to the air and gives a flatter trajectory. France was probably the first to use the pointed form, and Germany soon imitated her, producing in 1904 the S or Spitzer bullet, weighing 154 grains for the 7·9 mm. Mauser rifle and being projected from the muzzle with an initial velocity of 2,800 ft. a second. The British Mark VII bullet is of this type ; it weighs 174 grains for the ·303 (7·7 mm.) Service rifle, and has an initial velocity of 2,440 ft. a second, tubular cordite being employed for the charge. It has a hard lead core with a skin of cupro-nickel and a plug of aluminium under the nose. The length of the complete cartridge is 3·05 inches with this bullet, the same as with the older round-nosed bullet. The employment of projectiles weighing less than 400 grammes which are explosive or are charged with fulminating or inflammable substances was renounced by the Declaration of St. Petersburg, 1868, and reports of the use of rifle bullets of this kind should generally be treated with reserve. However, on April 17, 1915, *The Times* published an illustrated description of a composite bullet 8 mm. in diameter, which was one of a number captured by the Serbians from Austrian troops, and in which there was a chamber containing about 8 grains of a chlorate mixture which was arranged to be exploded on the bullet striking. The Mannlicher rifle employed by Austria, who acceded to the Declaration, has a bore of 8 mm. and the standard bullet for it weighs less than 16 grammes.

Of the projectiles used for larger weapons than rifles two main varieties may be distinguished—armour-piercing shot and shell which are intended to penetrate armour without breaking up, and shell which is intended to destroy men or material and which breaks up into pieces or emits a shower of bullets either on impact or when still in flight. Both these classes of projectile require to be provided with an arrangement to enable them to " take " the rifling of the guns from which they are fired—a function which in the rifle bullet is performed by the cupro-nickel envelope—and an effective device is found for the purpose in the " driving band " of copper introduced by Vavasseur. This band is forced by hydraulic presses into a groove cut towards the base of the shell, waved ribs being provided in the

groove to prevent the band from slipping round the body. The edges of the band are also undercut or dovetailed to keep it in place. This band as it is squeezed into the rifling not only causes the projectile to rotate and prevents the escape of gas, but also, owing to the resistance it offers to the forcing of the shell through the gun, gives time for the charge of powder to burn properly.

Modern armour-piercing shell is the result of the continual struggle between armour and projectile—a struggle in which now one now the other has gained the superiority. The plating of the first iron ships was found not to be proof against cast-iron projectiles, and accordingly a protection of wrought-iron armour was provided. This in turn was defeated by Sir William Palliser, who discovered that it could be pierced by a cast-iron shot the point of which had been hardened by being cast in an iron mould, whereby it was suddenly chilled. Then forms of armour were introduced against which the Palliser shot was ineffective, and the makers of projectiles turned to ordinary carbon steel and later to special steels containing nickel or chromium or both. One of their greatest triumphs was the discovery that

FRENCH SHELLS AT THE CREUSOT WORKS.

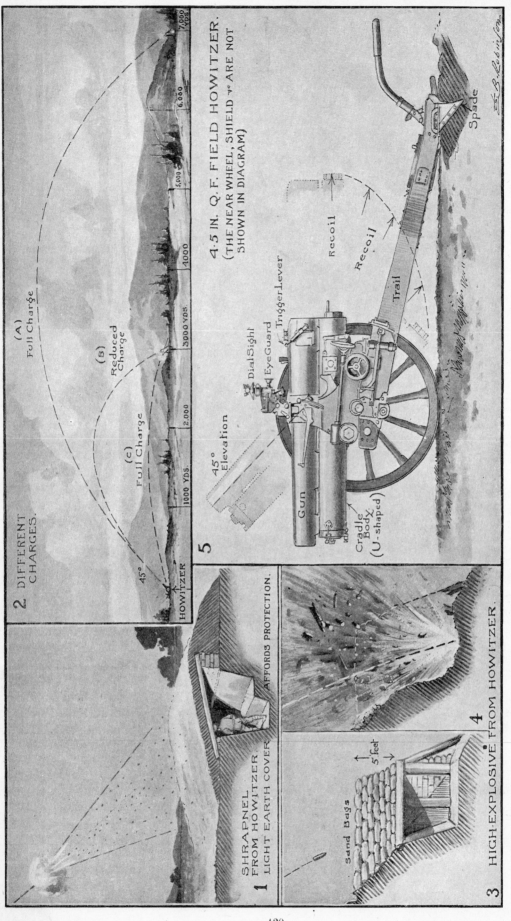

2 DIFFERENT CHARGES.

(A) Full Charge

(B) Reduced Charge

(C) Full Charge

45°

HOWITZER   1000 YDS.   2,000   3000 YDS.   4000   5,000   6,000   7,000 YDS.

4.5 IN. Q.F. FIELD HOWITZER.
(THE NEAR WHEEL, SHIELD ʸ ARE NOT SHOWN IN DIAGRAM)

45° Elevation

Dial Sight
Eye Guard
Trigger Lever
Gun
Cradle Body (U-shaped)
Trail
Recoil
Recoil
Spade

5

E. B. Robison.

1 SHRAPNEL FROM HOWITZER.

LIGHT EARTH COVER AFFORDS PROTECTION.

4 HIGH-EXPLOSIVE FROM HOWITZER.

3

Sand Bags

5 feet

A HOWITZER IN DIAGRAM SHOWING ITS GENERAL MECHANISM AND RANGES.

1. Light earth cover affords protection against shrapnel from howitzer. 2. (A) Represents a howitzer firing a full charge with 45 deg. elevation to 7,000 yards' range.
(B) Shows the trajectory at 3,000 yards with a reduced charge. (C) Shows a hit at 3,000 yards, with the full charge and reduced elevation. 3 and 4. Howitzer high-
explosive shells will go through the roof of a shelter covered with 5 feet of sandbags and burst inside the shelter. 5. The 4·5 in. Q.F. Field Howitzer.

the addition of a cap of soft steel much increases the penetrating power of a shell. In the course of experiments with a piece of compound armour plate it was found that a shell fired against the back or soft side was able to go right through, whereas when fired against the hardened and tempered front of the plate it was shattered and made only a comparatively small indentation. The inference was drawn that the fitting of a soft nose would enable a shell to pierce hardened armour and proved correct in practice. To give an example, showing the character of the results obtained, a projectile, weighing 100 lb. and having a velocity of 2,800 ft. a second, has perforated a 12-in. Vickers hardened steel plate, though an uncapped shell at the same velocity would penetrate only 3 inches.

There are two not very clearly distinguished types of armour-piercing shell. In one the design is directed towards securing the maximum of penetrative power, and the charge of high explosive is small, 2 or 3 per cent. of the weight of the complete projectile. In the other the penetrative power is less but a larger bursting charge is carried. In armour-piercing shot, of course, there is no charge of explosive. The results of experiments carried out on the carcase of the Jéna in 1909 confirmed the French naval authorities in the view that it was wrong to sacrifice perforating power in order to obtain a large charge of explosive and convinced them of the helplessness of shells containing 20 or even 10 per cent. of explosive against armour of any importance. But it would seem that the two requirements were to a great extent reconciled in the largest guns constructed for the British Navy in the period immediately preceding the outbreak of the war. Mr. Churchill, in introducing the Navy Estimates in March, 1914, stated that, whereas the 13·5-inch gun discharged a 1,400 lb. projectile, the 15-inch could hurl one weighing nearly a ton for a distance of 10 or 12 miles; that is, there was an increase of rather more than 30 per cent.—he was purposely vague on the point—in the weight of the projectile for an addition of 1½ inches to the calibre. This increase in the capacity of the shell, he asserted, produced results in far greater proportion in the explosive power, and the high explosive charge which the 15-inch gun could carry through and detonate inside the thickest armour afloat was very nearly half as large again as was the charge in the 13·5-inch. The

destructive effects claimed for these shells were vindicated when they were fired for the first time in warfare from the guns of the Queen Elizabeth in the bombardment of the Dardanelles.

In armour-piercing shells, in which penetrative power is of prime importance, the walls must possess enormous strength, and accordingly they are not only very thick, but are also made of the toughest and most resistant metal; on the other hand, in common shell the conditions are different, penetrative power becomes of minor account and chief importance is assumed by the explosive charge, for the damaging effect depends on the fragments formed by the bursting up of the walls, which

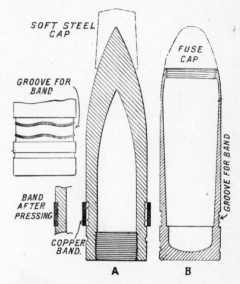

TWO TYPES OF SHELL.

The armour-piercing shell A has immensely thick and strong walls so that it may go through an armour plate without being broken up; the shrapnel B is only strong enough to withstand the explosion of the powder that projects the bullets from it.

accordingly only need be strong enough to withstand the shock of discharge without deformation and the shock of impact without breaking up. Cast-iron as a material for common shell fulfilled the first of these requirements so long as the guns had a comparatively low velocity, but as velocities increased steel had to be substituted. Cast-iron shells were also regarded as deficient in the second requirement, being apt to break up on impact before the fuse had time to act properly; the bursting charge was thus either ignited too late or not ignited at all, and in either case failed to carry out its function of hurling the fragments violently against the object of attack. Common

CAUGHT BY HIGH EXPLOSIVES.
The destruction of a German pontoon bridge in Northern France.

shell was filled with ordinary gunpowder, and owing to the comparatively feeble character of the explosion the pieces into which it was broken were somewhat large. They were projected mainly in and about the line of flight, and thus their effect was local; they were, however, capable of inflicting a good deal of damage on buildings and fortifications and on the unarmoured portions of ships, but were of little effect against troops.

Even before the war common shell had become practically obsolete, being superseded by what may be regarded as its lineal descendant, high explosive shell. The latter projectiles, indeed, are simply common shell of forged steel, filled with some high explosive such as lyddite and provided with arrangements to secure proper detonation of the charge. The superior power of the high explosive renders them much more effective instruments than common shell. The fragments into which they are broken are smaller and are thrown at high speed in every direction, while the blast or concussion in the air produced by the detonation of the charge sweeps away material in its path, men being killed at a considerable distance by the impact of the air wave without being touched by any fragment of the shell.

Shrapnel, the man-killing shell *par excellence,* was invented by an Englishman, Henry Shrapnel, in 1784, and improved later by Colonel Boxer. In its original form it was the spherical cast-iron shell of the period, having lead bullets mixed with the bursting charge, but it was defective in that the bullets were scattered in all directions when the shell burst. Boxer's improvement consisted in placing an iron diaphragm between the charge and the bullets, so that the flight of the latter was directed. When rifled guns came into use the shape of the shrapnel was changed and it was given an elongated form with an ogival nose. The bursting charge was placed in the base, separated by a diaphragm from the bullets which filled the body, while a tube down the centre conveyed the flash to the charge from the fuse in the nose. Substantially this remains the construction of modern shrapnel. The desideratum that the shell should contain as many bullets as possible while being strong enough to hold together on discharge and during flight could, however, be better fulfilled when cast-iron was displaced by steel, which permitted the walls to be made thinner. In this connexion it may be noted that so far as man-killing is concerned the bullets are regarded

GERMAN SHELL BURSTING IN THE ALLIES' TRENCHES IN FLANDERS.
In the foreground is a 150 mm. German shell which did not explode.

THE INTERIOR OF A SHRAPNEL SHELL.

A is the charge of powder which forces the bullets from the casing ; B the charge, exploded by the firing device E, which expels the shell from the gun.   The copper driving band is seen at C ; and D is the fuse head with timing apparatus.

as the only useful part of the projectile, and that the case is not intended to break up but to act as a gun propelling them from its mouth. After the charge has been fired in the air by the time-fuse which is fitted the bullets continue their flight for some distance in nearly the same direction as that in which the shell was travelling. The distance they travel depends on the velocity of the shell, though it may also be increased according to the strength of the black powder or high explosive bursting charge employed ; but at medium range they may cover a depth of some 350 yards with a high-velocity gun and about half that depth for one of low velocity. The greater depth is desirable in itself, but the high velocity required means a lighter projectile and the discharge of fewer bullets in a given time. As compared with earlier patterns of shrapnel, the number of bullets carried has also been increased by the expedient of making them smaller ; whereas they used to run from 18 to 34 in the pound the number per pound had increased to 45 or 50 in some field guns of about 3-inch calibre at the beginning of this century. For instance, in 1906 the bullets in the German 3·03-inch field gun shrapnel weighed 45 to the pound and numbered 300, while in the 2·95-inch guns of Italy and Belgium of about the same date they weighed 50 to the pound and numbered 360. The shells for the British 18-pounder (3·3-inch) contained 375 bullets weighing 41 to the pound. The effect of substituting steel for cast-iron in shrapnel may also be expressed in another way. When the latter was employed the bullets constituted about one-quarter of the total weight of the shell, whereas the use of steel enabled the ratio to be raised to about 50 per cent.

In order to secure accuracy of fire the gunner needs to be able to see the position where the burst occurs, and in certain conditions with the smaller shrapnel this is a matter of some difficulty. Accordingly to render the burst visible some smoke-producing device is employed. One method is to mix black powder with the bullets, and another, adopted in Russia, is to use a mixture of magnesium and antimony sulphide. In German shrapnel red amorphous phosphorus with gunpowder is included with the bullets and gives rise to dense white smoke. This inert form of phosphorus is by heating converted into the active yellow form, which is poisonous and has a highly injurious effect when it is carried into a wound by the bullet. On this account protests were raised, in the earlier stages of the war, against the German employment of phosphorus, but it should be noticed that the practice, however objectionable, had been followed, quite openly, years before the war started, and was not a device like asphyxiating gases introduced during the war.

For some years before the war attention had been paid to the production of a "universal shell," combining the characteristics of shrapnel and high explosive shell. It consists of an ordinary shrapnel body with the usual bursting or driving charge in the base, but in addition there is a second magazine in the head containing high explosive. When it is burst in the air by the time fuse, the flash is so arranged as not to affect the charge in the head, but ignites the base charge in the usual way and blows out the bullets, which are packed in the high explosive trinitrotoluene. Meanwhile the head continues its course until it strikes the ground or some hard object, and detonates on impact. If, however, the shell is burst by percussion, the high explosive in the head is detonated, and the fragments and bullets are blown out sideways, thus reaching men behind screens, etc. A sufficiently strong impact, as against a hard body, brings about the detonation of the trinitrotoluene among the bullets also, and the shell acts as a mine shell. An objection to universal shell regarded as shrapnel is that the number of bullets must be decreased. However, in a 14·3-pounder shell of this kind introduced by the Ehrhardt firm the bullets accounted for 42 per cent. of the weight of the fused shell, and in a similar projectile by Schneider for 43 per cent. The former contained 2·82 oz. of trinitrotoluene in the head, with 5 oz. among the bullets, and the latter 4·7 oz. in the head and 6·56 oz. among the bullets.

Before leaving the subject of shrapnel, reference may be made to two forms of projectile which resemble it—one because it is designed for a similar purpose, and the other because it is constructed on a similar principle. The first is case shot, which was obsolescent if not obsolete at the time of the war. It consisted of a cylindrical case of sheet iron containing sand shot or mixed metal balls. The envelope was so weak as to break up at the

muzzle of the gun and release the bullets, but not strong enough to " set up " when it was discharged, as in that case it would have taken the rifling, and the spin would have given the bullets great lateral dispersion with a small range to the front. Essentially a close-quarter projectile, it was of little use with field guns for ranges exceeding about 400 yards, though with larger guns it was effective up to about 1,000 yards. Star shell, the purpose of which is to give light, is made on the same lines as shrapnel, cylinders composed of light-giving composition being substituted for the bullets. It is designed to burst high in the air, the burst igniting and scattering the stars, which emit a bright light as they fall slowly to the ground.

In the preceding account of shells reference has frequently been made to fuses. These are devices employed in order to ensure the ignition of the explosive in the shell as and when required, and great variety is to be found in the details of their construction, though the principles upon which their design is based are comparatively few. Modern fuses may be divided into two kinds—percussion and time; they are placed in either the nose or the base of

SHELL READY TO BE LOADED INTO A FRENCH 220 mm. GUN.

SIXTEEN FORMS OF SHELL IN USE IN THE FRENCH ARMY.

the shell, but some varieties are not available for the one position and some not for the other.

The simplest form of percussion fuse is the direct action, the working of which depends entirely on the contact of the shell with the object struck. When the fuse comes up against the object a needle is forced in upon a mass of detonating composition, the explosion of which in turn explodes the magazine of the fuse and thence the charge of the shell ; by interposing a column of powder between the detonating material and the magazine the ignition of the charge may be delayed for a short time after impact, so that, for instance, the shell may have time to penetrate a piece of armour and explode behind it. No change takes place in fuses of this kind until the shell strikes, but in others the discharging of the gun prepares the fuse for action, and the action is completed when the shell strikes. In one fuse of this latter type the preparation is effected by the gases given off by the propelling charge of the gun. Pressing on a plate in the bottom of the fuse, they force it upwards, when a spindle attached to it releases a centrifugal bolt. This bolt in turn, under the rotation of the shell, releases a pellet or block of metal which is free to move forwards and backwards in a chamber, though its forward movement is restrained by a spring. When the shell strikes, the pellet is

carried forward against the resistance of the spring, and a needle on it detonates a cap. This fuse can be fitted only in the base. In others, which may be either base or nose, the freeing of the pellet is effected by the shock of the discharge of the gun, and the shock of impact throws the pellet with its needle against the detonator.

The purpose of time fuses is to enable a shell to be burst at a predetermined time after it has been fired, or, which is really the same thing, since the velocity of its flight is known, at a predetermined distance from the gun. They begin to act with the discharge of the gun, when a pellet with needle is set back on a detonating cap, as in the last percussion fuses mentioned. The cap ignites a train of slow-burning composition which is laid in two channels running round the inside of the fuse, and which ultimately leads to the magazine. The time of explosion is hastened or delayed by cutting out more or less of this composition, one of the channels consisting of a recessed ring which is made movable, so that a longer or shorter portion of its contents is put in the line of travel of the fire. The outside of the ring is graduated in time, and a safety position is provided in which communication between the detonator and the magazine is entirely shut off. A percussion fuse is commonly combined with the time fuse, the intention being to secure the explosion of the shell by impact should it hit the ground or other target sooner than was allowed for in the time setting.

As an account has already been given (Vol. IV., p. 371 *et seq.*,) of the grenades and other hand-thrown missiles used in trench warfare, reference need be made here only to the bombs dropped from airships and aeroplanes. These are of two kinds—explosive and incendiary. One that was dropped in Paris by a German airman in May, 1915, may be taken as an example of the former, though the mechanical features of its design were but lightly esteemed by those who picked it up unexploded. It consisted of a cast-iron cylinder rather more than $4\frac{1}{2}$ inches long and about $1\frac{3}{4}$ inches in diameter, with rounded pieces attached at each end. The top carried a cone or vane of thick fabric intended to make the cylinder maintain itself in a vertical position during its fall. The interior was filled with trinitrotoluene, and the walls were weakened with external grooves to aid fragmentation. The exploding mechanism was contained in a brass tube about $2\frac{1}{2}$ inches in length fixed to the lower end of the cylinder, and consisted substantially of a striking rod which was

pushed up as its bottom end hit the ground or a building, a needle at its top end being then forced into the detonating material embedded in the high explosive of the bomb proper. A heavy weight on the rod, aided by a spring, guarded the needle from being brought into premature contact with the detonator.

German incendiary bombs picked up in England and salved in a more or less damaged condition—one had been promptly dropped into a bucket of water—consisted, in one form, of a conical vessel about 10 inches in diameter at the base and over a foot in height. The body was made of metal pierced with holes and having an outer covering of an inflammable resinous material bound round with inflammable rope, which when ignited gave out a pungent smoke. Inside there was a mass of thermit, and generally some phosphorus in the base cup, while, as an additional luxury, celluloid chips and a little petrol were occasionally added. The igniting device and a handle were placed at the top. Thermit is the commercial name given to a patented mixture of granulated aluminium with some metallic oxide. When this mixture is ignited at one place a chemical reaction is started and spreads through the whole mass, the aluminium taking

A "JACK JOHNSON" BURSTING.

A FRENCH LAND-MINE EXPLODING UNDERNEATH A SECTION OF GERMAN TRENCHES.

the oxygen from the oxide, the metal of which is left in a molten condition owing to the very high temperature, of the order of 5,000° F., that is produced. German enterprise is commonly credited with the development and application of this reaction to practical purposes, such as welding tramway rails and repairing broken castings ; but, in fact, the first steps in this direction were taken in England.

After the foregoing survey of the different kinds of military ammunition we may turn to the engineering methods and processes employed for the production of the metal parts of shells and cartridges. Here only a general account is possible, for more than one reason. In the first place, a detailed description of all the methods adopted would be of interest only to professional engineers and would be unintelligible to anyone else. In the second place, an inordinate amount of space would be required, for it would be necessary to deal not only with the standard methods in use before the war began and with the various new arrangements which the makers of machine tools and other plant designed and brought forward, but also with the great number of what, without any disrespect, may be termed makeshift methods which hundreds of engineering manufacturers were forced to adopt in order to utilize their works. One of the most interesting features of the situation created by the war was indeed the manner in which plant and machinery designed for the manufacture of articles of peaceful commerce was adapted to the production of munitions. Examples might easily be multiplied, but three may be given from the western side of the Atlantic : one company whose normal occupation was the production of compressed air machinery was able to turn out large quantities of shrapnel with the addition of only one machine tool to its equipment ; another in the course of a few months transformed its bridge and bridge girder shops into a shell factory ; and the third made an arsenal out of works specially equipped for building railway locomotives and rolling stock.

The heaviest engineering operations in shell manufacture are those involved in the formation of the body or casing, and many of them can be performed in a variety of ways, sequences and groupings. The aim of the following account is to give a general idea of the character of the work and its results, and though it refers

mainly to the 18-pounder 3·3-in. shrapnel, it also applies in most respects to the larger calibres of the same type. Shrapnel shells are of special interest in that they possess a number of parts which are not required in armour-piercing and high explosive shells, but apart from these, and with due allowance for differences arising from size and function, the manufacture of the latter is broadly similar.

The 18-pounder shrapnel shell may be made from a solid bar of steel which is cut to a length about equal to that of the finished body and bored out internally by a drill, but forgings are generally regarded as preferable because, among other reasons, a smaller weight of metal

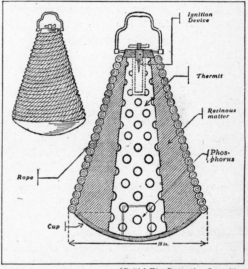

[*British Fire Prevention Committee.*

A GERMAN INCENDIARY BOMB.
The external appearance is seen on the left. The interior contains thermit, a chemical mixture which when ignited produces a quantity of molten metal at a very high temperature.

—less than one half—is required. In the latter case the shell begins as a billet or block of steel $3\frac{1}{2}$ inches in diameter, and of a length perhaps half as much again. The first operation is to pierce this block and form it into a deep cup. For this purpose, after being heated in a furnace to about 2,000° F., it is quickly put into a die, and a shaped punch is forced into it by a hydraulic or power press. The result is that the metal is squeezed out round the punch, and when the block is removed from the die it possesses a round hole in its centre extending nearly to its base, and is lengthened to about $7\frac{1}{2}$ inches. The next process is to draw it out to still greater length ; this again is effected in a press by means of shaped punches and dies working on the heated metal, and it emerges, about 10 or 11 inches long, in a shape bearing a recognizable resemblance to its final form, though without a curved end. How close the resemblance should be is to some extent a matter of opinion. Some are in favour of making the dimensions approximate as nearly as possible to those required in the finished shell, so as to reduce to a minimum the amount of metal left to be cut away by the machine tools subsequently, while others hold that the more economical plan is to be content with a somewhat rough approximation to the final size in the forging process, and to leave a comparatively large amount of metal to be dealt with in the lathes.

However this question is settled, the forging has next to undergo a series of machining operations. After it has been cut to a length of $9\frac{7}{8}$ inches the body is rough-turned to size and the taper formed, the base end finished, the powder chamber bored out in the base, the nose end turned, and the recess with its waved ribs cut near the base to receive the copper driving band. At this stage in its production a number of its dimensions are gauged, and if it passes the ordeal satisfactorily it undergoes a heat treatment, which is a most important part of its manufacture if it is to behave properly when it is actually being fired out of the gun. The diaphragm that separates the bullets from the powder charge, the seat for which has already been prepared, is next dropped inside the shell, and the following operations include closing up the nose to the required curve and diameter, turning it, and cutting in its interior a screw thread to take the fuse socket. The closing up is performed by heating the nose to a dull red heat and forcing a coned die over it by means of a press. After this the body, and especially the nose, are finished either by turning in a lathe or by grinding, the latter being the newer method. The copper driving band is then slipped over the base of the shell, forced by some form of press into the groove already prepared for it, and turned to its final shape.

This completes the machining operations on the case itself, but a number of accessory parts remain to be added before the shell is ready for delivery. In the first place, the tin box which holds the charge of powder has to be placed in the powder chamber below the diaphragm. As the diaphragm was put into the shell at an earlier stage, before the closing-up process, because its diameter is too large to permit it to pass the nose after the closing in of the latter, the tin box has to be jerked into position below it, and the operation requires some little dexterity. After it has been carried out and the two pieces have been driven home, the brass tube that is to convey the flash from the fuse in the head to the powder is screwed into a hole in the diaphragm, through which it protrudes into a hole in the upper part of the powder box. The next step is to fill the shell with bullets, which, by the turning of a tap, are run in from a receptacle like water. The shell is meanwhile shaken by a mechanical device so that they may settle down properly, or sometimes they are rammed into place. To prevent them from moving and to fill up the interstices between them, molten rosin is poured in, and immediately afterwards the shell is weighed. The margin of error allowed from the standard weight is very small, but a slight deficiency may be made up by adding buckshot. The top of the powder tube is next soldered to the fuse socket, which must be screwed in before the rosin has set, the superfluous solder cleared away, and the tube cleaned out if necessary. A protecting plug, which will be removed when the fuse body is inserted, having been screwed into the fuse socket, the shell undergoes its final inspection, and if it passes muster is painted and packed with others into boxes for transport. The duty of putting the charge of powder in place does not fall on the manufacturer of the shells.

As regards the manufacture of the accessory parts of the shrapnel, the powder chamber is formed of heavy tin plate in two pieces. The lower cup is cut out and formed to shape by means of a punch and die at a single operation, the rim being afterwards trimmed in a lathe. For the top part a blank is cut out from the sheet, its edges turned down, a hole pierced in the centre, and a small flange drawn round the hole, four operations being required. The two parts are then assembled and soldered together. The diaphragm, which in the finished shell is placed between the powder cup and the bullets, is made from a long strip of steel nearly half an inch thick. A circular disc is first punched out, and in subsequent operations, for which, as for the first, the metal is heated, is squeezed in dies to the required shape. The hole in the centre, into which the powder tube screws, is then drilled out, tapped and finished on lathes. Finally inspection follows, the requirements as to dimensions being fairly severe. At the other

THE GRENADE IN HAND-TO-HAND FIGHTING.

or nose end of the shell the fuse socket and plug are both forged at a dull red heat from a casting of brass alloy, and finished and threaded in a series of operations, which, like many of those required for the casings of the shells, are performed in groups on machines which are provided with a number of tools mounted in such a way that one of them after another may be brought to bear on the piece without

the latter being removed from the machine. The operations required for the production of the various parts of the fuse head are conducted on similar principles.

The bullets used in shrapnel are half an inch in diameter and usually spherical, though for the United States Army they are made with six flat faces with the object of enabling them to be packed more readily in the casing. They

NAVAL AMMUNITION.
Top.—Hoisting cordite charges for 12-inch guns.
Bottom. — Lowering a 12-inch shell into the magazine.

are composed of lead hardened with antimony, and may either be cast in iron moulds or struck between dies from a long thick wire fed forward continuously. For making the wire, molten metal is forced out from a cylinder through a die by a plunger; in another method the metal is used cold and is squeezed out of a hole of the required diameter by means of powerful hydraulic machinery. Any fins that may be formed on the bullets are removed by tumbling them together in a machine, when the rubbing of one upon another renders them quite smooth. Considerable exactitude is required in the manufacture, as 41 of them must weigh 1 lb., with an allowable error of only one dram.

The shells for the 18-pounder gun are fixed at one end of brass cartridge cases which contain the propelling charge and the arrangement for igniting it, and these are made by a series of operations consisting for the most part of cold-drawings. Brass composed of two parts of copper to one of zinc is found the most suitable material, because it possesses great strength and ductility, and when properly annealed will endure the maximum amount of work without rupture. It cannot be worked hot, and as the cold-drawings harden it and make it brittle its ductility has to be restored after each by annealing carried out at a temperature of about 1,200° F. The large number of drawings required is due to the fact that the metal will withstand only a certain amount of deformation without developing defects, and an attempt to form the case at a single operation would cause splitting.

The blank from which a 3·3-inch cartridge case is made is a disc about 6¼ inches in diameter, punched from a sheet of brass rather more than one-third of an inch thick, and it is gradually transformed into a cylinder about 11½ inches long in its final form and having the metal in its head, which has to bear an enormous pressure when the charge is fired, at least as thick as the original disc. In the case of a cartridge for a 6-inch gun the original disc is 14¼ inches in diameter and two-thirds of an inch thick, and in the course of manufacture it is drawn out to a length exceeding 42 inches. When an 18-pounder cartridge case is being made the first operation is to form the blank, in one or two stages, into a cup about 4 inches in diameter by pressing it into a die by means of a punch under a hydraulic pressure of from 1,000 to 1,500 lb. to the square inch. After the cupping, or after each cupping if there are two, it is annealed and then pickled in dilute sulphuric acid to remove scale. Six drawing or extending operations follow, carried out with dies and punches under great pressures, the effect of each being to make the brass cylinder a little narrower and a great deal longer, until after the last drawing it is less than 3¾ inches in diameter and over 13 inches long. In larger cartridges the number of drawings is greater. The sequence of drawings is interrupted at one or two points in order that the head may be indented—that is, have a small boss formed on its interior face for the primer, for which purpose it is squeezed between a punch having a recess similar to the boss that is to be formed and a die with a corresponding projection. After being trimmed to length it is next " headed." This operation, which is done in one or more stages, thickens and hardens the metal at the closed end, at the same time spreading it to form a narrow external flange. Very high pressures are required, and again the head is squeezed between a die and punches of suitable contours. In tapering, the cases are forced between dies of hardened steel, which in two or more operations reduce the diameter of the open end to 3⅜ inches, and complete the gradual tapering of the case back to the head. A series of machining operations on the two ends, including the formation of a hole for the primer, completes the case.

The cartridge cases for rifle ammunition are solid-drawn by methods similar to those described above, as also are the envelopes of their bullets, though the number of drawings required is smaller. The ordinary bullet consists of a lead core enclosed in an envelope or case composed of an alloy containing about 85 per cent. of copper with 15 per cent. of nickel. In making the cases blanks are cut from a long strip of metal at the rate of some 300 a minute, and are then cupped and drawn. The noses of

FRENCH INFANTRYMAN
Throwing a Hand-Grenade into the German Trenches.

the cases are given their proper shape in presses, and the cores are inserted automatically by machinery and pressed home. In order that the bullets may be held securely in the cartridge cases, they are grooved or " cannelured," the groove being rolled as they are carried in a rotating wheel past a stationary segment. The slight distortion which is produced by this operation is corrected by pushing them through dies, which restore them to their proper size. The cases are made by a process similar to that described in connexion with shrapnel bullets, being swaged to shape between punches and dies from a wire composed of 30 parts of lead with one of tin, and formed by squirting.

Although for some reason or other the part taken by the chemical industry in producing the ammunition required for the war did not gain so much public recognition, it was quite as important as that played by the engineering manufacturers. A shell when it leaves the hands of the engineer is merely an inert mass

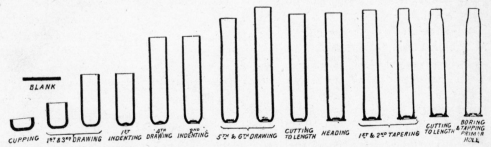

BLANK

CUPPING 1ST & 3RD DRAWING 1ST INDENTING 4TH DRAWING 2ND INDENTING 5TH & 6TH DRAWING CUTTING TO LENGTH HEADING 1ST & 2ND TAPERING CUTTING TO LENGTH BORING & TAPPING PRIMER HOLE

THE LIFE HISTORY OF A BRASS CARTRIDGE CASE.
Starting as a flat disc of metal, it is gradually drawn out and shaped by machines until it assumes the final form, ready to be loaded.

GERMAN 42 cm. GUN AND AUSTRIAN HOWITZER.

of metal, useless for the purpose it is intended to serve until it is, as it were, vivified by the substances which the chemist provides to drive it from the gun and rend it into fragments when it reaches its objective ; and the labour which the engineer bestows on fashioning it, his unremitting attention to the quality and treatment of the metals which compose it, his huge power-presses, his batteries of complicated machine tools, the delicate gauges which enable him to turn out his work true to the desired dimensions within a minute fraction of an inch, would all be wasted and unavailing were they not supplemented by the efforts of the chemist. An account of the nature and production of explosives must, therefore, form an essential part of a description of the manufacture of ammunition.

The explosives used in connexion with the projectiles fired from firearms are divided into the two broad classes of propellants and disruptives, according as they are required to force the projectile from the gun or to cause it to burst violently after it has been fired. Yet no definite line of demarcation can be drawn between the two classes ; indeed, the substances that compose the modern smokeless powders used as propellants act as disruptives

under certain conditions. An explosive is a chemical compound or mixture of compounds that is capable of undergoing a chemical reaction which sets free large volumes of heated gas, and the rapidity with which this reaction is completed determines whether the substance is to be called a propellant or a disruptive. When the reaction proceeds quite slowly it is no more than combustion ; at a quicker rate it becomes explosion and the substance in which it occurs may be regarded as a propellant ; while at the quickest rate, when it is completed almost instantaneously throughout the mass, it is detonation, and the action is disruptive, corresponding to a " high explosive." A rod of cordite, for example, ignited by an ordinary match, burns quietly and steadily in the open, giving one of the most beautiful yellow flames known to chemists, without smoke and without solid residue ; while a mass of the same powder exploded under the conditions that obtain in a gun projects a heavy shell with an initial velocity of half a mile a second. Similarly, a flake of gun-cotton burns quietly in the open, but if the reaction is started by means of a charge of mercury fulminate a dry, compressed mass of it detonates with a velocity of 18,000 ft. a second. The rapidity of the reaction depends on such factors as the chemical nature of the explosive, its physical conditions, the conditions under which it is burnt (e.g., whether in the open or confined), and the methods of firing employed, and it may be started in a variety of ways, as by heat, friction, an electric spark or current, percussion, or the shock from another explosion.

The propellant adopted in both the British Army and Navy is cordite, which is a mixture of nitroglycerine and gun-cotton, with a little vaseline or mineral jelly, and one of its most remarkable features is that, though both of its components are so violent, in their ordinary condition, that they cannot be utilized for artillery purposes, yet the product of their union is extraordinarily docile and amenable. Means have indeed been found, after many disastrous attempts, to moderate the explosion of gun-cotton in such a way that it can be used in firing guns, and it forms the basis of the nitro-cotton powders adopted by many continental Powers ; but nitroglycerine remains untamed so far as guns and shells are concerned, except

as regards cordite and similar powders. The advantage of cordite as compared with nitro-cotton powders not containing nitroglycerine is that, weight for weight, it yields more energy, so that smaller charges are required to do the same work. Accordingly the powder chambers of the guns can be made smaller and less magazine space is required. Considerations of this kind have led to the employment of nitro-glycerine powders closely resembling cordite for German and Austrian naval guns.

Cordite as originally devised by Sir Frederick Abel and Sir James Dewar about 1890 contained 58 per cent. of nitroglycerine, 37 per cent. of gun-cotton and 5 per cent. of mineral jelly, but as the result of experience in the South African War a modified form known as " Cordite M.D." was introduced, containing 35 per cent. of nitroglycerine and 60 per cent. of gun-cotton with the same amount of mineral jelly, which has a great value in preserving the stability of the powder. The advantage of the modified cordite is that it causes less erosion in the barrels of the guns. In making it the

NATURAL MUNITIONS.
Austrians rolling rocks and boulders down the mountains upon Italian troops in the Alps.

A BRITISH ADVANCED OBSERVATION POST.
Watching the effect of shells exploding over the German trenches.

proper proportions of dried gun-cotton and nitroglycerine are roughly mixed together and placed in an incorporating machine with the addition of acetone to act as a solvent and promote gelatinization. Subsequently the mineral jelly is added, and when all these ingredients are thoroughly mixed together the resulting product, known as "cordite dough," is removed from the machine. The next operation is to form it into cords varying in diameter from 1 to 5 mm. or more. For this purpose it is placed in a steel cylinder having at one end a hole of the required size, through which it is forced by a plunger worked by mechanical or hydraulic power. Before reaching the hole it has to pass through a filter, which prevents any small pieces of foreign substances such as sand or bits of wood or metal from reaching the die. The cord which issues from the press is either cut up into lengths or, in the smaller diameters, wound upon reels, and then taken to heated rooms, where it is freed from acetone and any moisture that it may contain. It is desirable that the drying process be slow, and the time required normally varies from a few days for the smaller sizes to several weeks for the larger ones. The acetone that is driven off is carried away by a current of air passing through the rooms and recovered by a chemical process so that it may be used over again.

Different batches of the same size of cords are next blended, the object being to secure uniformity and neutralize any slight differences that may arise from the raw materials or in the process of manufacture. Finally the cordite is packed in wooden boxes for transport. Various tests are applied, including heat tests intended to determine its capability of keeping without undergoing alterations in its chemical or ballistic properties.

Of the two main ingredients of cordite, nitroglycerine is a heavy oily liquid of a pale yellow colour and having a pungent aromatic flavour. It is made by the action of a mixture of strong nitric and sulphuric acids on glycerine, which is obtainable from most animal and vegetable fats and oils. In one process the acids are contained in a lead tank and the glycerine is injected by compressed air, which is also used to agitate the contents. The contents are kept cool by cold water circulated in lead pipes. The temperature is carefully watched, and should it be found impossible to keep it below a certain point, indicating decomposition and danger of explosion, the contents are quickly run off into a drowning tank containing cold water. When the action is complete the charge is run into another lead tank, when the nitroglycerine gradually separates and floats on the surface of the acids, whence it is removed through a side tap. In a later process the nitroglycerine is allowed to separate in the tank in which it is made, and waste acid is made to enter the bottom of the vessel, gradually raising the level of the contents till the floating nitroglycerine flows out by a pipe at the top. This arrangement dispenses with stop-cocks, the friction of which introduces an element of danger. The nitroglycerine is then washed repeatedly with soda solution to remove any traces of acid and with water only to remove the alkali, and is finally filtered.

Gun-cotton, the second component of cordite, is also made by the aid of a mixture of the strongest nitric and sulphuric acids acting on cotton waste. Chemically it is usually described as trinitrocellulose, and accordingly it may be made from anything containing cellulose. But the point to be remembered in connexion with the agitation which ended in cotton waste and yarn being declared contraband in August 1915 is that, though many materials have been tried, none has been found to be so satisfactory as the waste, or to yield quite the same quality of trinitrocellulose. For instance, cotton that has been strongly bleached or mercerized takes up less nitrogen and is more difficult to render stable. It follows that gun-cotton made from substitutes such as wood must at least be different from, and almost certainly inferior to, that made from cotton waste, and that powder containing it must give different results when

used in a gun, all the calculations for which are based on the assumption that the product from cotton waste is to be employed.

In the process of manufacture the cotton waste is picked over to remove impurities, teased in a machine and dried in hot air. For the actual nitration there are several processes. In that devised by Abel a charge of 1¼ lb. is immersed in the acids for five or six minutes and then after being squeezed is placed in an earthenware pot, where it remains for twenty-four hours while the nitration is completed. When the cotton is taken out it is put into centrifugal machines which remove much of the acid, and is subsequently washed in abundance of fresh water. In another process developed in Germany it is charged into perforated iron baskets which are rotated in the acid bath by a centrifugal machine. In a still newer arrangement it is pushed below the surface of the acids contained in a large earthenware pan, and a layer of water is run in over them ; when nitration is finished the acids are allowed to run out slowly while an equal quantity of water is distributed over their surface, ultimately running through the gun-cotton, which is left containing only a little acid. It has next to be freed from various impurities which if not removed would render it unstable, and for this purpose it undergoes a number of successive boilings extending over many hours. Pulping follows, carried out in water that is constantly

GERMAN GAS SHELLS COLLECTED BY THE FRENCH AFTER A BATTLE.

FRENCH SOLDIERS
Wearing metal masks to protect them from the
poisonous gases used by the Germans.

renewed, by a beating engine which breaks down
the fibres of the cotton, so that grit and other
impurities are set free. The pulp is next
washed several times in large tanks or
" poachers," continually agitated by a paddle-
wheel, in which also different batches are
mixed to secure uniformity of product. After
being fished out of the poachers the pulp is
lightly compressed into cylinders three inches
in diameter, in which form it is employed for
making cordite ; but if it is wanted for use in
mines or torpedoes it is moulded into slabs
under hydraulic pressure of 5 or 6 tons to the
square inch. Such slabs of wet gun-cotton
can be sawn or turned in a lathe, and are not
inflammable, so that they can be stored with
safety, yet they can be detonated with the aid
of a primer of dry gun-cotton. The hole to
receive the mercury fulminate detonating tube
which is necessary for this purpose is bored in
the primer before it is dried.

The fibrous structure of cotton is not sufficiently destroyed in the ordinary process of
making gun-cotton to permit the latter to be
used as a propellant, and no matter how
strongly it is compressed the minute tubes of
the fibres convey the igniting flame into the
interior of the mass and cause extremely rapid
combustion of the whole charge, the result
being, not the progressive burning required,

but an almost instantaneous production of great
volumes of gas which strain the gun without
giving much velocity to the projectile. No
success in utilizing gun-cotton as a propellant
was therefore obtained until it was found that
the original structure of the cotton can be
destroyed by gelatinizing the gun-cotton with
the aid of a solvent, so that it burns regularly
from the surface. It is on this principle that
the nitro-cotton powders used by Germany and
other countries are made. They are composed
either of true gun-cotton (trinitrocellulose) or
of collodion cotton (dinitrocellulose), which is
less highly nitrated, or of a mixture of the two
varieties.

We now come to two substances used solely
as high explosives—picric acid and the still
more notorious trinitrotoluene, variously known
as trotyl, trinol, tolite, trilit, and T.N.A. Both
are obtained ultimately from coal. The former,
trinitrophenol, is made by the nitration of carbolic acid, a product of the fractional distillation of coal tar ; the latter by the nitration of
toluene, a hydrocarbon contained in the crude
benzol also distilled from coal tar and washed
out from coal gas. Picric acid is the older of
the two. It was introduced into the French
service as a high explosive for shells in 1886
by Turpin, whose melinite, so called from its
honey-like colour, was in its final form simply
the fused acid. When the news of Turpin's
shells reached this country the nature of the
substance was soon realized, and after experiments at Lydd it was introduced into the
British service as lyddite, poured directly into
the shells in a molten condition. It can be made
and transported without danger, is very stable,
insensitive to percussion, and not liable to be
exploded by the shock of discharge of large
guns. It is extremely powerful with thorough
detonation, but for that a very strong detonator
is required. One of its drawbacks is that its
melting point is rather high, and another is that
in contact with metals it forms salts which in
some cases are very sensitive to heat, percussion
and friction ; for this reason the interiors of
shells filled with it are coated with varnish, and
in the course of manufacture it is carefully kept
from contact with metallic surfaces.

T.N.T., on the other hand, has a low melting
point, does not attack metals, and is very
stable. It is poured into shells in the molten
state like picric acid, but is not quite so powerful. The practice of compressing it in the
shells has given rise to serious accidents in

Germany, and has the further disadvantage that it increases the difficulty of detonation. Owing to the fact that the explosive does not contain within itself sufficient oxygen for complete combustion, the bursting of T.N.T. shells is accompanied by great volumes of heavy dense smoke ; hence such appellations as " Black Marias," " Jack Johnsons " and " Coal Boxes " given them by our soldiers.

It may have been noticed that the chemical names of the explosives which have been described all contain the word " nitro," showing that nitrogen is a constituent of each, although it is not to be found in the original materials— glycerine, cotton, carbolic acid and toluene— from which they are made. Now nitrogen accounts for roughly four-fifths of the air we breathe, and is therefore an extremely abundant substance ; but unfortunately the chemist cannot make much use of it in the form in which it exists in the atmosphere, because it is so inert as to refuse to take part in his operations. But it is more accommodating when it is already " fixed " or combined with some other element, and the combination which is generally best suited to his needs as regards the manufacture of explosives is nitric acid, one of its compounds with oxygen. Nitric acid is therefore of great importance, indeed is essential, for the production of explosives, and it is interesting to enquire from what source Germany and other countries obtain their supplies.

The great bulk of the nitric acid used in the industries of the world is made from the caliche containing Chile saltpetre (nitrate of soda), of which there are immense deposits along the coasts of Chile and Peru, and of the total exports of nitrate Germany before the war took more than any other country, her proportion being about one-third, or more than 800,000 tons annually. From it she made about 100,000 tons of nitric acid, though some was used among other purposes for converting the potassium chloride of her Stassfurt salt deposits into ordinary saltpetre (potassium nitrate), required in the manufacture of black gunpowder. When her mercantile marine was swept from the seas, her supplies of nitrate were presumably cut off, and the question presents itself how she managed to get the nitric acid necessary for making her explosives.

Apart from accumulated stores, there were two sources of supply open to her. Towards the end of the eighteenth century the great English natural philosopher Henry Cavendish

discovered that the nitrogen of the air could be made to combine with oxygen under the influence of the electric spark, and about 120 years later this method of producing nitric acid and nitrates became practical. Cheap electricity being essential for commercial success, the manufacture was established in Norway, where water-power is abundant, and German capital took a large part in its development. It has been calculated that if all the power available in Scandinavia, with a smaller amount

A HIGHLANDER
Wearing his gas mask.

in other parts of Europe, were utilized in making nitrate from the air, some fifty million tons could be produced every year, though before the war the annual production was far below 200,000 tons. But Germany had still another string to her bow, and the fact that the Badische Aniline Company, one of her most important chemical manufacturing concerns, withdrew all the capital it had sunk in the Norwegian industry suggests that she thought it a better one. Ammonia, a compound of nitrogen and hydrogen, is obtainable in abundance from a number of sources, as from the distillation of peat (of which there are enormous deposits in Prussia), from the coal used in blast furnaces and in making metallurgical coke and coal gas, and from the direct combination of atmospheric nitrogen with hydrogen by the aid of electricity, and when obtained it can be oxidized to nitric acid by a process worked out by the German chemist Ostwald. In this way one German colliery alone made as a by-product some 2,000 tons of nitric acid in 1912, besides other nitrate, and there is little doubt that after that date works were erected in Germany for carrying out the process on a much larger scale.

In conclusion a reference may be made to asphyxiating gases, which, although not ammunition in the ordinary sense, were used to produce the same effects as ammunition in killing or disabling men. Heralding their resort to this breach of the recognized rules of war by wholly false accusations that such gases had been used by the Allies, the Germans first adopted them towards the end of April 1915 in an attack on a portion of the Allied front held by the French to the north-east of the Ypres salient. Although various substances appear to have been employed, the chief was probably chlorine, a heavy greenish-yellow gas, which physically fulfils the conditions required for the purpose and is capable of producing the asphyxiation (spasm of the glottis) and subsequent bronchitis which were the symptoms observed. The preparation of this gas, which can readily be reduced to the liquid form by moderate pressure at ordinary temperatures, was a large industry in Germany before the war. Much of it was exported to other countries, and, as this trade was cut off, the manufacturers, among whom the above-mentioned Badische Aniline Company was prominent, had an abundant surplus of it to spare for murdering purposes, and also possessed ample supplies of tanks and vessels for its transportation. Receptacles filled with the liquid being brought up to the trenches, it could be squirted from hose by its own pressure in the required direction, resuming its gaseous form when relieved from that pressure. Equipments were also employed designed to be carried on the back of a man, who was supplied with oxygen-breathing apparatus so that he himself was unaffected by the gas. Poisonous and "lachrimatory" gases were also sometimes fired in large shells.

The Allies took successful measures to combat the effects of the gases by providing their men with masks and respirators, and on May 18 Lord Kitchener in the House of Lords foreshadowed the use of gas by the Allied forces to remove the "enormous and unjustifiable disadvantage" which must exist for them if nothing were done to meet the enemy with his own methods. Accordingly gas was employed by the Allies for the first time towards the end of September 1915. As was to be expected of them, the Germans complained, with characteristic lack of humour, that their loss of ground was due "not to any soldierly qualities of the English, but to a successful surprise by gas attack."

CHAPTER XCIV.

THE DARDANELLES CAMPAIGN (II.): THE GREAT LANDING.

ON April 25, 1915, the mighty Battle of the Landing was fought at the Dardanelles. Under cover of darkness, and under the protection of the Fleet, a great army was conveyed towards the rocky and desolate shores of the Gallipoli Peninsula. In the dim light of dawn landings were made at half a dozen points, and by nightfall the exploit which the Turks and their German mentors had deemed impossible was actually accomplished. The army was ashore, and by desperate valour had made good its position. Its foothold was scanty, its peril still seemed great, its losses had been heavy ; but it had landed, and the heroism of its assault had added fresh glories to the military annals of the British Empire. The amazing gallantry of the troops rang throughout the world, and for a time eclipsed all thought of the possible ultimate dangers and difficulties of the enterprise. It seemed to those watching from afar that further and complete success could not be denied to the men who had dared and done so much already. Throughout all the subsequent tragic episodes of the Dardanelles campaign the glowing triumph of the Battle of the Landing still shone with a light which was never dimmed. The memory of its glory remained a powerful influence when months afterwards men began to ask whether the attack upon the Dardanelles could ever be carried to a successful conclusion. No one cared even to suggest that the dogged bravery of the immortal 29th Division, and the undaunted devotion of the indomitable Australian and New Zealand Corps, might have been in vain. But their sacrifices were never made in vain. The good Australian and New Zealand blood shed at Gallipoli sealed and glorified for ever the patriotism of the Commonwealth and the Dominion, just as surely as if the impetuous heroes had died on Sydney Heads or on the shores of the Hauraki Gulf. At the gateway to Constantinople the men of the younger nations were fighting for the safety of their own fair lands, and from their graves sprang imperishable ideals which inspired their sorrowing kinsmen with renewed determination. Upon Englishmen the stubborn resistance encountered at the Dardanelles had a like effect, for it deepened the national resolve to pursue the war unflinchingly until Germany and her subordinate Allies were overthrown.

The Battle of the Landing was in certain respects unlike any other battle of modern times, by reason of the peculiar disabilities imposed upon the soldier who directed it, General Sir Ian Hamilton. He was in an extraordinary position. He had not planned the

441

ON BOARD H.M.S. "QUEEN ELIZABETH" AT MUDROS.

campaign. He had no intimate local knowledge of the scene of the operations. He was told to undertake a task for which the number of troops supposed to be required had been prescribed by others with even less knowledge than himself. He had no chance of effecting a real surprise attack. The guns of the Fleet had been sedulously advertising the intention of the Allies for many weeks. He was only sent out to take command after the earlier attempts to break down the defences of the Dardanelles by naval power alone had been conspicuously unsuccessful. He found upon his arrival that, though a force of troops had been assembled, it was impotent because the transports had been wrongly laden, a mistake for which he was in no sense responsible. Within twenty-four hours he had the mortification of helplessly witnessing a further great naval attack (and the loss of three battleships), when all his instincts must have told him that such a blow should only have been attempted in conjunction with his own land forces. He was imperatively compelled to remove his troops to Egypt in order that the transports might be laden afresh, although he knew full well that

every day's delay enabled the enemy to prepare still further for his onslaught. When at length he was ready, he had very little real choice in selecting the points at which to strike. It would have been extremely difficult for him, without ever having landed a man or a gun, to declare that he did not think a land attack upon the Gallipoli Peninsula was likely to succeed. He could not, at so late a stage, suggest an entirely new campaign against the Turks at some new and distant spot, such as the coast of Syria. All his past training, all the traditions in which he had been bred, impelled him at least to try at the appointed place. Sir Ian Hamilton was, in short, very much in the position in which Lord Cardigan found himself at the battle of Balaclava, when Captain Nolan rode up to him and said, according to the accepted version of the words :—"There are the enemy, and there are the guns." Moreover, he knew that reluctance to conduct an enterprise so carelessly and thoughtlessly conceived would probably only have resulted in the appointment of another general in his stead.

But he was not reluctant. He believed that in spite of the delays success was possible ; and he proved that at least the initial stages were possible, though at a great price.

The primary blame for the original mistakes of the Dardanelles Expedition rests in great measure, though by no means exclusively, upon the soldiers and sailors upon whose advice, and with whose concurrence, the British Ministry sanctioned the enterprise. No plea of preoccupations elsewhere can condone their errors and their faults. No excuse based upon the persuasive influence of civilian Ministers can suffice to free them from responsibility. Sir Ian Hamilton's share of responsibility only began after his arrival, when he found himself confronted by the handicaps which have been described. The utmost change he could have made in the original plan would have been to recommend a landing either at Enos or at some point on the coast of Asia Minor near the Dardanelles. Both these alternatives were probably excluded by the limited number of troops at his disposal.

Sir Ian Hamilton never seriously contemplated either alternative. Soon after he reached the island of Tenedos on March 17 he made by sea a preliminary reconnaissance of the outer or north-western shore of the Gallipoli Peninsula, from the Bulair isthmus to Cape Helles. The physical characteristics of the peninsula have already been broadly described in Chapter XCII. Sir Ian came very quickly to certain broad conclusions. He saw that the northern coast of the northern half of the peninsula, from Suvla Bay to Bulair, was useless for his purpose. It consisted of a chain of hills whose sides sloped steeply into the sea. "The precipitous fall of these hills," he afterwards wrote, "precludes landing, except at a few narrow gullies, far too restricted for any serious military movements." His choice was, therefore, confined to the coast between Cape Suvla, at the northern extremity of Suvla Bay, and the toe of the promontory at the entrance to the Dardanelles. The possible advantages of a landing at Suvla Bay were not considered attractive at the time, not only because the beach was wrongly supposed to be too exposed to bad weather, but also because the whole plan of

BRITISH TROOPS LEAVING THE SS. "NILE"
For the Landing Beach.

FRENCH TROOPS IN EGYPT.
General d'Amade addressing the troops before presenting the colours to a French regiment near Ramleh.

the landing was largely influenced by a contemplation of the principal positions in the interior of the peninsula.

These were three in number, and they must be described afresh in order to make clear the subsequent operations. There was first the height of Achi Baba, which was noted by Sir Ian Hamilton as 600 feet high, though some maps credit it with another 100 feet. There was next the Kilid Bahr plateau, or Pasha Dagh, a tableland commanding The Narrows, and lying in a transverse position across the peninsula. There was, thirdly, the Sari Bair mountain, nearly a thousand feet high, commanding the point of the Australian landing, a point which came to be known afterwards as "Anzac" (from the name of the attacking force, the Australian and New Zealand Army Corps). Sir Ian Hamilton wrote that the sides of Sari Bair ran up in a succession of almost perpendicular escarpments, and that "the whole mountain seemed to be a network of ravines and covered with thick jungle." As to the ground between Achi Baba and the tip of the peninsula, he wrote the following :

A peculiarity to be noted as regards this last southern sector is that from Achi Babi to Cape Helles the ground is hollowed out like a spoon, presenting only its outer edges to direct fire from the sea. The inside of the spoon

appears to be open and undulating, but actually it is full of spurs, nullahs, and confused under-features.

When he came to look for landing-places on the selected strip of coast, he found that they were few in number, and that the general character of the shore was precipitous. There were good landing-places to the north of Gaba Tepe. There were practicable beaches at various points around the end of the peninsula, from a spot opposite the village of Krithia to Morto Bay, on the other side, within the entrance to the Straits. Every beach seemed to be protected by trenches and wire entanglements, and even from his warship Sir Ian Hamilton could descry the semblance of gun emplacements. The prospects looked grim, for the enemy were well prepared. In his dispatch he stated the problem thus :

Altogether the result of this and subsequent reconnaissances was to convince me that nothing but a thorough and systematic scheme for flinging the whole of the troops under my command very rapidly ashore could be expected to meet with success ; whereas, on the other hand, a tentative or piecemeal programme was bound to lead to disaster. The landing of an army upon the theatre of operations I have described—a theatre strongly garrisoned throughout and prepared for any such attempt—involved difficulties for which no precedent was forthcoming in military history except possibly in the sinister legends of Xerxes. The beaches were either so well defended by works and guns or else so restricted by Nature that it did not seem possible, even by two or three simultaneous landings, to pass the troops ashore quickly enough to enable them to maintain themselves against the rapid concentration and counter-attack which the enemy was bound in such a case to attempt. It became necessary, therefore, not only to land simultaneously at as many points as possible, but to threaten to land at other points as well. The first of these necessities involved another unavoidable if awkward contingency—the separation by considerable intervals of the force.

The weather was also bound to play a vital part in my landing. Had it been British weather there would have been no alternative but instantly to give up the adventure. To land two or three thousand men, and then to have to break off and leave them exposed for a week to the attacks of 34,000 regular troops, with a hundred guns at their back, was not an eventuality to be lightly envisaged. Whatever happened, the weather must always remain an incalculable factor, but at least by delay till the end of April we had a fair chance of several days of consecutive calm.

Before finally working out the plan of the attack, however, it was necessary to redistribute the troops on the transports, and also to arrange afresh the stores and supplies upon the vessels. The harbour of Mudros, on the island of Lemnos, was packed with the vessels of the British and French Expeditionary Forces. A British soldier thus described the scene :

This place is most weird and interesting just now, with the Army that has gathered—Frenchmen in their blue tunics and red trousers, Chasseurs d'Afrique, with their exquisite Arab horses, Senegalese Infantry, black as my hat, with funny little tents, 8 ft. long, 4 ft. wide, and

2 ft. high, in the middle of which six men sleep. The tents are in six pieces, buttoning together, two each side and one each end ; each man carries one piece. During the day they lift up one side and make a sort of shade with it, under which they sit.

Their officers are all Frenchmen, of course ; fine, sun-burnt, big men ; some dark-haired from the south, and some quite fair, very nice to talk to.

Then there are ordinary French soldiers in khaki, and Australians, big men these, too ; loose-limbed and big-jawed, riding carelessly rough-coated, ugly horses, looking all the time as if they might easily fall off. Then there are British Regulars, Territorials, Marines, Artillery Flying Wing, Sappers, Army Service Corps, and all sorts Greek soldiers and sailors, peasants—men and women but very few of the latter, all wearing the *yashmak*.

Wooden shops springing up in all directions run by loud-voiced Greeks selling fruit, sweets, postcards, sponges, tinned stuff of all sorts, whisky, brandy, beer (at 2s. 6d. a bottle), their little wooden shops half the size of our motor shed, with " Bon Marché " chalked over the

GENERAL SIR IAN HAMILTON REVIEWING THE AUSTRALIANS AT ZEITUN.
The Australian Infantry marching past. Inset : General Sir Ian Hamilton.

64—2

KIT INSPECTION BEFORE LANDING AT THE DARDANELLES.

entrance or " Grill-room " ; mules staggering about under huge loads of fodder, supplies, &c., ammunition carts, Red Cross wagons, and small boys in hundreds crying " Pennie, Signor, pennie," diving in and out in imminent danger of their lives. And out in the bay battleships, cruisers, destroyers, transport supply ships, colliers, hospital ships, Greek trading schooners by the score, huge flat barges laden with fodder, and everywhere, like the small boys on shore, dash the little, fussing, puffing French picket boats or the more dignified English ones.

All the transports, except those of the Australian Infantry Brigade and the details encamped at Lemnos, were ordered to Egypt. Sir Ian Hamilton, accompanied by his Staff, proceeded to Alexandria on March 24, and remained there until April 7, " working out the allocation of troops to transports in minutest detail as a prelude to the forthcoming dis- embarcation." The rest of the Headquarters Staff came out direct from England to Alexan- dria, arriving on April 1. General d'Amade also went to Egypt, where the French force had been quartered at Ramleh, a popular watering-place near Alexandria.

The French camp was most extensive, and stretched for several miles to the east of Alex- andria. On April 5 (Easter Monday) General d'Amade presented new colours to two of the regiments, and Sir Ian Hamilton reviewed part of the French force. The review was held in

the desert on a great plateau surrounded by sand dunes. Regiment after regiment of infantry marched past in full formation ; the artillery, including the popular 75's, made a fine show ; and the cavalry rode by with the traditional dash and brilliance of the French mounted arm. The Cairo correspondent of *The Times* after- wards wrote that " the conduct on duty of the French troops has been as exemplary as their bearing at the Easter Monday review was dignified and creditable." There was a great gathering of spectators at the review, and in reply to a speech by M. Albert Defrance, the French Agent, Sir Ian Hamilton said that Frenchmen " ought to be proud of their nationality, when they realized that their country possessed troops like those that had just passed before him."

The inspiriting address delivered by General d'Amade in presenting the colours is worthy of preservation. It was as follows :

In the name of the President of the Republic I place these flags in your hands.

It is your native land, all of whose children are to-day under arms ; it is France, the well-beloved, who lives in these emblems, and beats with hope in their sacred folds. To-day you become their valiant guardians, courageous, stubborn and disciplined. You swear with me to defend them until death.

You swear before our Chief, the Commander-in-Chief

A SEAPLANE AT TENEDOS.

of the Allied Forces before the Minister of France, before the crowd of our compatriots and our friends gathered together to salute the presentation of these colours under the Egyptian sky.

You swear, finally, as upon an altar, before their three colours—the blue of the waves, the white of the city, the red of the blood of our sons and our brothers who have died for our country. And from to-day your soldiers' vow confers on these flags the glory with which they shine.

To-morrow, in their turn, it is they that will pour upon you their sublime radiance when you have planted them upon the enemy's shore.

Under their folds we shall march to battle hand in hand with our brave allies. We are fighting for the same cause.

By your courage you will write the names of victories on these flags.

In her turn, France will write the 1st Régiment de Marche d'Afrique, and the 6th Régiment mixte Colonial in her Book of Glory.

Colonels, I hand you these flags. They are entrusted by France to the bravery of your regiments.

When the time came to embark once more for Gallipoli, General d'Amade issued the following General Order dated April 15 :

The First Division of the Eastern Expeditionary Force will shortly disembark and establish itself by force on the enemy's shore.

From this very first contact with the enemy we must impress upon him our superiority and our will to conquer.

If we fall back we shall inevitably be pinned to the sea without a possible line of retreat.

But if we advance along the whole line, that will be the defeat of the enemy, our dead avenged, our soil freed—in a word, the definite victory of France.

Your choice between the two is made. Forward !

On April 7 Sir Ian Hamilton returned with his Staff to Lemnos, where he completed the

Return to a cruiser of a Seaplane after making a flight over the Turkish fortifications.
Inset: An Observation Balloon ascending.

AIR SCOUTING AT THE DARDANELLES.

SIR IAN HAMILTON,
General Commanding Mediterranean Expeditionary
Force.

preparation of his plans in conjunction with
Admiral de Robeck. The force he had at his
disposal was very varied. Its basis was the
29th Division, one of the last available regular
divisions of the original British Army. It had
only been brought up to full divisional strength
by the inclusion of a Territorial battalion of
excellent quality. The Surrey Yeomanry fur-

nished a squadron which served as divisional
cavalry, and the artillery included two batteries
of the 4th (Highland) Mounted Brigade. The
29th Division was chiefly composed of units
drawn from various overseas stations, which had
not worked together before in divisional formation. Hastily collected, the Division nevertheless covered itself with glory, and earned a
fame which can never die. It was constituted
as follows :

86th Infantry Brigade : 2nd Royal Fusiliers, 1st
Lancashire Fusiliers, 1st Royal Munster Fusiliers, and
1st Royal Dublin Fusiliers.
87th Infantry Brigade : 2nd South Wales Borderers,
1st King's Own Scottish Borderers, 1st Royal Innis-
killing Fusiliers, and 1st Border Regiment.
88th Infantry Brigade : 2nd Hampshires, 4th Worcesters, 1st Essex, and the 5th Royal Scots, the last-
named battalion being Territorials.

The 29th Division was commanded by
Major-General (afterwards Lieutenant-General)
A. G. Hunter-Weston, who had originally been
in charge of the 11th Brigade of the 3rd Corps
in France and Flanders.

There was next the East Lancashire Territorial Division, which had been undergoing
training in Egypt during the winter. The
following was its composition :

Lancashire Fusiliers Brigade : 5th, 6th, 7th and 8th
Lancashire Fusiliers.
East Lancashire Brigade   4th and 5th East Lanca-
shires, 9th and 10th Manchesters.
Manchester Brigade : 5th, 6th, 7th and 8th Man-
chesters.

The next section of the force was represented
by the Royal Naval Division, consisting of two
Naval Brigades and one Brigade of Royal
Marines. A portion of these troops had par-
ticipated in the unsuccessful Antwerp Expedition. The Division was accompanied by an
armoured-car section. Next came a considerable portion of the Indian troops from
Egypt, some of whom had already been engaged in repelling the attack upon the Suez
Canal. Finally, there was the magnificent
Australian and New Zealand Army Corps,
which had been wintering in Egypt, within
sight of the Pyramids, under the command of
Lieutenant-General Sir William Riddell Birdwood. It included sixteen battalions of Australian Infantry, and four battalions of New
Zealanders, with artillery and engineers.

General Birdwood was an able and experienced
soldier who had seen much service, and enjoyed
the special confidence of Lord Kitchener.
He had been Lord Dundonald's galloper at the
relief of Ladysmith, and was one of the first
officers to enter the beleaguered town. He was

Lord Kitchener's Military Secretary during the later stages of the South African War, and served him devotedly in the same capacity during the seven years of his tenure of the command in India. Afterwards he was appointed to a brigade on the North-West Frontier, but in 1912 became Quartermaster-General in India, a post he soon exchanged for the difficult and thankless office of Secretary to the Government of India in the Army Department. He had always proved himself equally competent at the desk and in the field. He had seen a good deal of frontier fighting, and served through the Tirah War of 1897–98. He was severely wounded in South Africa, and had been many times mentioned in dispatches. He held the Orders of the Bath, the Star of India, the Indian Empire, and the D.S.O., the last-named having been won in the Mohmand Expedition in 1908. He gained the confidence of the Australian troops from the outset, and Sir Ian Hamilton declared in the following August that he had been "the soul of Anzac."

The Australians were very tired of being cooped up on the transports, and were said to be "anxious to get ashore and stretch their limbs in a real fight, when their temporary

[Elliott & Fry

LIEUT.-GEN. SIR W. R. BIRDWOOD,
Commander of the Australian and New Zealand
Army Corps.

discomforts will be forgotten." One of them wrote home :

We are having an iron time ; we live in an iron ship, sleep on an iron floor, have nothing to eat but iron rations, and now, to crown all, I hear we are commanded by a fellow called " Iron " Hamilton.

The French Expeditionary Force was composed of Fusiliers Marins, battalions of the excellent Colonial Army (consisting partly of white troops, and partly of Senegal Tirailleurs and other native troops), and other units chiefly drawn from the garrisons of the French possessions in North Africa. General Joffre had been unwilling to weaken his forces by detaching men from his reserves in France, but General d'Amade had an admirable body of troops, who did valiant service when the great day of the landing arrived. The nominal total of the force at Sir Ian Hamilton's disposal represented three somewhat weak and diversified army corps (120,000 men). Considerably fewer than the number named actually took part in the Battle of the Landing.

The precise number of the Turkish forces concentrated in the Gallipoli Peninsula at the time of the attack on April 25 remained unknown. Sir Ian Hamilton spoke of " 34,000 regular troops with a hundred guns at their

LIEUT.-GEN. A. G. HUNTER-WESTON,
Commander of the 29th Division.

A VIEW OF ONE OF THE ANZAC LANDING-PLACES.
Quantities of stores are stacked on the beach.

back," but the remark apparently related either to the forces in position at the time of his first reconnaissance or to the strength of the resistance likely to be expected at the extreme end of the peninsula. A correspondent, writing from Constantinople on March 8, said that there were "supposed to be" 35,000 Turkish troops at the Dardanelles, but that within the preceding fortnight many more had been sent down, while more were being brought from Smyrna. On March 29 the Sultan of Turkey issued a decree constituting the German General Liman von Sanders Commander-in-Chief of the forces at the Dardanelles, which were designated the Fifth Army. Marshal von der Goltz, an old and famous friend of the Turks, was given the control of another Army concentrated around Constantinople. There can be no doubt that throughout the early weeks of April the Turks, who were fully informed of what was going on at Mudros and in Egypt, constantly sent reinforcements to the Dardanelles. They also developed their defences with feverish haste throughout the same period. A Special Correspondent of *The Times* at Athens estimated that the total number of effectives upon which the Turks could actually draw at this period for the Dardanelles amounted to about 275,000. This included the Army stationed near Constantinople, and certain units at Smyrna. What proportion of these was definitely sent to the Dardanelles before the Battle of the Landing was not known. There was no question that the assailants found the Turks in stronger force and better posted than they expected. They also found that they included substantial German contingents of picked men, who greatly strengthened the Turkish opposition. It may be noted that Sir Ian Hamilton stated that the Australians alone were being attacked near Gaba Tepe by 20,000 Turks by 11 a.m. on the morning of the 25th ; and this number was afterwards increased to 24,000. A Sofia report, dated April 30, put the total Turkish forces "assembled to oppose the invading troops on the European side" at over 150,000.

In all the circumstances set forth in this chapter and in Chapter XCII., ought the Allied attack of April 25 to have been delivered at all ? The question will probably be disputed by military historians for centuries to come. It is equally probable that in the majority of cases the verdict will be that the attempt should not have been made.

One of the great misfortunes of this isolated campaign at the Dardanelles, so remote from the other earlier theatres of the war, was that it originated with, and was pressed forward by, men who had no clear notion of the local difficulties. Ministers in England looked constantly to the end which was sought, and never to the means by which it was to be attained. Some of them were thinking of policy, others were attracted by the mere glamour of the prospect of capturing Constantinople by British prowess. No one appeared to think that failure was possible, and there was no one at hand to give expert advice. Lord Kitchener, already overwhelmed with other work, seems to have given the expedition his blessing, but to have given it very little thought in the earlier stages. There was virtually no General Staff in existence. No one even cared to inquire.

The Dardanelles campaign showed two things. It showed that at the beginning of 1915 there was a very grave lack of co-ordination in the strategy of the Allies, for it was soon no secret that both General Joffre and Sir John French disliked the scheme. It further showed that those in London who were responsible for the higher strategy of the British share in the war were not acting with sufficient prudence or foresight, or even with reasonable skill. They could see political visions, but they paid small heed to the more prosaic side of grand strategy. They flung the Fleet against the Dardanelles in defiance of the salutary doctrine that ships should not attack forts unless they were assured of land support. They then, having committed nearly every conceivable error at sea, proceeded to endeavour to take one of the most formidable positions encountered by the Allies during the war with a hotch-potch Army. The description implies not the slightest reflection upon the extraordinarily gallant troops who fought at the Dardanelles. Their courage was sublime, but their organization as an attacking force was makeshift and piecemeal. The troops were hurriedly collected. The Staff was selected almost at random. The Army did not know the Staff, the Staff did not know the Army. It may be said that these conditions were inevitable, and that no other course was possible at the moment. The argument is just, but it does not answer the criticism that in ordering the attack no thought was given to the inadequacy of the means employed. The proper

LANDING PARTY IN BOATS GOING ASHORE.

line of original inquiry should have been not "Can we take the Dardanelles ? " but " Can we take the Dardanelles with the forces now at our disposal ? " The authorities in London were right when they argued at the beginning of 1915 that they must not weaken Sir John French. They were wrong when they tacitly decided that any inexperienced units would do for the Dardanelles. They did, in fact, eventually weaken Sir John French, not in men, but in munitions ; for there was one period, though it did not last very long, when supplies needed in France were going to the Mediterranean.

The argument afterwards advanced that the attack on the Dardanelles relieved the pressure upon Egypt and upon our troops in Mesopotamia was never admissible. There was no pressure upon Egypt when the new campaign was ordered. One of the very reasons put forward in favour of the Dardanelles adventure was that the Army in Egypt was wasting its time. There was no serious pressure upon the Army in Mesopotamia. It had established itself at Kurna, at the junction of the Tigris with the old channel of the Euphrates, and it might very well have stayed there. No Minister and no expert dreamed in the first months of 1915 of suggesting that the needs of either Egypt or Mesopotamia required an attack upon the Dardanelles. The campaign was decided on for entirely different reasons,

which were sufficiently recounted in Chapter XCII.

The only other observation which it is necessary to make at this stage of the narrative is that after the failure of the great naval attack on March 18 the whole question of the Dardanelles should have been carefully reconsidered by experts in London. The repulse of the battleships, the revelation of the strength of the defences, the mistake about the transports, all furnished convincing reasons for discussing afresh whether the enterprise should be prosecuted further or abandoned. The Allies could have changed their plans at the end of March without serious loss of prestige, and without creating any gravely unfavourable impression in Asia. Apparently there was never any such serious reconsideration. " Bull-at-a-gate " theories of attack still held the field. Mr. Winston Churchill was at the height of his ardour, and most of the other Ministers were acquiescent without inquiry. The " compartment " system of control continued to prevail in the Cabinet. The only marked development was the formulation of new and still wilder schemes of naval attack, which fortunately came to naught.

Sir Ian Hamilton's final plan for the Battle of the Landing can be very simply stated. He resolved to effect his principal landings at the very tip of the peninsula, upon either side of Cape Helles. The troops were to advance against the village of Krithia, and afterwards to carry the height of Achi Baba. A second main landing was to be made by the Australians and New Zealanders a little to the north of Gaba Tepe. They were to advance over the divide between Sari Bair and the Kilid Bahr plateau (Pasha Dagh) in the direction of the town of Maidos. It was hoped that the force advancing by way of Krithia and Achi Baba would get into touch with the Australians, and that positions would be won from which the Narrows could be dominated. So greatly was the strength of the enemy's defences underestimated that it was seriously expected by many officers that Achi Baba would be crowned by nightfall on the first day. Six months later the expedition was still contemplating the slopes of Achi Baba from afar, while no union had been effected by land between the southern force and the Australians.

The different landing-places selected must be further described in greater detail. There were five around the end of the peninsula, named respectively S, V, W, X, and Y. The Australian landing-place was lettered Z. Of the five

beaches near Cape Helles, V, W, and X were to be main landings, while the attacks at S and Y were described by Sir Ian Hamilton as being intended "mainly to protect the flanks, to disseminate the forces of the enemy, and to interrupt the landing of his reinforcements."

Beach S was near Eski Hissarlik, at the eastern extremity of Morto Bay. It was small, was practically within the entrance to the Straits, and was at first commanded by guns on the Asiatic side. Just above the beach, on the high ground at Eski Hissarlik Point, stood the ruined fortifications known as De Tott's Battery, built in the eighteenth century.

Beach V was close to Cape Helles, and near the battery of Sedd-el-Bahr. It was described by Sir Ian Hamilton as " a sandy beach, about 300 yards across, facing a semi-circle of steeply rising ground, as the flat bottom of a half-saucer faces the rim, a rim flanked on one side by an old castle, on the other by a modern fort." The "old castle " was, of course, the ancient structure known to the Turks as "the New Castle of Europe." The castle stood at the south-eastern end of the beach,

LANDING TROOPS AND HORSES AT BEACH V.
[From a photograph taken from the SS. "Clyde."]

WITH THE AUSTRALIANS.
A telephone station. An operator is at work on the right.

near the village of Sedd-el-Bahr, which was on a bluff. The modern fort, known as Fort No. 1, was on another bluff at the other end. The bombardment had already reduced the castle to a battered ruin, while the fort was badly knocked about, its guns being out of action. The ruins of both buildings afforded excellent shelter for sharpshooters, who were able to command the whole scene of the landing at this spot. The beach itself was ten yards wide and 350 yards long, afterwards rising in a low sandy escarpment four feet high, and almost sheer, which afforded shelter of priceless value in the battle. Beyond were slightly concave grassy slopes, reaching a height of about a hundred feet, and having a radius of three or four hundred yards. Beach and slopes were commanded from the ruins and from trenches, and the whole position proved to be a veritable amphitheatre of death.

Beach W was a small sandy bay, between Cape Helles and Cape Tekke. It consisted, according to Sir Ian Hamilton, of "a strip of deep, powdery sand some 350 yards long and from fifteen to forty yards wide, situated immediately south of Tekke Burnu, where a small gully running down to the sea opens out a break in the cliffs. On either flank of the

beach the ground rises precipitously, but in the centre a number of sand dunes afford a more gradual access to the ridge overlooking the sea." The Turks turned Beach W into a regular death-trap by a cunning system of trenches and wire entanglements. The ridge near the beach was in its turn commanded by two strong infantry redoubts near the point marked 138 on the map.

Beach X was on the northern side of Cape Tekke, and was distinguished by a small break in the cliffs. It consisted of "a strip of sand some 200 yards long by eight yards wide at the foot of a low cliff." It was to some extent commanded by Turkish trenches on the adjacent hill marked 114.

Beach Y was immediately to the west of Krithia, and was merely "a narrow strip of sand at the foot of a crumbling scrub-covered cliff some 200 feet high." From the sea the cliff had looked to Sir Ian Hamilton not unlike the heights of Abraham, near Quebec. A number of small gullies running down the face of the cliff gave access to the summit, but they were so difficult that the Turks never thought them practicable. The consequence was that they did not defend Beach Y at all. They had a strong force of infantry, backed by machine guns, posted at Beach Y2, midway between X and Y ; but Y2 was not attacked by the British.

The original Beach Z near Gaba Tepe, the point selected as the landing-place for the Australians, was not attacked owing to a fortunate mistake. It was described as a rugged and difficult part of the coast, so rugged that it was not expected to be defended. Sir Ian Hamilton, in describing the landing of the Australians and New Zealanders, stated :

Owing to the tows having failed to maintain their exact direction the actual point of disembarcation was rather more than a mile north of that which I had selected, and was more closely overhung by steeper cliffs. Although this accident increased the initial difficulty of driving the enemy off the heights inland, it has since proved itself to have been a blessing in disguise, inasmuch as the actual base of the force of occupation has been much better defiladed from shell fire.

The beach on which the landing was actually effected is a very narrow strip of sand, about 1,000 yards in length, bounded on the north and the south by two small promontories. At its southern extremity a deep ravine, with exceedingly steep, scrub-clad sides, runs inland in a north-easterly direction. Near the northern end of the beach a small but steep gully runs up into the hills at right angles to the shore. Between the ravine and the gully the whole of the beach is backed by the seaward face of the spur which forms the north-western side of the ravine. From the top of the spur the ground falls almost sheer except near the southern limit of the beach, where gentler slopes give access to the mouth of the ravine behind. Farther inland lie in a tangled knot the under-features of Sari Bair, separated by deep ravines, which take a most confusing diversity of direction. Sharp spurs, covered with dense scrub, and falling away in many places in precipitous sandy cliffs, radiate from the principal mass of the mountain, from which they run north-west, west, south-west, and south to the coast.

It will be observed that the plan of attack included two feints, those at Beaches S and Y. A French regiment also contributed a feint by landing at Kum Kale, on the Asiatic side, an exploit which will be dealt with in due course. A much more imposing feint was made a day or two earlier near Enos, close to the mouth of the Maritza River and only twelve miles from Bulgarian territory. A squadron of warships covered a sham landing which resulted in several casualties. The feint had the desired result, for it was enormously exaggerated in the Press, and led to doubts about the real intention of the Allies.

The doubts did not long continue, for the demonstration near Enos was the prelude to the appearance of a vast armada. Mudros Bay had been once more packed with shipping. There were dozens of transports crammed with troops, and a great array of battleships and cruisers. At five o'clock on the afternoon of April 23 the first of the mighty liners steamed

slowly through the maze of vessels and out of the bay. Transport after transport followed. The bands of the Fleet played them out, the bluejackets lined up and cheered with wild enthusiasm, and the eager troops answered with a will. It was an inspiring scene, and every heart was full of hope.

The whole of the Fleet and the transports had been constituted into five divisions, and it required great skill to get the whole immense assemblage out of the bay and in position on the open sea. The next rendezvous was the island of Tenedos, which was reached on April 24. There the troops designated for the

12-INCH SHELLS ON BOARD A BRITISH BATTLESHIP.

attack were transferred to the battleships and mine-sweepers from which they were to land. Some of the battleships were detailed to cover the landing, others were to steam closer inshore and land the troops in small boats. Every detail had been worked out and rehearsed, each officer and man knew his post and the duties assigned to him. The landing operations were in charge of the Royal Navy, under the direction of Admiral de Robeck. On most of the warships, during the afternoon of the 24th, the ship's company and the troops were assembled on the quarterdeck to hear the captain read out Admiral de Robeck's proclamation to the combined forces. This was followed by a last service before battle, in which the chaplain

2nd Lieut. H. V. H. THROSSELL, of the Australian 10th Light Horse, who won the V.C.

offered a prayer for victory and asked for the divine blessing on the expedition. The blue-jackets and troops stood with uncovered and bowed heads during these solemn moments of intercession.

The night was calm and the sea unruffled. Towards midnight the ships bearing the troops quietly left Tenedos, each towing cutters and other small craft, and steamed slowly towards Cape Helles, which was the final rendezvous. They drew close to the Gallipoli Peninsula just before daybreak. "The morning," said Sir Ian Hamilton, "was absolutely still; there was no sign of life on the shore; a thin veil of mist hung motionless over the promontory; the surface of the sea was as smooth as glass."

The honour of being the first men to land on the Gallipoli Peninsula on the morning of the great battle rests with the Australians. Their first boat was close to the beach beyond Gaba Tepe when it was greeted with a sharp outburst of rifle fire at 4.53 a.m., the light being still dim. The next moment the boat was grating on the sand, and a Special Correspondent with the Australians afterwards wrote that the first Ottoman Turk to receive Anglo-Saxon steel since the last Crusade was bayonetted at 5.5 a.m. The statement was not strictly accurate, for the bayonet was used in the earlier naval landings; but the hour deserves

record. The Australian landing must, however, be described in detail later. Attention must first be paid to the various landings at the end of the Peninsula. Of these, the two feints at Beaches S and Y were timed for dawn, while the first troops for Beaches V, W and X were to reach the shore at 5.30 a.m., after half an hour's preliminary bombardment by the Fleet. The time fixed could not in all cases be strictly adhered to.

The landings at the end of the Peninsula were under the immediate direction of Rear-Admiral R. E. Wemyss, C.M.G., M.V.O., whose squadron consisted of the following :

Battleships : Swiftsure, Implacable, Cornwallis, Albion, Vengeance, Lord Nelson, and Prince George. Cruisers : Euryalus, Talbot, Minerva, and Dublin ; 6 fleet sweepers and 14 trawlers.

Punctually at 5 a.m. the covering battleships began to bombard the enemy's positions at various points on the promontory. Simultaneously the first feint was delivered at S Beach, close to De Tott's ruined battery. The force designated for this purpose consisted of the 2nd South Wales Borderers (less one company) and a detachment of the 2nd London Field Company R.E., the whole numbering about 700 rank and file. The force was commanded by Lieut.-Colonel Casson, and was carried in trawlers convoyed by H.M.S. Cornwallis. The trawlers were conducted into Morto Bay by Lieutenant-Commander Ralph B. Janvrin, R.N. They were carried astray by the swift current flowing out of the Straits, and it required much skill to bring the vessels into the necessary station and to effect the transhipment of the troops into small boats. The force was not only under fire from the shore near Eski Hissarlik Point, but also from guns posted on the Asiatic side of the Straits, though the latter were ultimately diverted by the French landing at Kum Kale. For his services at this juncture Lieutenant-Commander Janvrin received the Distinguished Service Order, and Admiral de Robeck noted in his dispatch that " he showed great judgment and coolness under fire, and carried out a difficult task with much success." By 7.30 a.m. the whole party was ashore, with a loss of about 50 killed and wounded. The enemy had a trench on the beach, which was quickly carried. The gallant Borderers gradually made their way up the cliffs, and by 10 a.m. had reached De Tott's Battery. There they entrenched themselves across the bluff, and by the afternoon they felt

SOME MEN OF THE AUSTRALIAN 10th LIGHT HORSE IN THEIR TRENCHES.

well able to hold their own against the 2,000 Turks who were opposing them. Towards evening the Turks attacked, but were repulsed with the aid of fire from the Cornwallis and the Lord Nelson. Next day the enemy again tried to dislodge them, but were again driven back with the help of the warships. On the 27th the French took over the position.

The first feint was, therefore, productive of even better results than had been anticipated, for the right wing of the landing was securely held from the outset. The naval fire was particularly helpful at this landing.

The other feint at Beach Y, on the other side of the peninsula, opposite Krithia, proved to be a far stiffer task. The landing force consisted of the 1st King's Own Scottish Borderers, and the Plymouth (Marine) Battalion of the Royal Naval Division. It was commanded by Lieutenant-Colonel Koe, and had great good luck at the outset. The troops were carried on the cruisers Amethyst and Sapphire, and the transports Braemar Castle and Southland. The little squadron was escorted by the battleship Goliath, and all were off Cape Tekke, about 7,000 yards south-west of Beach Y,

BRITISH TROOPS ENCAMPED ON BEACH W.

some time before daylight. The Turks, as has been already stated, never foresaw a landing at Beach Y at all. They had a large force of infantry, with machine and Hotchkiss guns, entrenched at Beach Y2, a couple of miles nearer Cape Tekke. The consequence was that Colonel Koe was able to get all his men on shore without any opposition. They were rowed and towed for a considerable distance from the actual landing-point. Half the Scottish Borderers were taken ashore at the first trip, and the other half followed at the second trip, the Marines being landed directly afterwards. The landing was very smartly carried out, and was an admirable piece of organization, which earned special praise from Admiral de Robeck. There was, indeed, great need for rapidity. The Turks were less than an hour's march away, and the cliffs were so steep that there had always been a doubt whether they were really scaleable at all. Had the beach been defended there can be little doubt that the heights would never have been reached. Had there been slowness in landing, the force might have been thrown into confusion when the Turks came hurrying up. As it was, the men swarmed up the gullies like cats, and were soon hauling reserves of water, food, and ammunition to the top. The Goliath began a bombardment in order to cover them, but at that stage little help from the sea was needed.

The orders to Colonel Koe were that if he effected a landing safely he was at once to march back along the coast and try to effect a junction with the force which was coming ashore at Beach X, near Cape Tekke. As soon as he had got both his battalions on the heights, therefore, he set out in the prescribed direction. Before he had gone very far, however, he en-

countered the Turkish infantry from Beach Y2, whom he immediately attacked. A vigorous engagement developed, and it was rapidly made plain that more than two battalions would be required to force a path southwards at that particular juncture. Nor was that all. Later in the day a large force of Turks was seen advancing towards Beach Y from the direction of the village of Krithia. Colonel Koe gave the order to entrench, and about this time received a wound which subsequently caused his death. The force was now almost outflanked, and was in a very perilous position. The enemy were in greatly superior numbers, and they brought up some field guns which did much execution. The warships could give small aid. From the top of the cliffs the ground sloped downwards. The British were beginning to discover the disadvantages of the scooped-out spoon-like formation of the ground near the end of the peninsula. Both they and their foes had become invisible to the anxious watchers on the ships, who did their best, but could not see their target. The Turks attacked again and again during the afternoon and evening, in ever-increasing strength. They threw bombs into the British trenches, their field guns maintained an incessant fire, and their vigorous tactics showed unmistakable signs of German direction. The Borderers and Marines fought valiantly like the heroes they were. They charged repeatedly with the bayonet, and drove back the Turks time after time. Great gaps were made in their own ranks, but their indomitable spirit never quailed against the heavy odds.

All night long the unequal fight continued. The Turks were no contemptible foes. They were full of daring and resource. Under cover of the darkness they actually managed to lead a pony with a machine-gun on its back into the middle of the British defences. They were just about to bring the gun into action, with consequences which might have been disastrous, when their presence was discovered, and they were swiftly bayoneted. Dawn broke on a mournful sight. The losses had been great, and Sir Ian Hamilton afterwards acknowledged that they were "deplorable." Many officers had gone down. The Scottish Borderers had been reduced by half their strength. It was true that the Turks had also suffered heavily, but they were constantly able to bring up more men. The position of the British had become desperate. They were completely worn out by continuous fighting. They were no longer able to man their trenches in sufficient numbers. The question of reinforcements was considered, but by 7 a.m. it seemed possible that they might be overwhelmed before further help could arrive. Reluctantly, therefore, the order to re-embark them as quickly as possible was given. The attendant warships were the Goliath, and the cruisers Talbot, Dublin, Sapphire, and Amethyst. They shelled the ground behind the top of the cliffs, and prevented the eager Turks from advancing to the edge. The result was that only a few snipers were able to harass the re-embarking troops. A small and devoted rearguard of the Scottish Borderers also greatly helped to keep the enemy at bay, and did not

[*Russell.*

REAR-ADMIRAL R. E. WEMYSS,
Who directed the landings at the end of the Peninsula.

descend the cliffs until the last possible moment. The really surprising thing was that all the wounded, as well as the stores and ammunition, were ever got away at all. The force which

AFTER ONE OF THE LANDINGS.
British Field Ambulance Men dressing the wounds of Turkish Soldiers.

VIEW OF SEDD-EL-BAHR BEACH SHOWING THE SS. "CLYDE" ON RIGHT.

landed at Beach Y probably owed its rescue as much to the courage and energy of Lieut.-Commander Adrian St. Vincent Keyes, R.N., as to anybody. He was chiefly responsible for the smartness of the original landing and for the efficiency of the subsequent re-embarcation. Sir Ian Hamilton thus acknowledged his services :

Lieutenant-Commander Keyes showed great coolness, gallantry, and ability. The success of the landing on Beach Y was largely due to his good services. When circumstances compelled the force landed there to re-embark, this officer showed exceptional resource and leadership in successfully conducting that difficult operation.

Admiral de Robeck expressed his entire concurrence, and Lieut.-Commander Keyes was rewarded with the Distinguished Service Order.

In estimating the action at Beach Y, it has to be remembered that it was largely a feint, and that its principal objects were to protect the flanks, to disseminate the enemy's forces, and to delay his reinforcements. To this extent it was at least partially successful, for it held up a large number of Turks who might otherwise have been thrown against the main attacks at the end of the peninsula. It may be reasonably said that too much was expected of it. That the enemy would have been massed in considerable strength upon Krithia was always fairly obvious, and that these two extremely isolated battalions would thus be exposed to a strong flank attack was also fairly plain. The order to march on Beach X, which apparently ignored the strong force of the enemy posted at Beach Y2, suggested inadequate air scouting. It also suggested a great danger that the column might have been cut off from any beach at all. This would almost inevitably have happened had not Colonel Koe come to blows so speedily with the Turks from Beach Y2. The landing at Beach Y was the only attack which failed, but though Sir Ian Hamilton afterwards observed that the tactical failure to make good the ground won was unfortunate, the right conclusion appears to be that the force was too weak for its allotted task, and that its weakness should have been foreseen. Considering its plight, arrangements should have been made earlier for its relief ; but it must also be noted that its partial failure had no adverse effect upon the main operations.

Of the main landings, that at Beach X, just north of Cape Tekke, was the most immediately successful, because it was accomplished with hardly any loss. The beach was narrow and

THE TRANSPORT "RIVER CLYDE" AS "THE NEW HORSE OF TROY."
She landed British troops on Gallipoli by running ashore, and poured out her cargo of men from doors cut in her side.

the cliff was low, so that the guns of the warships could be used with excellent effect. The first landing force consisted of two companies and a machine-gun section of the 1st Royal Fusiliers, who had been embarked on the battleship Implacable. The Turks were entrenched on the cliff, and they had constructed bomb-proof shelters. At dawn H.M.S. Swiftsure (Captain C. Maxwell-Lefroy, R.N.), which was the covering ship, began a fierce bombardment of the cliff. At 5.52 a.m. Captain H. C. Lockyer, R.N., took the Implacable, with an anchor down, to within 500 yards of the beach, this being the six-fathom limit. Sir Ian Hamilton remarked that " the Implacable's boldness was much admired by the Army." She smothered the cliff with her 12-inch shells, and the foreshore with 6-inch shrapnel. The storm of fire was so intense that not a Turk dared show his head. It was afterwards found that the shells had done very little damage to the trenches, though the ground around them was full of craters. But the bombardment served its purpose, and in two trips the Fusiliers were safely ferried ashore. They were accompanied by a beach working party furnished by the Anson Battalion of the Royal Naval Division. The landing was completed by 7 a.m. The beach master was Major W. T. C. Jones, D.S.O., R.M.L.I., who was commended in dispatches for his services. Admiral de Robeck said that " the manner in which this landing was carried out might well serve as a model."

Brigadier-General Marshall, commanding the 87th Brigade, was in control of the military operations undertaken from Beach X. His task was to endeavour to get into touch with the force which was simultaneously landing on Beach W. But the Beach W force was temporarily held up, and meanwhile Hill 114, on which the Turks were entrenched, intervened and was found to be a difficult obstacle. The Royal Fusiliers advanced firmly for a thousand yards or so, and were then heavily counterattacked by the Turks. Their right wing was rather badly exposed, and came under strong fire from a field battery established near Krithia. The position of the battery was made out, and signals were sent to the Implacable, which swiftly silenced it ; but meanwhile the Turkish counter-attack had forced the Royal Fusiliers to give ground. Two more battalions (of the 87th Brigade) were hurried ashore, and Hill 114 was then cleared of the enemy. At 11.30 a.m. the Royal Fusiliers joyfully joined hands with a portion of the splendid 1st Battalion of the Lancashire Fusiliers, from Beach W, on the slopes of the hill. Yet the Turks remained undaunted, and counter-attacked again from positions farther inland. They could not break the union between the two forces, but they pressed back General Marshall's brave troops almost to the edge of the cliffs. Nothing on that great day ever dismayed any of the units of the 29th Division. The men, with their backs to the sea and their faces to the foe, were incomparably resolute. They hastily dug themselves into shelter trenches, determined to hang on at any cost. When night fell they were holding the ground for half a mile round their landing-place, and their lines reached as far as

Hill 114. General Marshall was wounded during the day, but did not relinquish his command.

Beach W had meanwhile been the scene of one of the most wonderful and heroic exploits ever accomplished by the British Army. Sir Ian Hamilton wrote in his dispatch :

So strong, in fact, were the defences of Beach W that the Turks may well have considered them impregnable, and it is my firm conviction that no finer feat of arms has ever been achieved by the British soldier—or any other soldier—than the storming of these trenches from open boats on the morning of April 25.

The beach was practically in a bay enclosed by hills, and the way out of it led through a rather narrow gully. The Turks had fully expected a landing at this point, and had prepared for it with every device at their command. They had laid both land mines and sea mines. On the edge of the sea they had constructed a broad wire entanglement along the whole length of the beach. They had even stretched concealed barbed wire in the shallow waters. The heights overlooking the beach were covered with entrenchments, to which the gully gave sheltered access. Machine guns, which the naval fire could not search out, had been concealed in holes in the cliffs and trained on the hedge of barbed wire. Once the assailants had emerged from the cup-like bay, they were instantly exposed to fire from two strong infantry redoubts near Hill 138. The redoubts were in turn protected by wire entanglements 20 ft. broad, and their fire swept a bare open zone which had to be crossed in attacking them. From these redoubts another strong wire entanglement had been carried to the edge of the cliff, thus making communication between Beach W and the adjacent Beach V impossible until the redoubts had been taken. Add to these defences a host of snipers concealed behind every sand dune and every tuft of grass, and it was not surprising that the Turks firmly believed Beach W to be able to resist any attack. The position had one very slight weakness. There were rocks at the two ends of the bay which gave just a small foothold. From these rocks, and especially from those on the left under Cape Tekke, it was possible partially to enfilade the defences. To this tiny loophole the success eventually achieved against enormously heavy odds was in great measure due.

The battalion which won undying fame at the storming of Beach W was the 1st Battalion Lancashire Fusiliers, which was commanded by Major Bishop. Sir Ian Hamilton wrote that

"it was to the complete lack of the senses of danger or of fear of this daring battalion that we owed our astonishing success." The battalion was carried to Cape Helles in the cruiser Euryalus, and, as early as 4 a.m. had got into the ship's cutters and picket-boats designated for the duty of carrying the men ashore. At 5 a.m. the covering battleships opened a terrific fire on the beach and the whole of the defences, which was continued for nearly an hour. The result was disappointing, for it was afterwards found that neither the wire entanglements nor the trenches had suffered serious damage.

At 6 a.m. the great moment arrived. Eight picket-boats started for the shore in line abreast, each drawing four cutters packed with troops. In shallow water the picket-boats cast off, and the cutters were rowed to the beach. The central lines of boats made straight for the middle of the beach. A few swerved slightly to the right, nearer Cape Helles, while eight boats pulled direct for the rocks under Cape Tekke. With this last party was Brigadier-General Hare, commanding the 88th Brigade. All this time the Turks had held their fire, and had made no sound. As the first boat reached the beach a tremendous converging fusillade burst upon the dauntless men of Lancashire. They were swept with gusts of lead from rifles and machine-guns, and with a rain of small shells from hidden pom-poms. Almost the whole of the first lines of men who threw themselves upon the wire entanglements were swept away. In a few moments the edge of the sea was strewn with prostrate forms. So rapid was the slaughter that the watchers on the distant warships could not realize what was happening "Why are our men resting?" they exclaimed. The gallant fellows were resting, it was true, but theirs was already the long last rest of death in far too many cases. Yet those who still lived in the midst of the leaden hail never blenched. Led by their brave officers, they hacked their way fiercely and breathlessly through the wire entanglements. Few replied at this stage to the fire of the enemy. Their one thought was to burst the barrier, and to seek a less exposed position upon that death-strewn beach. It was at this terrible moment that the company which had deviated to the rocks beneath Cape Tekke helped to save a menacing situation. They had to a great extent escaped the cross-fire, and had been skilfully landed on the rocks. Some men

VIEW IN FRONT OF GABA TEPE.
A ravine lined with dug-outs and walls of sandbags.

clambered up the cliff-side, searched out the machine-gun sections in burrowed holes, and bayoneted the gunners to a man. Others turned the end of the wire entanglements and began a rapid enfilading fire upon the Turks. The slaughter on the main beach was slightly checked. The survivors of the three exposed companies tore their way through the barbed wire, and hurried right and left to the sheltering cliffs at the sides of the bay. Most of them made for the Cape Tekke side, and there the decimated companies were hurriedly but quite calmly re-formed by such officers as were still able to lead. There was no time to lose. The depleted ranks moved a short way inland and began clambering up the slopes in the direction of Hill 114, driving the Turks before them as they went, and clearing out the snipers. A smaller party had gathered under Cape Helles, and it painfully crept up to the crest of

BRITISH TROOPS RESTING UNDER THE SHADOW OF THE OLD FORT AT SEDD-EL-BAHR.

the cliffs near the lighthouse, only to be stopped by the line of wire entanglement stretching from the infantry redoubts to the edge of the cliff.

Soon after 9 a.m. the majority of the battalion had with extraordinary boldness made good their attempt to seize the Cape Tekke cliffs. Another regiment of infantry was landing, together with a detachment of the 2nd London Field Company, R.E., and a beach party composed of a platoon of the Anson Battalion. The beach master in charge of this party was Captain C. S. Townsend, R.N., and the assistant beach master was Commander (now Captain) B. St. G. Collard, R.N. Both remained on the beach all day under a galling fire superintending the further landing of men and stores, and both were commended in dispatches. The new arrivals had wisely landed under Cape Tekke. Hearing the shouts of the Lancashire Fusiliers above, they clambered up after them. The reinforcements enabled further progress to be made, and by ten o'clock three lines of Turkish trenches had been won. The beach was in British hands, and thenceforward the issue of the day at that particular point was never in doubt. Yet much had still to be done. The small party on Cape Helles was clinging tenaciously, but could make no progress. Major

Frankland, Brigade-Major of the 86th Infantry Brigade, went to its aid, and was shot dead. General Hare had been wounded at Cape Tekke, and his place had to be filled. Colonel Wolley-Dod, of the General Staff of the 29th Division, was sent ashore in his stead, with orders to organize a further advance. The position then was that the beach and the gully had been cleared of the enemy, and by 11.30 the force moving inland from Cape Tekke had got into touch with the Royal Fusiliers on Hill 114. But the redoubts near Hill 138 were still unassailed, and they formed the next objective.

About one o'clock the ground near Hill 138, and the infantry redoubts, were vigorously bombarded from the sea. At 2 p.m. the fine 4th Battalion of the Worcester Regiment advanced to assault the redoubts. The battalion, which was commanded by Lieutenant-Colonel D. E. Cayley, proved itself on this and on many later occasions to be animated by an admirable spirit of discipline and devotion. The men, who had to march a considerable distance, rushed impetuously up the bare glacis, and began to cut the barbed wire entanglement, heedless of the streams of bullets. Many were shot down, but their comrades persevered. With irresistible ardour they forced their way through the entanglements and leaped into the redoubts, bayoneting the stubborn defenders; but it was not until 4 p.m. that the hill and the field works were completely conquered.

With the capture of Hill 138, it seemed as though the exhausted troops who had landed on Beach W had done all that mortal man could do. Yet further demands were perforce made upon them. The landing on Beach V, on the other side of Cape Helles, had for the time being failed. Men were dying there in heaps. Could the Worcesters and some of the Lancashire Fusiliers get across the high ground on Cape Helles and help them by enfilading their assailants? No appeal was ever made to the men of the 29th Division to which they failed to respond. They began to attempt a rescue with quick cheerfulness. But for that day, at least, the fresh task was beyond their powers. The wire entanglement stretching from the captured redoubts to the edge of Cape Helles was not the only obstacle which barred their path. Beyond it lay the shattered ruins of the modern battery known as Fort No. 1. Its guns were silent, but the ruins were packed with Turkish riflemen, who poured in

a devastating fire upon the Worcesters and the other troops advancing against the new line of wire entanglement. The British soldiers were undismayed. "Through glasses," said Sir Ian Hamilton, "they could be seen quietly sniping away under a hellish fire as if they were pruning a vineyard." Yet they could not work miracles. The fire from Fort No. 1 grew heavier. Some of the troops which could not be landed on Beach V were diverted to Beach W. More of the 86th Brigade moved forward to strengthen the attack. But the Turks had been steadily sending up reinforcements from the direction of Krithia and Achi Baba. They were pressing hard all the way from Beach X to Fort No. 1. When night fell they were counter-attacking vigorously, and the British decided to be content to hold the ground they had won until the morning.

At the end of the day, therefore, the British position on this section of the peninsula extended from the lighthouse on Cape Helles, across Hill 138, then to Hill 114, and so to the low cliff at Beach X. The Turks gave the invaders no rest. They attacked repeatedly during the night, but were always driven back.

FRENCH TROOPS AT MUDROS.

The British line was thin, but it held. Every man on the beach was ordered into the trenches to assist. Officers and men alike, Engineers, Anson Marines, bluejackets, anybody and everybody who could pick up a rifle hurried forward. It was so dark that many of the beach working party could find no rifles, but those without weapons gallantly carried ammunition into the firing-line. One midshipman covered himself with bandoliers and groped his way up the gully. As he reached the trenches he was struck three times full in the chest. The impact of the bullets knocked him over, but he rose unhurt, for the bandoliers had saved him. During the night more troops were landed on Beaches W and X, and in the morning the British line was still unbroken.

Two more points must be recorded before leaving this phase of the Battle of the Landing. The first is that, in the opinion of the onlookers, there was not a man of the 1st Battalion Lancashire Fusiliers who had not earned the Victoria Cross half a dozen times on that murderous beach. The authorities thought the same, and in accordance with precedents set in the Indian Mutiny, the officers, non-commissioned officers, and men were each asked to select one of their number to receive the decoration. Their choice fell upon Captain Richard Raymond Willis, Sergeant Alfred Richards, and Private William Keneally, and the bestowal of the honours was thus recorded in the *London Gazette*:

On April 25, 1915, three companies and the headquarters of the 1st Batt. Lancashire Fusiliers, in effecting a landing on the Gallipoli Peninsula to the west of Cape Helles, were met by a very deadly fire from hidden machine-guns which caused a great number of casualties. The survivors, however, rushed up to and cut the wire entanglements, notwithstanding the terrific fire from the enemy, and, after overcoming supreme difficulties, the cliffs were gained and the position maintained.

Amongst the many very gallant officers and men engaged in this most hazardous undertaking, Captain Willis, Sergt. Richards, and Private Keneally have been selected by their comrades as having performed the most signal acts of bravery and devotion to duty.

The other point is that the Worcesters, who showed such determination in capturing the

LANDING TROOPS IN THE DARDANELLES.
The 6th Lancashire Fusiliers leaving the S.S. "Nile."
Inset: Major Bishop, Commander of the 1st Battalion Lancashire Fusiliers.

INDIAN TROOPS MARCHING AWAY FROM THE BEACH.

redoubts and in later actions, were specially commended for their general demeanour in a Brigade Order as follows :

The Brigade Commander wishes to place on record the great gallantry and devotion to duty displayed by Lieutenant-Colonel D. E. Cayley, officers, and men of the 4th Batt. Worcestershire Regiment during the operations since landing was effected on the Gallipoli Peninsula. The battalion has always been well in hand, and not a single straggler has been reported. They are a splendid example to the brigade.

It might be thought that no landing could have been more terrible than the storming of Beach W, but the scenes at Beach V, which lay between Cape Helles and the castle and village of Sedd-el-Bahr, were even worse. Beach V reproduced all the defensive characteristics of Beach W, with several formidable additions, and it was without the advantage of ledges of rocks at each end on which a foothold could be gained. On the contrary, the cliffs at the Cape Helles end were so perpendicular that it was impossible to think of climbing them ; while had they been scaled, the adventurous climbers would immediately have found themselves confronted by Fort No. 1 and an impassable zone of rifle fire. The bluff at the eastern end was crowned by the ruins of the castle and village, a nest of sharpshooters most difficult to dislodge. There were other important defensive positions which Beach W had lacked. There was a massive old ruined fort at the eastern end, between the shore and the village, which gave useful cover to the Turks. On the ridge which backed the bay, and commanding the whole amphitheatre, stood a ruined barrack, another

well-placed refuge for snipers. Then on the grassy terraces all around the amphitheatre riflemen were posted in snug concealment. Barbed wire had been extensively used, as at Beach W. Fifty yards back from the verge of the sea a great entanglement had been constructed, stretching from the ruined fort right across to Cape Helles. Sir Ian Hamilton declared that it was " made of heavier metal and longer barbs that I have ever seen elsewhere." Higher up the amphitheatre was traversed by another entanglement, which passed in front of the barrack and ended at the village. Yet a third entanglement ran at right angles to these two, at the eastern end of the beach. It went up the hill, and gave extra protection to the village and castle. The crests of the amphitheatre were scored with trenches, and were also provided with gun emplacements bearing four pom-poms. There were dummy pom-poms at other points to mislead the assailants. The ruined buildings, especially those on the flank, contained machine guns cleverly concealed. It was possible for the enemy to pour upon the beach a rain of rifle bullets and small shells surpassing in intensity any fire encountered at the other landings. The marvel was, not that the British attack was so long held up as in the event proved to be the case, but that it ever succeeded at all. The glorious annals of the British Army present no example of a position carried against more dreadful odds. Even this catalogue of defences does not exhaust the advantages which rested with the Turks,

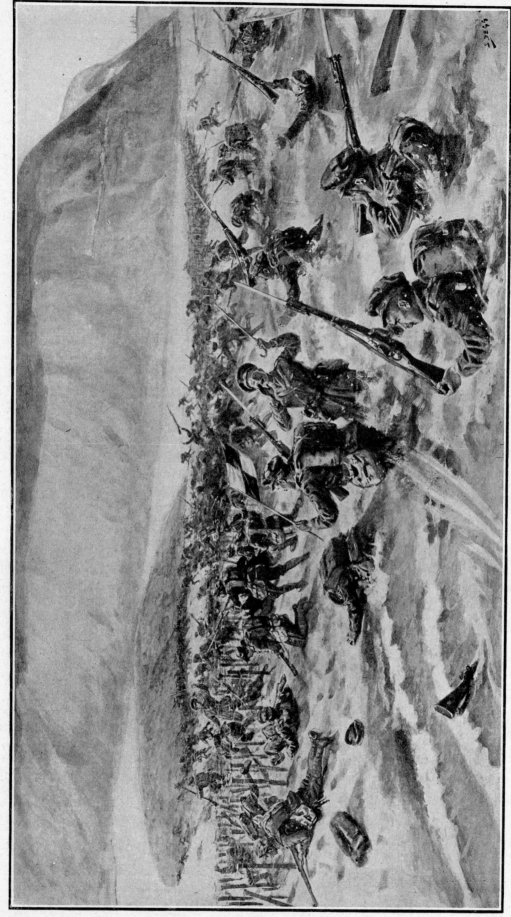

THE ASSAULT AT "LANCASHIRE LANDING," GALLIPOLI.

The opening phase of the Lancashire Fusiliers' attack which won three Victoria Crosses for the 1st Battalion at Beach W, April 25, 1915.

Behind amphitheatre and village the whole position was further dominated by Hill 141, a swelling height covered with entrenchments and entanglements. When all the amphitheatre and its adjuncts were overcome the hill had still to be won before the British position was in the least secure.

There was only one scanty advantage to be set against all these deterrent elements. Where the beach joined the grassy slopes, ten yards from the water's edge, the low escarpment four feet high gave slight shelter to men lying prone behind it. Many who survived the bloody conflict at Beach V owed their lives to those fifty inches of loose sandy soil.

It was recognized from the outset that Beach V was going to be the toughest task of all, and special and ingenious arrangements were made for the attack. It was decided that, as at the other landings, the first assault should be delivered by men sent ashore in open boats. It was also arranged, however, to endeavour to beach a steamer containing the bulk of the attacking force, who were to remain concealed within the steel hull of the vessel until the moment came for them to issue forth. The stratagem was a seaman's variation of the Wooden Horse of Troy. A stout collier, the River Clyde, was selected for the experiment, and she was specially prepared under the direction of Commander Edward Unwin, R.N. Great doors were cut in her sides, giving access to long gang-planks slung by ropes and sloping gradually to the bows. If the water proved to be sufficiently shallow, the men were to wade ashore from the gang-planks; but, if not, they were to pass into lighters which were to be placed between the steamer and the beach so as to form a bridge. From the beginning it was foreseen that the lighters would almost certainly be required. The bridge of the River Clyde was protected by steel plates. Twelve maxims, in rough casemates guarded by sandbags, were mounted in her bows and on the lower bridge.

The troops designated for this perilous enterprise were, in the first place, three companies of the 1st Royal Dublin Fusiliers, who were to go ashore in open boats. The River Clyde was packed with the rest of the Dublin Fusiliers, the 1st Royal Munster Fusiliers, half the 2nd Hampshire Regiment, the West Riding Field Company, R.E., and other details. She also carried Brigadier-General Napier, who was in immediate direction of the land attack, as well as several Staff officers. The total number of troops on board the collier was well over 2,000.

The attack began at dawn with a rapid bombardment from the battleship Albion, which made little real impression upon the defences. Then the plucky little picket-boats, eight in number, headed for the shore, each towing four cutters full of the Munsters. The River Clyde was already slowly approaching the beach, although the plan was that she was not to take the ground until the men in the open boats had delivered their attack. The Turks gave no sign. They never fired a single shot until the picket boats had cast off, and the first cutter slid on to the beach. Then burst forth, as though at a preconcerted signal, a fearful storm of projectiles, and in an instant the margin of sea and shore was transformed into a hell of destruction.

All the boats had made straight for the beach, for no protection was available on the flanks of the bay. The fire was so murderous that very few, either soldiers or bluejackets, survived it. The attack from the boats was practically wiped out. One boat entirely disappeared, with its occupants. Others were filled with killed and wounded before any attempt could be made to disembark. In a boat which continued to float only two men were left alive. Those of the Munsters who were able to jump out and wade ashore found themselves entangled in submerged barbed wire. As they emerged from the water, they were shot down until the beach was strewn with dead and dying. A few of the wounded, and one or two who miraculously passed through the terrible ordeal unscathed, managed to run or crawl up the beach to the shelter of the low escarpment, where they hastily dug themselves in. But the fate of most was either death or severe wounds. Nearly all the bluejackets shared the lot of the Munsters, and were destroyed where they stood. Not a boat ever got back. In all the records of the Navy and Army, there is no like tale of slaughter so instant and complete under such conditions. Few names have been associated with this epic exploit, but the memory of Lewis Jacobs, a brave able seaman of the Lord Nelson, must be preserved. He took his boat in to the beach unaided, after every soldier and seaman aboard had been either killed or wounded. To the end he pursued his appointed task undaunted. When last seen he was still trying to pole his

BRITISH OFFICERS WATCHING THE EFFECT OF A BOMBARDMENT.

cutter, with its tragic freight, towards the shore. While thus engaged he was shot down, and no man died that day more worthily. Other men of the Lord Nelson who behaved with conspicuous devotion were Leading-Seamen Colin McKechnie and Stanley E. Cullum, and Able Seamen Frederick T. M. Hyde, William E. Rowland, and Albert E. Bex. The first three were killed, the other two wounded. Bex received the Distinguished Service Medal.

The River Clyde had meanwhile moved ahead more rapidly than had been planned. "As often happens in war," wrote Sir Ian Hamilton afterwards, " the actual course of events did not quite correspond with the intentions of the Commander." The swift currents swirling round from the Dardanelles had affected the vessel's course, and she was beached, bows on, close to a reef of rock, and rather to the east of the point selected. The Turks had fully divined her significance, and a tornado of missiles was directed against her. It was at once seen by those on board that the water was too deep for wading ashore, and the two lighters which had been brought to form a bridge were quickly requisitioned. They were run out ahead of the collier, and

Lieutenant John A. V. Morse, R.N., at great peril to himself, helped to secure them at the bows. Unfortunately, owing to the current, they did not reach their proper stations, and a gap was left between the two. Seamen gallantly went ashore with lines to get them into position. Able Seaman William Charles Williams held on to a line in the water, despite the tremendous fusillade, for over an hour, until he was killed. For this devoted action he was posthumously decorated with the Victoria Cross.

The seamen on the reef called out to the soldiers to come ashore. One of the wooden gangways had been shot away, but it was still possible to reach the first lighter. A company of the Munster Fusiliers responded to the call. They came through the great holes in the vessel's side, and boldly faced the bullets which were rattling like hailstones against the hull. Running down the gangway, they leaped into the lighter, and tried to reach the shore. The gap between the two lighters was too broad to jump. The men scrambled into the sea, and those who were hit were mostly drowned, for their heavy equipment gave them no chance of escape. Those who got ashore rushed for the shelter of the low sandy bank. Many were shot when they reached the lighter, which was soon piled high with the dead and wounded. Just as a second company of the Munsters was endeavouring to disembark, the confusion was increased because the lighters drifted into a still more unfavourable position.

Then it was that Commander Unwin did the brave deed which won him the Victoria Cross. Observing from the ship that the lighters were becoming unmanageable, he entered the sea and stood up to his waist in water endeavouring to restore the bridge. He was assisted by Midshipman George L. Drewry, R.N.R., Midshipman Wilfrid St. A. Malleson, R.N., Able Seaman William Charles Williams (already mentioned), and Seaman George McKenzie Samson, R.N.R., upon all of whom the Victoria Cross was afterwards bestowed. Commander Unwin's work was thus described by Admiral de Robeck :

He worked on until, suffering from the effects of cold and immersion, he was obliged to return to the ship, where he was wrapped up in blankets. Having in some degree recovered, he returned to his work against the doctor's order and completed it. He was later again attended by the doctor for three abrasions caused by bullets, after which he once more left the ship, this time in a lifeboat, to save some wounded men who were lying in shallow water near the beach. He continued at this heroic labour under continuous fire, until forced to stop through pure physical exhaustion.

Midshipman Drewry, who doggedly helped with a cheerful disregard of the rifle and machine-gun fire, was wounded in the head, but still toiled on. Twice after he was hit he tried to swim from lighter to lighter with a line, and only gave up when he was completely exhausted. Thereupon Midshipman Malleson took the line, swam to the second lighter, and succeeded. The line broke, and twice again Malleson tried to repeat his exploit, but was unsuccessful. Seaman Samson stuck to the lighters all day, attending wounded and getting out lines, and was eventually dangerously hit.

Midshipman Malleson's work had meanwhile enabled the disembarcation to be continued, and a third company of the Munsters made a dash for the beach. The Turks had brought bigger guns to bear on the luckless collier and the lighters, and the company suffered so much from shrapnel that its losses were terrible. For a time further landings were forbidden. The battleships Albion and Cornwallis, and even the Queen Elizabeth herself, tried the effect of a further bombardment. Then the River Clyde disgorged more troops. Brigadier-General Napier, his Brigade-Major, Captain Costeker, and a number of men of the Hampshire Regiment, got into the lighters. Before they could land the line broke, and the unwieldy vessels swung again into deep water. The troops were ordered to lie down, but they were very much exposed, and both General

Napier and Captain Costeker were killed. General Napier was struck by three bullets, but was conscious for some time before he died. According to one published version, he sent a message to his men, saying that he would like to kiss the entire Fusilier Brigade. The Albion sent in a launch and pinnace, manned by volunteer crews, who offered to try to restore the lighters once more to their right positions, but by this time it was realized that further slaughter would be futile, and the boats were not used until after dark.

The general position at Beach V between 10 and 11 a.m. was sufficiently disconcerting. One way and another, about 1,000 men had left the River Clyde. Nearly half of these had been killed, wounded, or drowned. Most of the remainder were lying huddled under the sandy escarpment on the beach, many with wounds. More than 1,000 men were still cooped up on the collier, unable to land. The Turkish fire had grown in intensity, and it was almost certain death to pass down the gangway. The lighters had been pulled back into position once again, though a gap still separated them from the land. The British were held up, and it was even expected that the Turks would counter-attack. Had it not been for the screaming machine-gun battery on the River Clyde they would probably have done so ; but the maxims held off the enemy, and also helped to protect the men under cover on the beach. Any continuance of the landing while daylight lasted was held to be sheer sacrifice of life. Word was passed round

THE ROLL CALL.

that no more men were to attempt to go ashore until after dark.

Yet the efforts to succour the unfortunate wounded were not stayed. At various times during the day the work of rescue produced acts of great heroism. Surgeon Peter Burrows Kelly, R.N., attached to the Royal Naval Air Service, had been wounded in the foot during the morning. He remained in the River Clyde until the morning of the 27th, and during that time attended 750 wounded men, " although in great pain and unable to walk during the last twenty-four hours." He was given the Distinguished Service Order.

Commander Unwin's share in the noble work of saving the wounded has been already noted. Petty Officer Geoffrey Charlton Paine Rummings, of the Royal Naval Air Service, was specially commended for assisting Commander Unwin in these labours, and received the Conspicuous Gallantry Medal. The same medal was bestowed upon another Petty Officer of the Air Service, John Hepburn Russell, who was wounded " in gallantly going to

Commander Unwin's assistance." Two other recipients were Second-Class Petty Officer Frederick Gibson and Ordinary Seaman Jesse Lovelock, both of the Albion. Gibson took wounded to the River Clyde under heavy fire, having previously jumped overboard with a line and got his boat beached to complete the bridge to the shore. Lovelock assisted in getting a pontoon into position, and also helped in conveying wounded from the beach and the boats to the collier, " displaying great gallantry and coolness under fire."

When it was seen to be hopeless to try to gain more ground on Beach V that day, it became a question what to do with the remainder of the troops still on the battleships, who had been selected to reinforce the assault at that spot. At first it was proposed to send them round to Beach Y, where they were certainly sorely needed ; but eventually, as already explained, they were sent to Beach W. The River Clyde still drew at intervals the fire of the Turkish artillery. She was even shelled by big howitzers from the Asiatic side, but this battery was quickly suppressed by the battleships, though not before her sides had been pierced by four large shells, none of which exploded. The rifle and machine-gun fire of the Turks continued unceasingly until sunset, when it gradually died away. At dusk several small parties of the troops lying under the bank

BRITISH TROOPS LANDING GUNS.

Inset : An Australian gun entrenched on the Peninsula.

HORSES IN THEIR DUG-OUTS.

on the beach were able to creep under the lee of the old fort at the eastern end of the bay, quite near the River Clyde.

After dark there occurred perhaps the greatest miracle of this strange day. About 8 p.m. the whole of the thousand men still on board the River Clyde came out and quietly walked down the gangway without a single casualty. Not a shot was fired against them.

Efforts were then made to clear the old fort and the outskirts of the village, but on each occasion the British were repulsed. The moon was bright, the enemy were still able to fire accurately, and there was no chance of an effective advance. It was necessary to await the dawn, which seemed to come slowly enough. The men had very few senior officers with them, for most of these had been killed or wounded. Lieutenant-Colonel Carrington Smith, commanding the 2nd Hampshires, was amongst those who had fallen, and his adjutant had been wounded, as well as the adjutant of the Munsters. Two officers of the General Staff, Lieutenant-Colonel Doughty-Wylie and Lieutenant-Colonel Williams, had landed from the River Clyde and remained on

the beach all night, heartening the scattered units for the next morning's work. At daybreak they began to collect the survivors of the Dublin and Munster Fusiliers, and to form them with the two companies of the Hampshires into a force capable of a fresh attack. Those also at work included Captain R. C. K. Lambert, R.N., the beach master, and Commander N. W. Diggle, assistant beach master.

The whole of the episodes on April 25 on Beach V had formed an epitome of both the madness and the glory of the attack upon the Dardanelles.

One other incident in this area must be related to complete the narrative. A half-company of the Dublin Fusiliers had been landed at a camber just round the corner on the other side of Sedd-el-Bahr, where they were quite cut off from the rest of the operations. They tried to make their way across to Beach V, but the fire was too hot, and they had to desist. The little handful then made several attempts to enter the village of Sedd-el-Bahr, but were driven back. By noon they had only 25 effectives left, and as they were collected at a sheltered spot, they were got away.

LIEUT.-COL. KOE,
Commander of the landing force at Beach Y.

The wonderful deeds already related only became gradually known to the public, and it implies no slight upon the brave English soldiers and sailors who fought at the end of the peninsula to say that the chief preliminary interest of the whole Empire in the Battle of the Landing lay in the great attack delivered north of Gaba Tepe by the Australian and New Zealand Corps. Stirring accounts of the fighting qualities of the Divisions from the Antipodes had already reached England. Much had been written about their fine physique, their intense ardour, their happy adaptability, and their anxious desire to show to the world the stuff of which they were made. For the great Commonwealth and for the distant Dominion the moment was specially historic. Their sons were fighting in the greatest of all wars for the first time, and they were fighting not only for the Empire as a whole, but still more for the great heritage they had acquired and developed across the seas. Upon the Australians and New Zealanders a very special responsibility rested that day. It rested with them to prove that they were worthy to hold and to keep their own vast lands. More was at stake than a battle with the Turks on the rugged heights which lay before them. The future of the world was at stake, and they were striking their first great blows in the mighty struggle into which all mankind was gradually

being drawn. The Empire was watching eagerly to see how they acquitted themselves. Right nobly did they respond to the call. No one who knew them had ever doubted the valour of the Australians and New Zealanders. When night fell upon the Gallipoli Peninsula on April 25 the impression was confirmed that, as fighting men, the Australians and New Zealanders were second to none in the Empire. Throughout all the weary months which followed that impression was strengthened.

The attack delivered by the Australian and New Zealand Army Corps was by far the greatest of all the assaults made at the Battle of the Landing. The force immediately sent ashore numbered over 4,000, and by 2 p.m. this number had been increased to 12,000. The landing was under the direction of Rear-Admiral C. F. Thursby, C.M.G., whose squadron consisted of the following ships :

Battleships : Queen, London, Prince of Wales, Triumph, and Majestic.
Cruiser : Bacchante.
Destroyers : Beagle, Bulldog, Foxhound, Scourge, Colne, Usk, Chelmer, and Ribble.
Seaplane Carrier : Ark Royal.
Balloon Ship : Manica.
Fifteen Trawlers.

There were also a number of transports. About 1,500 of the troops were placed on the Queen, the London, and the Prince of Wales before leaving Mudros Bay, and these were to land first. The whole squadron left Mudros Bay on the afternoon of April 24, and steamed slowly through the night with all lights extinguished towards its destination. The appointed rendezvous was five miles from the landing-place, and it was reached at 1 a.m. The moonlight was very brilliant, and as the moon did not set until 3 a.m. it was afterwards thought that the watchers on the hillsides may have become early aware of the nearness of the flotilla. The soldiers on the battleships, who were mostly sleeping calmly, were aroused and served with a hot meal. A visitor to the mess decks wrote that " the Australians, the majority of whom were about to go into action for the first time under the most trying circumstances, possessed at 1 o'clock in the morning courage to be cheerful, quiet, and confident. There was no sign of nerves or undue excitement, such as one might reasonably have expected." At 1.20 a.m. H.M.S. Queen, the flagship, gave the order to lower the boats. The picket-boats were also lowered to take them in tow. The troops fell in on the quarter-decks of the battleships, and at 2.5 a.m. the signal was made for the 1,500 men to embark. As at the other landings, each picket-boat towed four cutters. Another 2,500 men were transferred from the transports to destroyers, which were to stand in as close to the shore as possible. The cutters, after landing their first loads, were to make for the destroyers and bring the rest of the men ashore.

The transfer of the troops to the small craft was effected very rapidly and in complete silence. The decks of the battleships were cleared for action, the crews went to general quarters, and at 2.58 a.m. the squadron approached the shore at a speed of five knots. The intention was to make the first landing just before daybreak.

At 4.10 a.m. the battleships Triumph and Majestic, and the cruiser Bacchante, were 2,500 yards from the shore, in line abreast, and four cables apart. The outline of the coast could just dimly be seen. The picket-boats were ordered to go ahead, and steamed slowly past the battleships, towing the heavily-laden boats. There was no preliminary bombardment, as it was hoped to effect a surprise. At 4.50 a.m. the enemy showed a light on shore, and three minutes later a strong fusillade broke out from rifles and a machine gun, wounding a number of the men in the boats.

The blood of the Australians was up. They saw a battalion of Turks running forward. The moment the keels touched the beach they leaped into the water. They waited for no orders. They fired no shots. Before the astonished Turks quite realized what was happening they were into them with the cold steel. The first Turk was bayoneted, as has been already noted, exactly at five minutes past five.

The Turks broke and fled, though some of them had no chance to escape, and were slain in their trenches. The first entrenchments were taken, and with them a machine-gun.

SUPPLYING TURKISH PRISONERS WITH WATER.
Inset : Drawing water through filter-pumps.

THE OLD FORT NEAR THE BEACH AT SEDD-EL-BAHR
After the landing of the British Force.

Then the Australians found themselves confronted with the steep cliff covered with thick scrub. The enemy had another trench half-way up, and were pouring in a galling fire. They had sharpshooters behind every bush, and were harassing not only the men on the beach, but still more the fresh boat-loads coming ashore from the destroyers. Three boats broke away from their tows, and drifted along the coast, helpless under a rain of bullets. The determined men at the base of the cliffs only paused to charge their magazines, and to throw aside their packs. Then they clambered with desperate haste up the cliff-side, cleared the second trench within a quarter of an hour, and pursued the startled Ottomans to the top. There was no semblance of order in that first wild rush, for there was no chance of keeping rank. Every man fought for himself, but the one universal object was to get forward.

The units of the first attack formed the 3rd Australian Infantry Brigade, and they were commanded by Colonel E. G. Sinclair Maclagan, D.S.O. Both Sir Ian Hamilton and Admiral de Robeck afterwards testified to the extraordinary gallantry and devotion of the Brigade, and of its admirable commander. The 1st and 2nd Brigades were rapidly following, and as they neared the beach they saw " a glass flat sea covered with a shallow mist, and beyond, the tops of green hills peering through the vapour, dim shapes of warships and transports, and a fleeting glimpse of a seaplane as it winged its way over the Turkish position." Nearer in

they could hear the continuous crackle of rifle-fire, which developed into a roar as they leaped into the water up to their armpits, and waded ashore, to be immediately hurried forward up the cliff to reinforce the 1st Brigade. The Turks by this time were bringing field-guns and howitzers into position at a respectful distance. They had even summoned warships to the Narrows, and were emulating the exploits of the Queen Elizabeth by firing shells right across the peninsula at the Australian landing-place. It became necessary to order the transhipment from the transports to be effected farther out, and this caused considerable delay. Captain E. K. Loring, R.N., was in charge of the naval transport arrangements, while Captain A. A. Vyvyan, R.N., and Commander C. C. Dix, R.N., acted as beach master and assistant beach master respectively. The beach was very narrow and was constantly under shell-fire. The landing, as has been mentioned, was made a mile north of the point originally selected. In the end the mistake proved a boon to Anzac, but on the first day it eventually brought about much confusion, owing to the small space available. The beach was crowded with fighting men and wounded, and the units became very mixed. The covering warships were strenuously bombarding the enemy, but they could distinguish few definite targets.

No better men than the Australians and New Zealanders could be found for extricating order out of such chaos. The attack had got out of hand, chiefly by reason of the headlong pursuit undertaken by the forces early ashore. They had broken into groups and were ardently chasing the Turks without much regard for concerted operations. The ground was very broken and diversified, and the undergrowth made it difficult for the detachments to keep in touch with each other. Some small bodies of Australians pressed a very long way indeed. It was even said, though the statement was never fully established, that some of them almost crossed the peninsula, and came in sight of Maidos and the Narrows. What is certain is that many were killed, others overpowered, and that the breaks in the ground hid the remains of some who had to be written down as missing. The Turks at this period were fighting in equally irregular order. They had become very numerous, and had recovered their balance, but presented small resemblance to military array. What they did with great effect was to keep up a constant fire, which wrought considerable execution. It was afterwards acknowledged to be practically impossible to give a consecutive account of these stages of the battle. Isolated episodes can only be selected and strung together. Thus it was found that the Turks were enfilading the beach with shrapnel from guns, some of which were posted on Gaba Tepe, and others far to the north. The worst series of casualties of the day were due to this shrapnel fire. Parties of the 9th

and 10th Battalions daringly charged three Krupp guns and put them out of action. One Australian fell over a cliff 100 feet high and was picked up little the worse. A New Zealander was slipping down a stone gully, and was warned that there was a land mine at the bottom. " Catch me when I come up ! " was his nonchalant response. A wounded man had his mouth shattered. " Got it where the chicken got the axe," he gasped with a contorted smile, and then he fainted as the stretcher-bearers arrived.

The battle on the heights and ridges was really pulled into a more coherent form by the steady arrival of strong reinforcements on both sides. At 2 p.m. about 12,000 Australians had landed, and more were coming ashore. Two batteries of Indian Mountain Artillery had also been landed. The enemy had already reached considerably greater numbers. Troops from Maidos were pouring across the peninsula through Eski-keui, and it was estimated that before noon there must have been 20,000 Turks in or near the firing-line. They checked the tendency to make isolated dashes, and they also compelled the formation of a more definite line. The Anzacs eventually found themselves posted in good strength on a semi-circular front, of which the left was on the high ground over Fisherman's Hut, while the right touched the cliffs about a mile north of Gaba Tepe. They

SEDD-EL-BAHR FORT.
A corner of wire entanglements round Sedd-el-Bahr Fort.

AN AUSTRALIAN IN THE TRENCHES.
Note the gramophone on right.

knew then full well that what they held they could keep. They had " made good."

The Turks counter-attacked repeatedly during the afternoon. They came on in swarms, especially against the 3rd Brigade and the left of the 2nd Brigade. The Anzacs never budged, and once or twice even charged in their turn. They had discovered early on that first day that though the Turk was a stubborn man behind a rifle, he seemed to dread cold steel more than death itself. The British warships had got a better range, and their fire greatly helped to check the counter-attacks. The Anzacs said afterwards that the roar of the ships' guns was so shattering that they had to tear up their " pull-through " rags in order to stuff their ears. General Birdwood and his staff went ashore in the course of the afternoon to devise further measures for holding the position, and also to arrange for the landing of some field guns next morning.

Soon after 5 p.m. the Turks hurled the most determined counter-attack of the day against the 3rd Brigade, which resolutely refused to be dislodged, and retaliated with the utmost vigour. The Turks lost heavily in this advance, as in all their counter-attacks. Their losses throughout the day were very great, especially after the Anzacs got up some machine-guns. The enemy came on in close formation, and were so slaughtered that long afterwards, according to Sir Ian Hamilton, the whole surrounding country was strewn with their dead. The guns to the north and on Gaba Tepe, which had been enfilading the beach, were silenced by the covering ships late in the afternoon ; but the more distant Turkish artillery was still difficult to deal with.

The position towards sunset was that the Turks were still bringing up more men, and their guns were pounding the Anzacs hard. It was therefore deemed advisable to contract the line for the night.

A Special Correspondent who witnessed the first day's conflict afterwards wrote :

Some idea of the difficulty to be faced may be gathered when it is remembered that every round of ammunition, all water, and all supplies had to be landed on a narrow beach and then carried up pathless hills, valleys, and bluffs several hundred feet high, to the firing line. The whole of this mass of troops, concentrated on a very small area, and unable to reply, were exposed to a relentless and incessant shrapnel fire, which swept every yard of the ground, although fortunately a great deal of it was badly aimed or burst too high. The reserves were engaged in road making and carrying supplies to the crests, and in answering the calls for more ammunition.

A serious problem was getting away the wounded from the shore, where it was impossible to keep them. All those who were unable to hobble to the beach had to be carried down from the hills on stretchers, then hastily dressed and carried to the boats. The boat and beach parties never stopped working throughout the entire day and night.

The courage displayed by these wounded Australians will never be forgotten. Hastily dressed and placed in trawlers, lighters, and ships' boats, they were towed to the ships. I saw some lighters full of bad cases. As they passed the battleship, some of those on board recognized her as the ship they had left that morning, whereupon, in spite of their sufferings and discomforts, they set up a cheer, which was answered by a deafening shout of encouragement from our crew.

I have, in fact, never seen the like of these wounded Australians in war before, for as they were towed amongst the ships, whilst accommodation was being found for them, although many were shot to bits and without hope of recovery, their cheers resounded through the night and you could just see, amidst a mass of suffering humanity, arms being waved in greeting to the crews of the warships. They were happy because they knew they had been tried for the first time in the war and had not been found wanting. They had been told to occupy the heights and hold on, and this they had done for 15 mortal hours under an incessant shell fire, without the moral and material support of a single gun ashore, and subjected the whole time to the violent counter-attacks of a brave enemy, led by skilled leaders, whilst his snipers, hidden in caves and thickets and amongst the dense scrub, made a deliberate practice of picking off every officer who endeavoured to give a word of command or to lead his men forward.

No finer feat of arms has been performed during the war than this sudden landing in the dark, this storming of the heights, and, above all, the holding on to the position thus won whilst reinforcements were being poured from the transports.

During the night the Turks continued to attack, and on one occasion even charged the 8th Battalion with the bayonet. The Australians were equally good with the bayonet by night and by day. They responded in kind, and there were no more Turkish bayonet charges that night. When dawn broke the Anzacs had firmly held a good square mile of the Gallipoli Peninsula, and it was clear they meant to go on holding it.

While the Anzacs were engaged near Gaba Tepe, some transports containing a portion of the Royal Naval Division were taken up the coast towards Bulair, in order to distract the enemy's attention. There was no attempt to land, and it was doubtful whether the demonstration served any really useful purpose.

The task of the French Expeditionary Force on the first day of the Battle of the Landing was confined to an attack by one regiment upon the positions on the Asiatic side of the entrance to the Straits. The regiment selected was three battalions strong, and numbered 2,800 rank and file. It met with fierce opposition, had very heavy losses, and displayed in its assault a courage and dash which made its onslaught worthy to be compared to the full with the desperate struggles on the other side

of the Straits. The object of the French landing was to prevent the enemy from making effective use of the Asiatic shore, and from attacking by gun-fire the transports at the end of the peninsula. In this our Allies very largely succeeded, but in drawing the fire of the Turkish guns they suffered greatly themselves. It was never intended that they should permanently make good the footing they quickly secured.

The French attack began with a heavy bombardment from the French warships, which were assisted by the Russian cruiser Askold (Captain Ivanoff). Contre-Amiral E. P. A. Guepratte was in general control of the operations, of which Sir Ian Hamilton rightly wrote that, "They contributed largely to the success of the British landings." The disembarcation was effected about 9.30 a.m., on the western side of the River Mendere, and immediately under the battered citadel of Kum Kale. The landing was begun under a terrific fire. One boat was completely smashed, and in others many men were wounded. A captain was the first to leap overboard and wade ashore, and the dauntless troops followed him with irresistible ardour. The castle was quickly stormed, the men paying no heed to the bullets which streamed upon them from machine guns. They cleared the interior of the castle, bayoneting the Turks as they went, and fought their way through the little village to its southern

A BRITISH SOLDIER SLEEPING ON A BED OF LIVE SHELLS.

side. Their next objective was the village of Yeni Shehr, but they were held up by three Turkish regiments which were strongly entrenched, and could get no farther that day. Four times during the succeeding night the Turks made powerful counter-attacks, led by German officers, but each time they were driven back with the bayonet, until the ground intervening was strewn with the enemy's dead. At one period 400 Turks were cut off from their comrades by the fire of the battleships, and were made prisoners. Next morning, however, it was plain that further progress was impossible without heavy reinforcements, and the troops were ordered to re-embark. They did so under the guns of the French warships without suffering further opposition. They had performed their task gallantly, but at a great cost. In that one day and night the regiment had lost one-fourth of its effective strength, having suffered 754 casualties. These were : killed, 167 ; wounded, 459 ; missing, 116.

The Battle of the Landing has now been described up to the morning of the second day. The forces at Beach Y and at Kum Kale had been, or were being, withdrawn. The isolated Anzacs were holding a shortened semicircular line against the gathering masses of the enemy. The little force at De Tott's Battery was holding its ground, but was still far from any other body. The exhausted troops at Beach V

were isolated also, and remained clustering under the old fort and the sandy bank, not having yet advanced to the attack of the village and castle of Sedd-el-Bahr, and Hill 141. The only two forces which had effected a junction were those landed at Beaches W and X, and they held a very narrow strip of the south-western corner of the peninsula. A tremendous further effort was necessary if the slender foothold obtained was to be made good. With what vigour and determination the advance was made, and at what price, must in turn be related. After 24 hours the British were ashore, but that was all. Their position continued to be precarious and seriously menaced.

The great fault of the plan of the Battle of the Landing was that the attacking forces were too dispersed, and that too many landings were attempted, in some cases in insufficient strength. The landing of the Anzacs north of Gaba Tepe was probably a mistake from first to last. It was a repetition of the episode of Beach Y on a larger scale, and was doubtless due to an underestimation of the strength of the enemy's positions farther south. Had the splendid Australian and New Zealand troops been thrown into the scale before Krithia and Achi Baba the first stages of the attack upon the Gallipoli Peninsula might have reached a different conclusion.

CHAPTER XCV.

THE ADVANCE FROM WARSAW: LAST STAGES OF THE SUMMER CAMPAIGN.

ON August 5 the German troops entered Warsaw. On September 18 followed the fall of Vilna. The intervening forty-four days form practically the conclusion of the great Austro-German offensive against Russia which, having begun on May 2 with the battle of Gorlitse and Tarnoff, was throughout the summer of 1915 the main, we might almost say, the absorbing, concern of the enemy.

From the point of view of strategy, two distinct phases can be distinguished in the advance from Warsaw to Vilna ; the fall of Brest Litovsk on August 25 can be taken as the landmark between them. The military operations of the first period carried to its logical conclusion the concentric movement against Eastern Poland. From the north across the Nareff, from the west across the Vistula, from the south past Lublin and Cholm, the enemy was advancing against the strategic centre and main railway junction of the *place d'armes* of Western Russia, the fortress of Brest Litovsk. On the day of its fall the Germans gained also possession of Bielostok, the junction of five railway lines, from Warsaw, Ossovets, Grodno, Volkovysk, and Brest Litovsk. Two days earlier Austrian troops had entered Kovel, where the railway

line leading from Warsaw to Kieff crosses that which unites Brest Litovsk with Rovno. The advance of the Austro-German armies during the three weeks which followed on the fall of Warsaw, carried them thus from the circumference of the semi-circle Ossovets-Lomza-Warsaw-Ivangorod-Cholm to its diameter, of which the railway line Bielostok-Kovel is the most essential part ; Brest Litovsk lies exactly half-way between Bielostok and Kovel and is the centre of that sector. Whilst the Austro-German armies, under Mackensen and Prince Leopold, of Warsaw fame, were forcing the line of the Bug, the northern group under Hindenburg was mainly engaged in reducing the Russian fortresses on the Niemen. On August 17 fell Kovno, on August 26 our Allies evacuated Olita, in the first days of September they had to abandon Grodno, their last stronghold on the River Niemen.

Thus four weeks after the fall of Warsaw, the Austro-German armies were in possession of the entire Bug-Niemen line. The supposition had been frequently expressed in previous strategic speculations that that line formed the ultimate goal of the enemy's endeavours in the Eastern theatre of war, and that having reached it, he would pass to the defensive, transferring his

GENERAL IVANOFF.

main forces to some other front. Yet, even after the fall of Brest, the Austro-German offensive showed no sign of slackening. Evidently the goal of the Germanic armies lay still farther east. What was it ? Was it Kieff or was it Petrograd ? It now appears that neither the oldest, sacred capital of East-European Slavdom, nor the centre of the modern Russian State, was the immediate objective of the Germanic commanders. They seem to have been aiming at something far less impressive from the point of view of the layman, but far more important from that of the strategist : at the railway line which crosses the Pripet Marshes between Baranovitchy and Sarny, and connects Vilna with Rovno. The skilful retreat of the Russian armies had, time after time, deprived the German commanders of the "crowning mercy," which they were hoping for and seeking after; they never achieved their second Sedan on an infinitely bigger scale, which would have settled the war in so far as Eastern Europe was concerned. But if they could not capture the Russian army, they hoped to reduce it to practical impotence by forcing it to abandon the railway line across the Pripet Marshes, the biggest and most impassable area of morasses in Europe. Had our Allies been forced to abandon that railway connecting Vilna and Rovno, their armies would have been cut in two by the swamps of Polesie ; all direct communication between the troops operating to the north of them and those

concentrated in the southern area would have ceased. Not a single other railway line crosses from north to south the 180 miles of marshland which lie between the Vilna-Baranovitchy-Luniniets-Sarny-Rovno line and the River Dnieper. Even beyond it there is no direct line connecting the northern and the southern area ; it is more than 100 miles east of the Dnieper that the two railway systems join at a small railway-station in the government of Tchernihoff.

With the fall of Brest Litovsk on August 25, the central sector of the western of the two railway lines which run from Vilna to Rovno passed into the hands of the enemy. A further advance in force due east of Brest, through the marshes against Luniniets, would have been a most hazardous undertaking ; in fact, it would hardly have been practicable. It was but natural to start the operations against the eastern line by an offensive against the two termini, Vilna and Rovno. Having captured these two points, the Austro-German forces might have tried a converging movement against Luniniets along the three railway lines leading towards it from the north, west and south. Even then they would still have been confronted by a very difficult task. No big numbers of troops can operate in that region of swamps ; nor is it probable that their offensive could have been supported by flanking movements against the Luniniets-Gomel line, either from the north or the south.

Preparatory operations for an attack in the direction of Vilna had been carried on ever since the fall of Warsaw ; in the last week of August these operations assumed the character of a general · offensive. In front of Rovno, where since the beginning of July the Bug and the Zlota Lipa had been in the main the dividing line between the two armies, the Austro-German forces reopened their offensive on August 27. Thus after the fall of Brest Litovsk three separate zones came into existence in the Eastern theatre of war. Lithuania and the Baltic Provinces formed the northern division. Vilna was in it the immediate objective of the German armies, the Vilna-Dvinsk front forming, for the time being, a secondary area of operations. The central district lay in the region of the Pripet Marshes.

The strategical centre of the southern zone was Rovno ; the front between the Zlochoff-Tarnopol-Volotchisk railway line and the Dniester formed at the southern end of that zone a less important though by no means negligible extension of the battle line ; it became in September the scene of severe fighting and of some marked Russian victories.

Considering the supreme importance of the Vilna-Rovno line, one cannot wonder at the extreme stubbornness with which our Allies defended its two decisive areas. There was hardly any need for explaining the change in strategy by the changes which had taken place in the highest Russian commands. There is no exaggeration in the statement that, since the days when under the still immediate influence of recent, unexpected, staggering defeats, our

CROSS-EXAMINATION AT THE FRONT.
An officer of the Austrian Intelligence Department endeavouring to elicit information from captured Russian soldiers.

65—2

Allies had to abandon the line of the San, the link between the Vistula and the Dniester— never since those days had so much been at stake as was at stake in the battles fought for the Vilna-Luniniets-Rovno line. Vilna was held by the Russian armies to the very last, perhaps even longer than was prudent. Their retreat from that district, executed at a moment when they seemed surrounded by the enemy, was a piece of supreme strategic skill; but only the enormous importance of that region justifies the delay in the retreat which had rendered necessary acro- batic feats in strategy. With the capture of Vilna, however, only one-half was accomplished of the task with which the Austro-German armies were confronted; and few things are more embarrassing and more costly than partial successes. The German armies suc- ceeded in their attempt against Vilna; the Austrian troops failed in front of Rovno. It is

AN AUSTRIAN ARMOURED TRAIN.

easy to guess how German generals or military writers explained that difference in results, but it seems more than doubtful whether impartial history can accept their explanation. The task of the German armies was from the very outset incomparably easier than that of the Austrians, the forces at their disposal were considerably bigger, and their work was half done when the Austro-Hungarian troops had only just opened their offensive against the line of the Bug and the Zlota Lipa. Once the line of the Niemen was forced, Vilna was bare of any strong natural lines of resistance; the broken ground, the lakes and the dense forests of Lithuania did not work altogether in favour of the defending troops. The forces of our Allies were not sufficient for establishing a con- tinuous line of defence; in the absence of such a line the country offered to the attacking side exceptional facilities for strategic man-

œuvres, especially as the distances over which these evolutions could be carried out were very considerable. A circle drawn round Vilna at a radius of one hundred miles hardly touches the two nearest powerful obstacles to the move- ments of the German armies, the Dvina in the north-east and the Pripet Marshes in the south-east; the country which intervenes between Vilna and Dvinsk, Minsk and Barano vitchy offered full scope to attempts at envelop- ing the central position of the Russian armies.

Very different were the conditions in the southern zone. The front between the Kovel- Sarny railway line and the Dniester is more or less equal in length to that extending between Dvinsk and the railway-junction of Barano- vitchy, both measuring about 200 miles in length. The nature of the southern zone limits, however, all offensive against it to frontal attacks. The main courses of practically all the rivers in that district tend due north or south, and offer a number of consecutive, powerful lines of defence. The wooded hills between Zlochoff and Teofilpol form the watershed between the basins of the Pripet and the Dniester. In that region the upper courses of their confluents wind in different directions, adding to the defensive strength of that narrow centre. North of Lutsk and Rovno the Styr and Horyn are surrounded by wide swamps; in fact, in that region the Marshes of the Pripet extend in the valleys of its con- fluents for a considerable distance south of the Kovel-Kieff railway. South of the Zlochoff- Tarnopol line the numerous tributaries of the Dniester, the Zlota Lipa, the Strypa, and the Sereth, and even minor streams like the Koro- piec and the Dzuryn, offer excellent positions for defence. The marshes which line their upper courses cease only where these rivers enter the region of deep cañons; in fact, the two systems of natural defence, which attain their highest development along the Pripet and the Dniester, extend to a minor degree throughout the area of their tributaries. However well deserved was the praise which the Russian armies under General Ivanoff received for their brilliant defence of Rovno and their victories in Austrian Podolia, it would hardly be fair to blame the Austrian armies for their failure, as is often done by their German " friends " and allies.

The end of the summer, as indicated by the calendar, may be also taken as the real close of the Austro-German summer campaign against

DEFEAT OF VON BELOW'S CAVALRY RAIDERS.
Russian Cavalry successfully expelling the Germans from Molodetchna.

THE RUSSIAN RETREAT.
Russian troops removing the points on a railway.

Russia. Three weeks after the fall of Vilna the centre of interest shifted from the north-eastern front to the new theatre of war in the Balkans. What was at that time the position of the Austro-German armies with regard to the Dvinsk-Vilna-Rovno railway line ? It can be described in few words. In the northern zone, from a point a few miles south of Dvinsk to one lying a similar distance to the south of Baranovitchy, the railway had passed into the hands of the enemy ; the entire southern portion, east of the rivers Jasiolda and the Horyn, had remained in the possession of our Allies. Thus the Austro-German campaign beyond the Niemen and the Bug, during the late summer of 1915, failed to achieve its main strategic object.

The weeks which followed on the fall of Warsaw were perhaps the most critical in the history of the Eastern campaign, and never did the leadership of the Russian generals and the fighting power of the Russian soldier show themselves in a more brilliant manner. The task of withdrawing the armies from the Polish salient was formidable in itself ; it was rendered still more difficult by the necessity of guarding the immensely long north-eastern flank against the attacks of the enemy. On the line Ossovets-Riga, extending over a distance of about 300 miles, the German forces were standing hardly anywhere more than 50 miles, and in most cases considerably less, from the Warsaw-Bielostok-

Vilna-Dvinsk-Petrograd railway. The cutting of that line at any point before the withdrawal of the Russian armies from Poland had been effected would undoubtedly have had a most serious effect on the retreat. The points of the greatest danger were, however, naturally those in which the Prussian railways join the main Russian trunk-line. At Novo-Georgievsk the Mlava-Warsaw line crosses the Vistula ; although the capture of that line would not have carried the Germans into the rear of the main bodies of the retreating armies, it would have nevertheless interfered very seriously with their operations. It would have enabled the Germans to get round the Russian troops which were covering the right flank on the line Vyshkoff-Ostroff-Lomza. The second point of danger was Ossovets, on the Königsberg-Bielostok-Brest Litovsk railway, the third Kovno on the Königsberg - Vilna line. Finally, the capture of Riga and of the Riga-Dvinsk front by the Germans would have been considered at that time a serious threat to the Russian retreat. Exaggerated ideas were then current concerning the possibilities of establishing a German naval base at Riga. The full extent to which the Russian Navy and the British submarines dominated the Baltic was hardly realized, and apprehensions were entertained that the Germans might profit considerably by gaining possession of the Riga-Dvinsk railway and of the River Dvina between these two towns.

Attacks against the Riga-Dvinsk front, against Kovno and against Ossovets, were carried out by the Germans simultaneously with operations in Poland; but it was only gradually, as the successive attempts at cutting the Russian retreat in the western salient met with failure, that the offensive farther to the north-east was gaining in weight and in importance. The attempts at breaking through the Warsaw-Bielostok front seemed to offer at first the best chances of encircling the Russian armies. However serious the cutting of the Petrograd-Warsaw line might have been for our Allies, in itself it would not necessarily have been disastrous. They had two other railway-lines north of the Pripet marshes to rely upon, and the farther we go to the north-east the greater is the distance which separates them from what was at that time the zone of danger from enemy attacks. The narrow Polish salient forms the head of a

parabola, of which the Warsaw-Dvinsk and Warsaw-Kieff railways are the arms; all the lines run in it close to one another. On the northern flank of the Polish salient the German forces had broken through the Nareff line full ten days before the fall of Warsaw, and in the first days of August hardly more than 10 miles intervened between them and the Warsaw-Bielostok-Petrograd railway. Moreover, a powerful group of Austro-German armies was pressing forward from the south, past Lublin and Cholm. The first "pair of pincers," aiming at cutting off the Russian retreat, was directed against the region of Siedlets; a quick concentric advance from the north against Siedlets and from the south against Lukoff would have spelt disaster to the armies of our Allies. Whilst the main forces of the armies of Generals von Gallwitz and von Scholtz were thus trying to break through across the Bug and Nareff

AN ATTEMPT TO FORCE A WAY THROUGH THE ENEMY'S BARBED WIRE.
Russian troops who fell amidst entanglements while making a charge.

(above Ostrolenka) and Mackensen's armies were pressing from the direction of Lublin and Cholm, the new-fangled " group of armies " of Prince Leopold of Bavaria* was advancing from the Vistula. The extreme slowness of the advance of the latter forces in face of comparatively weak Russian rearguards was probably due partly to the difficulties of transport with which it was faced (all the bridges across the Vistula had been blown up by the Russians, and it was not until the end of August that the construction of the first permanent bridge across the river was completed by the German engineers), and partly because the Germans,

crossed the Nareff, our Allies were still offering successful resistance to their onslaughts in front of the line of the Bug. " Ostroff is still in the hands of the enemy," remarks the German official *communiqué* of the following day. On August 7 the Germans forced the passage across the Bug, a few miles above Novo-Georgievsk, and two days later the fortress was surrounded from all sides. Yet it. resisted ; contrary to their usual tactics, our Allies left behind a garrison in that advanced outpost at the junction of the Bug and the Vistula. General von Beseler, the German specialist in siege-operations, was sent against it with a powerful

RUSSIAN PRISONERS WITH THEIR MACHINE GUNS BEING MARCHED OFF THE
BATTLEFIELD BY THEIR CAPTORS.

hoping for the success of the " pincing " movement, may have thought it preferable not to accelerate the Russian retreat by exercising pressure from the west.

The defence put up by our Allies between the Nareff and the Bug surpassed anything the Germans had expected. On August 9, more than a fortnight after the troops of Gallwitz had

train of the heaviest siege-artillery, but the Russian garrison held out sufficiently long to deprive the fall of the fortress and the opening of the road to the Germans of practically all strategic importance. The impossibility of forcing the Vyshkoff-Ostroff line, whilst an advance from that direction could still have exercised a serious influence on the Russian retreat, caused the German commanders in the Nareff region to transfer their main attention to the sector between Ostrolenka and Vizna. After several unsuccessful attempts, the troops of General von Scholtz broke at last on August 9 through the front of the Lomza line and stormed Fort 4 of the outer defences of Lomza ; on the next morning they entered the fortress itself. But even after the fall of Lomza their advance did

---

* The German *communiqués* never made public the composition of that mysterious group of armies. General von Woyrsch seems to have been the only star in Prince Leopold's solar system, and even that star had its " extra-tours " ; it revolved round Mackensen rather than round its own presumptive sun. But the son-in-law of the Austrian Emperor, the brother of the King of Bavaria, who as the effect of a lame compromise between the Central Powers had become the " conqueror of Warsaw," had to have his " group of armies," even if it had to resemble a bishopric *in partibus infidelium.*

The Southern approach to the Citadel, showing the bridge which was destroyed by the Russians before evacuation. Inset: General Von Beseler, the captor of the Fortress.

Russian prisoners leaving the fortress.

SCENES AFTER THE FALL OF NOVO-GEORGIEVSK.

THE CAPTURE OF NOVO- GEORGIEVSK.
German troops entering into possession of the Citadel.

not gain considerably in speed, however hard the German *communiqués* tried to convey that impression. The position can best be gathered from a sentence in their report of August 13. Its wording is interesting. "*On it goes between Nareff and Bug,*"* says the German *communiqué* of August 13, "though the enemy brings up all the time fresh forces to that front, and his resistance must be broken at point after point." One seems to hear in the first part of the sentence the clattering hoofs of the hosts of modern Huns; the ending amounts to a polite apology for not being able to advance by more than a very few miles a day. At last, on August 15, the Germans reached the heights of Briansk; "the brave troops" of "the victorious German armies" pursuing "the fleeing enemy" reached the line of the Nurzets, approximately three weeks after they had first crossed the Nareff; the distance between these two rivers amounts to about 30 miles. But by that time practically the entire Russian force had withdrawn on to the line of Bielostok, Brest Litovsk and Kovel, and the strategic problem which confronted the German armies had changed in most of its aspects.

Whilst in the north the armies of Gallwitz and Scholtz were advancing from the Nareff towards the Bug and Nurzets, fighting of an even

* "Zwischen Narew und Bug ging es weiter vorwärts . . "

more desperate character was developing along the southern front. The armies under Mackensen's command stood at the time of the fall of Warsaw along a line from five to ten miles north of the Lublin-Cholm railway. It was here that was to be found the most powerful concentration of the enemy's forces. The operations of the Fourth Austro-Hungarian and the Eleventh German Army extended over a front of not more than 60 miles; these two armies comprised, including their strategic reserves, probably not less than from twelve to fourteen army corps. In the first half of July they had received reinforcements from practically all the armies which were holding farther south the line of the Bug and the Zlota Lipa. Moreover, they had on their two outer flanks the support of two armies, the movements of which were practically subordinated and subsidiary to their own. On the Vistula, between Garvolin and Ivangorod, stood the army of General von Woyrsch (it included the Austro-Hungarian troops of General von Kövess); on the Bug, opposite Vladimir Volynsky, operated the army-group of General von Puhallo.

The Austro-German advance from the south was, however, met by some of the best Russian troops under the leadership of generals whose ability had been sufficiently proved during the month which intervened between the second

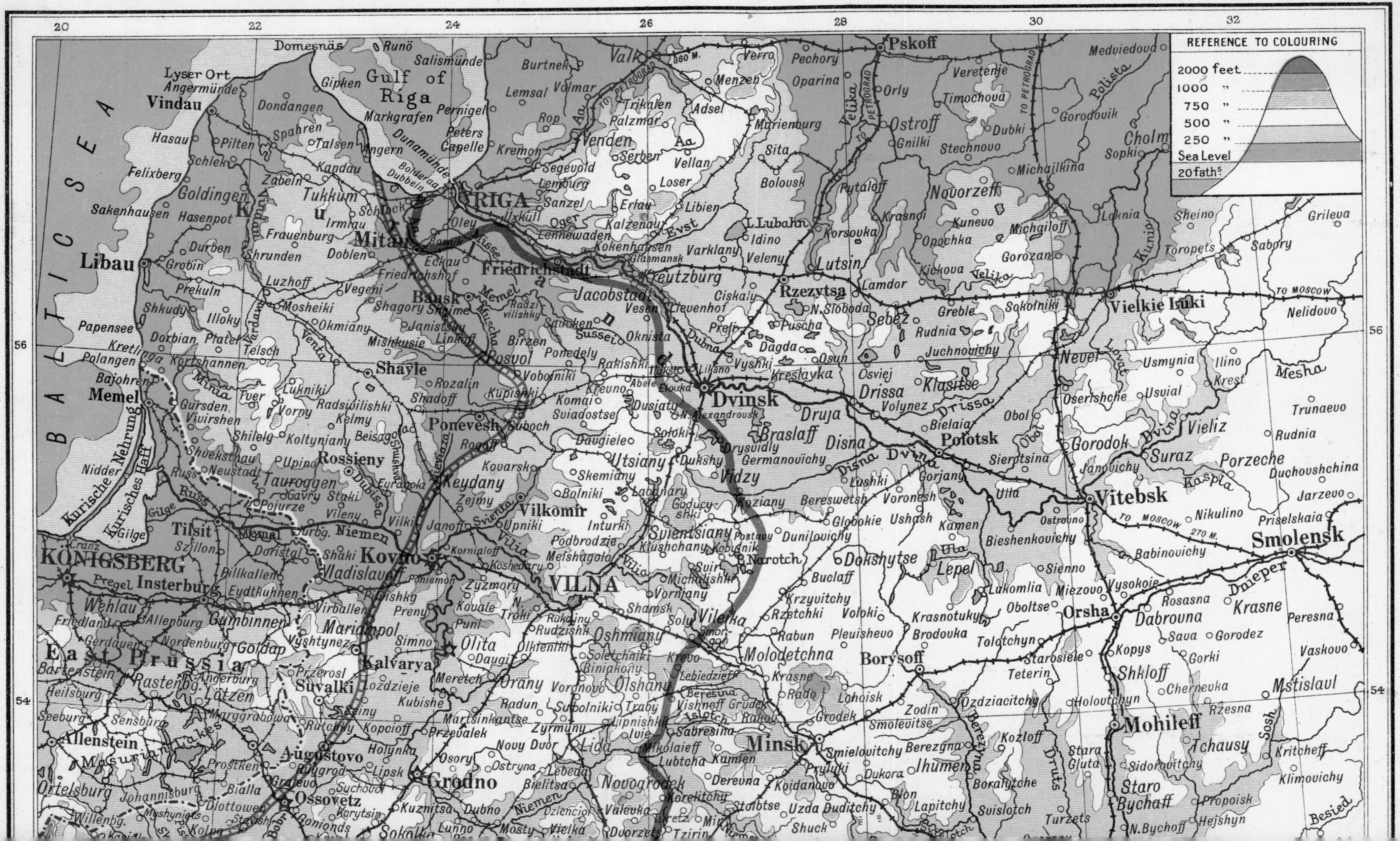

REFERENCE TO COLOURING

2000 feet	
1000 "	
750 "	
500 "	
250 "	
Sea Level	
20 fath?	

BALTIC SEA

Gulf of Riga

E A S T P R U S S I A

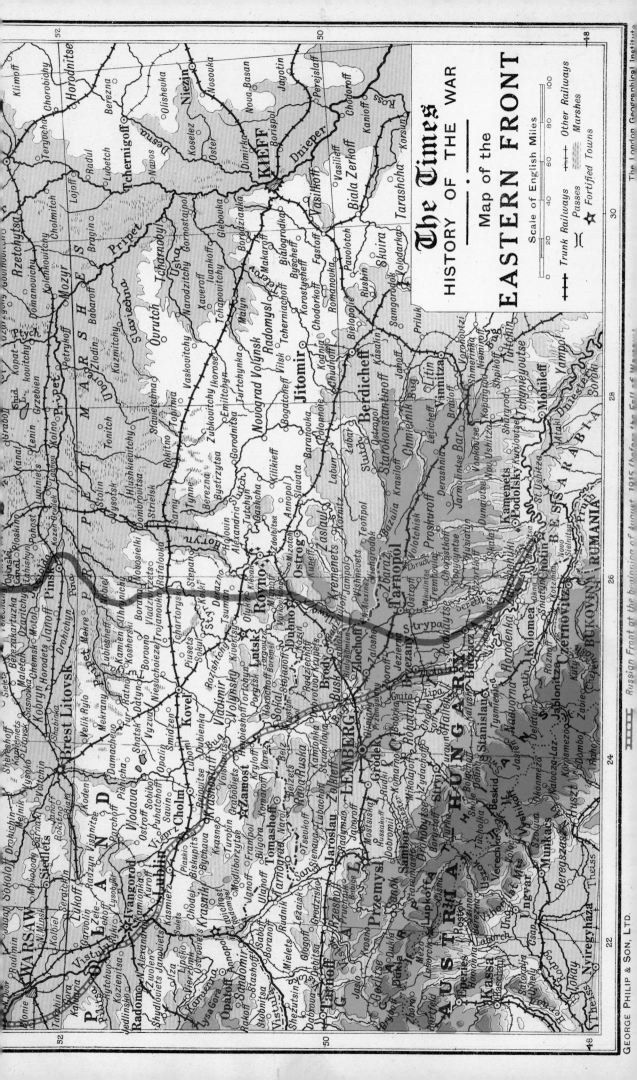

The Times

HISTORY OF THE WAR

Map of the

EASTERN FRONT

Scale of English Miles

+——+ Trunk Railways   +——+ Other Railways
)—(Passes   ⊥⊥⊥⊥ Marshes
★ Fortified Towns

The London Geographical Institute

GEORGE PHILIP & SON, LTD.

Russian Front at the beginning of August 1915 (before the Fall of Warsaw)

battle of Krasnik and the fall of Warsaw. At the time when the last Russian troops were leaving the capital of Poland, a pitched battle was being fought between the River Vieprz and Savin. A supreme effort of Mackensen to break through the Russian lines met at first with complete failure ; only after a few days of fighting of the most severe character, and by using all his locally available forces, was he able to force our Allies to withdraw a few miles to the north. It was the same kind of advance as had been that from Krasnostaff to Cholm.

On August 6 the main weight of the Austro-German offensive in south-eastern Poland shifted to the district of Lubartoff. It is at that point that the Lublin-Parchoff-Lukoff railway crosses the marshy valley of the Vieprz. Could a quick advance have been carried out along that line, some parts at least of the retreating Russian armies might have been cut off from their immediate goal, the line of the Bug round Brest Litovsk. South-west of Lubartoff the broad, flat ridge of Hill 183 served our Allies as their main *point d'appui ;* on the

opposite bank of the Vieprz their rearguards had entrenched themselves in the hilly region of Vola Russka. A considerable number of heavy batteries were collected by the Austrians in front of Hill 183, and on August 6 a bombardment " of the approved type " was opened against the positions of our Allies, who, still short of guns and ammunition, were unable to answer it in an adequate manner. At 9.15 a.m. the Austrian infantry began its advance. The Russian positions were held by forces far weaker in numbers and still more inferior in artillery, but their garrison was composed of excellent Siberian regiments, whereas practically all the Austrian regiments which carried out the attack belonged to the Fourteenth Army Corps under General Roth. This army corps was composed almost entirely of regiments which drew their recruits from the Alpine provinces, especially from the Tyrol ; throughout the present war the Austrian troops from the German-speaking provinces had proved inferior as fighters either to the Magyar or the Galician regiments. The Austrian attack against Hill 183, notwithstand-

AFTER THE GERMAN OCCUPATION OF BREST LITOVSK.
German troops carrying bags of grain from the blazing Citadel. 65—3

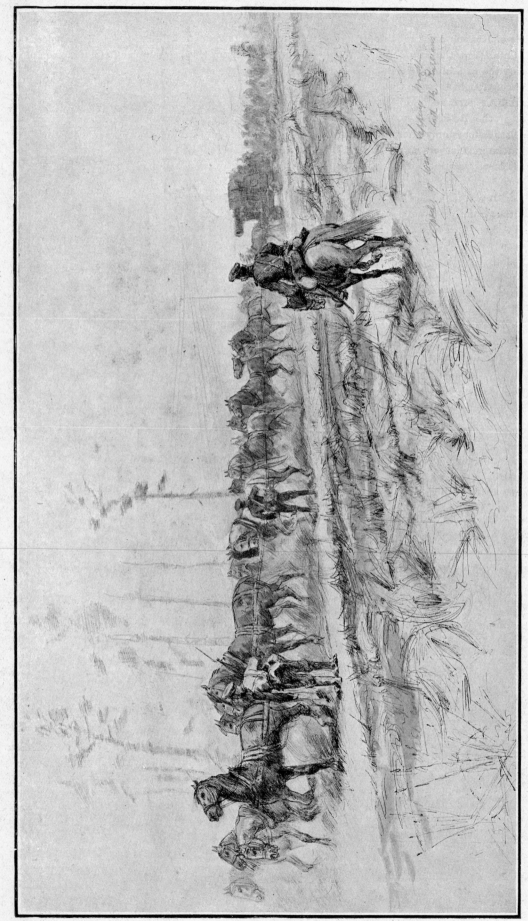

A CAPTURED GERMAN HEAVY HOWITZER BEING CARTED OFF UNDER ESCORT OF RUSSIAN SOLDIERS.

ing the powerful support of the artillery, broke down almost completely. After a whole day of bombardment and of repeated, violent attacks, the Austrians had not yet reached the main Russian positions. About 8.30 p.m. the infantry attacks stopped and the bombardment of the Russian positions recommenced with full violence. It was again followed up by infantry attacks; the fighting continued throughout the night. Meantime the Germans had succeeded in capturing the main positions of the Russian rearguards, east of the Vieprz. On August 7 the " Edelweiss Corps "* entered the trenches on Hill 183, after they had been evacuated by the Siberian regiments, which had to withdraw in accordance with the retreat on their left. By the night of August 8-9 our Allies evacuated the entire left bank of the Vieprz.

About the same time the last Russian troops were withdrawn from the region of Zelechoff and Garvolin, their main forces having already reached the district of Lukoff and Siedlets. The retreat from the Polish salient was secured; by August 15 it was practically completed. Mackensen left it to the " group of armies " under Prince Leopold to occupy the abandoned districts of Siedlets and Lukoff. If any encircling movement was still to be carried out to the west of the Pripet Marshes and the Lithuanian forests it had to be attempted against Brest Litovsk. After heavy, long-drawn fighting, Mackensen gained on August 15 the crossing over the Bug at Vlodava.

The first stage of the retreat from the *place d'armes* in south-eastern Poland thus closes, about August 15, ten days after the fall of Warsaw. The next ten days form a stage of transition between it and the offensive against Vilna and Rovno. The fall of Brest Litovsk on August 25, with which the last traces disappear of the " Polish salient,"† and the eastern theatre of war breaks up into three separate zones, forms nevertheless the visible landmark between the two stages of the Austro-German advance from Warsaw against the Vilna-Rovno line.

The retreat of the Russians south of the Pripet Marshes was comparatively easy; there

was hardly any danger of their armies being in any way outflanked by the enemy. But the main body of the Russian armies had to retire to the north of the marshes; the southern area, at least west of the Dnieper, is of less vital importance than the north, and being, moreover, easier to defend, required far smaller numbers of troops. The main body of the Russian armies had to retire through the long corridor in which the railway lines Bielostok-Vilna-Dvinsk and Brest Litovsk-Baranovitchy-Minsk form the outer lines of communication.

During the ten days August 15-25 a corresponding regroupment took place in the distribution of the German forces; by the time of the fall of Brest Litovsk the main concentration of the enemy armies was gathered in

GENERAL VON BESELER
(in centre) and members of his staff.

front of the south-western gate to the " corridor." The German armies standing along the Riga-Ponevesh-Kovno-Ossovets front were continuing their attempts at battering down its western wall. The armies of von Gallwitz and von Scholtz, which at the time of the fall of Warsaw had been attacking the line between Novo-Georgievsk and Ossovets, executed during the ten days of August 15-25 a wheel to the east; that movement was accompanied by a contraction of their front. On the day of the fall of Brest they were holding the Ossovets-Bielostok-Bielsk line. The two armies which in the beginning of August had stood between Novo-Georgievsk and Ivangorod advanced by Siedlets and Lukoff against the front extending between the Nurzets and the Bug. The Fourth Austro-Hungarian Army, under

---

* The Fourteenth Army Corps was called in the jargon of Austrian journalists by the name of this favourite flower of sentimental Viennese burghers, when on their holidays they disguise themselves as Alpine mountaineers.

† Bielostok, Brest Litovsk and Kovel are not geographically or politically part of Russian Poland; strategically they must, however, be included in the system of Eastern Poland.

AT THE GRAVESIDE OF THE ENEMY.
Austrian troops honour the graves of the heroic Russians.

Archduke Joseph-Ferdinand, approached Brest Litovsk from the west. The Eleventh German Army, which remained under the immediate command of Mackensen, and included considerable parts of Linsingen's army, was attacking the fortress from the south. If it is admissible to speak of armies after four months of the most severe fighting and after several regroupments as if they were still the same, it might be said that all the armies which in the early days of May, at the outset of the great Austro-German offensive, had stood between Ossovets and the angle of the Carpathian front south of Gorlitse, were now gathered in the space between the Bobr and the Pripet Marshes.

Not all of them were, however, meant to continue the offensive beyond the Bug. The centre of the Austro-German armies, which had to be kept in full strength whilst a strong Russian resistance was expected in the sector of Brest Litovsk, was depleted as soon as that fortress had been abandoned by our Allies and the Pripet Marshes were reached. Soon after the fall of Brest news was given out by the enemy concerning an impending separation of the Austro-Hungarian and the German

forces. This statement was a half-truth, which was meant to cover the withdrawal of troops to the Serbian frontier. These were naturally taken from the centre, which, with the fall of Brest, had accomplished its task, and it was just there that the mixture of German and Austro-Hungarian troops was greatest. There were very few Austrian troops north of the Nurzets, and those consisted mainly of cavalry and artillery. There were only about two or three German army corps south of Vladimir Volynsky (most of them were included in the German army-group of Count Bothmer; it was the remainder of the original army Linsingen, and still kept its position between the Austro-Hungarian armies of Boehm-Ermolli and of Pflanzer-Baltin). On the other hand, each of the three central armies was more or less mixed. The army of General von Woyrsch contained a whole group of Austro-Hungarian regiments under General Kövess von Kövesshaza. The army of Archduke Joseph-Ferdinand included ever since the end of April the German Division of General von Besser. The Eleventh German Army stood in between the Austro-Hungarian troops of the Archduke in the north and those of General Puhallo in the south, and contained the Fourth Austro-Hungarian Army Corps under General Arz von Straussenberg. Thus, through the withdrawal of the army-group Kövess and the army Mackensen to the Serbian front, and also of a certain number of regiments to the Western front, the amount of heterogeneous enclaves was indeed reduced in number and importance. It is, moreover, interesting to mark that before the Fourth Austro-Hungarian Army was entrusted with the task of advancing into the wilderness of the Pripet Marshes the German Division of General von Besser was withdrawn from it and transferred to a more favourable climate.

It had originally been expected, and the German commanders seem to have entertained the idea almost to the last, that the Russians would attempt to hang on to the district of Brest Litovsk as long as possible. Not that any considerable value was ascribed to its once formidable defences. The inner part of the stronghold was by now obsolete, and even the six new forts were placed, in view of the long range of the modern siege artillery, too close to the centre. Yet the district

presented in itself such unusual facilities for defence that a stubborn resistance was expected, similar to that which our Allies had kept up for so long in front of the Vistula line Events took a different turn; it was some 200 miles north of Brest Litovsk, round Kovno, that the fate of that stronghold was decided.

About July 20 German troops had got within twelve miles from Kovno; in the first days of August the Tenth German Army, under General von Eichhorn, had drawn up close to the south-western front of the fortress. On August 6 preparations were begun for an assault against it.

The town of Kovno lies on the left—*i.e.,* the northern—bank of the Niemen at its junction with the River Vilia, and a short distance below the junction of the Niemen and Jessia (a tributary which it receives from the south). The ring of forts round Kovno encircles the two river junctions, the town, and the railway bridge of the Königsberg-Vilna line across the Niemen. The main forts were eleven in number, and were situated at distances varying from two to four miles from the centre of the town. Three of the forts guarded it on the east, one covered the

RUSSIAN DEFENCE WORK.
Dug-outs and trenches in Poland.

A SHELL-SWEPT CROSSING.—GERMAN RED CROSS CONTINGENT.

Vilna bridge, seven protected the approaches from the south and west. Besides these there was a girdle of minor works round the town.

For the first attack the enemy selected the south-western section between the Niemen and the Jessia. The battle began at 1 a.m. on August 8 by a bombardment in which guns of all calibre up to 16 inches were employed. "The hurricane fire of the enemy," says the official Russian *communiqué* of August 10, "lasted not less than two hours, and our batteries replied vigorously. About three in the morning assaulting columns in close formation marched against our positions. By concentrated fire, the explosion of land mines, and gallant counter-attacks by our troops the enemy was thrown back by five in the morning along the whole front attacked. The exhausted Germans, who had suffered enormous losses, were hurled back into the neighbouring ravines, where apparently they began to prepare for a fresh assault.

"At noon on August 8 the enemy fire increased to a terrible intensity, but this protracted and destructive hurricane of fire from the most powerful guns failed to shake our troops, who firmly withstood the hail of projectiles showered upon them. Our artillery valiantly supported our heroes with its fire. This incessant cannonade lasted all day.

"At nightfall the enemy columns which had been continuously massing in front of our positions again rushed to the assault, their attacks lasting for two hours. The enemy succeeded in taking a part of the trenches on the line of the advanced positions which his fire had swept, but afterwards, by the heroic efforts of our reserves which had been brought up, the Germans were once more repulsed with enormous losses.

"The enemy only retained the works near the village of Piple which he had won at the cost of enormous efforts and losses."

The failure of this first attempt to take the fortress by assault was followed by a week of bombardment, accompanied by almost daily infantry attacks against particular sectors of the fortifications. About August 15 the siege entered on its final, culminating stage. For two days a most violent bombardment by siege artillery of all calibre was kept up, and on August 16 the enemy launched a series of violent attacks with his full strength, with the object of storming the fortifications on the

left bank of the Niemen. "Towards the evening of yesterday," says the official Russian *communiqué* of August 17, "he succeeded in carrying a small fort which had been greatly damaged by artillery fire, and in breaking into the intervening spaces between some other forts in the western sector. Fighting continues."

It continued throughout the night and the following day ; the enemy entered the town and established himself in the adjoining district which forms an isthmus between the Niemen and the Vilia. Notwithstanding the most tenacious resistance of the Russian garrison, the German troops of the army of General von Eichhorn, commanded by General

GENERAL LITZMANN.
Victor of Kovno.

von Litzmann, captured by the night of August 17 the last forts of Kovno.

The most powerful fortress on the Niemen had fallen ; the line of the Niemen and Bug was pierced. This was no time for half-hearted decisions ; the fall of Kovno settled the fate of Brest Litovsk. A powerful group of armies had been collected by the supreme Russian Command round Vilna ; forces sufficient to withstand for some time the pressure from the west were gathered between Vilna and Grodno. Yet this was no longer a position of stable balance. The Germans could be detained in the river defiles of the Niemen and its tributaries, and in the mighty forests of Lithuania, but there was no hope of soon driving them back across the Niemen or of checking their advance indefinitely. Had our Allies under these circumstances persisted in hanging on to the line Grodno-

Bielostok-Brest Litovsk, they would have been courting disaster. A withdrawal from the threatened western front was necessary in order that the line might be saved from the danger of being broken up, and the armies from the threat of envelopment and capture.

On August 16 General Leiming, the Russian commander of Brest Litovsk, issued orders for the complete evacuation of the town by the civilian population. On August 17 a German aviator reported to the commander of the Sixth Army, which was advancing against Brest, that a stream of people twenty miles long was moving out of the town. These were not preparations for a siege—the town of Brest lay outside the ring of fortifications ; they were the preliminaries of a retreat in the style of 1812.

On the entire front from Ossovets to Vladimir Volynsky the garrisons were drawn in from the outlying positions. The district of Vladimir Volynsky was evacuated about August 20 ; three days later cavalry belonging to the army of General von Puhallo entered Kovel. At the northern end of the line the Russians withdrew on August 22 from Ossovets, that unique fortress in the present war which could not be reduced by the fire even of the heaviest siege-artillery, by a

fire to which infinitely more powerful strongholds, both on the western and the eastern fronts, had succumbed in a few weeks, if not days. On August 24 the Russian rearguards withdrew within the ring of fortifications of Brest Litovsk. The Austrian *communiqués* of those days carefully kept up the appearance of operations in a grand style ; the effect of the fall of one of the best-known European fortresses was not to be lost because the Russians did not play the game, or rather refused to play the game which would have suited their enemies. Finally the Austrian report of August 26 announced to the world in an appropriately dramatic style the capture of the stronghold. " The fortress of Brest-Litovsk has fallen. The Hungarian Landwehr, under General von Arz, captured the village of Kobylany, south-west of the fortress, and thereby broke through the outer line of forts. The West Galician, Silesian and North Moravian infantry at the same time stormed the fort to the south of the village of Koroshtchyn. German troops captured the citadel near the railway bridge." A similar statement was issued from Berlin, except that the 22nd Brandenburg Reserve army corps appears in it as the decid-

AFTER THE RUSSIAN RETREAT.
German engineers rebuilding a bridge destroyed by the Russians.

THE GERMAN ARMY IN RUSSIA.
Difficulties of transport: A cavalry regiment crossing marshy ground.

ing factor on that great day. Neither *communiqué* speaks of booty or prisoners.

The correspondent of the *Nieuwe Rotterdamsche Courant*, who was with the Austro-Hungarian troops on their entry into Brest, describes the town as " a sea of fire." The town lay—it can hardly be said to exist any longer—to the east of the fortress, on the main road by which the Russians had to retire. Whilst the Austro-German troops were entering Brest, our Allies were taking up new positions beyond the fiery waves, among the lazy, silent, stagnant waters of the Pripet Marshes.

Six days before the fall of Brest "the advanced sentinel" in the west, Novo-Georgievsk, had fallen. This was the only fortress in which our Allies left a garrison after their line had been withdrawn ; that had to be done in this one case in order to secure the safe retreat of the main forces. When the Germans entered Novo-Georgievsk the Russian armies were already some 80 miles away, and the Kaiser had an opportunity of inspecting fresh carnage without any danger to his august person. Having done so, he held a review.

This was how the correspondent of the Berlin *Lokalanzeiger* saw the Kaiser's review at Novo-Georgievsk. " With gigantic, mighty strides he advanced upon the parade ground, with a thick stick in his hand. The Kaiser comes close in front of me. He looks at me sharply. I know the look. To-day there

is something immensely joyous, almost humorous, in the keen eyes. Oh, you stupid Quadruple Ententists ! If you only had an idea. . . .! His Majesty went with the same powerful strides from battalion to battalion. . . . In his customary short, sharp tones he thanked his troops in the name of all Germany, . . . and distributed numerous Iron Crosses."

During the remaining week of August the fighting in the zone north of the Pripet continued without any very marked results. Round Brest itself the Austrians entered the region of the marshes. East of the line Bielostok-Brest the German troops reached the Forest of Bialoviez, practically the only remaining virgin forest in the plains of Europe, the last refuge of the almost extinct European bison. The scene of the more important strategic operations shifted now to the north and to the south of the Bielostok-Kovel sector.

From the tangle of isolated incidents which in the northern zone fill the week following on the fall of Brest two movements stand out as expressing the main strategic endeavours and preoccupations of the contending armies. Between Kovno and Vilna our Allies had succeeded in checking the advance of the enemy. They now undertook a counter-offensive in the district north of Vilna ; by compelling the Germans to withdraw beyond the River Svienta

AN AUSTRIAN TRENCH IN THE FLOODED AREA.

they gained a cover for their northern flank and put, for the time being, the armies round Vilna out of danger of an enveloping movement from the north. The Germans, on the other hand, attempted to drive a wedge between the Russian group round Vilna and that round Grodno. Having crossed the Niemen near Meretch, they tried to reach the Vilna-Grodno railway-line near Orany. On August 26 our Allies evacuated the fortress of Olita, falling back on Vilna. The movement against Orany was, however, held up sufficiently long to allow the main bodies of troops to withdraw from their advanced positions. Orany was reached by the Germans on August 31; on September 1-2 our Allies evacuated Grodno. "On the western front of Grodno," says the German report of September 2, "the outer line of forts has fallen. The North-German Landwehr took by storm yesterday Fort No. 4, situated north of the Dombrovo-Grodno high road. The garrison, consisting of 500 men, was captured. Late in the evening followed the capture by troops from Baden of Fort No. 4a, situated farther north. Here we took a garrison of 150. The other fortifications on the advanced western front were thereupon evacuated by the Russians." On the next day the capture of Grodno by the Germans was completed. "Near Grodno our attacking troops, by their quick action, succeeded in crossing the Niemen. After street fighting the town was occupied and 400 prisoners were taken." The modesty of the German claims concerning the number of prisoners by itself proves the skill with which the evacuation of Grodno was carried out, and indicates the nature of the retreat. Only at one point a more considerable body of Russian troops was in danger of being cut off. This danger was met and averted by a successful counter-offensive. "Near Grodno, on the morning of September 3," says the Russian official *communiqué* of the following day, "fierce fighting was resumed. Our troops entered the town, captured eight machine guns and about 150 prisoners, and by this success permitted the unmolested retirement of neighbouring troops whose positions formed too great a salient on our general front."

During the next few days the Germans attempted an advance towards Lida which would have driven a wedge between the armies round Vilna and those standing between the Upper Niemen and the Pripet Marshes. It failed; on September 7 the Russian line still extended unbroken from the region of Meretch,

by Piaski, Zelva, and Bereza Kartuska to Chemsk in the Pripet Marshes.

Meantime Austrian troops were trying to advance along the few roads and pathways which lead through the swamps in the direction of Drohichyn. It is necessary to form some idea of the character of that country in order fully to understand the nature of an advance through it.

The sources of the Pripet lie half-way between Brest Litovsk and Vladimir Volynsky; it joins the Dnieper some fifty miles north of Kieff. From its source to its mouth it measures about 340 miles in length; the entire difference in level between its two ends amounts to only about 150 feet—*i.e.*, its average fall is less than 6 inches to a mile; hence the marshy character of its wide, flat valley. The normal width of the Pripet amounts to about 40 yards near Pinsk, 200 yards near Mozyr, and 400 yards at its mouth. In spring and autumn the river changes, however, into a regular lake, widening out in many places to twelve miles and more. The width of the marshes varies considerably in different parts. Near Pinsk, where they are by no means widest, it exceeds 120 miles. The total area of the Pripet Marshes approaches 30,000 square miles. Into that wide depression flow the waters from the surrounding hills and high plateaus. As can be seen from the map enclosed in this chapter, in the north the ground rises more than 800 feet above the level of the marshland, in the west by about 600 feet, in the south by more than 1,200 feet. In recent years the Russian Government has been trying to lay dry some parts of the swamps and bring them under the plough. Its endeavours were supported by the inexhaustible patience of the Russian peasant. He has toiled on the higher ground, for the greater part of the year a prisoner on islands in a treacherous sea. A wrong step off the beaten track means death in those regions. The soft, slimy morass has swallowed up even many experienced inhabitants of the country. The heavy, poisonous air has killed many of those who dared to enter the district. Only in winter, when the waters freeze, can the inhabitants of those regions move about freely across the plain and through the forests between the scattered homesteads or villages; at present there is in the Pripet Marshes on the average only about one homestead to every three square miles.

There are pathways known only to the local population; there are others over which only men born and bred in the marshes can venture to walk. Both men and animals develop in those districts a peculiar step, they move quickly, throwing their weight forward. A slower, heavier step would break through the thin crust of firm soil which covers the morass. It is possible to adopt many a device for facilitating movements across the marshes. In the open marshes burdens may be drawn on sledges; in the forests pathways may be constructed by felling trees; or, where the marsh is shallow, by removing the slimy moss which covers the underlying sand. Footwear resembling the Canadian snow-shoes is useful; similarly a light long stick with a hook at the end ought to be carried. It helps to keep the balance, and when one begins to sink, by laying the stick on the ground, and thus distributing the weight over a wide surface, one may succeed in scrambling out of the marsh. Where there is wood one may succeed in reaching a tree with the hook and pulling oneself out of the grasp of the mud.

There are, of course, also firm roads leading through the marshes, along which even heavy guns can be drawn. But by keeping to those roads alone an army can hardly hope to conquer or retain a hold on the marshland. A story recounting some of the difficulties with which the Austrians were confronted in their advance was told about the middle of September by one of their officers to the war correspondent of the *Neue Freie Presse*: "An advance in the Rokitno Marshes presents incredible diffi-culties to our cavalry. The swamps and the rain which has been falling for weeks render it sometimes practically impossible. Neverthe-less, a strong line of cavalry and artillery moves through that zone, fighting incessantly with Cossacks and Tcherkessian horsemen. Mounted on their light horses these enemies are un-tiring, and it is difficult to get at them. The paths along which the squadrons and batteries can move are narrow, and it is necessary to search every piece of forest after Cossacks, so as not to leave behind patrols of those foolhardy fellows. . . . In a desperate guerilla warfare one piece of forest after another has to be cleared. Every day brings new cavalry fighting. With extreme tenacity the Cossacks oppose our advance through the marshes. They continually attempt surprise attacks. Everywhere their mobile swarms emerge from the moors, faithfully helped by the local

population, which knows all the pathways; . . . they can be withstood only by unrelenting watchfulness. They show great contempt of death; they much rather let themselves be killed than surrender. . . ."

This is the story of a successful survivor, presented to the anxious public at home. The dead have no voice, especially when drowned in a morass. Soon a new enemy was to arise for the invaders. After the fall of Vilna some of the Austrian troops from the centre seem to have been withdrawn to the south and replaced by Germans, who started to treat the local population in their usual manner. The peasants who at first had acted merely as guides for the Russian troops, exas-perated by outrages and atrocities committed by the enemy, took to arms. Bands were formed which earned for themselves the name of the "Marsh-Wolves." By the end of September the screen of the Austro-German forces was supposed to have reached the line of Pinsk. But at the same time the Cossacks and Marsh-Wolves are known to have been operating as far west as Kobryn and Mekrany.

The Germans had left the greatest part of the operations in the marshes to the Austrians; these, in a similar spirit of brotherly love, sent into that region the Polish Legions—*i.e.*, the Poles who, believing that the future of their country lay with the Central Powers, had volunteered for service with the Austrian Army. It was the story of San Domingo all over again; in the West Indies perished many of the best Polish legionaries of Napoleon I., in the Pripet Marshes many of their spiritual descendants. In an army order dated Sep-tember 13, 1915, Archduke Joseph-Ferdinand thanked the Polish legions for the services rendered in the clearing of the northern and eastern marshes. "I am convinced," wrote the Archduke, "that the legions, though separated, will also in future accomplish to an equal degree the most important task of offering a powerful *point d'appui* to the great cavalry corps." There was one thing which the Polish Legions had been demanding of the Austrian army command as a pledge for the future—to be united on Polish soil into a nucleus of a Polish army; they were broken up into separate detachments and sent into the Pripet Marshes.

At the time of the fall of Warsaw the Russian population was leaving Riga; only the Baltic

THE RUSSIAN RETREAT.
A railway destroyed by the Russians.

Germans were staying behind in anxious, joyful expectation of their kinsmen from the south. In the beginning of August hardly anyone thought that Riga could hold out more than a few days. Then the enemy suddenly ceased to ex.rcise any further pressure from the south. It seems that the Germans hoped to be able to force the line of the Dvina by means of a successful naval attack against Riga. Two attempts were made; one about August 9, the next ten days later. If the first one was unsuccessful, the second proved disastrous for the attacking side. The German Fleet suffered defeat at the hands of the Russian warships and the British submarines; it was compelled to retire, and was even reported to

have lost one battle cruiser, two light cruisers, and several torpedo boats and destroyers.

Thereupon the attacks by land were resumed. General von Below, having received reinforcements, advanced towards the Dvina, and opened an offensive against the bridgeheads of Lennewaden and Friedrichstadt. The Russians withdrew across the river and destroyed the bridges. At the same time an attempt was made by the enemy in the direction of Jacobstadt, where the Mitau-Moscow railway crosses the Dvina. The German attacks were vigorously countered by the Russian troops, and after September 8 practically 'no further movement was heard of on that front until late in October.

AUSTRIAN TRANSPORT ON THE MARCH.

AUSTRIAN CAVALRY CROSSING A RIVER IN POLAND.

It is just possible that the operations on the Dvina were in great part meant chiefly as a blind for the impending new movement farther south and as a plausible explanation for the concentration of troops in the district of Ponevesh. About the same time as the offensive in the north was weakening, the first news arrived of a vigorous German offensive across the River Svienta. Says the Russian official *communiqué* of September 11 :—" The enemy is advancing on the Dvinsk road and the neighbouring roads, directing his principal effort with the assistance of strong field and siege artillery south of the Dvinsk road. Simultaneously large forces of the enemy are advancing in the region east of Suirvinty (between Vilkomir and Vilna), their general direction being from Vilkomir toward Svientsiany (half-way between Vilna and Dvinsk)."

On the next day the Germans reached Utsiany on the Ponevesh-Svientsiany railway. At the same time other armies were pressing forward from the south ; a concentric offensive was undertaken from the districts of Meretch, Grodno and Zelva in the direction of Lida. From the north-west, in the district of Meishagola a direct offensive was attempted against Vilna. But it was from the north that threatened the greatest danger. " Near the station of Svientsiany," says the Petrograd report of September 13, " the railway has been cut by the enemy. Under the pressure of the enemy, who made a decisive attack in the region between the Svientsiany and Vilna districts, our troops retired to the vicinity of the railway station of Podbrodzie." The Germans had thus gained possession of an important junction on the Vilna-Dvinsk-Petrograd railway ; only the two branch lines leading to the south-east, the Lida-Baranovitchy and the Molodetchna-Minsk line remained open for the Russian troops which were gathered round Vilna. By these two branch lines they could still reach the two railways connecting them with their base in the north-east, the Lida-Molodetchna-Polotsk-Vielkie Luki and the Baranovitchy-Minsk-Smolensk line. It is clear that of the two branch lines the Vilna-Minsk line was the more important, as it lies farther away from the south-western front.

Soon even that was in danger. " Small detachments of German cavalry," says the Petrograd official report of September 16, " appeared near the railway between Molodetchna and Polotsk ; " and the report of the following day announces that enemy detachments had actually reached in several places the railway line Vilna-Molodetchna. The speed of the enemy's movements proves by itself that his main force consisted of cavalry. Its strength was estimated at 12 or 13 cavalry divisions, which would mean more than 40,000 men. This body of horse was said to have been supported by infantry conveyed by motor vehicles. They were followed by bigger bodies of troops which reached the line Vidzy-Godocyshki about September 20. It is quite likely that the strength of the raiding body was exaggerated. Yet the movement, executed with much initiative and dash, placed the Russian armies in a position of great difficulty and danger. The retreat from Vilna could no longer be delayed, especially not as from the south-west the armies of von Gallwitz, von Scholtz and Prince Leopold were, with a total disregard to losses, pressing their advance towards Lida and across the Shara towards Baranovitchy. By September 22 the Germans had passed Lida and were approaching Baranovitchy.

On September 19 General Evert, the chief commander of the central group of Russian armies, ordered the complete evacuation of Vilna. Only a narrow passage remained open to the south-east of the town. Had the Russians chosen this for their retreat as being the line of least resistance, they might easily have been caught in the flank by the German armies advancing from the south. Holding back the enemy in the west and north, General Evert launched a counter-offensive to the east, against the Germans who were holding the Soly-Smorgon-Molodetchna railway. It met with complete success ; the railway line and road were cleared of the enemy and the opening to the east was widened. One by one the Russian army corps now slipped out from the German sling ; not a single one of them was intercepted and captured by the enemy. By October 1 our Allies had straightened out their line south of Dvinsk. The army was saved ; only Vilna was lost and so was the Vilna-Rovno railway line down to Baranovitchy. Yet that loss was deprived of real strategic importance by the success which our Allies had meantime scored in the southern zone, round Rovno and between the Sereth and the Strypa.

Two days before the fall of Brest Litovsk Austrian cavalry belonging to the army group of General von Puhallo had entered Kovel.

From here it continued its advance to the east, its left wing trying to push in between the big marshes and the triangle of the Volhynian fortresses, Lutsk, Dubno and Rovno, which were the centre and the pivot of General Ivanoff's armies; the right wing of Puhallo's army was meantime approaching the River Styr, in front of Lutsk.

With the fall of Kovel and Vladimir Volynsky the line of the Middle Bug was pierced and it was certain that that of the Upper Bug and of the Zlota Lipa in Galicia would have to be abandoned. The Austro-German offensive against that line recommenced on August 27. On that day the Fifth Austro-Hungarian army corps under FML. von Goglia (Army Boehm-Ermolli) broke through the Russian positions near Gologory, at the watershed between the Bug and the Zlota Lipa. Our Allies withdrew across the marshy valley of the Upper Bug towards Bialykamien. On the next day the enemy entered the town of Zlochoff. Whilst the Second Austro-Hungarian Army under General von Boehm-Ermolli was forcing the Upper Bug, the Austro-German Army under Count Bothmer crossed the Zlota Lipa round Brzezany, advancing towards the Zboroff-Podhaytse line. In the south the left wing of the Army of Pflanzer-Baltin was advancing from Nizniow and Koropiets towards Buczacz. Our Allies had to withdraw from the line of the Bug and Zlota Lipa not so much on account of the pressure brought on it from the west, but rather because it would have been risky to hang on to an advanced position in Eastern Galicia whilst there was as yet no certainty of their being able to maintain themselves in the Volhynian triangle. Had the Russians succeeded in holding out on the Zlota Lipa, but had they at the same time been compelled to abandon Rovno, their southern armies would have run a serious risk of being enveloped, especially as along the southern flank, on the Dniester, the Austrians had near Zaleshchyki a footing within the " belt of the Dniester."

Volhynia was clearly the decisive theatre of war in the southern zone. It was along the Lvoff-Brody-Rovno line that the Army of General von Boehm-Ermolli was exercising the main pressure. A concentric movement seems to have been planned against Rovno, from Kovel by Lutsk and from Galicia by way of Dubno. On August 29 a fierce battle began on the entire front extending from Bialykamien by Toporoff to Radziechoff (on the Lvoff-Stojanoff railway-line). Seven separate attacks were delivered on that day by the enemy against Hill 366, which dominates the district of Bialykamien, but each of them was beaten off with heavy losses. The fighting continued during the following days. On August 31 our Allies suffered a reverse ; the enemy captured Lutsk and crossed the Styr, the Russians slowly falling back on the Olyka-Radziviloff front. This retreat necessitated also a withdrawal of the line farther south. On September 1 the Austrians entered Brody.

South of the Lvoff-Krasne-Brody railway line our Allies had to withdraw from the line of the Zlota Lipa to that of the Strypa, and then to that of the Sereth. This retreat was carried out in a way resembling the previous withdrawals of these troops ;* though retiring, they succeeded in inflicting on the enemy more serious losses than they suffered themselves. A number of guns and about 10,000 prisoners were captured by them in skilful counter-attacks whilst they fell back some 30 miles to the east.

The advance of the enemy against Dubno continued during the first week of September, though it had to be paid for by extremely heavy losses. On September 7 the Austrian forces reached the Ikva ; on the same day they entered the fortress of Dubno, which had been previously evacuated by our Allies. But before they had time to celebrate that new success came the Russian counter-blow.

" In Galicia, near Tarnopol," says the Petrograd report of September 8, " we achieved yesterday a great success against the Germans. The German 3rd Guards Division and the 48th Reserves Division, reinforced by an Austrian Brigade and a great quantity of heavy and light artillery, according to statements made by prisoners, had been preparing for several days a decisive attack. This was fixed for the night of September 7-8.

" Forestalling the enemy, our troops took the offensive, and after a stubborn fight on the River Doljanka the Germans yesterday evening were completely defeated.

" At the end of the engagement the enemy developed artillery fire of the most extraordinary intensity. Only the impossibility of replying with the same weight of metal prevented us from further developing the success we had obtained.

" The Germans, besides enormous losses in

* For a description of the retreat to the Zlota-Lipa *cf.* Chapter XCI., page 338.

THE GERMAN ADVANCE.

Russian Maxim guns at work among the ruins of a Polish village.

killed and wounded, left as prisoners in our hands more than 200 officers and 8,000 men.

" We captured thirty guns, fourteen of which were of heavy calibre, many machine guns, gun-limbers, and other booty."

This victory was accompanied by one hardly less important in the district south-west of Trembovla.* The country to the north-west

* Trembovla itself lies deep in the valley of the Sereth ; on a wooded hill on its eastern bank stand the ruins of an old Polish castle. Trembovla is one of the oldest towns of " Red Russia," its castle was one of the Polish strongholds against the invasions of the Turks and the Tartars.

of that town is an undulating plain traversed by many small streams. South of the Buczacz-Chortkoff railway the high plateau is cut by many deep cañons. Between Trembovla and the heads of those cañons stretches wide, open ground. In its centre, to the west of the Trembovla-Buczacz high road, extends a complete plain, the so-called "steppe of Pantalicha." Not a single hill rises above its flat, even level; no river crosses it, no trees afford cover. Here and there in slight depressions extend small marshes. Some fifty years ago the steppe was still virgin soil, covered by high grass. Two generations ago * the land was brought under the plough, the marshes gradually shrunk in extent, wild water-fowl, which in former years swarmed in the steppe of Pantalicha, practically disappeared. The wide, open district became in recent times the favourite ground for Austrian cavalry manœuvres; the country south-west of Trembovla came to play the part of the Galician Salisbury Plain. It was to become now the scene of a great battle.

"On the Sereth, in the district south-west of Trembovla," says the official *communiqué* of September 9, "our assumption of the offensive, having been developed on the 7th, resulted in a success as important as that gained under Tarnopol.

"During the 7th and the 8th we took here 150 officers and 7,000 men prisoners, with three guns and thirty-six machine guns. Our losses were unimportant. Yesterday evening the enemy retreated in great haste pursued by our troops towards the River Strypa.

"Since September 3 our success on the whole front of the River Sereth has secured us the following trophies: 383 officers and over 17,000 rank and file prisoners, 14 heavy guns, 19 light guns, 66 machine guns, and 15 artillery limbers captured.

"Altogether our armies are firmly and resolutely carrying out the movement in conformity with the object assigned and contemplate the future with confidence."

On September 9 the battle was continued in the district between Trembovla and Chortkoff.

"The Austrians were forced to beat a precipitate retreat," says the Petrograd report; "according to a provisional estimate we took 5,000 prisoners with sixteen officers." On the next day the battle continued along the entire line from Tarnopol to Tluste, on a front of about fifty miles.

Tluste, a wretchedly poor little town on the Zaleshchyki-Chortkoff railway, is the junction of four first-class high roads and three secondary roads. From the north-west an excellent, wide high-road leads from Buczacz by way of Koszylovtse through Tluste to Ustsie Biskupie; from Zaleshchyki another high road crosses Tluste in a northerly direction, leading by Chortkoff and Trembovla to Tarnopol.* The troops of General von Pflanzer-Baltin were standing in the beginning of September in a semicircle round the important railway junction near Chortkoff. A converging movement from Buczacz and Tluste was intended against it; it was countered by our Allies, and on September 10 the Austrians had to beat a speedy retreat from Tluste to Zaleshchyki.

The fighting between the Sereth and the Strypa was continued during the following weeks, bringing in for our Allies heavy "bags" of prisoners. The total number captured by the armies of General Ivanoff during the month of September exceeded 100,000.

Meantime in Volhynia our Allies not only completely arrested the advance of the enemy, but after some heavy fighting recaptured, on September 23, the fortress of Lutsk, taking prisoners eighty officers and about 4,000 men.

On September 5 the following Army Order was issued by the Tsar:

To-day I have taken the supreme command of all the forces of the sea and land armies operating in the theatre of war.

With firm faith in the clemency of God, with unshakable assurance in final victory, we shall fulfil our sacred duty to defend our country to the last. We will not dishonour the Russian land.

(Signed)   Nicholas,
General Headquarters.

In assuming the supreme command of his fleets and armies the Emperor of Russia expressed in a deed the determination which he shared with his entire nation and with the Governments and peoples of his Allies.

---

* Though Eastern Galicia has by now attained a surprising level of modern development, for things previous to, say, 1880, there apply still certain primitive methods of calculation. The nearest one can get to know is that Pantalicha was first ploughed by "our grandfathers."

* Tluste is not on the Sereth. No high roads follow the rivers south of the Buczacz-Chortkoff line. The open high plateau between the rivers is preferable to their winding, deep cañons.

END OF VOLUME FIVE.

INDEX TO VOLUME V.

ILLUSTRATIONS IN VOLUME V.

PORTRAITS.

PLACES.

MAPS AND PLANS.